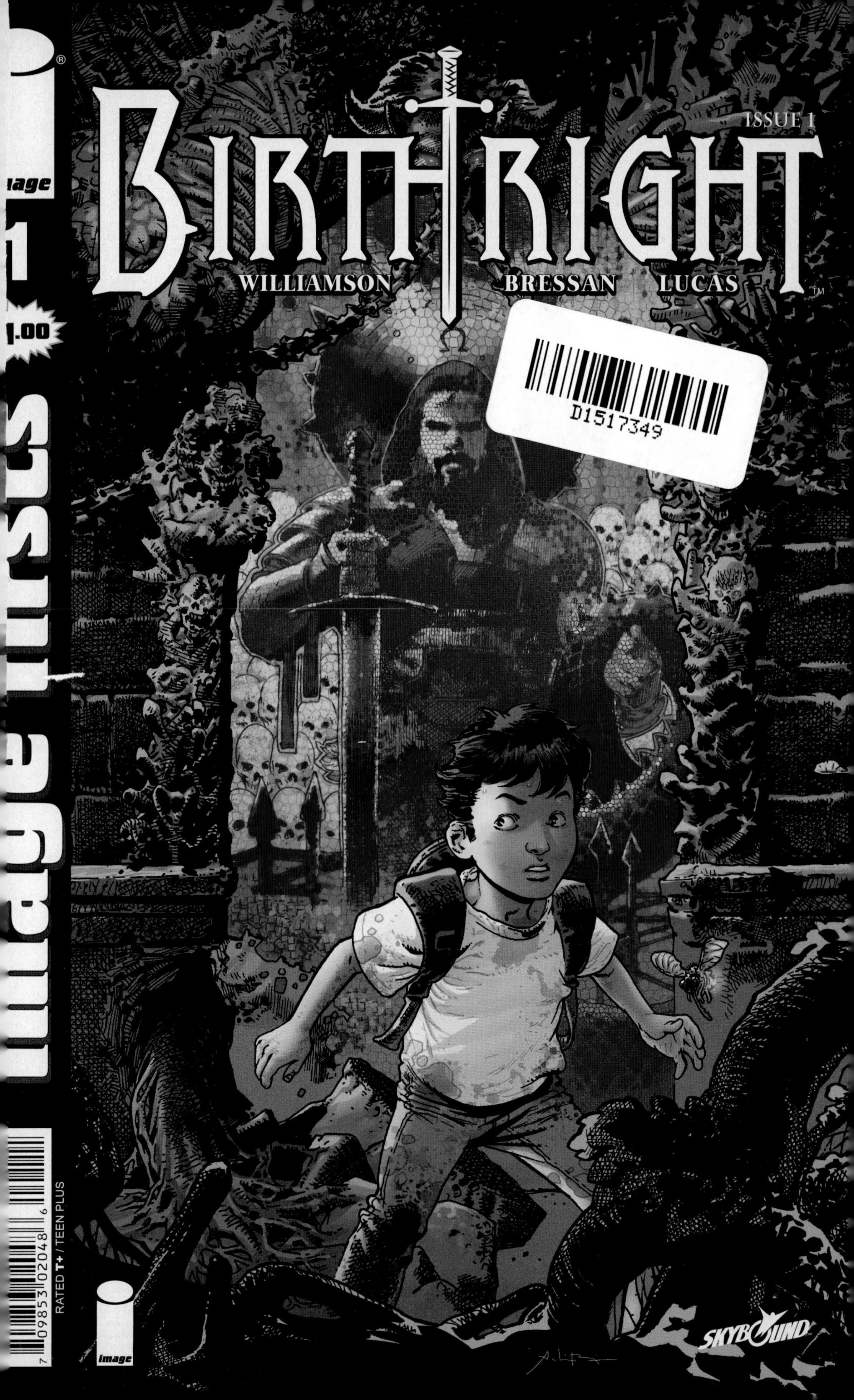
ISSUE 1
BIRTHRIGHT
WILLIAMSON
BRESSAN
LUCAS
image firsts
RATED T+ / TEEN PLUS
SKYBOUND
image

Joshua Williamson
creator, writer

Andrei Bressan
creator, artist

Adriano Lucas
colorist

Pat Brosseau
letterer

Helen Leigh
assistant editor

Sean Mackiewicz
editor

cover by
Andrei Bressan &
Adriano Lucas

Rian Hughes
logo design

map by
Joshua Williamson &
Jason Ho

IMAGE COMICS, INC.
Robert Kirkman *Chief Operating Officer*
Erik Larsen *Chief Financial Officer*
Todd McFarlane *President*
Marc Silvestri *Chief Executive Officer*
Jim Valentino *Vice-President*

Eric Stephenson *Publisher*
Corey Murphy *Director of Sales*
Jeff Boison *Director of Publishing Planning & Book Trade Sales*
Jeremy Sullivan *Director of Digital Sales*
Kat Salazar *Director of PR & Marketing*
Emily Miller *Director of Operations*
Branwyn Bigglestone *Senior Accounts Manager*
Sarah Mello *Accounts Manager*

Drew Gill *Art Director*
Jonathan Chan *Production Manager*
Meredith Wallace *Print Manager*
Briah Skelly *Publicity Assistant*
Randy Okamura *Marketing Production Designer*
David Brothers *Branding Manager*
Ally Power *Content Manager*
Addison Duke *Production Artist*
Vincent Kukua *Production Artist*
Sasha Head *Production Artist*
Jeff Stang *Direct Market Sales Representative*
Emilio Bautista *Digital Sales Associate*
Chloe Ramos-Peterson *Administrative Assistant*

www.imagecomics.com

www.skybound.com

Robert Kirkman *CEO*
David Alpert *President*
Sean Mackiewicz *Editorial Director*
Shawn Kirkham *Director of Business Developm*
Brian Huntington *Online Editorial Director*
June Alian *Publicity Director*
Rachel Skidmore *Director of Media Developme*
Jon Moisan *Editor*
Arielle Basich *Assistant Editor*
Dan Petersen *Operations Manager*
Sarah Effinger *Office Manager*
Nick Palmer *Operations Coordinator*
Genevieve Jones *Production Coordinator*
Andres Juarez *Graphic Designer*
Stephan Murillo *Administrative Assistant*

International inquiries: *foreign@skybound.com*
Licensing inquiries: *contact@skybound.com*

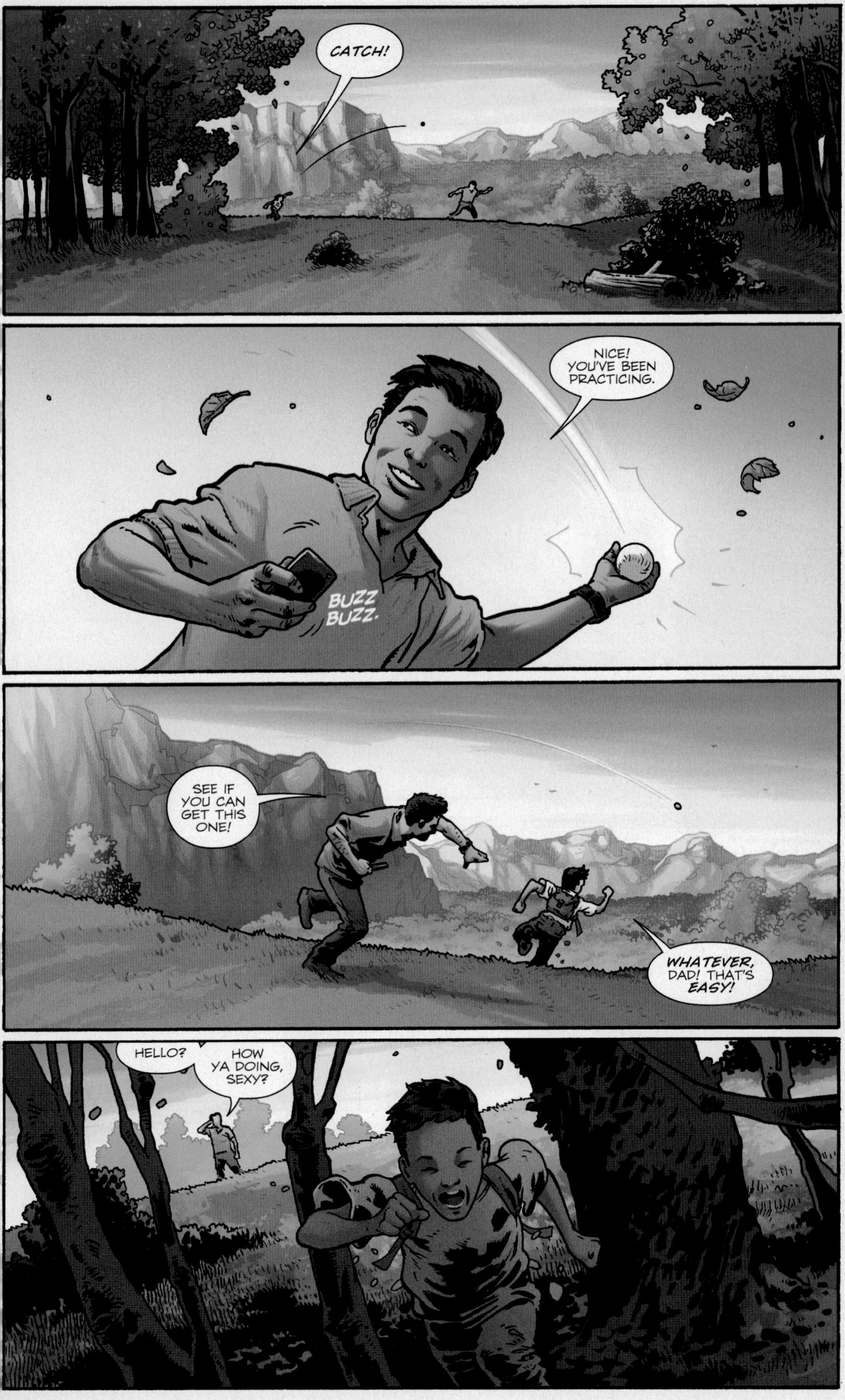
CATCH!
NICE! YOU'VE BEEN PRACTICING.
BUZZ BUZZ.
SEE IF YOU CAN GET THIS ONE!
WHATEVER, DAD! THAT'S EASY!
HELLO?
HOW YA DOING, SEXY?

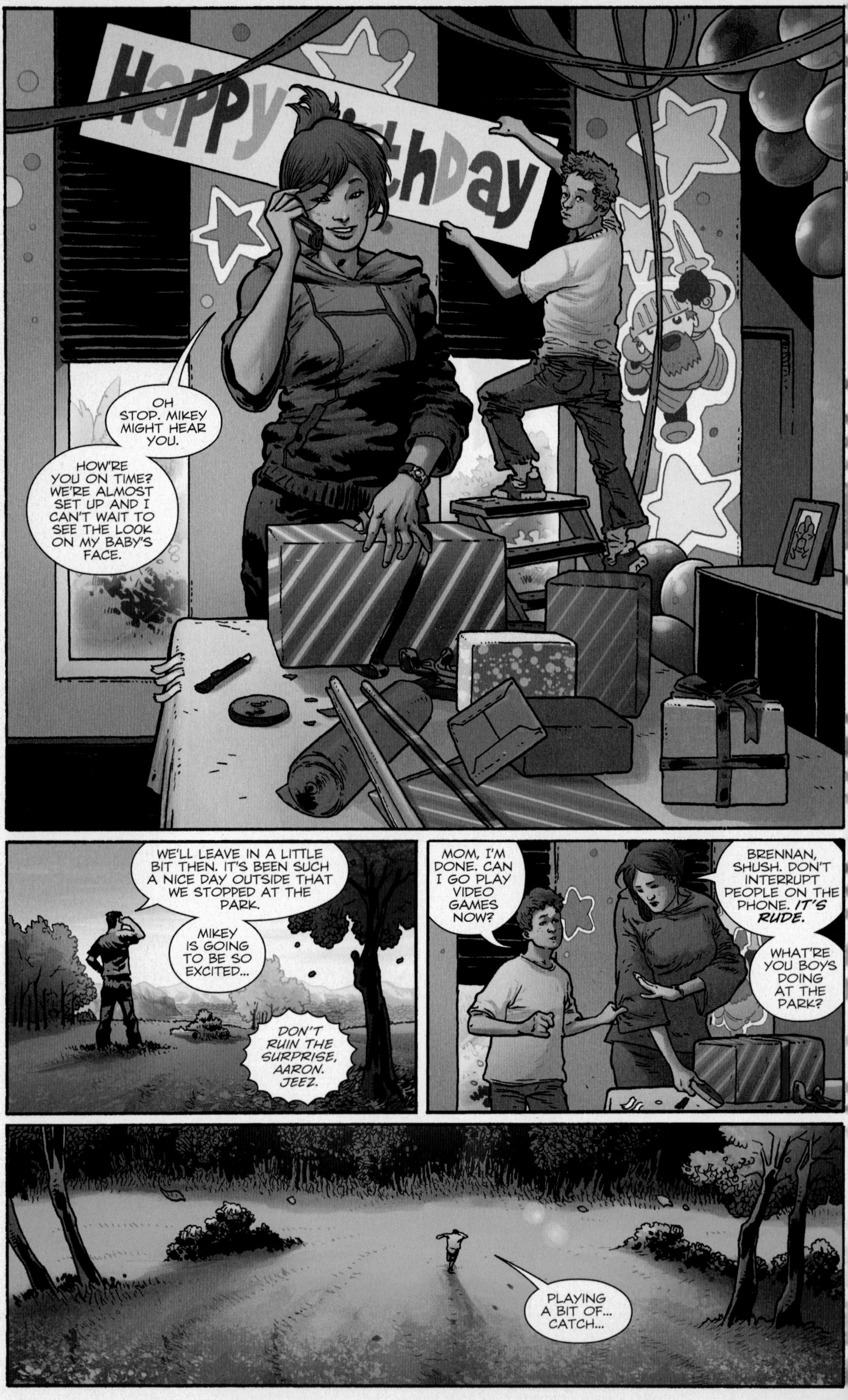
OH STOP. MIKEY MIGHT HEAR YOU.
HOW'RE YOU ON TIME? WE'RE ALMOST SET UP AND I CAN'T WAIT TO SEE THE LOOK ON MY BABY'S FACE.
WE'LL LEAVE IN A LITTLE BIT THEN. IT'S BEEN SUCH A NICE DAY OUTSIDE THAT WE STOPPED AT THE PARK.
MIKEY IS GOING TO BE SO EXCITED...
DON'T RUIN THE SURPRISE, AARON. JEEZ.
MOM, I'M DONE. CAN I GO PLAY VIDEO GAMES NOW?
BRENNAN, SHUSH. DON'T INTERRUPT PEOPLE ON THE PHONE. *IT'S RUDE.*
WHAT'RE YOU BOYS DOING AT THE PARK?
PLAYING A BIT OF... CATCH...

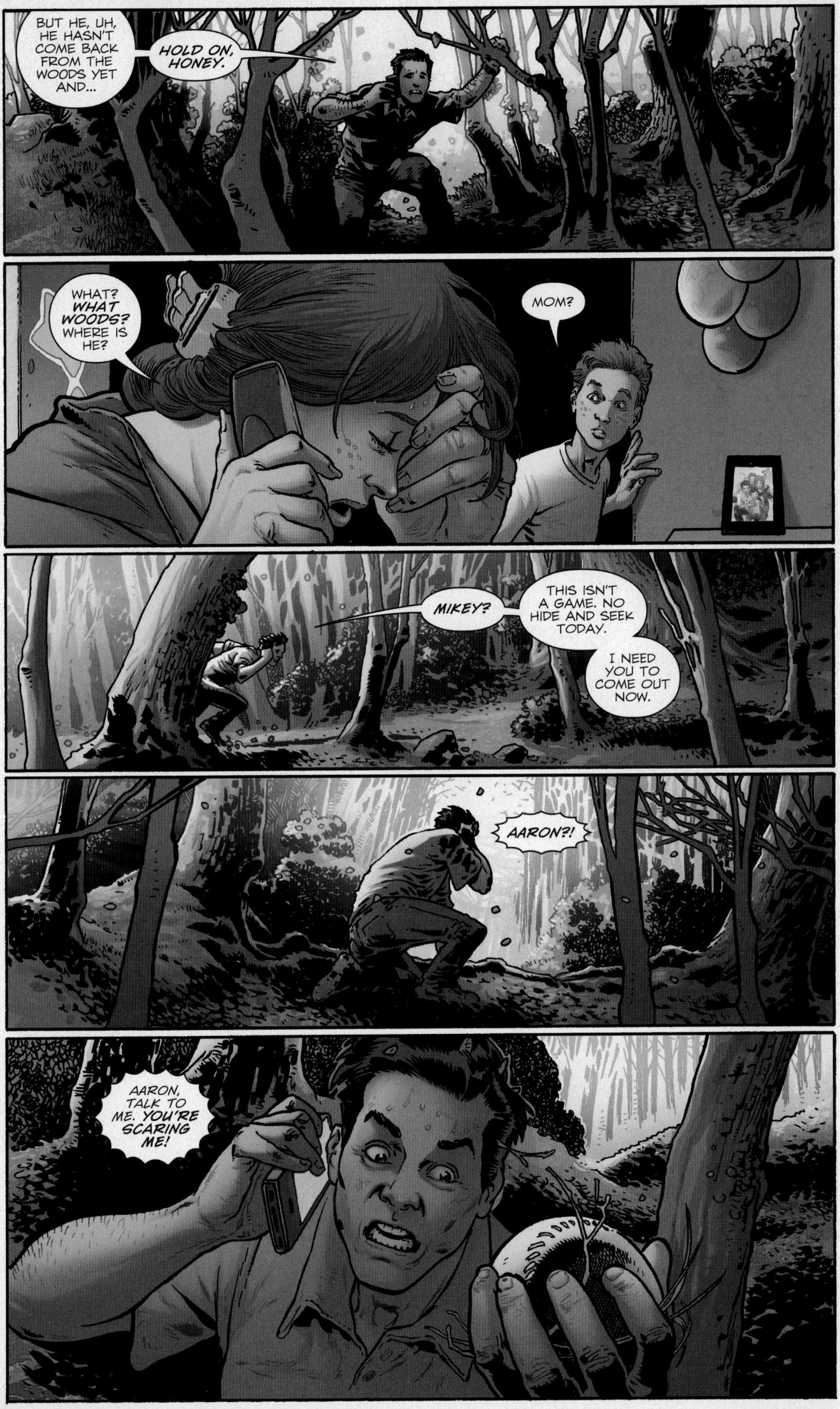
BUT HE, UH, HE HASN'T COME BACK FROM THE WOODS YET AND...
HOLD ON, HONEY.
WHAT? WHAT WOODS? WHERE IS HE?
MOM?
MIKEY?
THIS ISN'T A GAME. NO HIDE AND SEEK TODAY.
I NEED YOU TO COME OUT NOW.
AARON?!
AARON, TALK TO ME. YOU'RE SCARING ME!

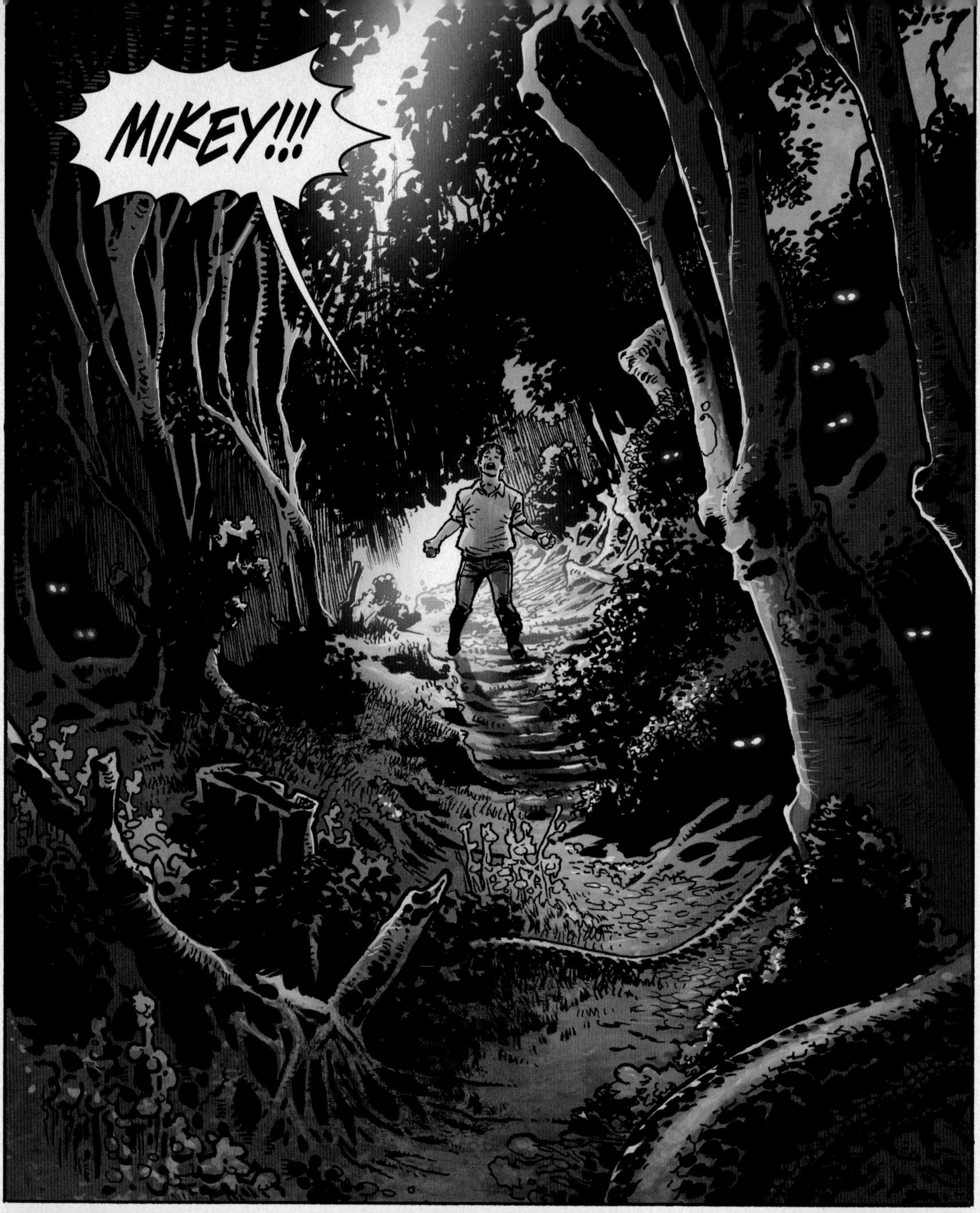
MIKEY!!!

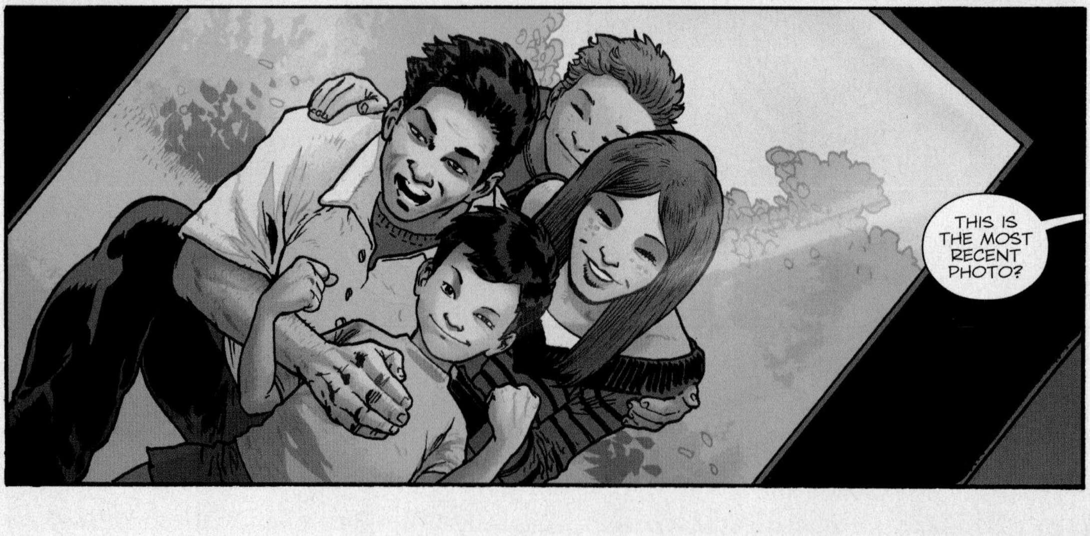
THIS IS THE MOST RECENT PHOTO?

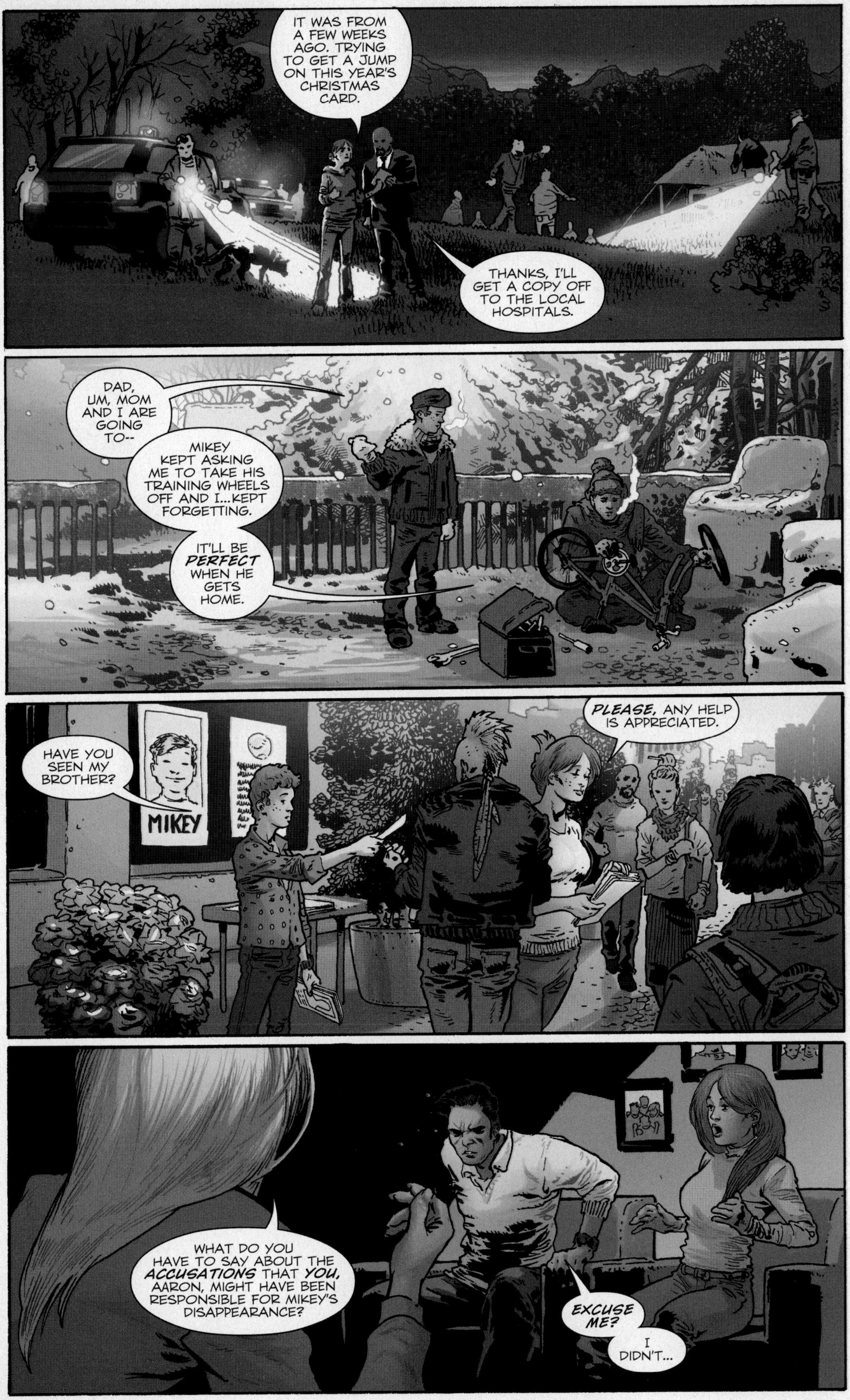
IT WAS FROM A FEW WEEKS AGO. TRYING TO GET A JUMP ON THIS YEAR'S CHRISTMAS CARD.
THANKS, I'LL GET A COPY OFF TO THE LOCAL HOSPITALS.
DAD, UM, MOM AND I ARE GOING TO--
MIKEY KEPT ASKING ME TO TAKE HIS TRAINING WHEELS OFF AND I...KEPT FORGETTING.
IT'LL BE *PERFECT* WHEN HE GETS HOME.
HAVE YOU SEEN MY BROTHER?
MIKEY
PLEASE, ANY HELP IS APPRECIATED.
WHAT DO YOU HAVE TO SAY ABOUT THE *ACCUSATIONS* THAT *YOU,* AARON, MIGHT HAVE BEEN RESPONSIBLE FOR MIKEY'S DISAPPEARANCE?
EXCUSE ME?
I DIDN'T...

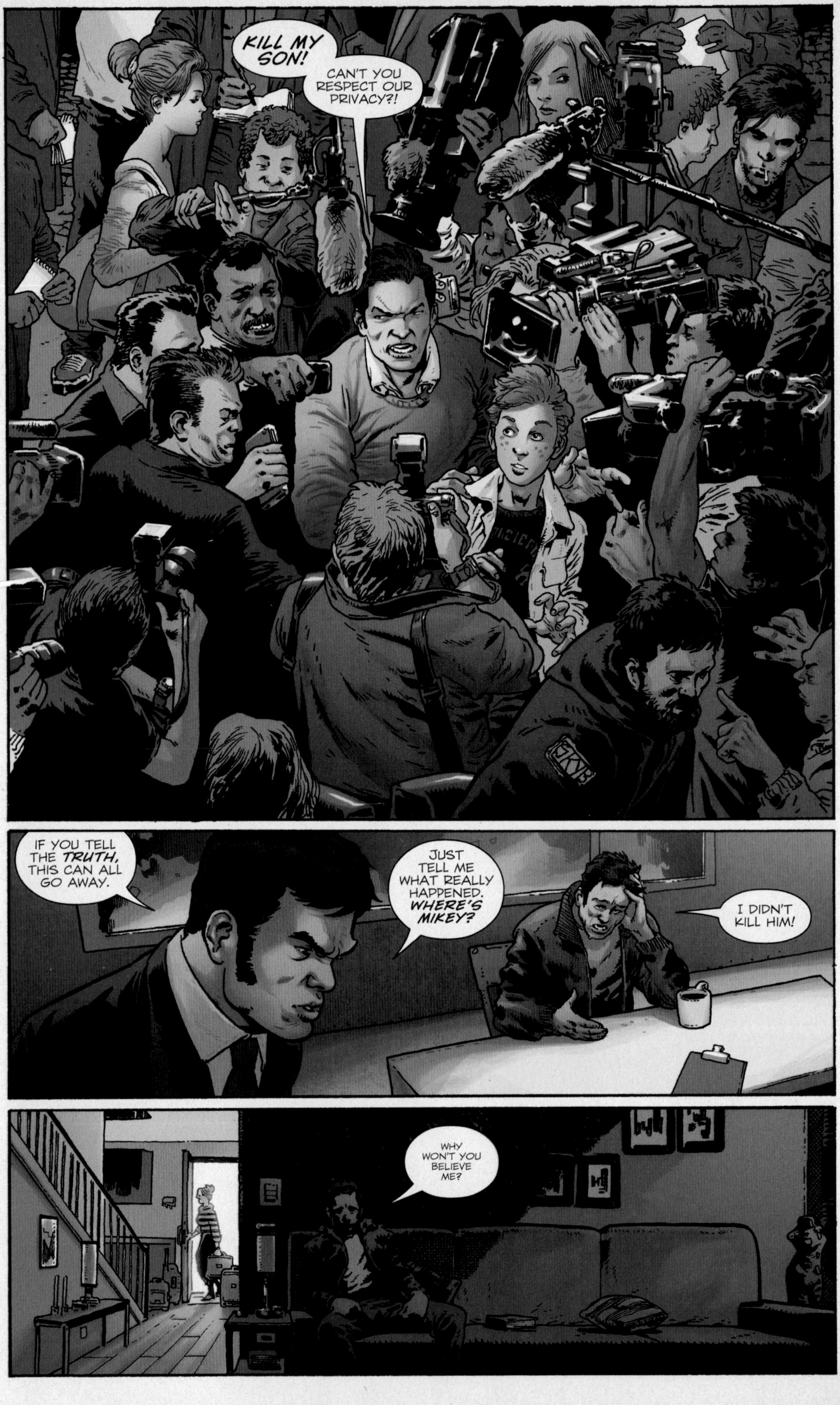
KILL MY SON!
CAN'T YOU RESPECT OUR PRIVACY?!
IF YOU TELL THE *TRUTH,* THIS CAN ALL GO AWAY.
JUST TELL ME WHAT REALLY HAPPENED. *WHERE'S MIKEY?*
I DIDN'T KILL HIM!
WHY WON'T YOU BELIEVE ME?

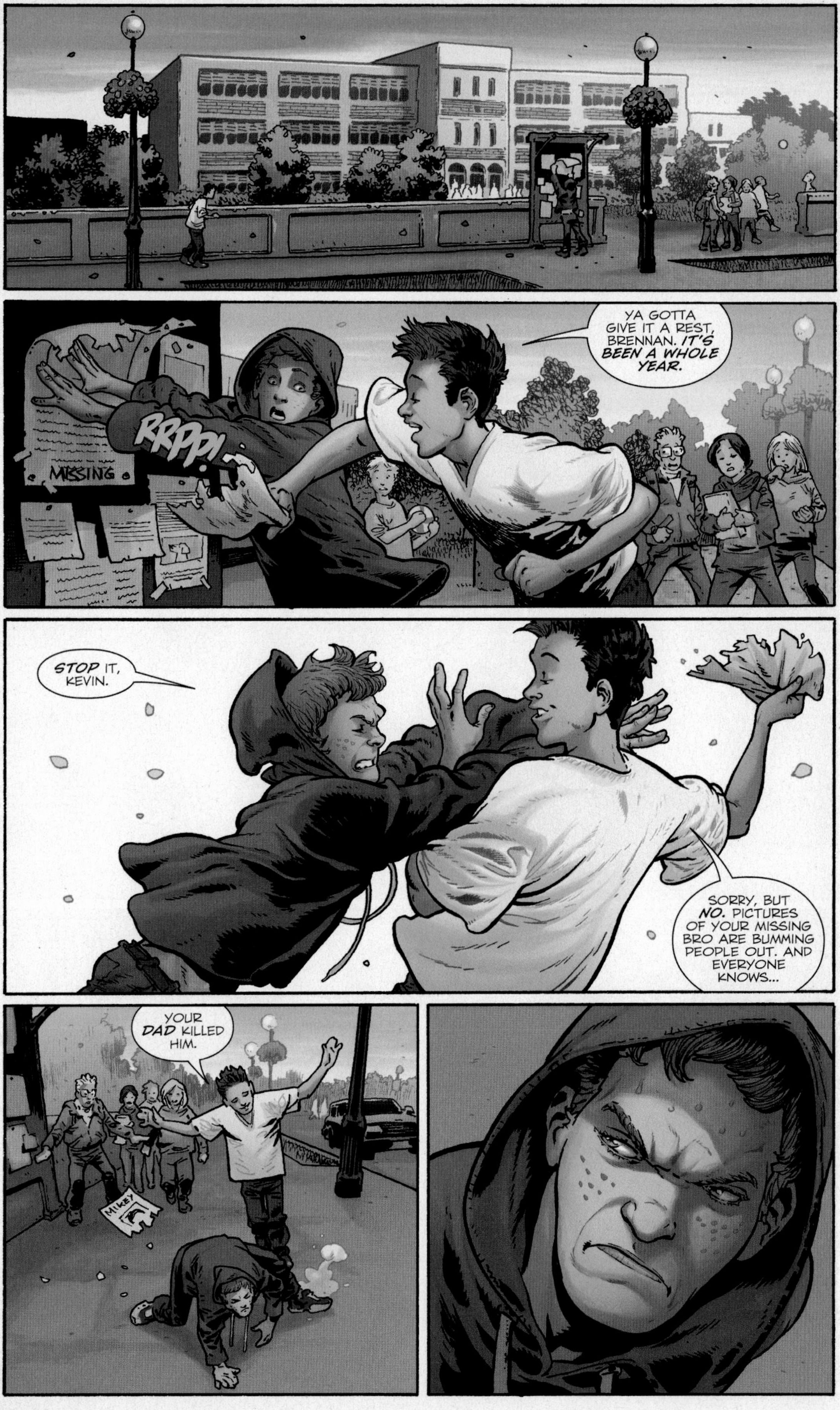
YA GOTTA GIVE IT A REST, BRENNAN. IT'S BEEN A WHOLE YEAR.
RRPP!
MISSING
STOP IT, KEVIN.
SORRY, BUT NO. PICTURES OF YOUR MISSING BRO ARE BUMMING PEOPLE OUT. AND EVERYONE KNOWS...
YOUR DAD KILLED HIM.
MIKEY

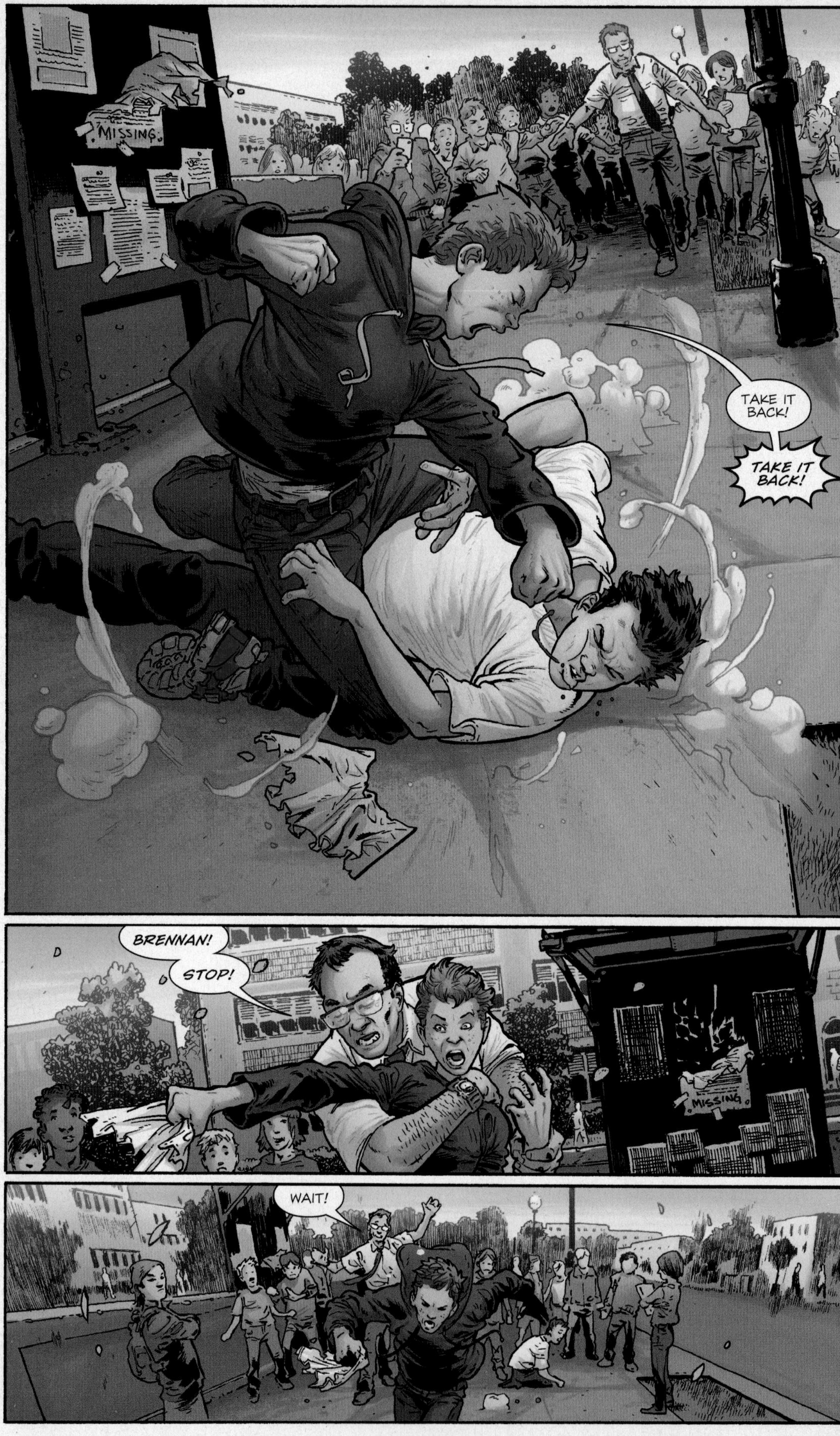
MISSING
TAKE IT BACK!
TAKE IT BACK!
BRENNAN!
STOP!
MISSING
WAIT!

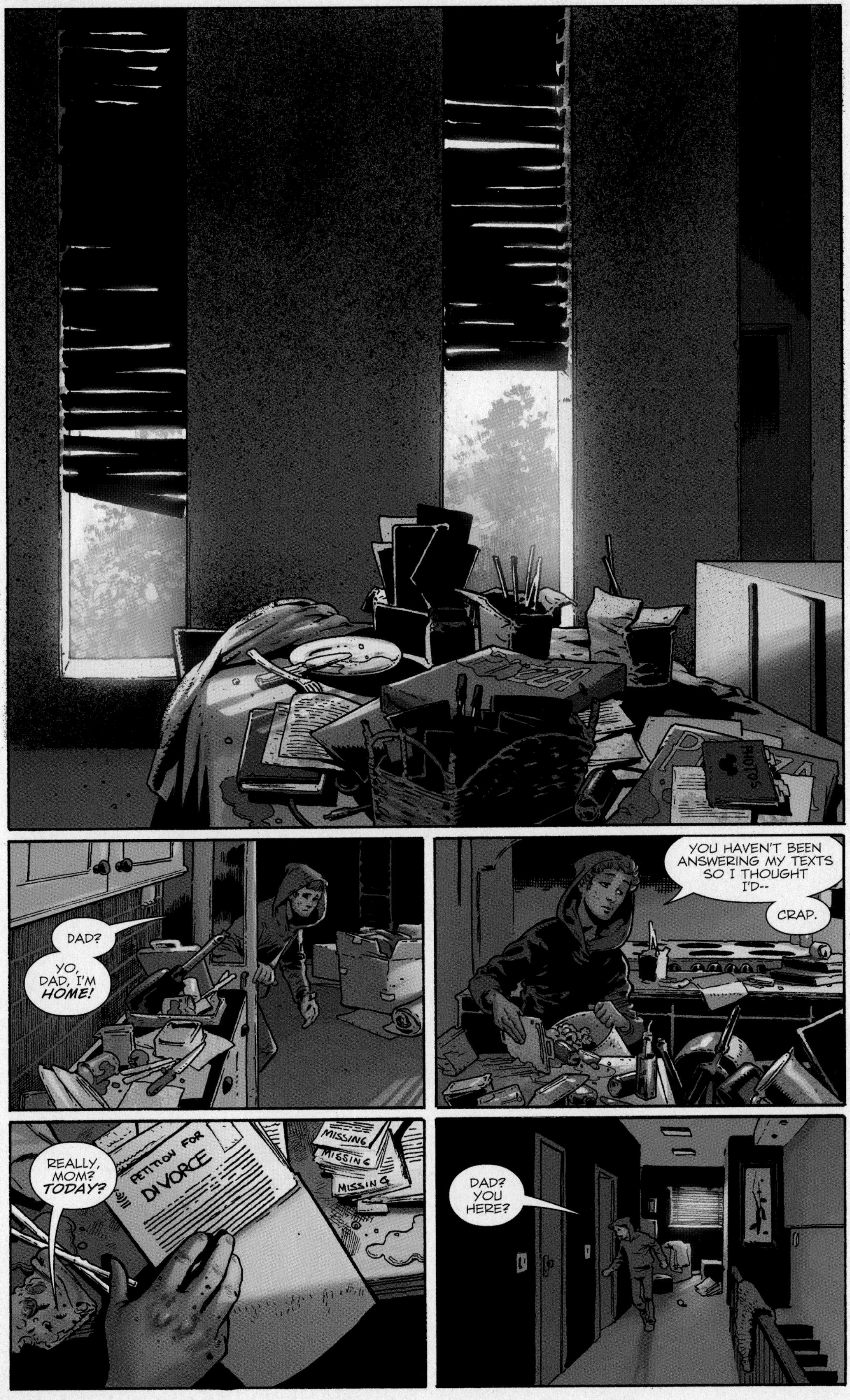
DAD?
YO, DAD, I'M *HOME!*
YOU HAVEN'T BEEN ANSWERING MY TEXTS SO I THOUGHT I'D--
CRAP.
REALLY, MOM? *TODAY?*
PETITION FOR DIVORCE
MISSING
MISSING
MISSING
DAD? YOU HERE?

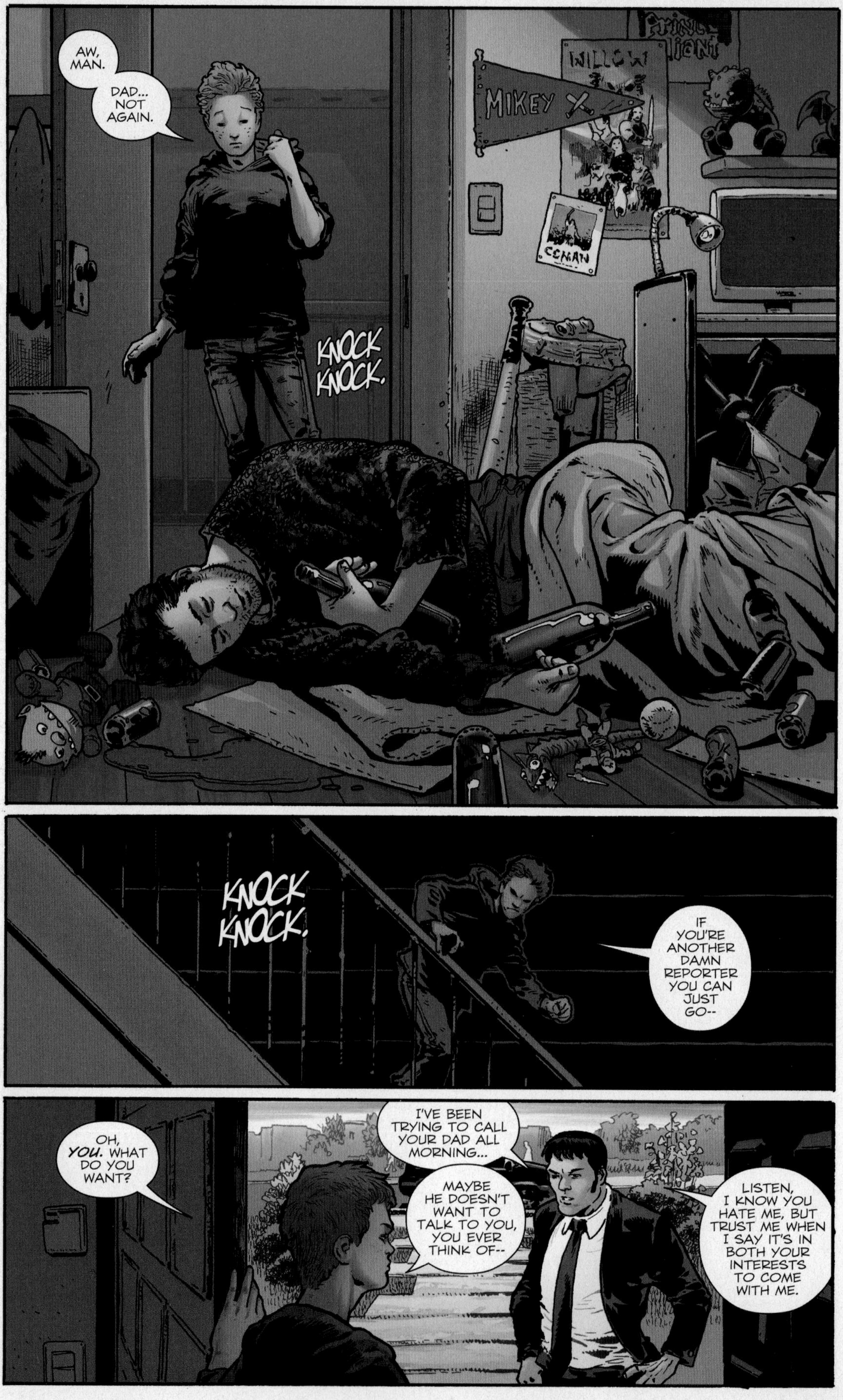
AW, MAN.
DAD... NOT AGAIN.
MIKEY
WILLOW
CONAN
KNOCK KNOCK.
KNOCK KNOCK.
IF YOU'RE ANOTHER DAMN REPORTER YOU CAN JUST GO--
OH, *YOU.* WHAT DO YOU WANT?
I'VE BEEN TRYING TO CALL YOUR DAD ALL MORNING...
MAYBE HE DOESN'T WANT TO TALK TO YOU, YOU EVER THINK OF--
LISTEN, I KNOW YOU HATE ME, BUT TRUST ME WHEN I SAY IT'S IN BOTH YOUR INTERESTS TO COME WITH ME.

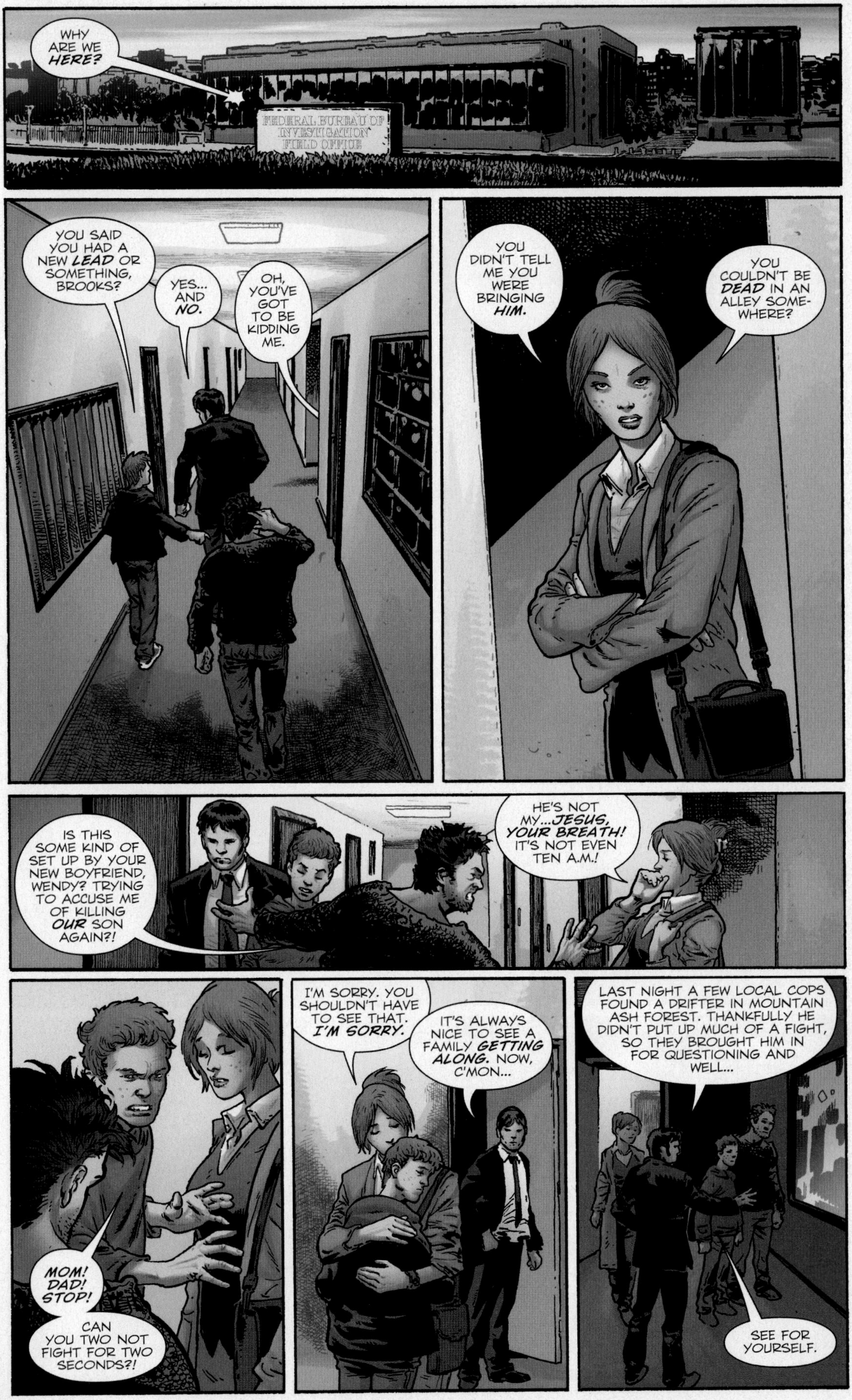
WHY ARE WE HERE?
FEDERAL BUREAU OF INVESTIGATION FIELD OFFICE
YOU SAID YOU HAD A NEW LEAD OR SOMETHING, BROOKS?
YES... AND NO.
OH, YOU'VE GOT TO BE KIDDING ME.
YOU DIDN'T TELL ME YOU WERE BRINGING HIM.
YOU COULDN'T BE DEAD IN AN ALLEY SOME-WHERE?
IS THIS SOME KIND OF SET UP BY YOUR NEW BOYFRIEND, WENDY? TRYING TO ACCUSE ME OF KILLING OUR SON AGAIN?!
HE'S NOT MY...JESUS, YOUR BREATH! IT'S NOT EVEN TEN A.M.!
MOM! DAD! STOP!
CAN YOU TWO NOT FIGHT FOR TWO SECONDS?!
I'M SORRY. YOU SHOULDN'T HAVE TO SEE THAT. I'M SORRY.
IT'S ALWAYS NICE TO SEE A FAMILY GETTING ALONG. NOW, C'MON...
LAST NIGHT A FEW LOCAL COPS FOUND A DRIFTER IN MOUNTAIN ASH FOREST. THANKFULLY HE DIDN'T PUT UP MUCH OF A FIGHT, SO THEY BROUGHT HIM IN FOR QUESTIONING AND WELL...
SEE FOR YOURSELF.

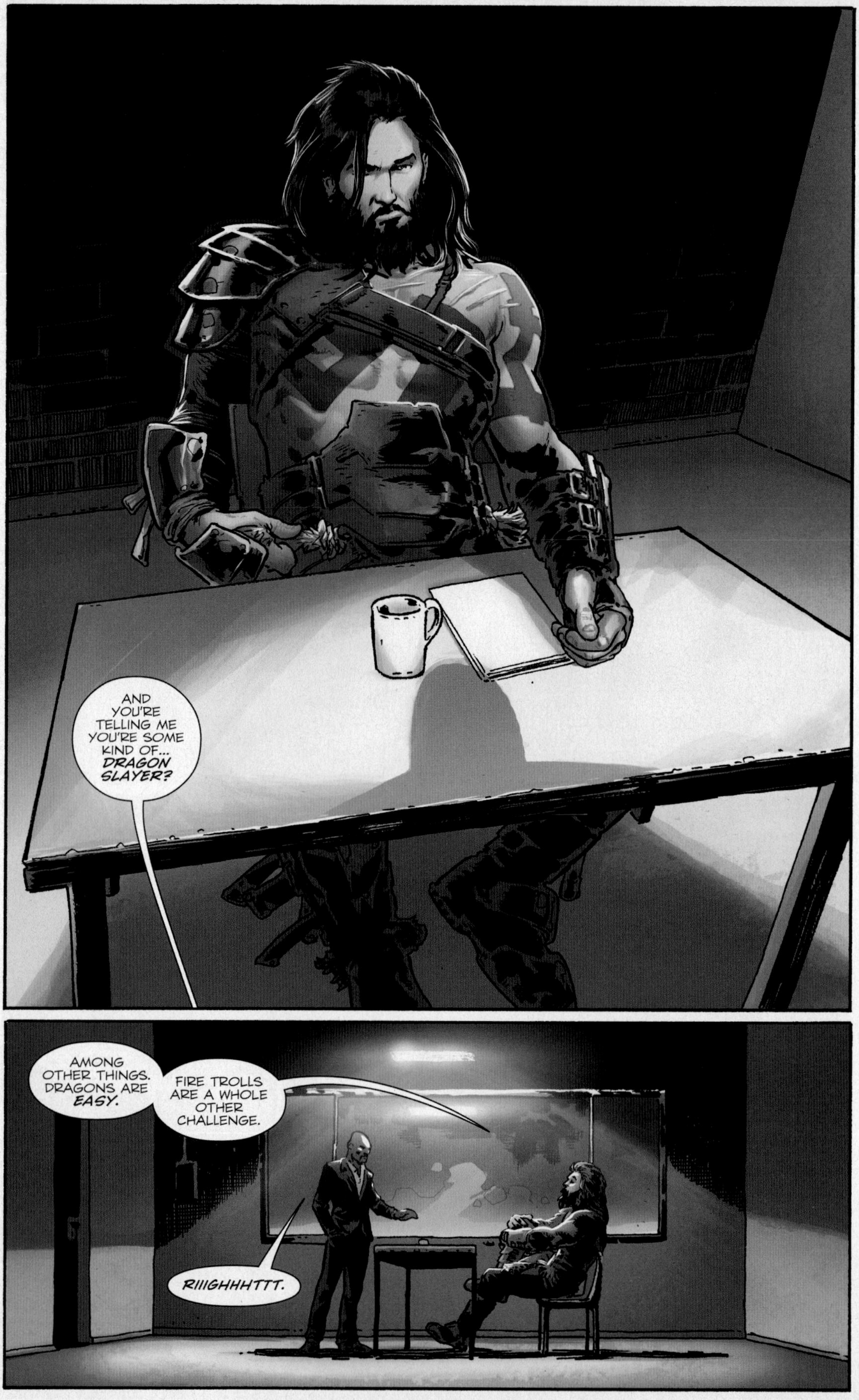
AND YOU'RE TELLING ME YOU'RE SOME KIND OF... DRAGON SLAYER?
AMONG OTHER THINGS. DRAGONS ARE EASY.
FIRE TROLLS ARE A WHOLE OTHER CHALLENGE.
RIIIGHHHTTT.

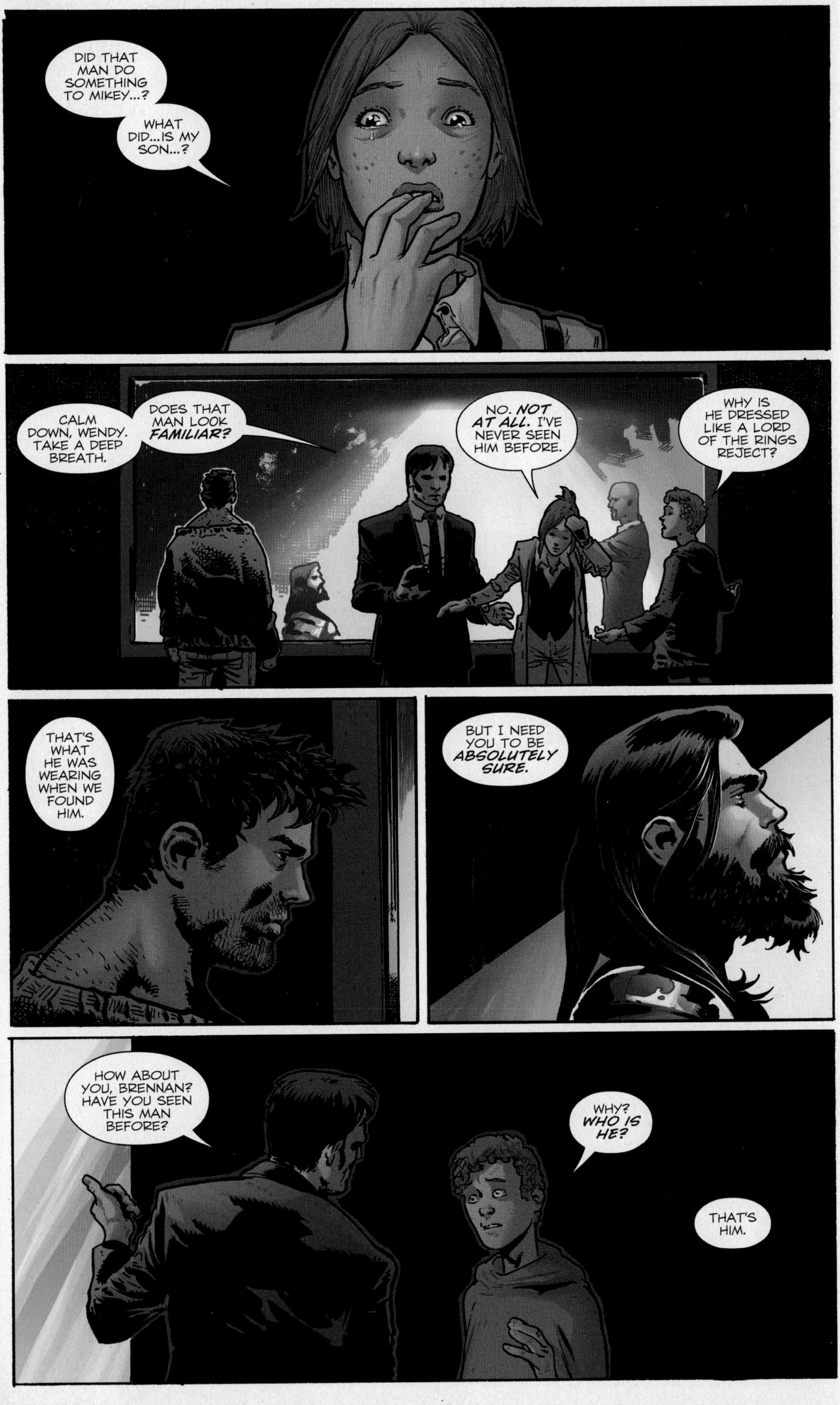
DID THAT MAN DO SOMETHING TO MIKEY...?
WHAT DID...IS MY SON...?
CALM DOWN, WENDY. TAKE A DEEP BREATH.
DOES THAT MAN LOOK FAMILIAR?
NO. NOT AT ALL. I'VE NEVER SEEN HIM BEFORE.
WHY IS HE DRESSED LIKE A LORD OF THE RINGS REJECT?
THAT'S WHAT HE WAS WEARING WHEN WE FOUND HIM.
BUT I NEED YOU TO BE ABSOLUTELY SURE.
HOW ABOUT YOU, BRENNAN? HAVE YOU SEEN THIS MAN BEFORE?
WHY? WHO IS HE?
THAT'S HIM.

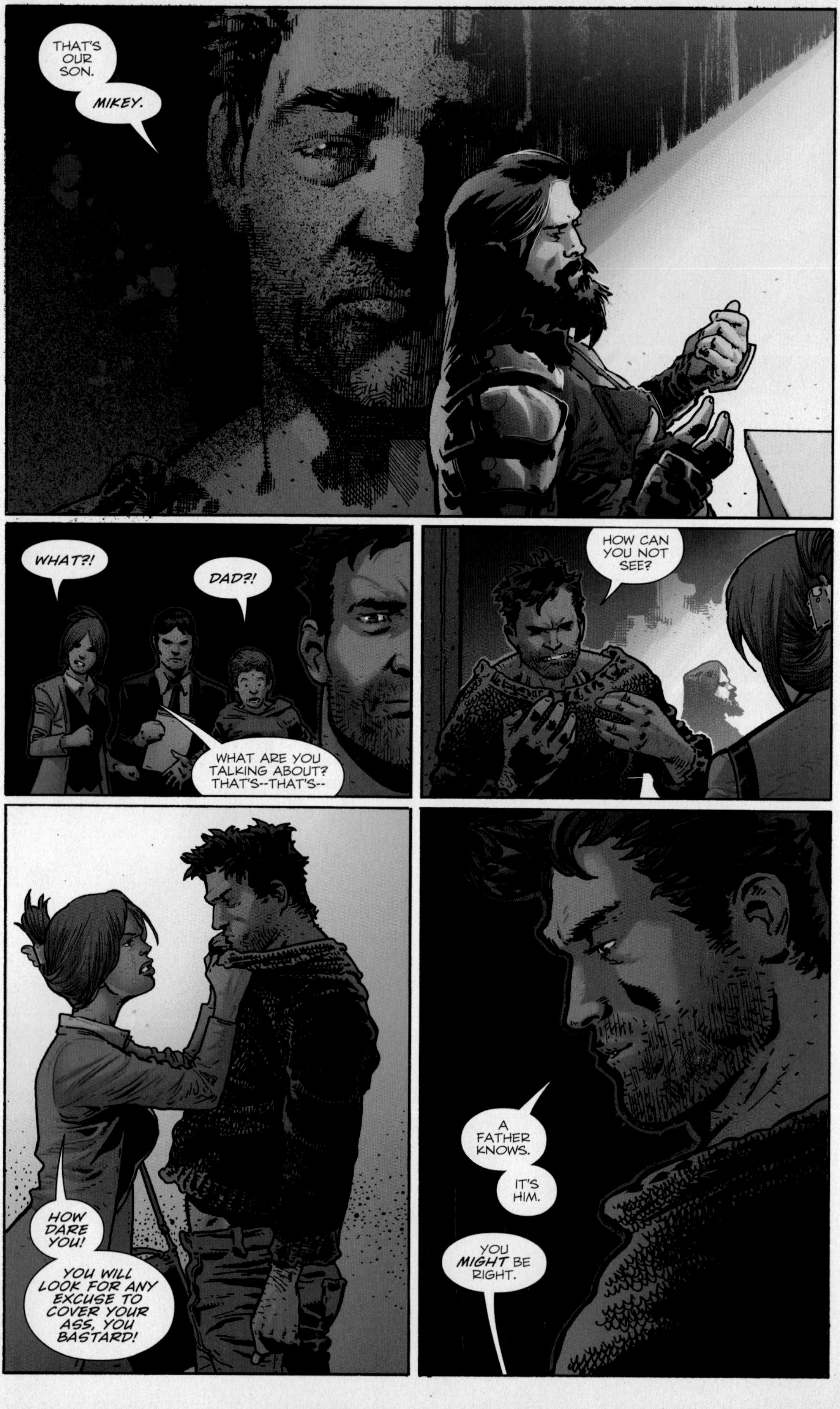
THAT'S OUR SON.
MIKEY.
WHAT?!
DAD?!
WHAT ARE YOU TALKING ABOUT? THAT'S--THAT'S--
HOW CAN YOU NOT SEE?
HOW DARE YOU!
YOU WILL LOOK FOR ANY EXCUSE TO COVER YOUR ASS, YOU BASTARD!
A FATHER KNOWS.
IT'S HIM.
YOU MIGHT BE RIGHT.

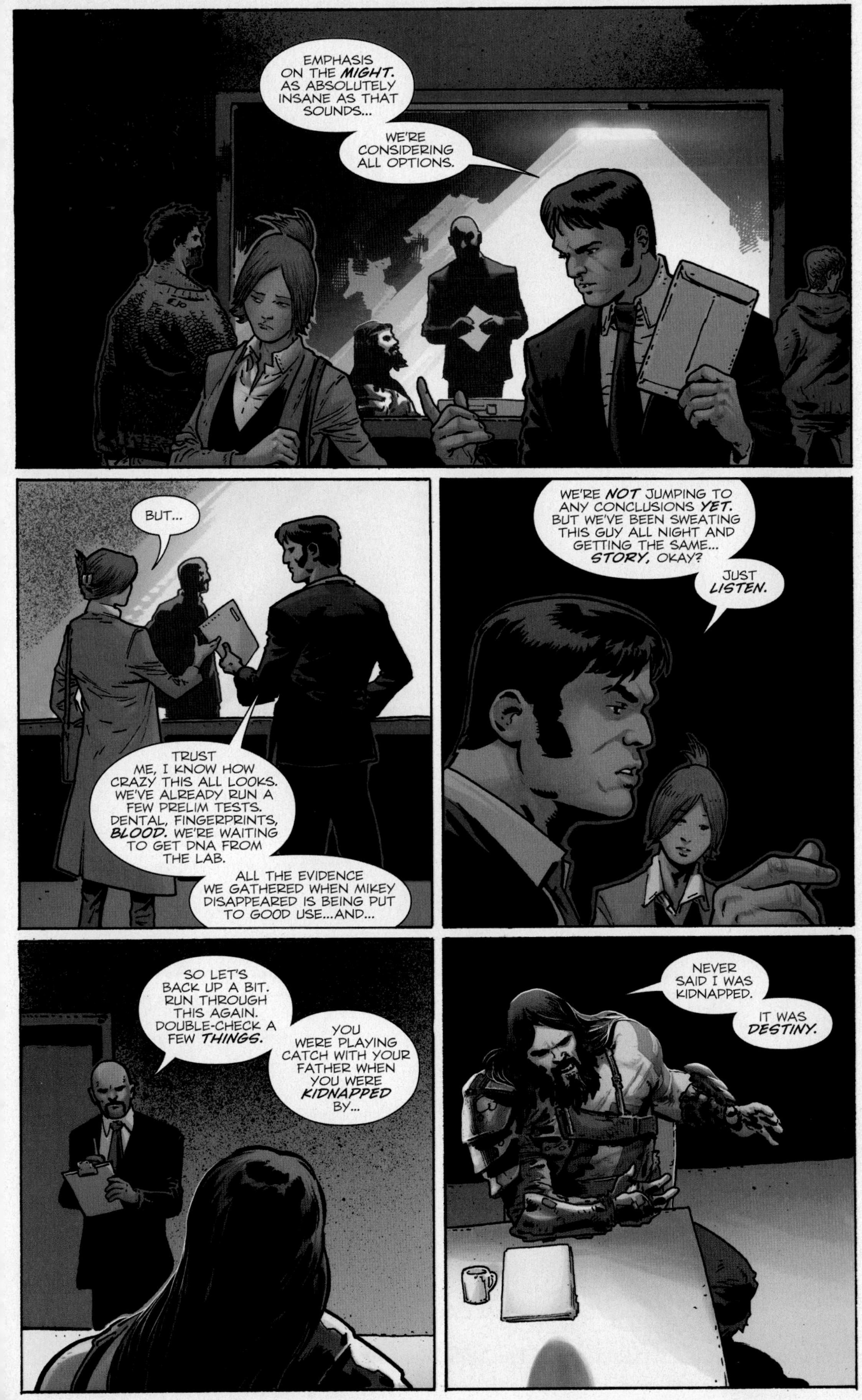
EMPHASIS ON THE MIGHT. AS ABSOLUTELY INSANE AS THAT SOUNDS...
WE'RE CONSIDERING ALL OPTIONS.
BUT...
TRUST ME, I KNOW HOW CRAZY THIS ALL LOOKS. WE'VE ALREADY RUN A FEW PRELIM TESTS. DENTAL, FINGERPRINTS, BLOOD. WE'RE WAITING TO GET DNA FROM THE LAB.
ALL THE EVIDENCE WE GATHERED WHEN MIKEY DISAPPEARED IS BEING PUT TO GOOD USE...AND...
WE'RE NOT JUMPING TO ANY CONCLUSIONS YET. BUT WE'VE BEEN SWEATING THIS GUY ALL NIGHT AND GETTING THE SAME... STORY, OKAY?
JUST LISTEN.
SO LET'S BACK UP A BIT. RUN THROUGH THIS AGAIN. DOUBLE-CHECK A FEW THINGS.
YOU WERE PLAYING CATCH WITH YOUR FATHER WHEN YOU WERE KIDNAPPED BY...
NEVER SAID I WAS KIDNAPPED.
IT WAS DESTINY.

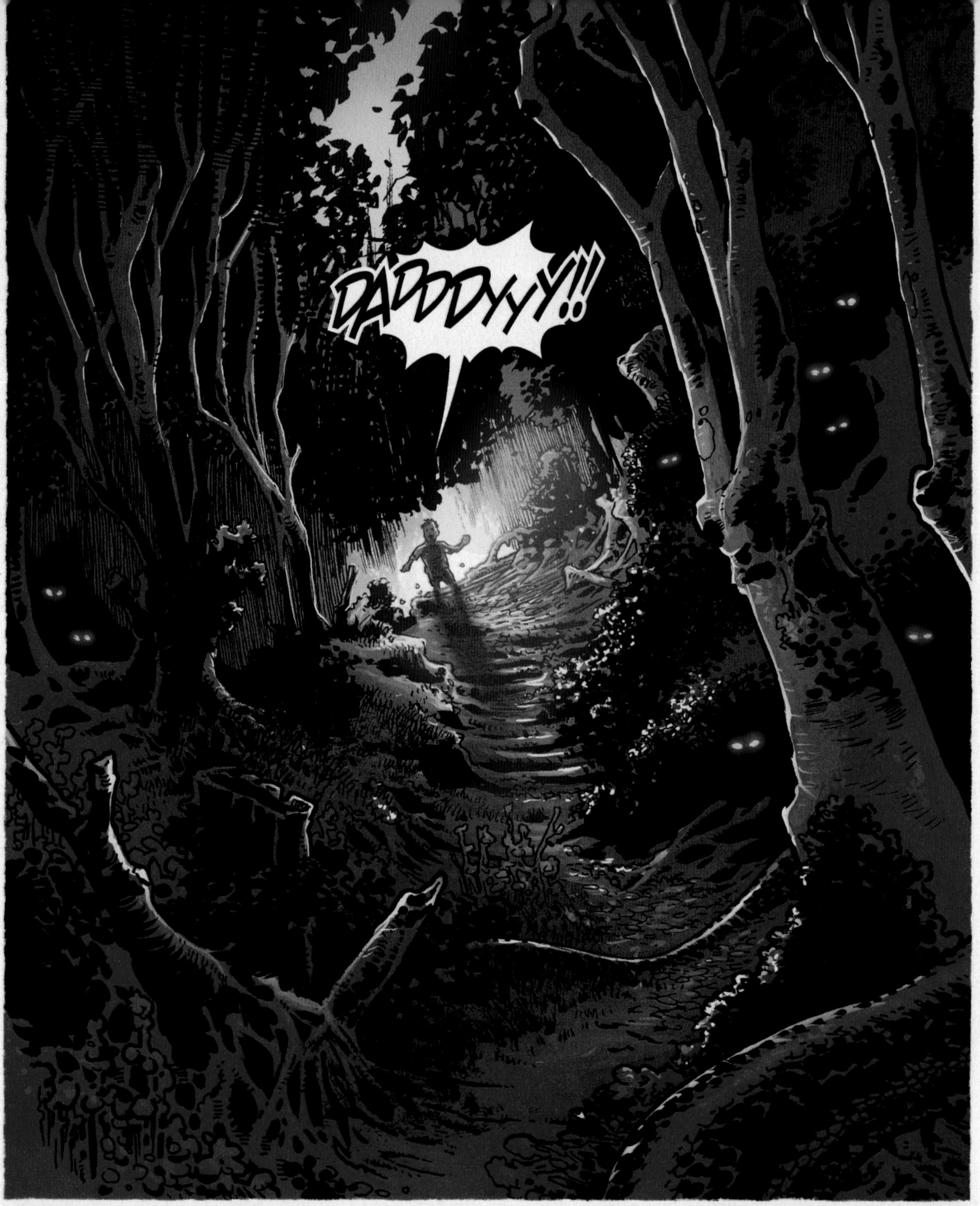
DADDDYYY!!

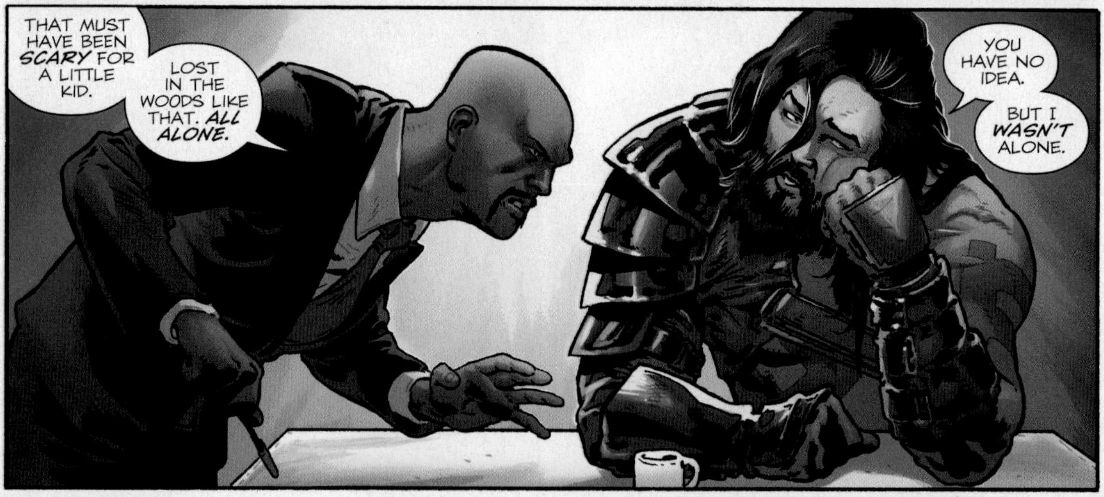
THAT MUST HAVE BEEN SCARY FOR A LITTLE KID.
LOST IN THE WOODS LIKE THAT. ALL ALONE.
YOU HAVE NO IDEA.
BUT I WASN'T ALONE.

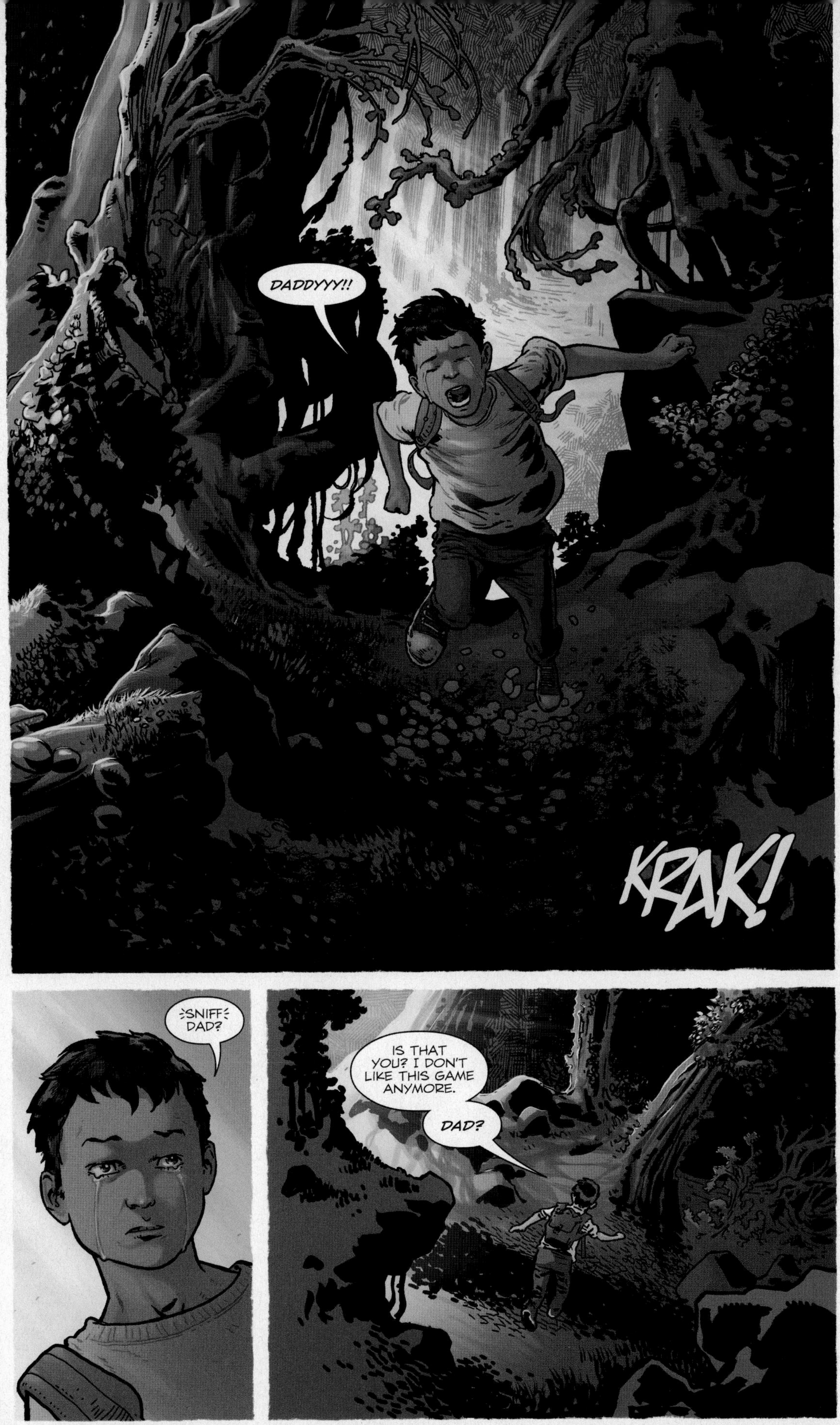
DADDYYY!!
KRAK!
SNIFF
DAD?
IS THAT YOU? I DON'T LIKE THIS GAME ANYMORE.
DAD?

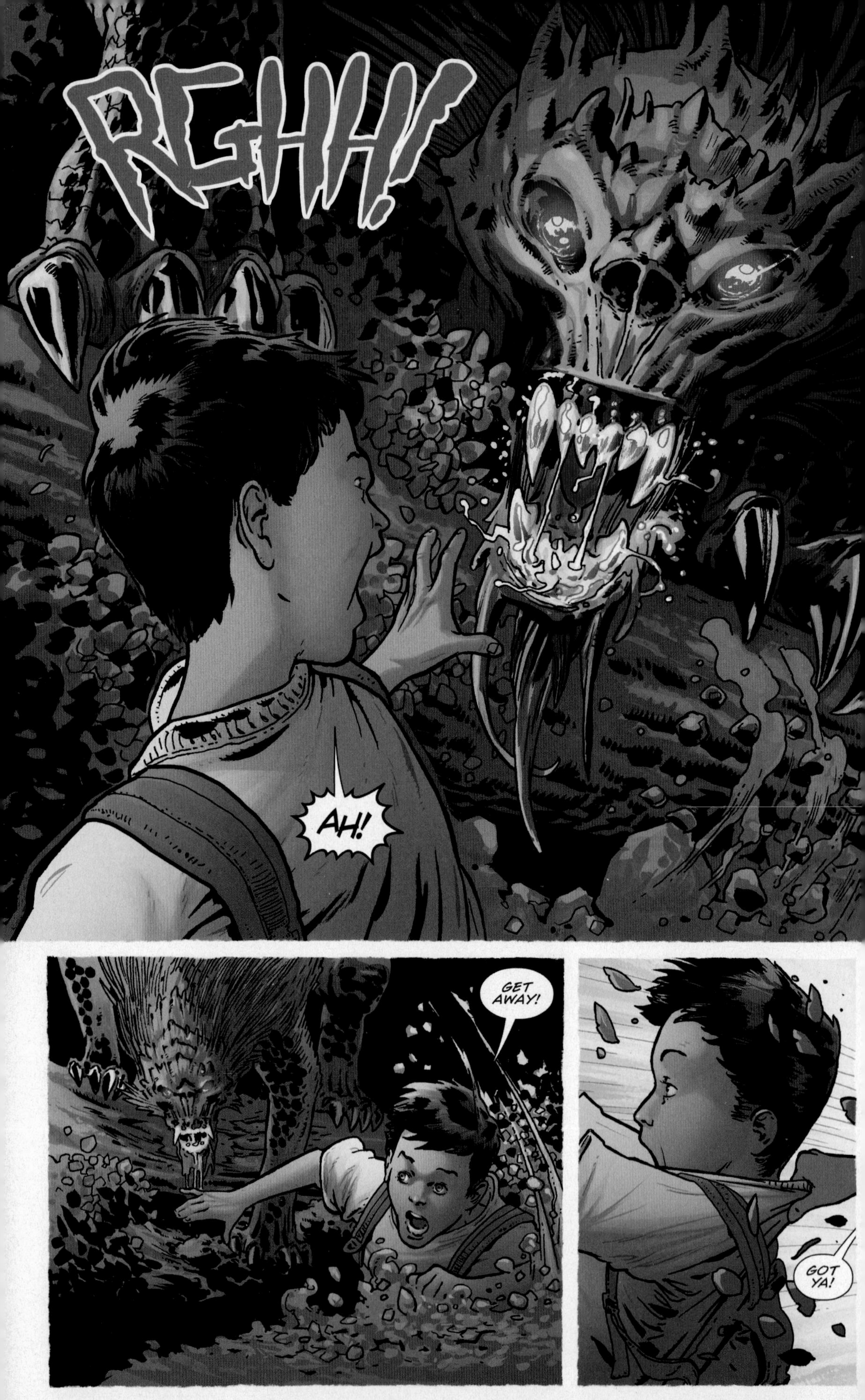
RGHH!
AH!
GET AWAY!
GOT YA!

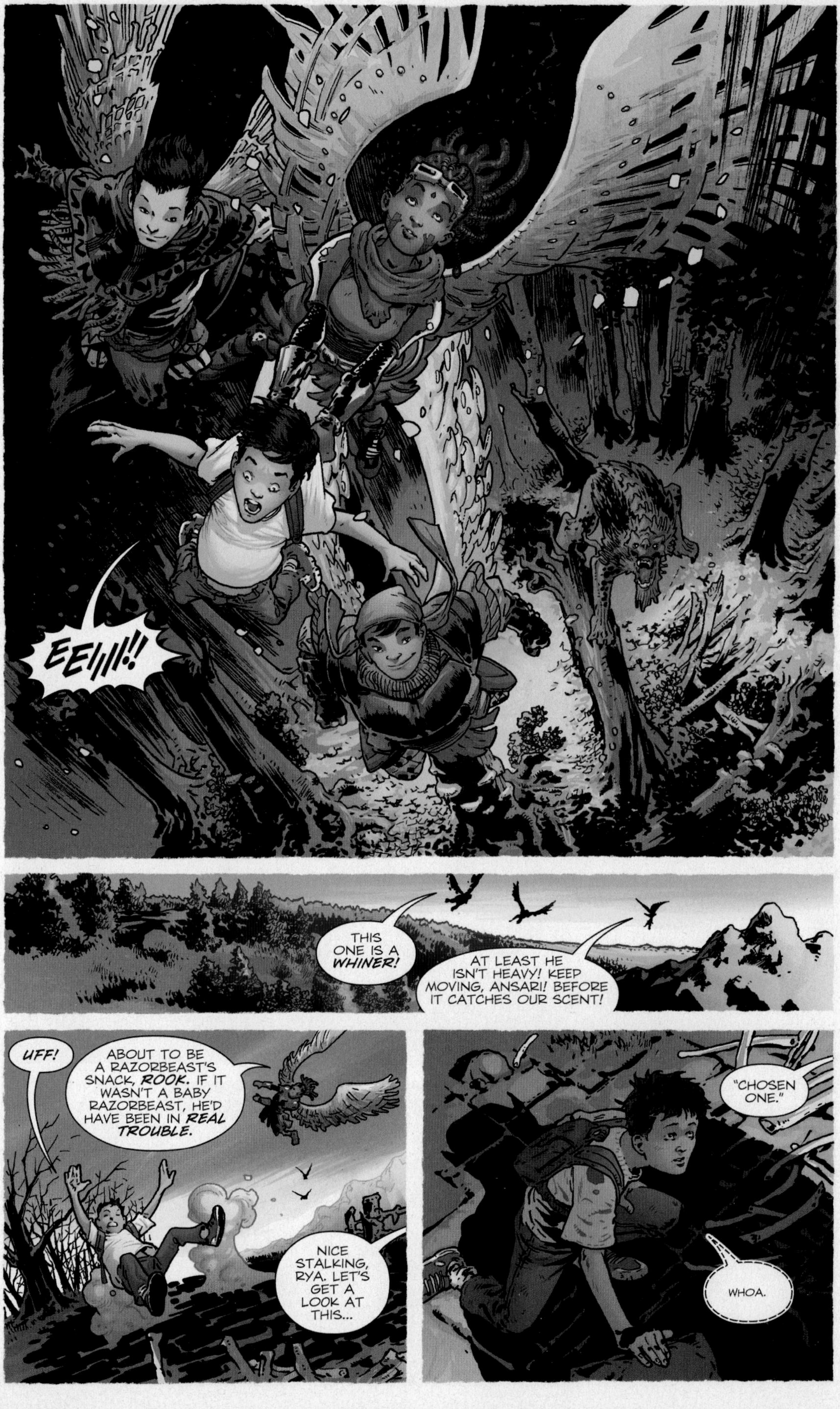
EEIIII!!
THIS ONE IS A WHINER!
AT LEAST HE ISN'T HEAVY! KEEP MOVING, ANSARI! BEFORE IT CATCHES OUR SCENT!
UFF!
ABOUT TO BE A RAZORBEAST'S SNACK, ROOK. IF IT WASN'T A BABY RAZORBEAST, HE'D HAVE BEEN IN REAL TROUBLE.
NICE STALKING, RYA. LET'S GET A LOOK AT THIS...
"CHOSEN ONE."
WHOA.

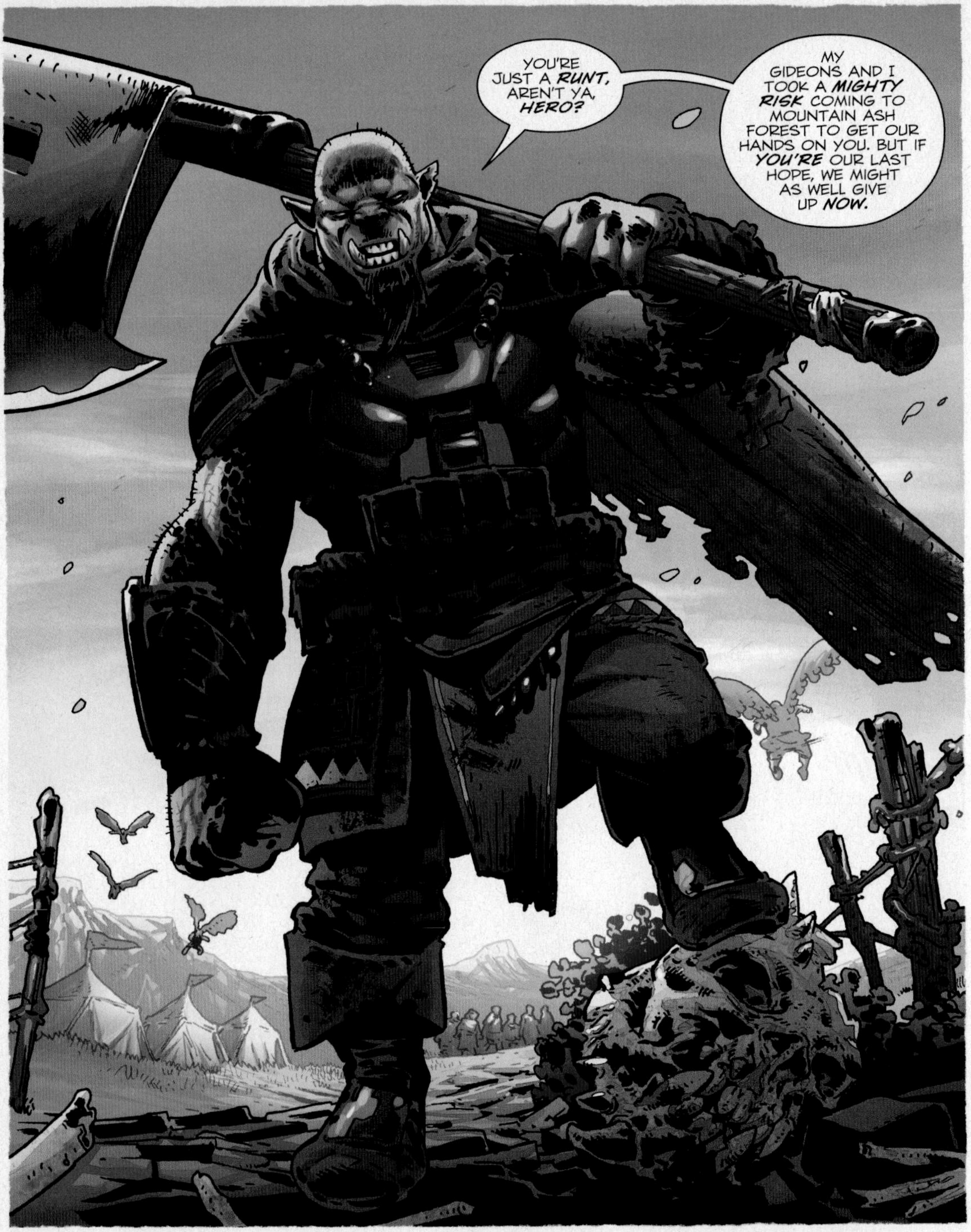
YOU'RE JUST A *RUNT,* AREN'T YA, *HERO?*
MY GIDEONS AND I TOOK A *MIGHTY RISK* COMING TO MOUNTAIN ASH FOREST TO GET OUR HANDS ON YOU. BUT IF *YOU'RE* OUR LAST HOPE, WE MIGHT AS WELL GIVE UP *NOW.*

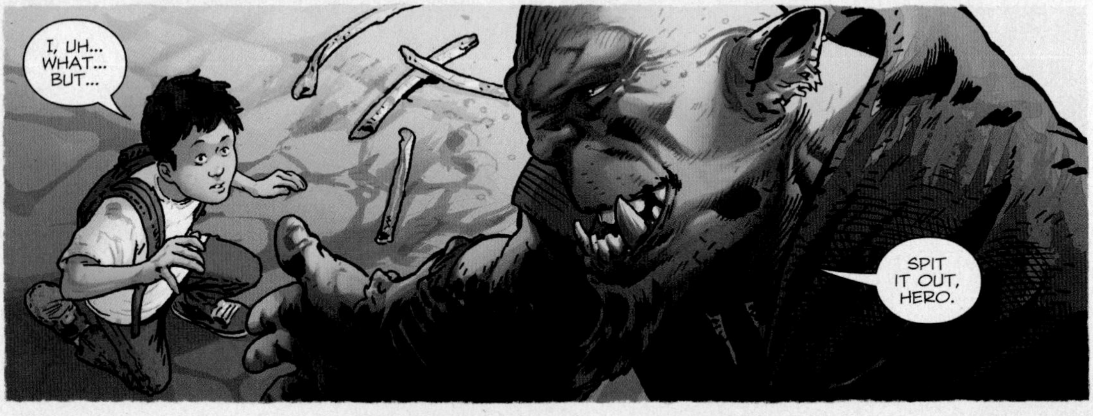
I, UH... WHAT... BUT...
SPIT IT OUT, HERO.

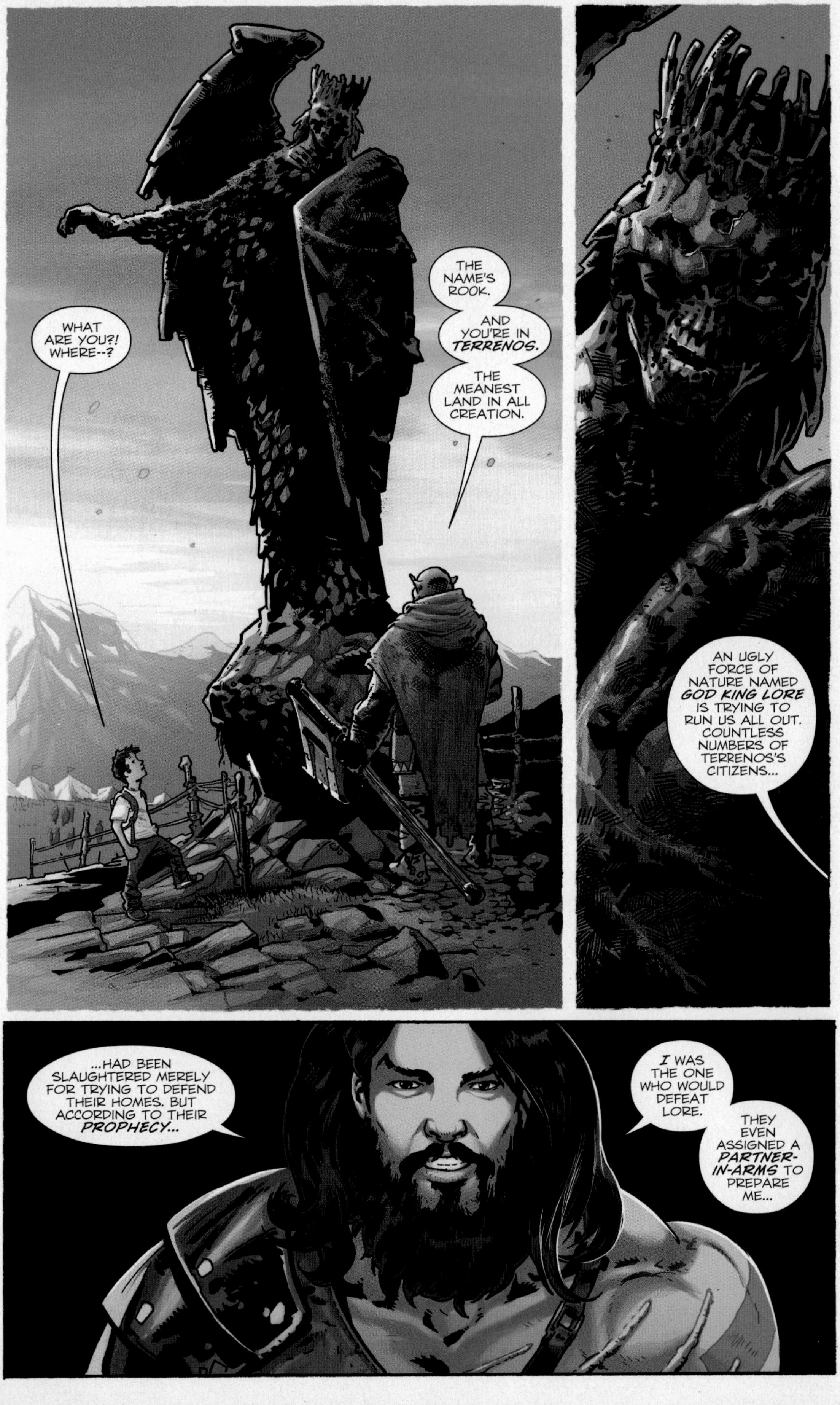
WHAT ARE YOU?! WHERE--?
THE NAME'S ROOK.
AND YOU'RE IN *TERRENOS.*
THE MEANEST LAND IN ALL CREATION.
AN UGLY FORCE OF NATURE NAMED **GOD KING LORE** IS TRYING TO RUN US ALL OUT. COUNTLESS NUMBERS OF TERRENOS'S CITIZENS...
...HAD BEEN SLAUGHTERED MERELY FOR TRYING TO DEFEND THEIR HOMES. BUT ACCORDING TO THEIR ***PROPHECY...***
I WAS THE ONE WHO WOULD DEFEAT LORE.
THEY EVEN ASSIGNED A ***PARTNER-IN-ARMS*** TO PREPARE ME...

RYA, YOU'RE ON SQUAB DUTY. MAKE SURE OUR LITTLE HERO HERE DOESN'T GET EATEN BEFORE WE GET TO THE SWAMPS OF SERENITY.
ROOK?! NO! WHY ME?? HE'LL ONLY SLOW ME DOWN!
I'M NOT SLOW! I CAN BEAT ANY GIRL IN A RACE! EASY!
HA. YOU HEARD THE LAD. HE'LL KEEP UP.

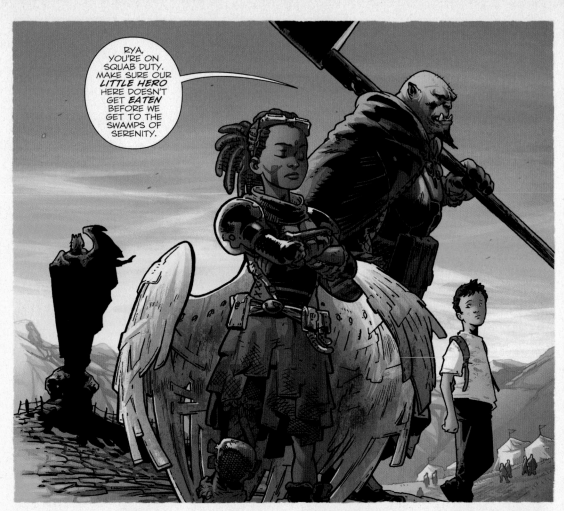

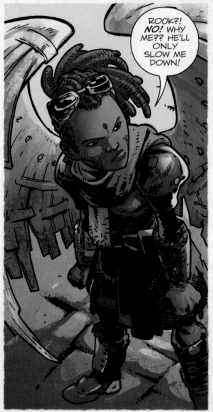

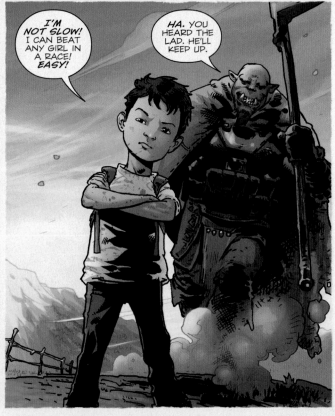

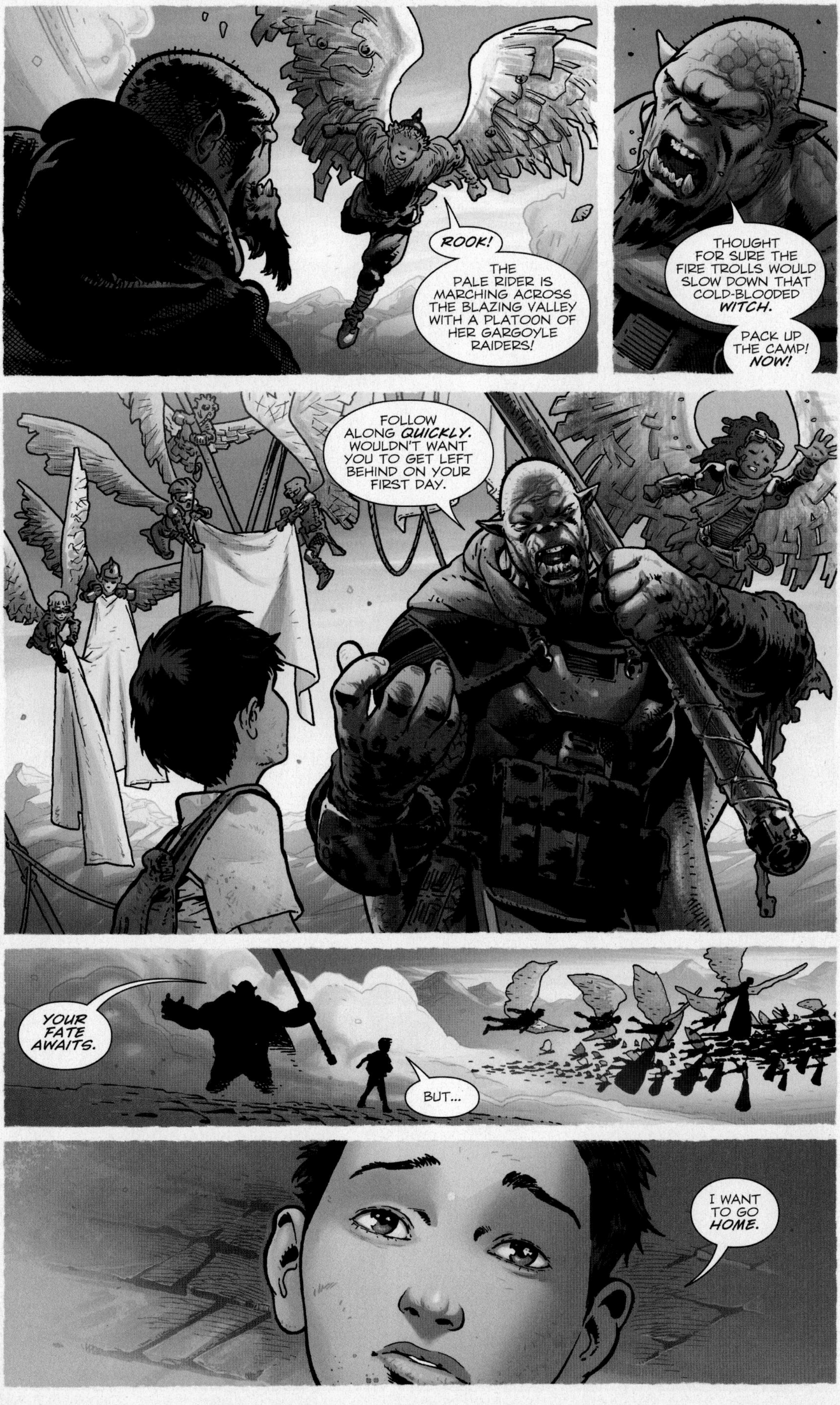
ROOK!
THE PALE RIDER IS MARCHING ACROSS THE BLAZING VALLEY WITH A PLATOON OF HER GARGOYLE RAIDERS!
THOUGHT FOR SURE THE FIRE TROLLS WOULD SLOW DOWN THAT COLD-BLOODED WITCH.
PACK UP THE CAMP! NOW!
FOLLOW ALONG QUICKLY. WOULDN'T WANT YOU TO GET LEFT BEHIND ON YOUR FIRST DAY.
YOUR FATE AWAITS.
BUT...
I WANT TO GO HOME.

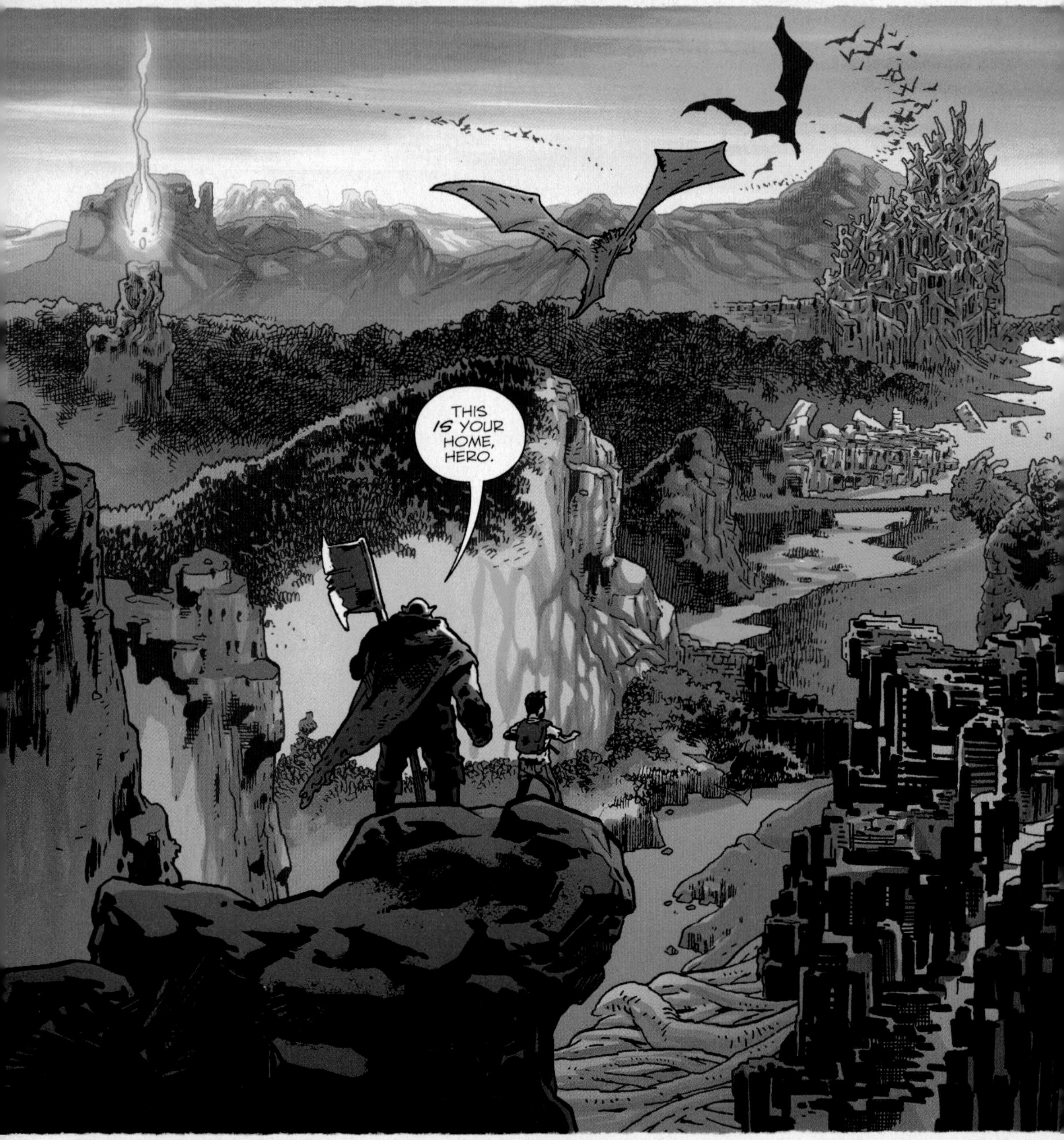
THIS IS YOUR HOME, HERO.

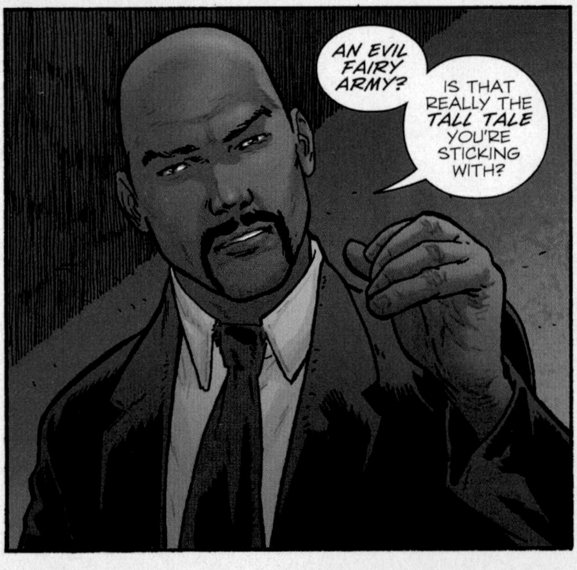
AN EVIL FAIRY ARMY?
IS THAT REALLY THE TALL TALE YOU'RE STICKING WITH?

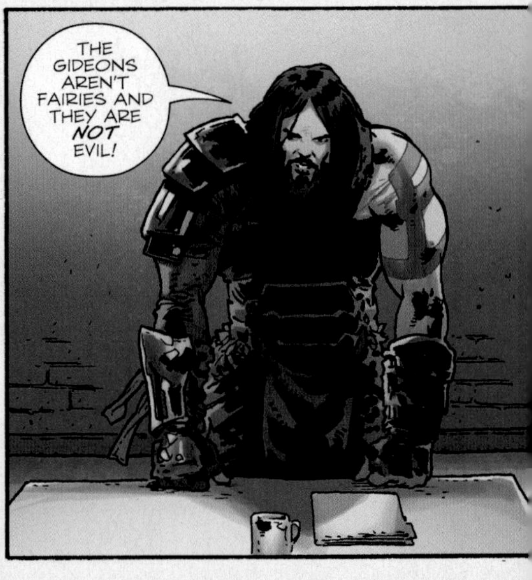
THE GIDEONS AREN'T FAIRIES AND THEY ARE NOT EVIL!

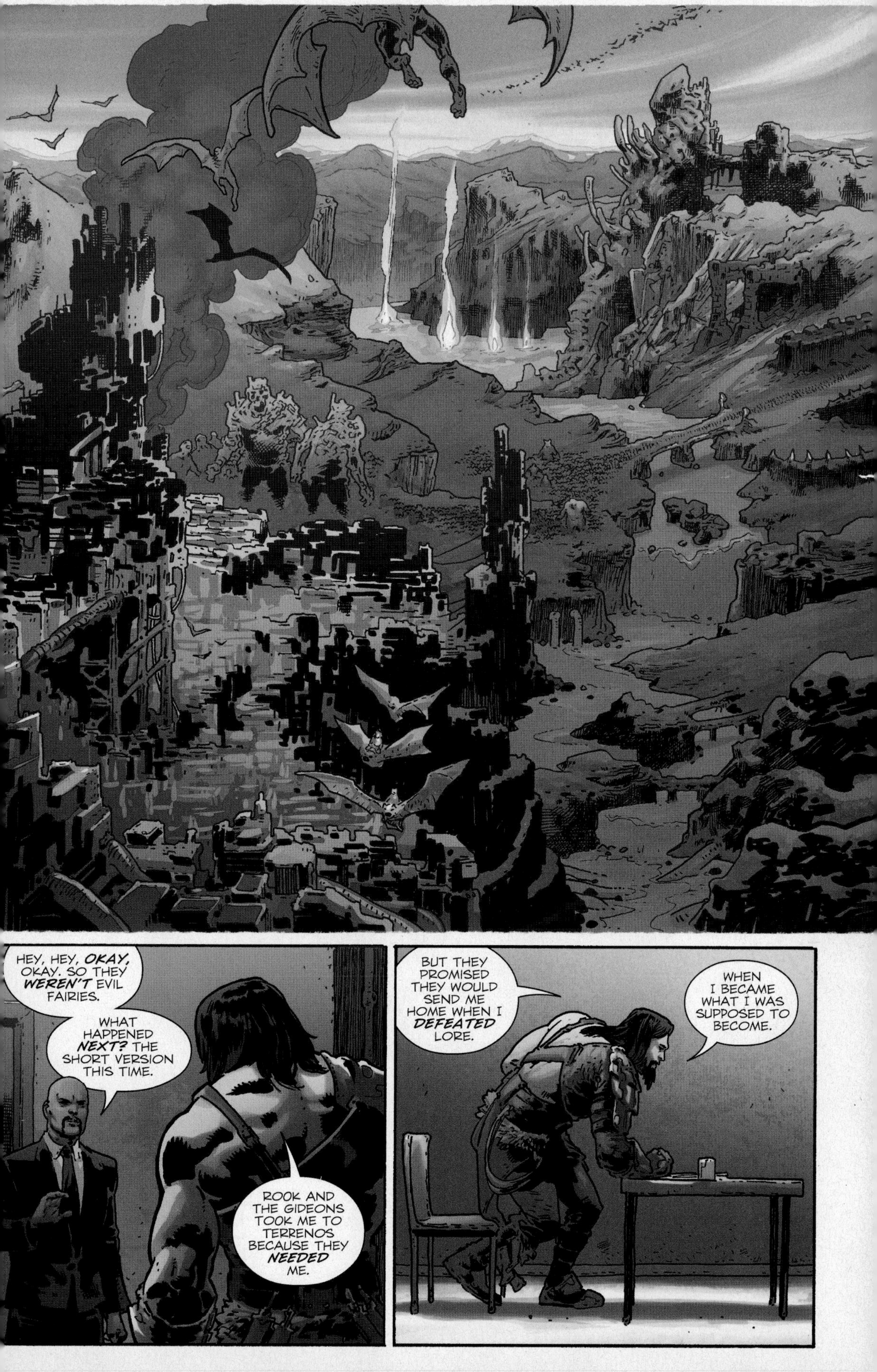
HEY, HEY, OKAY, OKAY. SO THEY WEREN'T EVIL FAIRIES.
WHAT HAPPENED NEXT? THE SHORT VERSION THIS TIME.
ROOK AND THE GIDEONS TOOK ME TO TERRENOS BECAUSE THEY NEEDED ME.
BUT THEY PROMISED THEY WOULD SEND ME HOME WHEN I DEFEATED LORE.
WHEN I BECAME WHAT I WAS SUPPOSED TO BECOME.

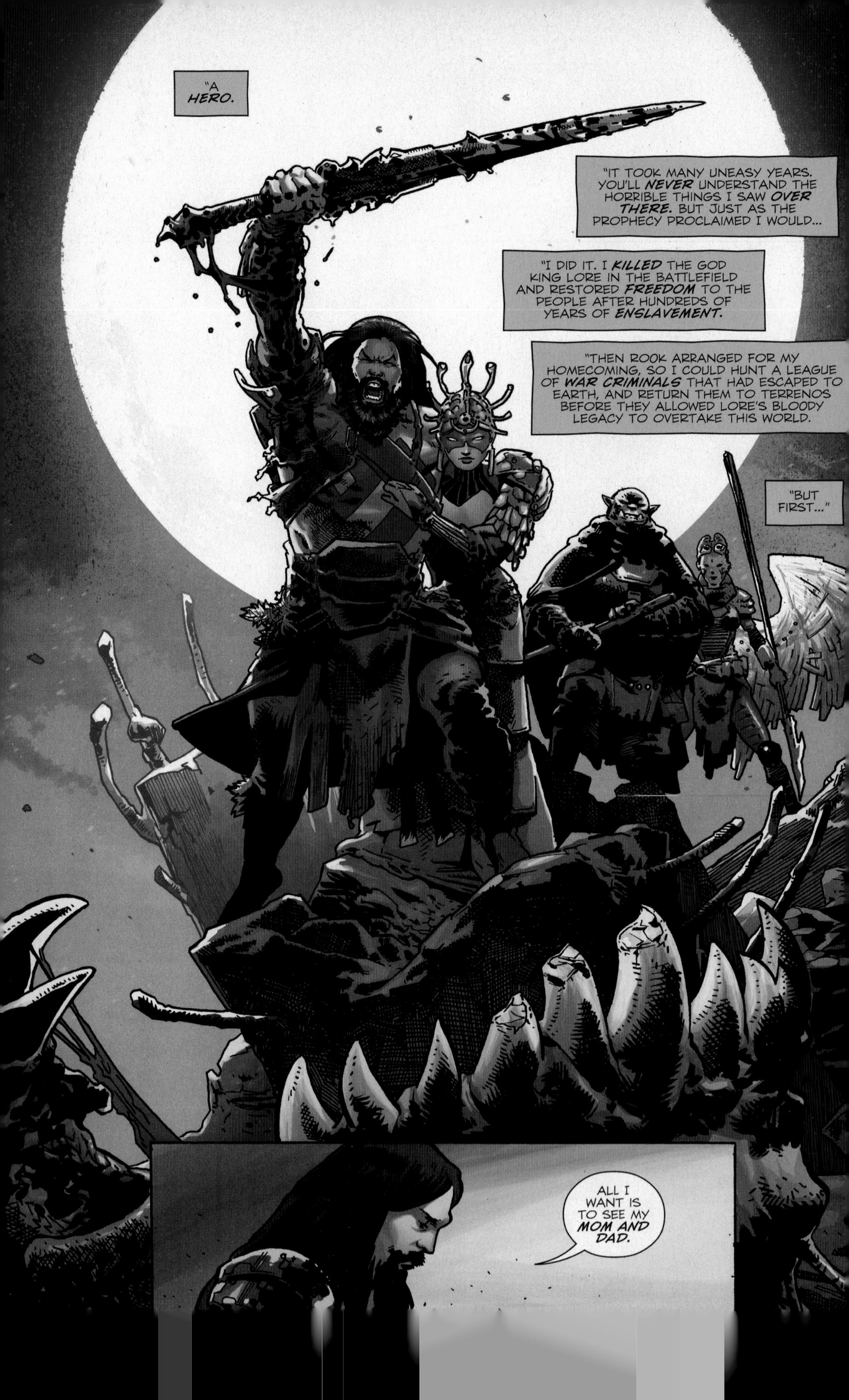
"A HERO.
"IT TOOK MANY UNEASY YEARS. YOU'LL NEVER UNDERSTAND THE HORRIBLE THINGS I SAW OVER THERE. BUT JUST AS THE PROPHECY PROCLAIMED I WOULD...
"I DID IT. I KILLED THE GOD KING LORE IN THE BATTLEFIELD AND RESTORED FREEDOM TO THE PEOPLE AFTER HUNDREDS OF YEARS OF ENSLAVEMENT.
"THEN ROOK ARRANGED FOR MY HOMECOMING, SO I COULD HUNT A LEAGUE OF WAR CRIMINALS THAT HAD ESCAPED TO EARTH, AND RETURN THEM TO TERRENOS BEFORE THEY ALLOWED LORE'S BLOODY LEGACY TO OVERTAKE THIS WORLD.
"BUT FIRST..."
ALL I WANT IS TO SEE MY MOM AND DAD.

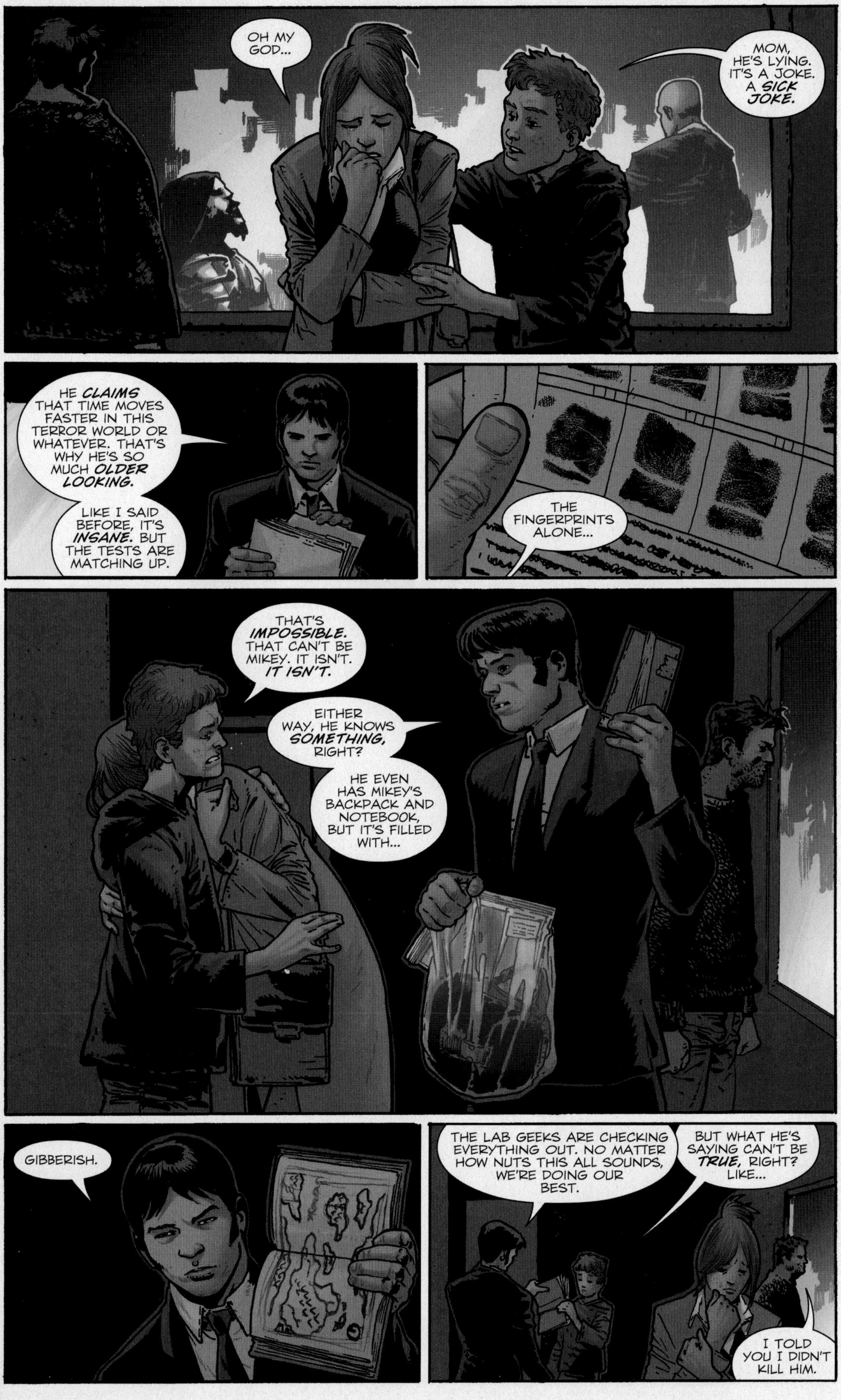
OH MY GOD...
MOM, HE'S LYING. IT'S A JOKE. A SICK JOKE.
HE CLAIMS THAT TIME MOVES FASTER IN THIS TERROR WORLD OR WHATEVER. THAT'S WHY HE'S SO MUCH OLDER LOOKING.
LIKE I SAID BEFORE, IT'S INSANE. BUT THE TESTS ARE MATCHING UP.
THE FINGERPRINTS ALONE...
THAT'S IMPOSSIBLE. THAT CAN'T BE MIKEY. IT ISN'T. IT ISN'T.
EITHER WAY, HE KNOWS SOMETHING, RIGHT?
HE EVEN HAS MIKEY'S BACKPACK AND NOTEBOOK, BUT IT'S FILLED WITH...
GIBBERISH.
THE LAB GEEKS ARE CHECKING EVERYTHING OUT. NO MATTER HOW NUTS THIS ALL SOUNDS, WE'RE DOING OUR BEST.
BUT WHAT HE'S SAYING CAN'T BE TRUE, RIGHT? LIKE...
I TOLD YOU I DIDN'T KILL HIM.

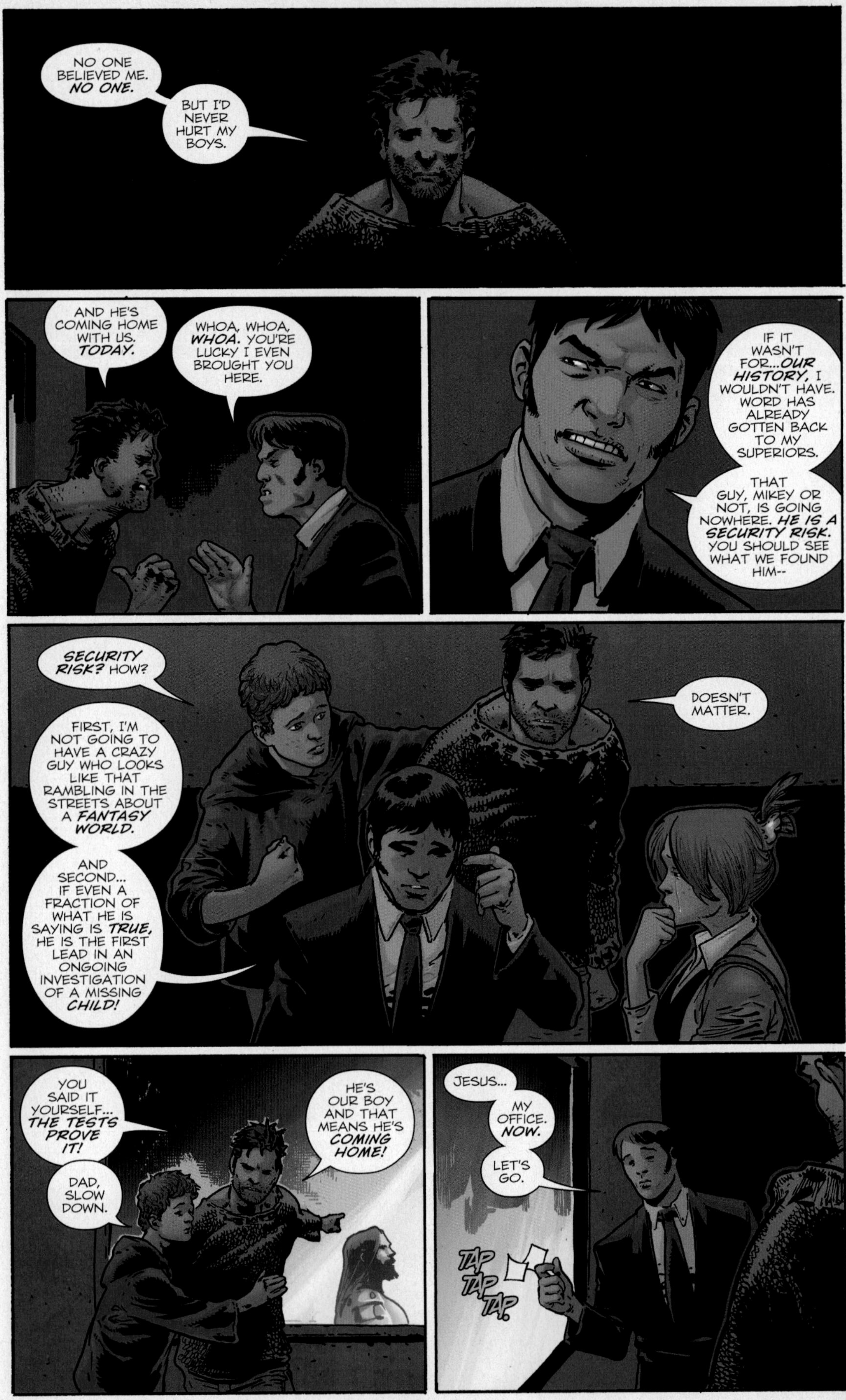
NO ONE BELIEVED ME. NO ONE.
BUT I'D NEVER HURT MY BOYS.
AND HE'S COMING HOME WITH US. TODAY.
WHOA, WHOA, WHOA. YOU'RE LUCKY I EVEN BROUGHT YOU HERE.
IF IT WASN'T FOR...OUR HISTORY, I WOULDN'T HAVE. WORD HAS ALREADY GOTTEN BACK TO MY SUPERIORS.
THAT GUY, MIKEY OR NOT, IS GOING NOWHERE. HE IS A SECURITY RISK. YOU SHOULD SEE WHAT WE FOUND HIM--
SECURITY RISK? HOW?
DOESN'T MATTER.
FIRST, I'M NOT GOING TO HAVE A CRAZY GUY WHO LOOKS LIKE THAT RAMBLING IN THE STREETS ABOUT A FANTASY WORLD.
AND SECOND... IF EVEN A FRACTION OF WHAT HE IS SAYING IS TRUE, HE IS THE FIRST LEAD IN AN ONGOING INVESTIGATION OF A MISSING CHILD!
YOU SAID IT YOURSELF... THE TESTS PROVE IT!
HE'S OUR BOY AND THAT MEANS HE'S COMING HOME!
DAD, SLOW DOWN.
JESUS...
MY OFFICE. NOW.
LET'S GO.
TAP TAP TAP.

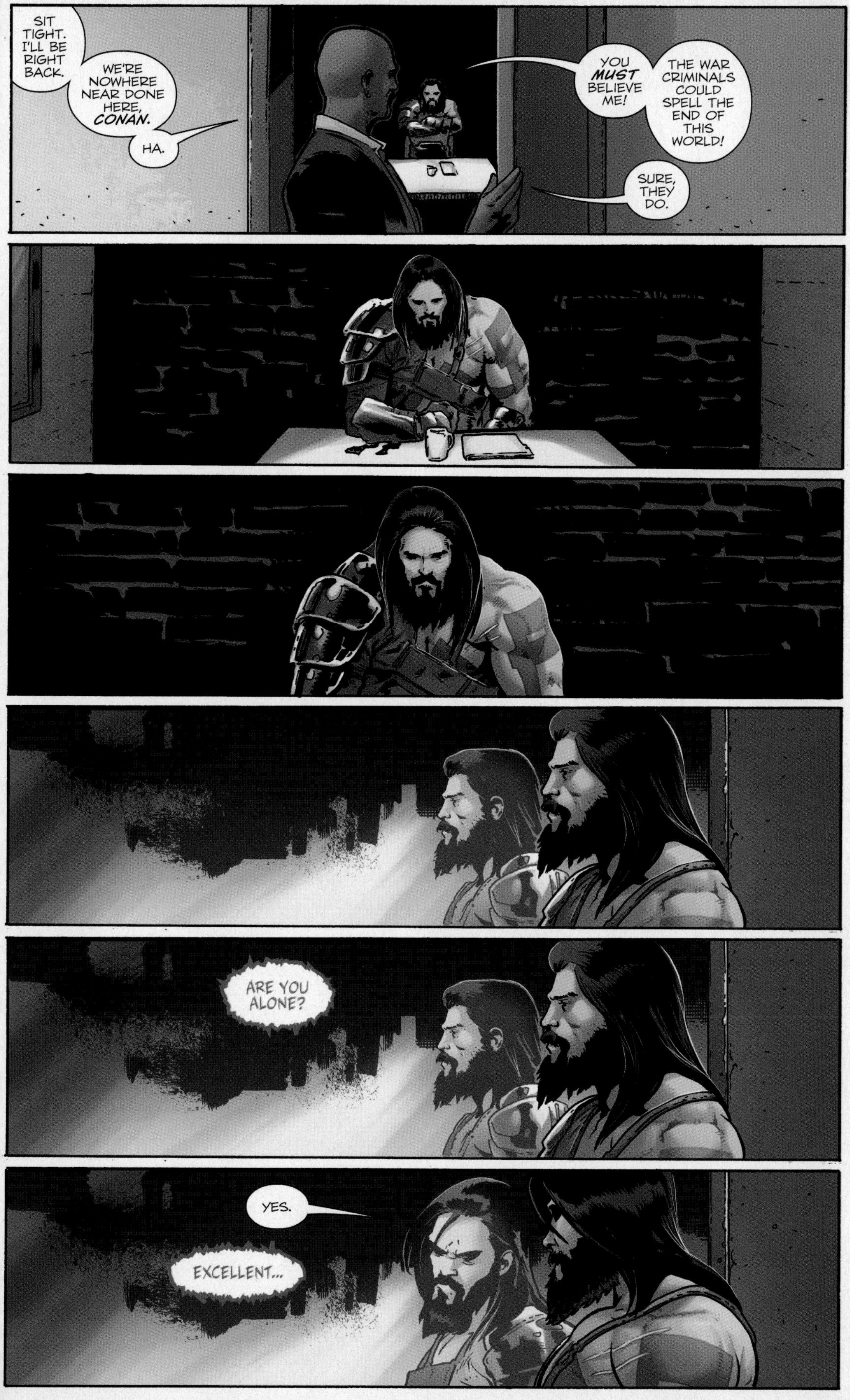
SIT TIGHT. I'LL BE RIGHT BACK.
WE'RE NOWHERE NEAR DONE HERE, CONAN.
HA.
YOU MUST BELIEVE ME!
THE WAR CRIMINALS COULD SPELL THE END OF THIS WORLD!
SURE, THEY DO.
ARE YOU ALONE?
YES.
EXCELLENT...

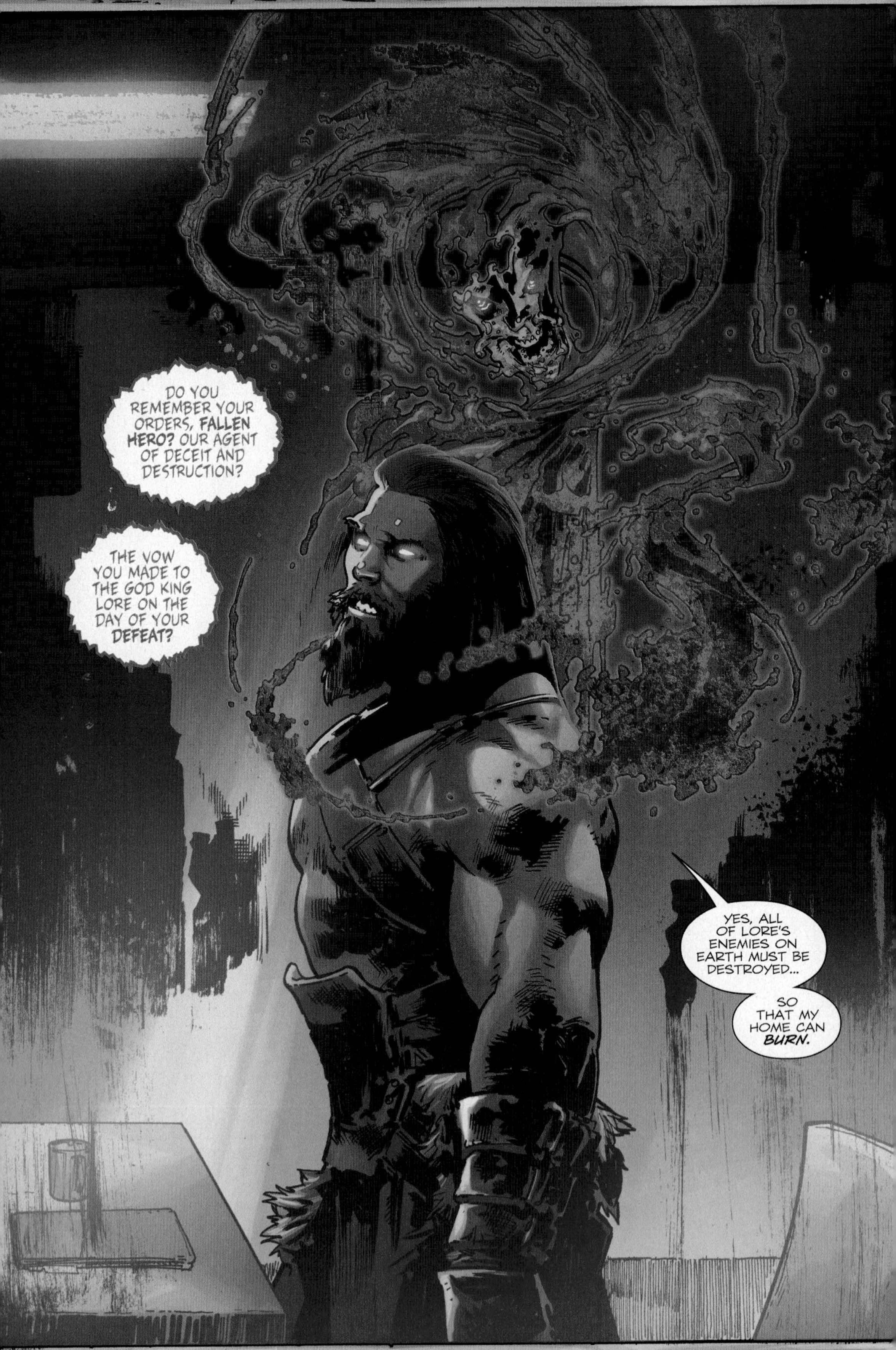
DO YOU REMEMBER YOUR ORDERS, **FALLEN HERO?** OUR AGENT OF DECEIT AND DESTRUCTION?
THE VOW YOU MADE TO THE GOD KING LORE ON THE DAY OF YOUR **DEFEAT?**
YES, ALL OF LORE'S ENEMIES ON EARTH MUST BE DESTROYED...
SO THAT MY HOME CAN ***BURN.***

send letters to BIRTHRIGHT@SKYBOUND.COM

WHEN I WAS A KID I GOT INTO TROUBLE ALL THE TIME.

he cause of this?

dventure.

Iy friends and I were always trying to relive Stand y Me. We wanted to be Goonies. We hoped there ould be monsters in the dark so we could be a real fe Monster Squad. We wanted to find urban legends. f we thought we had a treasure map, we'd follow it. If e heard about a castle, we'd find it. We were like this ecause of the stories of my youth:

he NeverEnding Story, Peter Pan, The Lion, the Vitch and the Wardrobe, Dark Crystal, Legend, abyrinth, Charlie and the Chocolate Factory, Vizard of Oz, E.T....

tories that took kids that were just like me and ent them to faraway lands full of more than just dventure... but the supernatural, the odd, and the ntastical.

ut there was one thing that always bugged me about ose stories...

hese kids would get to go on these great adventures... ut they never had to deal with the consequences. Ve never really got to see what happened when they ot home. How do you go back to living a normal life fter something like that? Go back to school when ou know there is a great big world out there? And ow do you sleep at night knowing that the stuff of ightmares is real? After you battle a dragon or sail ith pirates or defeat an evil witch... how do you go ack to just being a kid?

hat is how the idea of BIRTHRIGHT started. What happened after the adventure was over? What o you do next?

his is that story.

Ve've been working on this book for a long time. I rst started to put this book together back in 2007, ut it just never clicked. It was missing pieces. An ndercooked idea. Maybe I was just too young to ally grasp the size of the story I wanted to tell. And it wasn't until Skybound got involved that this really started to take shape. That was when the concepts of destiny started to play a larger part. If I told you that your entire life was about one moment—you were put on this world for one thing—and it's all you'd ever be... and you accomplished that one thing... what do you do next? It fit so well in our theme of the journey after the adventure that the book finally came together.

Then we got Andrei Bressan, who made the world come to life with his amazing pages and designs. The energy he brings to this book is unmatched and fueled us. Adriano Lucas came on with the colors and blew us all away. It's amazing, right?

To say that BIRTHRIGHT is a labor of love is an understatement.

Without hesitation, this is the most work I've ever put into a book. The amount of world building and character work has been intense. But I hope you agree that it's all been worth it.

But there is one thing I left out. As much as BIRTHRIGHT is about adventure and fantasy and the hero's journey... it's about family.

Fathers and sons, wives and sons, husbands and wives, and... brothers. The adventures we go on together as a family.

Making comics has been a dream come true for me. And BIRTHRIGHT is in a lot of ways the acumination of those dreams. Just look at the package we put together for this first issue! Skybound, myself and the rest of the creative team put a lot of work into this series... it was an investment in the story... and with you, the reader.

If you stick with us, we promise to always put this level of quality into every issue.

Go on this adventure with us.

Let's see if we can get into some trouble.

JOSHUA WILLIAMSON
Portland, Oregon
September 15th, 2014

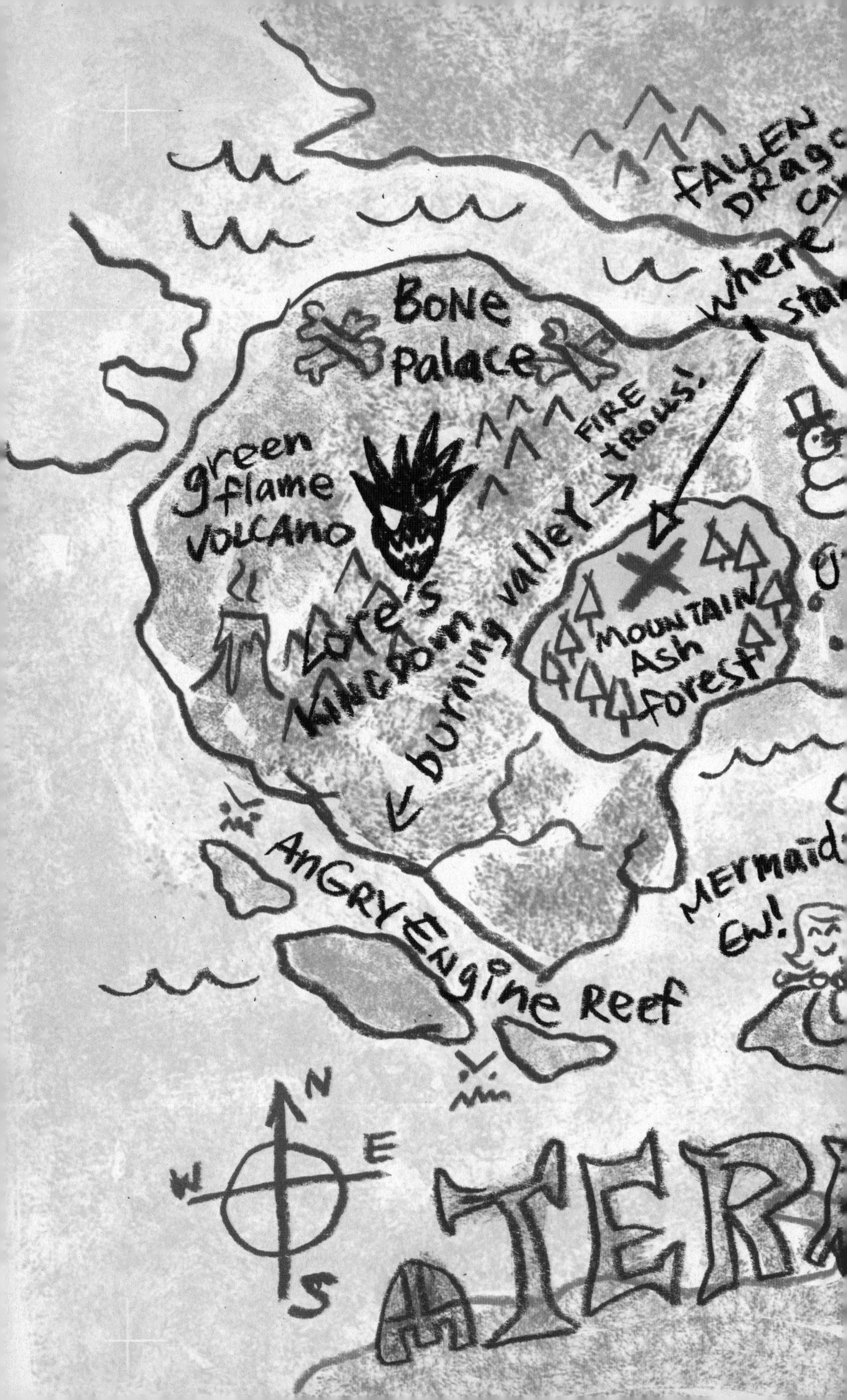
FALLEN DRAG
where I sta
BONE Palace
FIRE TROLLS!
green flame VOLCANO
Lore's KINGDOM
burning valley
MOUNTAIN Ash forest
ANGRY Engine Reef
MERMAID
Ew!
N
E
W
S
TER

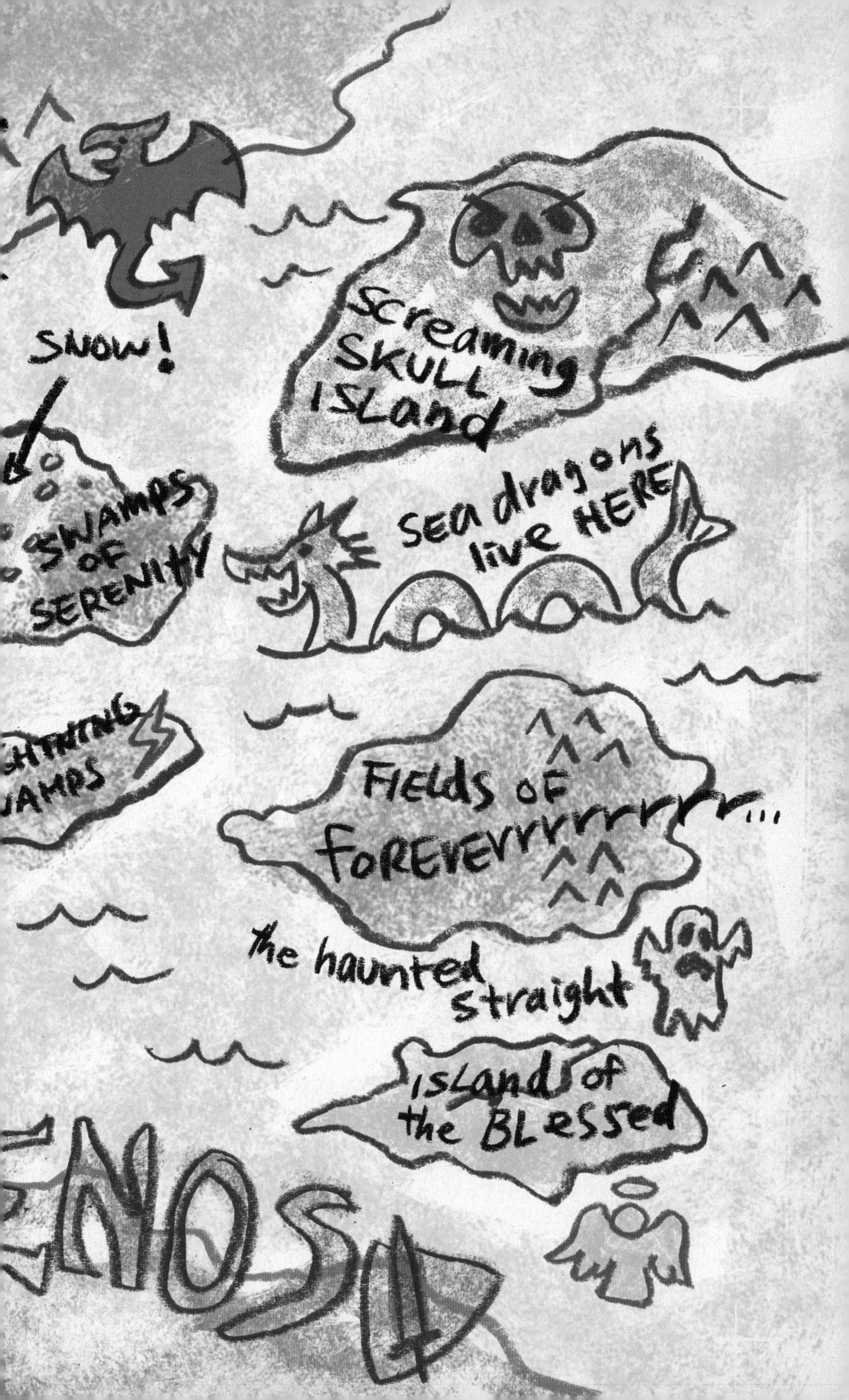
SNOW!
Screaming SKULL ISLand
SWAMPS OF SERENITY
Sea dragons live HERE
FIELDS OF foREverrrrrrrr...
the haunted straight
ISLand of the BLessed

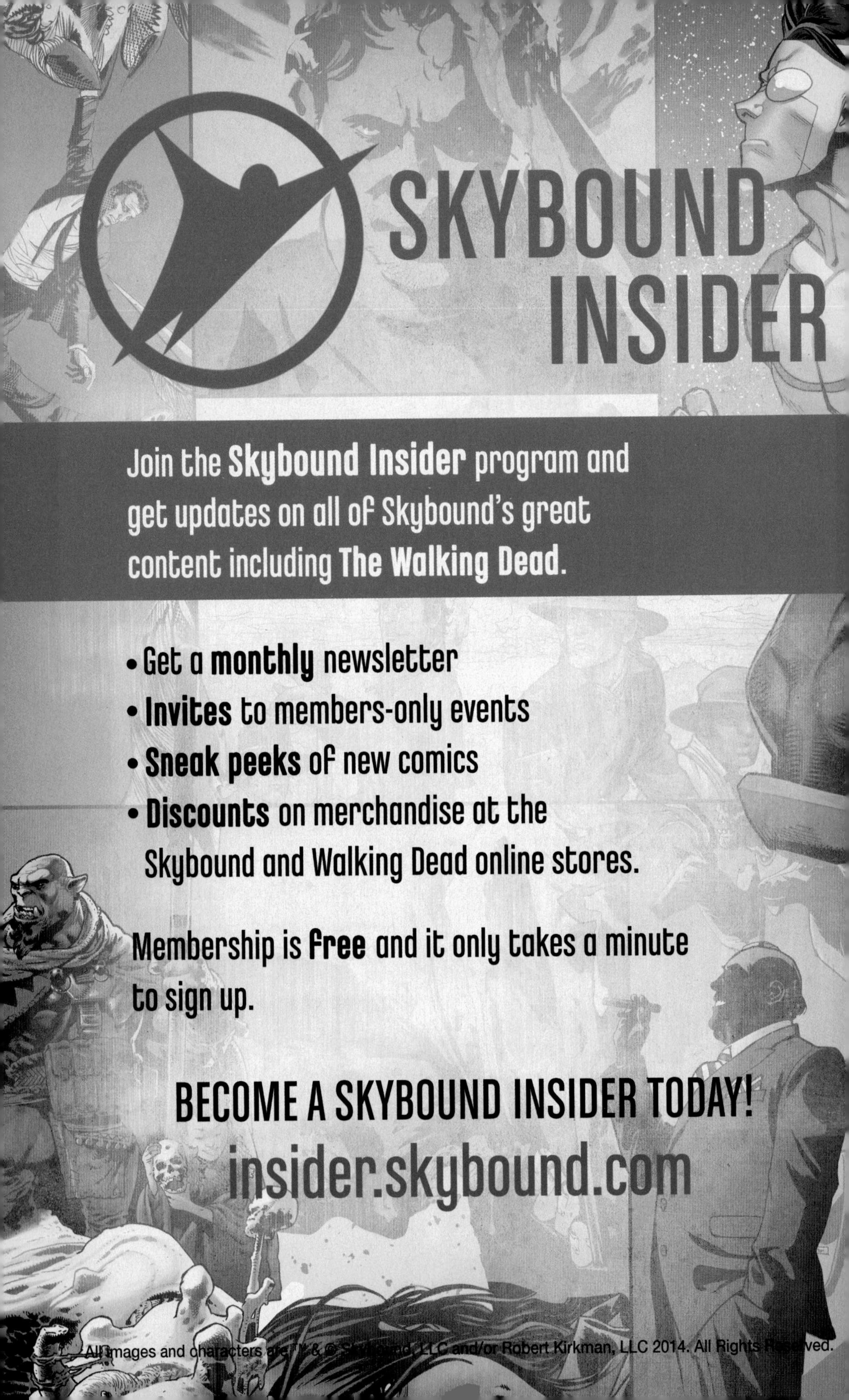
SKYBOUND
INSIDER
Join the Skybound Insider program and get updates on all of Skybound's great content including The Walking Dead.
• Get a monthly newsletter
• Invites to members-only events
• Sneak peeks of new comics
• Discounts on merchandise at the Skybound and Walking Dead online stores.
Membership is free and it only takes a minute to sign up.
BECOME A SKYBOUND INSIDER TODAY!
insider.skybound.com
All images and characters are ™ & © Skybound, LLC and/or Robert Kirkman, LLC 2014. All Rights Reserved.

COLLECTIONS BY JOSHUA WILLIAMSON

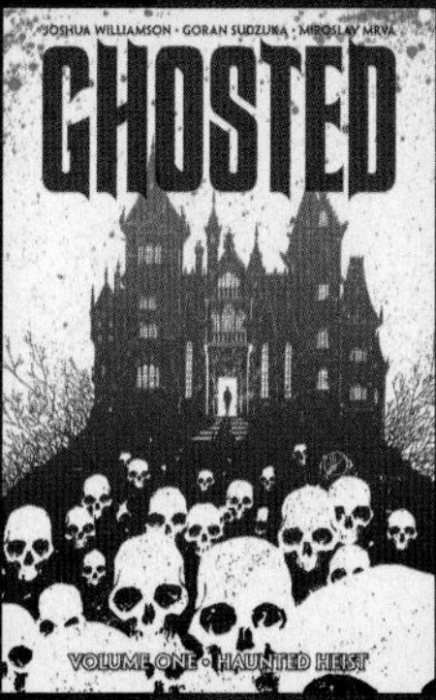
JOSHUA WILLIAMSON • GORAN SUDZUKA • MIROSLAV MRVA
GHOSTED
VOLUME ONE • HAUNTED HEIST

GHOSTED VOL. 1
978-1-60706-836-5
$9.99

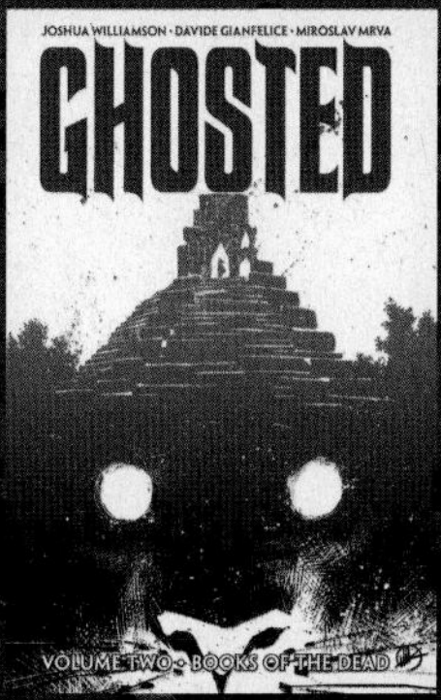
JOSHUA WILLIAMSON • DAVIDE GIANFELICE • MIROSLAV MRVA
GHOSTED
VOLUME TWO • BOOKS OF THE DEAD

GHOSTED VOL. 2
978-1-63215-046-2
$12.99

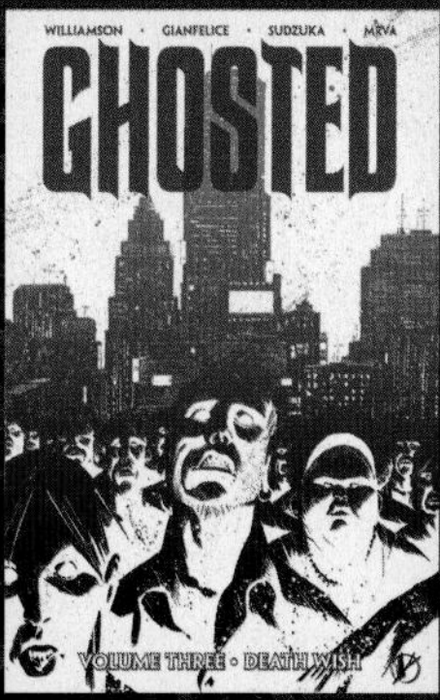
WILLIAMSON • GIANFELICE • SUDZUKA • MRVA
GHOSTED
VOLUME THREE • DEATH WISH

GHOSTED VOL. 3
978-1-60706-051-6
$12.99

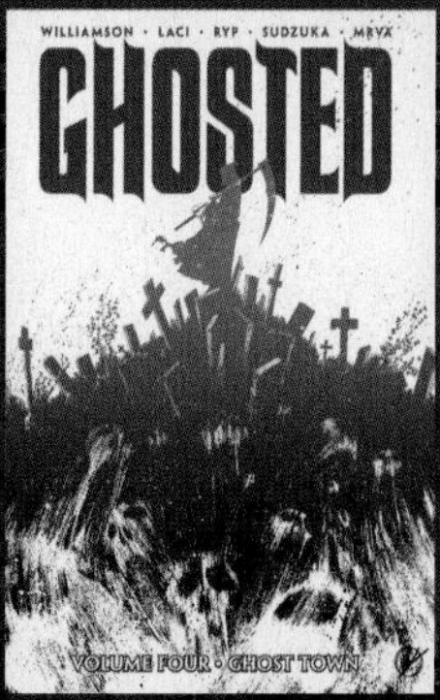
WILLIAMSON • LACI • RYP • SUDZUKA • MRVA
GHOSTED
VOLUME FOUR • GHOST TOWN

GHOSTED VOL. 4
978-1-63215-317-3
$12.99

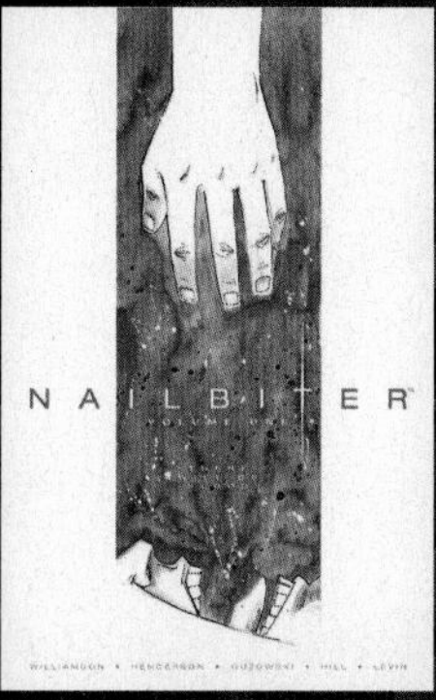
NAILBITER

NAILBITER VOL. 1
978-1-63215-112-4
$9.99

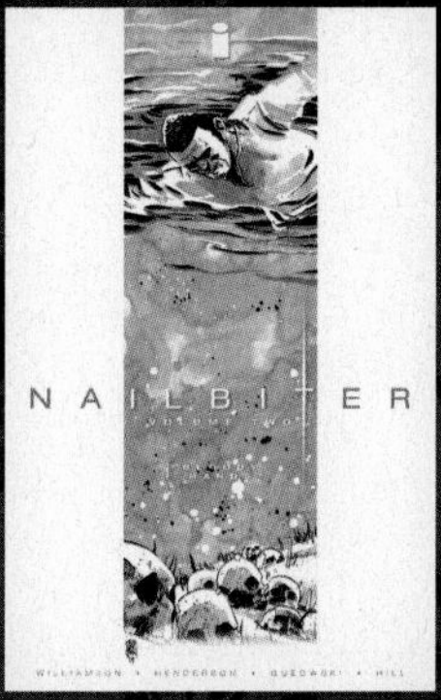
NAILBITER

NAILBITER VOL. 2
978-1-63215-232-9
$14.99

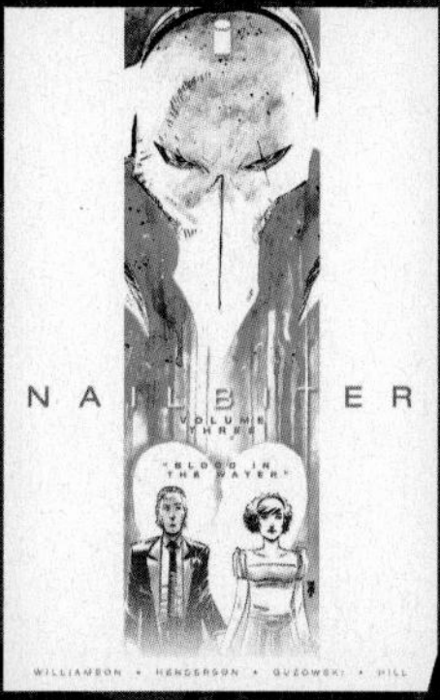
NAILBITER

NAILBITER VOL. 3
978-1-63215-485-9
$14.99

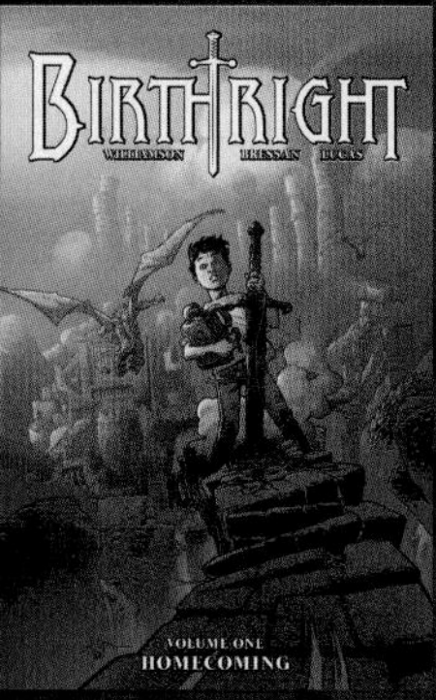
BIRTHRIGHT
WILLIAMSON BRESSAN LUCAS
VOLUME ONE
HOMECOMING

BIRTHRIGHT VOL. 1
978-1-63215-231-2
$9.99

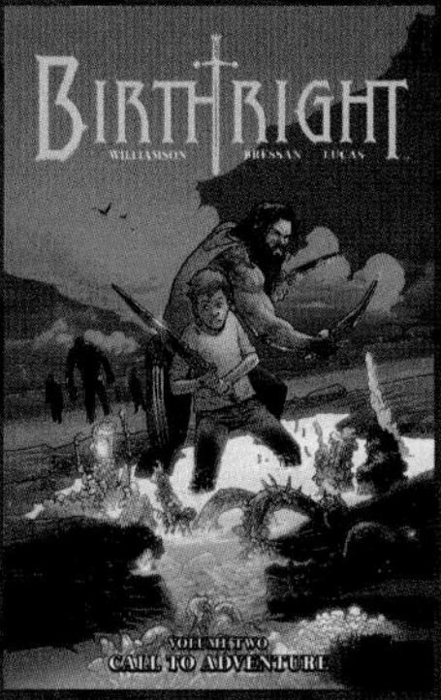
BIRTHRIGHT
WILLIAMSON BRESSAN LUCAS
VOLUME TWO
CALL TO ADVENTURE

BIRTHRIGHT VOL. 2
978-1-63215-446-0
$12.99

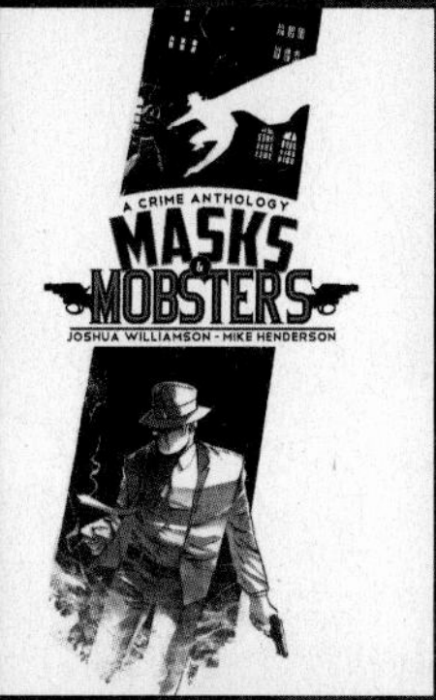
A CRIME ANTHOLOGY
MASKS & MOBSTERS
JOSHUA WILLIAMSON • MIKE HENDERSON

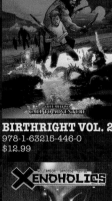

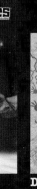

MASKS & MOBSTERS VOL. 1 HC
978-1-60706-765-8
$19.99

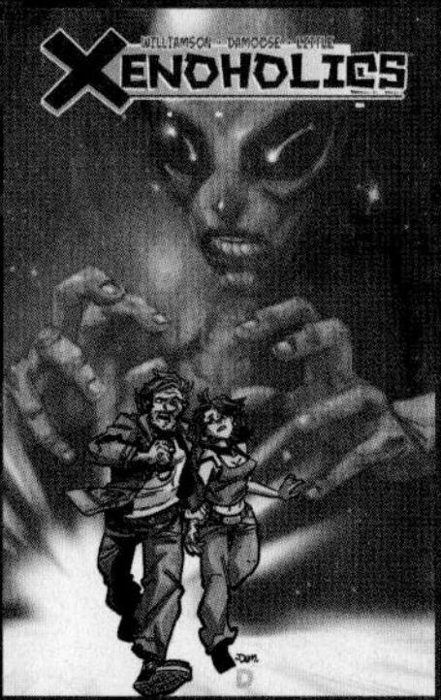
XENOHOLICS

XENOHOLICS
978-1-60706-557-9
$14.99

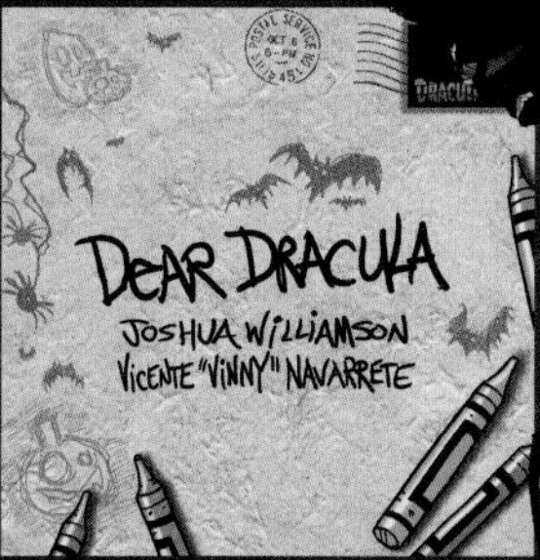
DEAR DRACULA
JOSHUA WILLIAMSON
VICENTE "VINNY" NAVARRETE

DEAR DRACULA
978-1-58240-970-2
$7.99

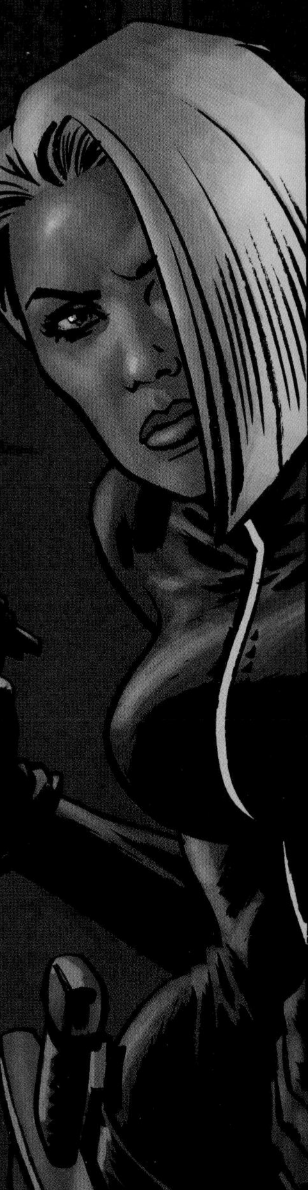

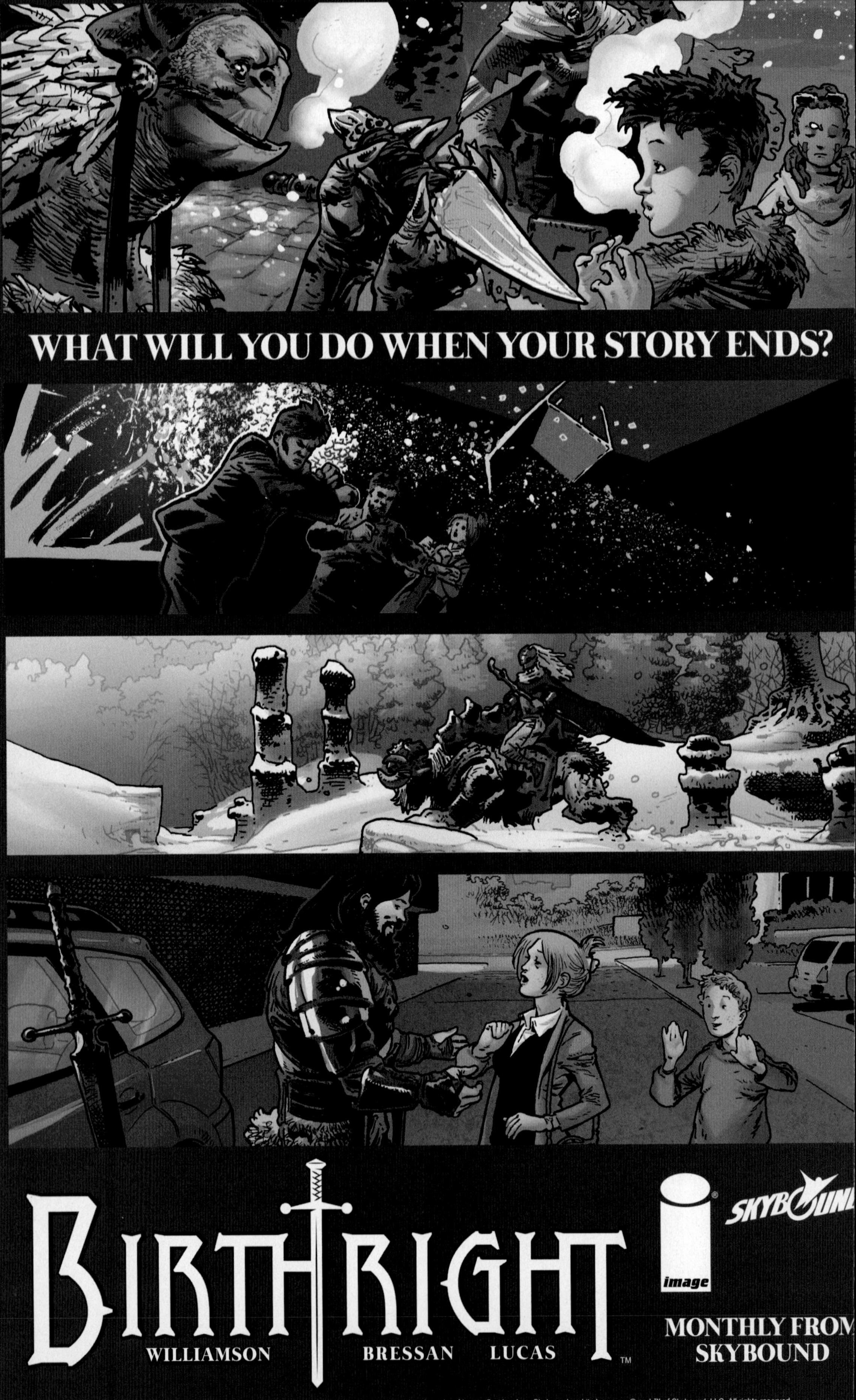
WHAT WILL YOU DO WHEN YOUR STORY ENDS?
BIRTHRIGHT
WILLIAMSON
BRESSAN
LUCAS
image
SKYBOUND
MONTHLY FROM SKYBOUND

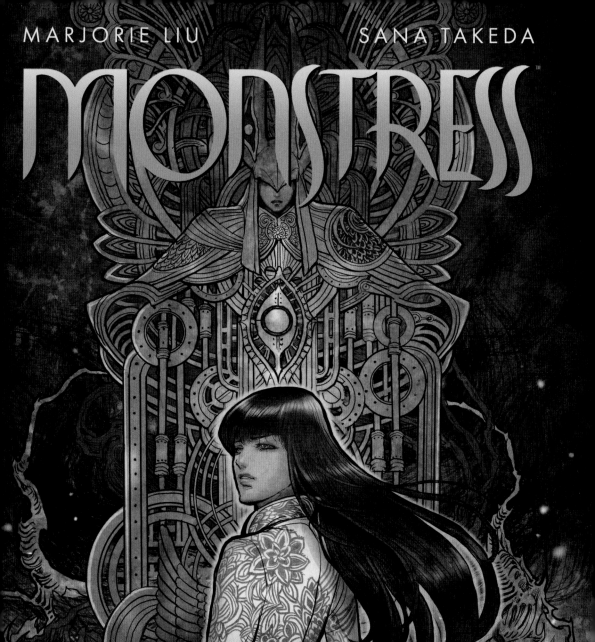

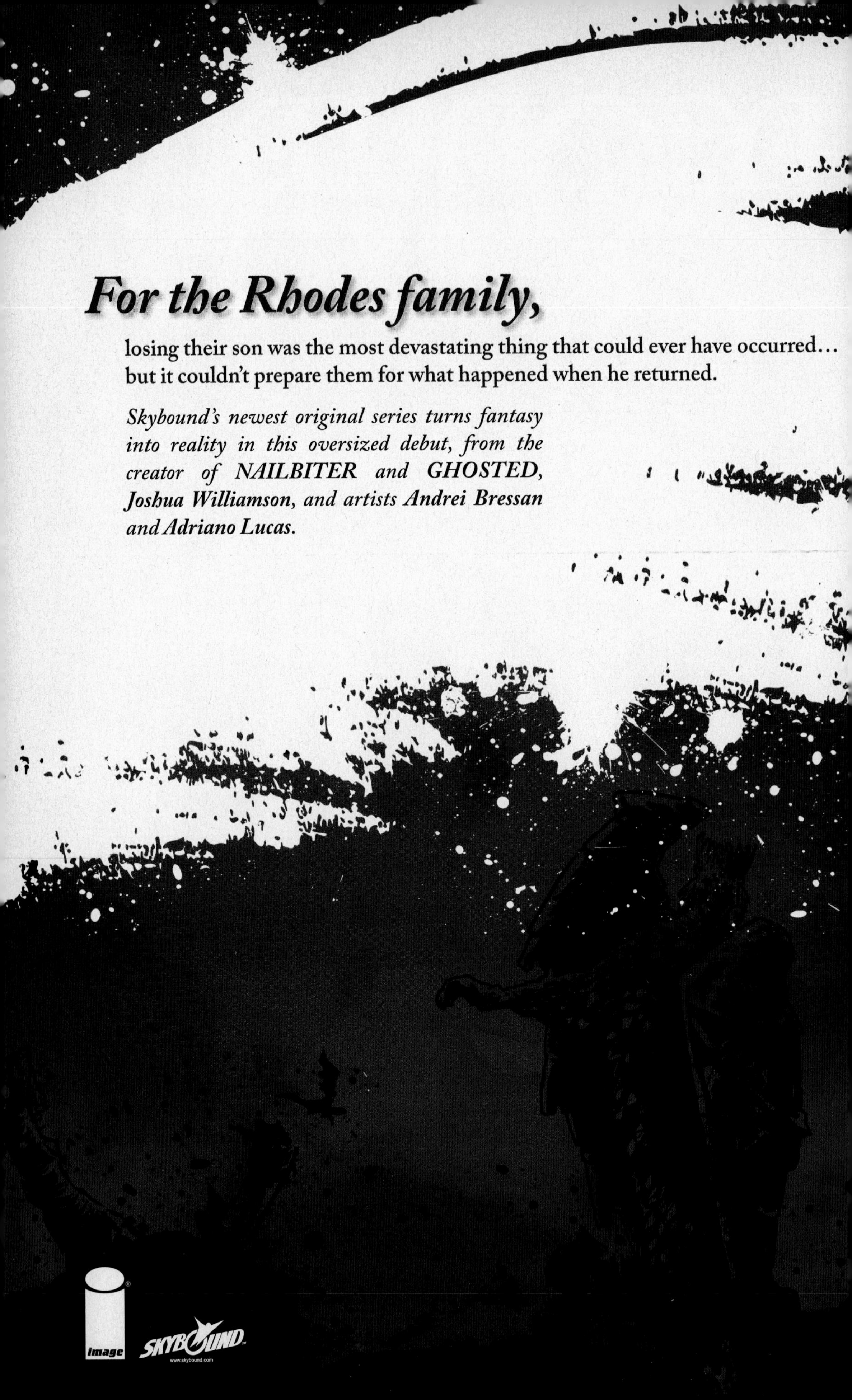
For the Rhodes family,
losing their son was the most devastating thing that could ever have occurred… but it couldn't prepare them for what happened when he returned.
Skybound's newest original series turns fantasy into reality in this oversized debut, from the creator of NAILBITER and GHOSTED, Joshua Williamson, and artists Andrei Bressan and Adriano Lucas.
image
SKYBOUND
www.skybound.com

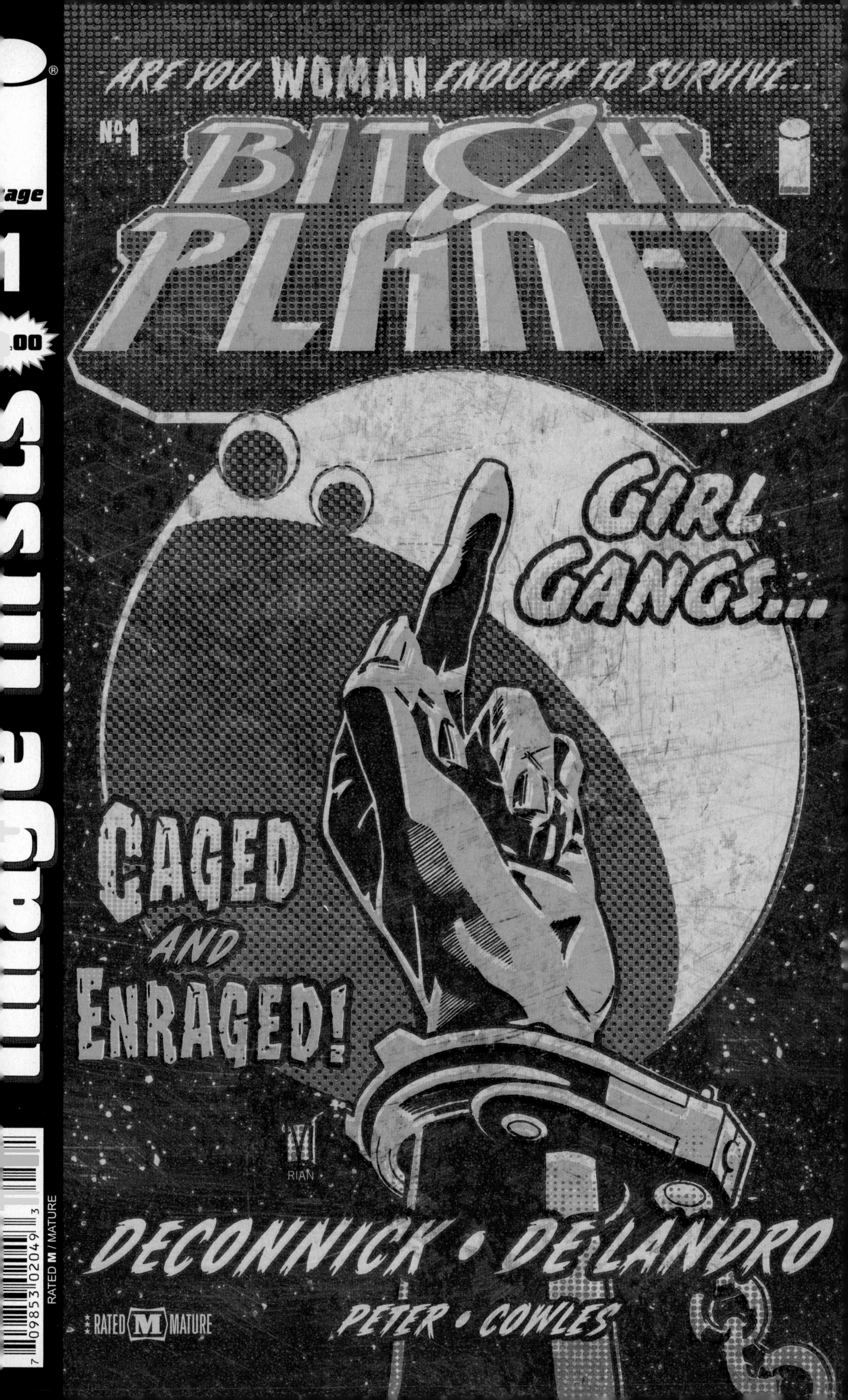
ARE YOU WOMAN ENOUGH TO SURVIVE...
Nº1
BITCH PLANET
GIRL GANGS...
CAGED AND ENRAGED!
RIAN
DECONNICK • DE LANDRO
PETER • COWLES
RATED M MATURE
image firsts
1
RATED M / MATURE

IMAGE COMICS, INC.

Robert Kirkman - Chief Operating Officer / Erik Larsen - Chief Financial Officer / Todd McFarlane - President / Marc Silvestri - Chief Executive Officer / Jim Valentino - Vice-President

Eric Stephenson - Publisher / Corey Murphy - Director of Sales / Jeff Boison - Director of Publishing Planning & Book Trade Sales / Jeremy Sullivan - Director of Digital Sales / Kat Salazar - Director of PR & Marketing / Emily Miller - Director of Operations / Branwyn Bigglestone - Senior Accounts Manager / Sarah Mello - Accounts Manager / Drew Gill - Art Director / Jonathan Chan - Production Manager / Meredith Wallace - Print Manager / Briah Skelly - Publicity Assistant / Randy Okamura - Marketing Production Designer / David Brothers - Branding Manager / Ally Power - Content Manager / Addison Duke - Production Artist / Vincent Kukua - Production Artist / Sasha Head - Production Artist / Tricia Ramos - Production Artist / Jeff Stang - Direct Market Sales Representative / Emilio Bautista - Digital Sales Associate / Chloe Ramos-Peterson - Administrative Assistant

IMAGECOMICS.COM

IMAGE FIRSTS: BITCH PLANET #1

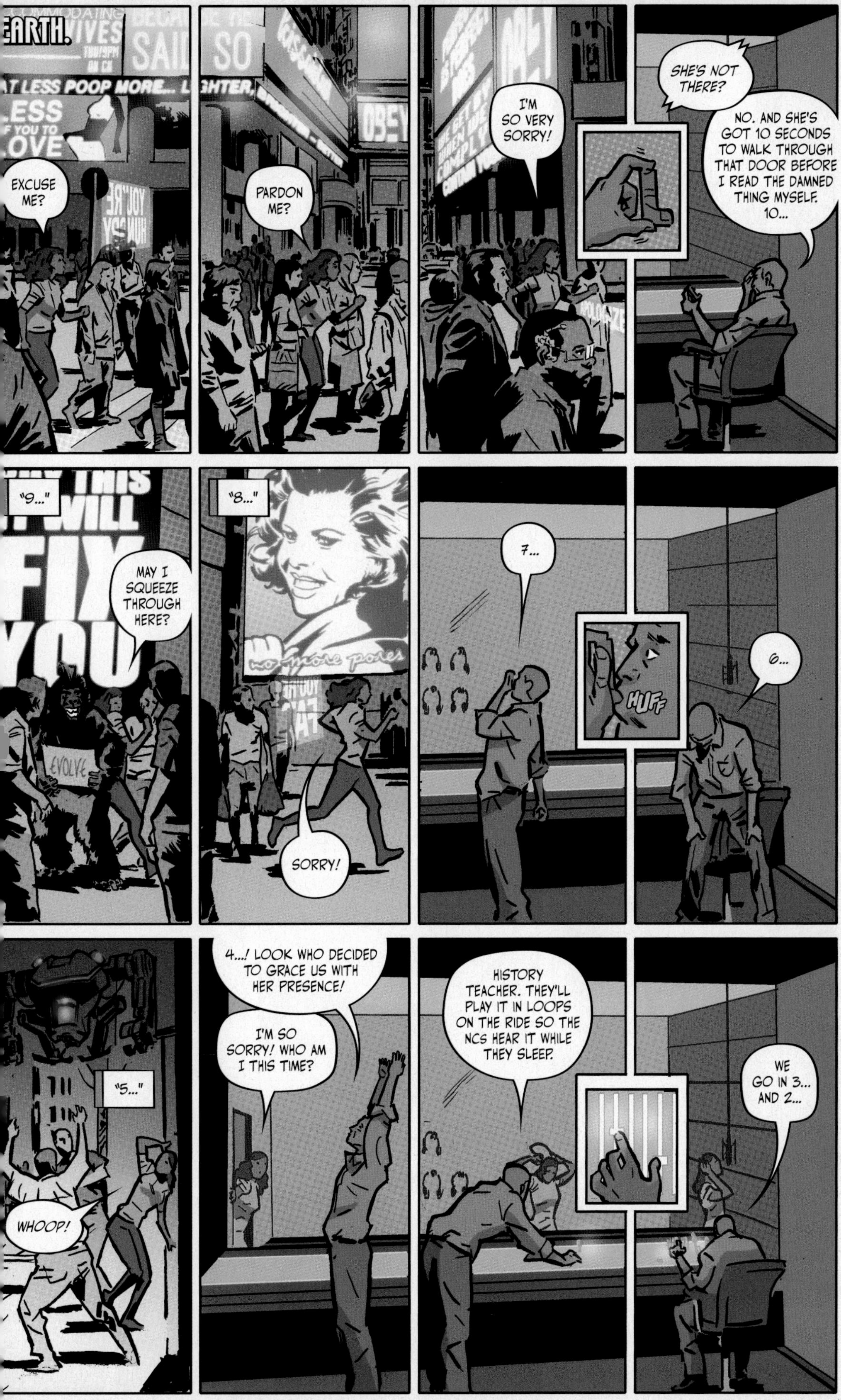

EARTH.
EXCUSE ME?
PARDON ME?
OBEY
I'M SO VERY SORRY!
APOLOGIZE
SHE'S NOT THERE?
NO. AND SHE'S GOT 10 SECONDS TO WALK THROUGH THAT DOOR BEFORE I READ THE DAMNED THING MYSELF. 10...
"9..."
FIX YOU
MAY I SQUEEZE THROUGH HERE?
EVOLVE
"8..."
no more pores
SORRY!
7...
HUFF
6...
"5..."
WHOOP!
4...! LOOK WHO DECIDED TO GRACE US WITH HER PRESENCE!
I'M SO SORRY! WHO AM I THIS TIME?
HISTORY TEACHER. THEY'LL PLAY IT IN LOOPS ON THE RIDE SO THE NCS HEAR IT WHILE THEY SLEEP.
WE GO IN 3... AND 2...

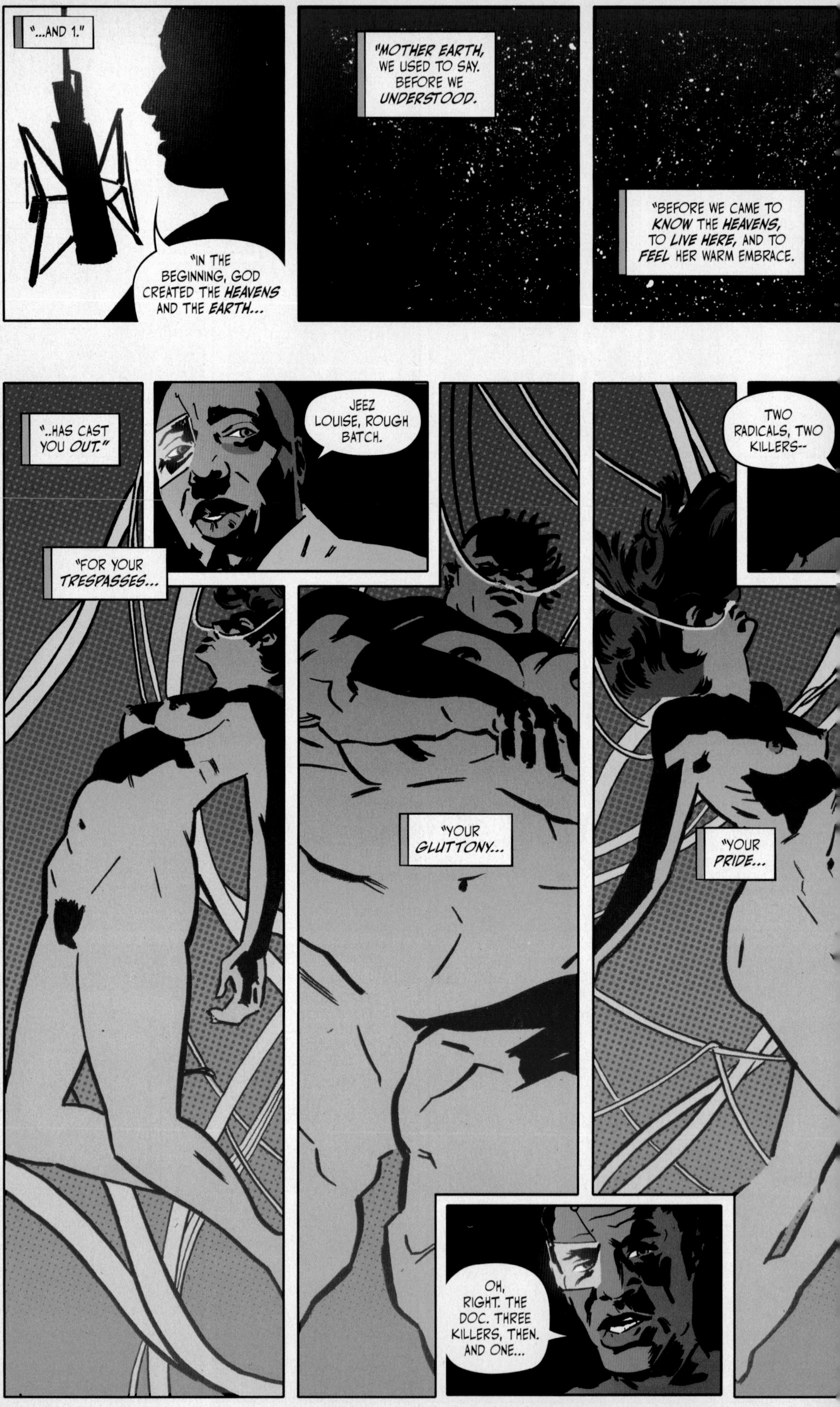
"...AND 1."
"IN THE BEGINNING, GOD CREATED THE HEAVENS AND THE EARTH...
"MOTHER EARTH, WE USED TO SAY. BEFORE WE UNDERSTOOD.
"BEFORE WE CAME TO KNOW THE HEAVENS, TO LIVE HERE, AND TO FEEL HER WARM EMBRACE.
"..HAS CAST YOU OUT."
JEEZ LOUISE, ROUGH BATCH.
TWO RADICALS, TWO KILLERS--
"FOR YOUR TRESPASSES...
"YOUR GLUTTONY...
"YOUR PRIDE...
OH, RIGHT. THE DOC. THREE KILLERS, THEN. AND ONE...

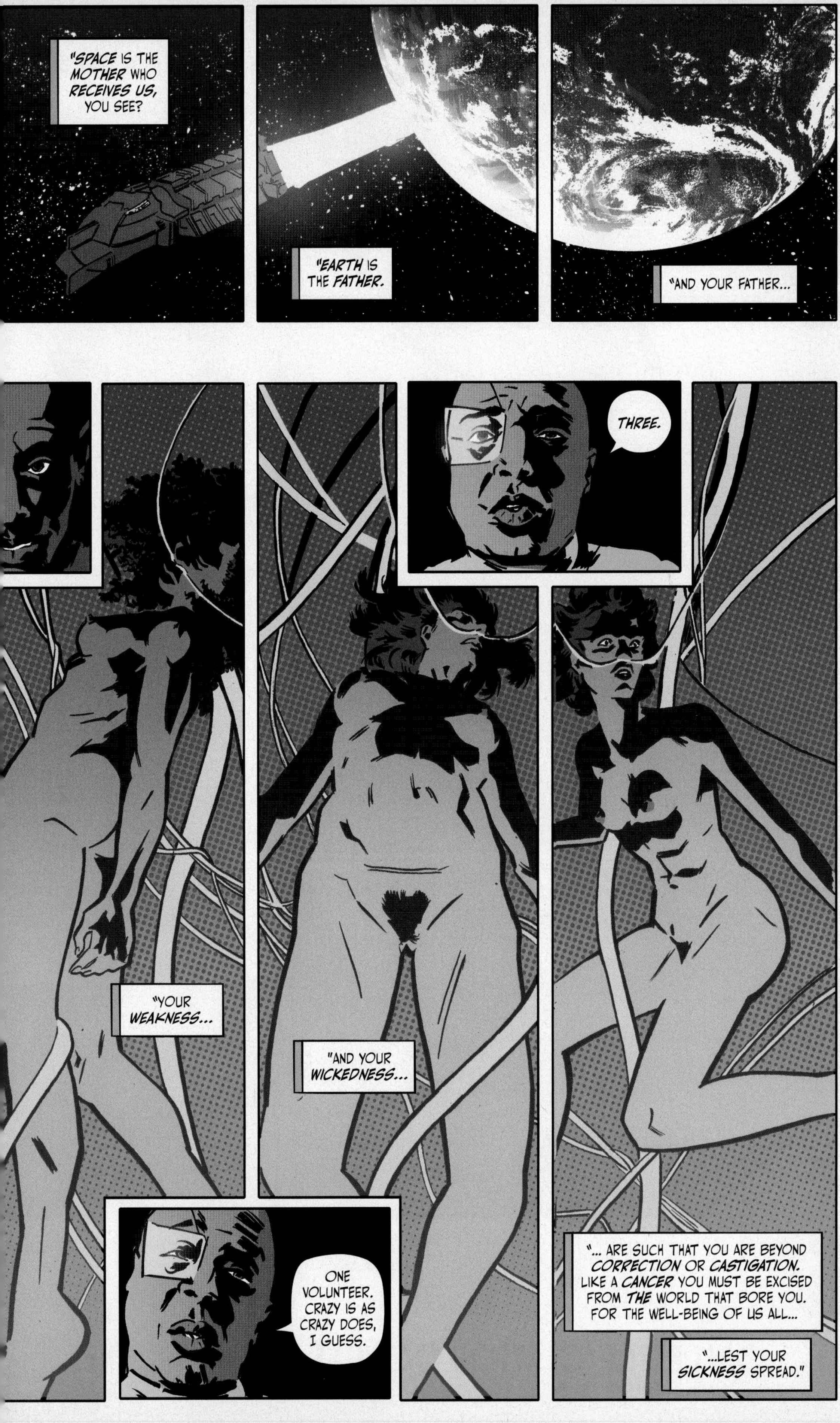
"SPACE IS THE MOTHER WHO RECEIVES US, YOU SEE?
"EARTH IS THE FATHER.
"AND YOUR FATHER...
THREE.
"YOUR WEAKNESS...
"AND YOUR WICKEDNESS...
"... ARE SUCH THAT YOU ARE BEYOND CORRECTION OR CASTIGATION. LIKE A CANCER YOU MUST BE EXCISED FROM THE WORLD THAT BORE YOU. FOR THE WELL-BEING OF US ALL...
ONE VOLUNTEER. CRAZY IS AS CRAZY DOES, I GUESS.
"...LEST YOUR SICKNESS SPREAD."

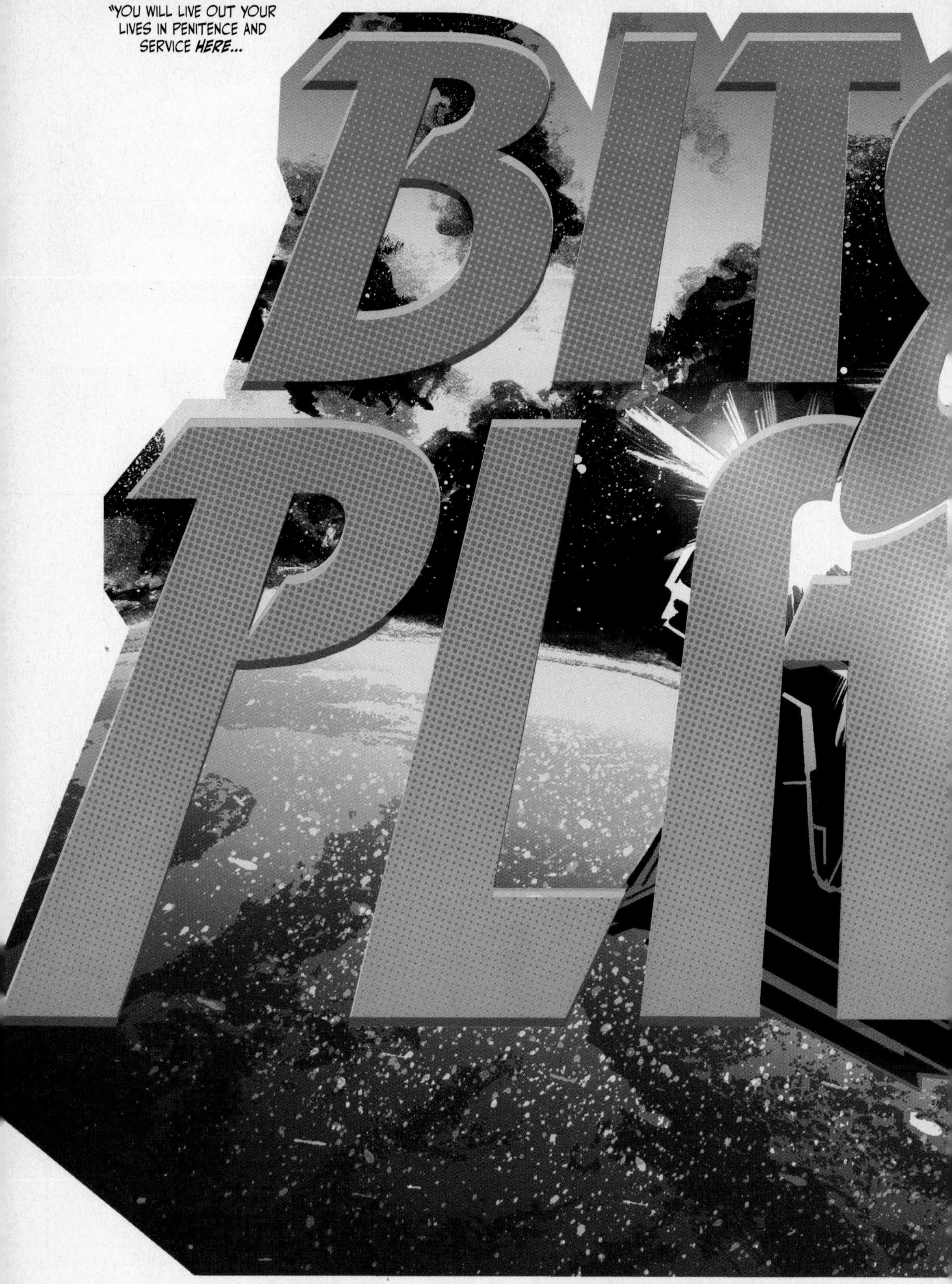
"YOU WILL LIVE OUT YOUR LIVES IN PENITENCE AND SERVICE *HERE*...

KELLY SUE DECONNICK
SCRIPT

CRIS PETER
COLORS

CLAYTON COWLES
LETTERS

RIAN HUGHES
COVER DESIGN & LOGO DESIGN

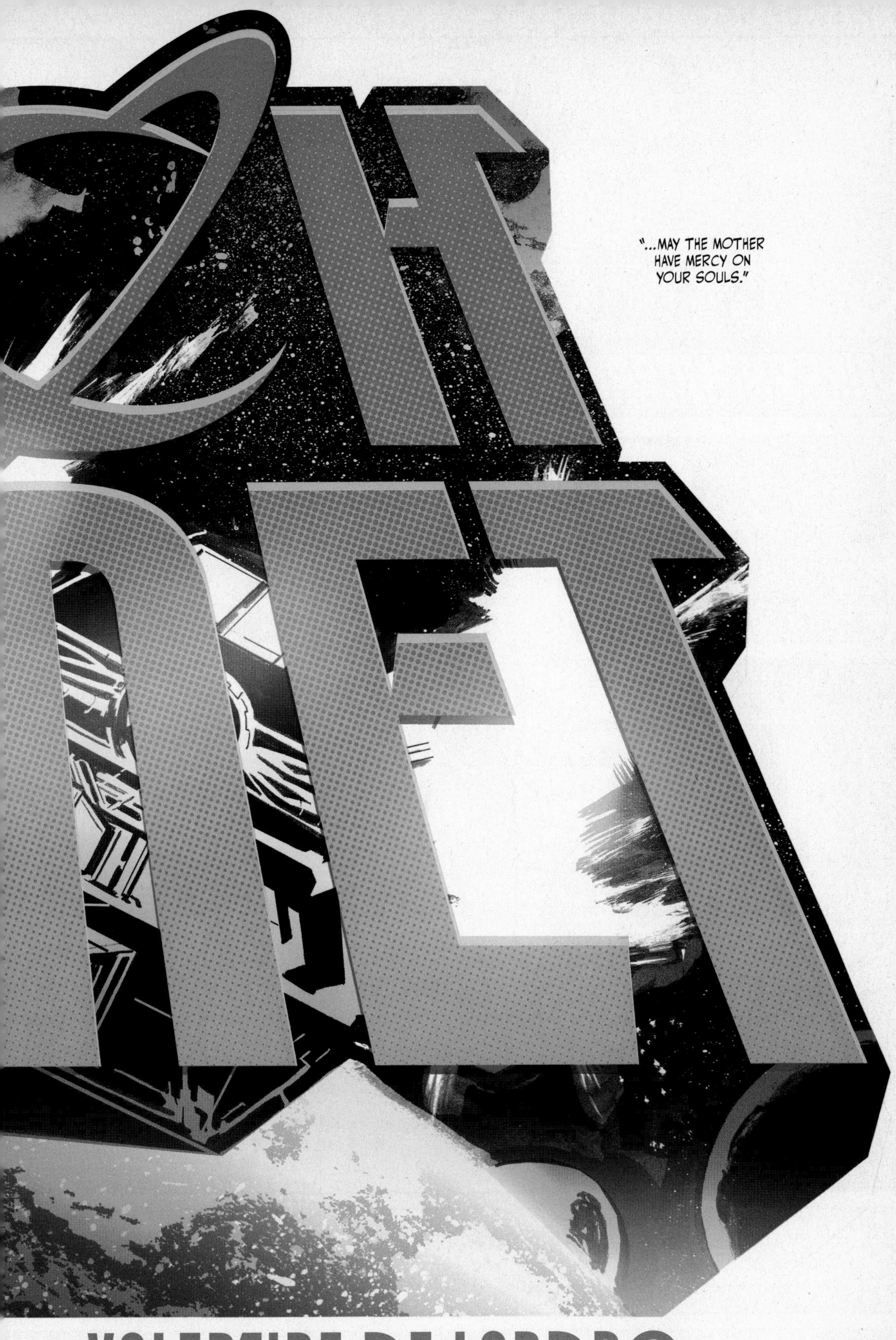
"...MAY THE MOTHER HAVE MERCY ON YOUR SOULS."

VALENTINE DE LANDRO
ART/COVERS

LAURENN McCUBBIN
BACKMATTER DESIGN

LAUREN SANKOVITCH
EDITOR

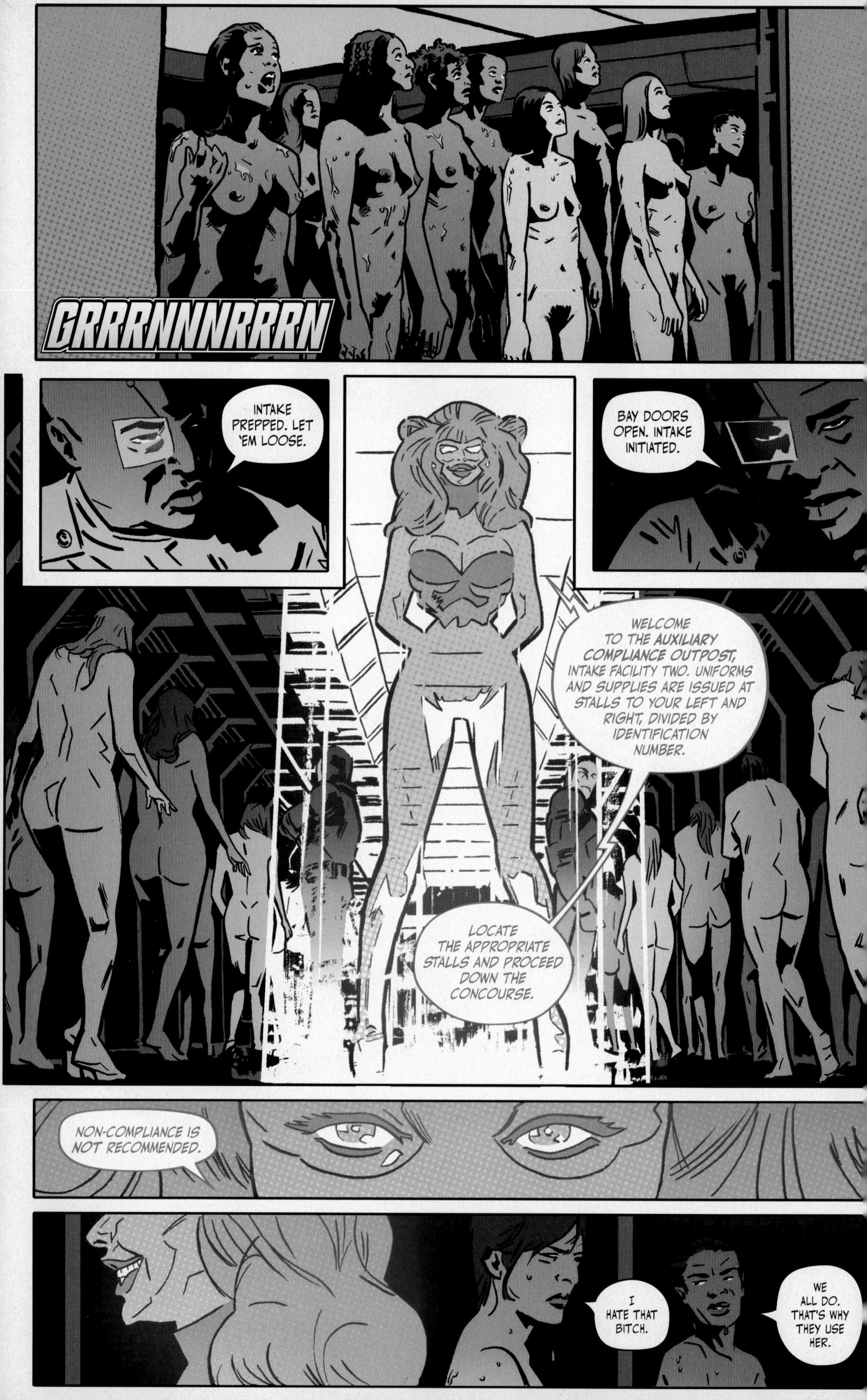
GRRRNNNRRRN
INTAKE PREPPED. LET 'EM LOOSE.
BAY DOORS OPEN. INTAKE INITIATED.
WELCOME TO THE AUXILIARY COMPLIANCE OUTPOST, INTAKE FACILITY TWO. UNIFORMS AND SUPPLIES ARE ISSUED AT STALLS TO YOUR LEFT AND RIGHT, DIVIDED BY IDENTIFICATION NUMBER.
LOCATE THE APPROPRIATE STALLS AND PROCEED DOWN THE CONCOURSE.
NON-COMPLIANCE IS NOT RECOMMENDED.
I HATE THAT BITCH.
WE ALL DO. THAT'S WHY THEY USE HER.

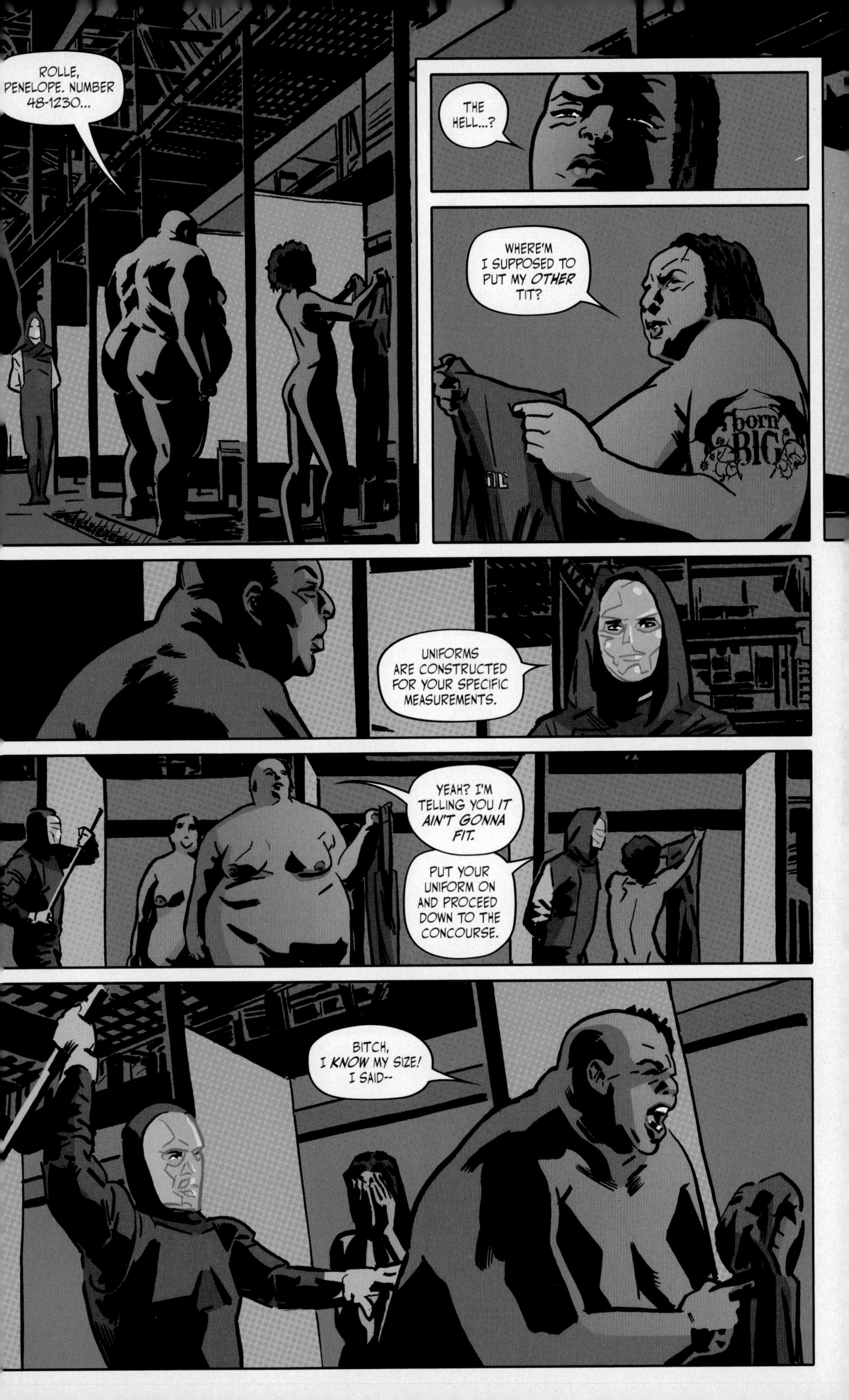
ROLLE, PENELOPE. NUMBER 48-1230...
THE HELL...?
WHERE'M I SUPPOSED TO PUT MY OTHER TIT?
UNIFORMS ARE CONSTRUCTED FOR YOUR SPECIFIC MEASUREMENTS.
YEAH? I'M TELLING YOU IT AIN'T GONNA FIT.
PUT YOUR UNIFORM ON AND PROCEED DOWN TO THE CONCOURSE.
BITCH, I KNOW MY SIZE! I SAID--
born BIG

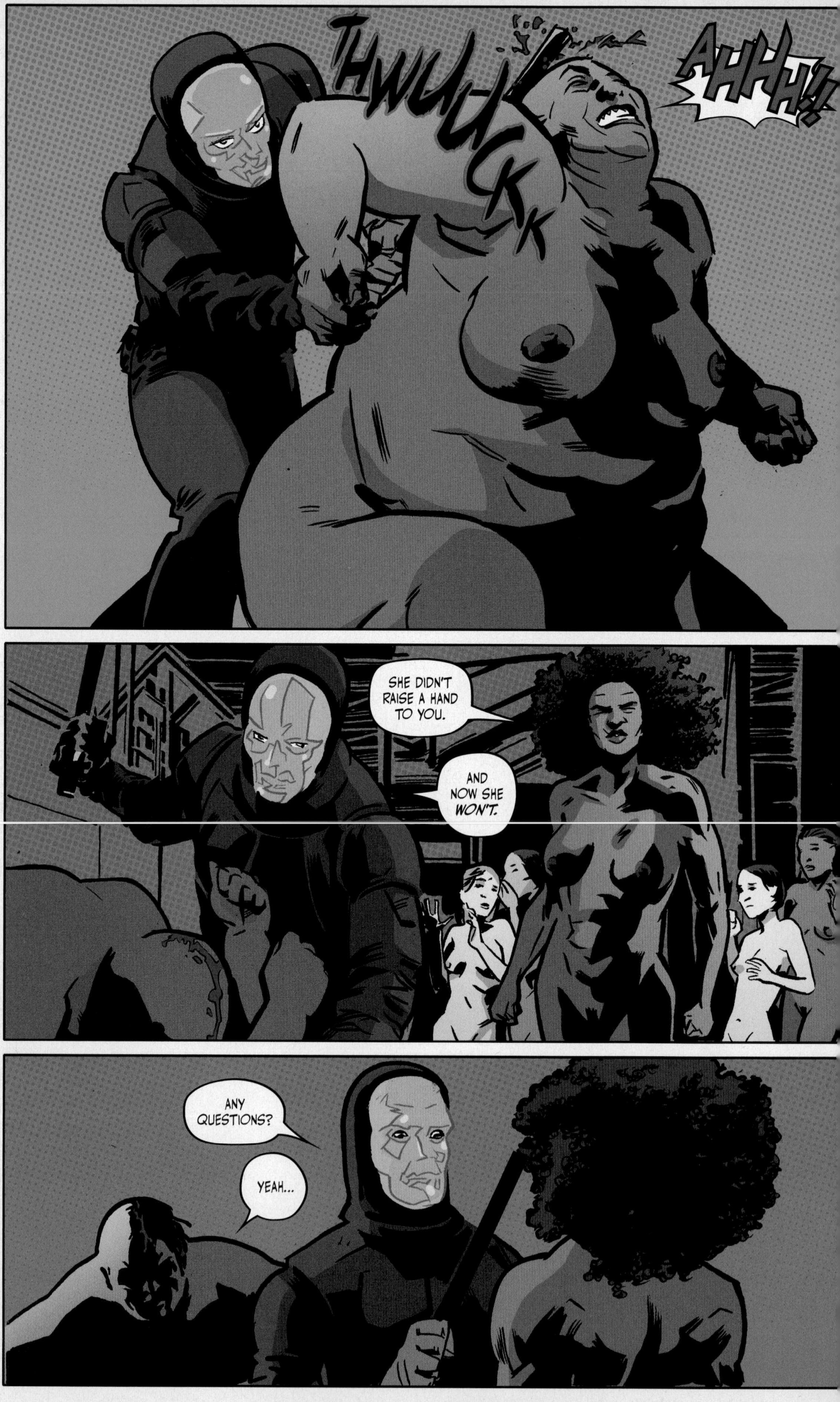
THWUUCKK
AHHH!!
SHE DIDN'T RAISE A HAND TO YOU.
AND NOW SHE *WON'T.*
ANY QUESTIONS?
YEAH...

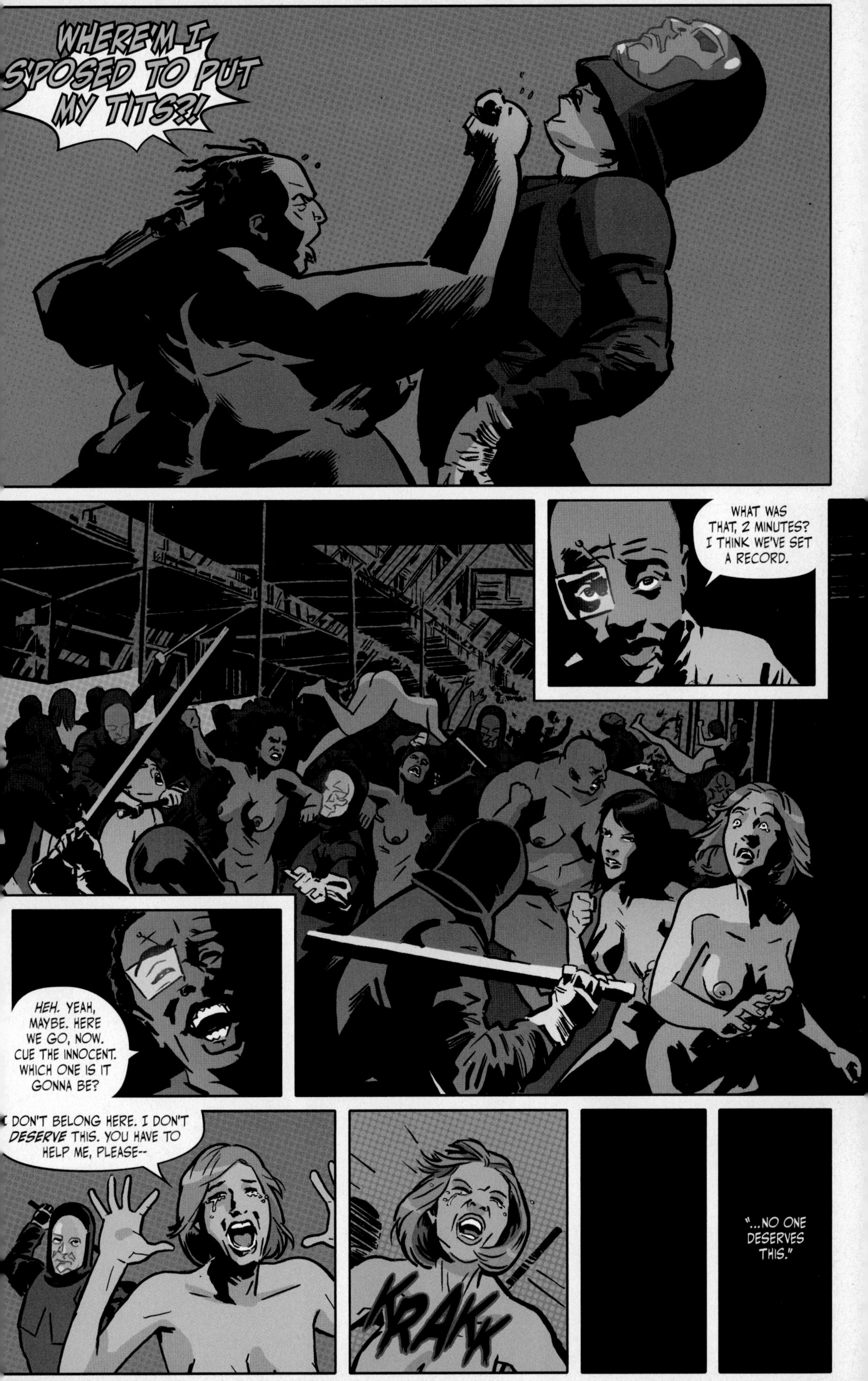
WHERE'M I S'POSED TO PUT MY TITS?!
WHAT WAS THAT, 2 MINUTES? I THINK WE'VE SET A RECORD.
HEH. YEAH, MAYBE. HERE WE GO, NOW. CUE THE INNOCENT. WHICH ONE IS IT GONNA BE?
DON'T BELONG HERE. I DON'T *DESERVE* THIS. YOU HAVE TO HELP ME, PLEASE--
KRAKK
"...NO ONE DESERVES THIS."

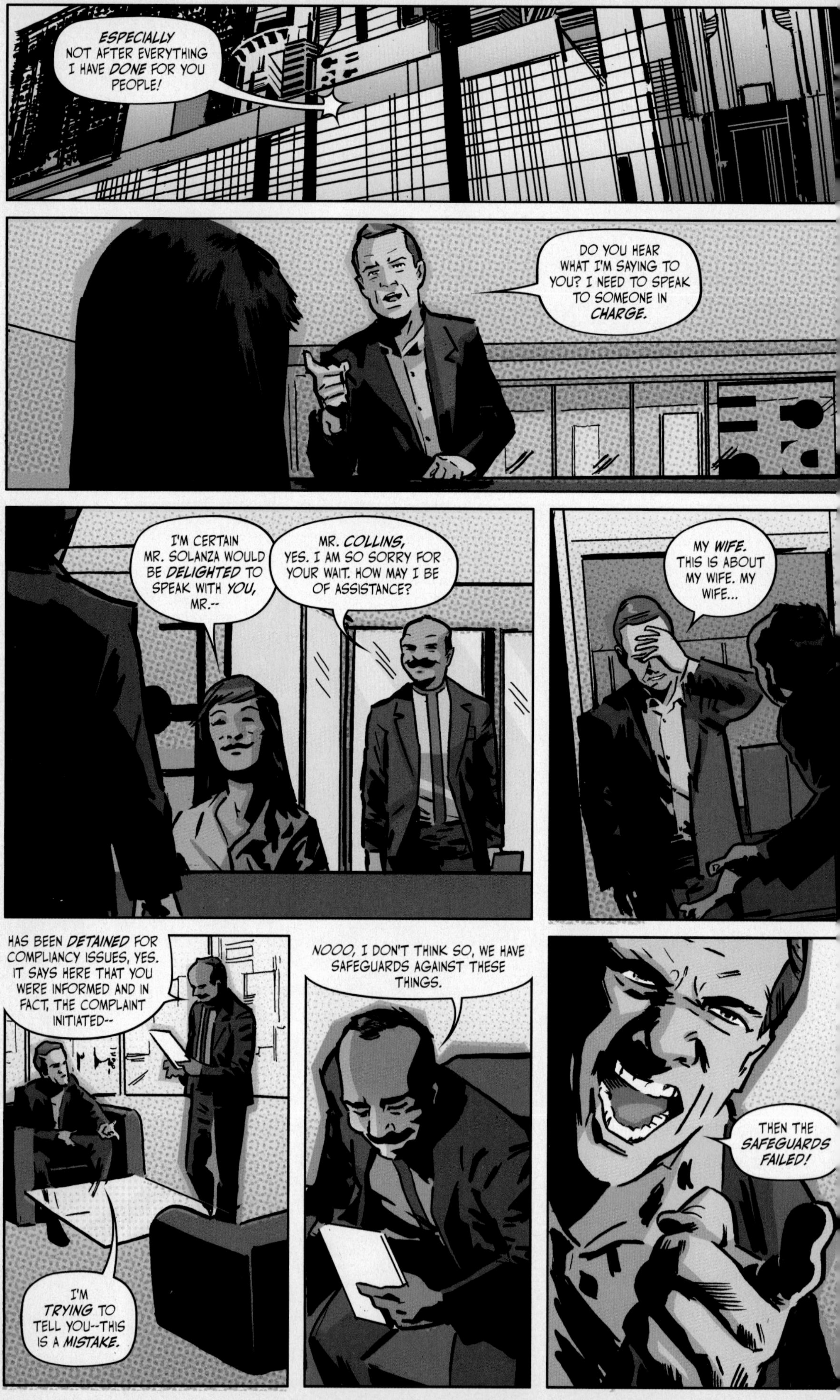
ESPECIALLY NOT AFTER EVERYTHING I HAVE DONE FOR YOU PEOPLE!
DO YOU HEAR WHAT I'M SAYING TO YOU? I NEED TO SPEAK TO SOMEONE IN CHARGE.
I'M CERTAIN MR. SOLANZA WOULD BE DELIGHTED TO SPEAK WITH YOU, MR.--
MR. COLLINS, YES. I AM SO SORRY FOR YOUR WAIT. HOW MAY I BE OF ASSISTANCE?
MY WIFE. THIS IS ABOUT MY WIFE. MY WIFE...
HAS BEEN DETAINED FOR COMPLIANCY ISSUES, YES. IT SAYS HERE THAT YOU WERE INFORMED AND IN FACT, THE COMPLAINT INITIATED--
I'M TRYING TO TELL YOU--THIS IS A MISTAKE.
NOOO, I DON'T THINK SO, WE HAVE SAFEGUARDS AGAINST THESE THINGS.
THEN THE SAFEGUARDS FAILED!

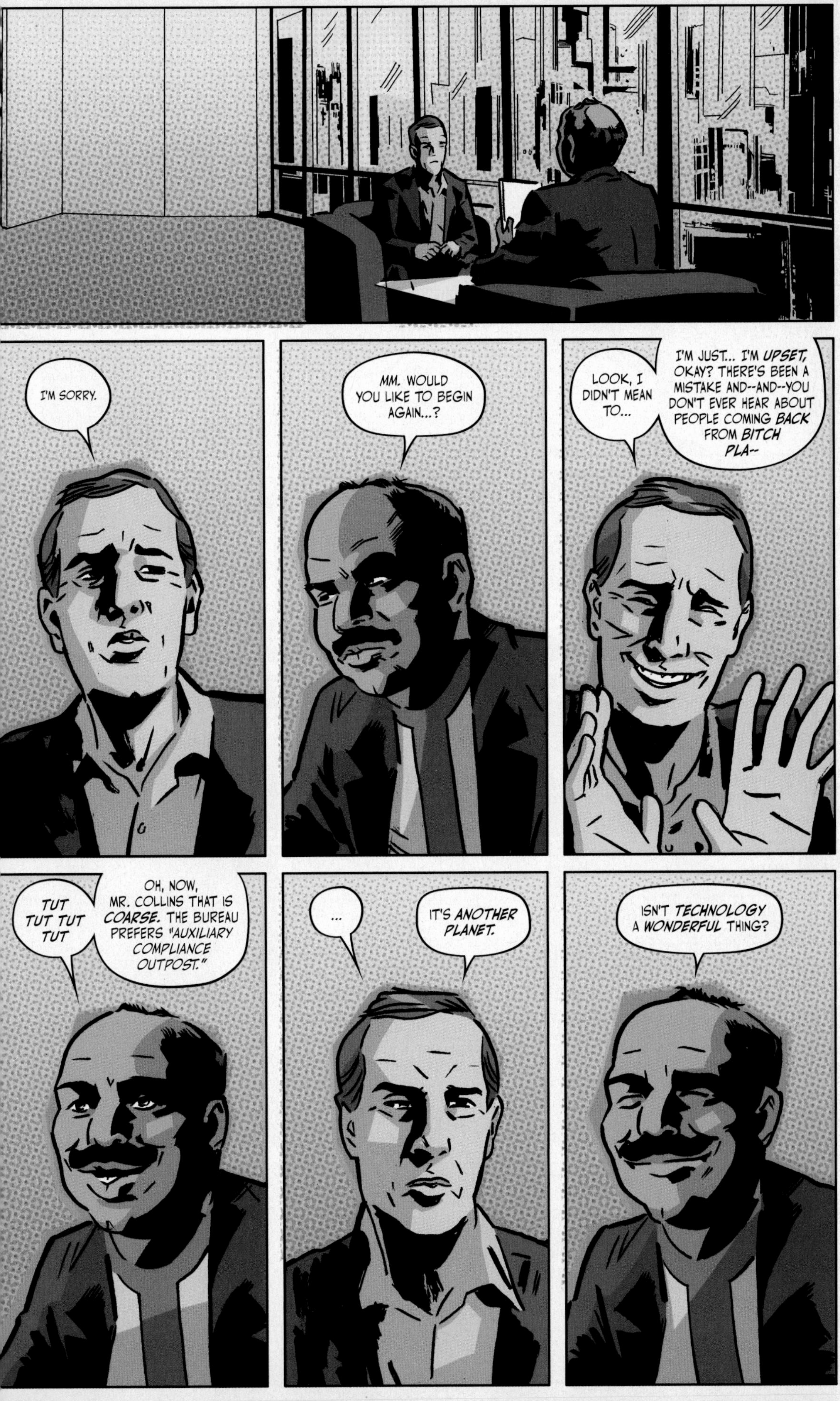
I'M SORRY.
MM. WOULD YOU LIKE TO BEGIN AGAIN...?
LOOK, I DIDN'T MEAN TO...
I'M JUST... I'M UPSET, OKAY? THERE'S BEEN A MISTAKE AND--AND--YOU DON'T EVER HEAR ABOUT PEOPLE COMING BACK FROM BITCH PLA--
TUT TUT TUT TUT
OH, NOW, MR. COLLINS THAT IS COARSE. THE BUREAU PREFERS "AUXILIARY COMPLIANCE OUTPOST."
...
IT'S ANOTHER PLANET.
ISN'T TECHNOLOGY A WONDERFUL THING?

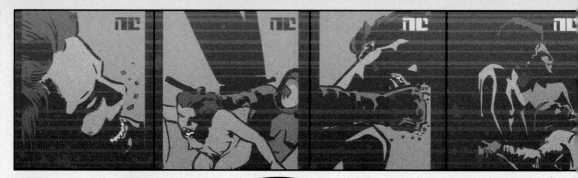

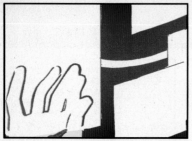

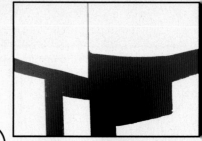

IT'S THEIR OWN *FAULT* THEY DON'T SEE IT COMING.

SOME OF THEM *MUST.*

THEY WON'T LET THEMSELVES! RUNS COUNTER TO EVERYTHING THEY BELIEVE.

AS FAR AS SHE'S CONCERNED, SHE'S DONE EVERYTHING RIGHT?

AYEP. IF ANYTHING, YOU'D THINK *WE'D* LEARN TO STOP BEING SURPRISED.

SO WHICH ONE IS IT?

WHITE GIRL.

OF COURSE.

NAME'S *MARIAN COLLINS.*

WELL, MARIAN COLLINS WANTS TO TALK TO "*SOMEONE IN CHARGE.*"

LET HER. LOAD THE MODEL. RUN 'THE CATHOLIC.'

I *LOVE* THE CATHOLIC!

I LOOK AFTER YOU, DON'T I?

YOU DO, YOU DO. RUNNING THE CATHOLIC... NOW...

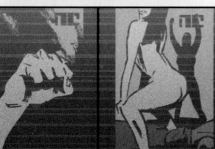

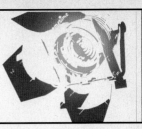

"LIGHTS UP!"

MARIAN COLLINS, MY ANGEL...

PLEASE STEP FORWARD AND CONFESS YOUR SINS.

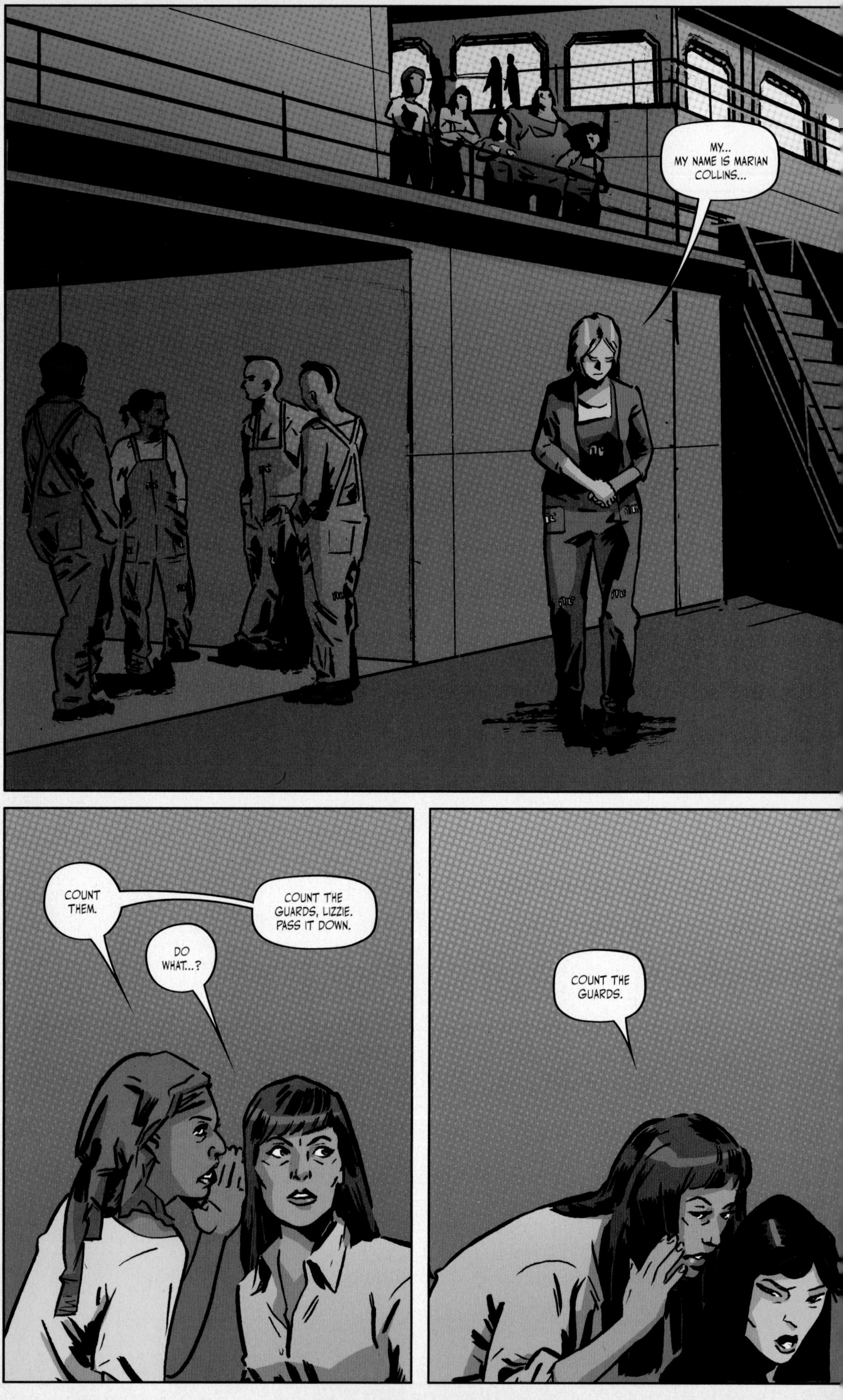
MY... MY NAME IS MARIAN COLLINS...
COUNT THEM.
COUNT THE GUARDS, LIZZIE. PASS IT DOWN.
DO WHAT...?
COUNT THE GUARDS.

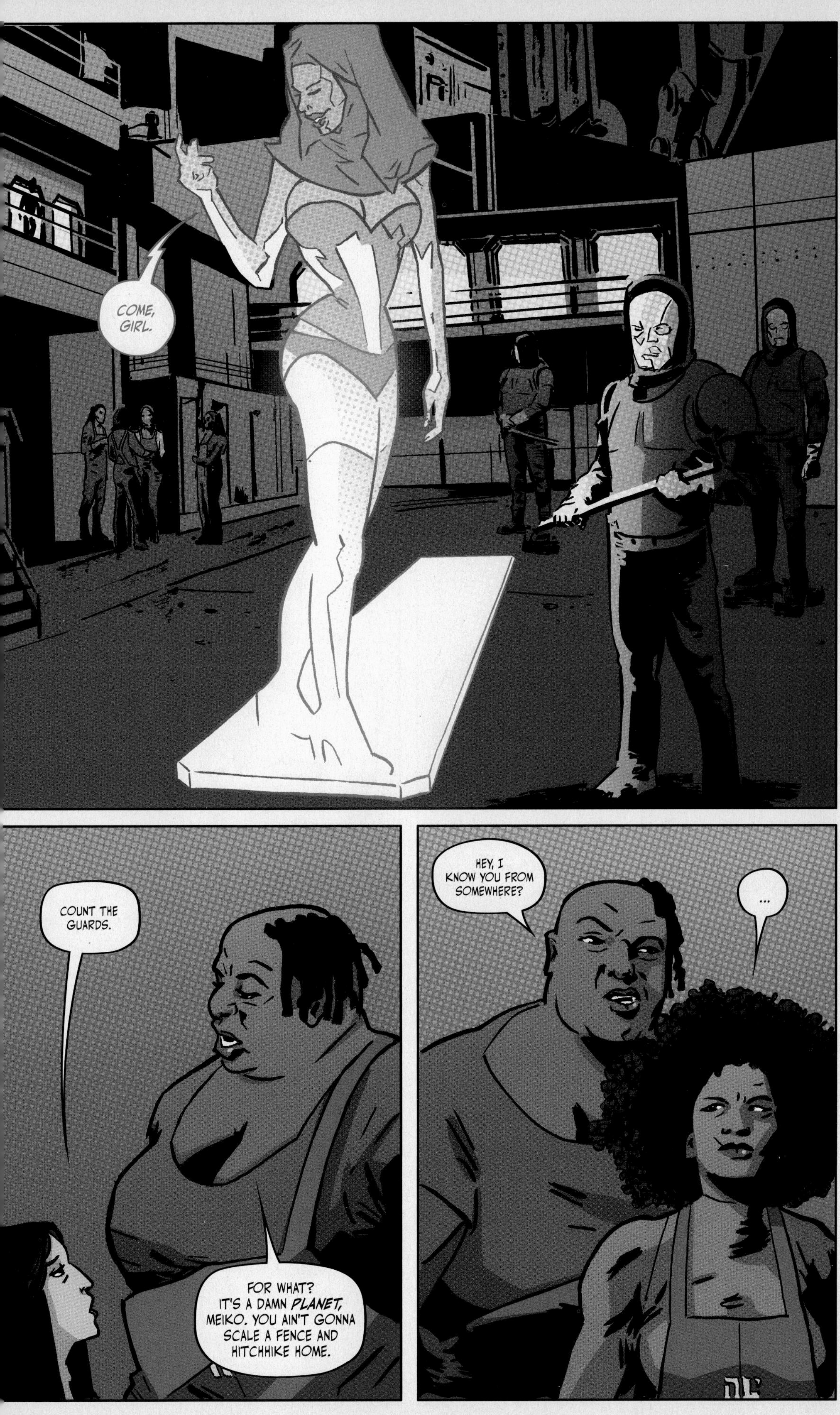
COME, GIRL.
COUNT THE GUARDS.
FOR WHAT? IT'S A DAMN *PLANET*, MEIKO. YOU AIN'T GONNA SCALE A FENCE AND HITCHHIKE HOME.
HEY, I KNOW YOU FROM SOMEWHERE?
...

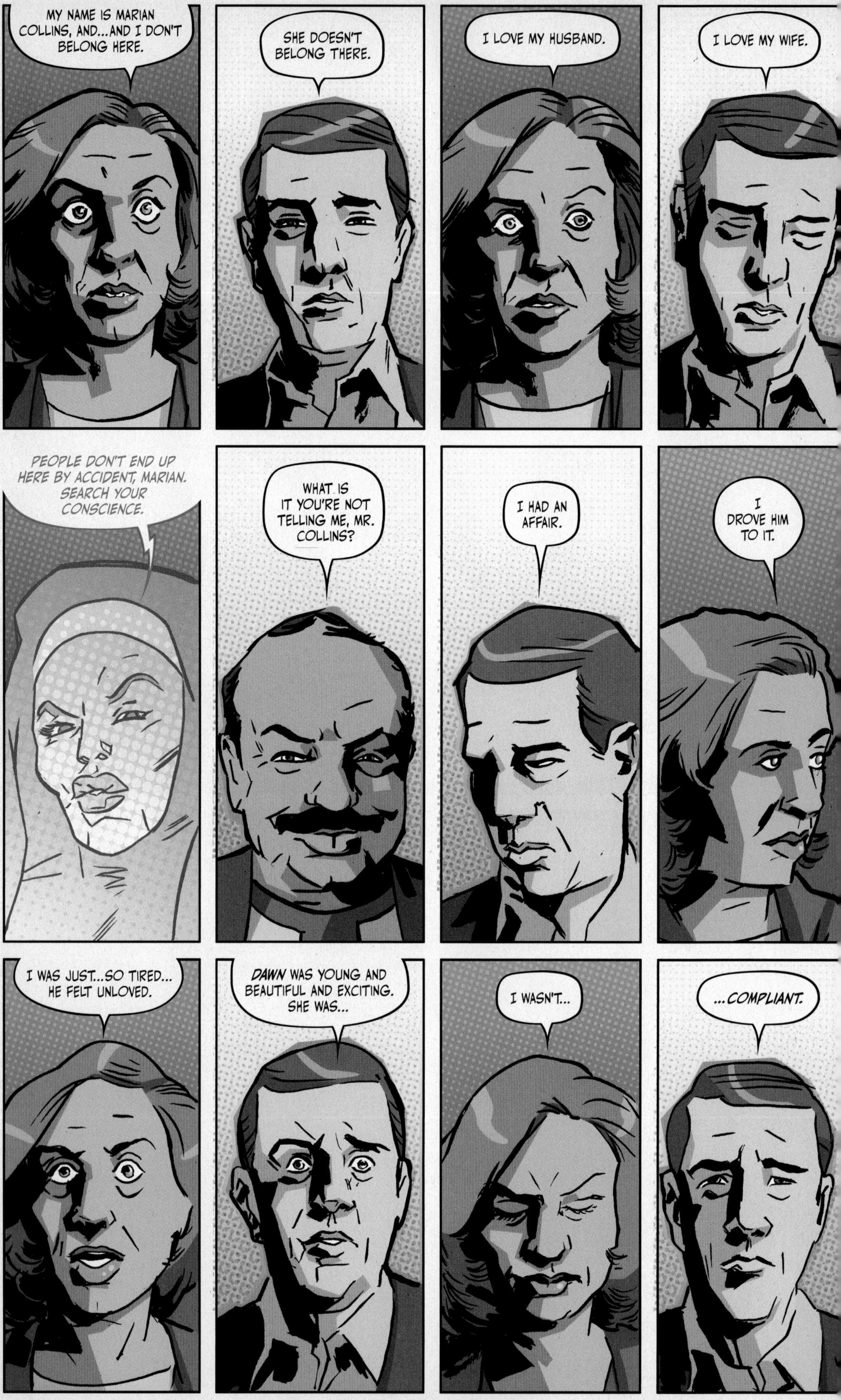
MY NAME IS MARIAN COLLINS, AND...AND I DON'T BELONG HERE.
SHE DOESN'T BELONG THERE.
I LOVE MY HUSBAND.
I LOVE MY WIFE.
PEOPLE DON'T END UP HERE BY ACCIDENT, MARIAN. SEARCH YOUR CONSCIENCE.
WHAT IS IT YOU'RE NOT TELLING ME, MR. COLLINS?
I HAD AN AFFAIR.
I DROVE HIM TO IT.
I WAS JUST...SO TIRED... HE FELT UNLOVED.
DAWN WAS YOUNG AND BEAUTIFUL AND EXCITING. SHE WAS...
I WASN'T...
...COMPLIANT.

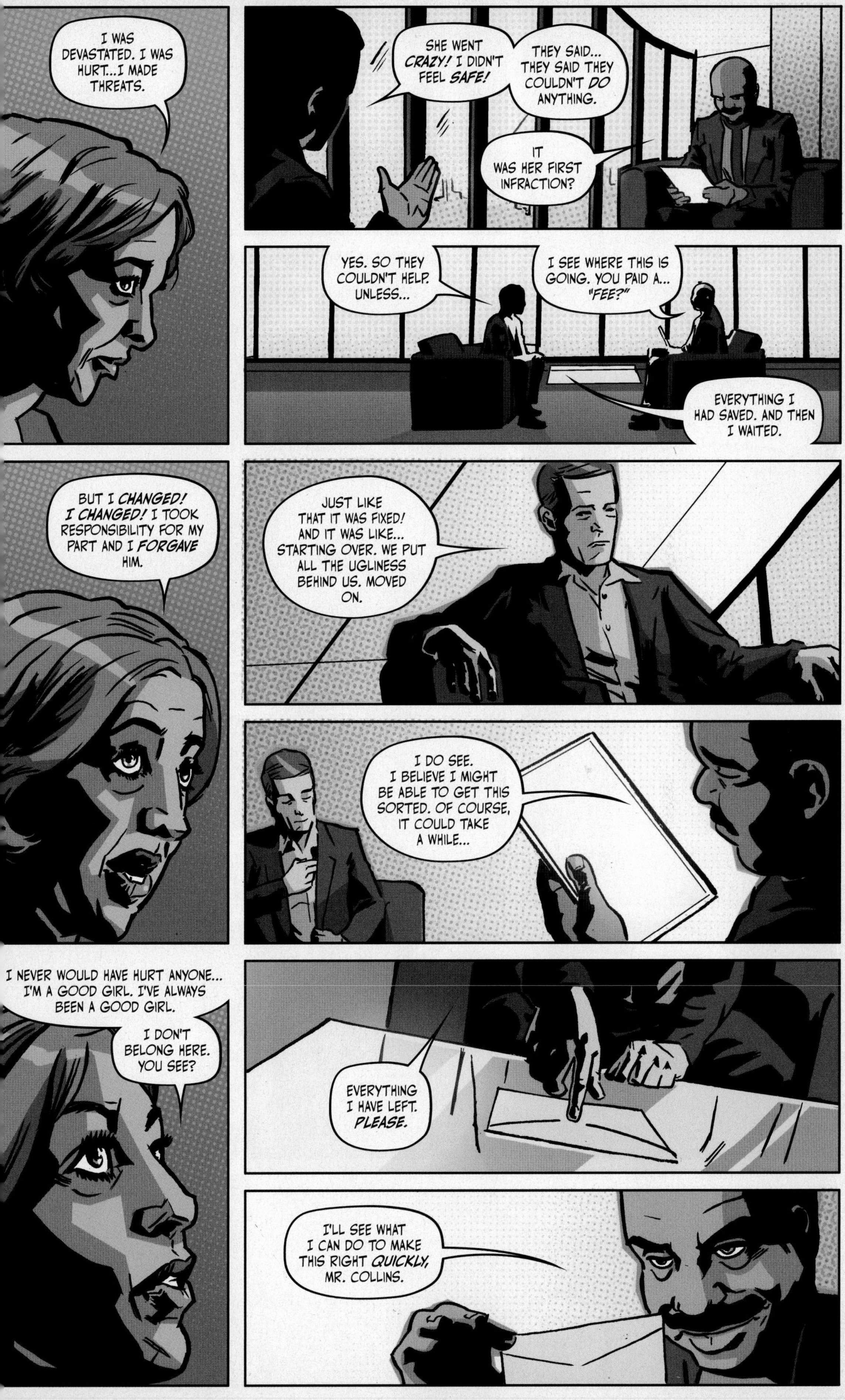

I WAS DEVASTATED. I WAS HURT...I MADE THREATS.
SHE WENT *CRAZY!* I DIDN'T FEEL *SAFE!*
THEY SAID... THEY SAID THEY COULDN'T *DO* ANYTHING.
IT WAS HER FIRST INFRACTION?
YES. SO THEY COULDN'T HELP. UNLESS...
I SEE WHERE THIS IS GOING. YOU PAID A... *"FEE?"*
EVERYTHING I HAD SAVED. AND THEN I WAITED.
BUT I *CHANGED! I CHANGED!* I TOOK RESPONSIBILITY FOR MY PART AND I *FORGAVE* HIM.
JUST LIKE THAT IT WAS FIXED! AND IT WAS LIKE... STARTING OVER. WE PUT ALL THE UGLINESS BEHIND US. MOVED ON.
I DO SEE. I BELIEVE I MIGHT BE ABLE TO GET THIS SORTED. OF COURSE, IT COULD TAKE A WHILE...
I NEVER WOULD HAVE HURT ANYONE... I'M A GOOD GIRL. I'VE ALWAYS BEEN A GOOD GIRL.
I DON'T BELONG HERE. YOU SEE?
EVERYTHING I HAVE LEFT. *PLEASE.*
I'LL SEE WHAT I CAN DO TO MAKE THIS RIGHT *QUICKLY,* MR. COLLINS.

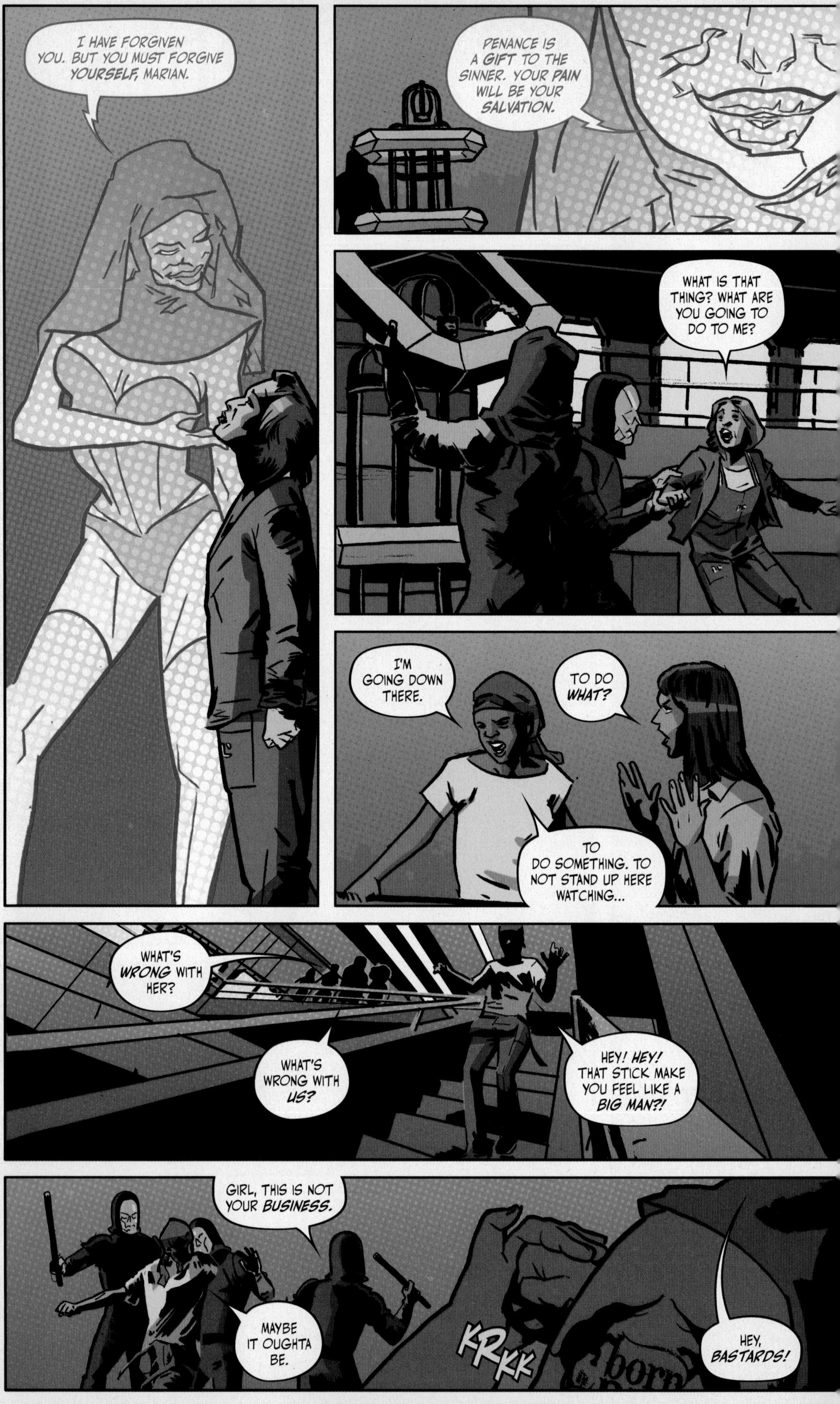
I HAVE FORGIVEN YOU. BUT YOU MUST FORGIVE *YOURSELF,* MARIAN.
PENANCE IS A *GIFT* TO THE SINNER. YOUR *PAIN* WILL BE YOUR *SALVATION.*
WHAT IS THAT THING? WHAT ARE YOU GOING TO DO TO ME?
I'M GOING DOWN THERE.
TO DO *WHAT?*
TO DO SOMETHING. TO NOT STAND UP HERE WATCHING...
WHAT'S *WRONG* WITH HER?
WHAT'S WRONG WITH *US?*
HEY! *HEY!* THAT STICK MAKE YOU FEEL LIKE A *BIG MAN?!*
GIRL, THIS IS NOT YOUR *BUSINESS.*
MAYBE IT OUGHTA BE.
KRKK
HEY, *BASTARDS!*

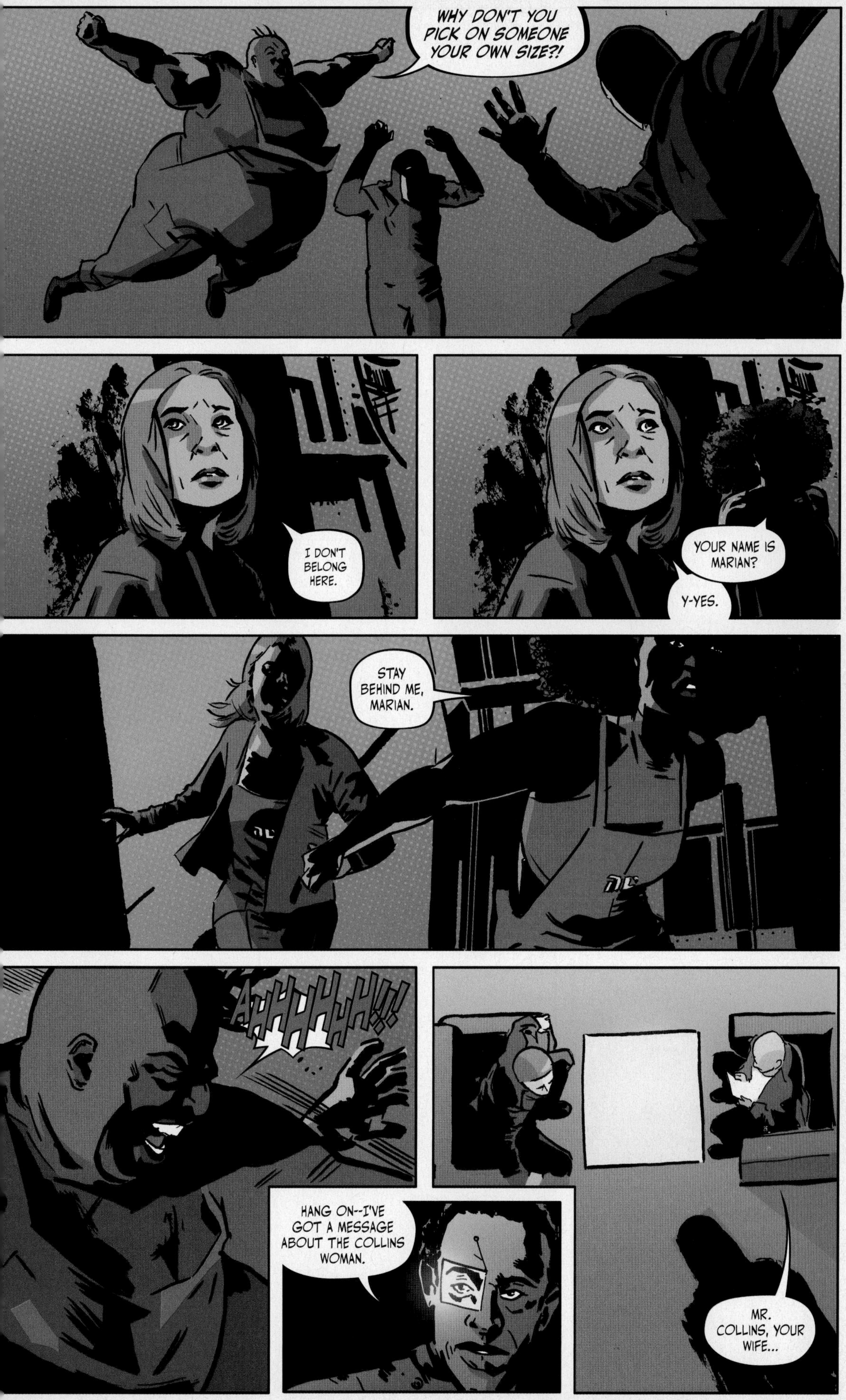
WHY DON'T YOU PICK ON SOMEONE YOUR OWN SIZE?!
I DON'T BELONG HERE.
YOUR NAME IS MARIAN?
Y-YES.
STAY BEHIND ME, MARIAN.
AHHHHHH!!!
HANG ON--I'VE GOT A MESSAGE ABOUT THE COLLINS WOMAN.
MR. COLLINS, YOUR WIFE...

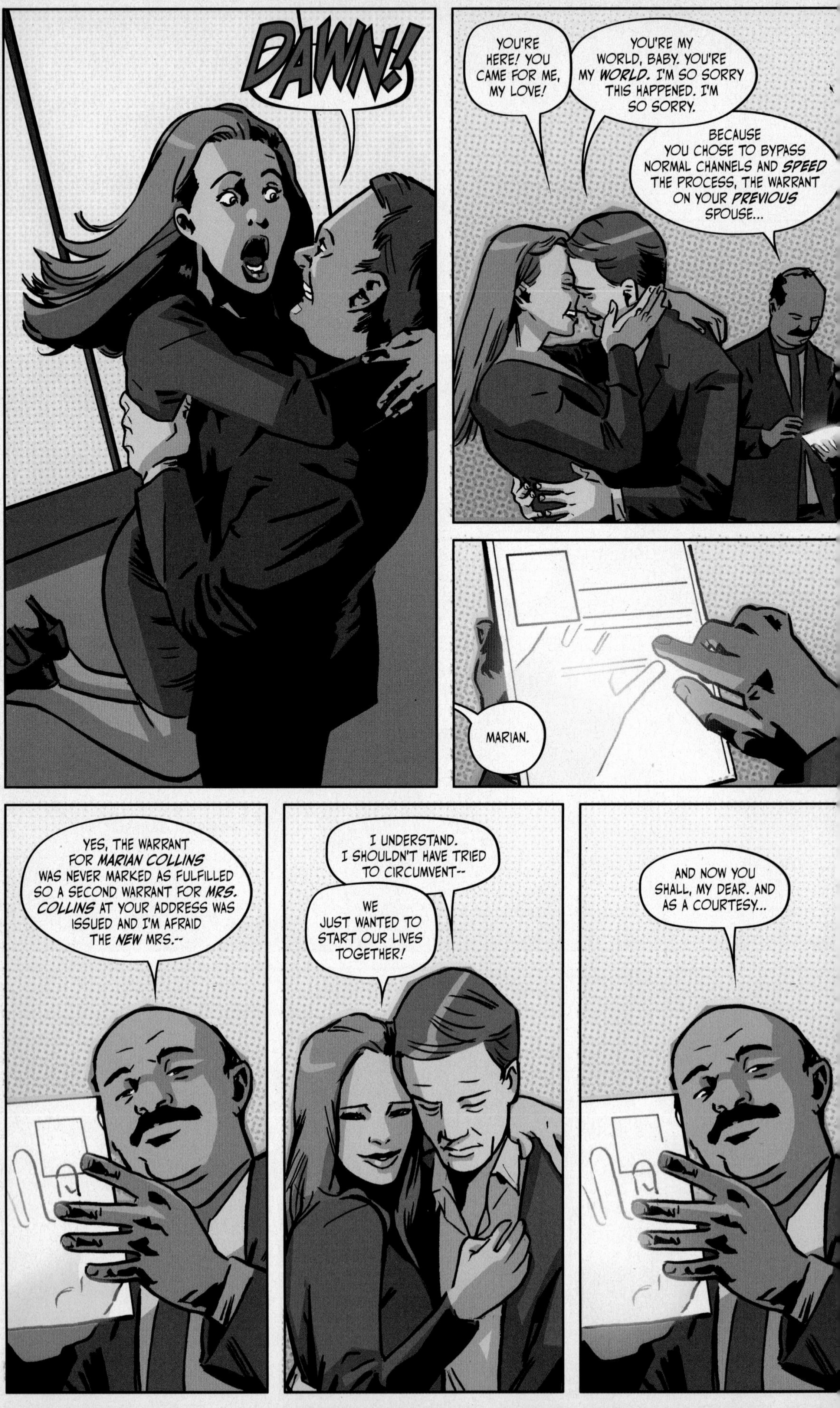
DAWN!
YOU'RE HERE! YOU CAME FOR ME, MY LOVE!
YOU'RE MY WORLD, BABY. YOU'RE MY WORLD. I'M SO SORRY THIS HAPPENED. I'M SO SORRY.
BECAUSE YOU CHOSE TO BYPASS NORMAL CHANNELS AND SPEED THE PROCESS, THE WARRANT ON YOUR PREVIOUS SPOUSE...
MARIAN.
YES, THE WARRANT FOR MARIAN COLLINS WAS NEVER MARKED AS FULFILLED SO A SECOND WARRANT FOR MRS. COLLINS AT YOUR ADDRESS WAS ISSUED AND I'M AFRAID THE NEW MRS.--
I UNDERSTAND. I SHOULDN'T HAVE TRIED TO CIRCUMVENT--
WE JUST WANTED TO START OUR LIVES TOGETHER!
AND NOW YOU SHALL, MY DEAR. AND AS A COURTESY...

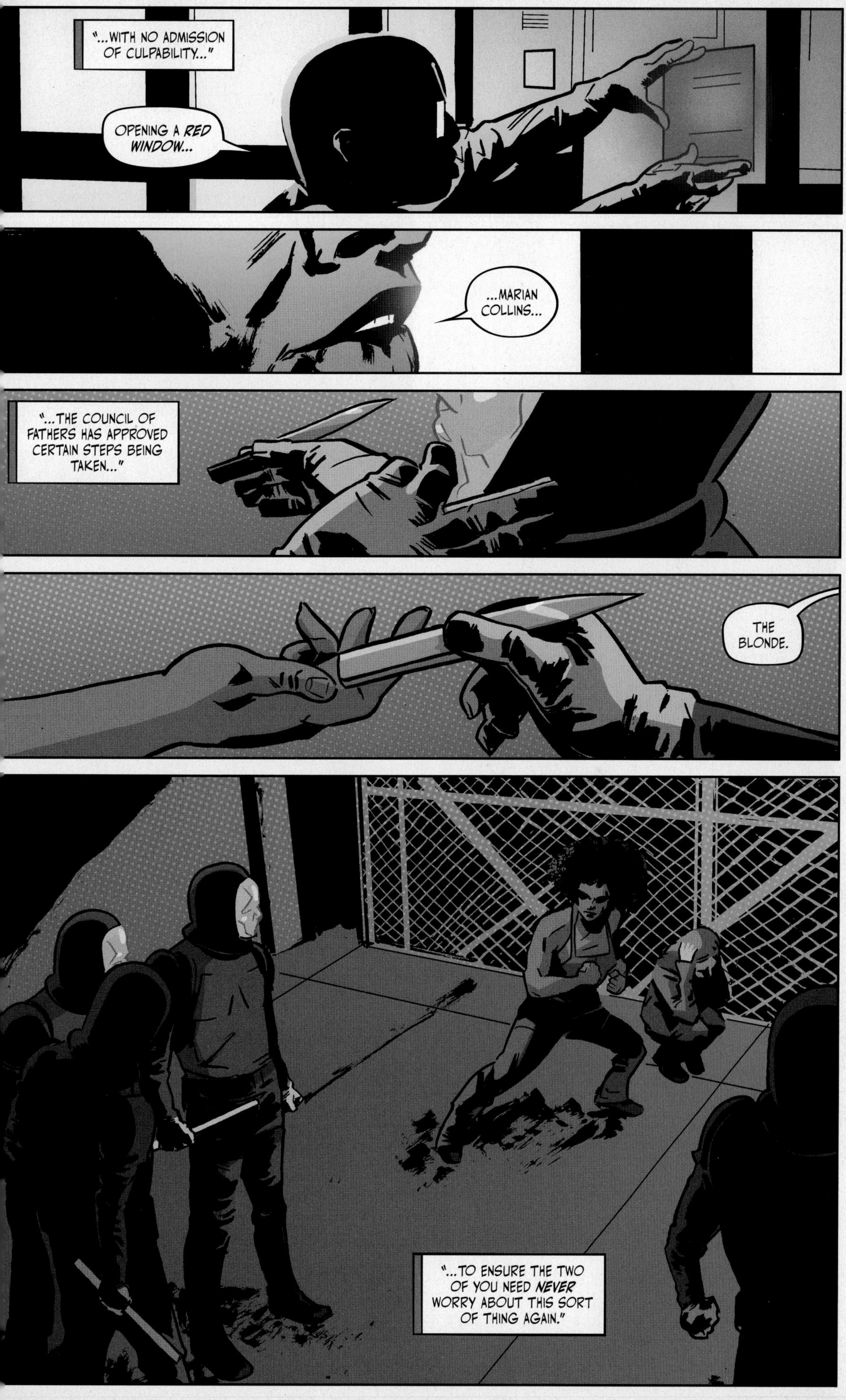
"...WITH NO ADMISSION OF CULPABILITY..."
OPENING A RED WINDOW...
...MARIAN COLLINS...
"...THE COUNCIL OF FATHERS HAS APPROVED CERTAIN STEPS BEING TAKEN..."
THE BLONDE.
"...TO ENSURE THE TWO OF YOU NEED NEVER WORRY ABOUT THIS SORT OF THING AGAIN."

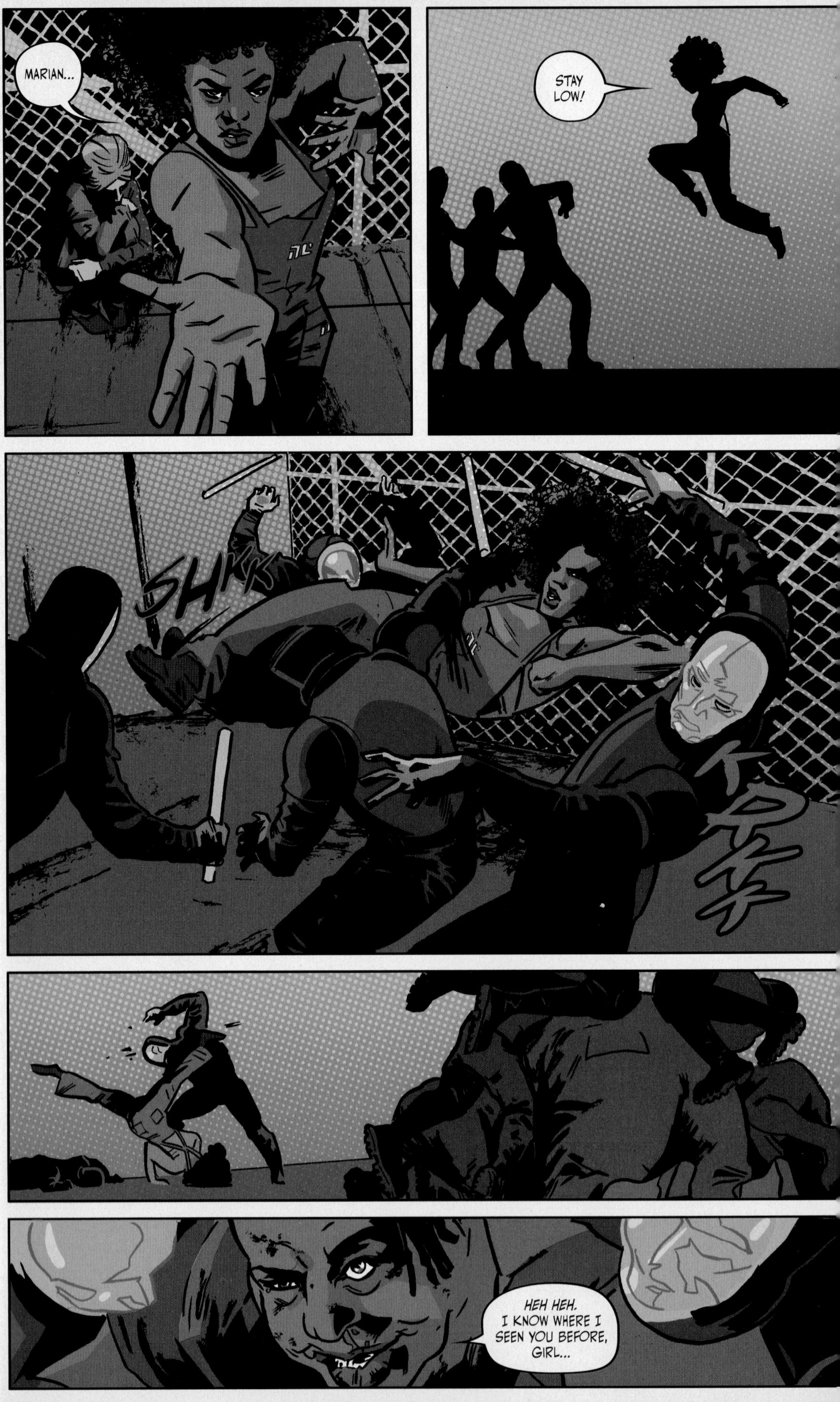
MARIAN...
STAY LOW!
SHKK
KRKK
HEH HEH.
I KNOW WHERE I SEEN YOU BEFORE, GIRL...

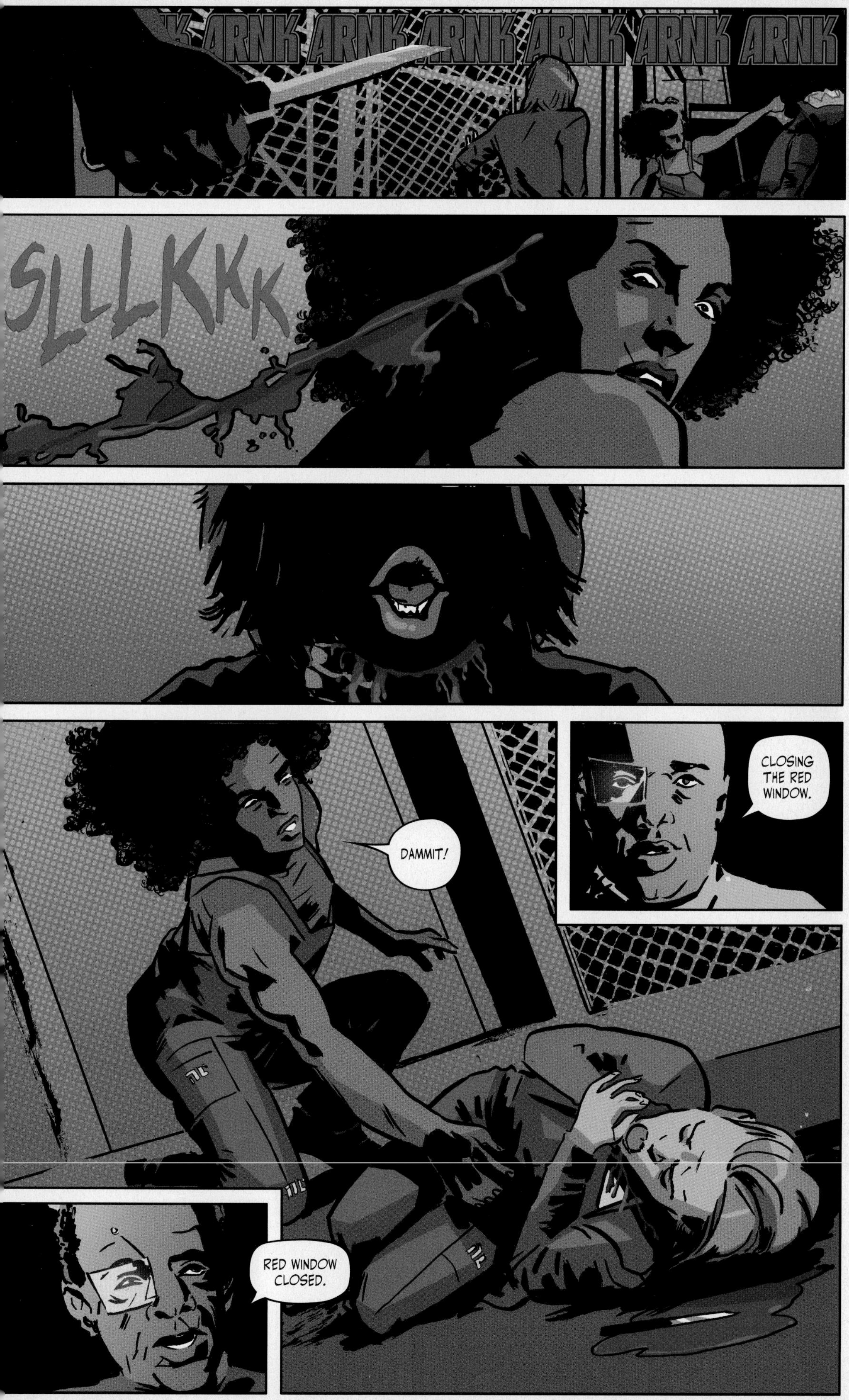
ARNK ARNK ARNK ARNK ARNK ARNK
SLLLKKK
DAMMIT!
CLOSING THE RED WINDOW.
RED WINDOW CLOSED.

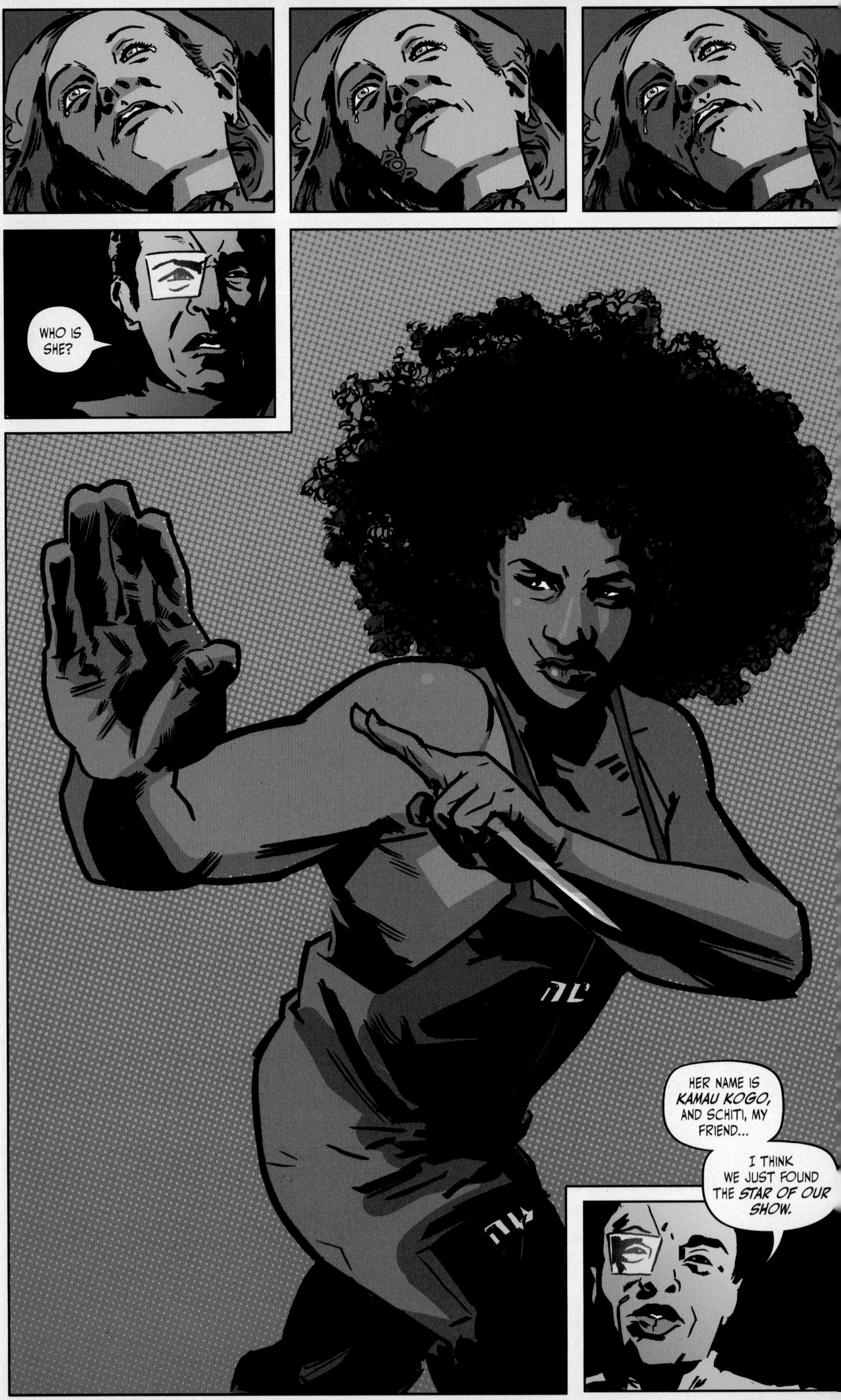
POP
WHO IS SHE?
HER NAME IS KAMAU KOGO, AND SCHITI, MY FRIEND...
I THINK WE JUST FOUND THE STAR OF OUR SHOW.

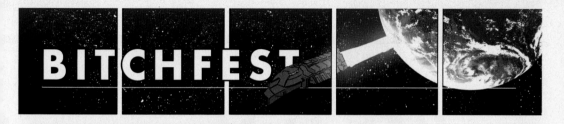

BITCHFEST

ONLINE BITCHPLA.NET | **E-MAIL** BLAHBLAHBLAH@BITCHPLA.NET | **SOCIAL** #BITCHPLANET

BITCH PLANET
PENNY ROLLE: FULL VIEW
born BIG
BITCH PLANET
KAMAU KOGO: FULL VIEW

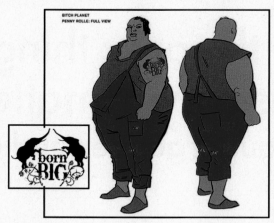

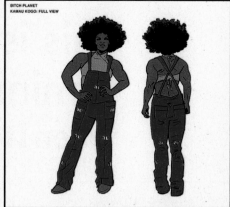

Designs by Valentine De Landro.

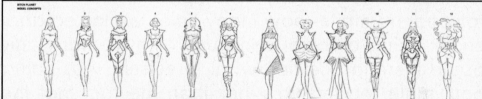

Danielle Henderson has been instrumental in the development of this book since its inception, even going so far as to drive in from Seattle to spend a Saturday with Laurenn McCubbin and me, scrawling ideas on a whiteboard and talking me down off various ledges as I confessed my many fears surrounding about this project—a feat she sometimes accomplishes with hard social science and sometimes with a powerful and challenging Girl-you-are-better-than-this-cowardly-shit-you-are-showing-me look. Danielle has got that look nailed and I am forever grateful for it.

And because she is unendingly generous, she also agreed to provide our first backmatter essay, which follows. Among her many other accomplishments, Danielle is the author of *Feminist Ryan Gosling*, which you want to own. Find her on the web at DanielleHenderson.net.

—KELLY SUE DECONNICK
NOVEMBER 4, 2014

"But I'm not

This is the only thing
feminism even matte
when I taught gender studie

No matter how many examples of misogyny I provided, no matter how many times we talked about gender being a social construct, or how many times I asked them to question what, precisely, was natural about male leadership other than the fact that they said it was natural, one person always held out, one person refused to believe that women were culturally oppressed. Most of the time they didn't want anyone insulting the important women in their lives, the ones who'd chosen to stay home and raise children, and it took some time for them to finally understand that feminism isn't about making women's choices invalid, but giving women the right to make any decision that they want. When they insisted that they weren't oppressed personally (even if they could see how it worked against others), I had a list of questions for them to answer: Have you ever been catcalled and felt helpless to defend yourself for fear of retribution? Do you feel like you have to wear makeup when you leave

ɔppressed."

eard more than "Does nymore?"

t a large Midwestern college.

the house? When you flip through magazines, do you automatically come up with a list of 50 things about yourself that you need to change?

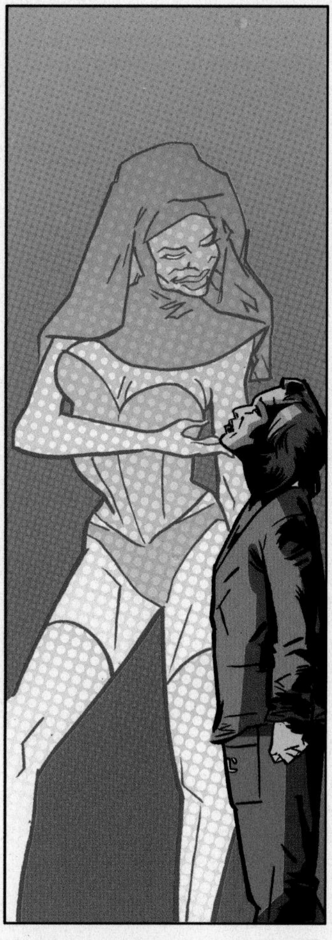

The striking thing about *Bitch Planet* is that we're already on it. We don't have to get thrown on a shuttle to be judged non-compliant — be a little overweight, talk too loud, have an opinion on the Internet — or be a woman of color. African American women are *three* times more likely to be incarcerated than white women[1], and most

1 Sayers, Shoshanna. "Mass Incarceration & People of Color." Southern Coalition for Social Justice, 14 Apr. 2014.

"I *guarantee* you know at least one woman who has *thought* about murdering someone for telling her she'd be prettier if she smiled."

often for offenses related to men–like how sex workers get inordinately more time in prison than their johns .[1] The scenarios you see on TV shows like "Orange is the New Black" are often based on actual events, but race issues aren't confined to women in prison. Race plays a huge factor in the rest of our lives, too. The standard of beauty prefers white women, so literally anyone non-white is non-compliant. (The bait-and-switch protagonist flip at the end of *Bitch Planet* #1 strikes me for that reason.)

White women don't fare much better in the culture of compliance; they're encouraged to pluck, snip, and tone their way down to a rough, whittled flesh stick to even be considered desirable (the relationship of a woman's perceived desirability to her perceived value is a whole other rage-inducing conversation). Penny Rolle might be my favorite Bitch so far; she's not white, but she physically embodies non-compliance and ends up being the toughest motherfucker in the group. Penny is not afraid to take up space, literally or figuratively. She hearkens back to conversations I've had with fat activists, women who are on a mission to prove that health comes at any size as a way of freeing women from the social mores that insist smaller is better.

In fact, many of the characters in this book are people you might already know. Okay, maybe you don't know any murderers, but I *guarantee* you know at least one woman who has *thought* about murdering someone for telling her she'd be prettier if she smiled.

And in light of the fact that "trading in for a better model" (BARF) has become standard rhetoric, it's not all that absurd to imagine someone's husband might sacrifice her for younger woman. We all either know, or are, the woman who treats eating a muffin or gaining two pounds like the end of the world. Perhaps the most messed up product of the cultural policing of women is that it creates an atmosphere where we police ourselves—think of the movie "Mean Girls," or any situation where young women are trying to live up to the social pressure of a queen bee.

We already live in a world where archaic Solanza-like politicians see us as wombs on legs, where social networks declare photos of breastfeeding to be obscene but won't judge fan pages dedicated to mass-killer Elliott Rodgers as hate speech, where a persistent and unequal valuing of beauty rewards the woman who is willing to diminish herself the most.

When my students asked me how feminism could possibly matter to them, I asked them questions with the hope of helping them reach an understanding of exactly what it might look like for them, individually. Are you content to live in a world that devalues you because you of your gender presentation? Are you willing to earn less for the same work just because that's the way it's always been? Are you going to wait for someone else to advocate for you, or are you ready to get out there and ask for what you want?

Are you compliant?

Danielle Henderson writes about film, television, and pop culture through the lens of race, gender, and class. She is a former editor and current staff writer for Rookie, and a book based on her popular website, *Feminist Ryan Gosling,* was released by Running Press in August 2012. She is very tall, and often forgets that she has freckles; strangers take every opportunity to remind her of both.

2 Steiner, Monica. "Are Prostitutes and 'Johns' Punished Equally? " Criminal Law, CriminalDefenseLawyer.com. Nolo, 2014. Web.

ITTY BITTY BITCHY
USE #BITCHPLANET

Ben Acker
@bnacker
#BitchPlanet: I have been waiting for this book ever since I broke the story by moderating the hell out of @kellysue

Mike Marlow
@MikeyGeek
@kellysue If #bitchplanet isn't a ripping yarn about the largest puppy mill in the galaxy, I don't know what I'll do.

James Leech
@jamesdleech
@kellysue I hope #bitchplanet results in the destruction of the patriarchy. Also Non-Compliant iPhone covers.

Envy Adams
@feminazgul
I really want #bitchplanet to not pull any punches. I want it to get in your face and never stop.

Schmelsea
@soundslikedead
@kellysue I really want #bitchplanet to be a comic that is about me, for me, but challenges me and is fucking awesome as all get out.

hannah banana :D
@hannahnoelle94
Dude I'm so excited for bitch planet to come out!!! #bitchplanet #comics

Jnet
@clam_slamz
@kellysue More bitches. Less planets. #bitchplanet

"GO FORTH AND BE NON-COMPLIANT."

BITCH FACE
TO BE FEATURED IN ITTY BITTY BITCHY OR BITCH FACE, BE SURE TO USE THE #BITCHPLANET HASHTAG ON TWITTER AND INSTAGRAM

1.
Kit Cox
@kitcox
i am #noncompliant - thanks
@samhumphries for the photo (with
guest appearance by beardo)

2.
jillwebb
@jillwebb
For @kellysue - looking forward to
#bitchplanet and new characters to
root for.

3.
Dog with a Blog
@motheroftrash
Hey @kellysue these temp tattoos are
real freakin rad!! #CarolCorps
#prettydeadly #noncompliant

4.
Rick Budd
@rbudd913
@kellysue Can't wait for this series.
#noncompliant

HEY KIDS, PATRIARCHY!

Missed Connection

ME: At the pool outside DESTINATIONS LOUNGE last Thursday night. I was wearing khakis, solid earning potential, a sparkling smile and a sincere desire for meaningful emotional connection beyond the usual small talk.
YOU: Hot, wet and mute

Are You Non-Compliant?

GIRLS, GIRLS, GIRLS!
You want that sexy, his-blood-in-a-bottle-around-your-neck **CRAZY CHICK** mystique? What says **DREAMY BAD GIRL** like a temporary tattoo??
PUT IT ON YOUR FACE.

X-RAY SPECS

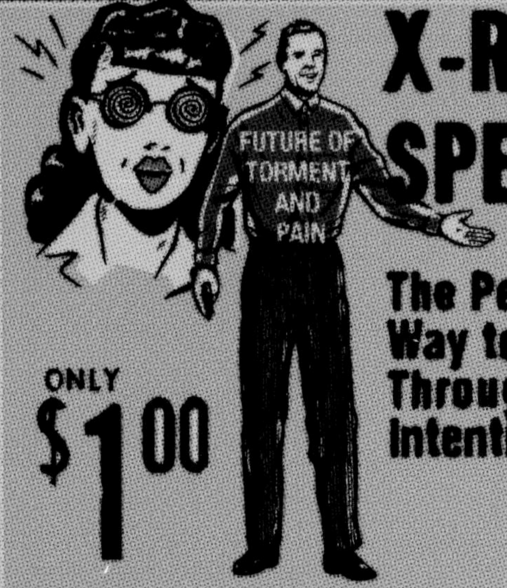
FUTURE OF TORMENT AND PAIN

The Perfect Way to See Through His Intentions

ONLY $1.00

AMAZING CLARITY INSTANTLY!
Surprise insight! Scientific obfuscation really works. Imagine—you put on the "X-Ray" Specs and hold his hand in front of you. You SEEM to be able to look right through him and see the truth! That guy in the black Taurus who followed you home? Is that really insecurity you "see" beneath his clothes? Or is it a gun? Is he probably going to murder you?
LOADS OF LAUGHS AND FUN AT PARTIES

Happy Anniversary!

Dawn, you are my light, my morning, my new beginning. Every day I wake with you, I am reborn. Every minute before we met was prologue — HALF my age and ALL of my heart! Let's stay young together forever as long as it feels good.
xxx Skip

RABBIT

I'm spending the only credits I have to place this ad. I need your help. There's no one else I can turn to and nowhere I can hide. **THE DUCHESS** said this was how to reach you. Tell me what to do. **— ALICE**

Let Us Change Your Personality (or at least your signature!)

Send us your full name and we'll craft **SIX UNIQUE SIGNATURES** for you to choose from, learn and pretend they express something real about you. Don't like your name? For an extra twenty-five cents, we'll change that too.

SIGN................3 for $3.00 w/shipping

PROTECT YOUR FACE

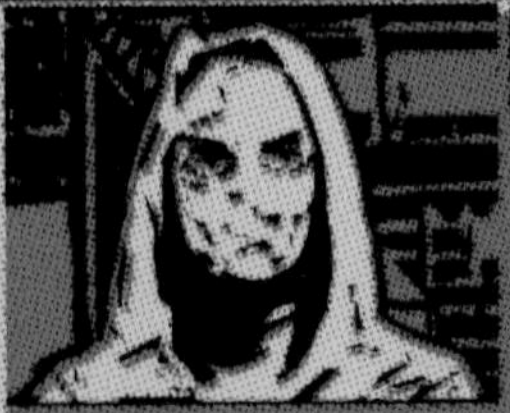

The sadistic staff on BITCH PLANET must shield their skin to protect themselves from the dampening effects of the alien environment. Who knew their prophylactic faces would be as FABULOUS as they are FREAKY? Now you can emulate the look! Be the first on your block to warp your face and call it FASHION.

FACE...............$3.00 w/shipping

ORDER BY MAIL

You know this is garbage, right? You're ordering garbage. Okay, well, you were warned. Send your dad's hard earned money to the address below and we'll keep the Postal Service alive a little longer by mailing you some crap. I'm not shipping international, so don't even try.

ITEM	HOW MANY	PRICE
SIGN		$3.00
FACE		$3.00
NON		$1.50
	TOTAL	

ALLOW 3-6 WEEKS FOR SHIPPING

SEND CHECK OR MONEY ORDER TO:
Milkfed Criminal Masterminds, Inc. PO Box 25662, Portland, OR 97298

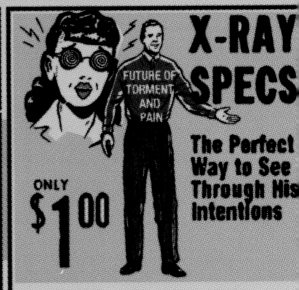

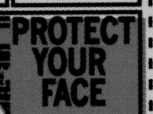

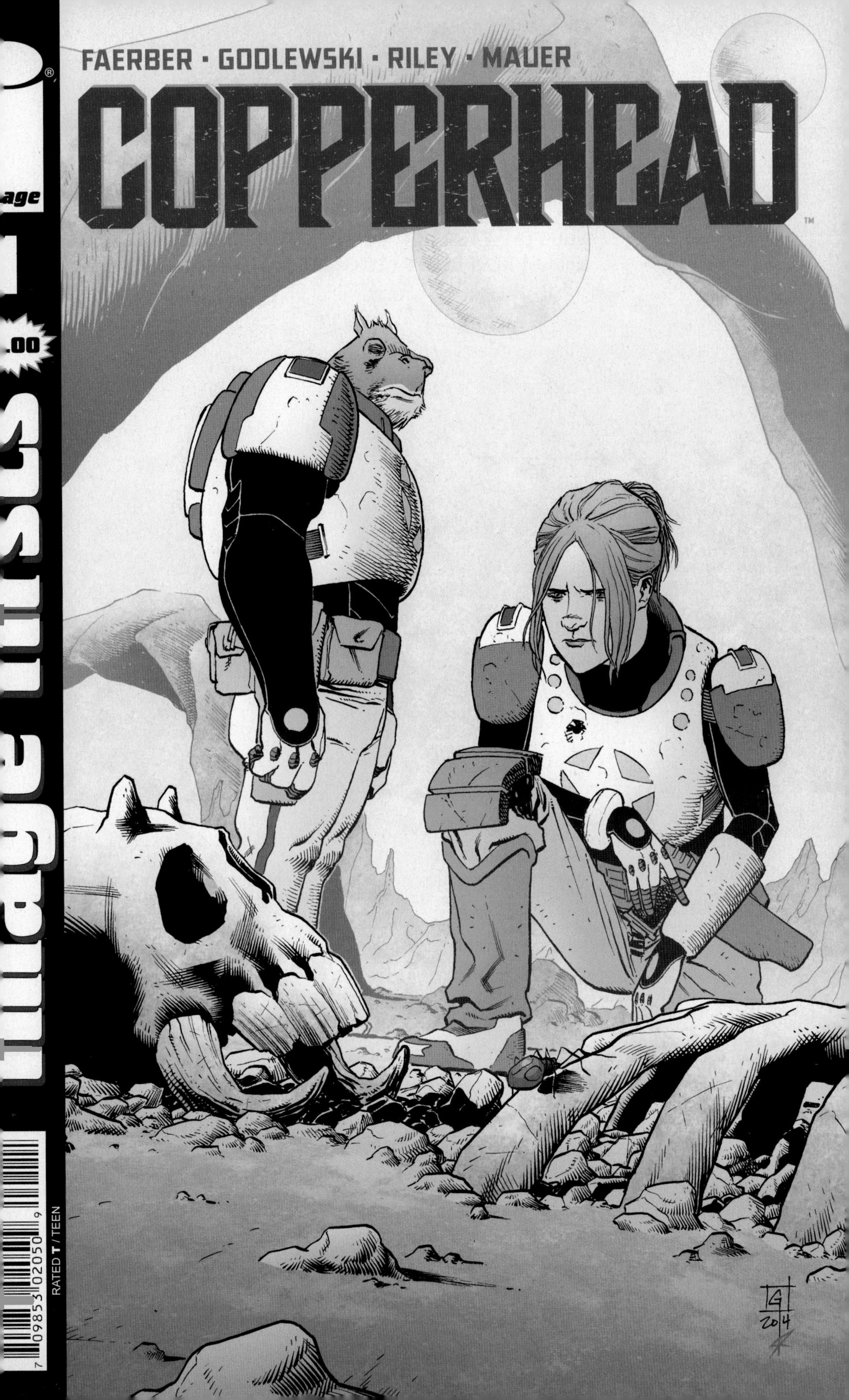

FAERBER · GODLEWSKI · RILEY · MAUER
COPPERHEAD
™
image firsts
.00
RATED T / TEEN
7 09853 02050 9

CREATED BY Jay Faerber & Scott Godlewski

COPPERHEAD™

writer **JAY FAERBER**   **SCOTT GODLEWSKI** artist
colorist **RON RILEY**   **THOMAS MAUER** letterer

Image Comics, Inc.

Robert Kirkman — Chief Operating Officer
Erik Larsen — Chief Financial Officer
Todd McFarlane — President
Marc Silvestri — Chief Executive Officer
Jim Valentino — Vice-President

Eric Stephenson — Publisher
Corey Murphy — Director of Sales
Jeff Boison — Director of Publishing Planning & Book Trade Sales
Jeremy Sullivan — Director of Digital Sales
Kat Salazar — Director of PR & Marketing
Emily Miller — Director of Operations
Branwyn Bigglestone — Senior Accounts Manager
Sarah Mello — Accounts Manager
Drew Gill — Art Director
Jonathan Chan — Production Manager
Meredith Wallace — Print Manager

Briah Skelly — Publicity Assistant
Randy Okamura — Marketing Production Designer
David Brothers — Branding Manager
Ally Power — Content Manager
Addison Duke — Production Artist
Vincent Kukua — Production Artist
Sasha Head — Production Artist
Tricia Ramos — Production Artist
Jeff Stang — Direct Market Sales Representative
Emilio Bautista — Digital Sales Associate
Chloe Ramos-Peterson — Administrative Assistant

imagecomics.com

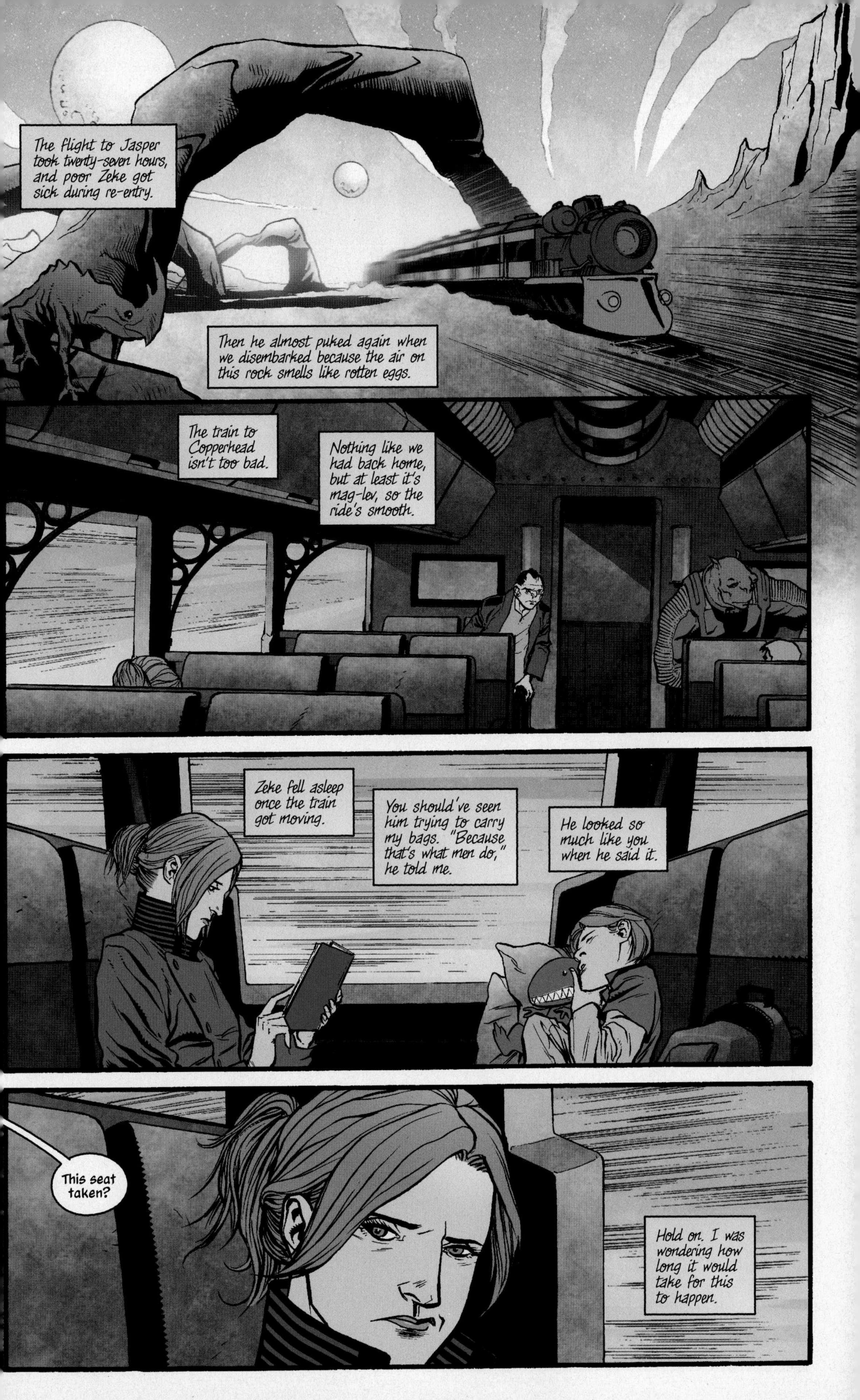
The flight to Jasper took twenty-seven hours, and poor Zeke got sick during re-entry.
Then he almost puked again when we disembarked because the air on this rock smells like rotten eggs.
The train to Copperhead isn't too bad.
Nothing like we had back home, but at least it's mag-lev, so the ride's smooth.
Zeke fell asleep once the train got moving.
You should've seen him trying to carry my bags. "Because that's what men do," he told me.
He looked so much like you when he said it.
This seat taken?
Hold on. I was wondering how long it would take for this to happen.

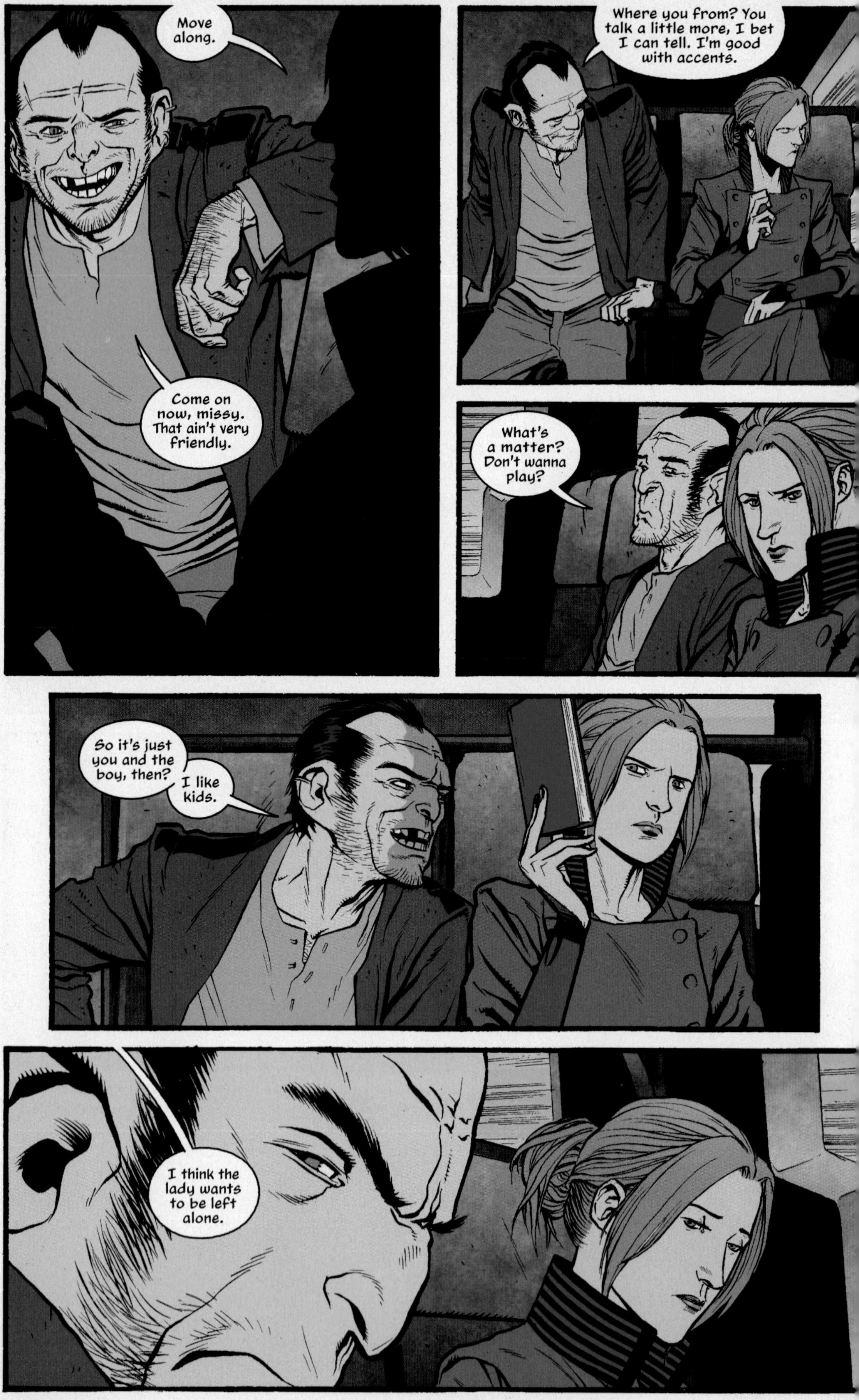
Move along.
Come on now, missy. That ain't very friendly.
Where you from? You talk a little more, I bet I can tell. I'm good with accents.
What's a matter? Don't wanna play?
So it's just you and the boy, then?
I like kids.
I think the lady wants to be left alone.

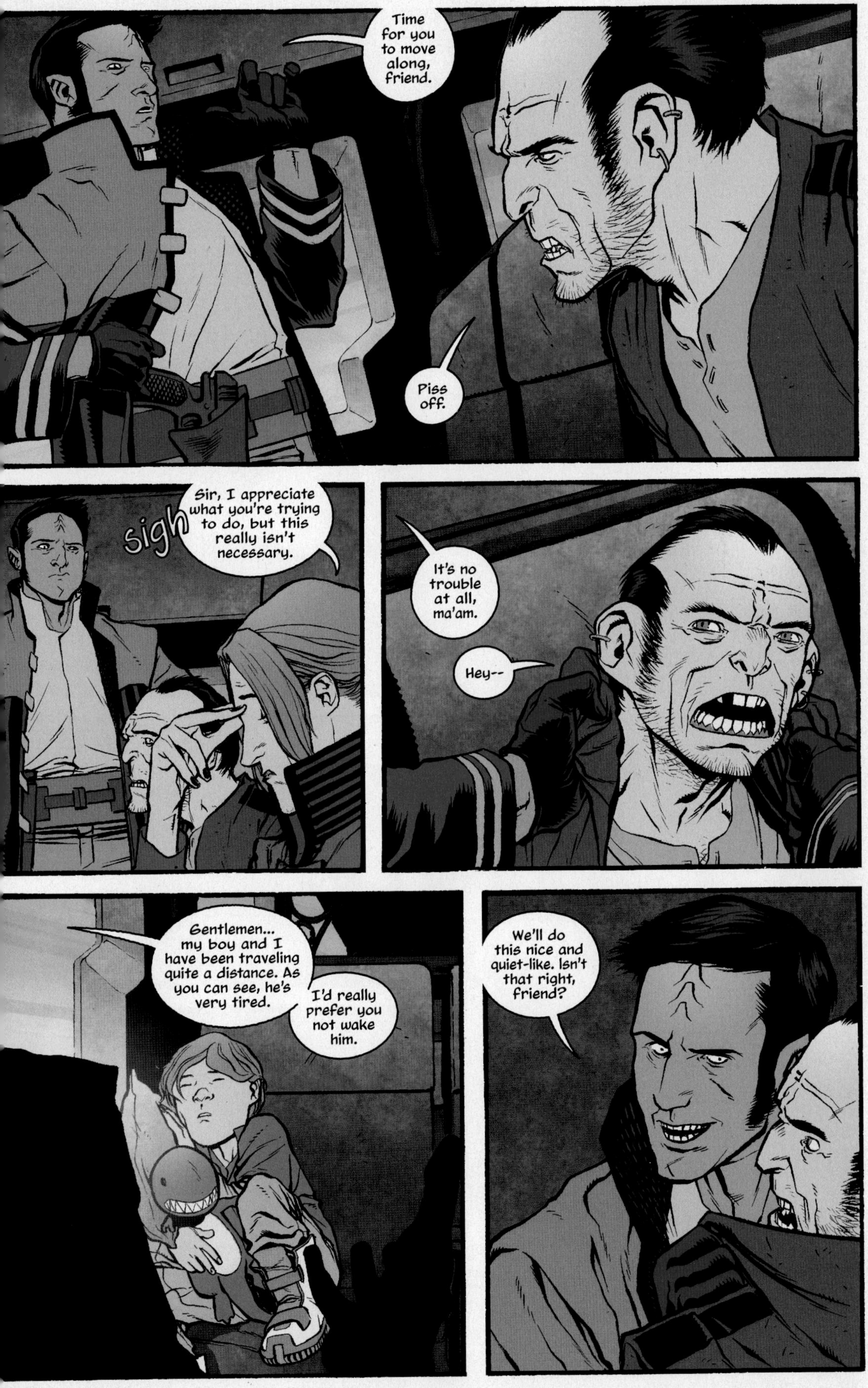
Time for you to move along, friend.
Piss off.
Sir, I appreciate what you're trying to do, but this really isn't necessary.
sigh
It's no trouble at all, ma'am.
Hey--
Gentlemen... my boy and I have been traveling quite a distance. As you can see, he's very tired.
I'd really prefer you not wake him.
We'll do this nice and quiet-like. Isn't that right, friend?

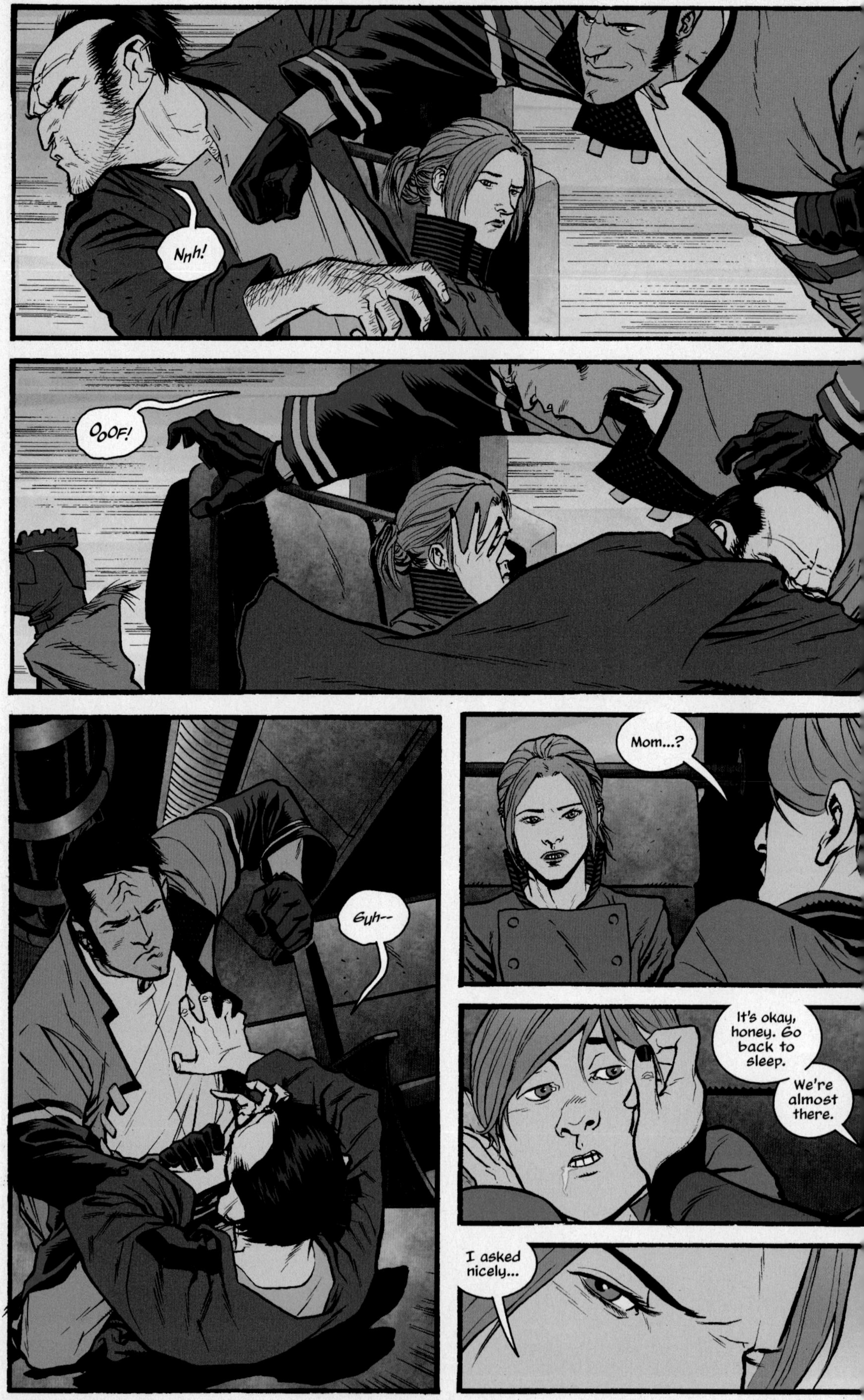
Nnh!
OOOF!
Guh--
Mom...?
It's okay, honey. Go back to sleep.
We're almost there.
I asked nicely...

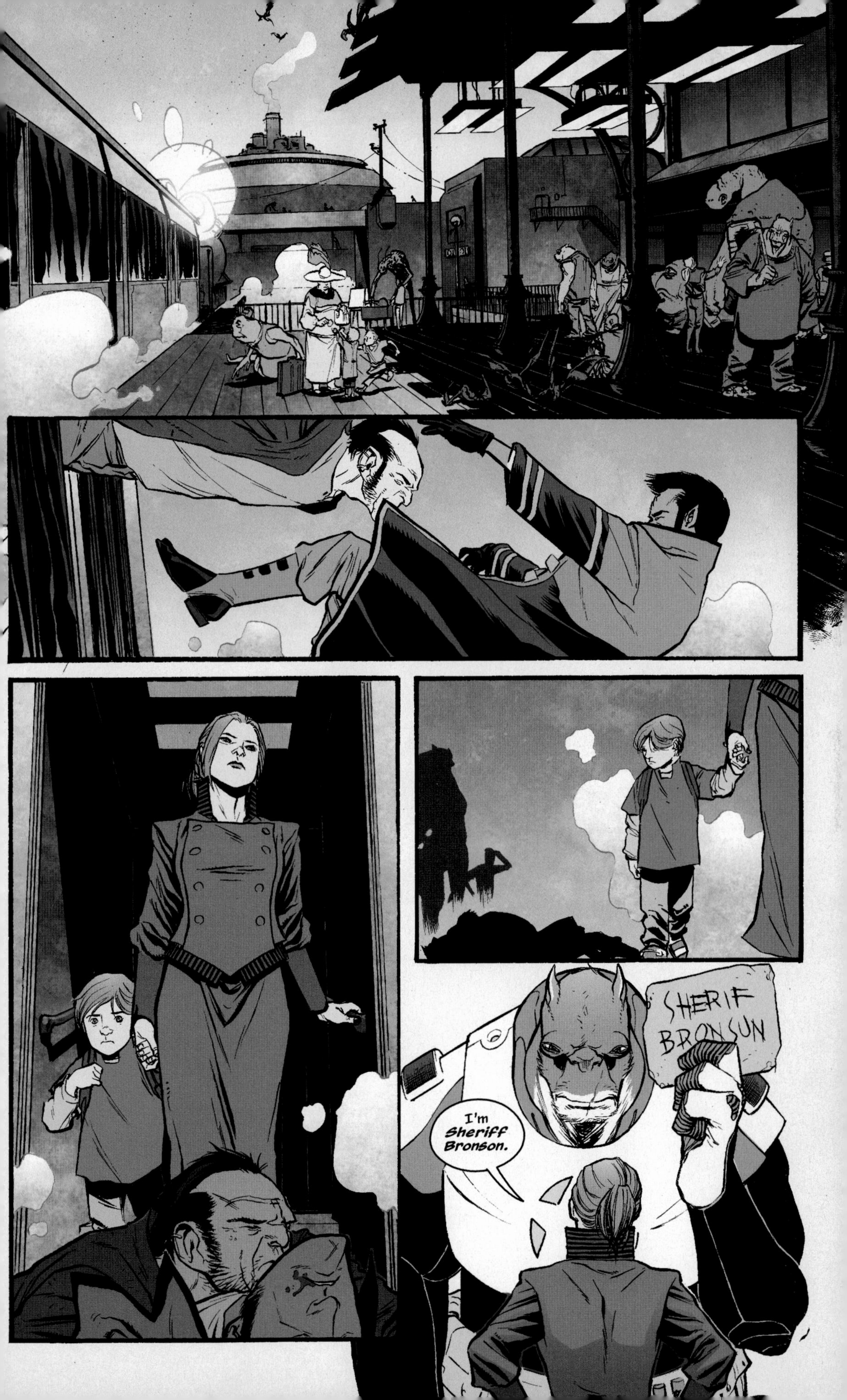
SHERIF BRONSUN
I'm Sheriff Bronson.

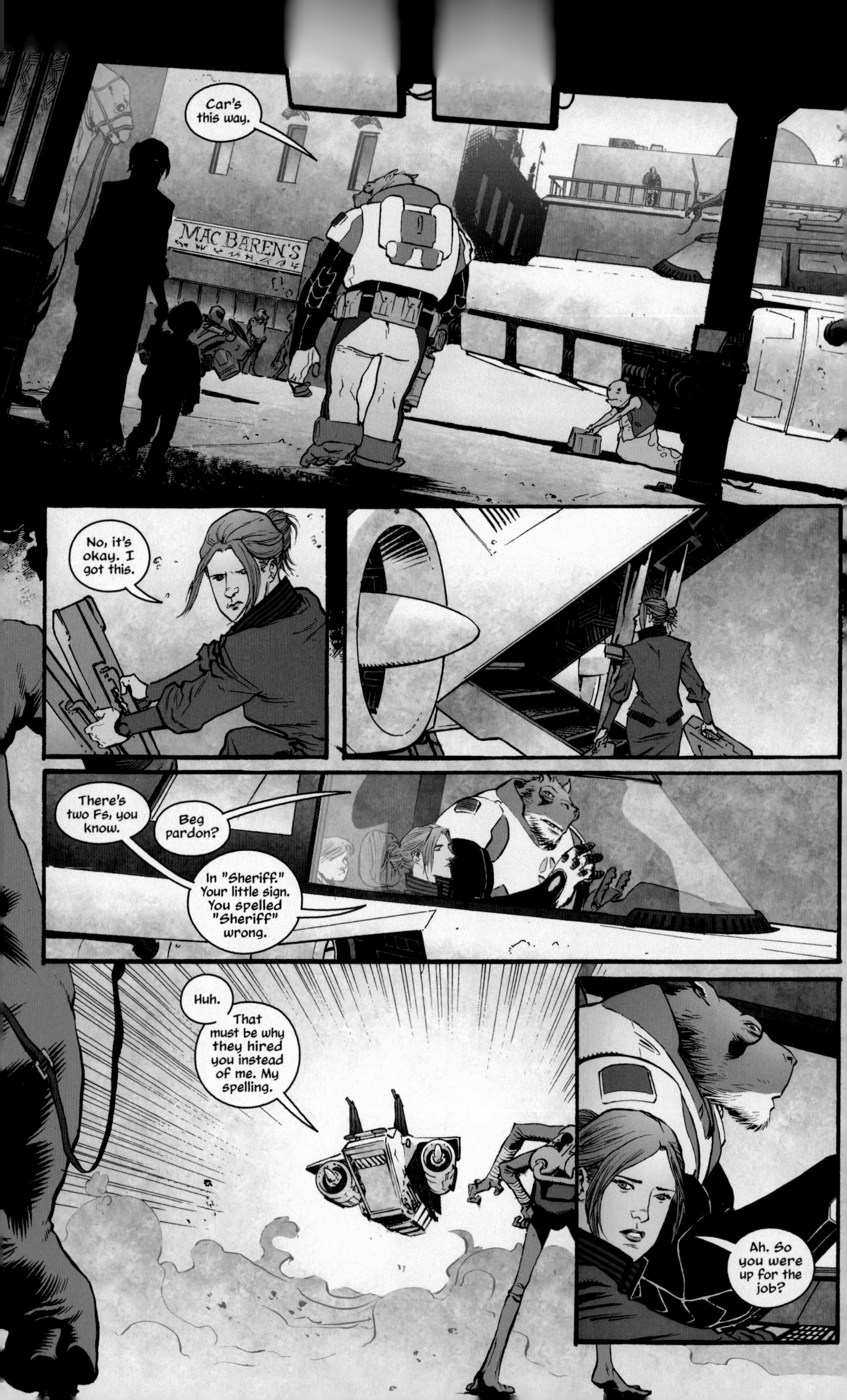

Car's this way.
MAC BAREN'S
No, it's okay. I got this.
There's two Fs, you know.
Beg pardon?
In "Sheriff." Your little sign. You spelled "Sheriff" wrong.
Huh.
That must be why they hired you instead of me. My spelling.
Ah. So you were up for the job?

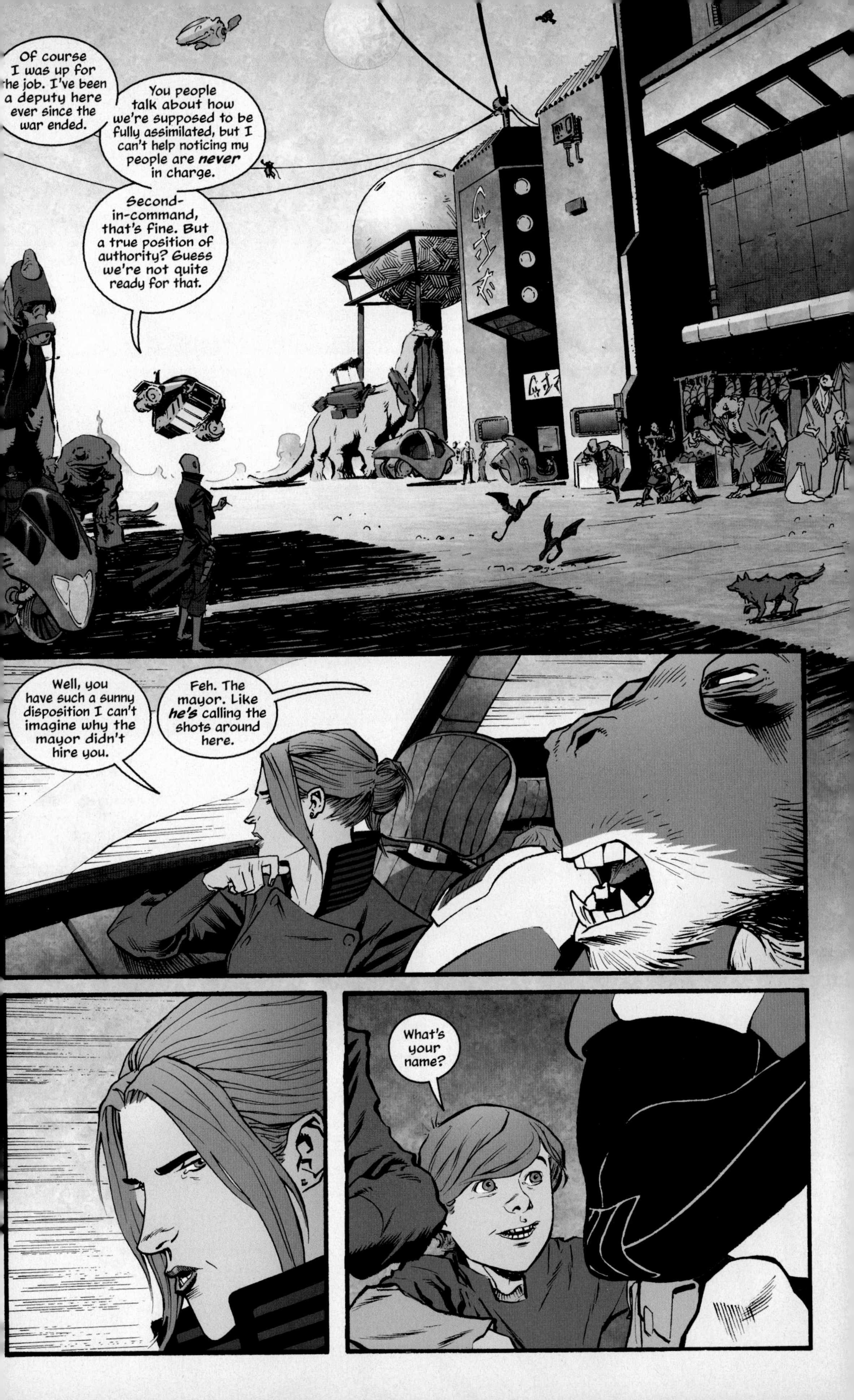
Of course I was up for he job. I've been a deputy here ever since the war ended.
You people talk about how we're supposed to be fully assimilated, but I can't help noticing my people are ***never*** in charge.
Second-in-command, that's fine. But a true position of authority? Guess we're not quite ready for that.
Well, you have such a sunny disposition I can't imagine why the mayor didn't hire you.
Feh. The mayor. Like ***he's*** calling the shots around here.
What's your name?

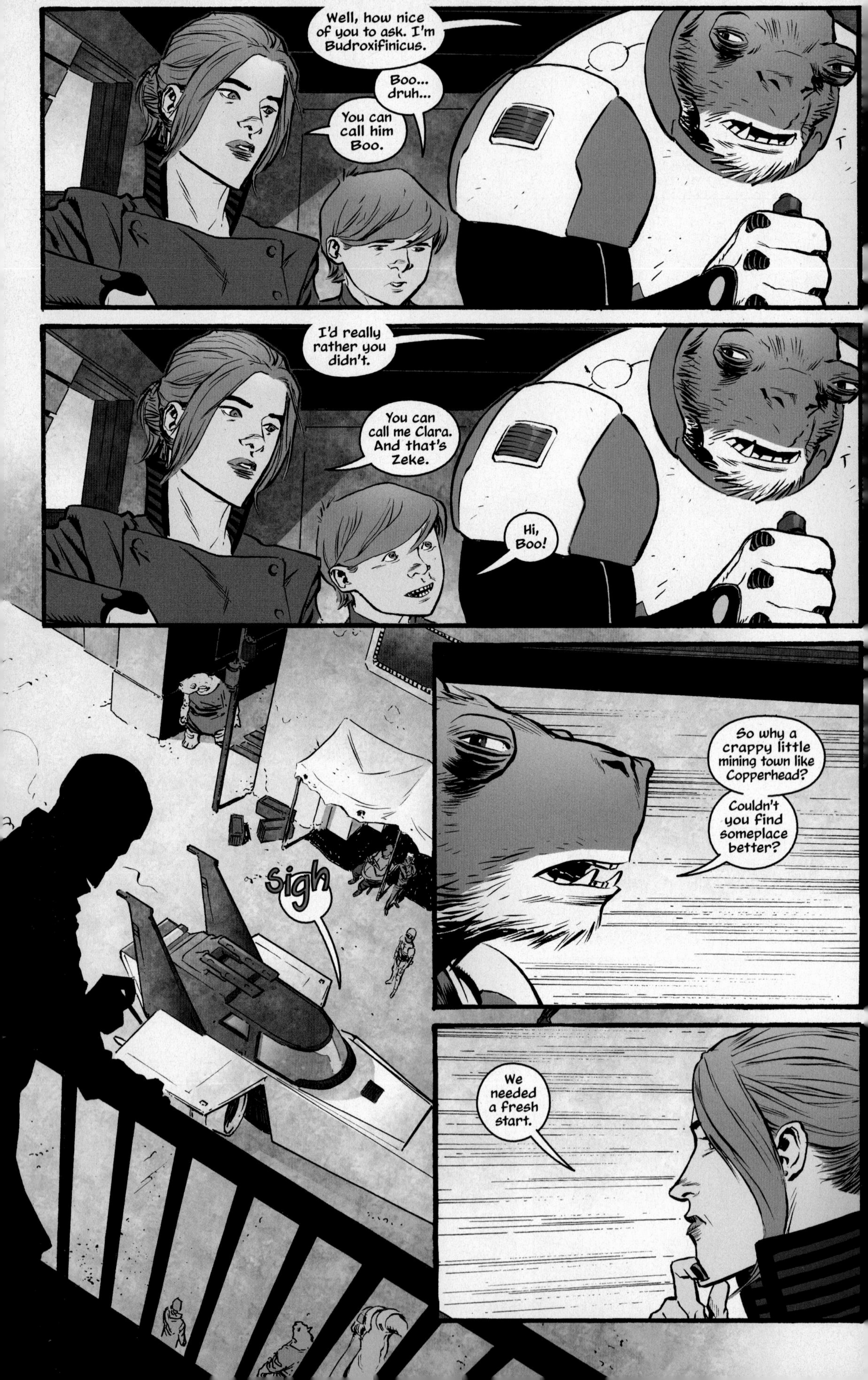
Well, how nice of you to ask. I'm Budroxifinicus.
Boo... druh...
You can call him Boo.
I'd really rather you didn't.
You can call me Clara. And that's Zeke.
Hi, Boo!
Sigh
So why a crappy little mining town like Copperhead?
Couldn't you find someplace better?
We needed a fresh start.

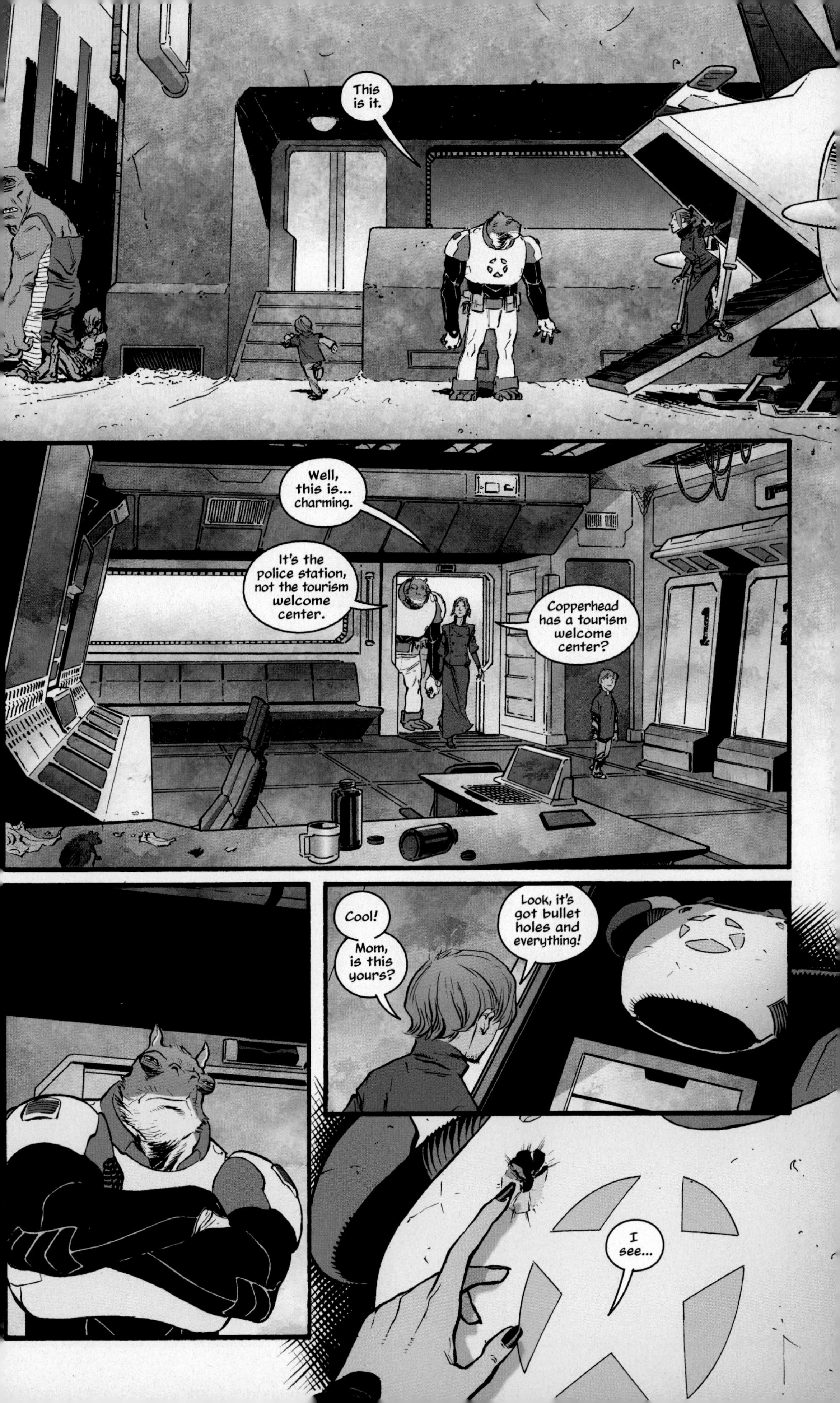
This is it.
Well, this is... charming.
It's the police station, not the tourism welcome center.
Copperhead has a tourism welcome center?
Cool!
Mom, is this yours?
Look, it's got bullet holes and everything!
I see...

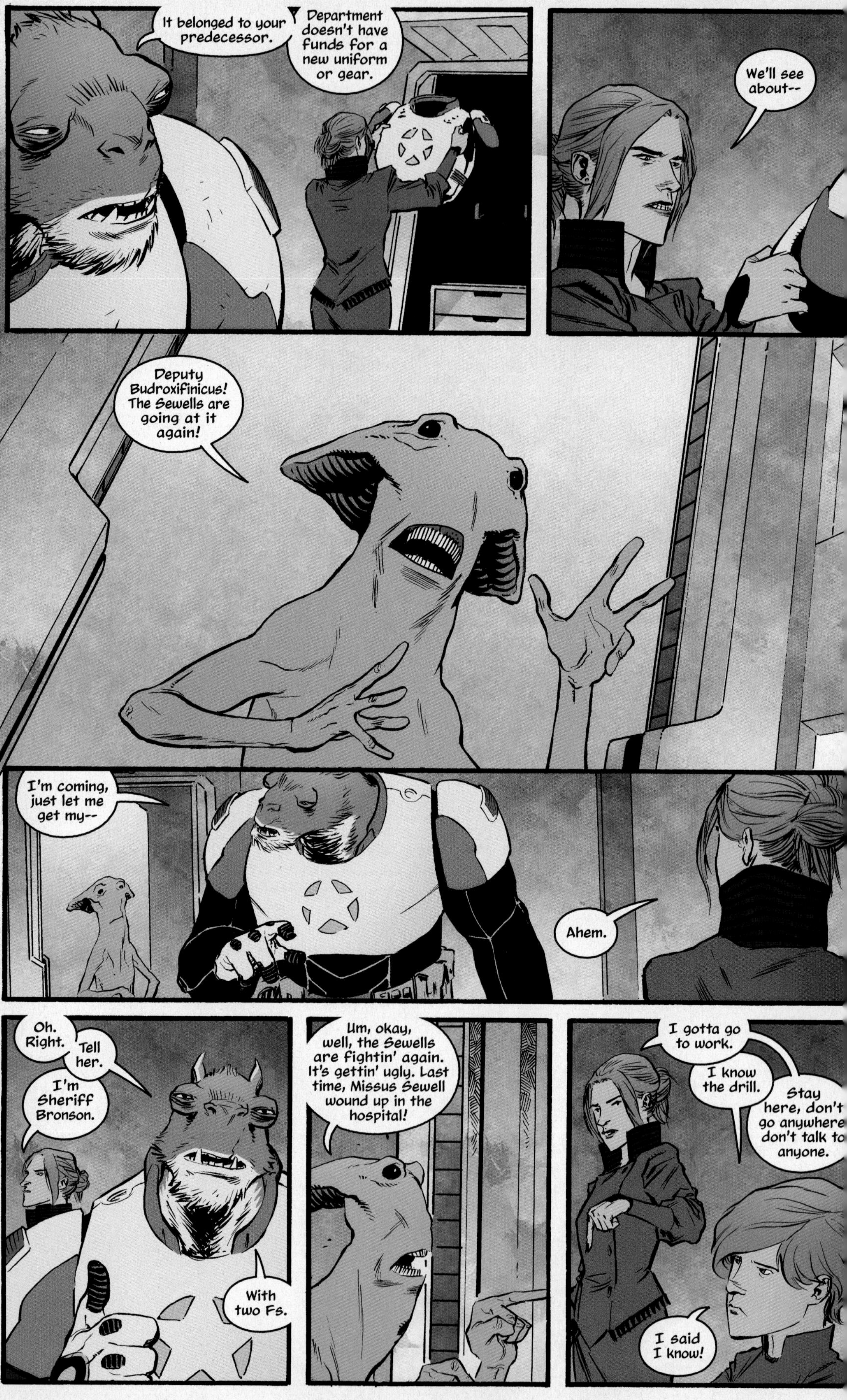
It belonged to your predecessor.
Department doesn't have funds for a new uniform or gear.
We'll see about--
Deputy Budroxifinicus! The Sewells are going at it again!
I'm coming, just let me get my--
Ahem.
Oh. Right.
Tell her.
I'm Sheriff Bronson.
With two Fs.
Um, okay, well, the Sewells are fightin' again. It's gettin' ugly. Last time, Missus Sewell wound up in the hospital!
I gotta go to work.
I know the drill.
Stay here, don't go anywhere don't talk to anyone.
I said I know!

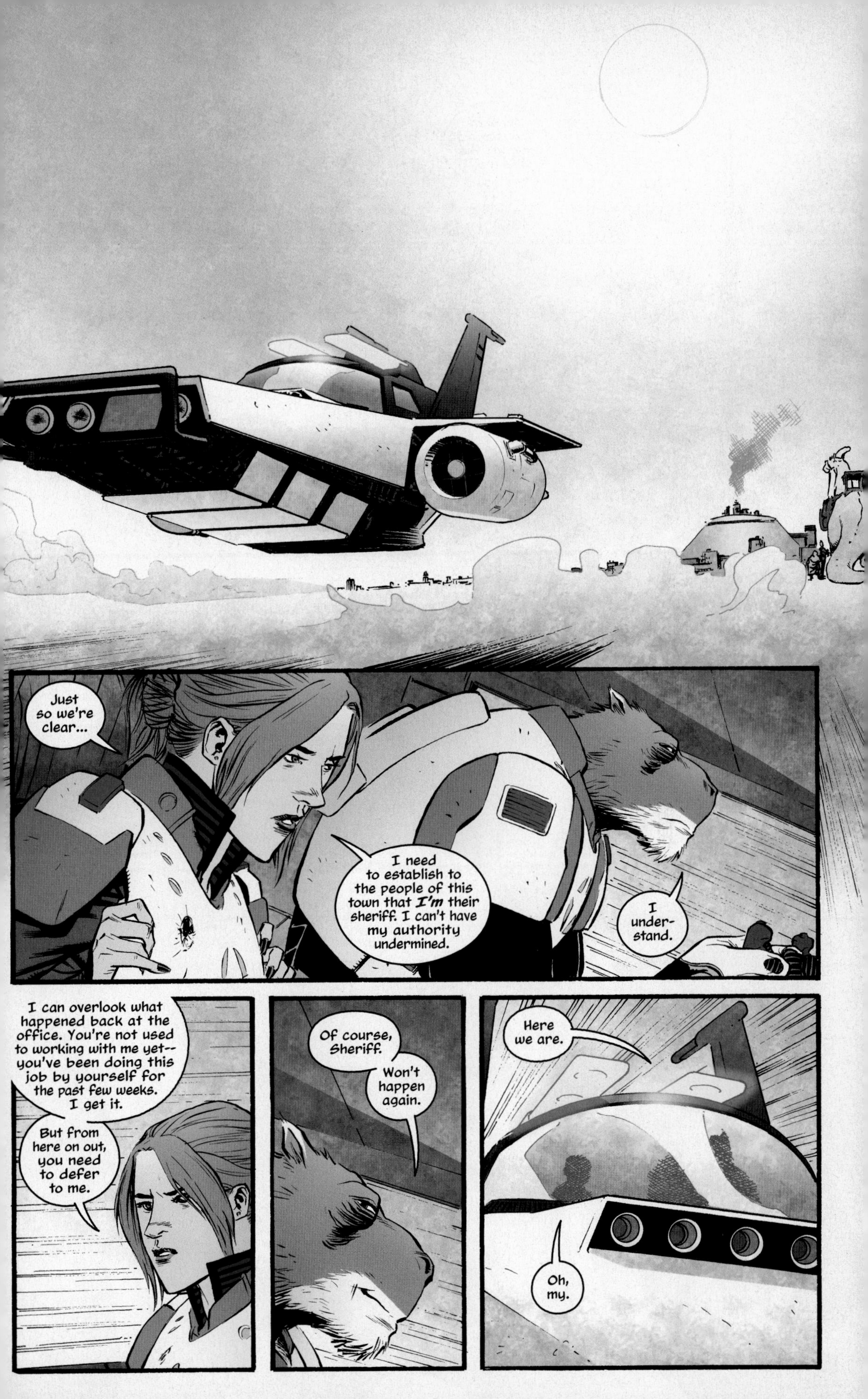

Just so we're clear...
I need to establish to the people of this town that I'm their sheriff. I can't have my authority undermined.
I under-stand.
I can overlook what happened back at the office. You're not used to working with me yet--you've been doing this job by yourself for the past few weeks. I get it.
But from here on out, you need to defer to me.
Of course, Sheriff.
Won't happen again.
Here we are.
Oh, my.

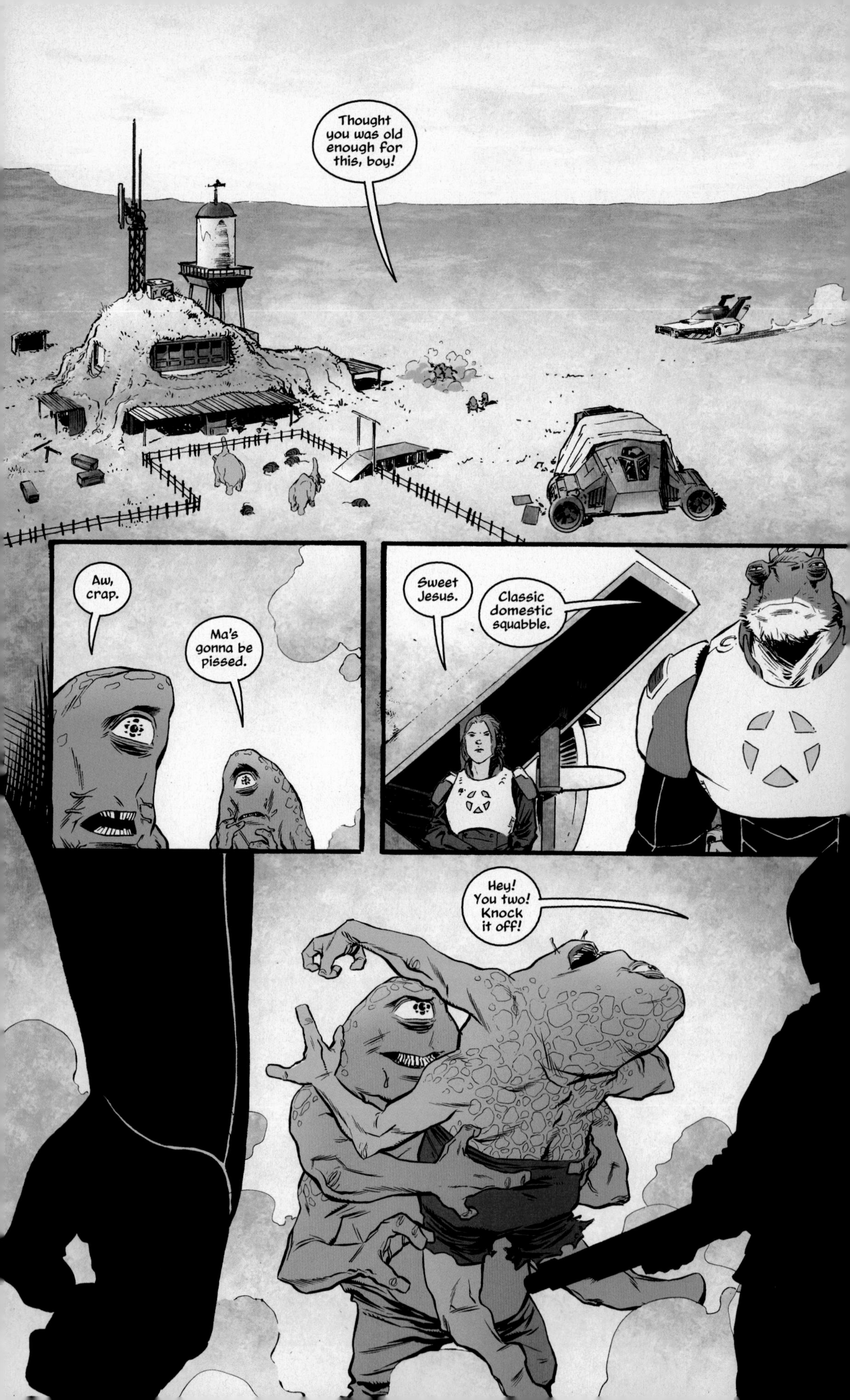
Thought you was old enough for this, boy!
Aw, crap.
Ma's gonna be pissed.
Sweet Jesus.
Classic domestic squabble.
Hey! You two! Knock it off!

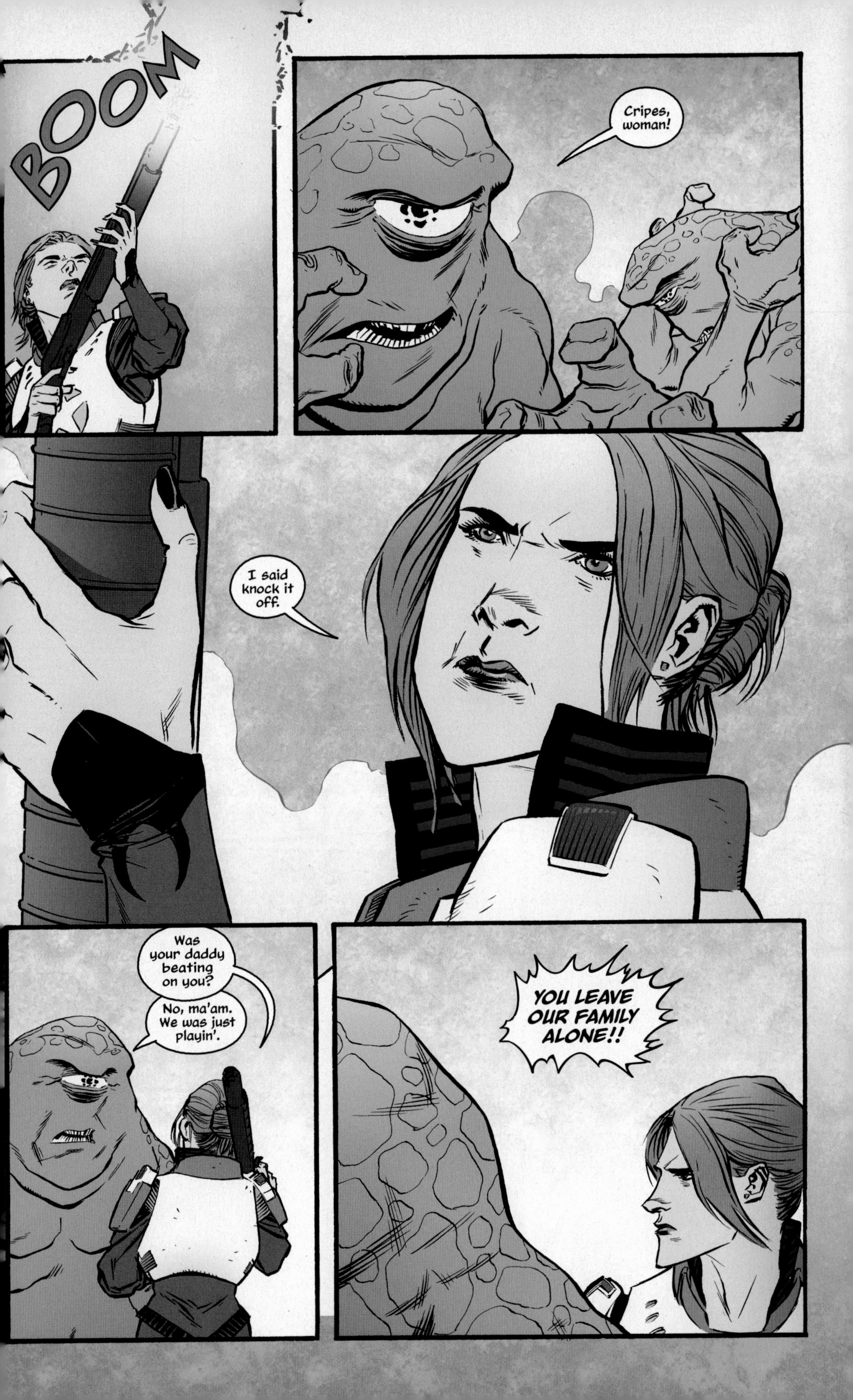
BOOM
Cripes, woman!
I said knock it off.
Was your daddy beating on you?
No, ma'am. We was just playin'.
YOU LEAVE OUR FAMILY ALONE!!

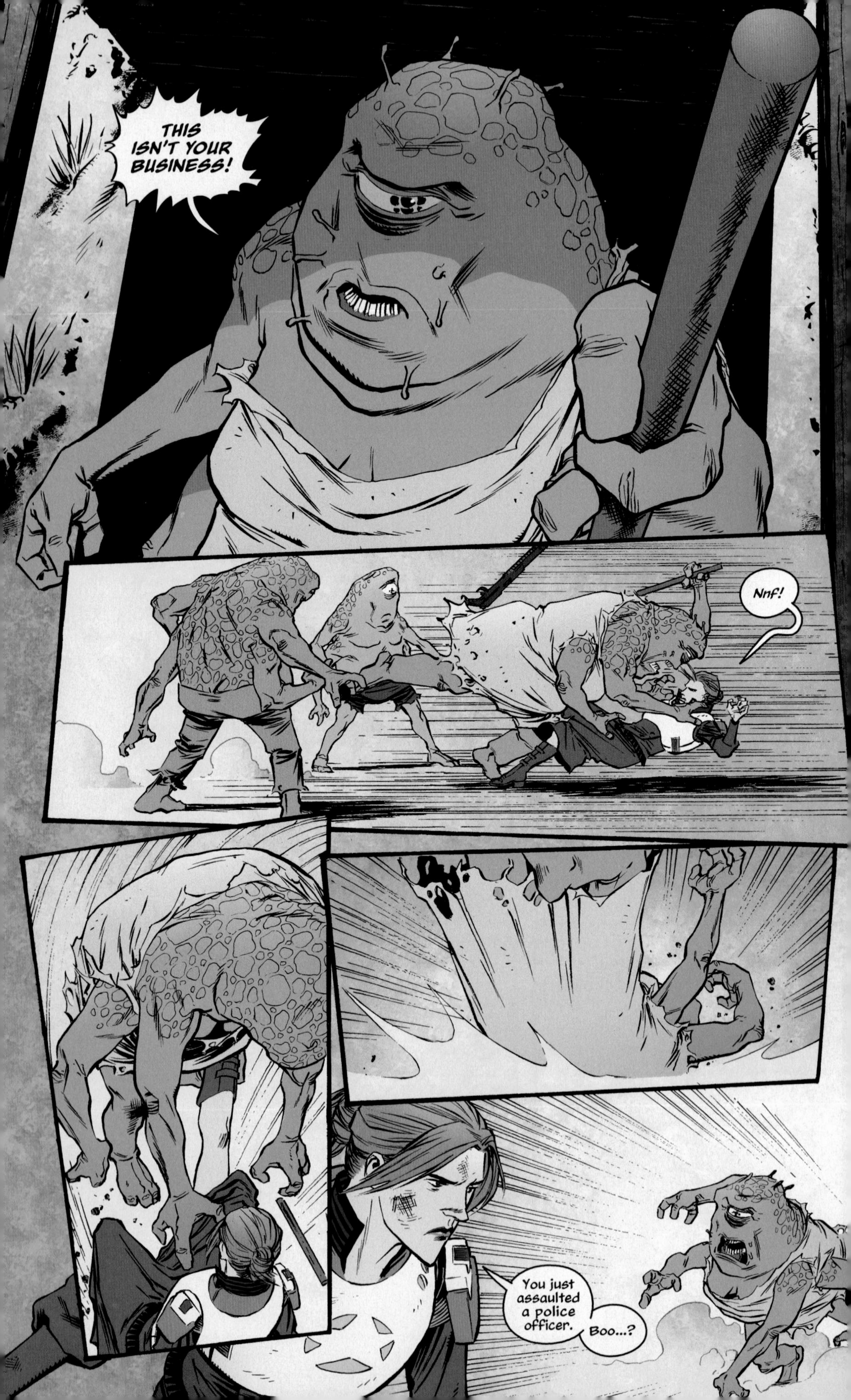
THIS ISN'T YOUR BUSINESS!
Nnf!
You just assaulted a police officer.
Boo...?

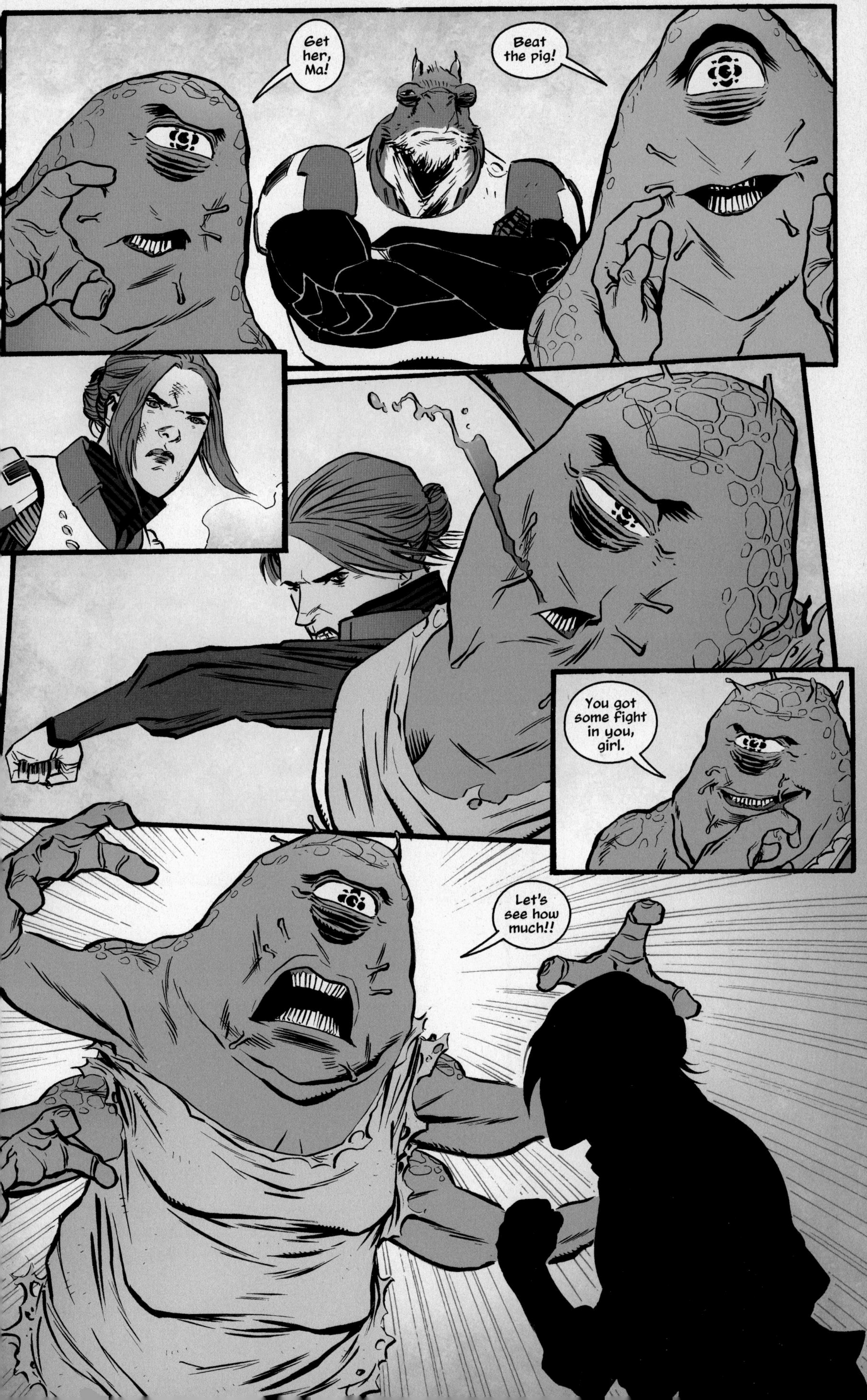
Get her, Ma!
Beat the pig!
You got some fight in you, girl.
Let's see how much!!

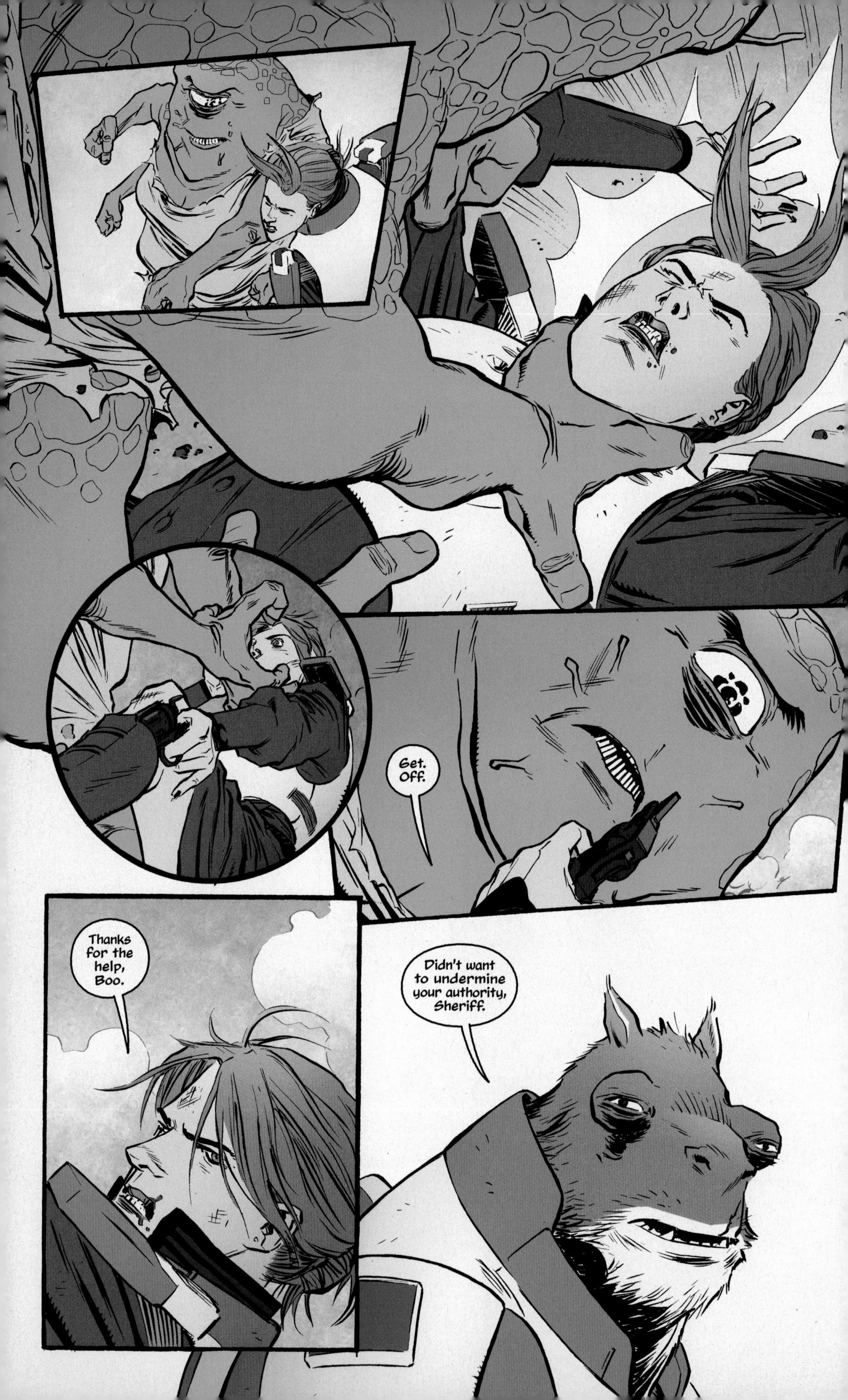
Get.
Off.
Thanks for the help, Boo.
Didn't want to undermine your authority, Sheriff.

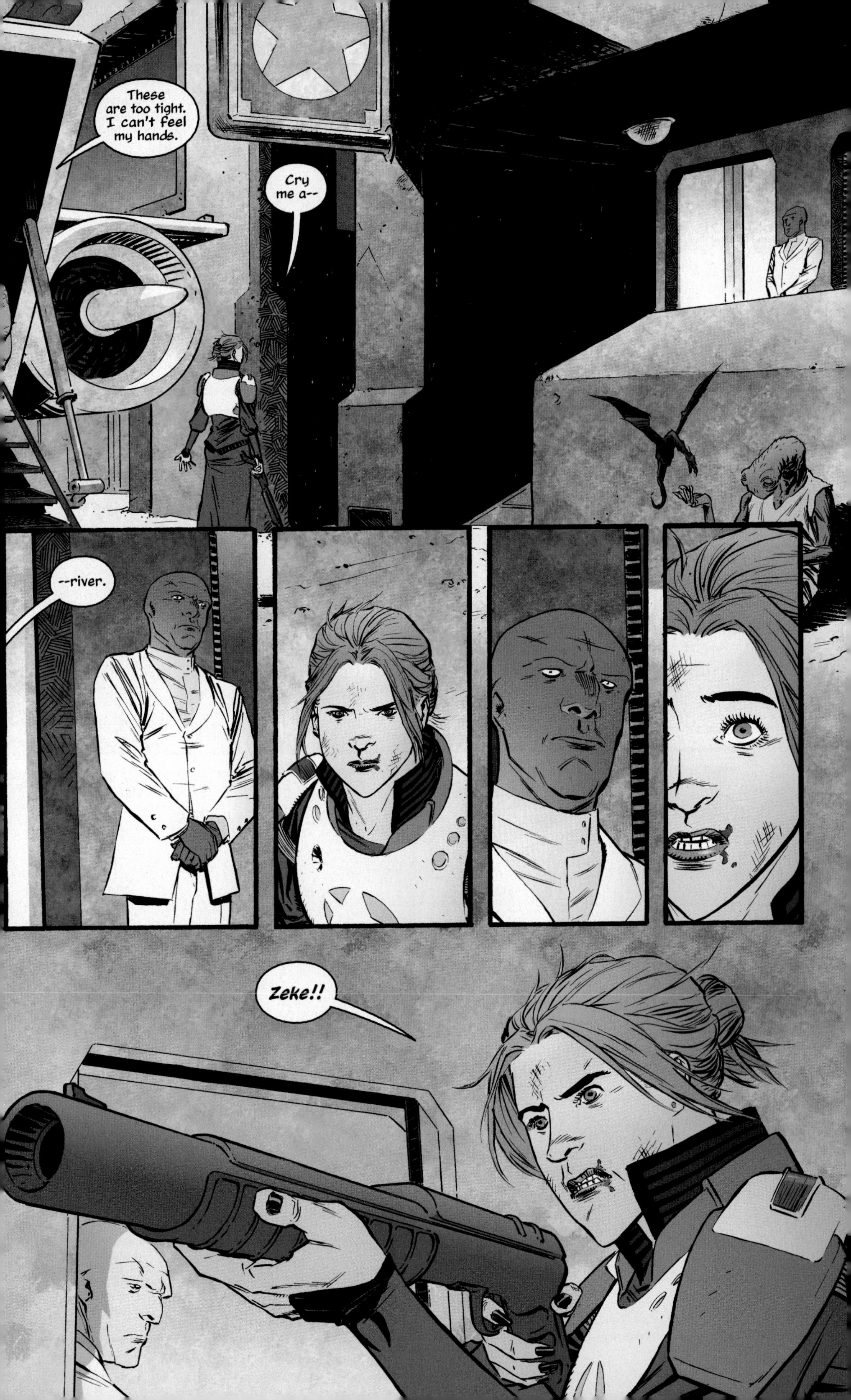
These are too tight. I can't feel my hands.
Cry me a--
--river.
Zeke!!

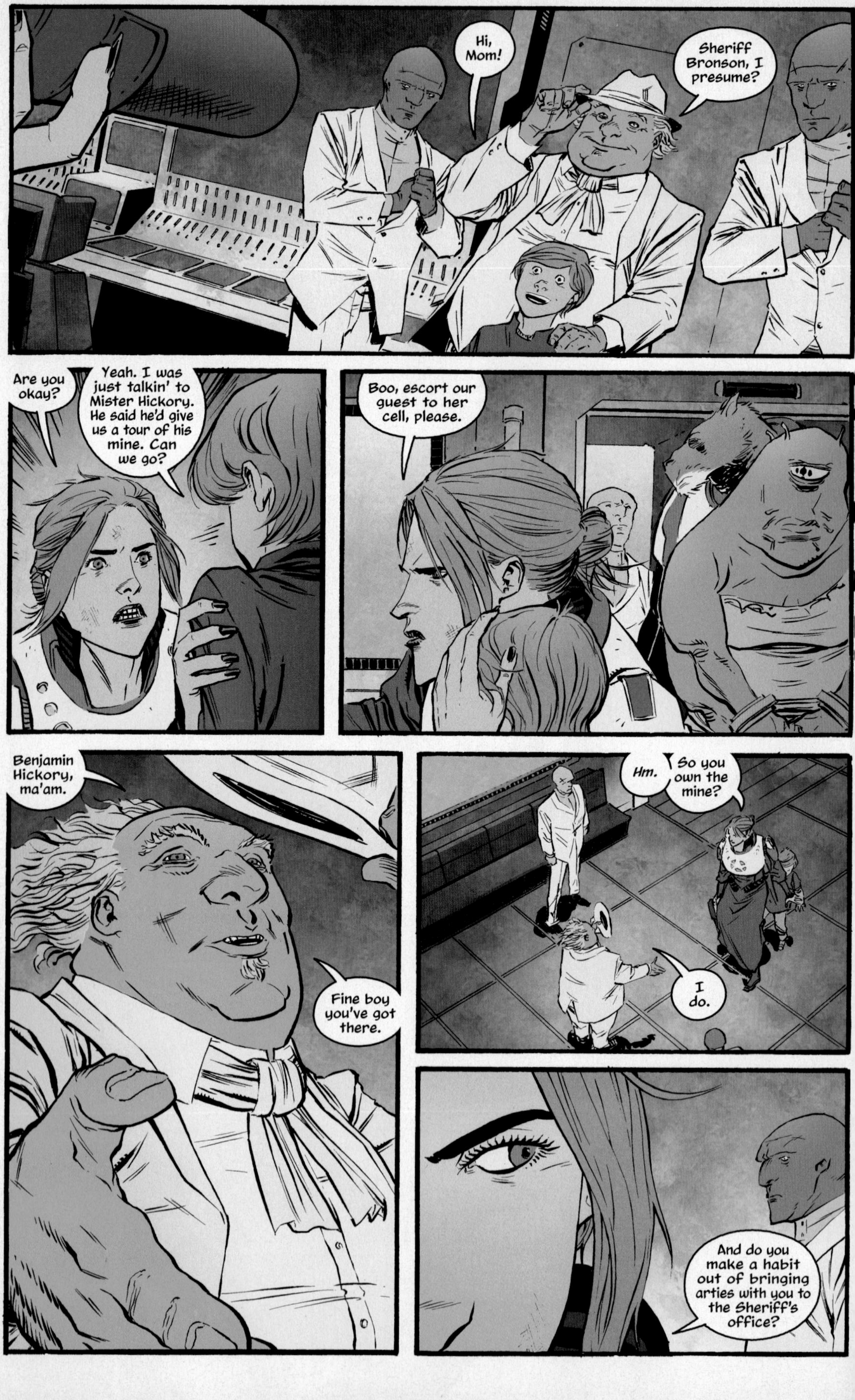
Hi, Mom!
Sheriff Bronson, I presume?
Are you okay?
Yeah. I was just talkin' to Mister Hickory. He said he'd give us a tour of his mine. Can we go?
Boo, escort our guest to her cell, please.
Benjamin Hickory, ma'am.
Fine boy you've got there.
Hm.
So you own the mine?
I do.
And do you make a habit out of bringing arties with you to the Sheriff's office?

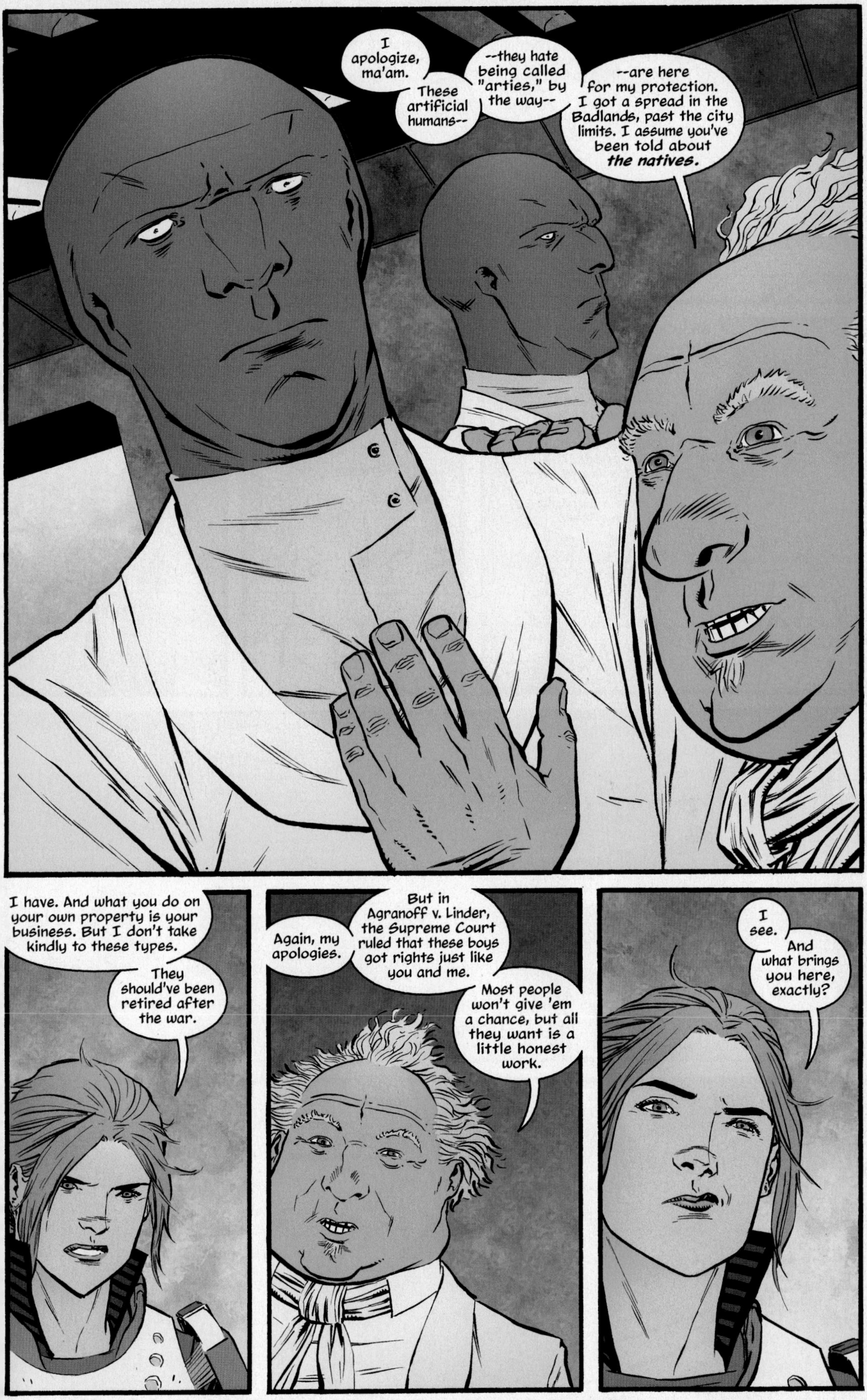
I apologize, ma'am.
These artificial humans--
--they hate being called "arties," by the way--
--are here for my protection. I got a spread in the Badlands, past the city limits. I assume you've been told about *the natives.*
I have. And what you do on your own property is your business. But I don't take kindly to these types.
They should've been retired after the war.
Again, my apologies.
But in Agranoff v. Linder, the Supreme Court ruled that these boys got rights just like you and me.
Most people won't give 'em a chance, but all they want is a little honest work.
I see.
And what brings you here, exactly?

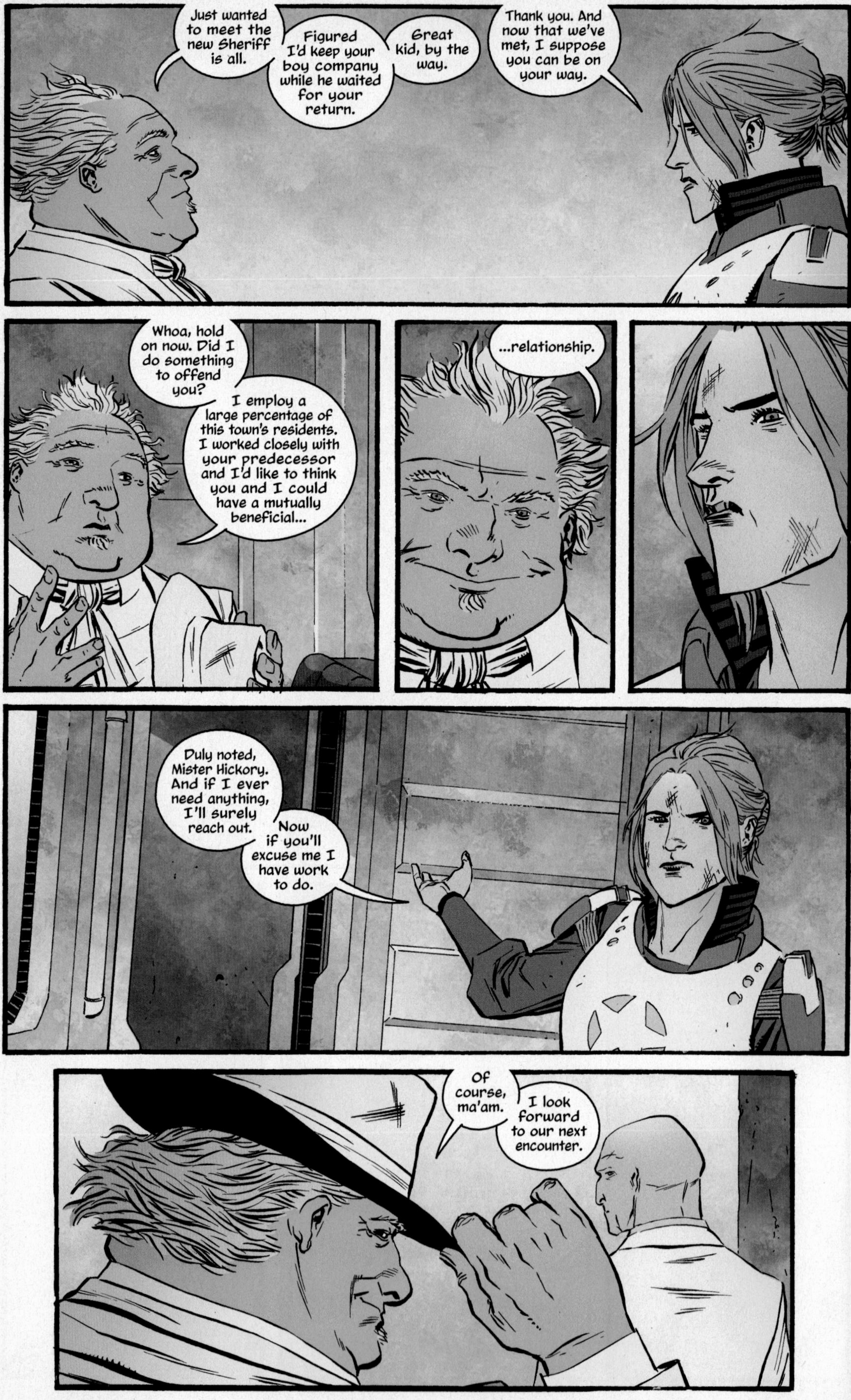
Just wanted to meet the new Sheriff is all.
Figured I'd keep your boy company while he waited for your return.
Great kid, by the way.
Thank you. And now that we've met, I suppose you can be on your way.
Whoa, hold on now. Did I do something to offend you?
I employ a large percentage of this town's residents. I worked closely with your predecessor and I'd like to think you and I could have a mutually beneficial...
...relationship.
Duly noted, Mister Hickory. And if I ever need anything, I'll surely reach out.
Now if you'll excuse me I have work to do.
Of course, ma'am.
I look forward to our next encounter.

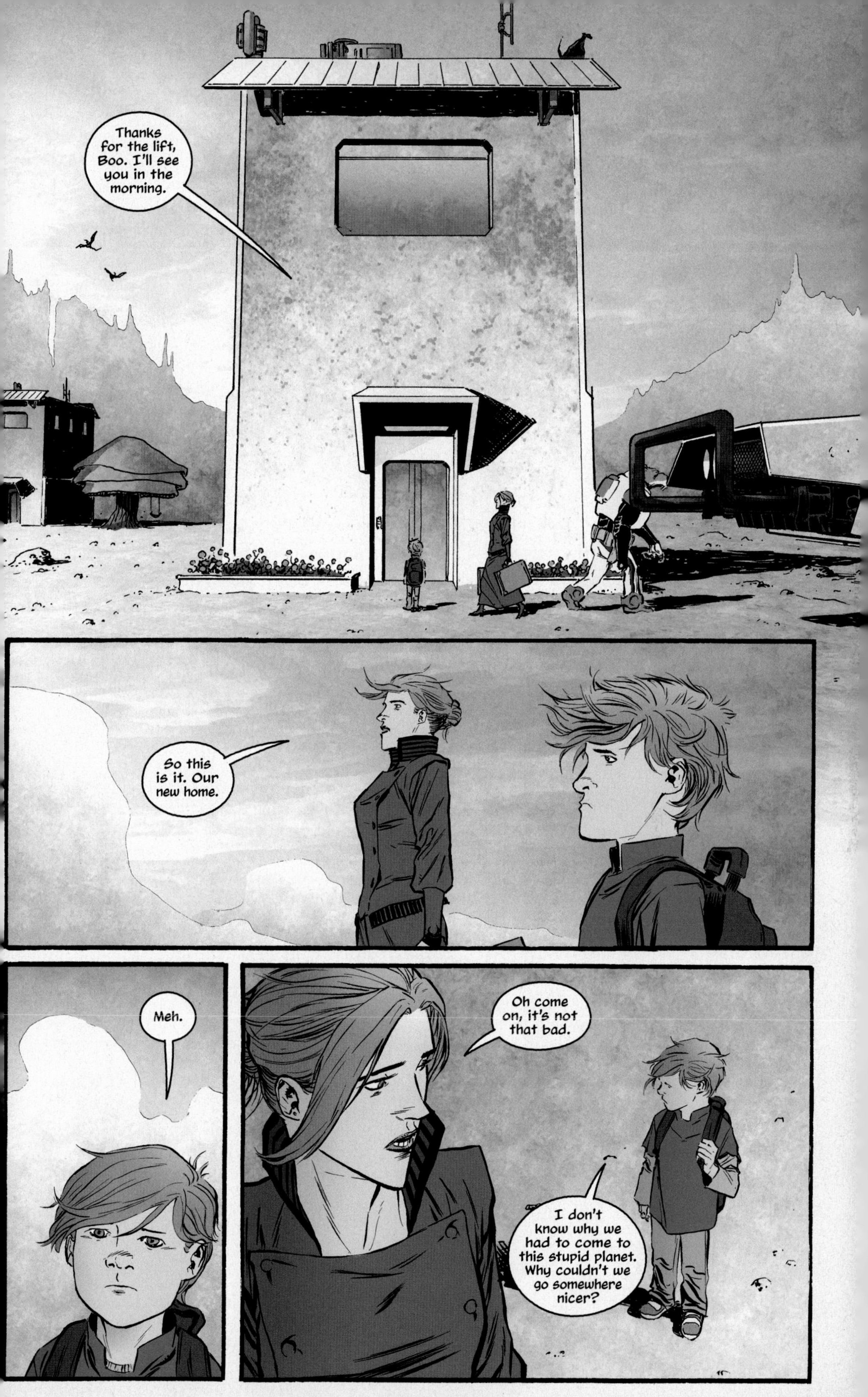
Thanks for the lift, Boo. I'll see you in the morning.
So this is it. Our new home.
Meh.
Oh come on, it's not that bad.
I don't know why we had to come to this stupid planet. Why couldn't we go somewhere nicer?

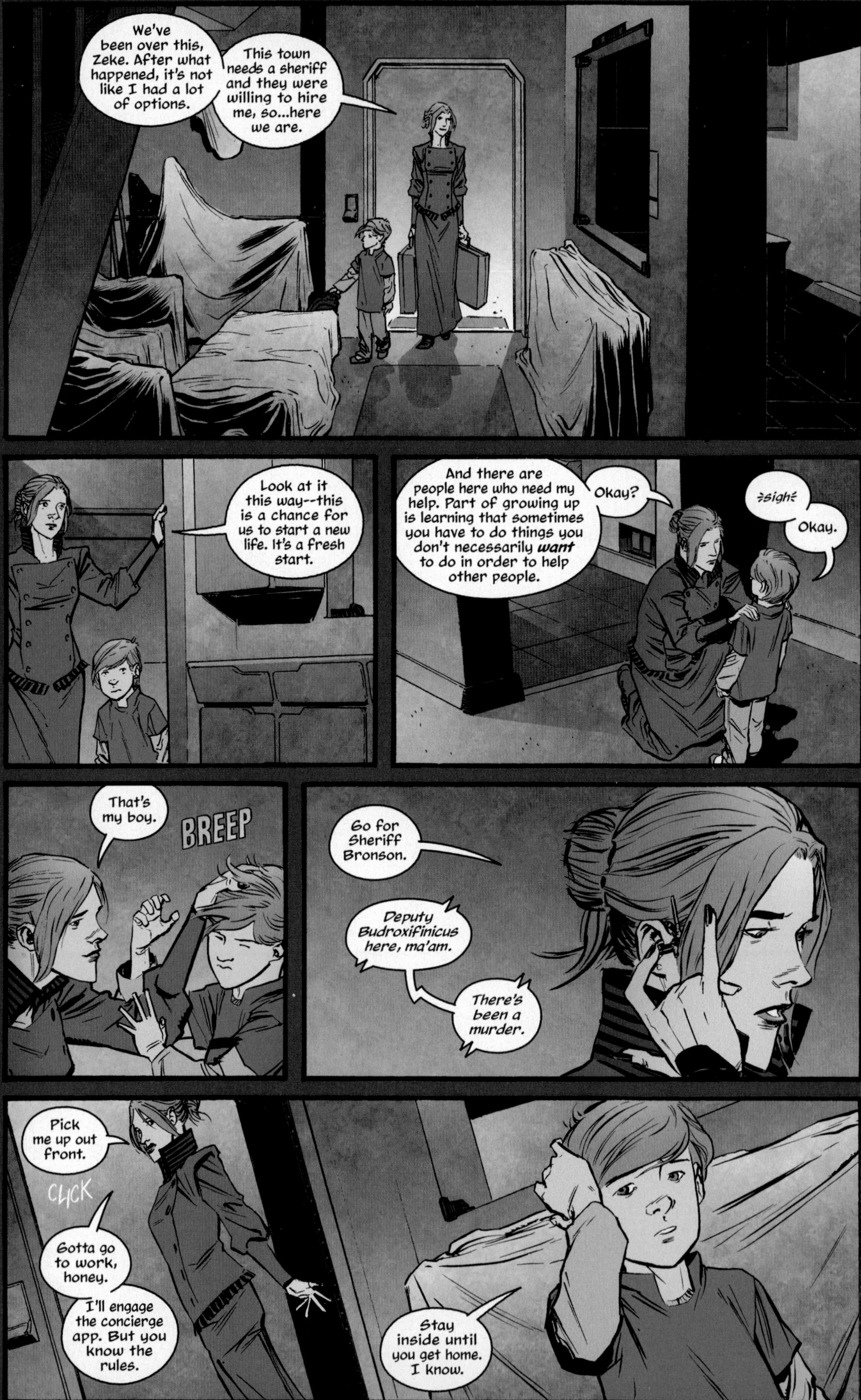
We've been over this, Zeke. After what happened, it's not like I had a lot of options.
This town needs a sheriff and they were willing to hire me, so...here we are.
Look at it this way--this is a chance for us to start a new life. It's a fresh start.
And there are people here who need my help. Part of growing up is learning that sometimes you have to do things you don't necessarily *want* to do in order to help other people.
Okay?
sigh
Okay.
That's my boy.
BREEP
Go for Sheriff Bronson.
Deputy Budroxifinicus here, ma'am.
There's been a murder.
Pick me up out front.
CLICK
Gotta go to work, honey.
I'll engage the concierge app. But you know the rules.
Stay inside until you get home. I know.

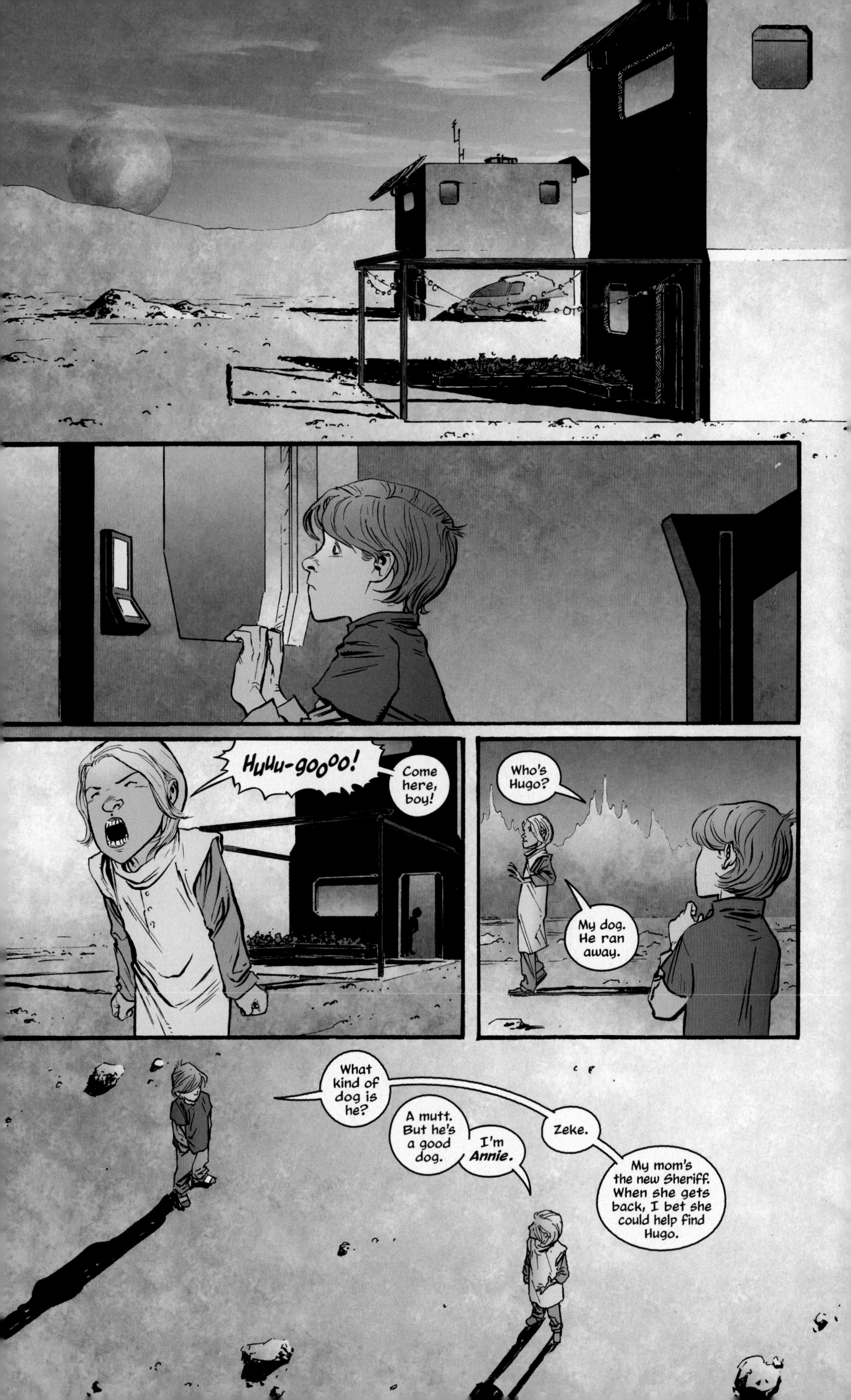
Huuu-gooooo!
Come here, boy!
Who's Hugo?
My dog. He ran away.
What kind of dog is he?
A mutt. But he's a good dog.
I'm *Annie.*
Zeke.
My mom's the new Sheriff. When she gets back, I bet she could help find Hugo.

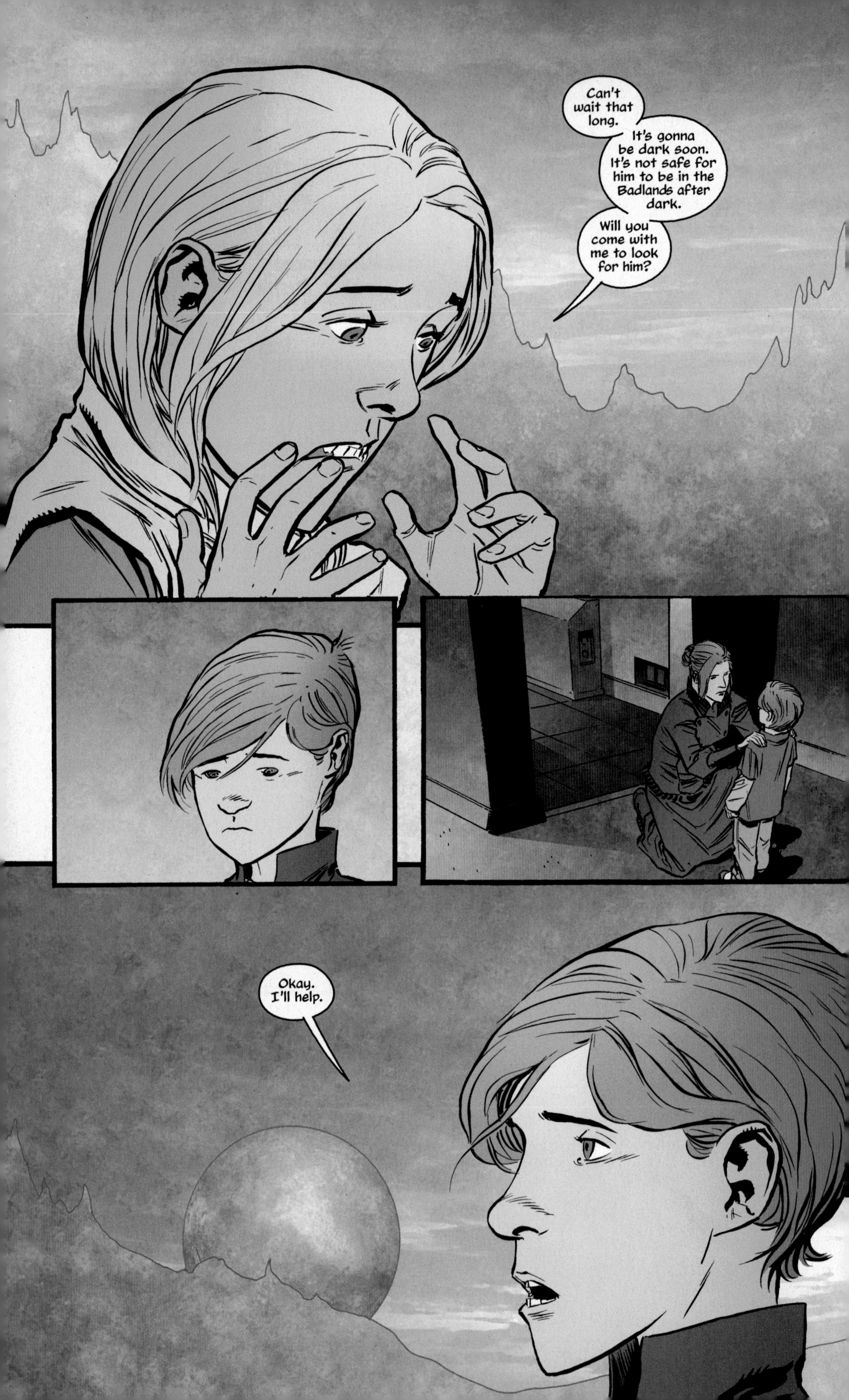
Can't wait that long.
It's gonna be dark soon. It's not safe for him to be in the Badlands after dark.
Will you come with me to look for him?
Okay. I'll help.

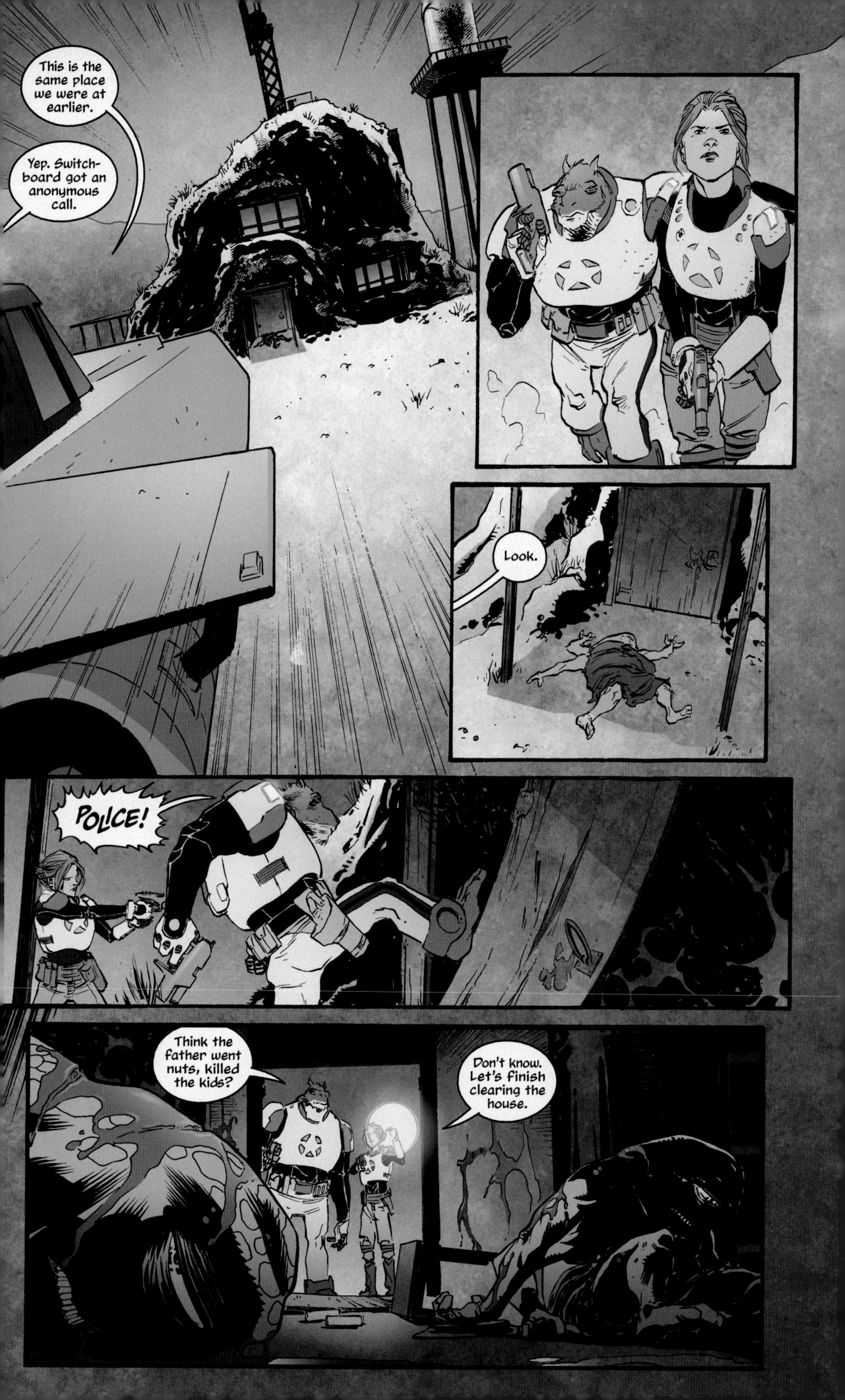
This is the same place we were at earlier.
Yep. Switch-board got an anonymous call.
Look.
POLICE!
Think the father went nuts, killed the kids?
Don't know. Let's finish clearing the house.

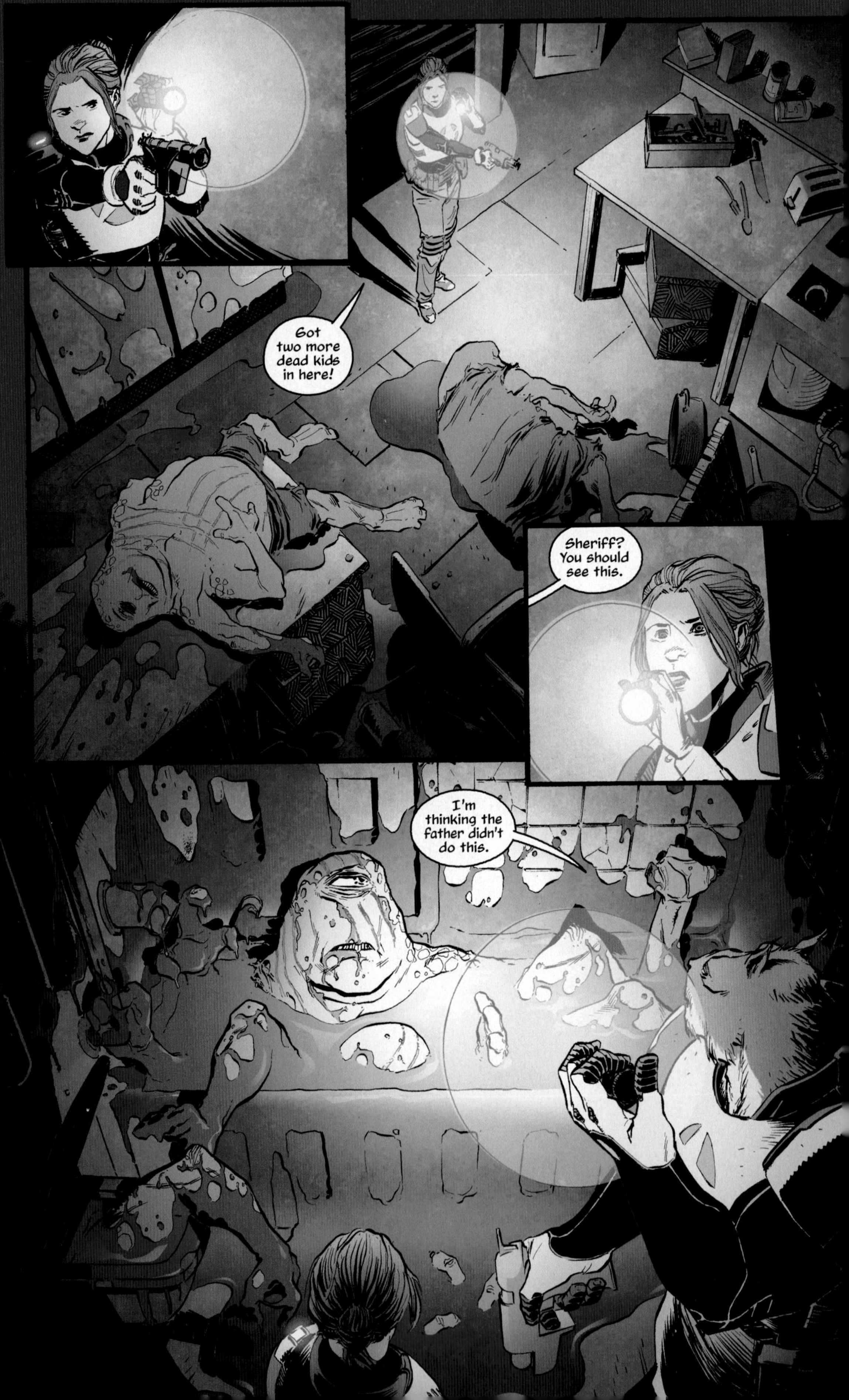
Got two more dead kids in here!
Sheriff? You should see this.
I'm thinking the father didn't do this.

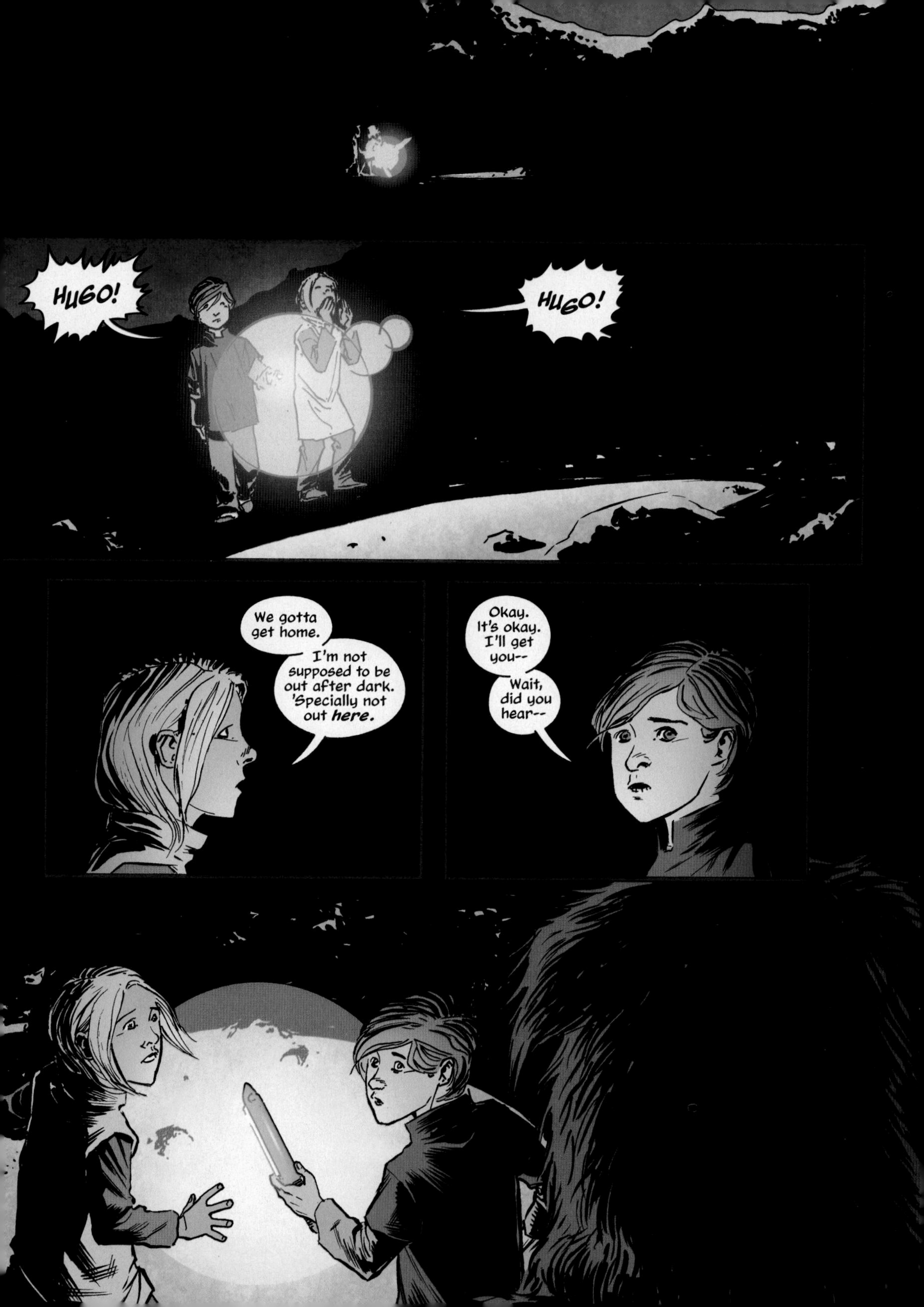
HUGO!
HUGO!
We gotta get home.
I'm not supposed to be out after dark. 'Specially not out *here.*
Okay. It's okay. I'll get you--
Wait, did you hear--

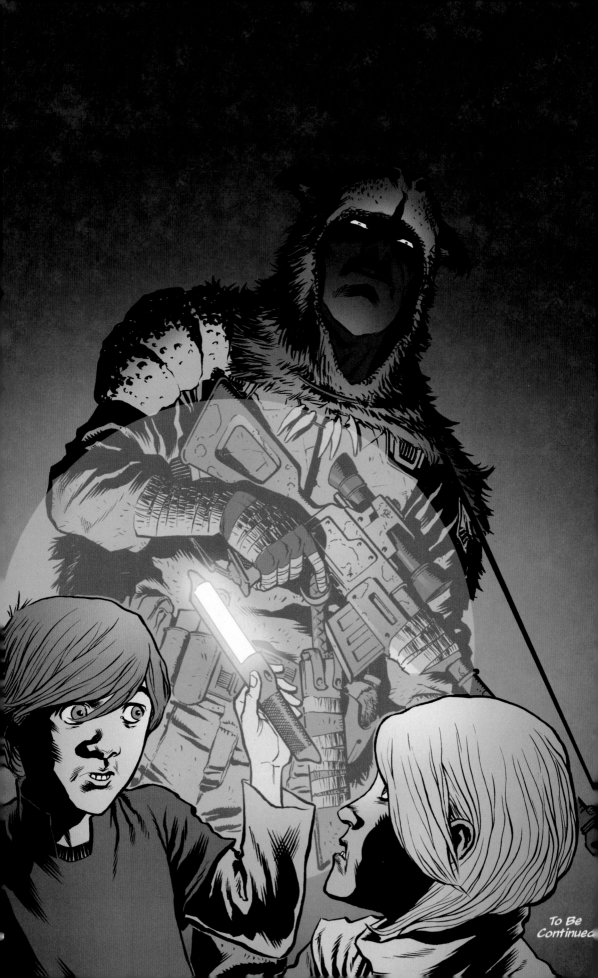

To Be
Continued

THE COPPERHEAD TELEGRAPH

send your messages to jay.faerber@gmail.com

'm not the first person to think of this.

Jot by a long shot. I don't know what the irst "space western" was. I've heard that Gene Roddenberry pitched STAR TREK as WAGON TRAIN in space." And of course here's Joss Whedon's FIREFLY. And back in he 80s, there were the cartoons GALAXY ANGERS (which I loved) and BRAVESTARR which I thought was dumb).

number of years ago, I got the itch to take ny own stab at this—to do a story about classic frontier town, but set on an alien lanet. "DEADWOOD in space" was all I had vritten in my ideas document (a file on my omputer where I jot down random ideas).

nd that's where it sat. Fast forward a few ears, and I came across ***Scott Godlewski's*** rt on Boom's DRACULA: THE COMPANY)F MONSTERS series. I was blown away. 've always got my eye out for new artists, nd Scott was among the best I'd seen. I eached out to him, and asked if he wanted o work on something together. I had his idea about a time travel series. We xchanged some emails, and agreed to team p.

was never able to get the time travel series remise to work, so we shelved that idea, nd I mentioned this "DEADWOOD in pace" idea to him. I don't seem to have that nitial correspondence, but I think that's all told him. Just that simple idea. But he was nto it, and what followed was a huge volley f emails, back and forth. Together, we built OPPERHEAD into what you're reading. Jot just the characters, but the town. The vorld. The history. The alien races. The war hat recently ended. All of it.

cott didn't just draw this series, he helped reate it in every way.

Ve approached ***Ron Riley*** about coloring he book. Ron is my go-to colorist. We tarted working together years and years go on NOBLE CAUSES, and we stayed ogether for DYNAMO 5 and NEAR DEATH.

With COPPERHEAD, Scott and I wanted a specific look—we wanted something that would stand out. Scott summed it up perfectly when he said "think of this book as a Western, not a sci-fi book." After hearing that simple instruction, Ron turned in the version of the colors that are in the book. The scratchy, desert look that everything has. I just love it.

Incidentally, Scott's instruction to "think of this book as a Western" helped solidify things for me, too. It's something I keep in the back of my mind whenever I'm working on an issue. It's a Western. It just happens to take place on an alien planet.

To letter the book, I approached someone I'd never worked with before—***Thomas Mauer,*** whose work really impressed me on UMBRAL and UNDERTOW. Our book didn't start with the letter "U," but I remained optimistic that he'd join the team. I wanted the book's letters to have a unique look—and Thomas manages to walk the fine line between making the letters distinct, without making them distracting. Comic book lettering is a bit like music in a film—you want people to appreciate it, but not notice it so much that it pulls you out of the experience. And Thomas manages to do that.

So that's the team. We're really pouring our blood, sweat, and tears into this thing. I hope it shows. I hope you enjoy spending time in the town of Copperhead as much as we do.

In future issues, we hope to run letters from you guys. If you don't feel like writing, that's cool. We'll find something to talk about.

See you in a month.

—Jay Faerber
July 2014

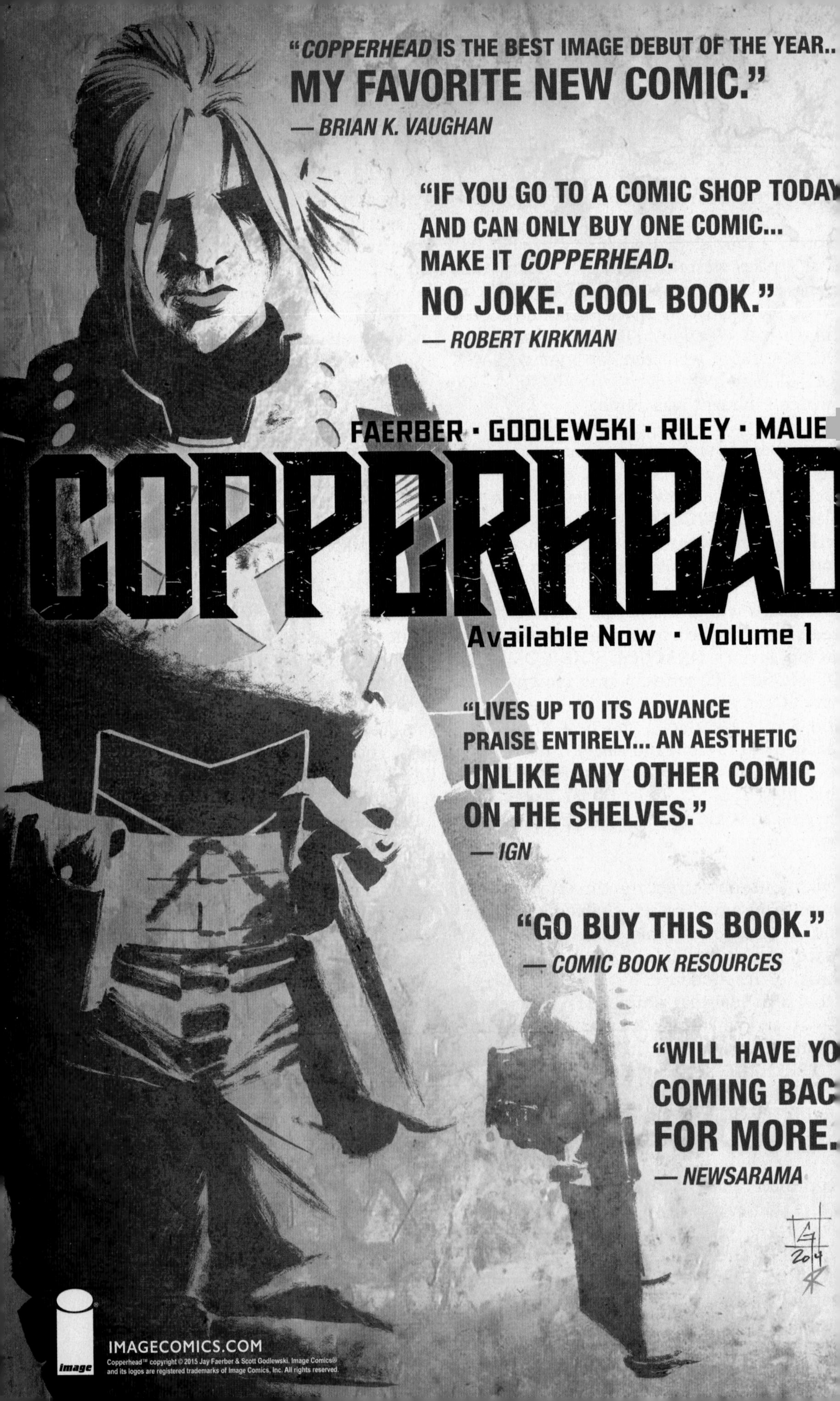

"COPPERHEAD IS THE BEST IMAGE DEBUT OF THE YEAR..
MY FAVORITE NEW COMIC."
— BRIAN K. VAUGHAN
"IF YOU GO TO A COMIC SHOP TODAY
AND CAN ONLY BUY ONE COMIC...
MAKE IT COPPERHEAD.
NO JOKE. COOL BOOK."
— ROBERT KIRKMAN
FAERBER · GODLEWSKI · RILEY · MAUE
COPPERHEAD
Available Now · Volume 1
"LIVES UP TO ITS ADVANCE
PRAISE ENTIRELY... AN AESTHETIC
UNLIKE ANY OTHER COMIC
ON THE SHELVES."
— IGN
"GO BUY THIS BOOK."
— COMIC BOOK RESOURCES
"WILL HAVE YO
COMING BAC
FOR MORE.
— NEWSARAMA
IMAGECOMICS.COM
Copperhead™ copyright © 2015 Jay Faerber & Scott Godlewski. Image Comics® and its logos are registered trademarks of Image Comics, Inc. All rights reserved.

DESCENDER

JEFF LEMIRE

DUSTIN NGUYEN

Image

1

$1.00

RATED M / MATURE

7 09853 02051 6

IMAGE COMICS Presents

DESCENDER: TIN STARS: PART

Written by JEFF LEMIRE

Illustrated by DUSTIN NGUYEN

Lettered and Designed by STEVE WANDS

Cover by DUSTIN NGUYEN

Descender Created by JEFF LEMIRE & DUSTIN NGUYEN

Special Thanks to CHRIS ROSS

Corey Murphy – Director of Sales
Jeff Boison – Director of Publishing Planning & Book Trade Sales
Jeremy Sullivan – Director of Digital Sales
Kat Salazar – Director of PR & Marketing
Emily Miller – Director of Operations
Branwyn Bigglestone – Senior Accounts Manager
Sarah Mello – Accounts Manager
Drew Gill – Art Director
Jonathan Chan – Production Manager
Meredith Wallace – Print Manager
Briah Skelly – Publicity Assistant
Randy Okamura – Marketing Production Designer
David Brothers – Branding Manager
Ally Power – Content Manager
Addison Duke – Production Artist
Vincent Kukua – Production Artist
Sasha Head – Production Artist
Tricia Ramos – Production Artist
Jeff Stang – Direct Market Sales Representative
Emilio Bautista – Digital Sales Associate
Chloe Ramos-Peterson – Administrative Assistant
IMAGECOMICS.COM

for IMAGE COMICS
ROBERT KIRKMAN chief operating officer
ERIK LARSEN chief financial officer
TODD MCFARLANE president
MARC SILVESTRI chief executive officer
JIM VALENTINO vice-president
ERIC STEPHENSON publisher

www.imagecomics.com

IMAGE FIRSTS: DESCENDER #1. DECEMBER 2015. Published by Image Comics, Inc. Office of publication: 2001 Center Street, 6th Floor, Berkeley, CA 94704. Copyright © 2015 171 Studios & Dustin Nguyen. All rights reserved. DESCENDER™ (including all prominent characters featured herein), its logo and all character likenesses are trademarks of 171 Studios & Dustin Nguyen, unless otherwise noted. Image Comics® and its logos are registered trademarks of Image Comics, Inc. No part of this publication may be reproduced or transmitted, in any form or by any means (except for short excerpts for review purposes) without the express written permission of Image Comics, Inc. All names, characters, events and locales in this publication are entirely fictional. Any resemblance to actual persons (living or dead), events or places, without satiric intent, is coincidental. Printed in the USA. For information regarding the CPSIA on this printed material call: 203-595-3636 and provide reference # RICH – 656680.

For international rights, please contact: foreignlicensing@imagecomics.com

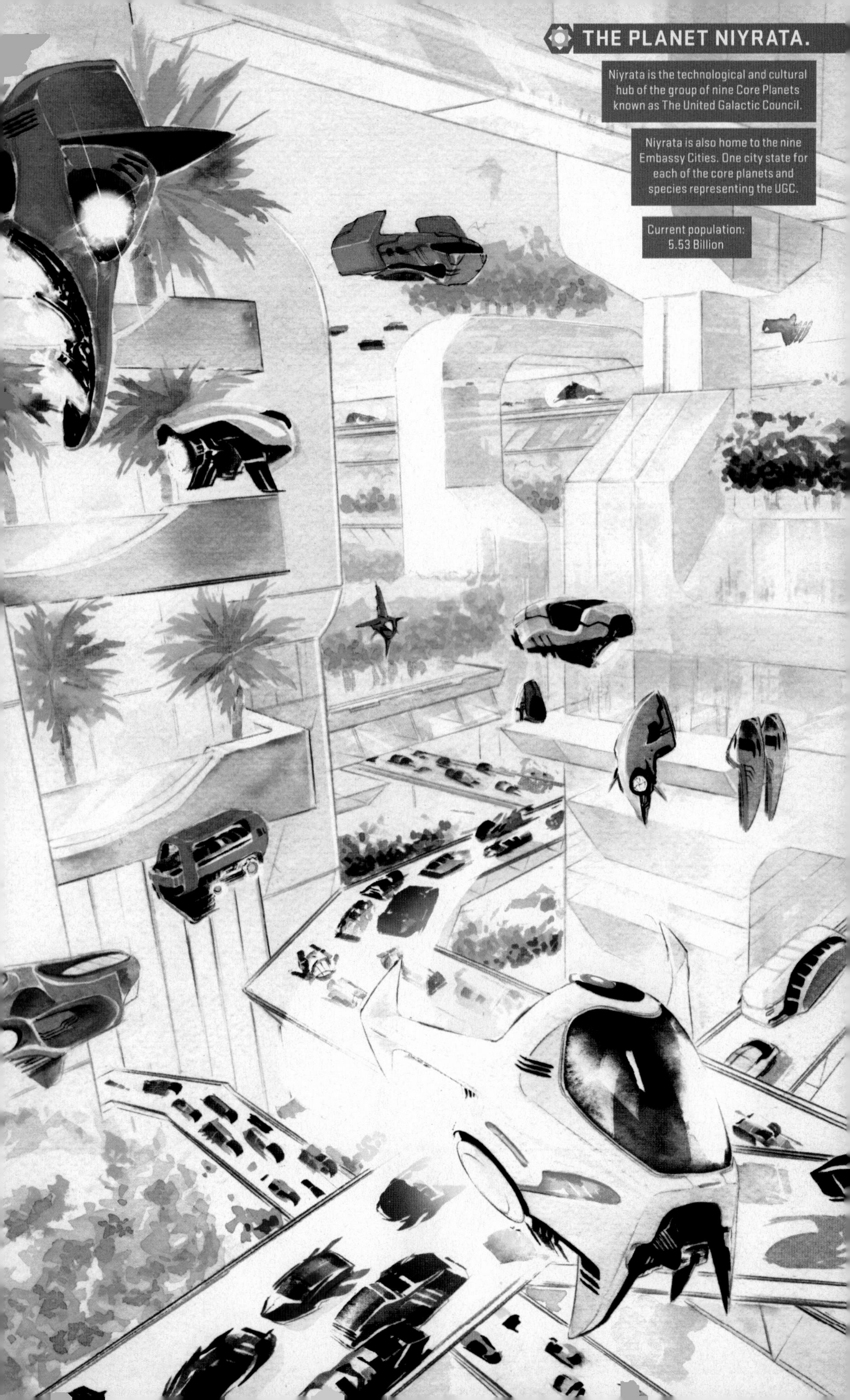
THE PLANET NIYRATA.
Niyrata is the technological and cultural hub of the group of nine Core Planets known as The United Galactic Council.
Niyrata is also home to the nine Embassy Cities. One city state for each of the core planets and species representing the UGC.
Current population: 5.53 Billion

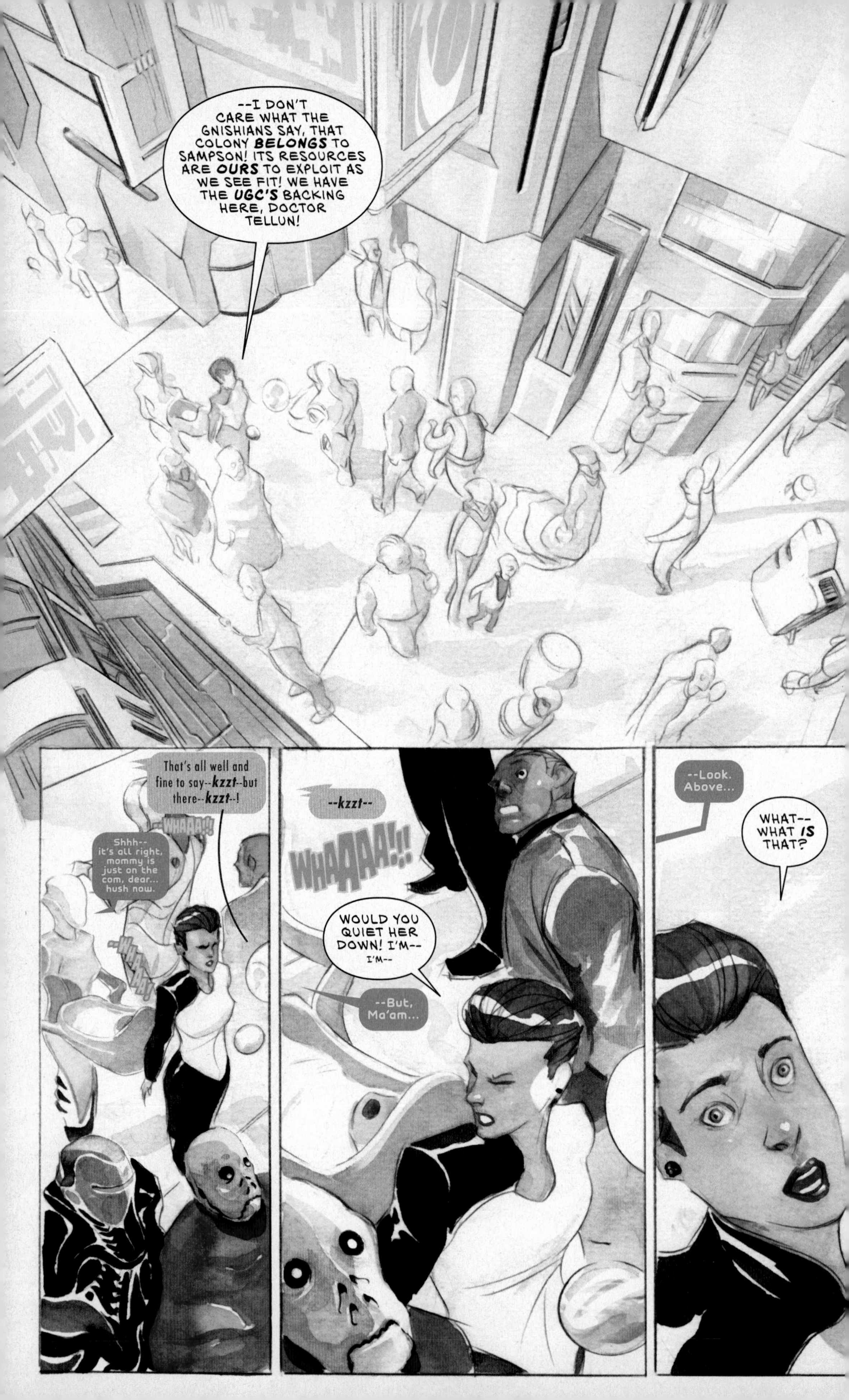
--I DON'T CARE WHAT THE GNISHIANS SAY, THAT COLONY BELONGS TO SAMPSON! ITS RESOURCES ARE OURS TO EXPLOIT AS WE SEE FIT! WE HAVE THE UGC'S BACKING HERE, DOCTOR TELLUN!
That's all well and fine to say--kzzt--but there--kzzt--!
WHAAA!!!
Shhh-- it's all right, mommy is just on the com, dear... hush now.
WHAAA!
--kzzt--
WHAAAA!!!
WOULD YOU QUIET HER DOWN! I'M-- I'M--
--But, Ma'am...
--Look. Above...
WHAT-- WHAT IS THAT?

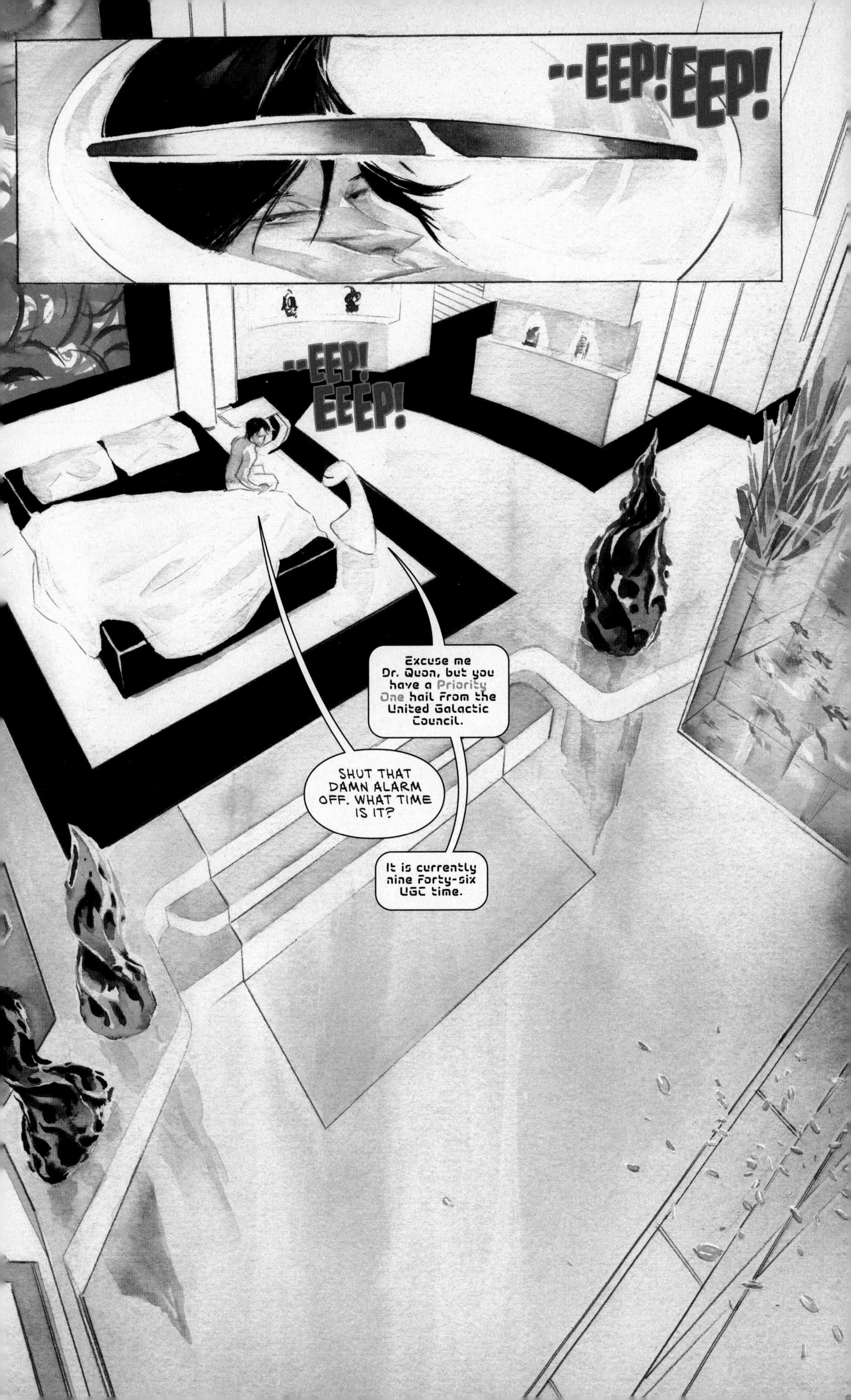
--EEP! EEP!
--EEP! EEEP!
SHUT THAT DAMN ALARM OFF. WHAT TIME IS IT?
Excuse me Dr. Quon, but you have a Priority One hail from the United Galactic Council.
It is currently nine forty-six UGC time.

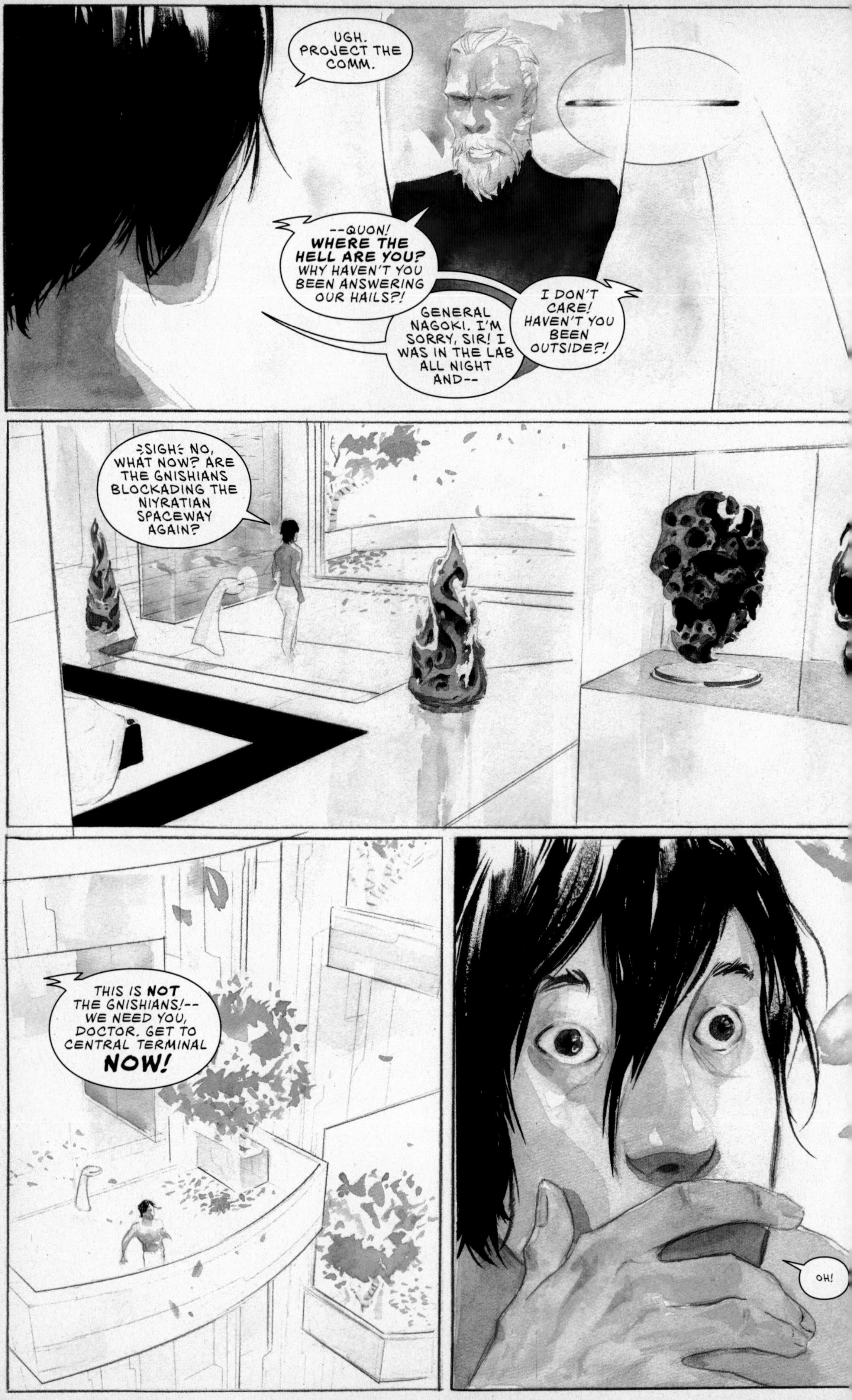
UGH. PROJECT THE COMM.
--QUON! **WHERE THE HELL ARE YOU?** WHY HAVEN'T YOU BEEN ANSWERING OUR HAILS?!
GENERAL NAGOKI. I'M SORRY, SIR! I WAS IN THE LAB ALL NIGHT AND--
I DON'T CARE! HAVEN'T YOU BEEN OUTSIDE?!
=SIGH= NO, WHAT NOW? ARE THE GNISHIANS BLOCKADING THE NIYRATIAN SPACEWAY AGAIN?
THIS IS **NOT** THE GNISHIANS!-- WE NEED YOU, DOCTOR. GET TO CENTRAL TERMINAL **NOW!**
OH!

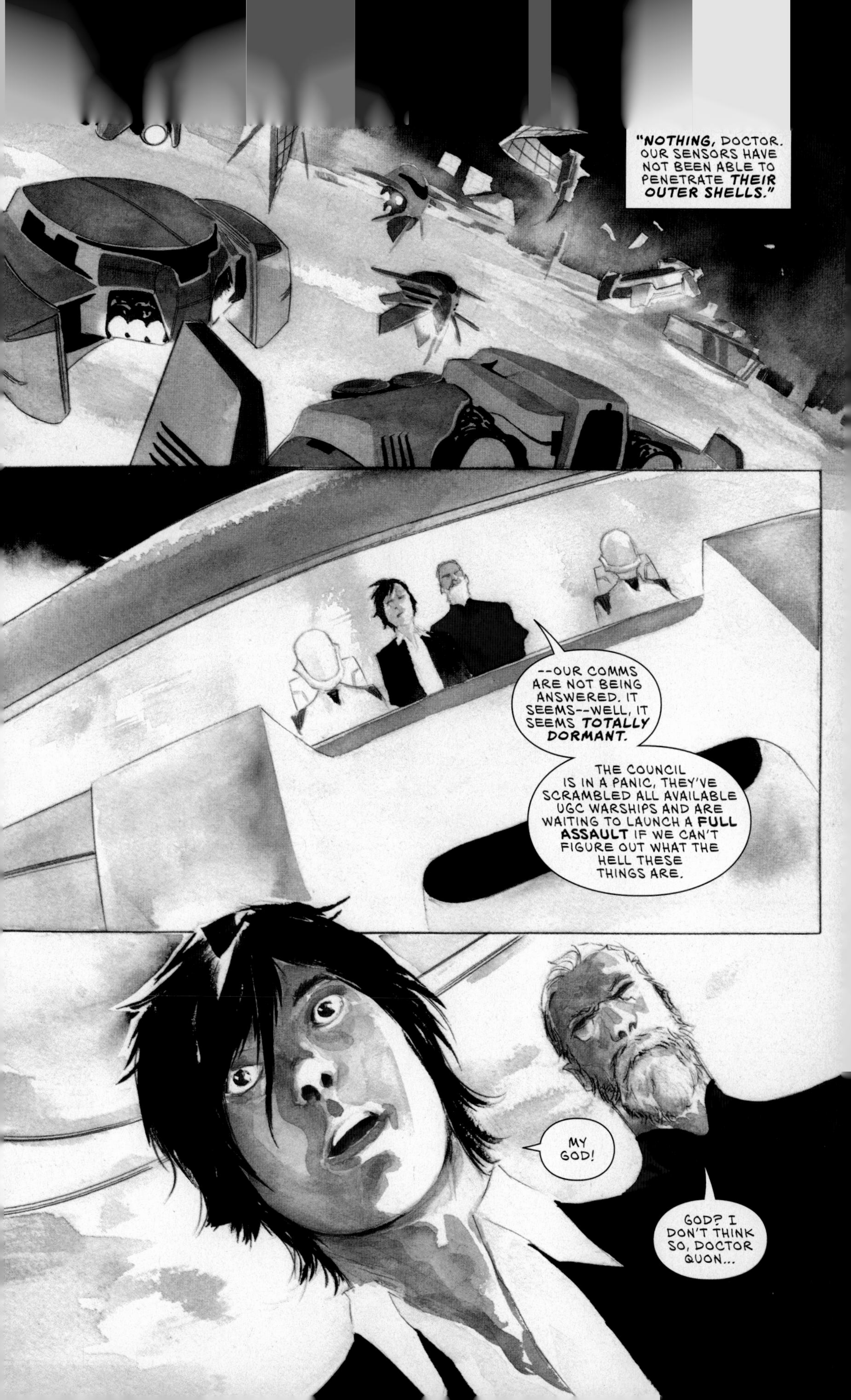
"NOTHING, DOCTOR. OUR SENSORS HAVE NOT BEEN ABLE TO PENETRATE THEIR OUTER SHELLS."
--OUR COMMS ARE NOT BEING ANSWERED. IT SEEMS--WELL, IT SEEMS TOTALLY DORMANT.
THE COUNCIL IS IN A PANIC, THEY'VE SCRAMBLED ALL AVAILABLE UGC WARSHIPS AND ARE WAITING TO LAUNCH A FULL ASSAULT IF WE CAN'T FIGURE OUT WHAT THE HELL THESE THINGS ARE.
MY GOD!
GOD? I DON'T THINK SO, DOCTOR QUON...

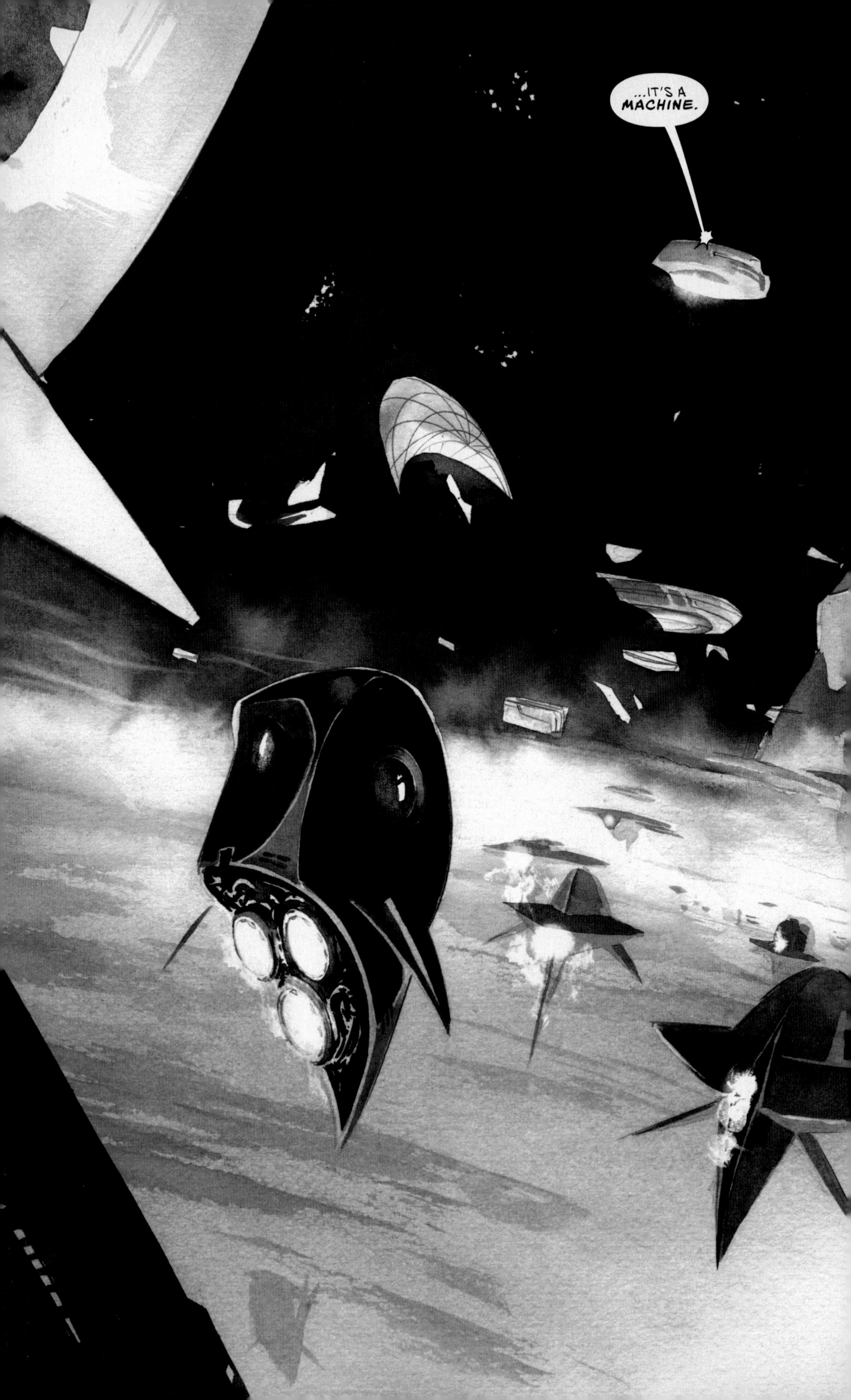
...IT'S A MACHINE.

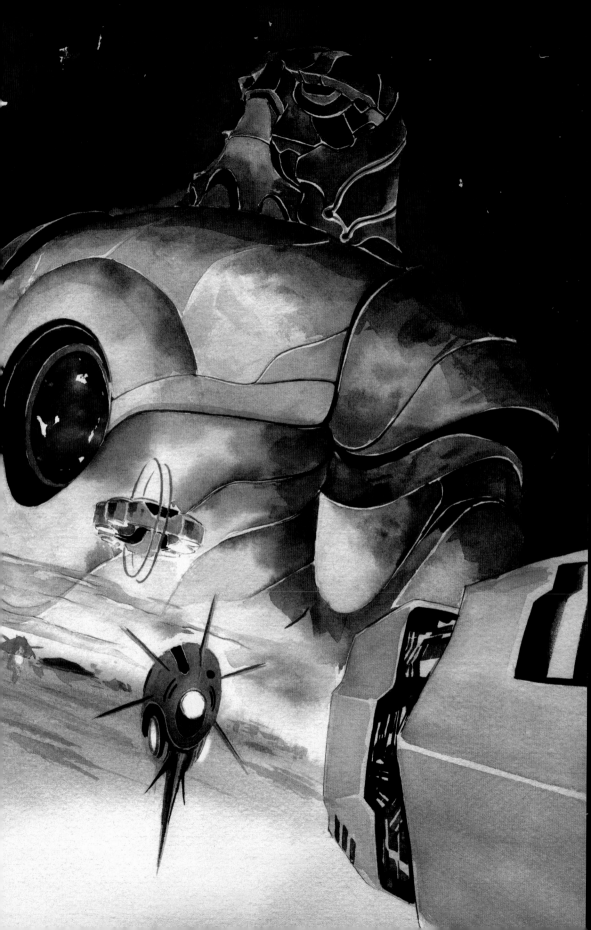

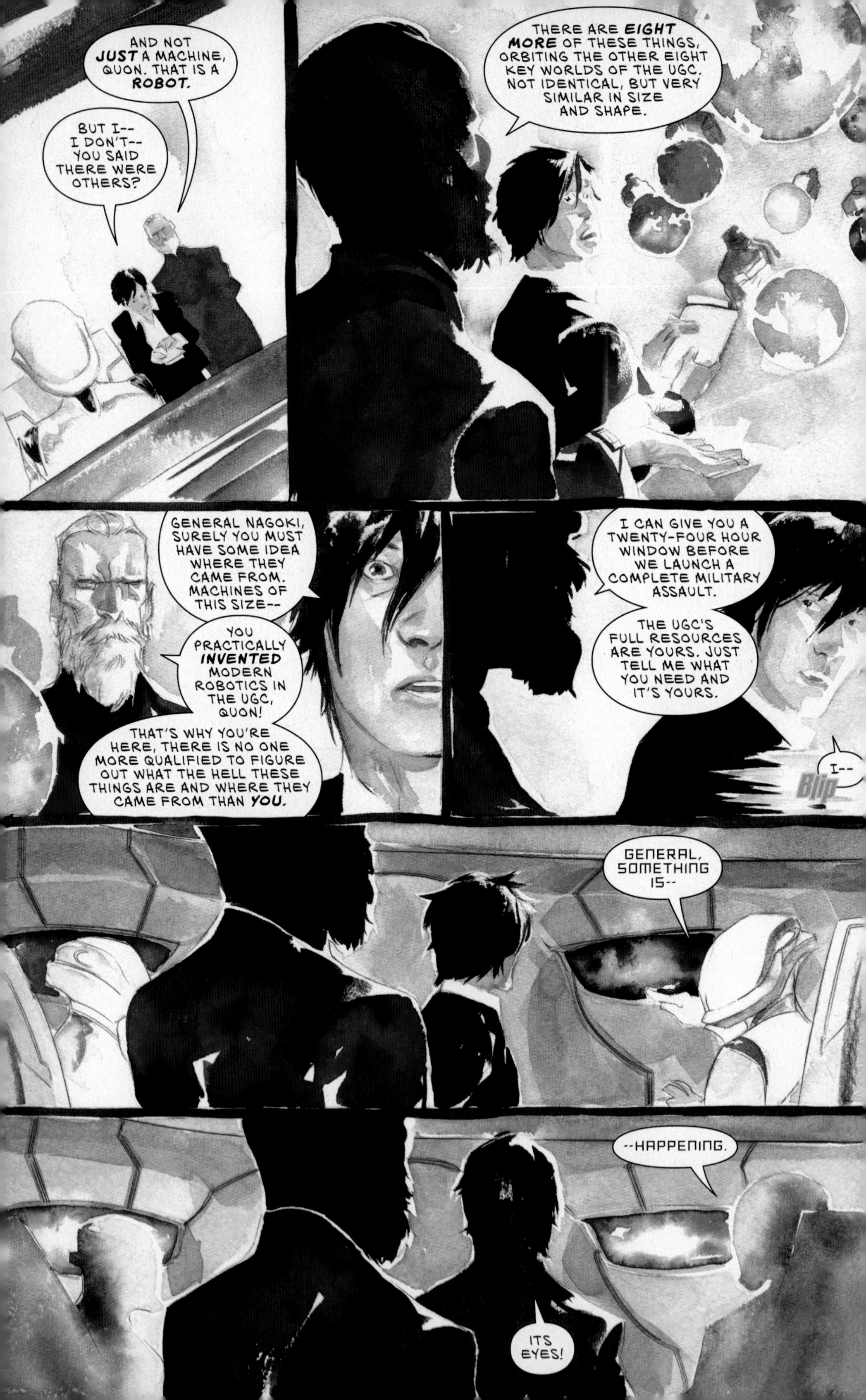
AND NOT JUST A MACHINE, QUON. THAT IS A ROBOT.
BUT I-- I DON'T-- YOU SAID THERE WERE OTHERS?
THERE ARE EIGHT MORE OF THESE THINGS, ORBITING THE OTHER EIGHT KEY WORLDS OF THE UGC. NOT IDENTICAL, BUT VERY SIMILAR IN SIZE AND SHAPE.
GENERAL NAGOKI, SURELY YOU MUST HAVE SOME IDEA WHERE THEY CAME FROM. MACHINES OF THIS SIZE--
YOU PRACTICALLY INVENTED MODERN ROBOTICS IN THE UGC, QUON!
THAT'S WHY YOU'RE HERE, THERE IS NO ONE MORE QUALIFIED TO FIGURE OUT WHAT THE HELL THESE THINGS ARE AND WHERE THEY CAME FROM THAN YOU.
I CAN GIVE YOU A TWENTY-FOUR HOUR WINDOW BEFORE WE LAUNCH A COMPLETE MILITARY ASSAULT.
THE UGC'S FULL RESOURCES ARE YOURS. JUST TELL ME WHAT YOU NEED AND IT'S YOURS.
I--
Blip
GENERAL, SOMETHING IS--
--HAPPENING.
ITS EYES!

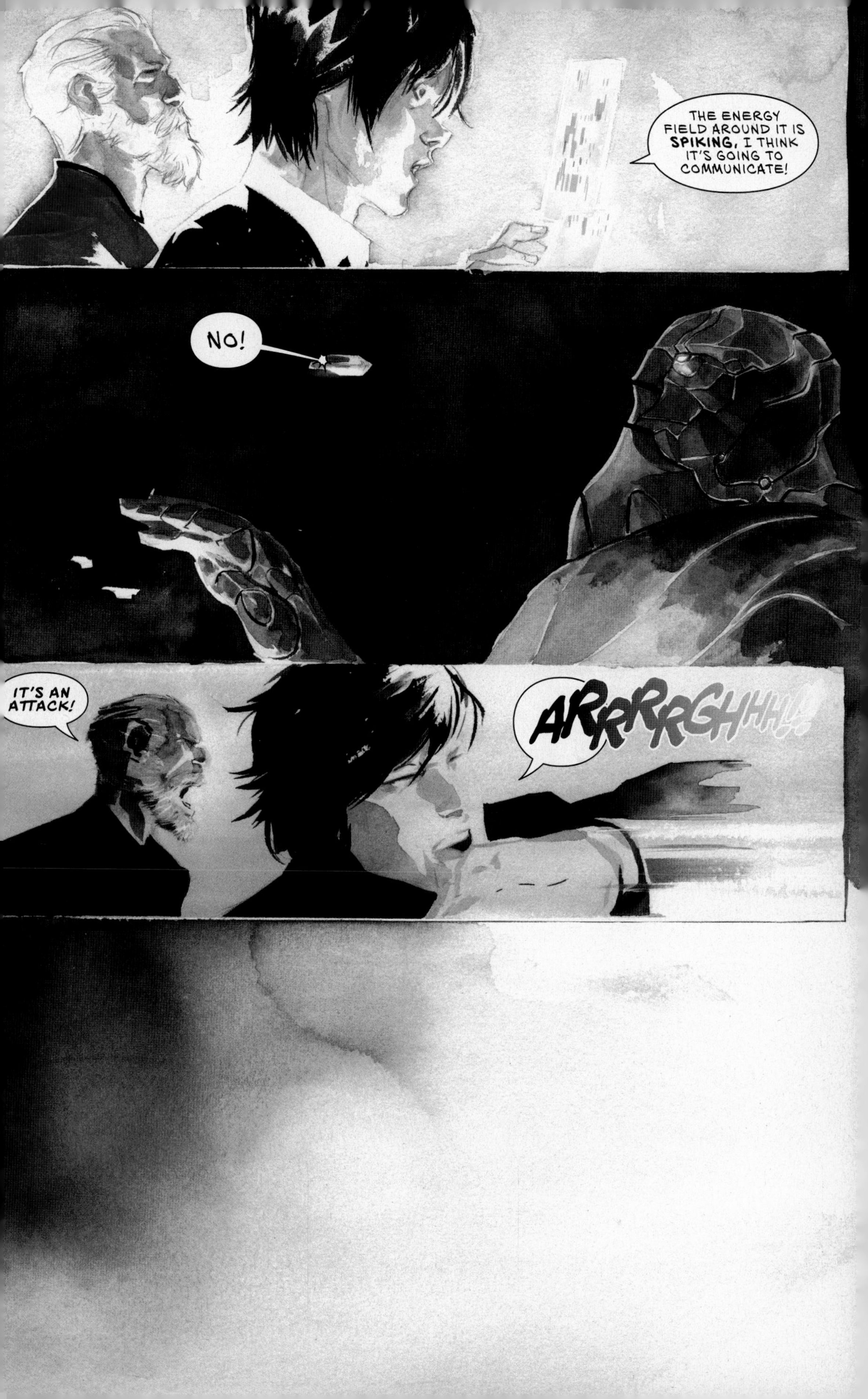
THE ENERGY FIELD AROUND IT IS SPIKING, I THINK IT'S GOING TO COMMUNICATE!
NO!
IT'S AN ATTACK!
ARRRRGHHH!!

DESC

NDER

BOOK I: TIN STARS

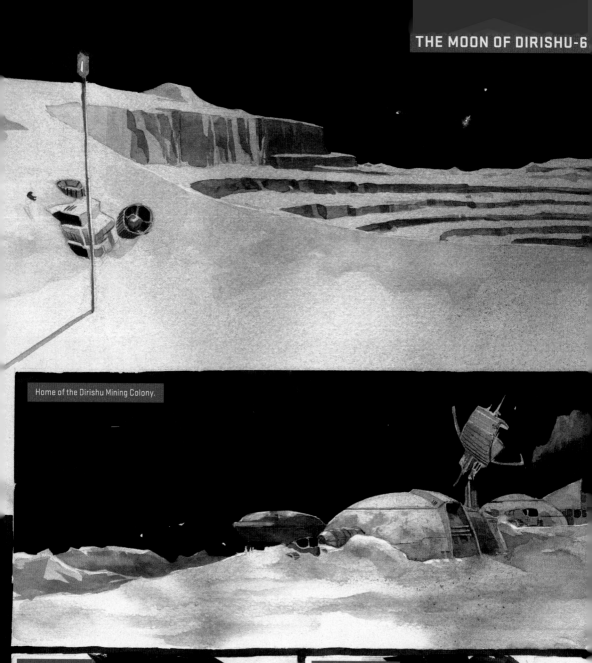

Home of the Dirishu Mining Colony.

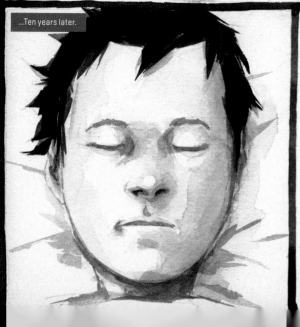

...Ten years later.

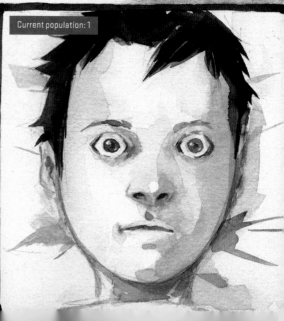

Current population: 1

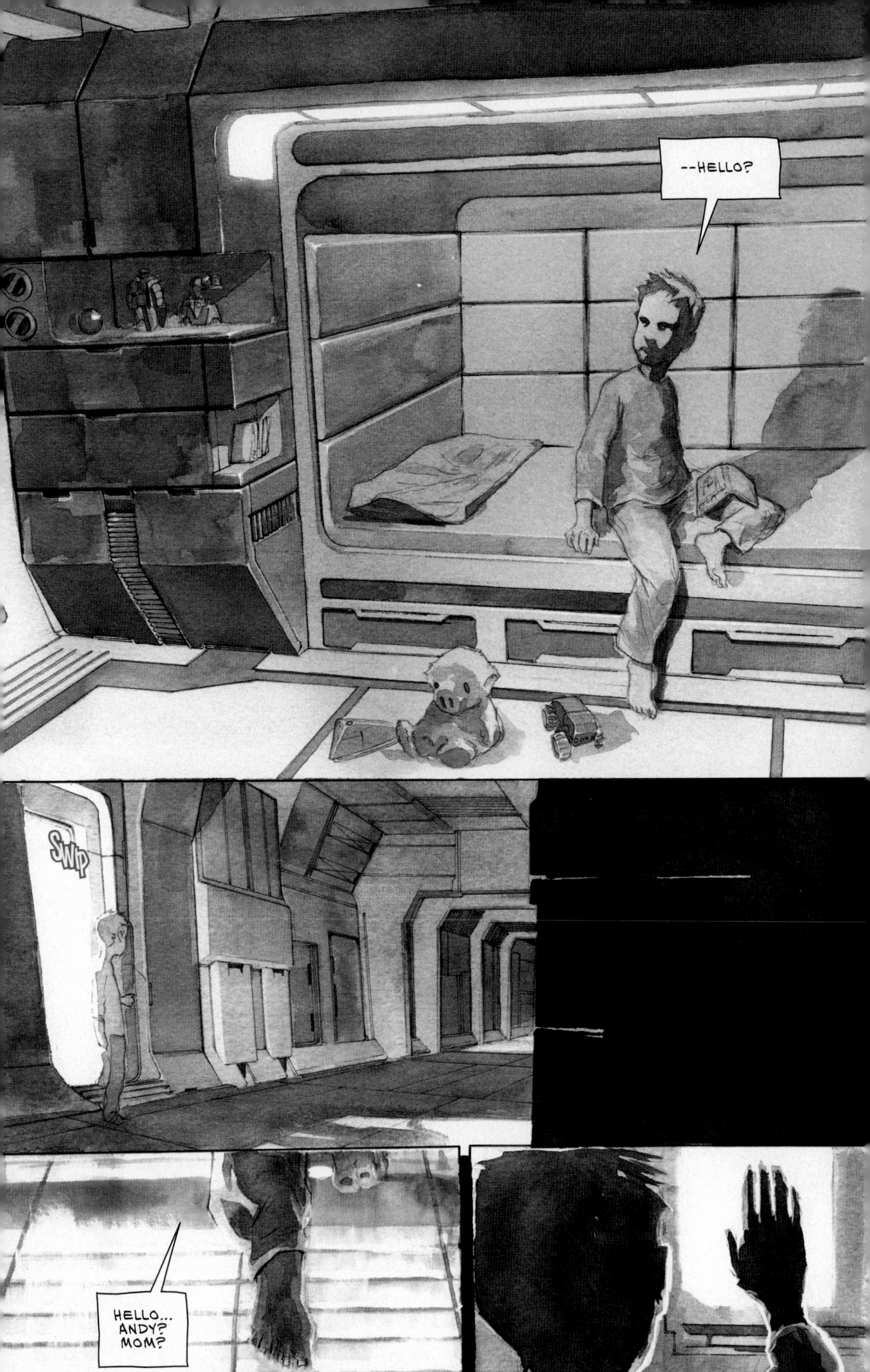
--HELLO?
SWIP
HELLO... ANDY? MOM?

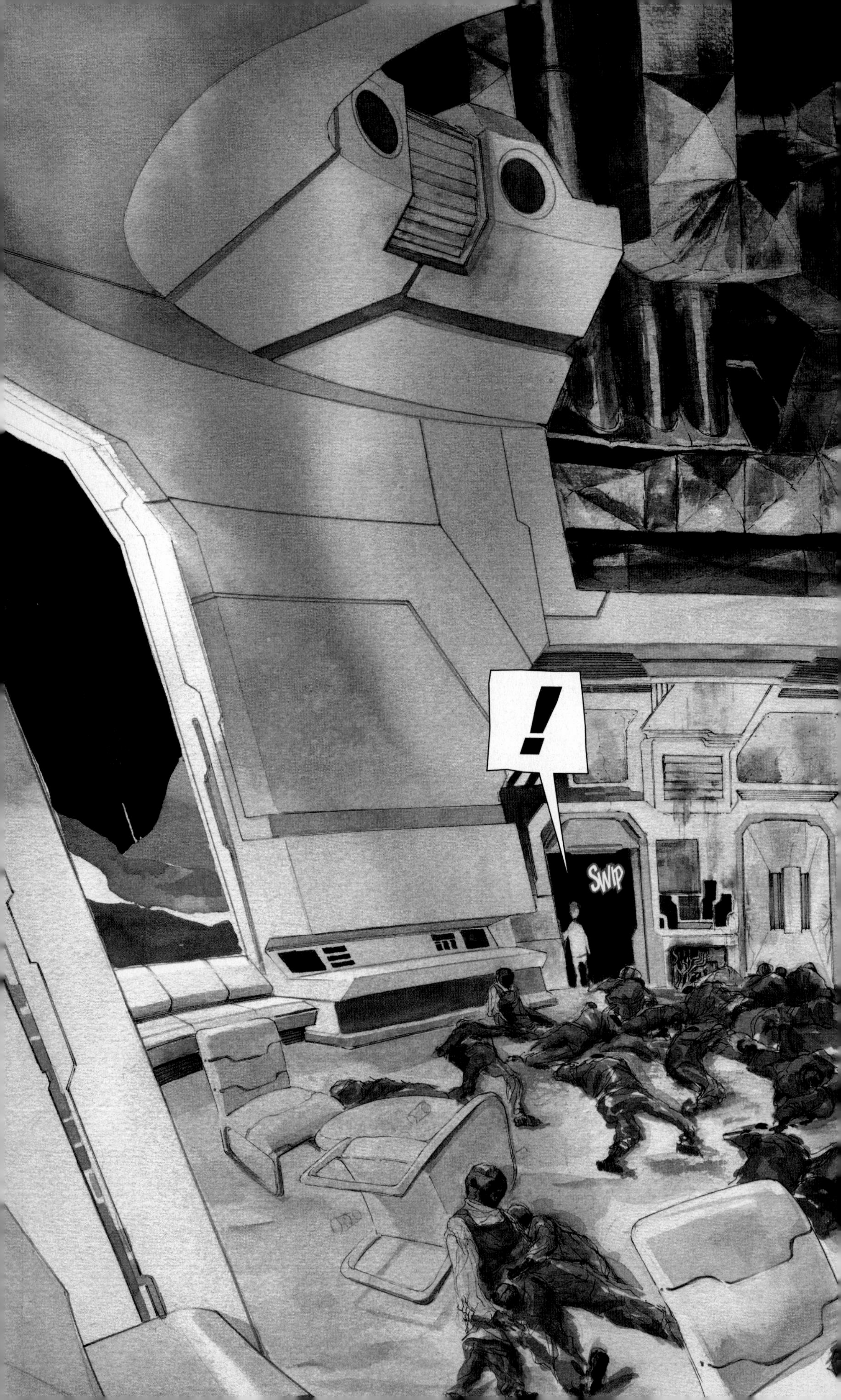
!
SWIP

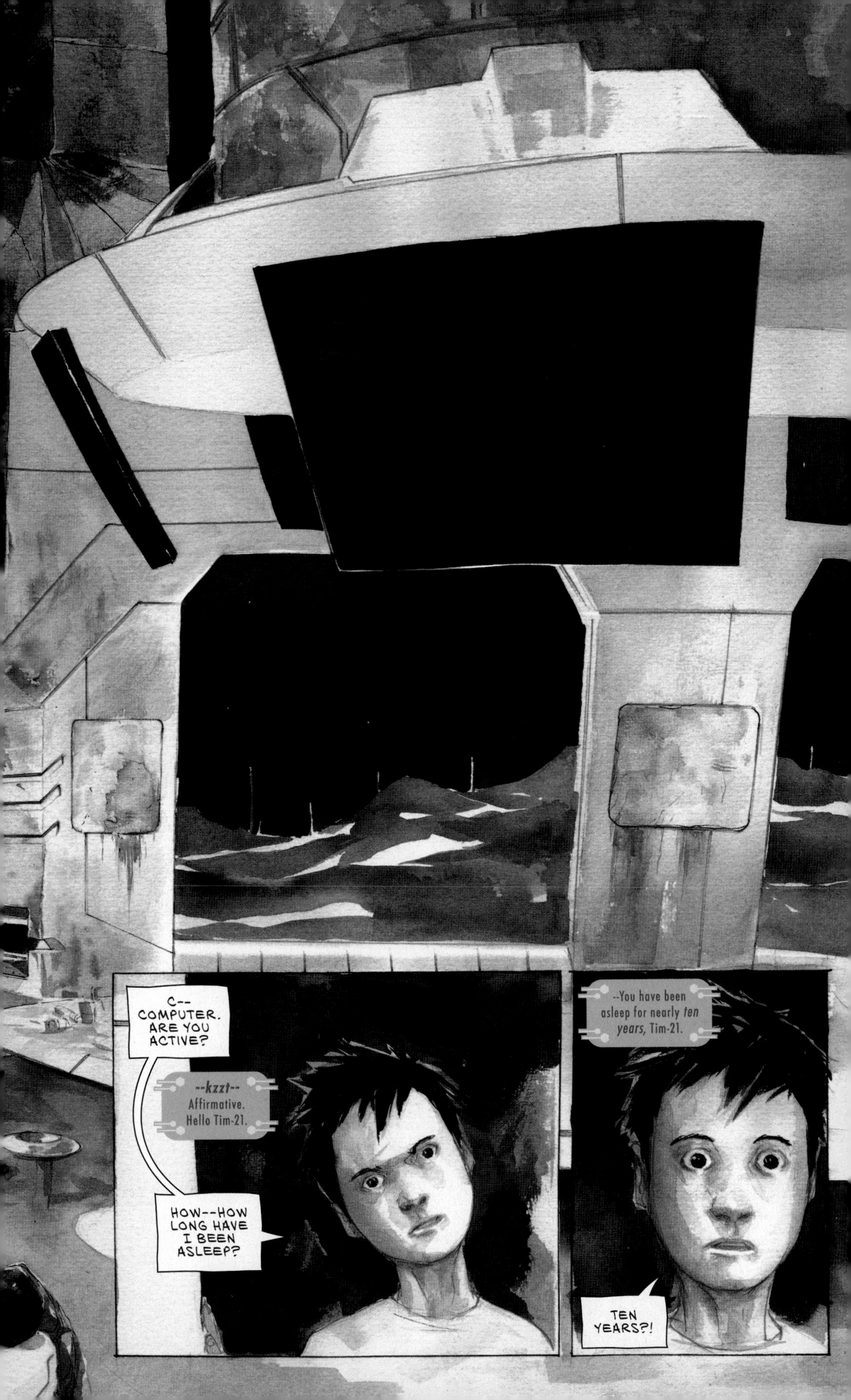
C--COMPUTER. ARE YOU ACTIVE?
--kzzt-- Affirmative. Hello Tim-21.
HOW--HOW LONG HAVE I BEEN ASLEEP?
--You have been asleep for nearly *ten years*, Tim-21.
TEN YEARS?!

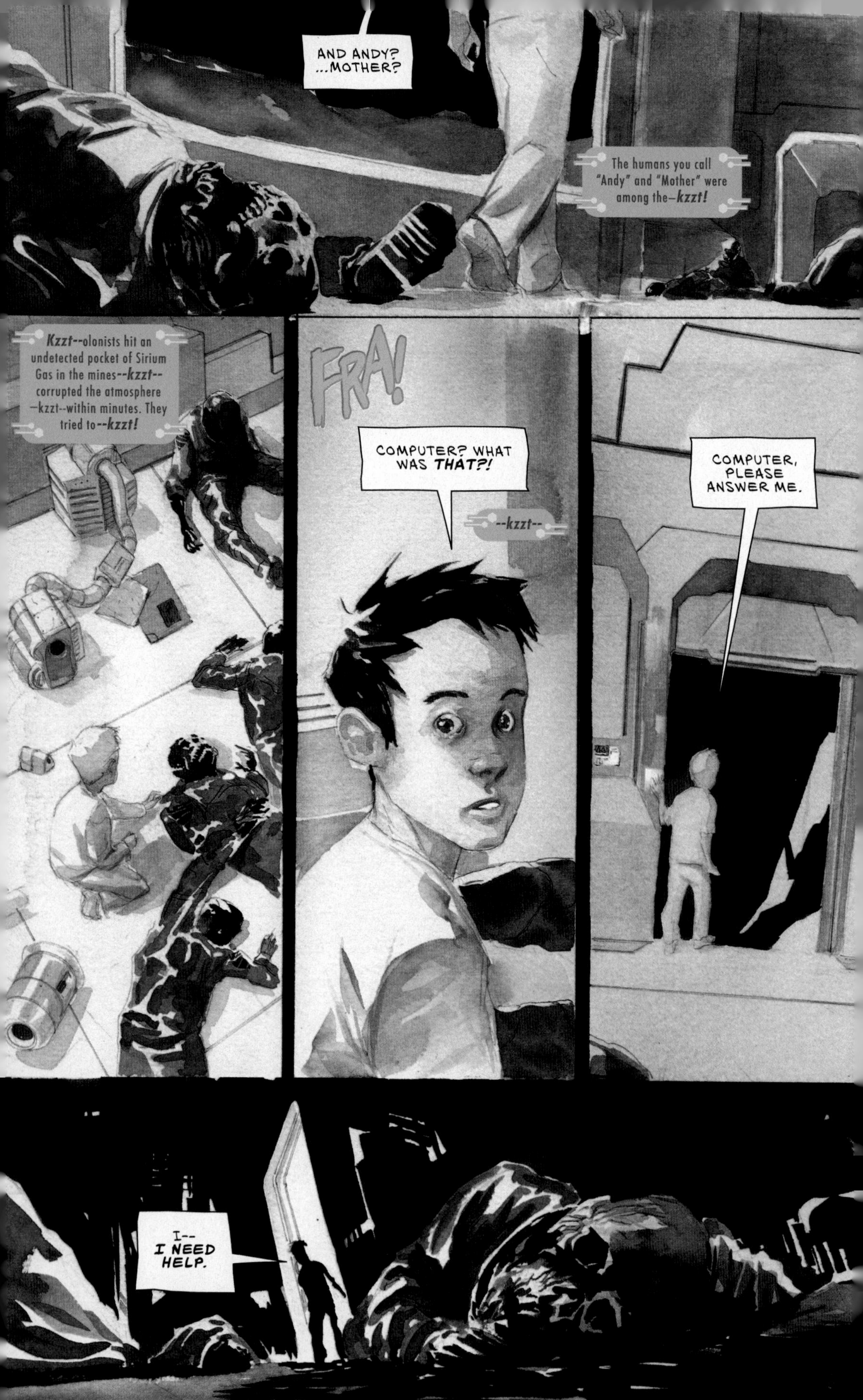
AND ANDY? ...MOTHER?
The humans you call "Andy" and "Mother" were among the–*kzzt!*
Kzzt--olonists hit an undetected pocket of Sirium Gas in the mines--*kzzt*--corrupted the atmosphere –kzzt--within minutes. They tried to--*kzzt!*
FRA!
COMPUTER? WHAT WAS *THAT?!*
--kzzt--
COMPUTER, PLEASE ANSWER ME.
I-- I NEED HELP.

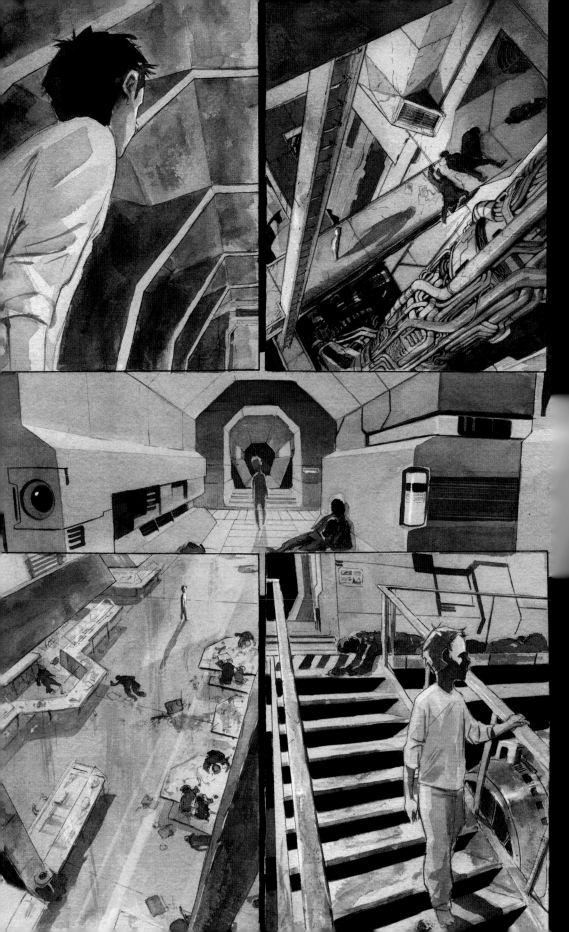

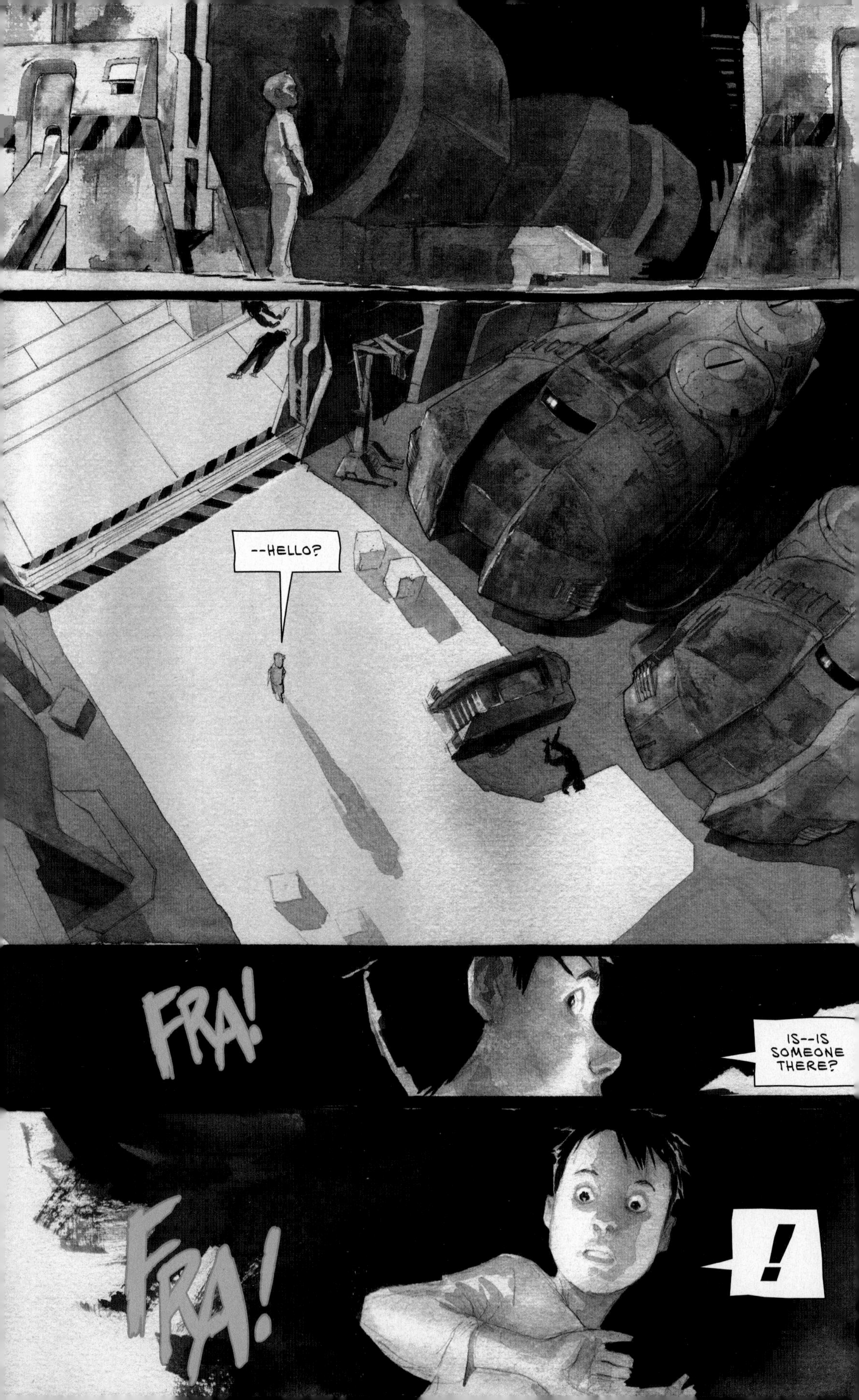
--HELLO?
FRA!
IS--IS SOMEONE THERE?
FRA!
!

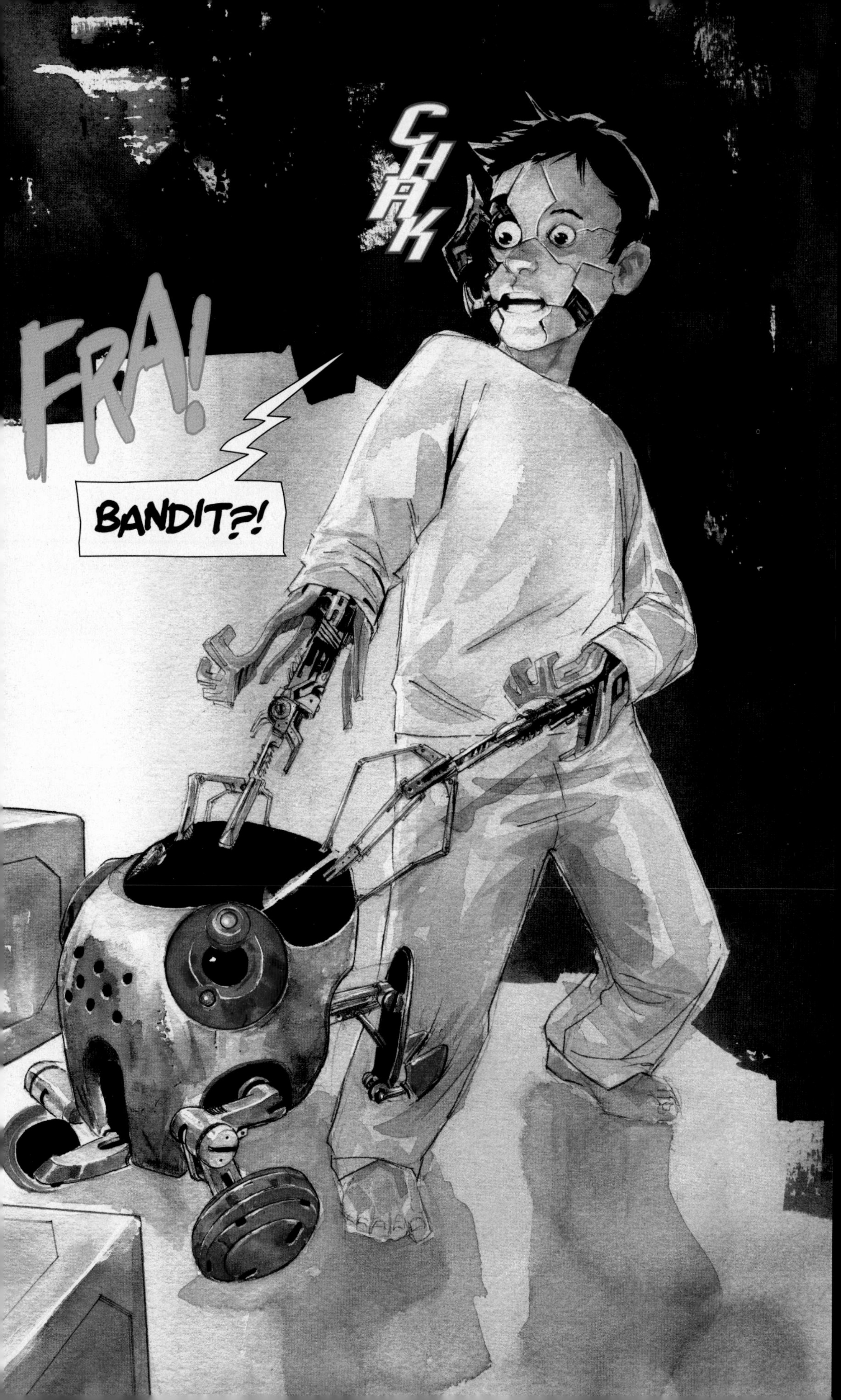
CHAK
FRA!
BANDIT?!

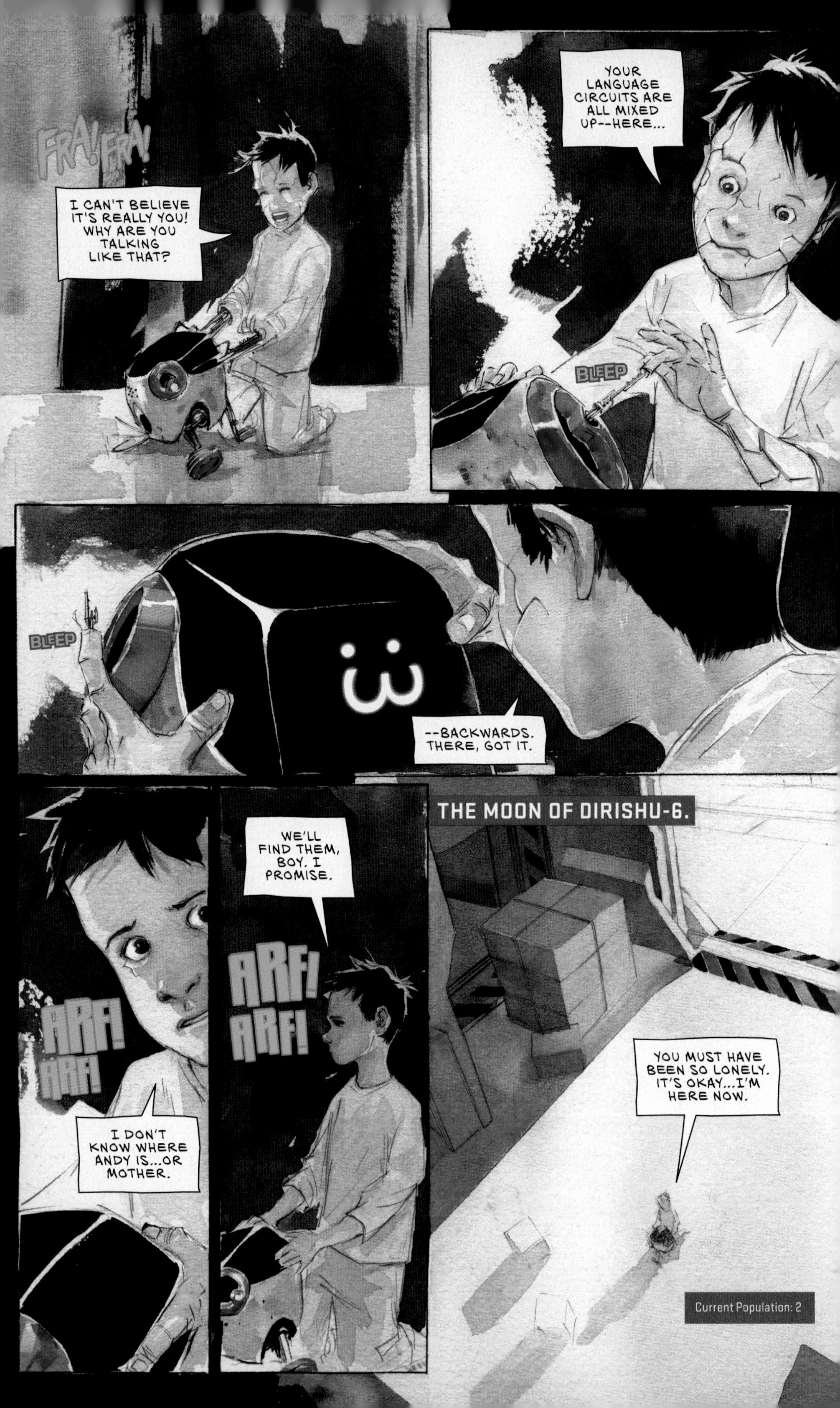
FRA! FRA!
I CAN'T BELIEVE IT'S REALLY YOU! WHY ARE YOU TALKING LIKE THAT?
YOUR LANGUAGE CIRCUITS ARE ALL MIXED UP--HERE...
BLEEP
BLEEP
--BACKWARDS. THERE, GOT IT.
ARF! ARF!
I DON'T KNOW WHERE ANDY IS...OR MOTHER.
WE'LL FIND THEM, BOY. I PROMISE.
ARF! ARF!
THE MOON OF DIRISHU-6.
YOU MUST HAVE BEEN SO LONELY. IT'S OKAY...I'M HERE NOW.
Current Population: 2

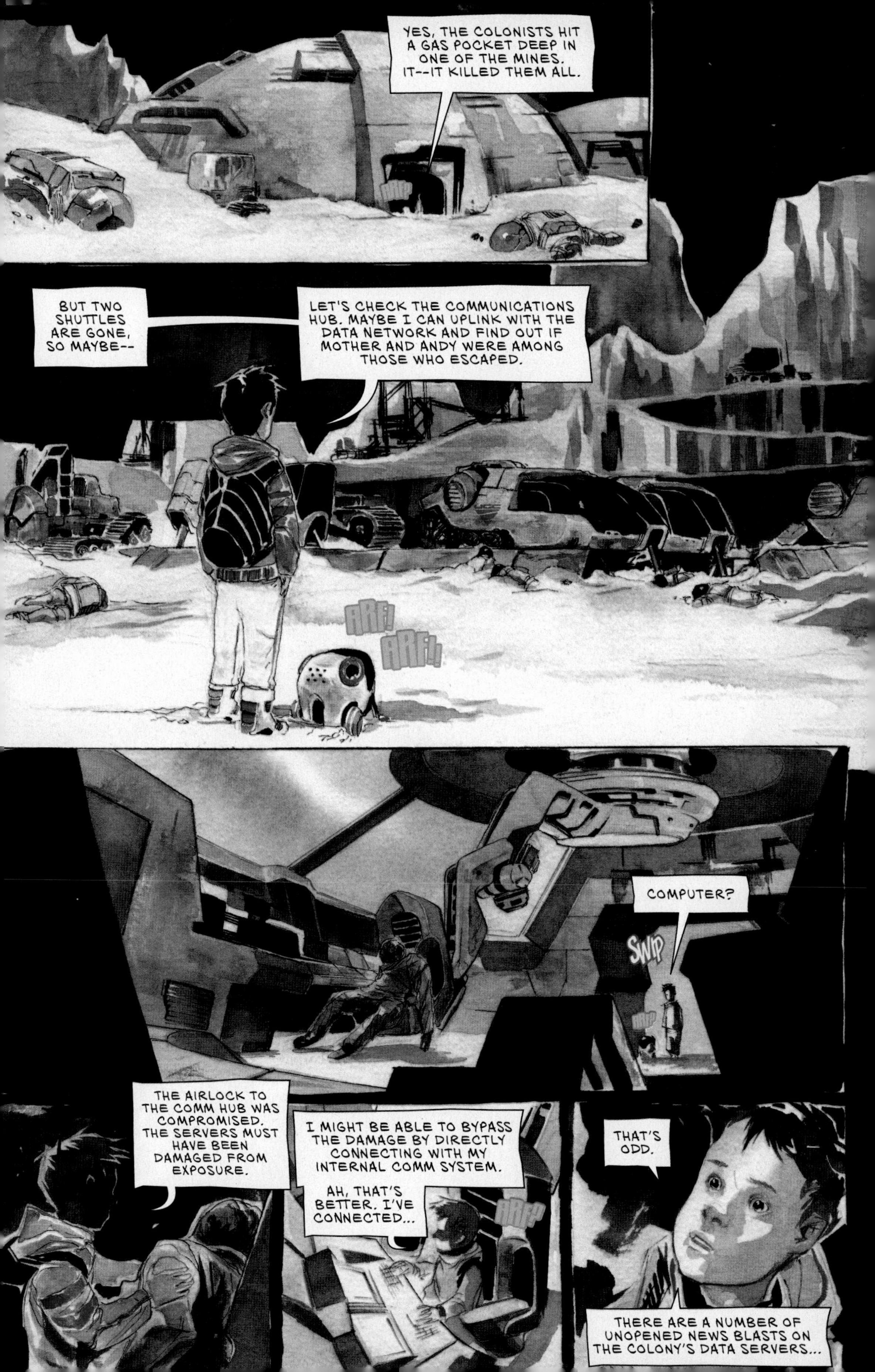
YES, THE COLONISTS HIT A GAS POCKET DEEP IN ONE OF THE MINES. IT--IT KILLED THEM ALL.
ARF!
BUT TWO SHUTTLES ARE GONE, SO MAYBE--
LET'S CHECK THE COMMUNICATIONS HUB. MAYBE I CAN UPLINK WITH THE DATA NETWORK AND FIND OUT IF MOTHER AND ANDY WERE AMONG THOSE WHO ESCAPED.
ARF! ARF!!
COMPUTER?
SWIP
ARF
THE AIRLOCK TO THE COMM HUB WAS COMPROMISED. THE SERVERS MUST HAVE BEEN DAMAGED FROM EXPOSURE.
I MIGHT BE ABLE TO BYPASS THE DAMAGE BY DIRECTLY CONNECTING WITH MY INTERNAL COMM SYSTEM.
AH, THAT'S BETTER. I'VE CONNECTED...
ARF?
THAT'S ODD.
THERE ARE A NUMBER OF UNOPENED NEWS BLASTS ON THE COLONY'S DATA SERVERS...

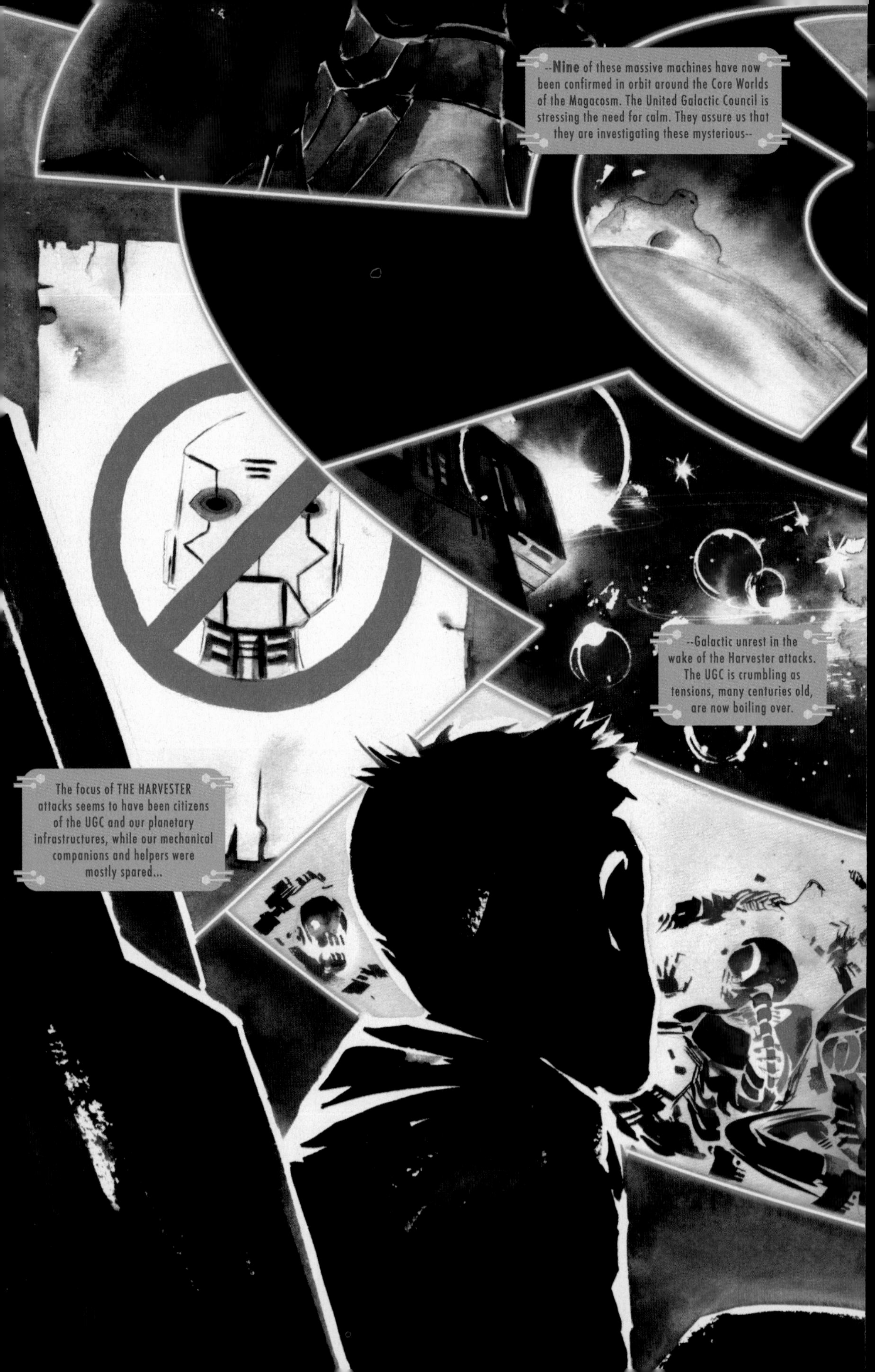
--Nine of these massive machines have now been confirmed in orbit around the Core Worlds of the Magacosm. The United Galactic Council is stressing the need for calm. They assure us that they are investigating these mysterious--
--Galactic unrest in the wake of the Harvester attacks. The UGC is crumbling as tensions, many centuries old, are now boiling over.
The focus of THE HARVESTER attacks seems to have been citizens of the UGC and our planetary infrastructures, while our mechanical companions and helpers were mostly spared...

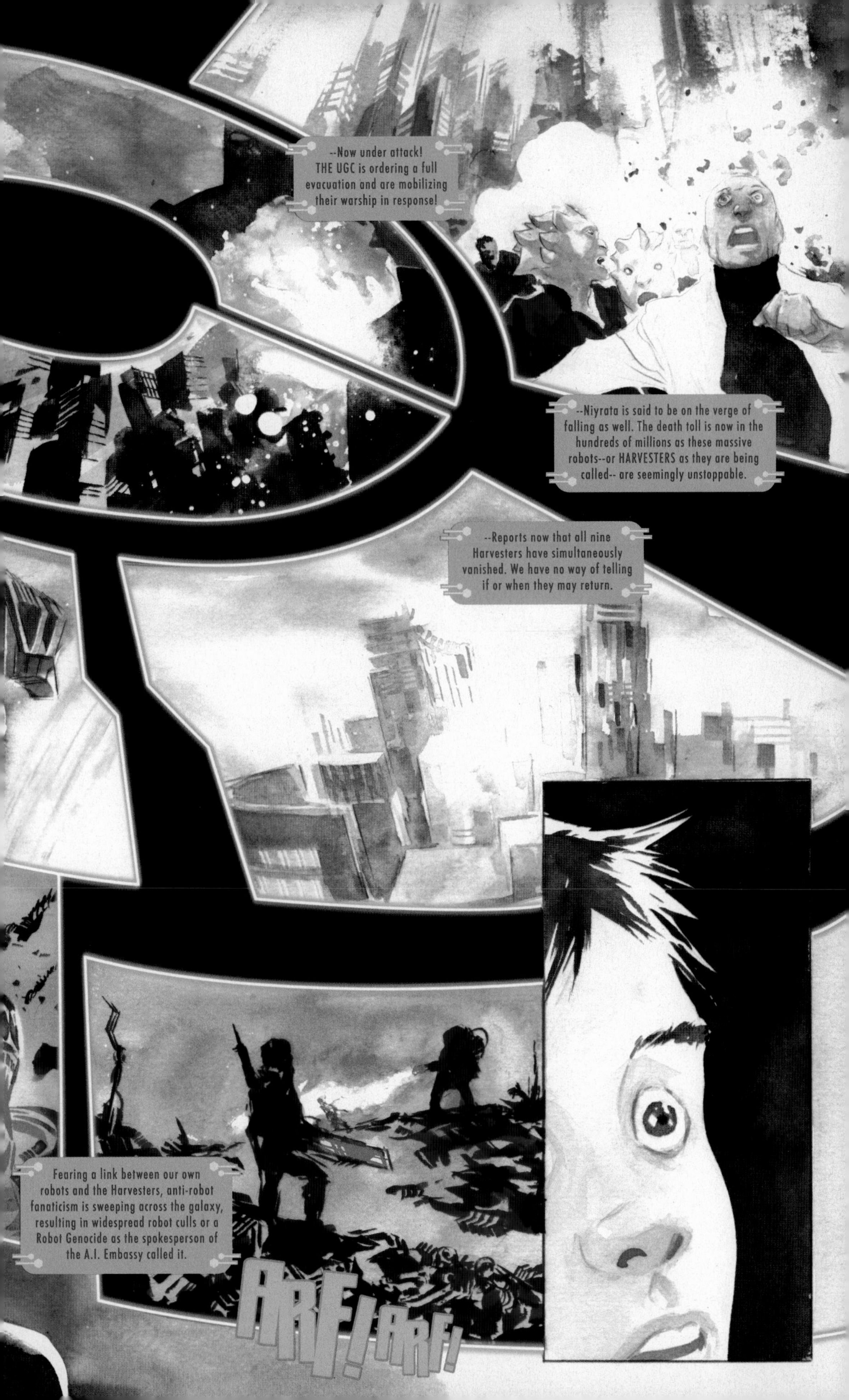
--Now under attack! THE UGC is ordering a full evacuation and are mobilizing their warship in response!
--Niyrata is said to be on the verge of falling as well. The death toll is now in the hundreds of millions as these massive robots--or HARVESTERS as they are being called-- are seemingly unstoppable.
--Reports now that all nine Harvesters have simultaneously vanished. We have no way of telling if or when they may return.
Fearing a link between our own robots and the Harvesters, anti-robot fanaticism is sweeping across the galaxy, resulting in widespread robot culls or a Robot Genocide as the spokesperson of the A.I. Embassy called it.
ARF! ARF!

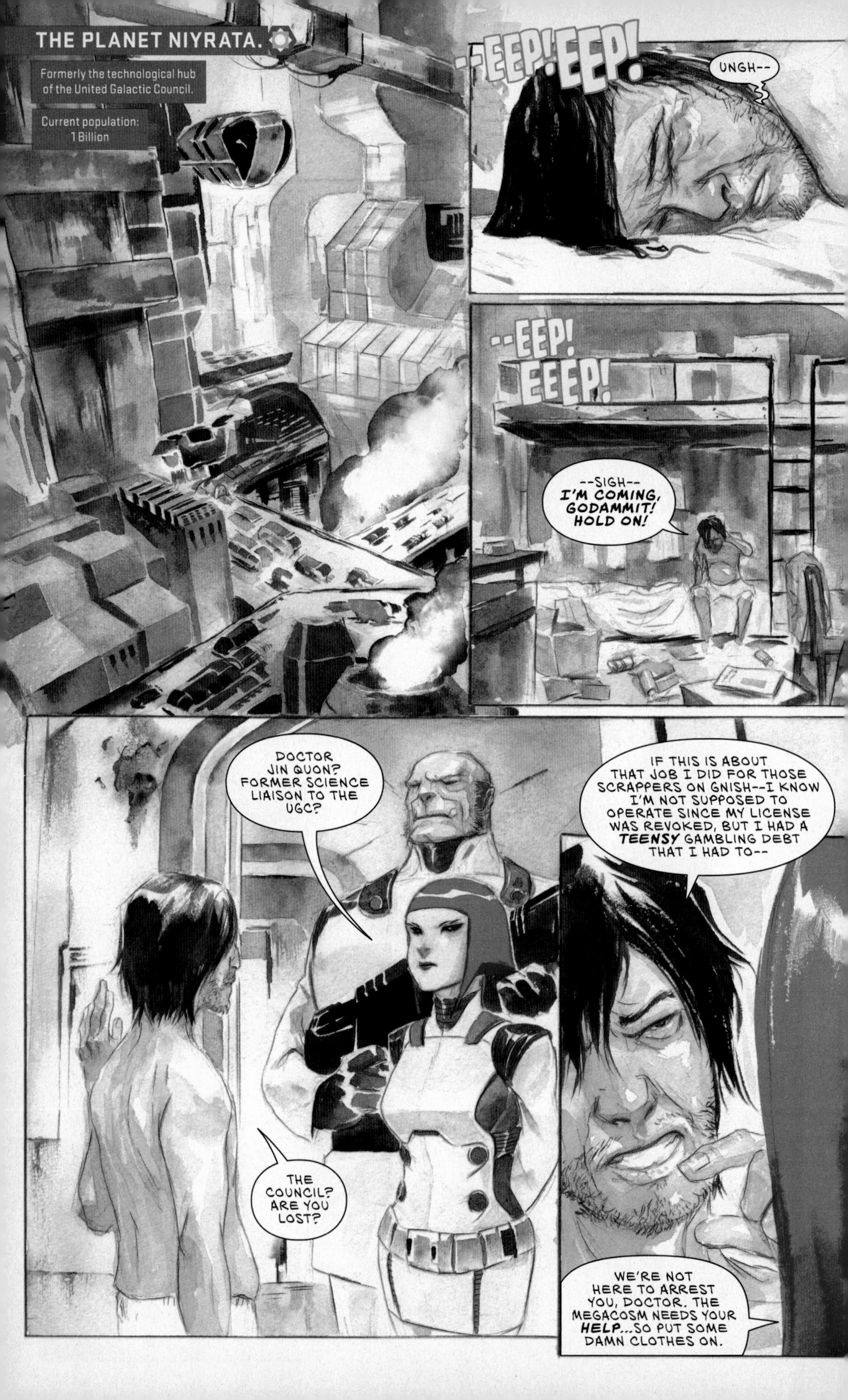
THE PLANET NIYRATA.
Formerly the technological hub of the United Galactic Council.
Current population: 1 Billion
--EEP! EEP!
UNGH--
--EEP! EEEP!
--SIGH-- I'M COMING, GODAMMIT! HOLD ON!
DOCTOR JIN QUON? FORMER SCIENCE LIAISON TO THE UGC?
THE COUNCIL? ARE YOU LOST?
IF THIS IS ABOUT THAT JOB I DID FOR THOSE SCRAPPERS ON GNISH--I KNOW I'M NOT SUPPOSED TO OPERATE SINCE MY LICENSE WAS REVOKED, BUT I HAD A TEENSY GAMBLING DEBT THAT I HAD TO--
WE'RE NOT HERE TO ARREST YOU, DOCTOR. THE MEGACOSM NEEDS YOUR HELP...SO PUT SOME DAMN CLOTHES ON.

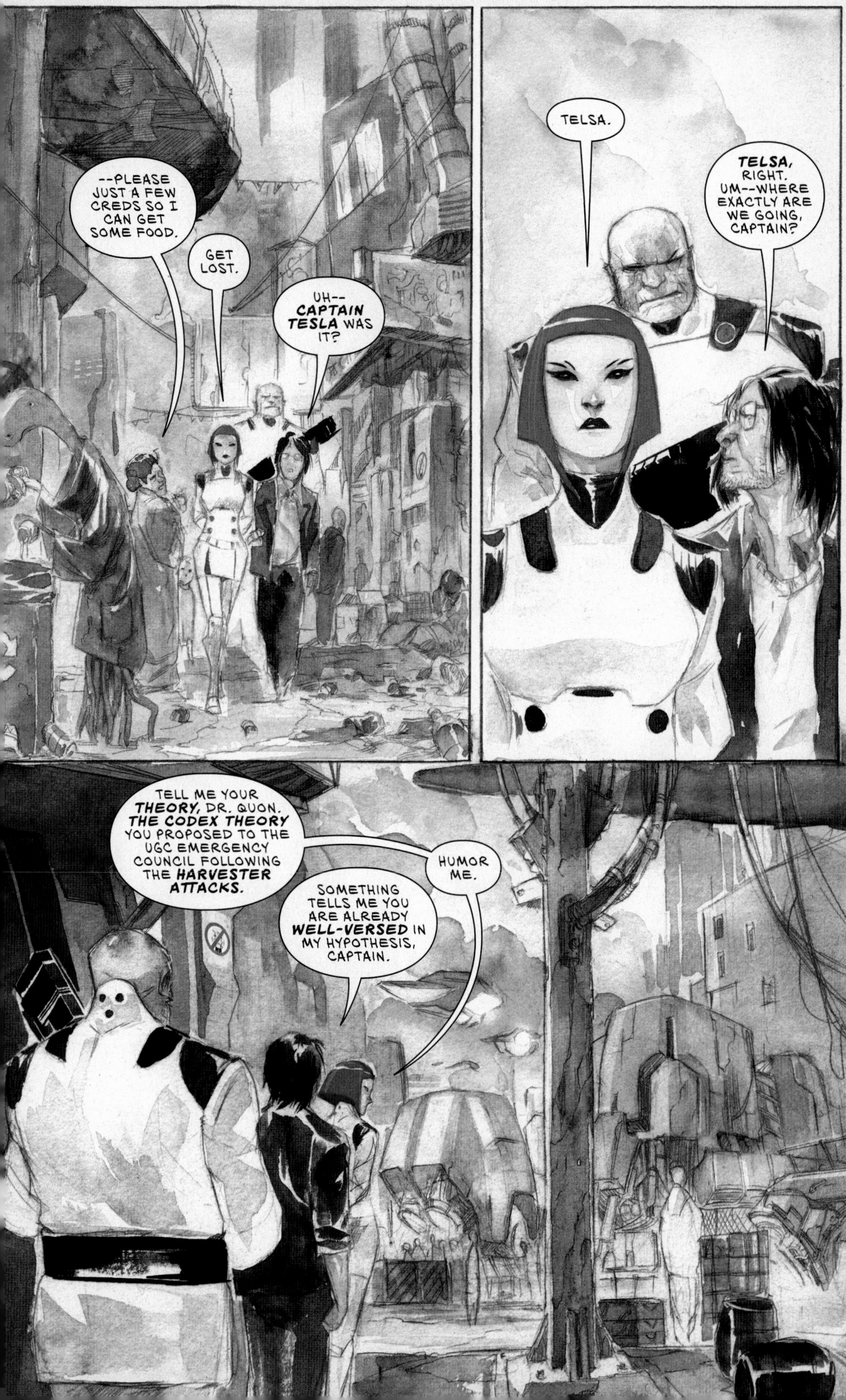
--PLEASE JUST A FEW CREDS SO I CAN GET SOME FOOD.
GET LOST.
UH-- **CAPTAIN TESLA** WAS IT?
TELSA.
TELSA, RIGHT. UM--WHERE EXACTLY ARE WE GOING, CAPTAIN?
TELL ME YOUR **THEORY,** DR. QUON. **THE CODEX THEORY** YOU PROPOSED TO THE UGC EMERGENCY COUNCIL FOLLOWING THE **HARVESTER ATTACKS.**
HUMOR ME.
SOMETHING TELLS ME YOU ARE ALREADY **WELL-VERSED** IN MY HYPOTHESIS, CAPTAIN.

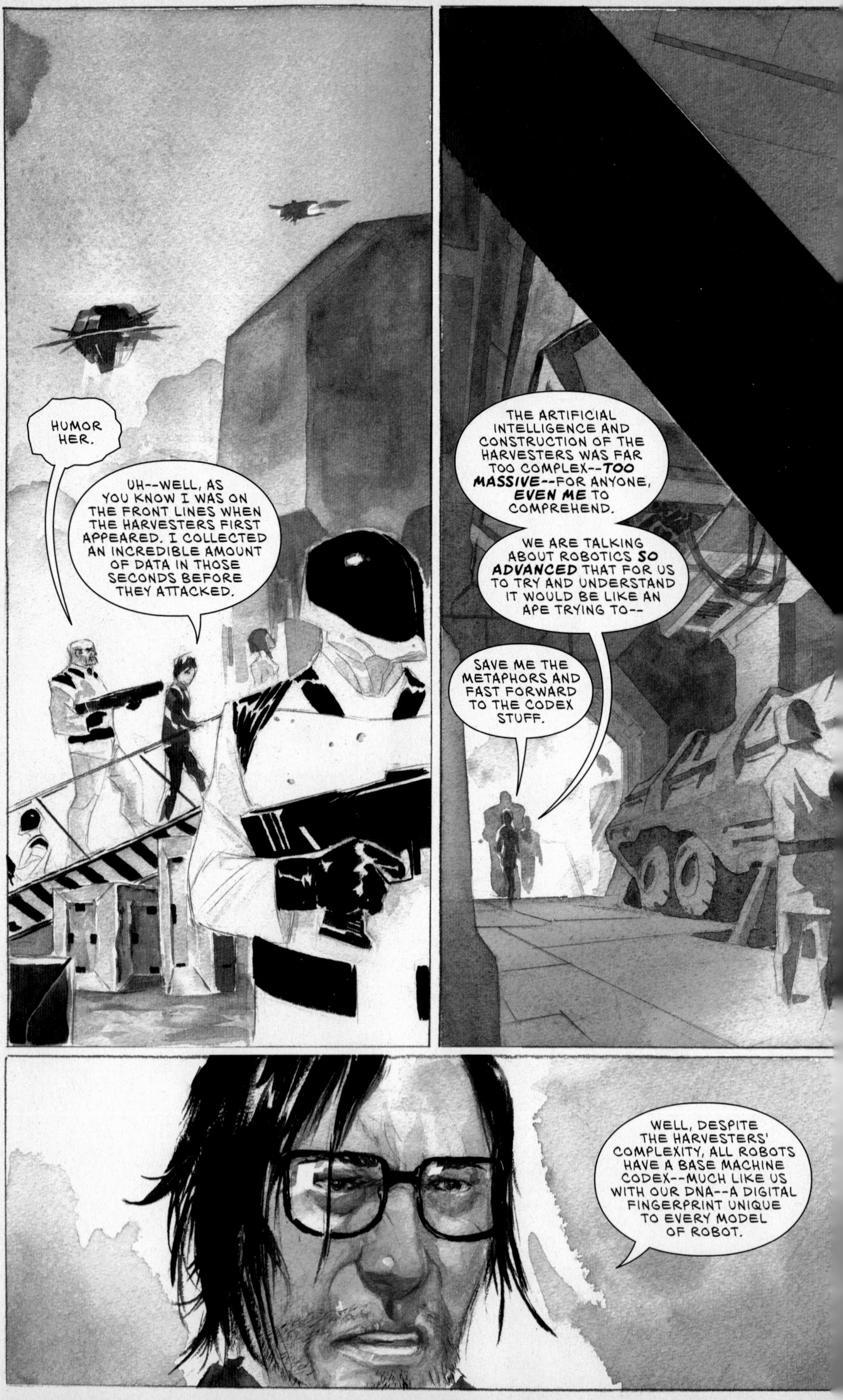
HUMOR HER.
UH--WELL, AS YOU KNOW I WAS ON THE FRONT LINES WHEN THE HARVESTERS FIRST APPEARED. I COLLECTED AN INCREDIBLE AMOUNT OF DATA IN THOSE SECONDS BEFORE THEY ATTACKED.
THE ARTIFICIAL INTELLIGENCE AND CONSTRUCTION OF THE HARVESTERS WAS FAR TOO COMPLEX--TOO MASSIVE--FOR ANYONE, EVEN ME TO COMPREHEND.
WE ARE TALKING ABOUT ROBOTICS SO ADVANCED THAT FOR US TO TRY AND UNDERSTAND IT WOULD BE LIKE AN APE TRYING TO--
SAVE ME THE METAPHORS AND FAST FORWARD TO THE CODEX STUFF.
WELL, DESPITE THE HARVESTERS' COMPLEXITY, ALL ROBOTS HAVE A BASE MACHINE CODEX--MUCH LIKE US WITH OUR DNA--A DIGITAL FINGERPRINT UNIQUE TO EVERY MODEL OF ROBOT.

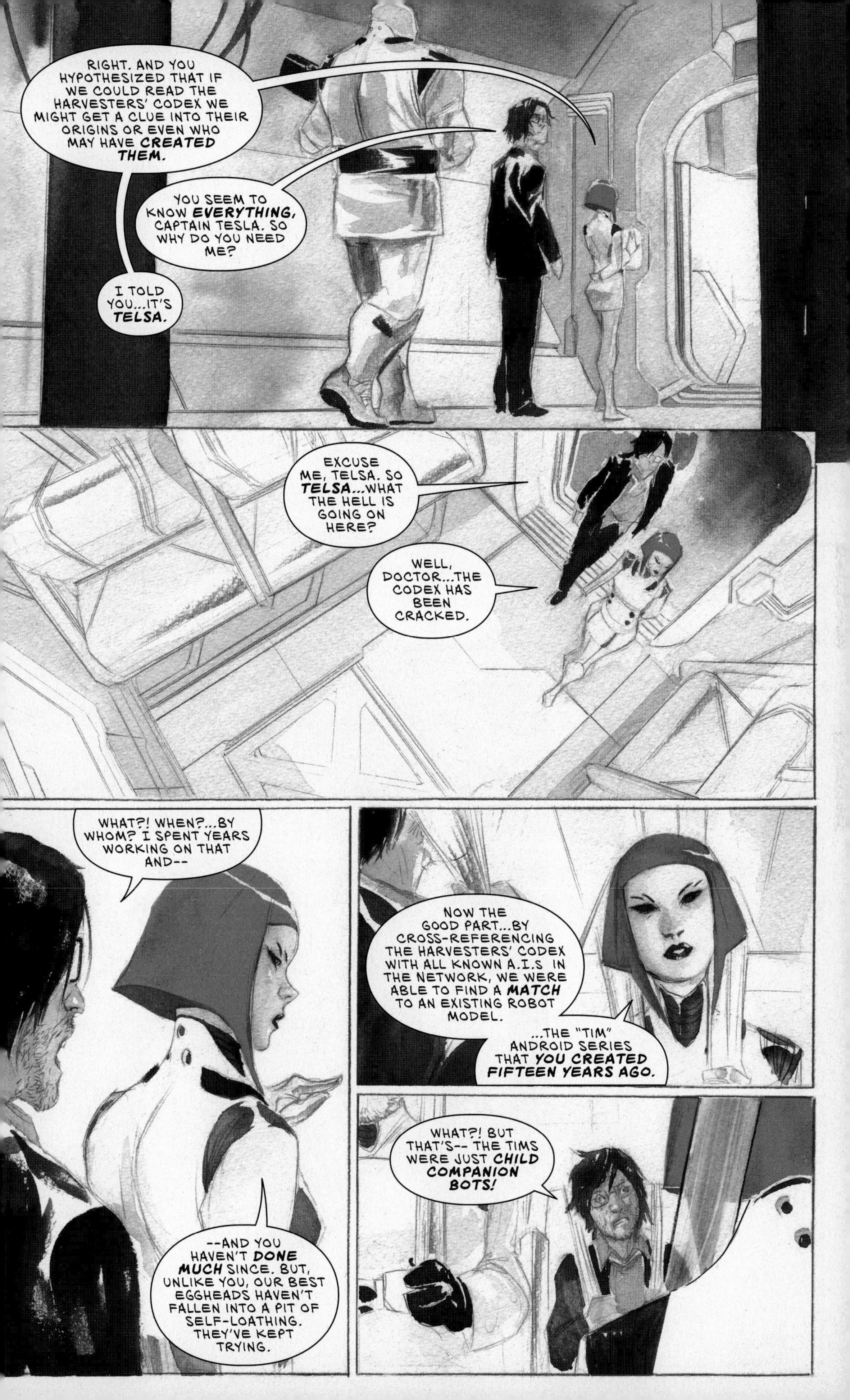
RIGHT. AND YOU HYPOTHESIZED THAT IF WE COULD READ THE HARVESTERS' CODEX WE MIGHT GET A CLUE INTO THEIR ORIGINS OR EVEN WHO MAY HAVE CREATED THEM.
YOU SEEM TO KNOW EVERYTHING, CAPTAIN TESLA. SO WHY DO YOU NEED ME?
I TOLD YOU...IT'S TELSA.
EXCUSE ME, TELSA. SO TELSA...WHAT THE HELL IS GOING ON HERE?
WELL, DOCTOR...THE CODEX HAS BEEN CRACKED.
WHAT?! WHEN?...BY WHOM? I SPENT YEARS WORKING ON THAT AND--
--AND YOU HAVEN'T DONE MUCH SINCE. BUT, UNLIKE YOU, OUR BEST EGGHEADS HAVEN'T FALLEN INTO A PIT OF SELF-LOATHING. THEY'VE KEPT TRYING.
NOW THE GOOD PART...BY CROSS-REFERENCING THE HARVESTERS' CODEX WITH ALL KNOWN A.I.S IN THE NETWORK, WE WERE ABLE TO FIND A MATCH TO AN EXISTING ROBOT MODEL.
...THE "TIM" ANDROID SERIES THAT YOU CREATED FIFTEEN YEARS AGO.
WHAT?! BUT THAT'S-- THE TIMS WERE JUST CHILD COMPANION BOTS!

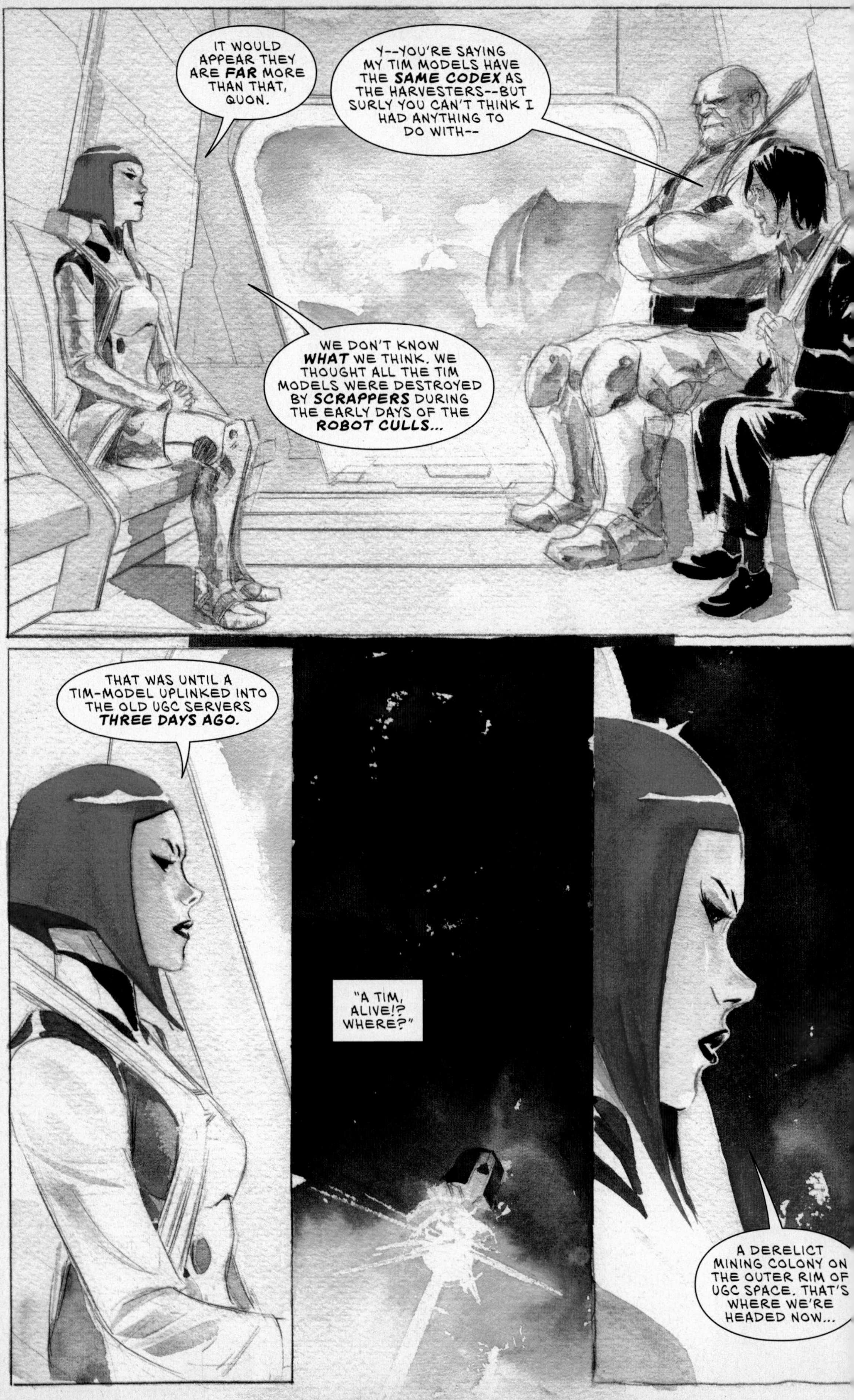
IT WOULD APPEAR THEY ARE FAR MORE THAN THAT, QUON.
Y--YOU'RE SAYING MY TIM MODELS HAVE THE SAME CODEX AS THE HARVESTERS--BUT SURLY YOU CAN'T THINK I HAD ANYTHING TO DO WITH--
WE DON'T KNOW WHAT WE THINK. WE THOUGHT ALL THE TIM MODELS WERE DESTROYED BY SCRAPPERS DURING THE EARLY DAYS OF THE ROBOT CULLS...
THAT WAS UNTIL A TIM-MODEL UPLINKED INTO THE OLD UGC SERVERS THREE DAYS AGO.
"A TIM, ALIVE!? WHERE?"
A DERELICT MINING COLONY ON THE OUTER RIM OF UGC SPACE. THAT'S WHERE WE'RE HEADED NOW...

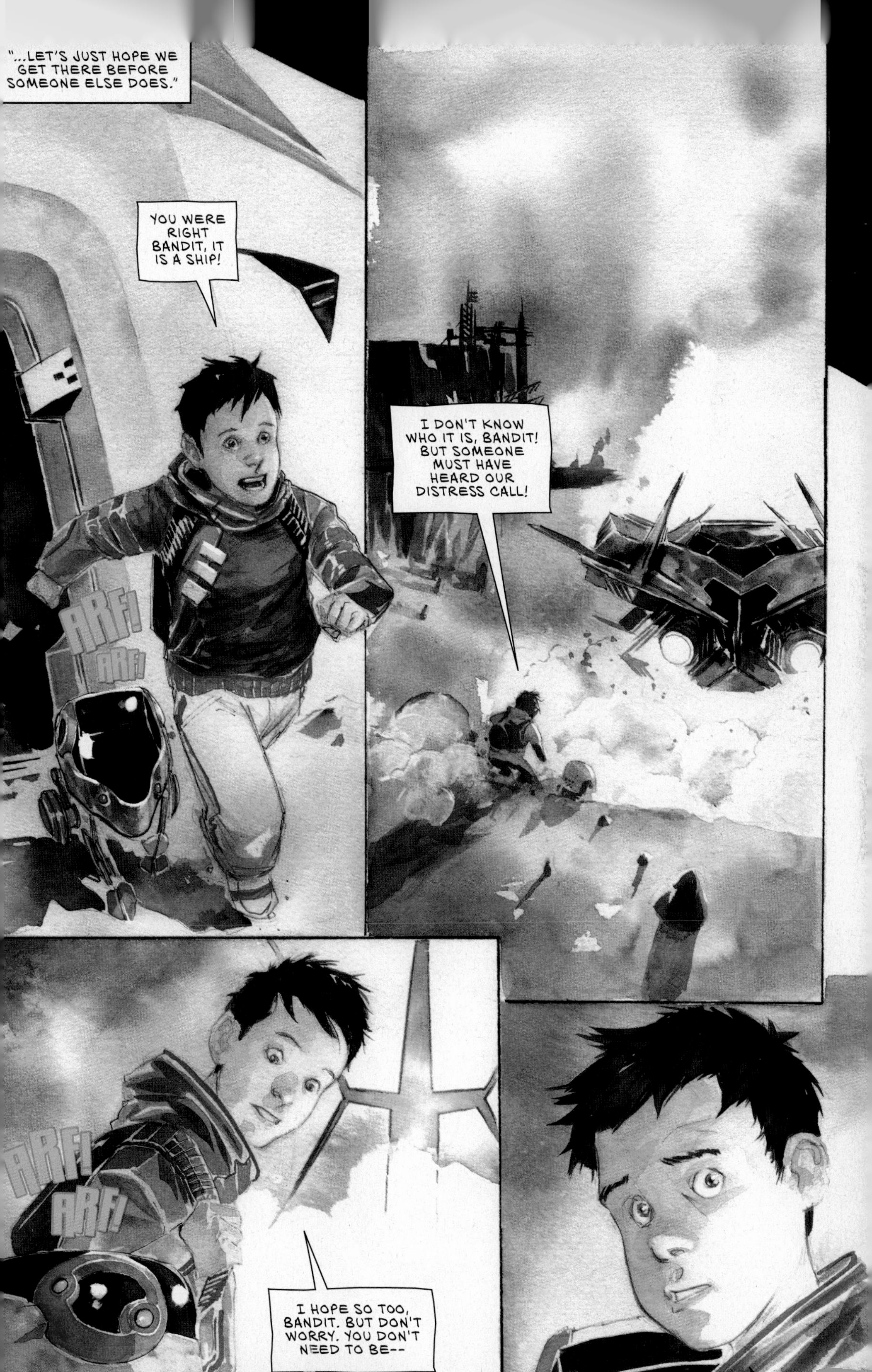
"...LET'S JUST HOPE WE GET THERE BEFORE SOMEONE ELSE DOES."
YOU WERE RIGHT BANDIT, IT IS A SHIP!
ARF! ARF!
I DON'T KNOW WHO IT IS, BANDIT! BUT SOMEONE MUST HAVE HEARD OUR DISTRESS CALL!
ARF! ARF!
I HOPE SO TOO, BANDIT. BUT DON'T WORRY. YOU DON'T NEED TO BE--

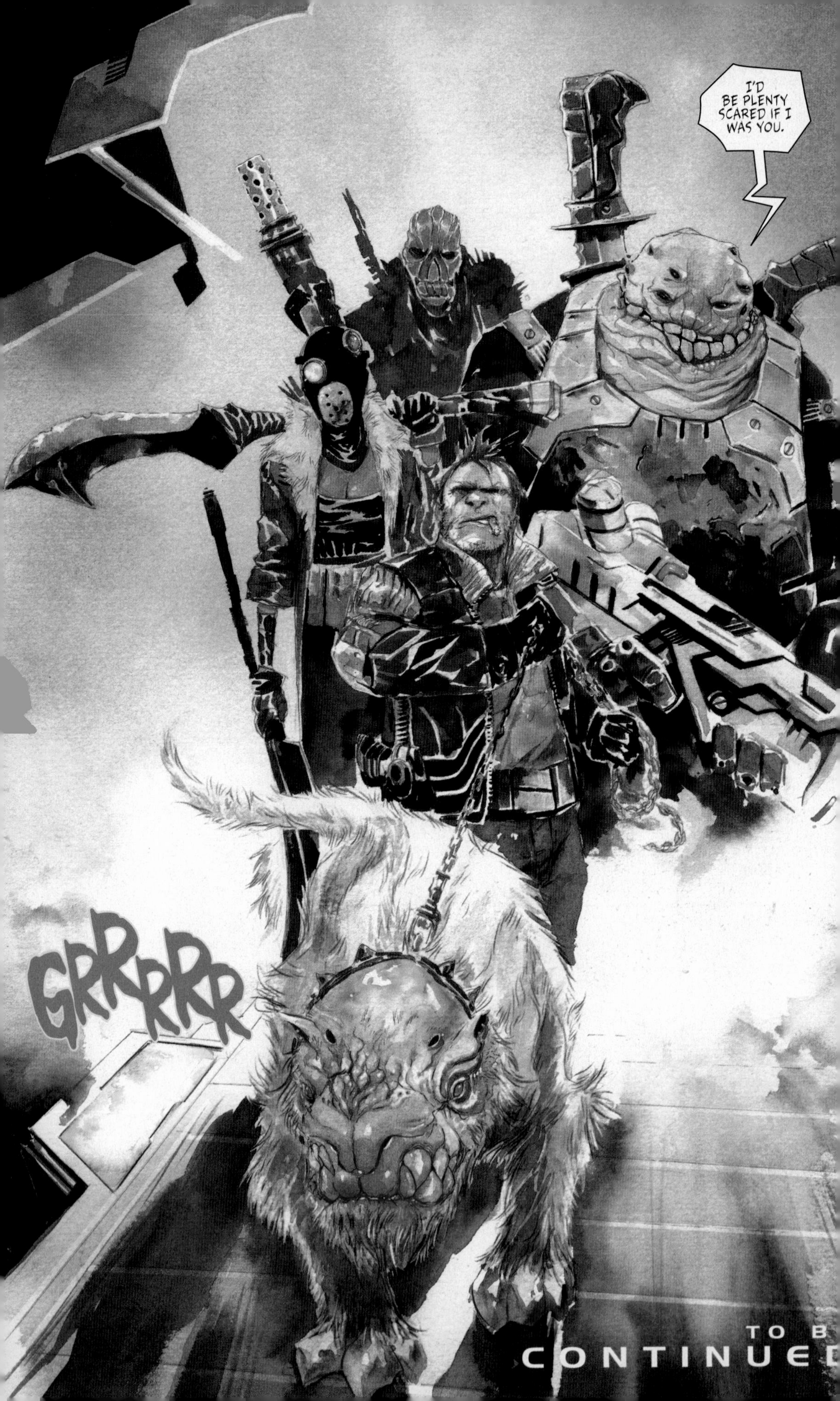
I'D BE PLENTY SCARED IF I WAS YOU.
GRRRRR
TO B
CONTINUED

ATLAS OF THE CORE PLANETS OF THE UNITED GALACTIC COUNCIL

NIYATA (THE HUB WORLD): Former technological and cultural hub of the UGC and former home of the nine Embassy Cities. One city state for each of the core planets and races representing UGC. Now a devastated world, what's left of the UGC still resides there, clinging to power. Home of the NIYRATAN MONARCHY that has guided the UGC for centuries.

PHAGES (THE GHOST WORLD/HAUNTED PLANET): Home to a gaseous race called THE PHAGES. Their spectral, ghost-like appearance scared early explorers into thinking the planet was haunted. Basically a world full of ghosts with no solid matter. Cities and aliens all made of gases. The only non-gaseous species are a race of hostile 20-foot tall giants.

MATA: An aquatic world. Was once home to a great empire and a baroque, almost renaissance-type world, but long ago was flooded and turned into a water-world. The descendants of this monarchy now survive on a floating, mobile kingdom. The ruins of the old cities still lay below the water.

SAMPSON: Home to the original colonists from Old Earth. Sampson is a massive city and the military center of the Megacosm and home of the largest human cities.

KNOSSOS:
The smallest Core planet in the Megacosm.

SILENOS: The unique atmosphere on Silenos makes all sound and vibration impossible, creating a totally silent world where the native race communicates by projecting telepathic hieroglyphs into the air.

AMUN: The greatest ally of the GNISHIANS. An insect-like race that live in underground hives.

GNISH: The largest planet and the home of the largest military force. Leaders in the anti-robot, anti-technology movement in the wake of the Harvesters. A race ruled by luddite zealots who preach independence and sovereignty for all worlds all the while working for more and more control of Megacosm space. Main funder of the Scrappers. Home to the MELTING PITS, massive gladitorial arenas were Robots are made to fight to the death.

OSTRAKON: A desert wasteland devoid of all life. Contains the ruins of an ancient civilization that has long since gone extinct.

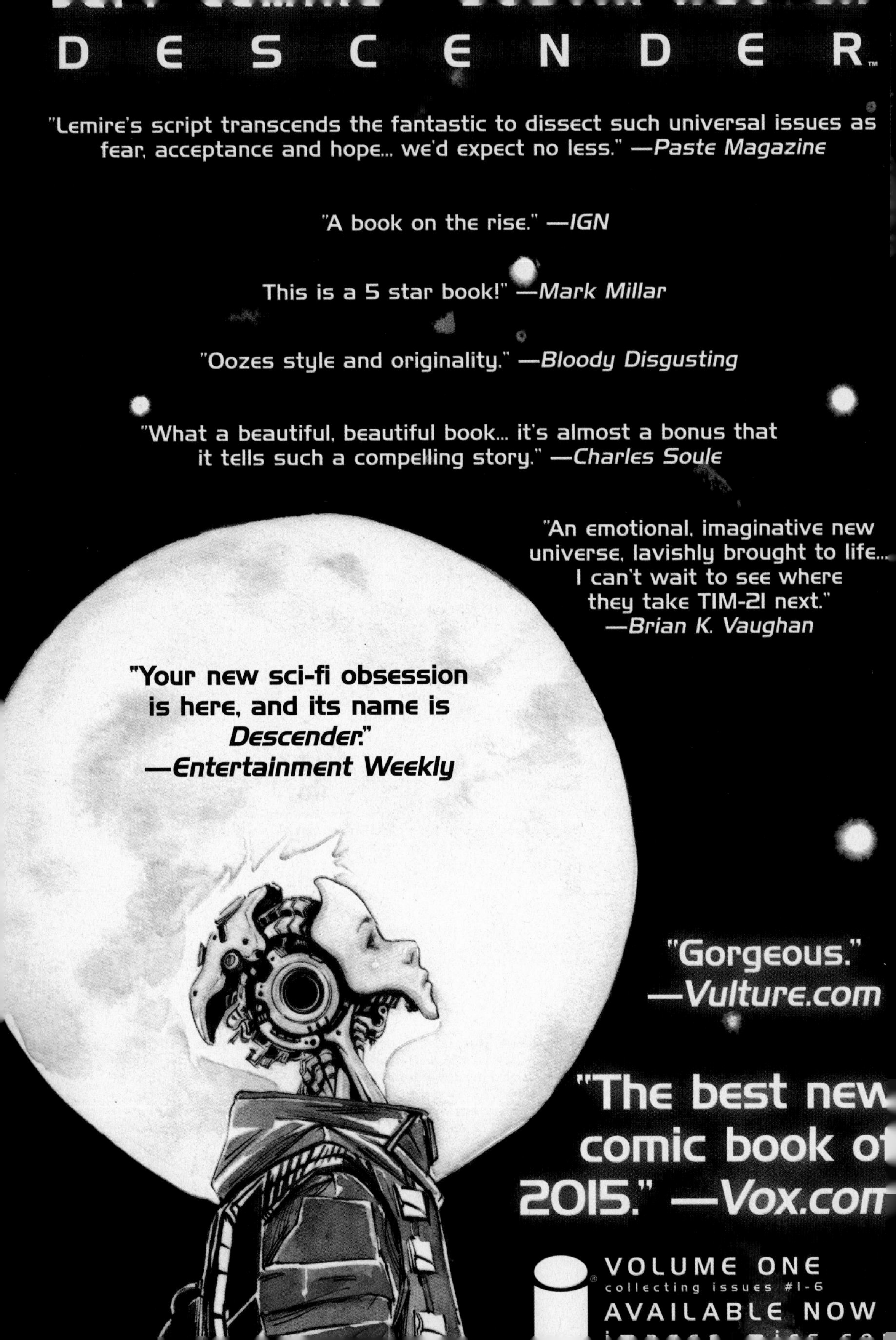

D E S C E N D E R™
"Lemire's script transcends the fantastic to dissect such universal issues as fear, acceptance and hope... we'd expect no less." —Paste Magazine
"A book on the rise." —IGN
This is a 5 star book!" —Mark Millar
"Oozes style and originality." —Bloody Disgusting
"What a beautiful, beautiful book... it's almost a bonus that it tells such a compelling story." —Charles Soule
"An emotional, imaginative new universe, lavishly brought to life... I can't wait to see where they take TIM-21 next." —Brian K. Vaughan
"Your new sci-fi obsession is here, and its name is Descender." —Entertainment Weekly
"Gorgeous." —Vulture.com
"The best new comic book of 2015." —Vox.com
VOLUME ONE
collecting issues #1-6
AVAILABLE NOW

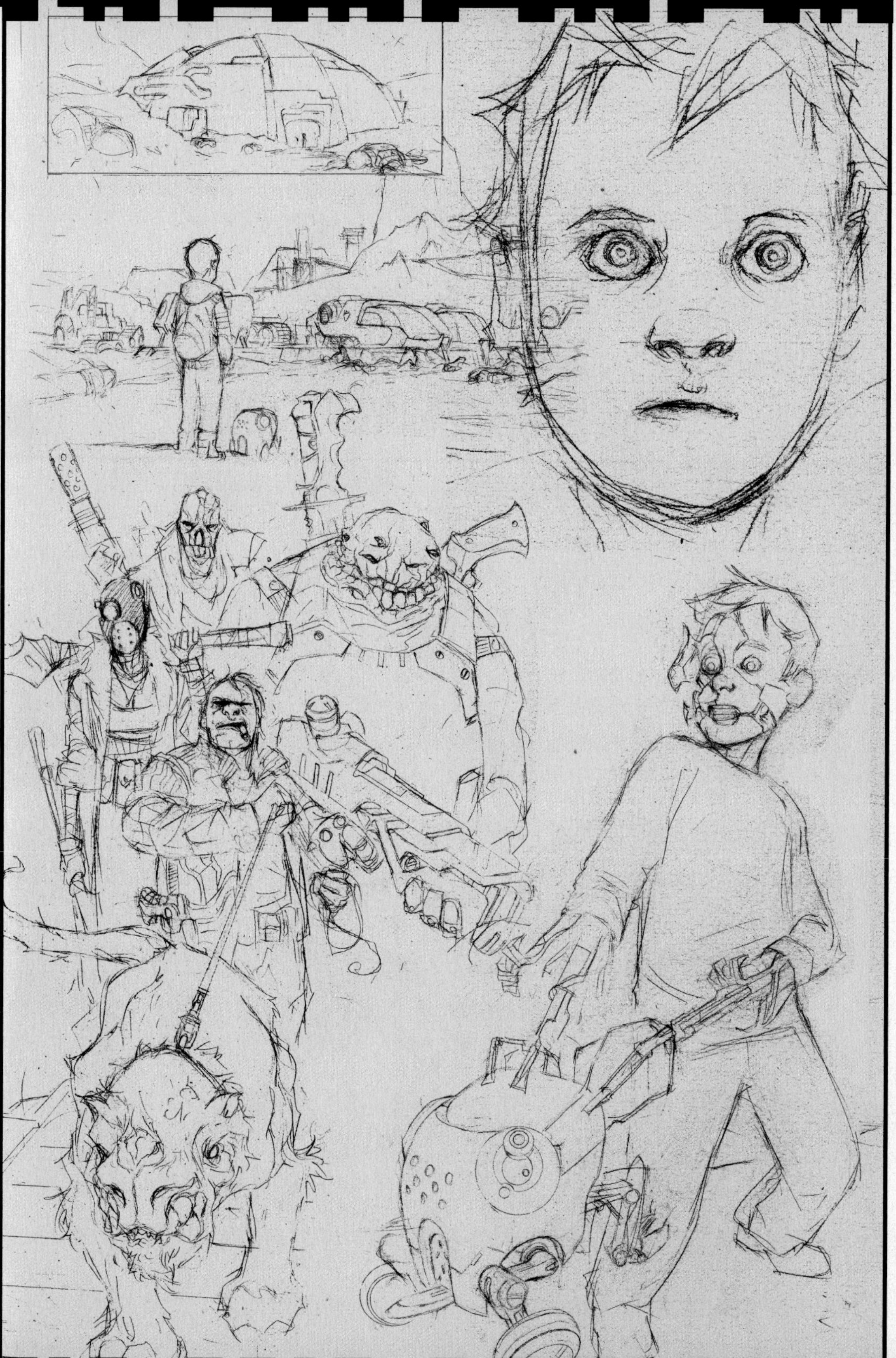

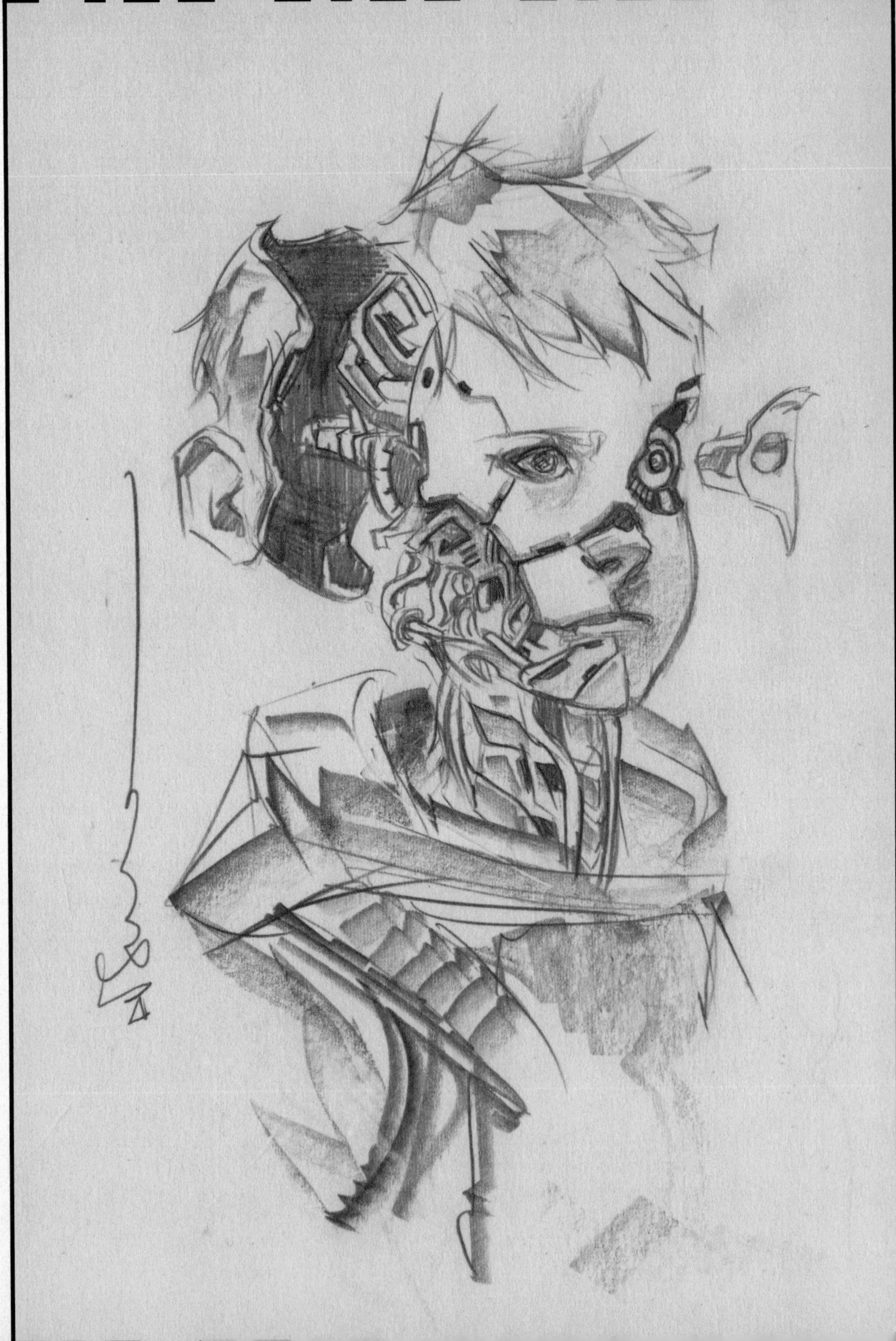

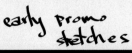

early promo sketches

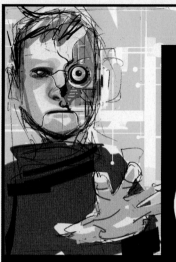

BANDIT

ROTATES FOR DIFF. THINGS

ARMS/FEET CARRY THINGS

hello Tim

VIEW FROM BEHIND

HOVERS (EASIER ON SOME TERRAIN & TO get into certain panels/shots)

WALKING MODE -MAYBE USES WHEN HE'S BROKEN, OR ON certain atmospheres?

SLEEP MODE?

U(₀·I·₀)U

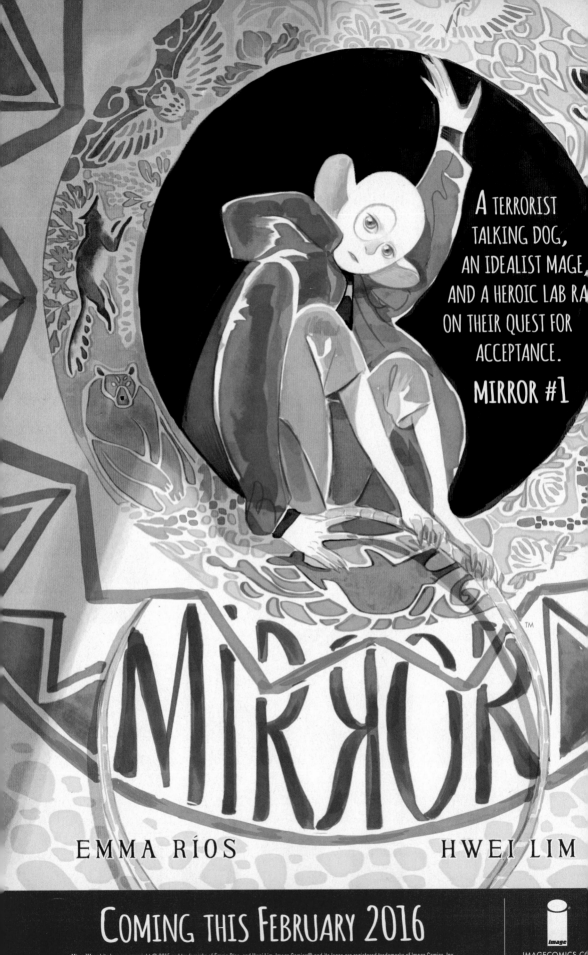

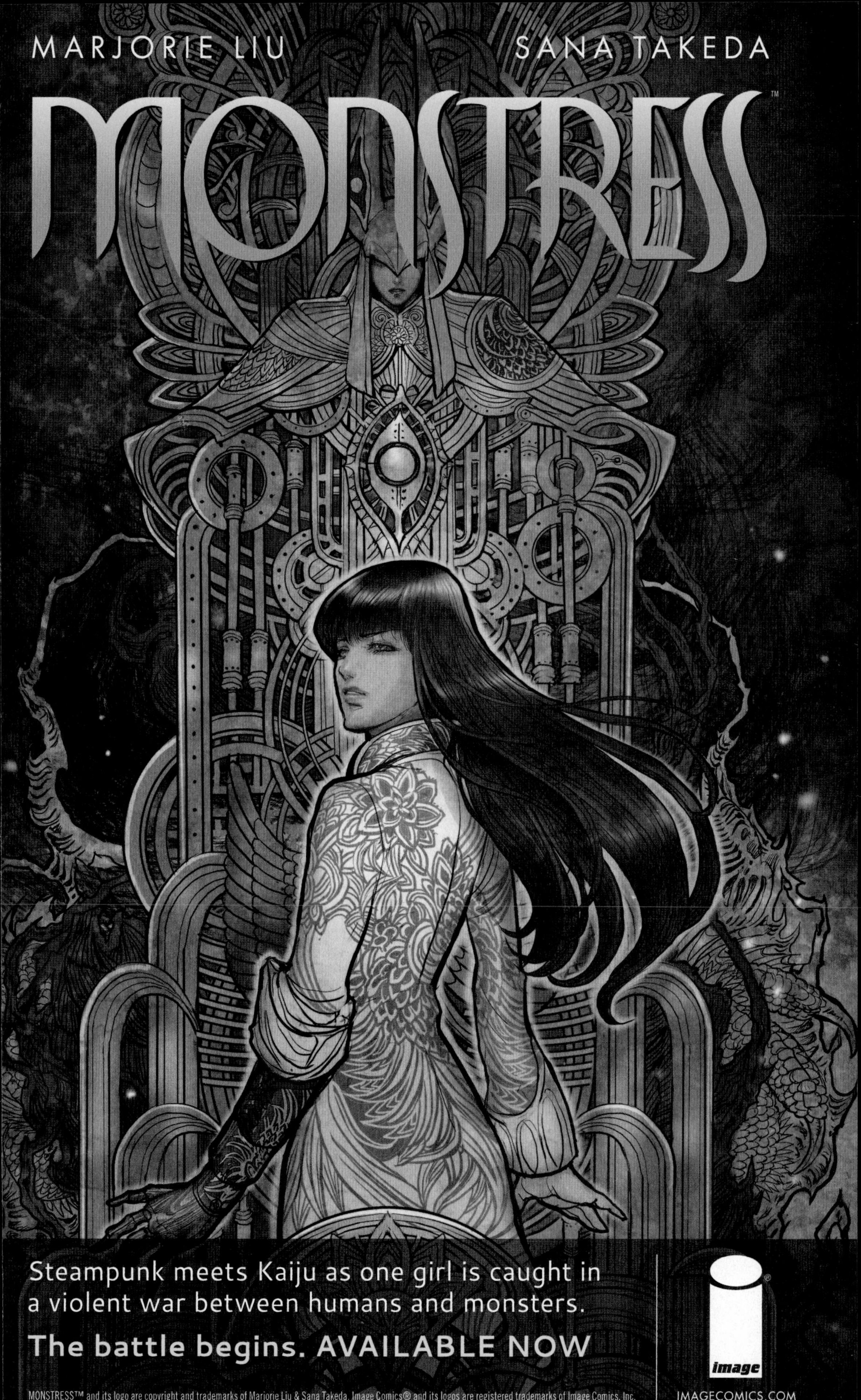
MARJORIE LIU
SANA TAKEDA
MONSTRESS™
Steampunk meets Kaiju as one girl is caught in a violent war between humans and monsters.
The battle begins. AVAILABLE NOW
image
MONSTRESS™ and its logo are copyright and trademarks of Marjorie Liu & Sana Takeda. Image Comics® and its logos are registered trademarks of Image Comics, Inc.
IMAGECOMICS.COM

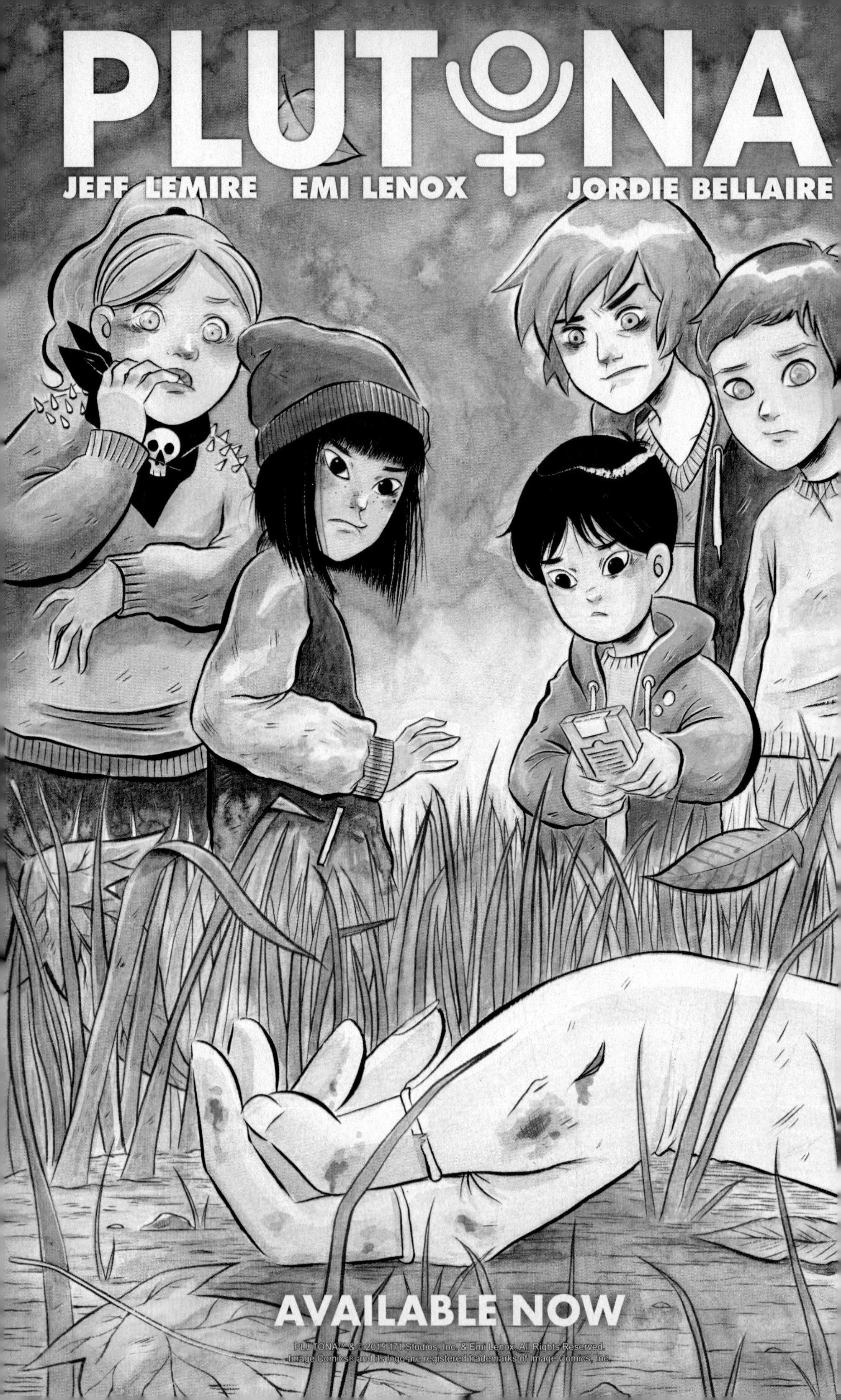

PLUTONA
JEFF LEMIRE
EMI LENOX
JORDIE BELLAIRE
AVAILABLE NOW
PLUTONA™ & © 2015 171 Studios, Inc. & Emi Lenox. All Rights Reserved.
Image Comics® and its logo are registered trademarks of Image Comics, Inc.

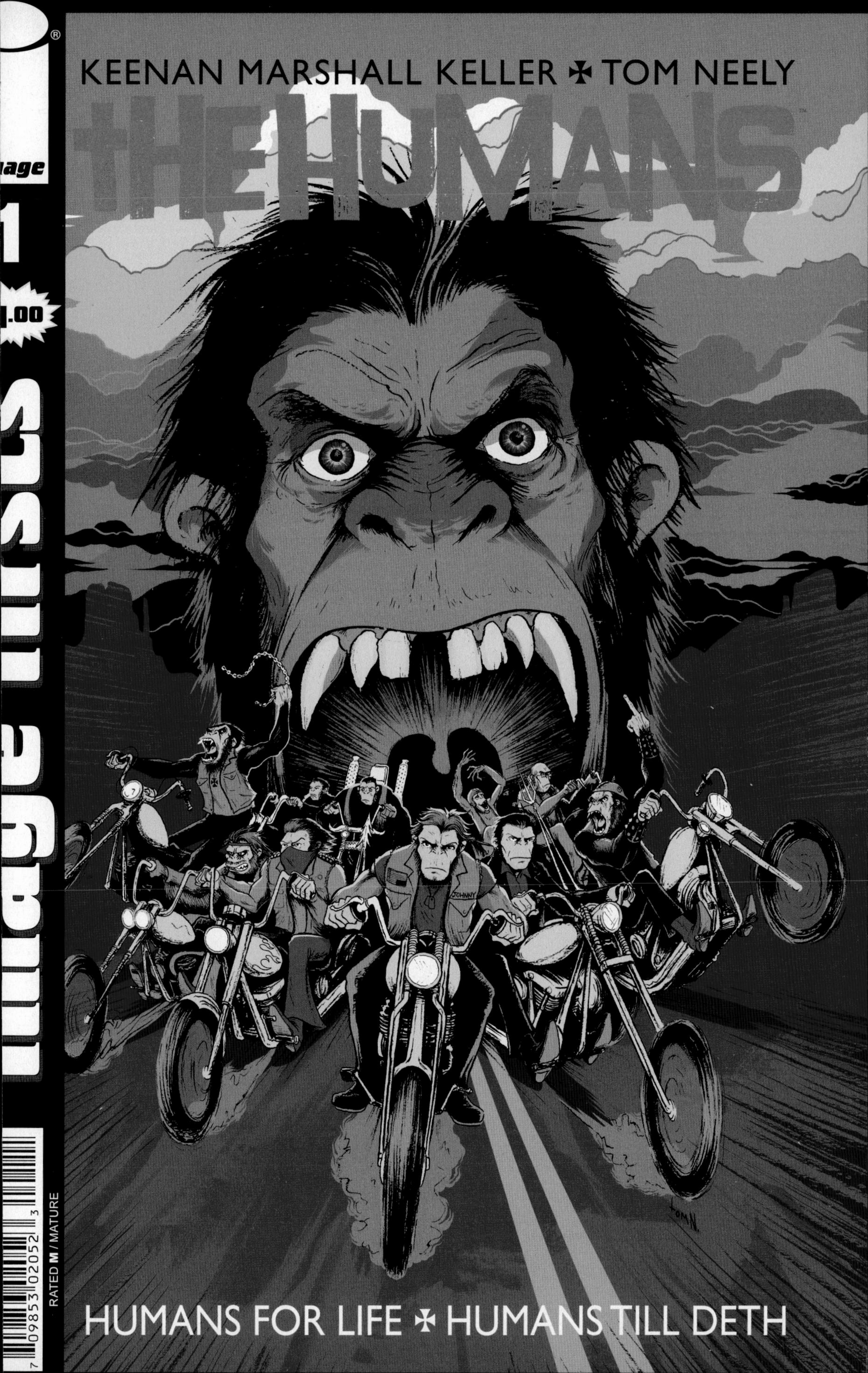
KEENAN MARSHALL KELLER ✠ TOM NEELY
THE HUMANS
JOHNNY
HUMANS FOR LIFE ✠ HUMANS TILL DETH

tHE HUMANS

CREATED BY KEENAN MARSHALL KELLER & TOM NEELY

Written by Keenan Marshall Keller
Drawn by Tom Neely
Color by Kristina Collantes
Back cover pin-up by Benjamin Marra

HUMANS FOR LIFE
HUMANS TILL DETH

IMAGE COMICS, INC.
Robert Kirkman – Chief Operating Officer
Erik Larsen – Chief Financial Officer
Todd McFarlane – President
Marc Silvestri – Chief Executive Officer
Jim Valentino – Vice-President
Eric Stephenson – Publisher
Corey Murphy – Director of Sales
Jeff Boison – Director of Publishing Planning & Book Trade
Jeremy Sullivan – Director of Digital Sales
Kat Salazar – Director of PR & Marketing
Emily Miller – Director of Operations
Branwyn Bigglestone – Senior Accounts Manager
Sarah Mello – Accounts Manager
Drew Gill – Art Director
Jonathan Chan – Production Manager
Meredith Wallace – Print Manager
Briah Skelly – Publicity Assistant
Randy Okamura – Marketing Production Designer
David Brothers – Branding Manager
Ally Power – Content Manager
Addison Duke – Production Artist
Vincent Kukua – Production Artist
Sasha Head – Production Artist
Tricia Ramos – Production Artist
Jeff Stang – Direct Market Sales Representative
Emilio Bautista – Digital Sales Associate
Chloe Ramos-Peterson – Administrative Assistant
IMAGECOMICS.COM

SEPTEMBER 22nd, 1970
SOMEWHERE OUTSIDE BAKERSFIELD, CA

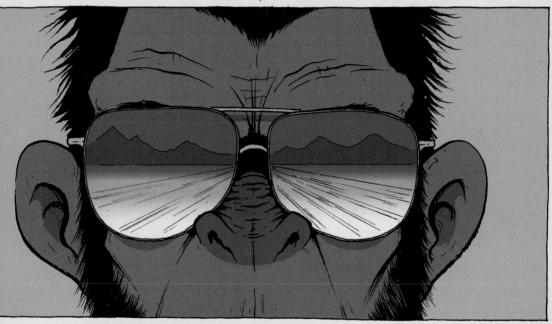

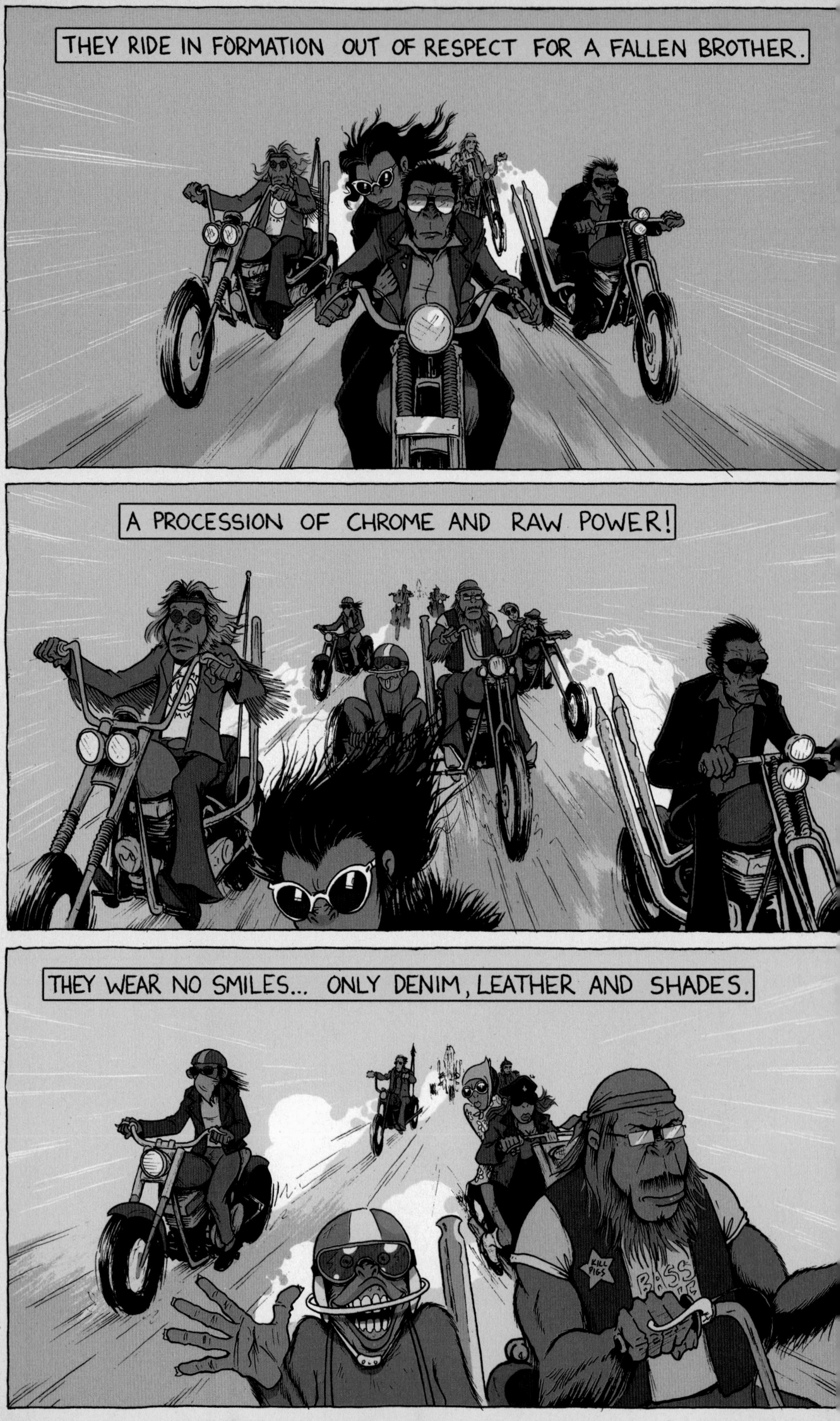
THEY RIDE IN FORMATION OUT OF RESPECT FOR A FALLEN BROTHER.
A PROCESSION OF CHROME AND RAW POWER!
THEY WEAR NO SMILES... ONLY DENIM, LEATHER AND SHADES.
KILL PIGS

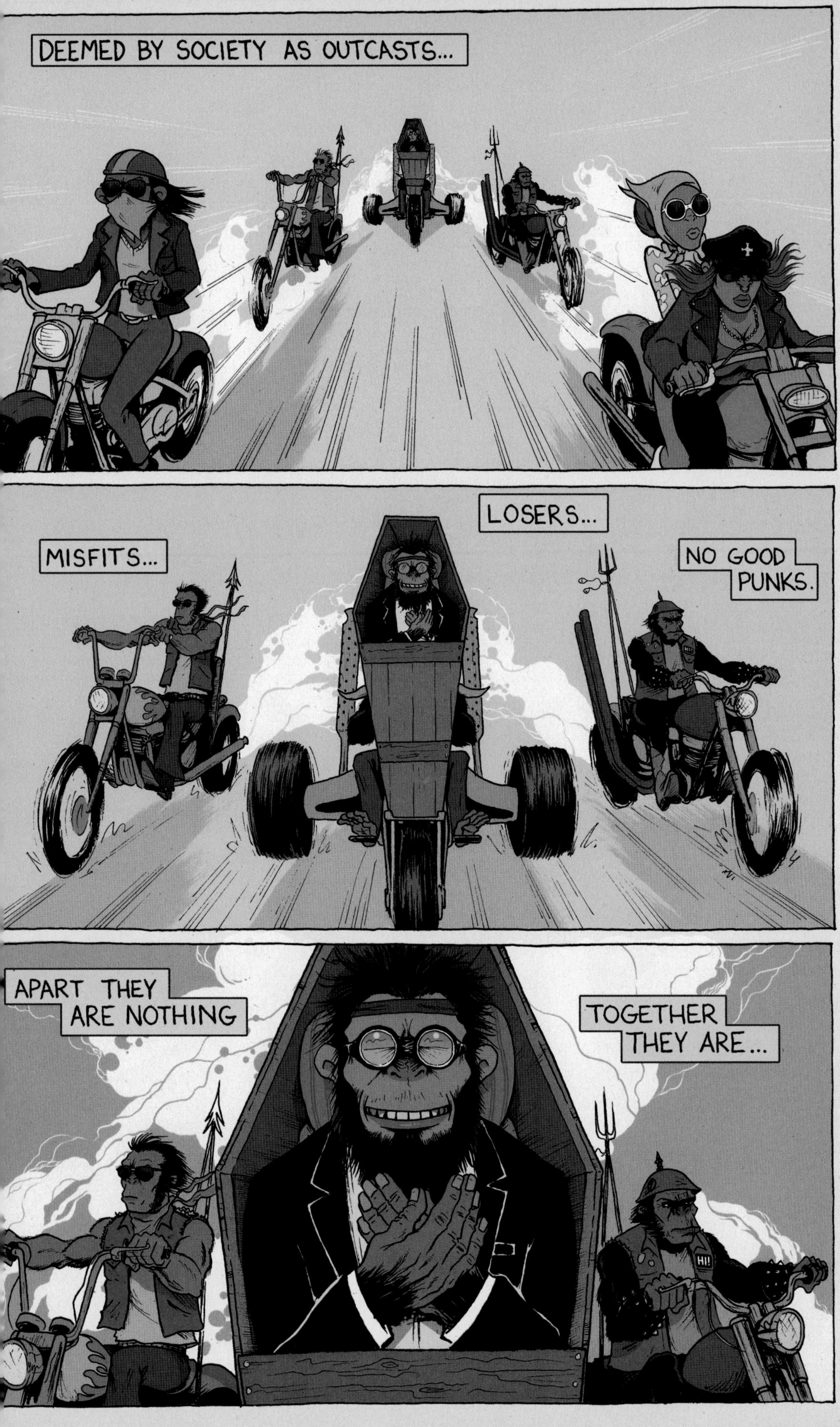
DEEMED BY SOCIETY AS OUTCASTS...
MISFITS...
LOSERS...
NO GOOD PUNKS.
APART THEY ARE NOTHING
TOGETHER THEY ARE...
HI!
HI!

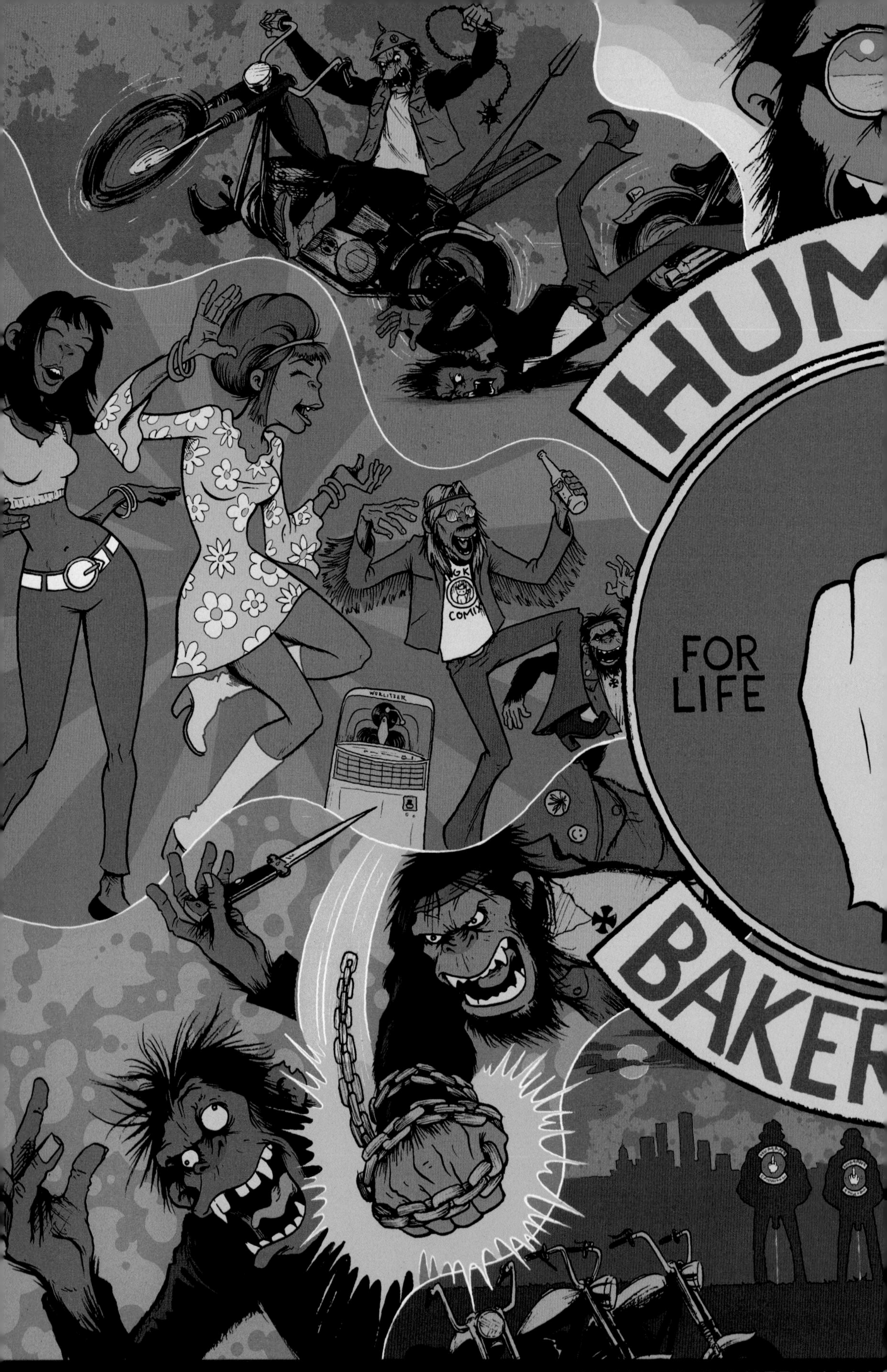
HUM
FOR LIFE
BAKER
WURLITZER
GK COMIX

CREATED BY KEENAN M

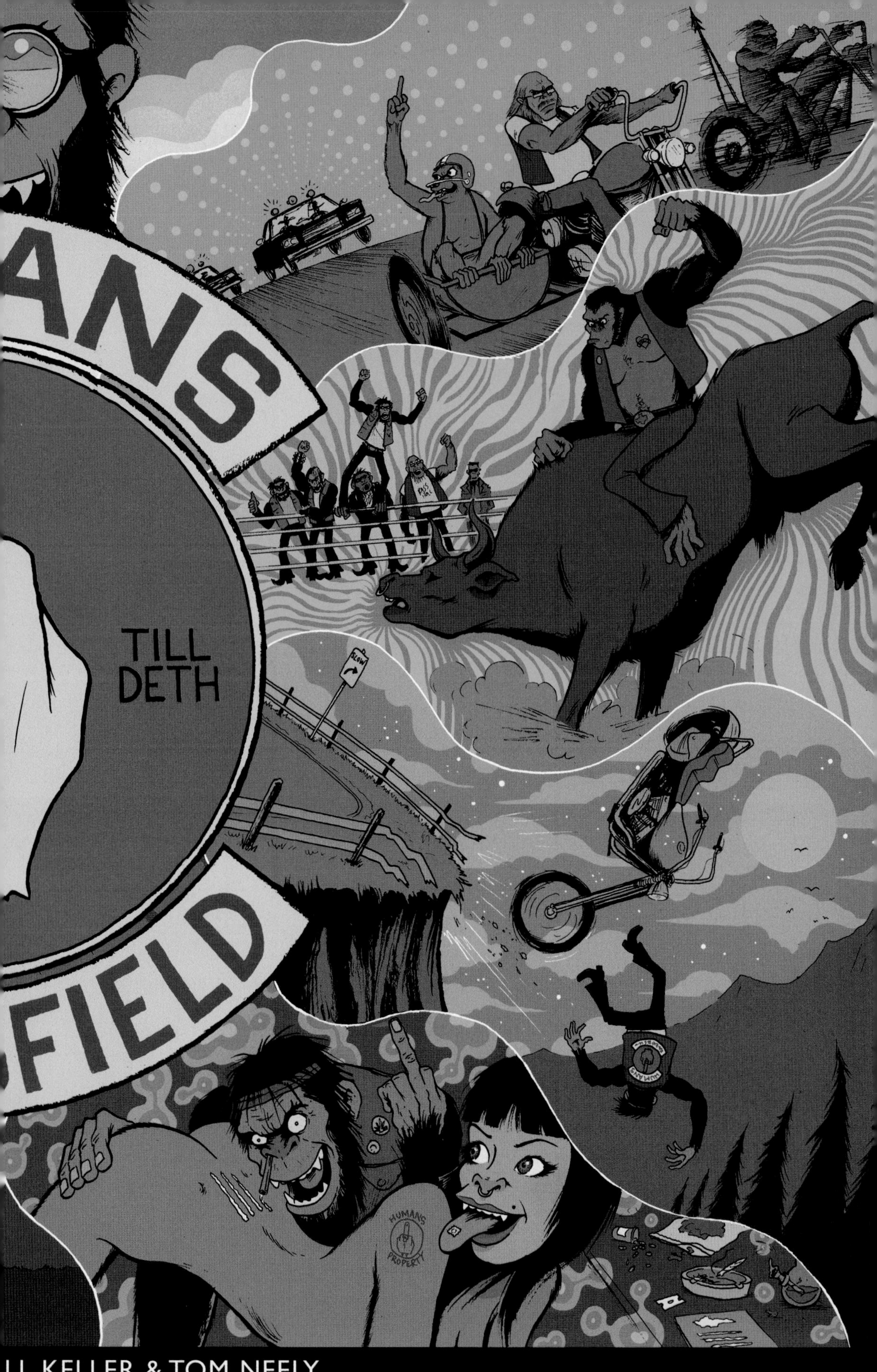
ANS
TILL
DETH
FIELD
SLOW
HUMANS
PROPERTY

LL KELLER & TOM NEELY

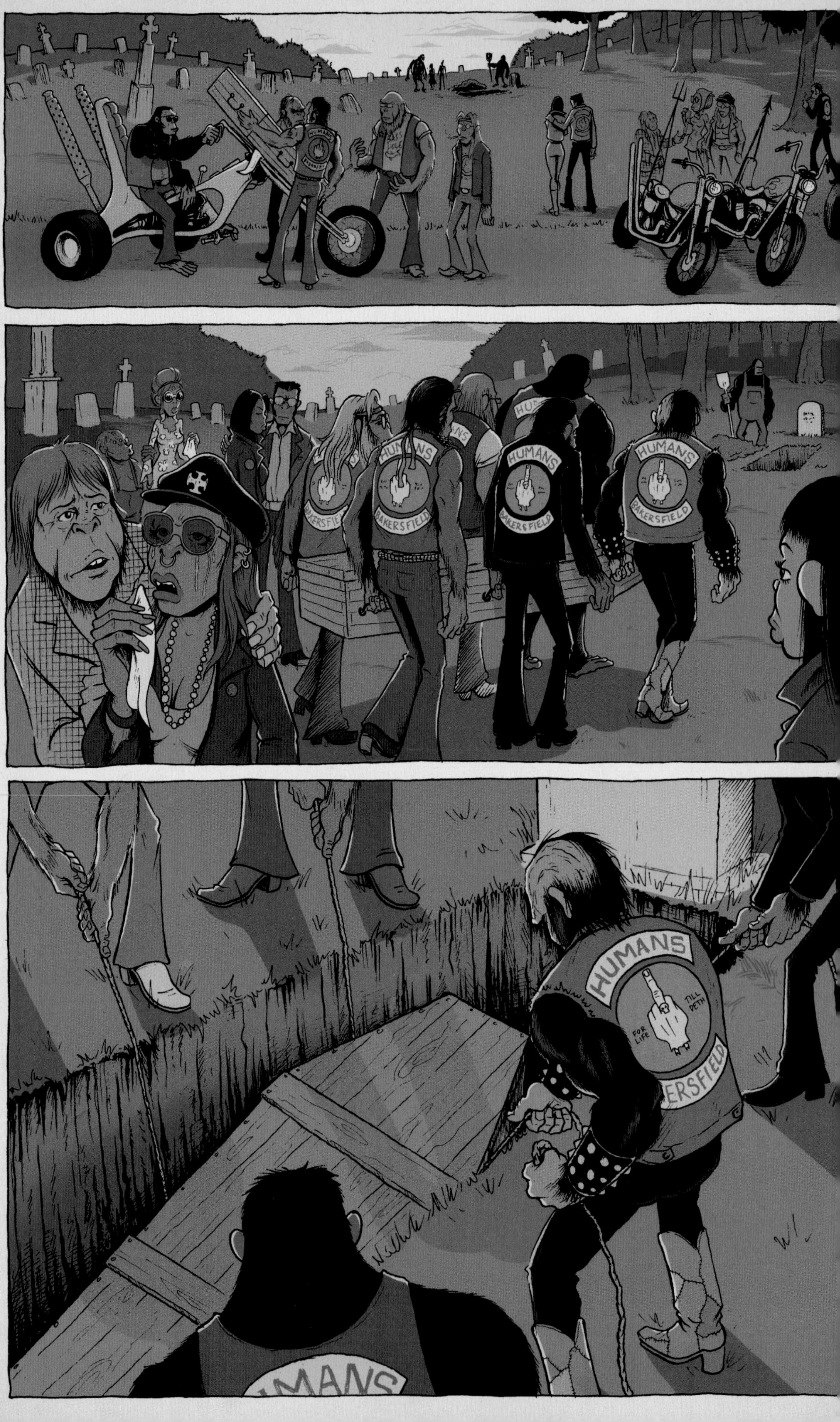
HUMANS
BAKERSFIELD
HUMANS
BAKERSFIELD
HUMANS
BAKERSFIELD
HUMANS
TILL DETH
FOR LIFE

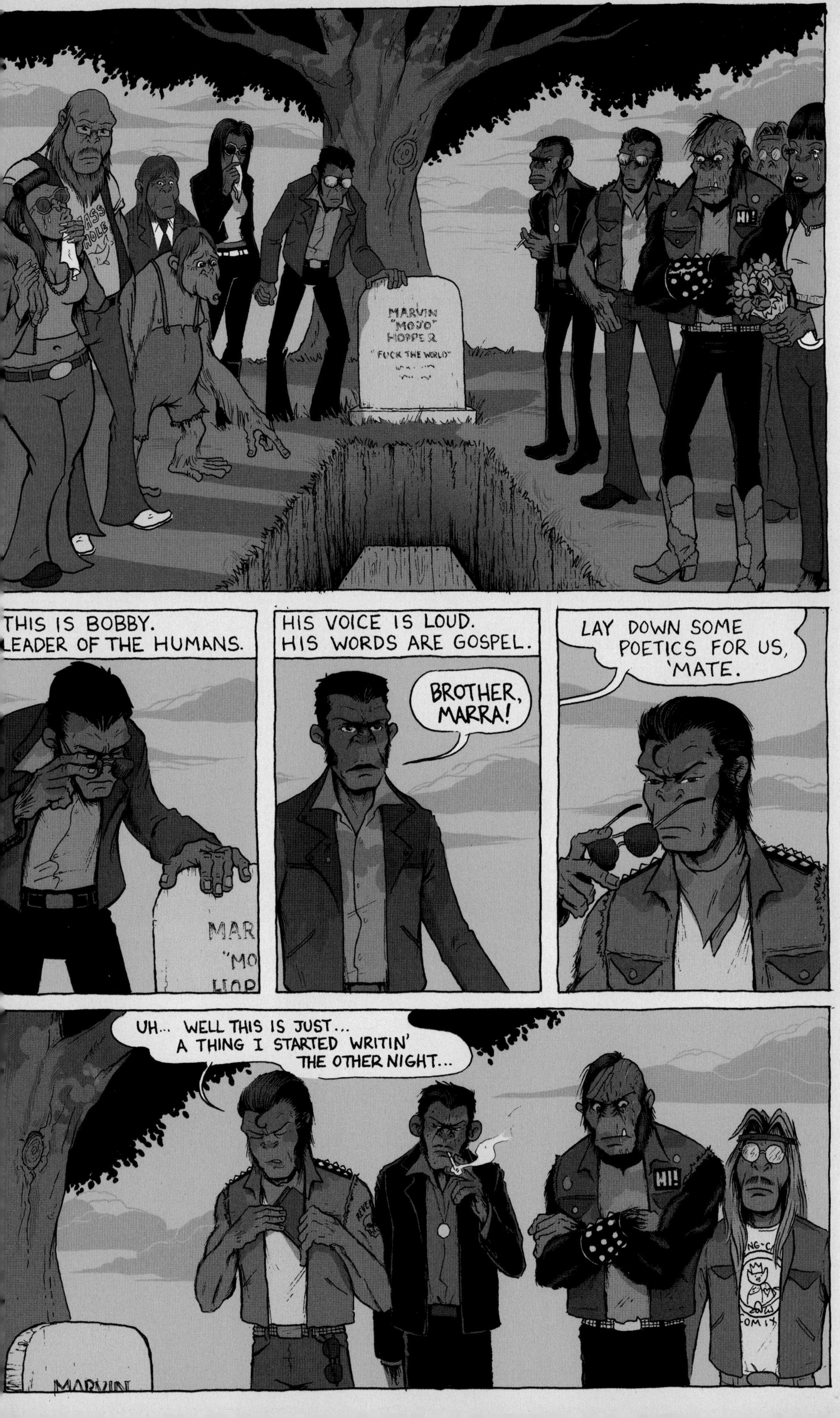
MARVIN "MOJO" HOPPER
"FUCK THE WORLD"
HI!
THIS IS BOBBY. LEADER OF THE HUMANS.
MAR "MO HOP
HIS VOICE IS LOUD. HIS WORDS ARE GOSPEL.
BROTHER, MARRA!
LAY DOWN SOME POETICS FOR US, 'MATE.
UH... WELL THIS IS JUST... A THING I STARTED WRITIN' THE OTHER NIGHT...
HI!
MARVIN

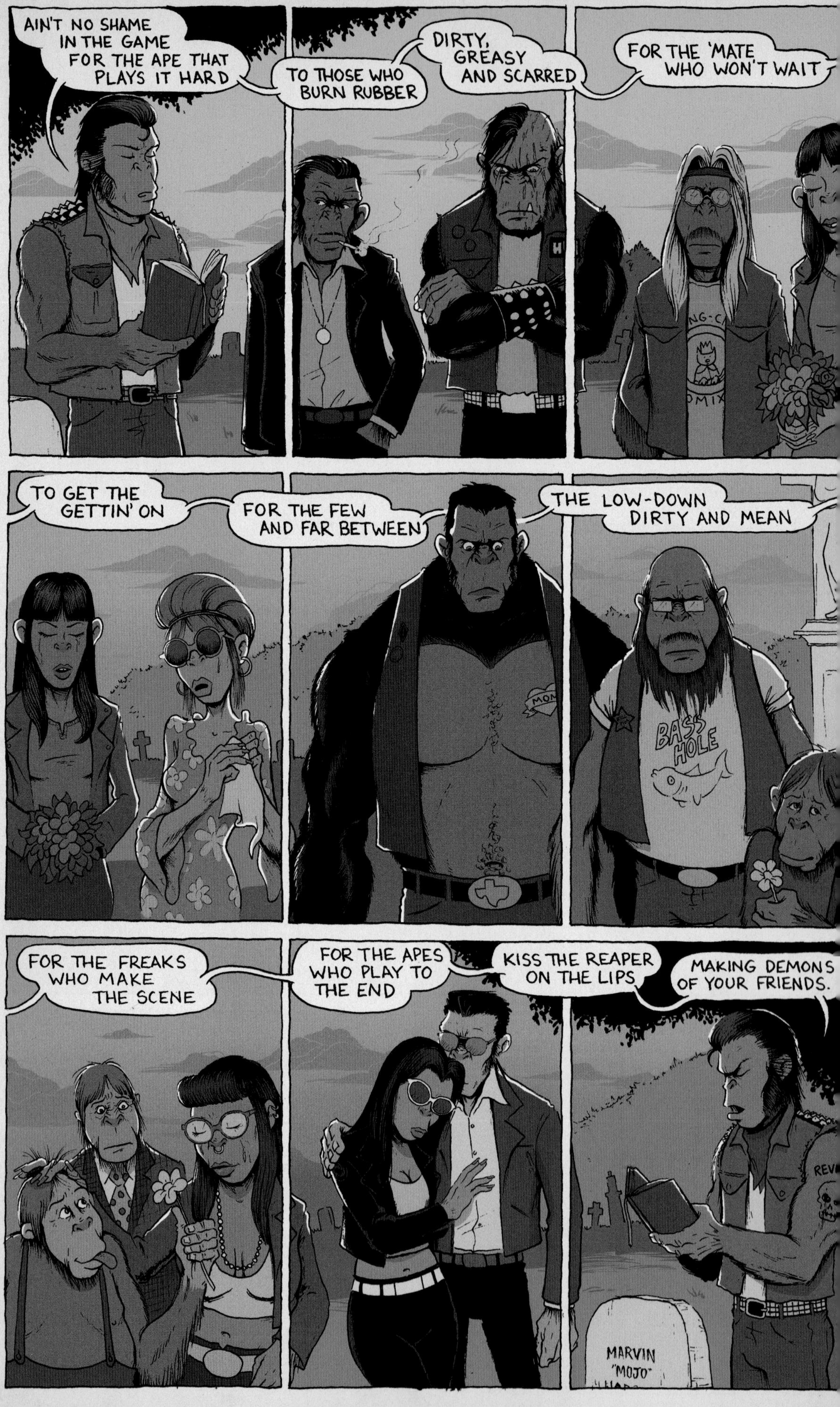
AIN'T NO SHAME IN THE GAME FOR THE APE THAT PLAYS IT HARD
TO THOSE WHO BURN RUBBER
DIRTY, GREASY AND SCARRED
FOR THE 'MATE WHO WON'T WAIT
TO GET THE GETTIN' ON
FOR THE FEW AND FAR BETWEEN
THE LOW-DOWN DIRTY AND MEAN
BASS HOLE
FOR THE FREAKS WHO MAKE THE SCENE
FOR THE APES WHO PLAY TO THE END
KISS THE REAPER ON THE LIPS
MAKING DEMONS OF YOUR FRIENDS.
MARVIN "MOJO"

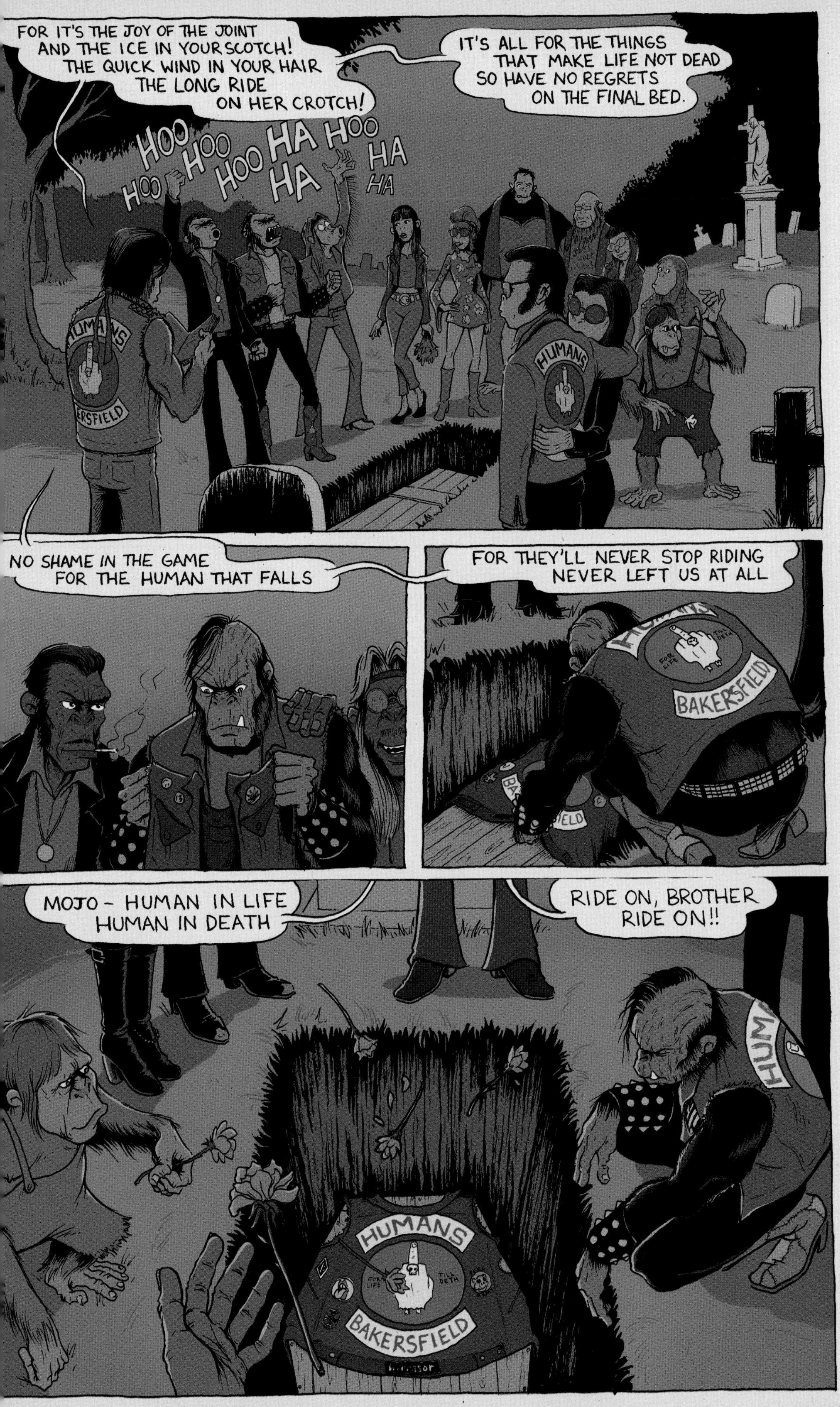
FOR IT'S THE JOY OF THE JOINT AND THE ICE IN YOUR SCOTCH! THE QUICK WIND IN YOUR HAIR THE LONG RIDE ON HER CROTCH!
IT'S ALL FOR THE THINGS THAT MAKE LIFE NOT DEAD SO HAVE NO REGRETS ON THE FINAL BED.
HOO HOO HOO HOO HA HOO HA HA HA
NO SHAME IN THE GAME FOR THE HUMAN THAT FALLS
FOR THEY'LL NEVER STOP RIDING NEVER LEFT US AT ALL
MOJO - HUMAN IN LIFE HUMAN IN DEATH
RIDE ON, BROTHER RIDE ON!!
HUMANS
BAKERSFIELD

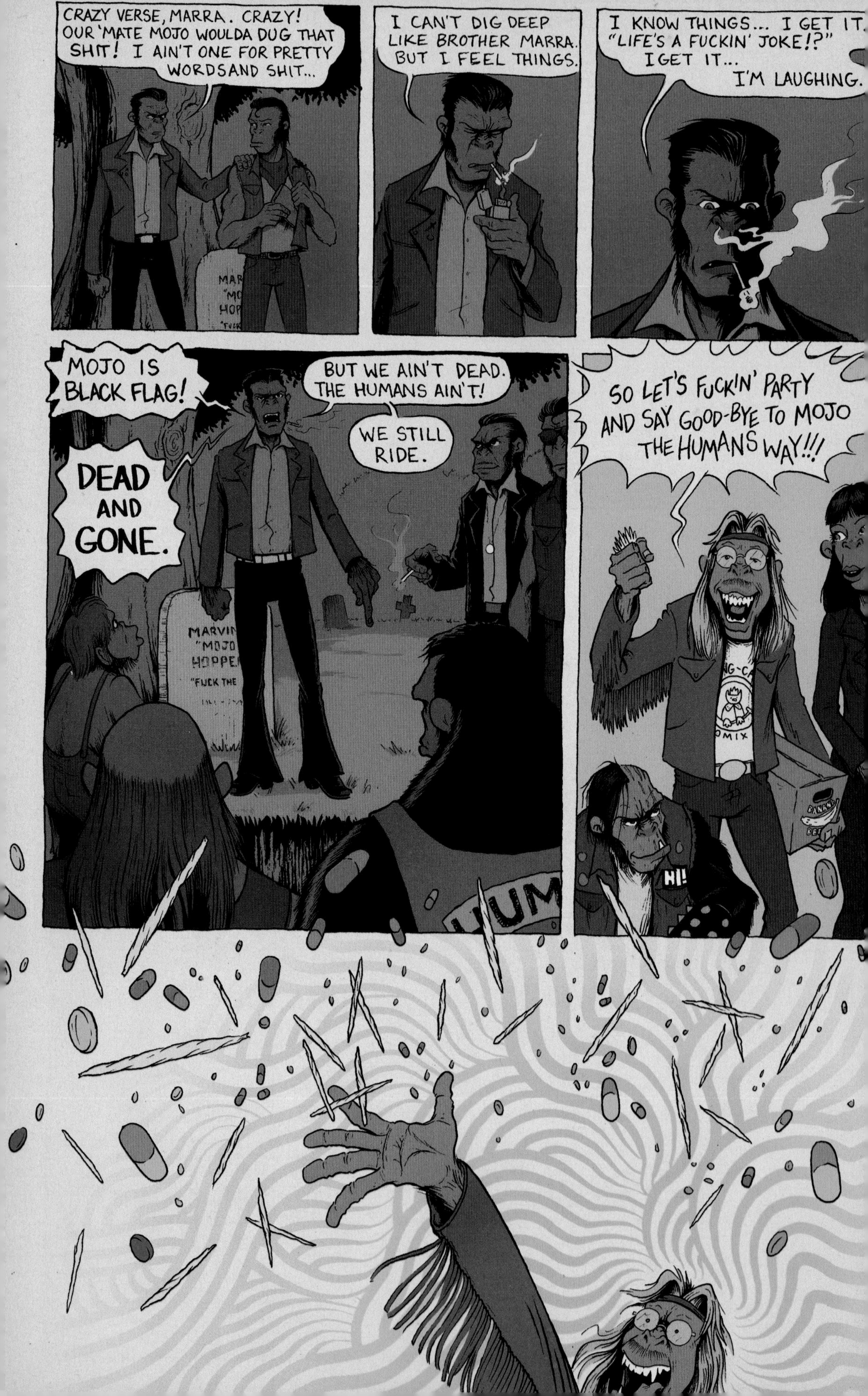
CRAZY VERSE, MARRA. CRAZY! OUR 'MATE MOJO WOULDA DUG THAT SHIT! I AIN'T ONE FOR PRETTY WORDSAND SHIT...
MAR "MO HOP "FUCK
I CAN'T DIG DEEP LIKE BROTHER MARRA. BUT I FEEL THINGS.
I KNOW THINGS... I GET IT. "LIFE'S A FUCKIN' JOKE!?" I GET IT... I'M LAUGHING.
MOJO IS BLACK FLAG!
DEAD AND GONE.
BUT WE AIN'T DEAD. THE HUMANS AIN'T!
WE STILL RIDE.
MARVIN "MOJO" HOPPER "FUCK THE
HUM
SO LET'S FUCKIN' PARTY AND SAY GOOD-BYE TO MOJO THE HUMANS WAY!!!
OMIX
HI!

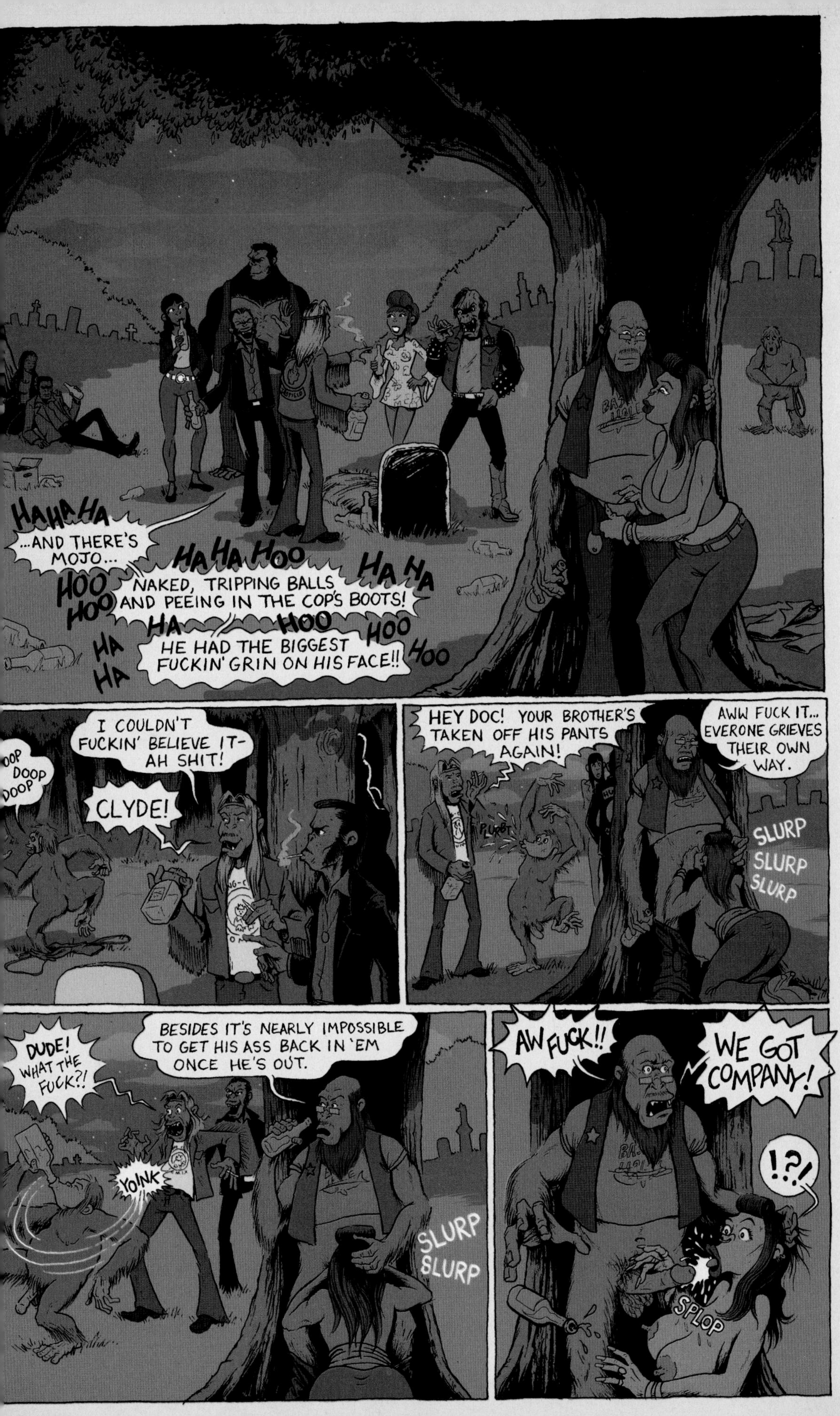

HAHAHA
...AND THERE'S MOJO...
HA HA HOO
HA HA
HOO HOO
NAKED, TRIPPING BALLS AND PEEING IN THE COP'S BOOTS!
HA
HOO
HOO
HA HA
HE HAD THE BIGGEST FUCKIN' GRIN ON HIS FACE!!
HOO
I COULDN'T FUCKIN' BELIEVE IT- AH SHIT!
OOP DOOP DOOP
CLYDE!
HEY DOC! YOUR BROTHER'S TAKEN OFF HIS PANTS AGAIN!
PLURBT
AWW FUCK IT... EVERONE GRIEVES THEIR OWN WAY.
SLURP
SLURP
SLURP
DUDE! WHAT THE FUCK?!
BESIDES IT'S NEARLY IMPOSSIBLE TO GET HIS ASS BACK IN 'EM ONCE HE'S OUT.
YOINK
SLURP
SLURP
AW FUCK!!
WE GOT COMPANY!
!?!
SPLOP

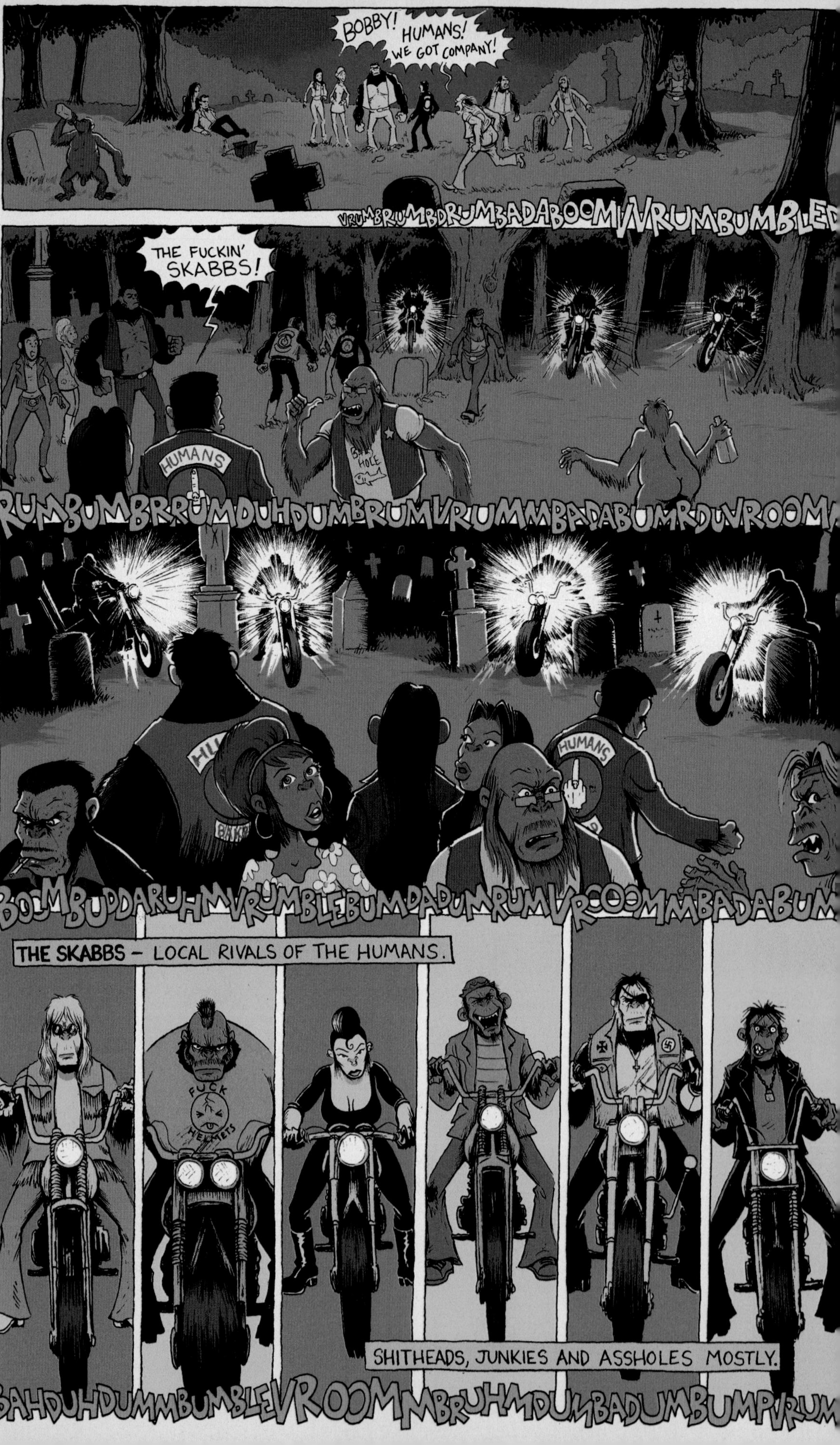
BOBBY! HUMANS! WE GOT COMPANY!
VRUMBRUMBDRUMBADABOOMVVRUMBUMBLED
THE FUCKIN' SKABBS!
HUMANS
BABY HOLE
RUMBUMBRRUMDUHDUMBRUMVRUMMMBADABUMRDUVROOM
HUMANS
BOOMBUDDARUHMVRUMBLEBUMDADUMRUMVROOMMBADABUM
THE SKABBS – LOCAL RIVALS OF THE HUMANS.
FUCK HELMETS
SHITHEADS, JUNKIES AND ASSHOLES MOSTLY.
BAHDUHDUMMBUMBLEVROOMMBRUHMDUMBADUMBUMPVRUM

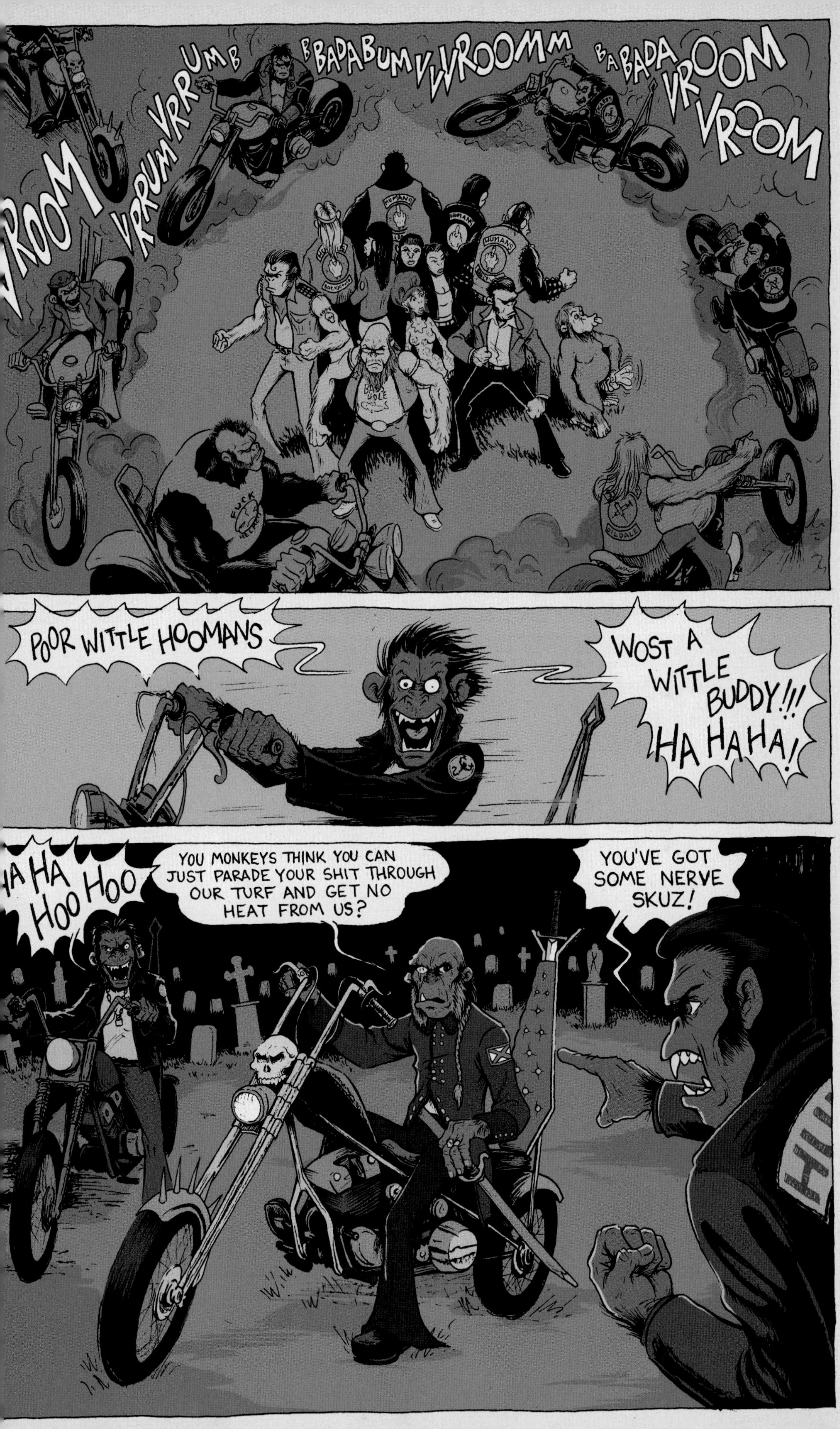

VROOM
VRRUM VRRUMB
BBADABUM VVVROOMM
BABADA VROOM
VROOM
POOR WITTLE HOOMANS
WOST A WITTLE BUDDY!!! HA HAHA!
HA HA HOO HOO
YOU MONKEYS THINK YOU CAN JUST PARADE YOUR SHIT THROUGH OUR TURF AND GET NO HEAT FROM US?
YOU'VE GOT SOME NERVE SKUZ!

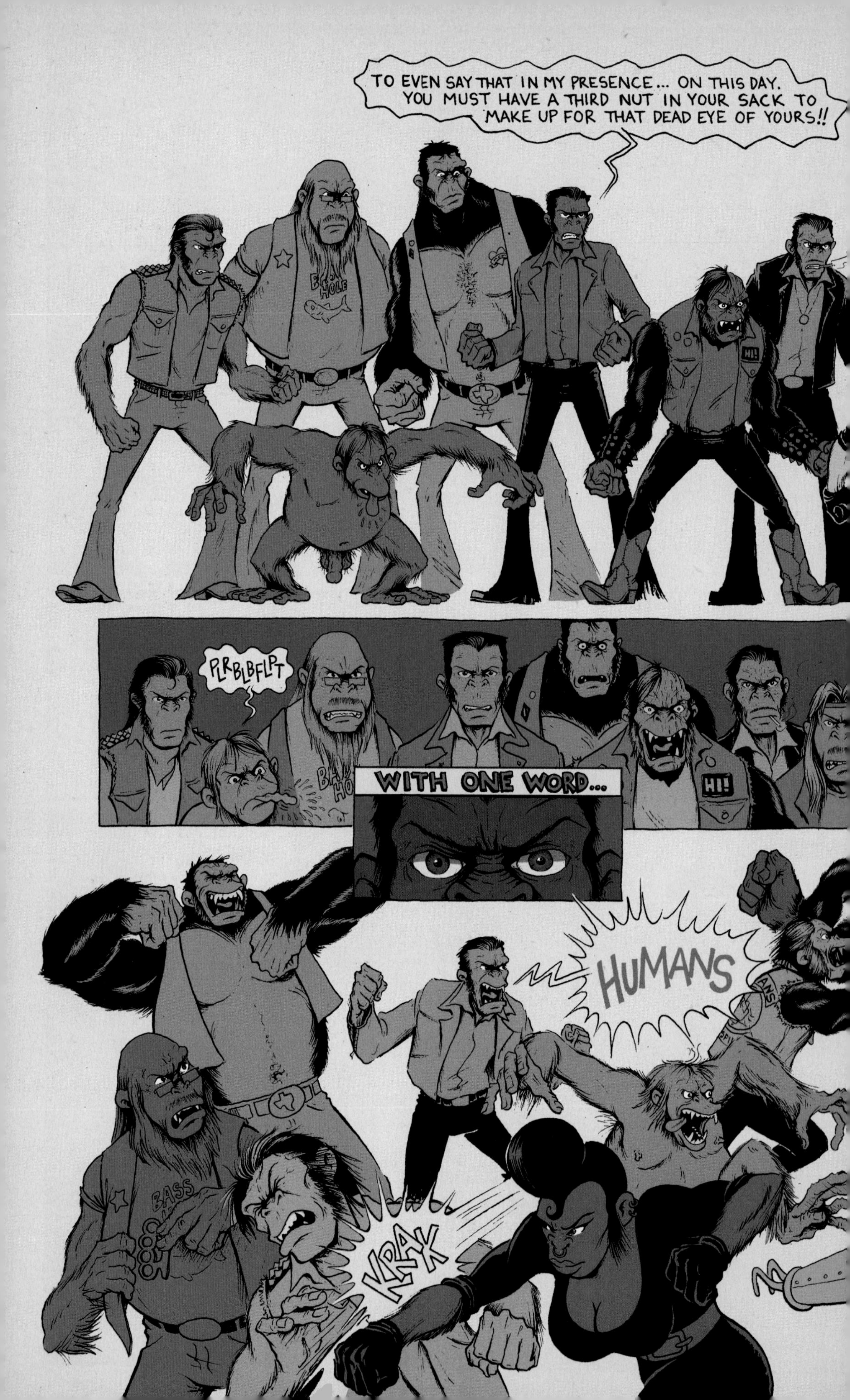
TO EVEN SAY THAT IN MY PRESENCE... ON THIS DAY. YOU MUST HAVE A THIRD NUT IN YOUR SACK TO MAKE UP FOR THAT DEAD EYE OF YOURS!!
PLRBLBFLPT
WITH ONE WORD...
HUMANS
KRAK

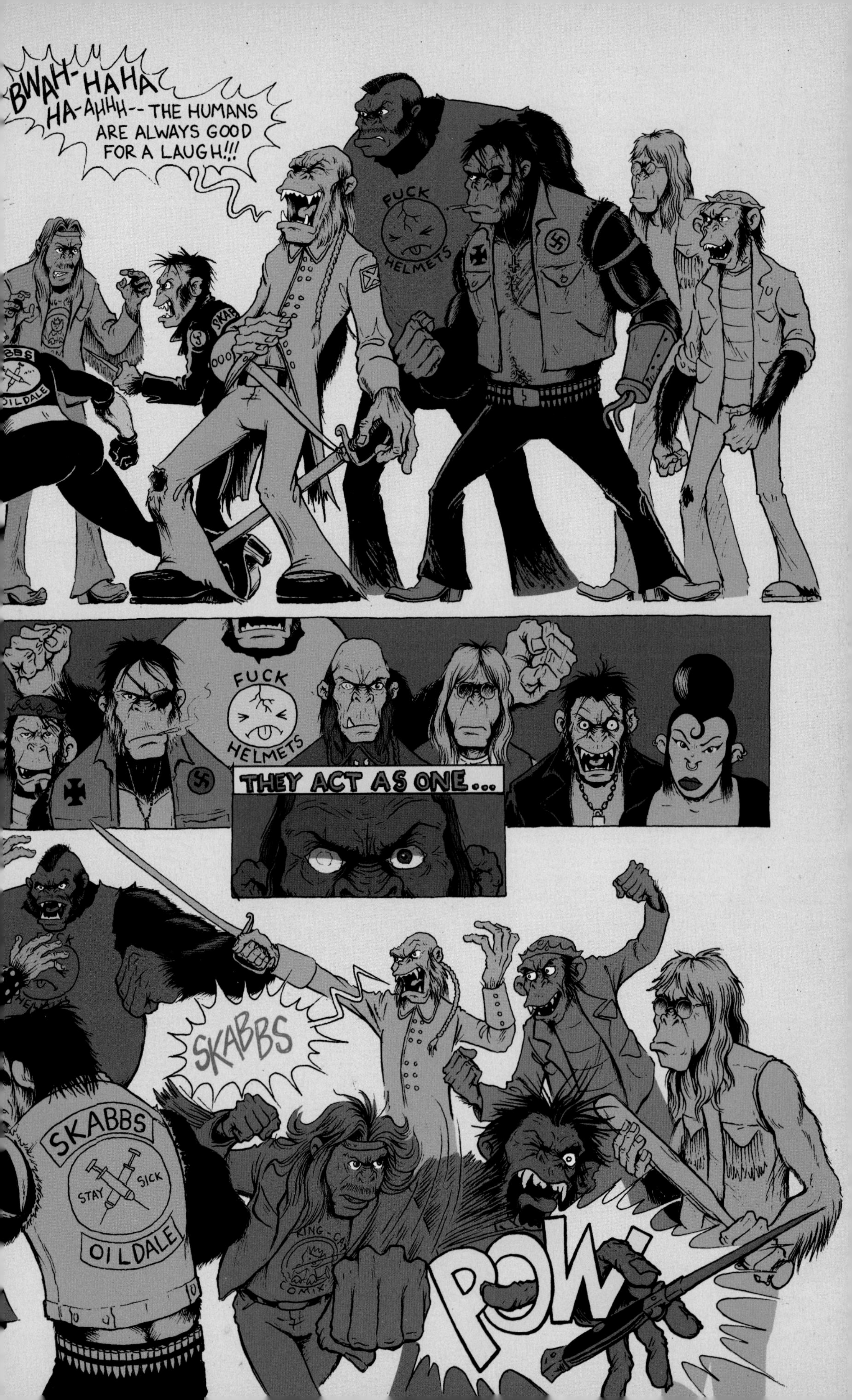
BWAH-HAHA HA-AHHH-- THE HUMANS ARE ALWAYS GOOD FOR A LAUGH!!!
FUCK HELMETS
SKABBS
OILDALE
FUCK HELMETS
THEY ACT AS ONE...
SKABBS
SKABBS
STAY SICK
OILDALE
KING-CAT COMIX
POW!

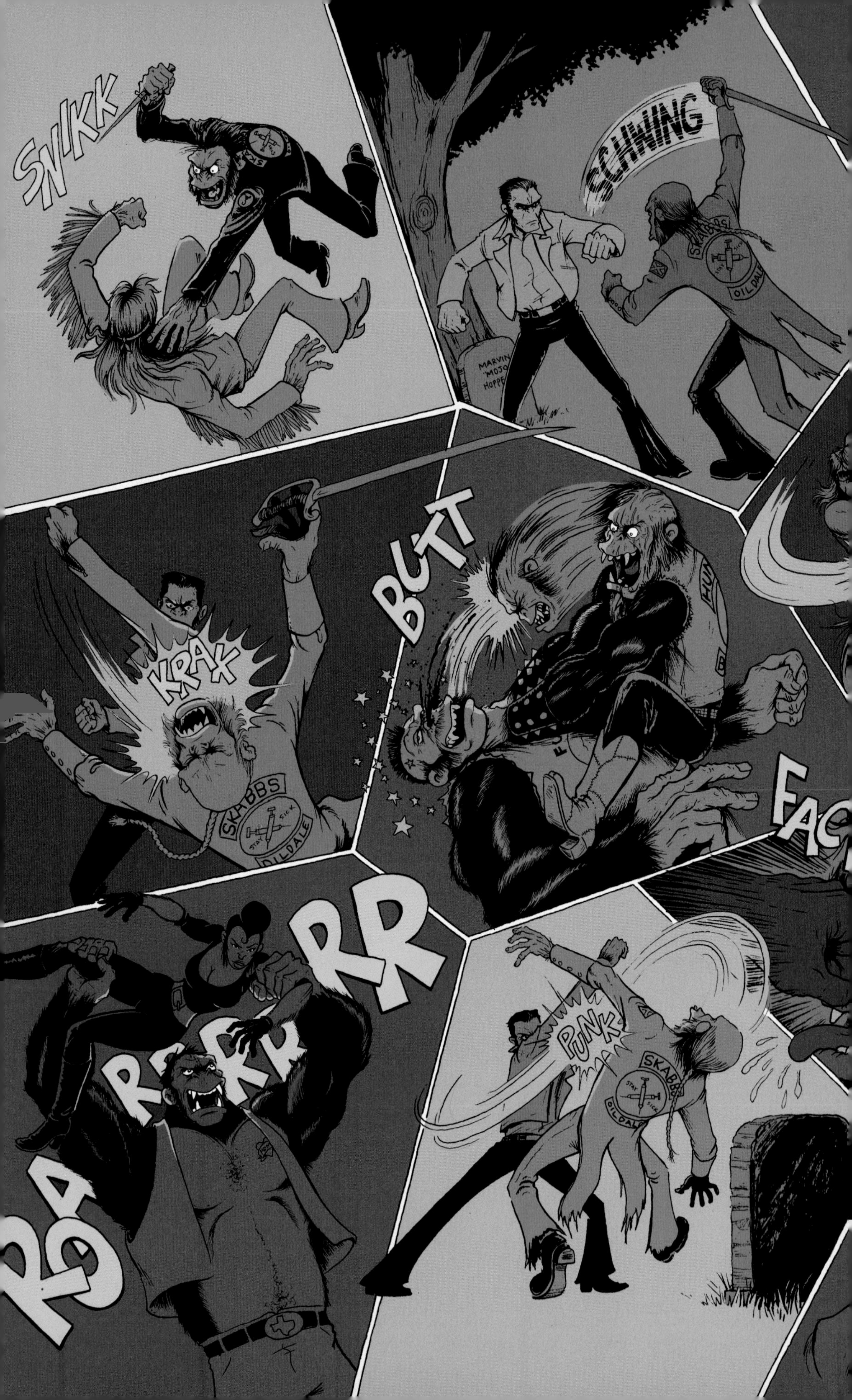
SNIKK
SCHWING
MARVIN "MOJO" HOPPE
SKABBS
OILDALE
KRAK
SKABBS
STAY SICK
OILDALE
BUTT
PUNK
SKABBS
OILDALE

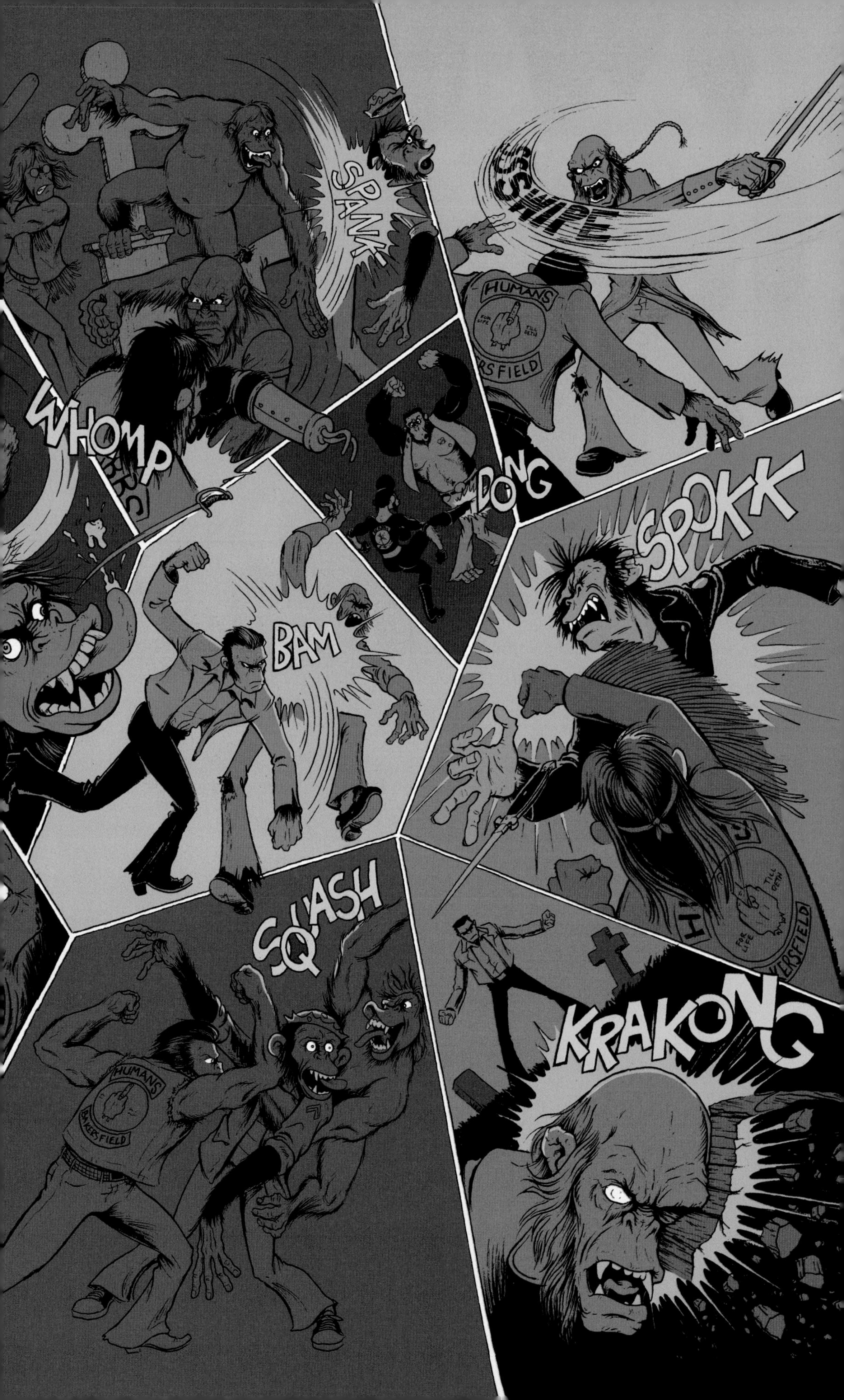
SPANK
SWIPE
HUMANS
FOR LIFE
TILL DETH
WHOMP
DONG
SPOKK
BAM
SQUASH
KRAKONG
HUMANS
BAKERSFIELD

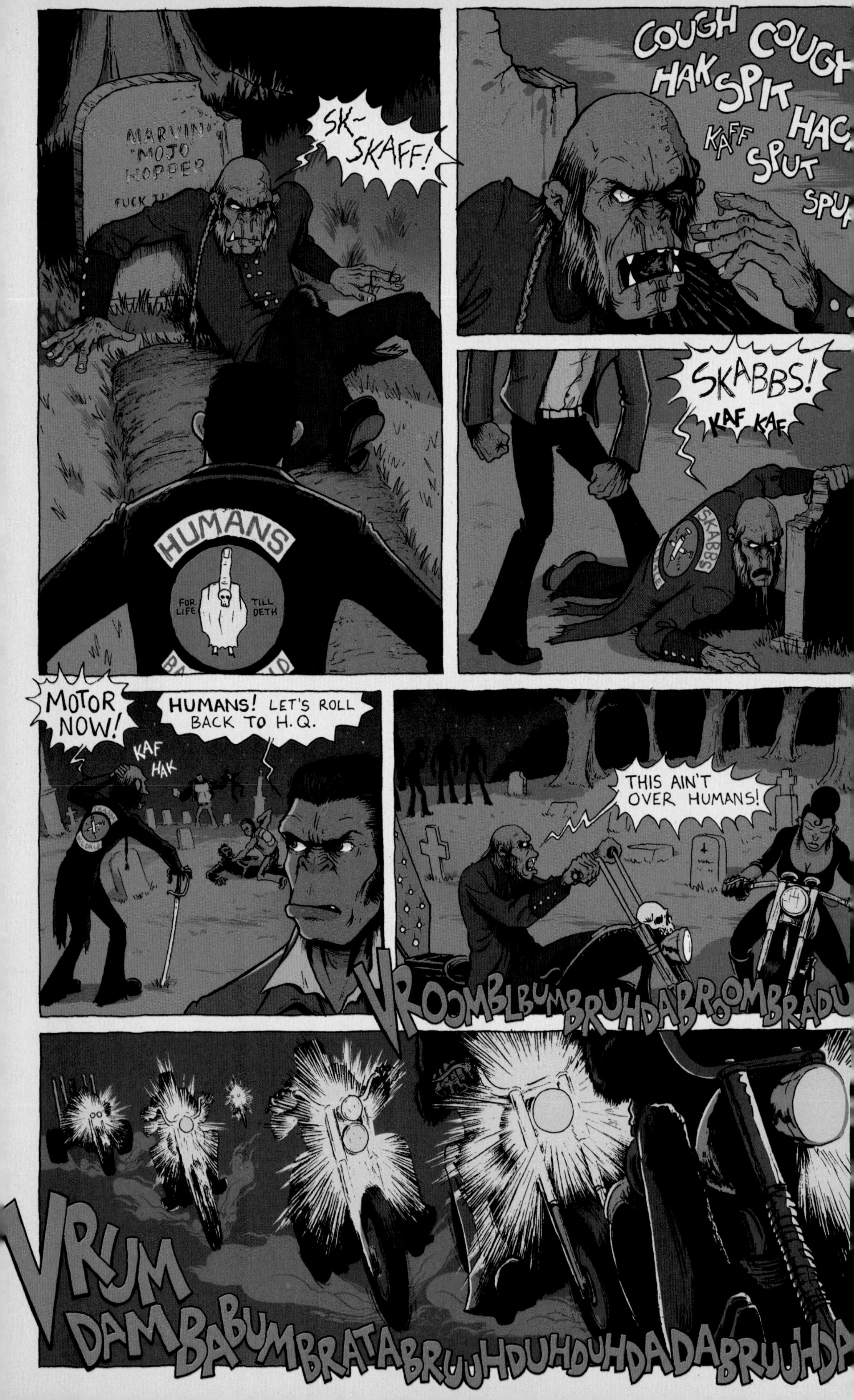

MARVIN "MOJO" HOPPER
SK- SKAFF!
HUMANS
FOR LIFE
TILL DETH
COUGH COUGH
HAK SPIT HAC
KAFF SPUT
SPU
SKABBS! KAF KAF
SKABBS
MOTOR NOW!
KAF HAK
HUMANS! LET'S ROLL BACK TO H.Q.
THIS AIN'T OVER HUMANS!
VROOMBLBUMBRUHDABROOMBRADU
VRUM DAMBABUMBRATABRUUHDUHDUHDADABRUUHDA

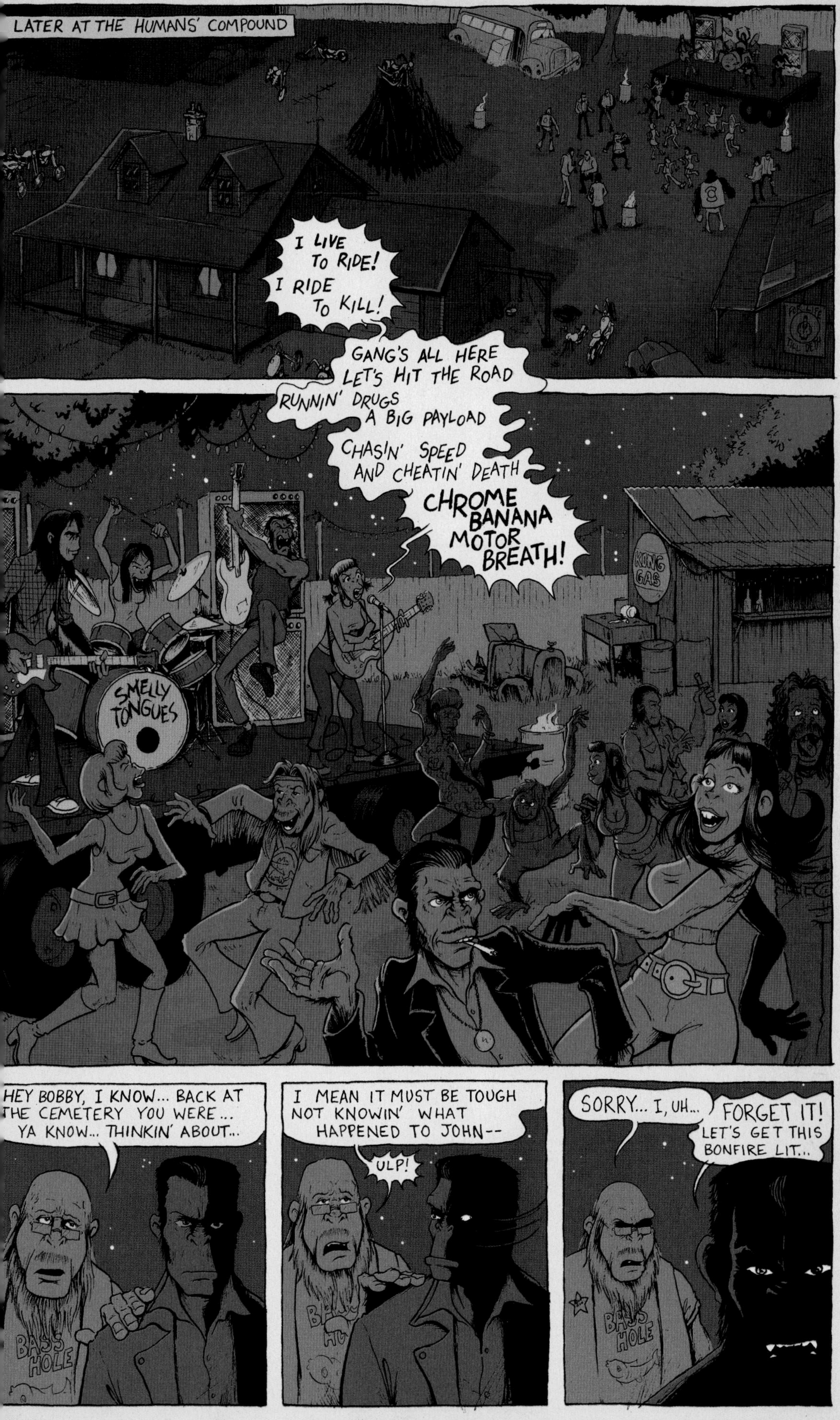
LATER AT THE HUMANS' COMPOUND
I LIVE TO RIDE! I RIDE TO KILL!
GANG'S ALL HERE LET'S HIT THE ROAD RUNNIN' DRUGS A BIG PAYLOAD CHASIN' SPEED AND CHEATIN' DEATH
CHROME BANANA MOTOR BREATH!
KONG GAS
SMELLY TONGUES
HEY BOBBY, I KNOW... BACK AT THE CEMETERY YOU WERE... YA KNOW... THINKIN' ABOUT...
BASS HOLE
I MEAN IT MUST BE TOUGH NOT KNOWIN' WHAT HAPPENED TO JOHN--
ULP!
SORRY... I, UH...
FORGET IT! LET'S GET THIS BONFIRE LIT...
BASS HOLE

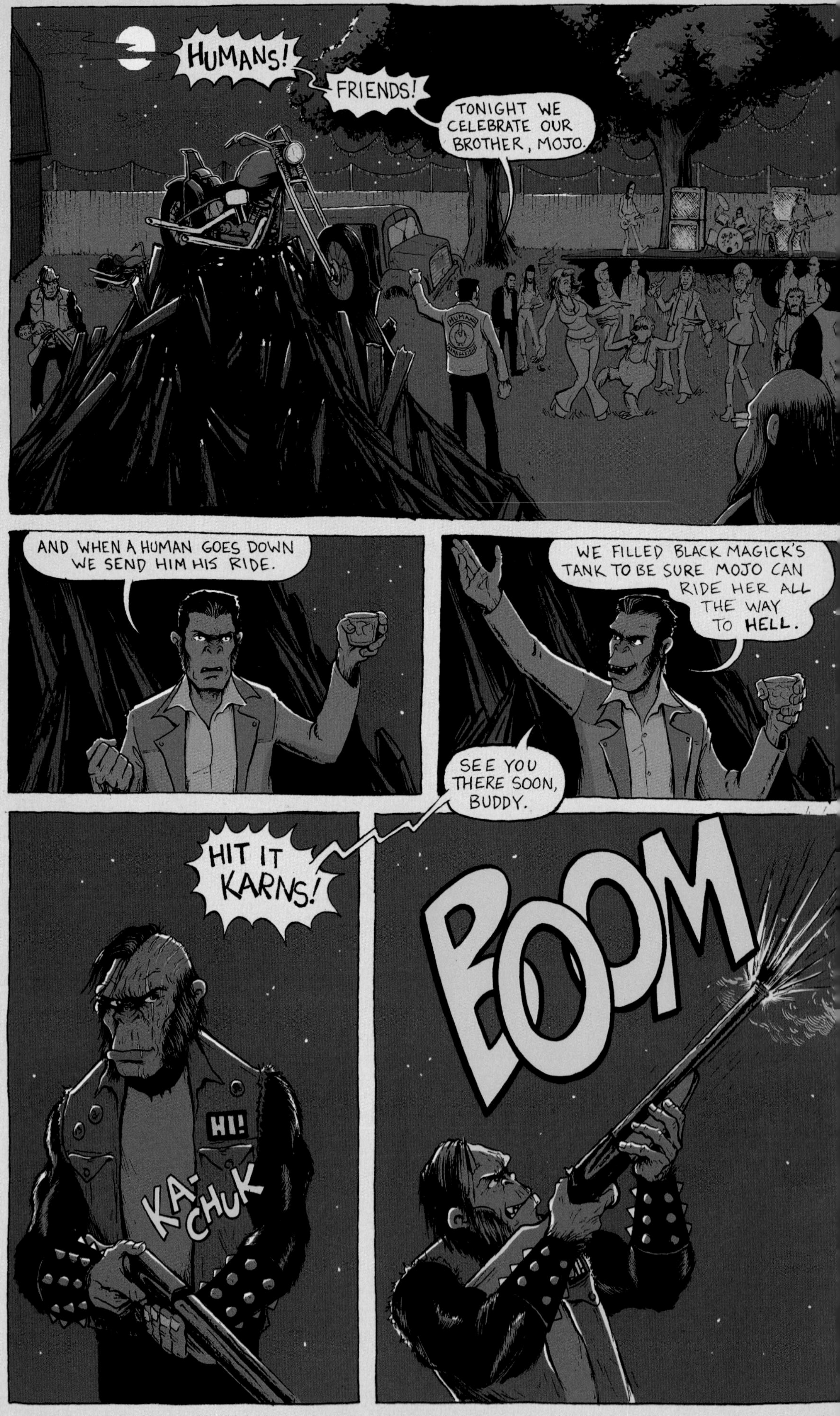
HUMANS!
FRIENDS!
TONIGHT WE CELEBRATE OUR BROTHER, MOJO.
AND WHEN A HUMAN GOES DOWN WE SEND HIM HIS RIDE.
WE FILLED BLACK MAGICK'S TANK TO BE SURE MOJO CAN RIDE HER ALL THE WAY TO HELL.
SEE YOU THERE SOON, BUDDY.
HIT IT KARNS!
HI!
KA-CHUK
BOOM

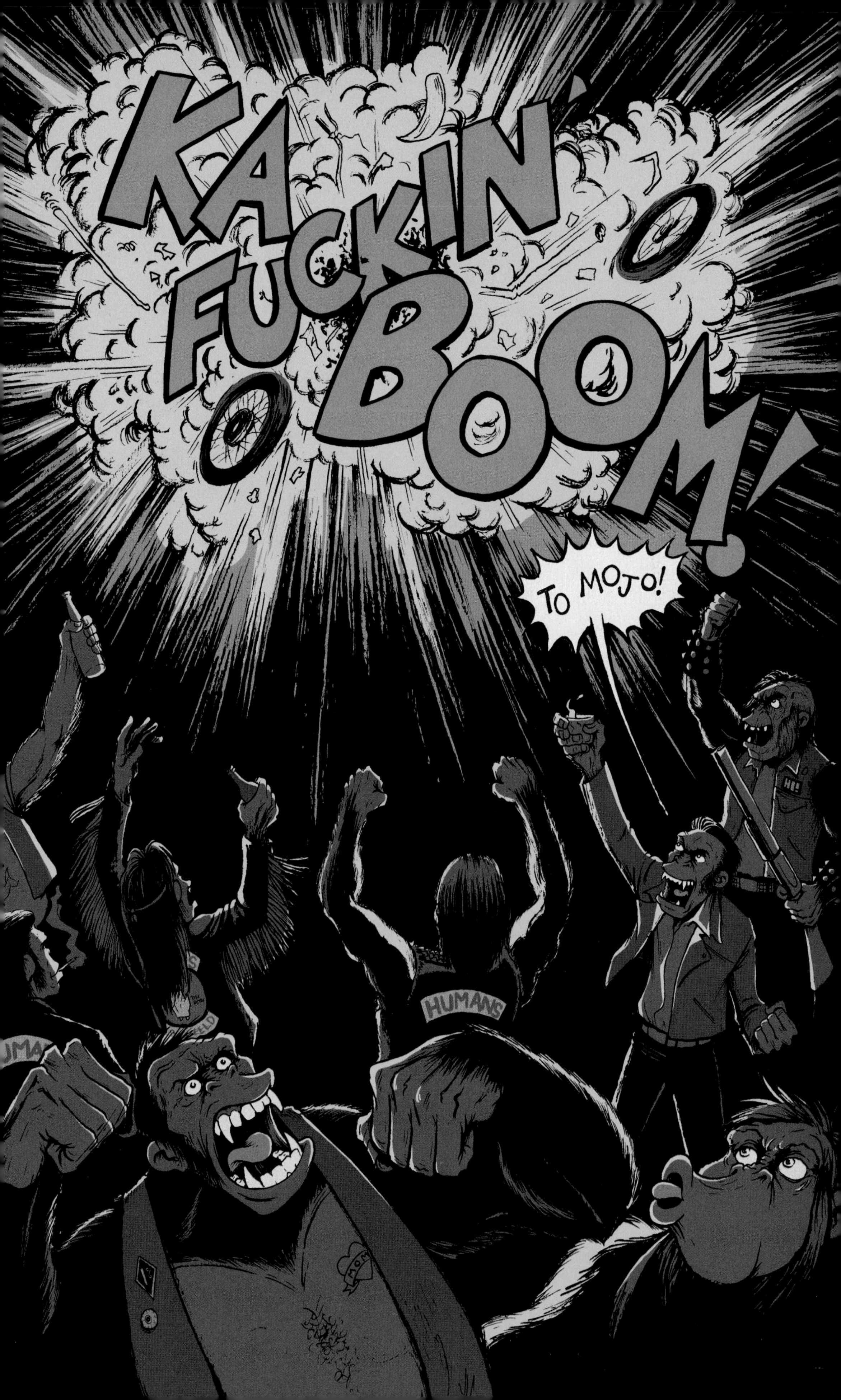
KA FUCKIN' BOOM!
TO MOJO!
HUMANS
MOM

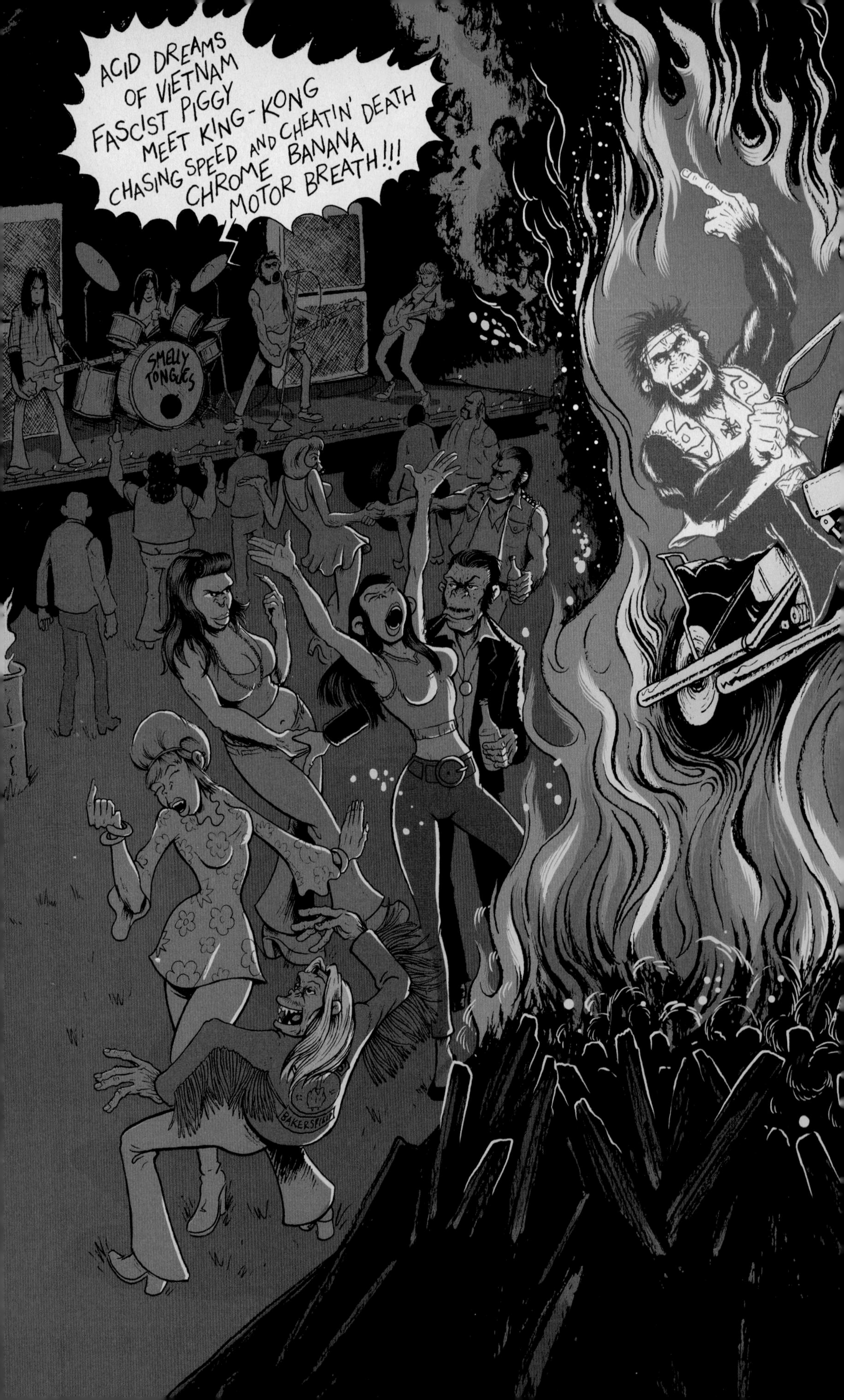
ACID DREAMS
OF VIETNAM
FASCIST PIGGY
MEET KING-KONG
CHASING SPEED AND CHEATIN' DEATH
CHROME BANANA
MOTOR BREATH!!!
SMELLY TONGUES
BAKERSFIELD

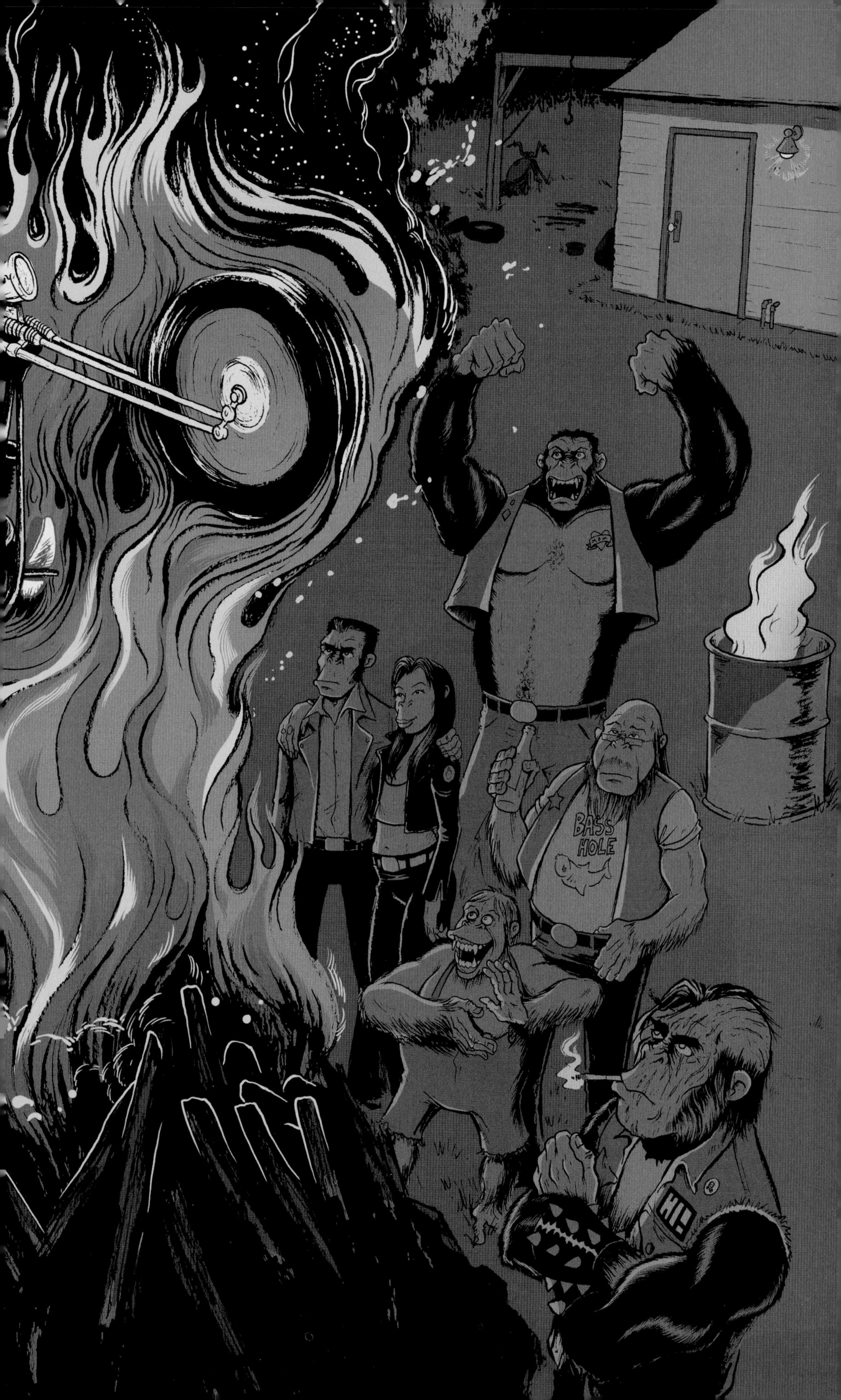
BASS HOLE

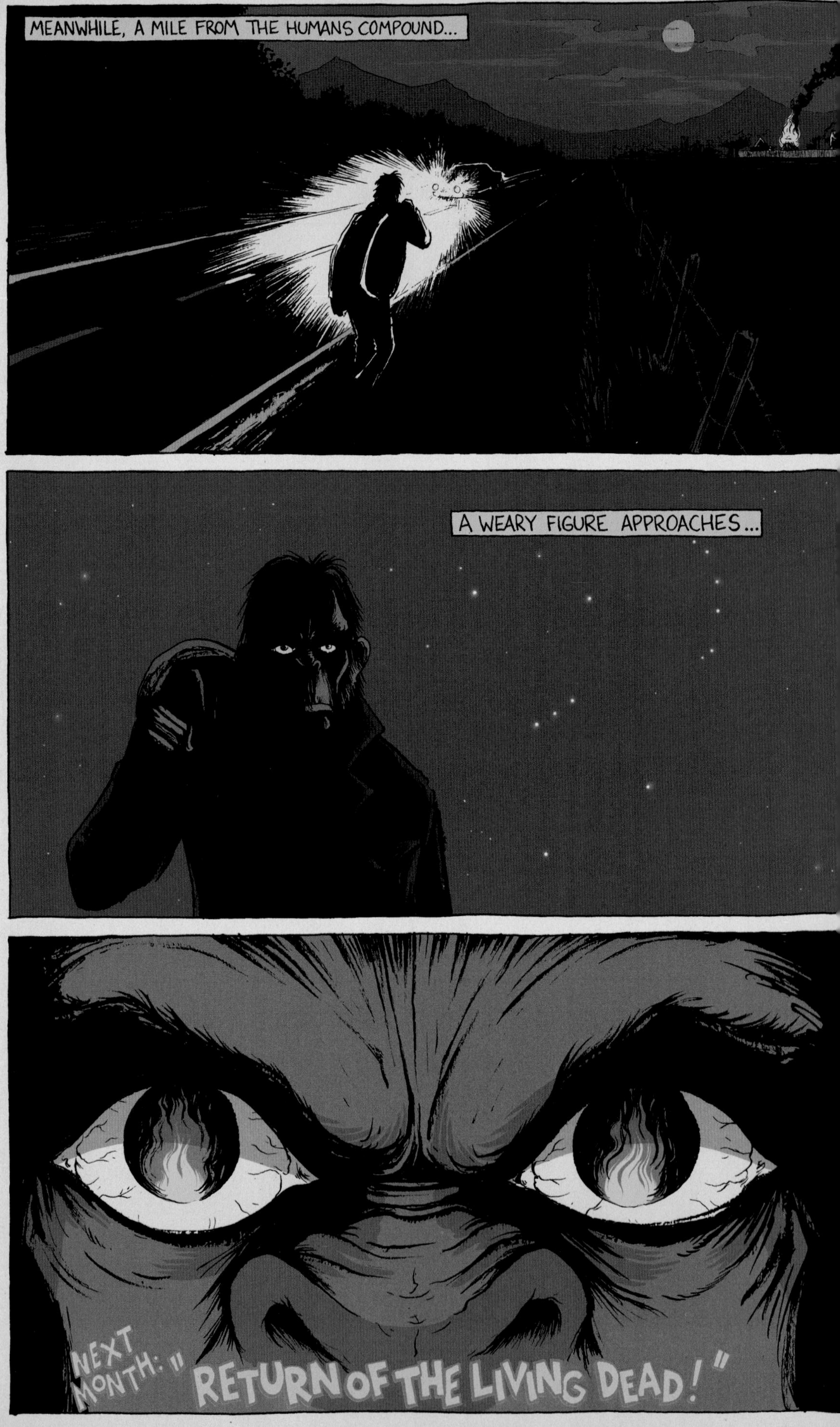
MEANWHILE, A MILE FROM THE HUMANS COMPOUND...
A WEARY FIGURE APPROACHES...
NEXT MONTH: "RETURN OF THE LIVING DEAD!"

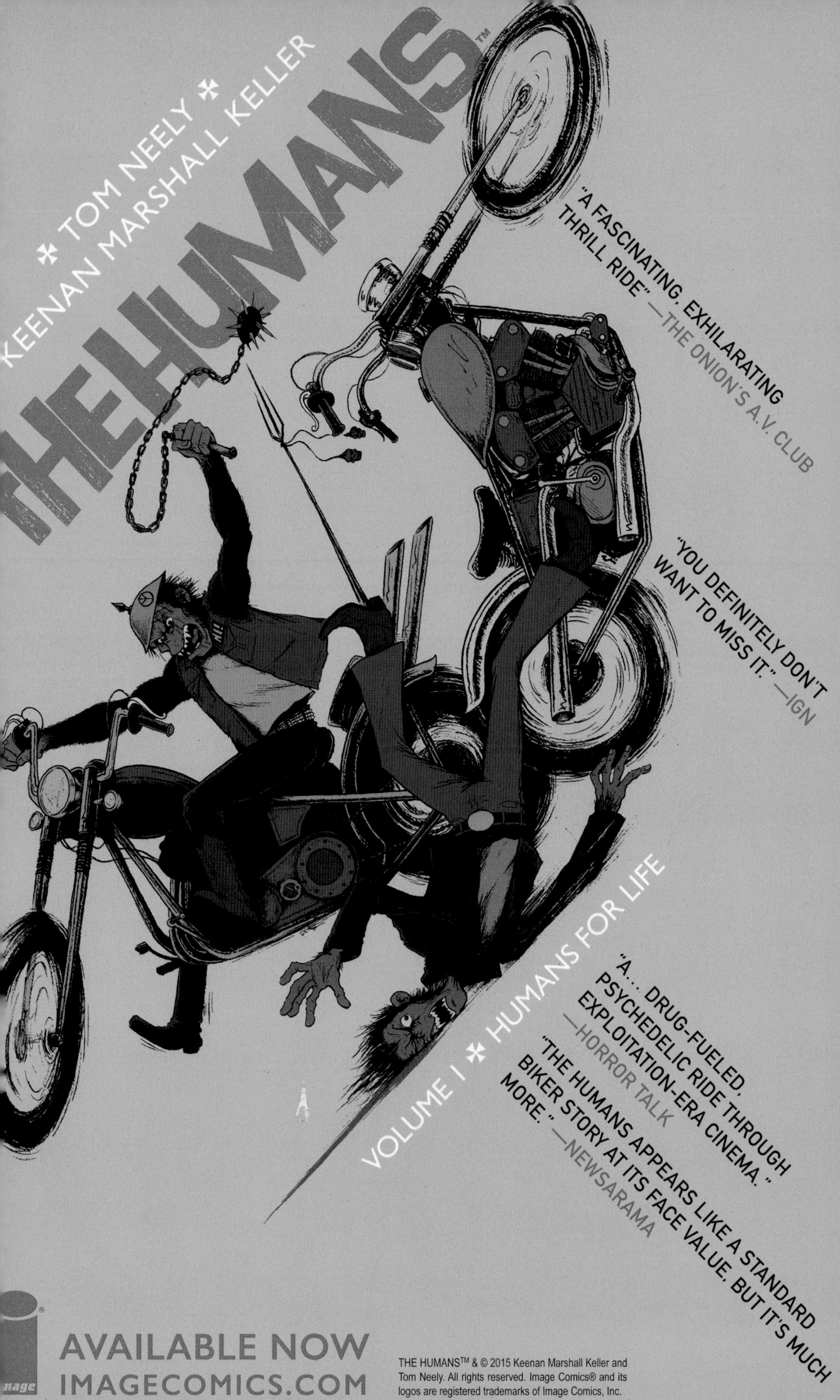

* TOM NEELY *
KEENAN MARSHALL KELLER
THE HUMANS™
"A FASCINATING, EXHILARATING THRILL RIDE" —THE ONION'S A.V. CLUB
"YOU DEFINITELY DON'T WANT TO MISS IT." —IGN
VOLUME 1 * HUMANS FOR LIFE
"A... DRUG-FUELED, PSYCHEDELIC RIDE THROUGH EXPLOITATION-ERA CINEMA." —HORROR TALK
"THE HUMANS APPEARS LIKE A STANDARD BIKER STORY AT ITS FACE VALUE, BUT IT'S MUCH MORE." —NEWSARAMA

APESHIT

THE HUMANS MOTORCYCLE CLUB OFFICIAL NEWSLETTER

NOV. 1970   BURN AFTER READING!   F.O.A.D.

KARNS' KORNER

Well, hello all you fleshy hairless pukes... This is Karns here. The tuffest, weirdest, gnarliest monkeyfucker in the HUMANS! And it my fuckin job to talk to you "Skins" about all the HUMANS happenings. I'm also being forced to answer any questions you nerds might come u with... I gotta do it, but I don't gotta like it! I don't know why they picke me... Can't read or write a lick... 'Cept some curse words... They could got Marra, but I bet they was afraid he'd get all poetic and star rhyming and shit... Can't hardly understand what he's going-on abou half the time anyhow... Poetry is for the guy who's not good with a knife. and I love me some pigstickers.

So, what the fuck you think, eh?? The comic's pretty fucking boss, right RIGHT???!!!! Poor Mojo... never got to ride in the funny papers wit. us... You'll never get to see how bad-ass that fucker was. (unless you're one of the luck few whom got the mysterious and hard t find issue #0). But The HUMANS don't have much time for mournin cause a killer party's gonna erupt when the "living dead" return from hell called Vietnam, 'mate. I guess you'll just have to grab a copy nex month to see what the fuck I'm talkin' bout...

So, get off your fleshy butts and write me a god-damned letter, or som deep symbolic breakdown of The HUMANS where you talk about th social and economic paradigms at play and the overall historica commentary of the 70s as it pertains to today and blah bah blah.... O you can tell me how kick ass Tom Neely's ape fights are or how bad th shit writing is...I don't care... Like I said. I'm half illiterate... and th other half just don't give a fuck...

- KARN

P.S. For all you hot skin gals out there... I'm always looking for a ne mama... I burn through em' REAL quick... So hit me up. Send me picture... But no APES! I don't do hair, ladies... I like em smooth.

Write to Karns or any of the Humans: P.O. Box 39674, Los Angeles, CA 90039, or humansforlife@gmail.com

MARRA'S NOTEBOOK

A couple of dudes have been riding with us late A writer named Keller and an artist named Ne They say they wanna chronicle our motorcycle as a comic book. We think that's pretty kille Here's a couple of early sketches of us Huma by chief art monkey, Tom Neely.

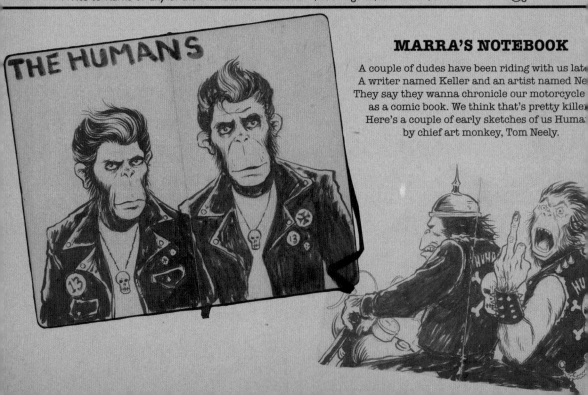

FROM THE ART MONKEY HAUS!

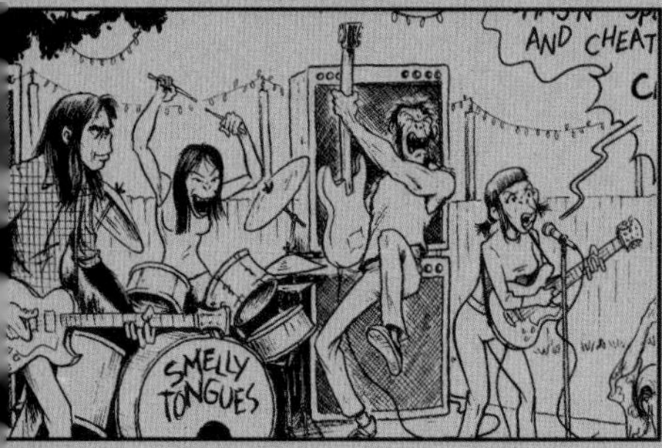
AND CHEAT
SMELLY TONGUES

The HUMANS SOUNDTRACK VOLUME: 1

Hello Kiddies! So this lil' section is where we will be offering you a free downloadable track with every issue. The idea is that by the end of the series, we'll have put out a soundtrack to accompany our book. Each issue will have with it a new song or two to download from our soundcloud site. So, now that you're caught up to speed; the first couple of songs available come from the limited edition HUMANS Soundtrack Vol 1, 7" vinyl we released this summer featuring two Los Angeles bands!

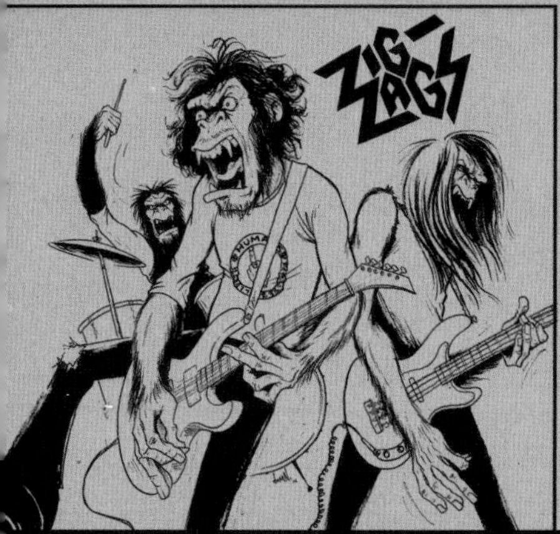
ZIG-ZAGS

Zig-Zags "Let's Die (The HUMANS March)!" Written as the anthem for the gang, this track is heavy, driving, sweaty and tuff. It screams of gang mayhem and is a killer kickstart to the HUMANS soundtrack!

Smelly Tongues "Live To Ride" is like a psychedelic headtrip through a desert on acid dancing around a bonfire, smokin' dope and worshipping Satan on a motorcycle. Sounds like a good time to me.

You can **download** this and all future tracks **FOR FREE** at : **https://soundcloud.com/the-humans-soundtrack**

Check out **Zig-Zags** and buy their other shit. They fuckin' rule. You will love them! **https://zigzags.bandcamp.com/**
Get their full length LP on In The Red Records

Get the **Smelly Tongues** full length LPs on Urinal Cake Records

PIN-UP ARTIST PROFILE!

O! Marra here, to spill a few words about another brother ho goes by the name of Marra... Ahem... Pardon my ego, ıt at first I was like - there's only one MARRA, bro! But ıis cartoonist who calls himself **Benjamin Marra** ecently rode with us Humans on a cross country trip, and gotta say that chimp is okay by me. He's a true artist, a ɔet, and he's good in a rumble, too. And anyone with a ıuck Bronson tattoo is okay in my book. So, he drew us a cture for the back cover of this here funny-book... I think ɔ's gotta thing for the skins like brother Karns, but do hat thou wilt, 'mate. He draws some pretty awesome omic books like **Night Business** and **Blades and Lazers**. omics from another planet man - that shit will blow your ind! I highly recommend you check them out **traditionalcomics.com**

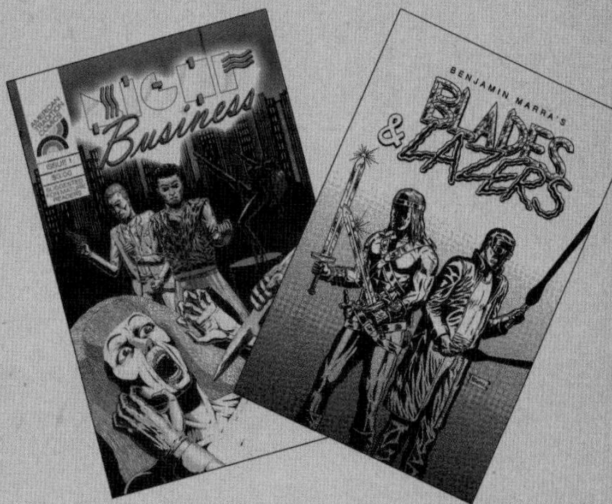
Night Business
BENJAMIN MARRA'S
BLADES & LAZERS

Thanks for riding with us Benji!
See ya next time.
- Marra

OUR COLORIST IS FIRED... AGAIN!

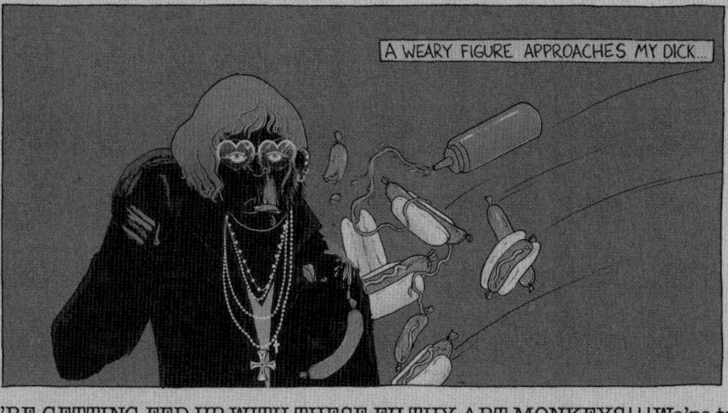
A WEARY FIGURE APPROACHES MY DICK...

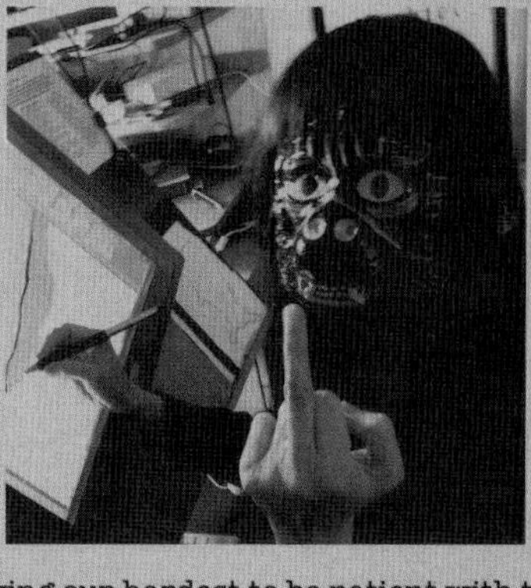

ʌE'RE GETTING FED UP WITH THESE FILTHY ART MONKEYS!!!We're trying our hardest to be patient with this ne. We caught her in Costa Rica and put her to work but she keeps drawing hot dogs and drag make-up on every page! Back to the banana-fields for this silly gibbon!

CREATORS' NOTES!

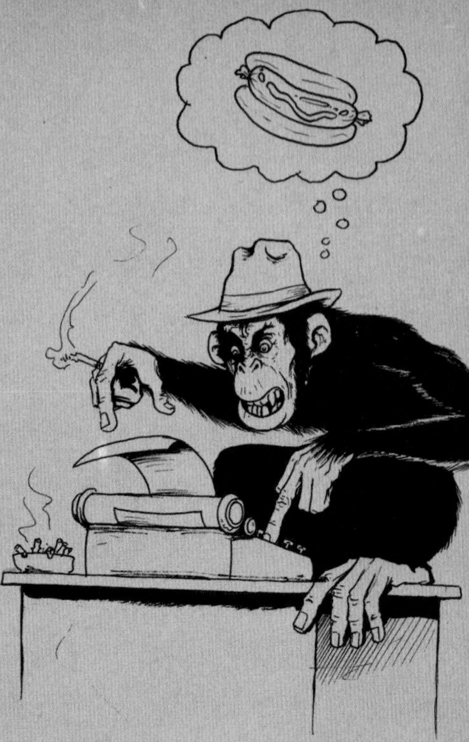

Hey everyone! Hope you dug issue #1!!!!
Sorry for Karns' language and the horrid grammar... He never finished the 5th grade and has always been filled with bile and pus ever since his momma left him as a child... That's why we love him so... But he did bring up some great points I'd like to talk about! One being: Please, write to Karns! He'll answer your letters at the back of each issue within his forum, APESHIT. You can ask him anything... Just be forewarned... He will answer in a crude and obscenely honest way... That's just how he does.

Also, please look for issue #2 a month from now on store shelves! We (Keenan, Tom and Kristina) are extremely psyched to bring you this series and hope you'll join us for the twisted road ahead for the HUMANS as the story and characters start to take shape. It's been a long haul for us to get to this point and now that we're here, we wanna keep the ride going!!!

The HUMANS Issue #2 "Return of the Living Dead" will bring with it a new major character and the beginnings of The HUMANS story!

So join the fanclub, buy the comics, glue hair to your body, and break a few laws... **Yer part of the HUMANS now.**

- Keenan Marshall Keller and Tom Neely

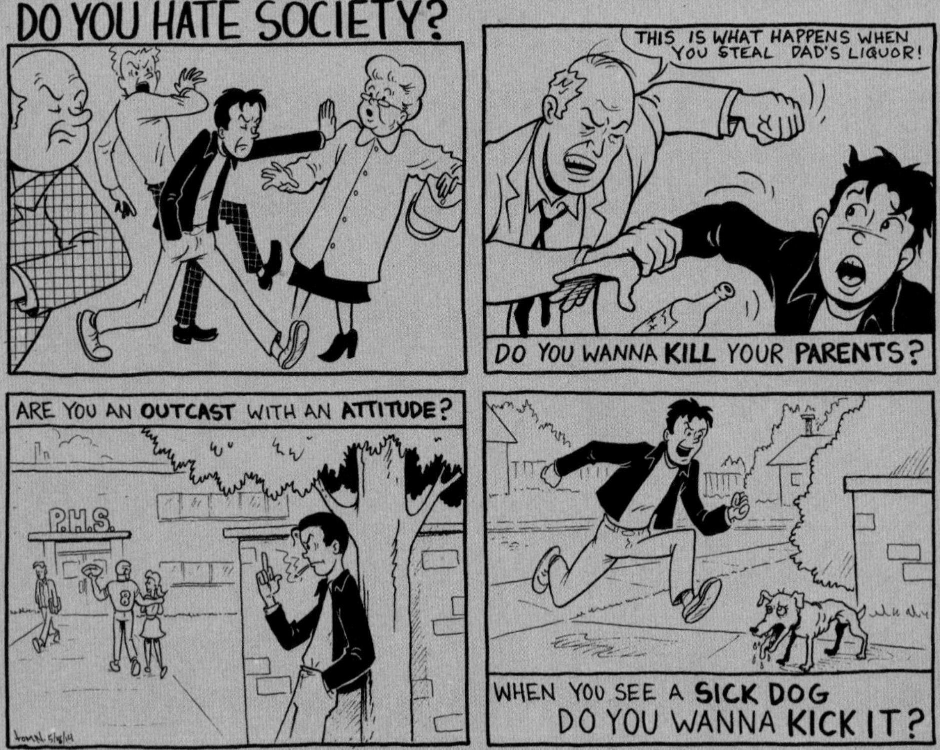
DO YOU HATE SOCIETY?
THIS IS WHAT HAPPENS WHEN YOU STEAL DAD'S LIQUOR!
DO YOU WANNA KILL YOUR PARENTS?
ARE YOU AN OUTCAST WITH AN ATTITUDE?
P.H.S.
WHEN YOU SEE A SICK DOG DO YOU WANNA KICK IT?

THEN... JOIN THE HUMANS FANCLUB!!!

Yes! I want to be a human slave!
Please send a 3" patch to:

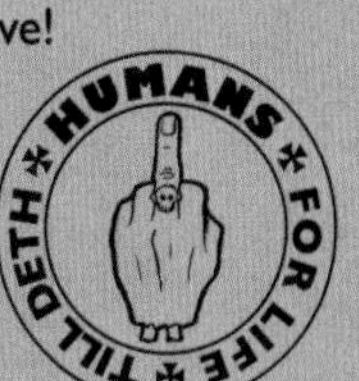
HUMANS
FOR LIFE
TILL DETH

____

____

____

Signature: ____________________

I understand that wearing this patch marks me as property of the Humans.

Humans Fanclub, P.O. Box 39674, LA, CA 90039

Show your colors
with your very own red, black and white HUMANS 3" patch! Let all your friends know who's got your back.

RIDE WITH STYLE AND FUCK SHIT UP THE HUMANS WAY!

Clip this form and send $6 along with a self-addressed, stamped envelope TODAY!

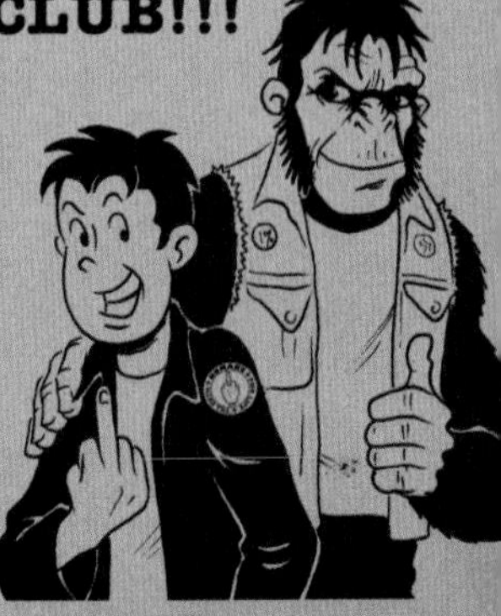

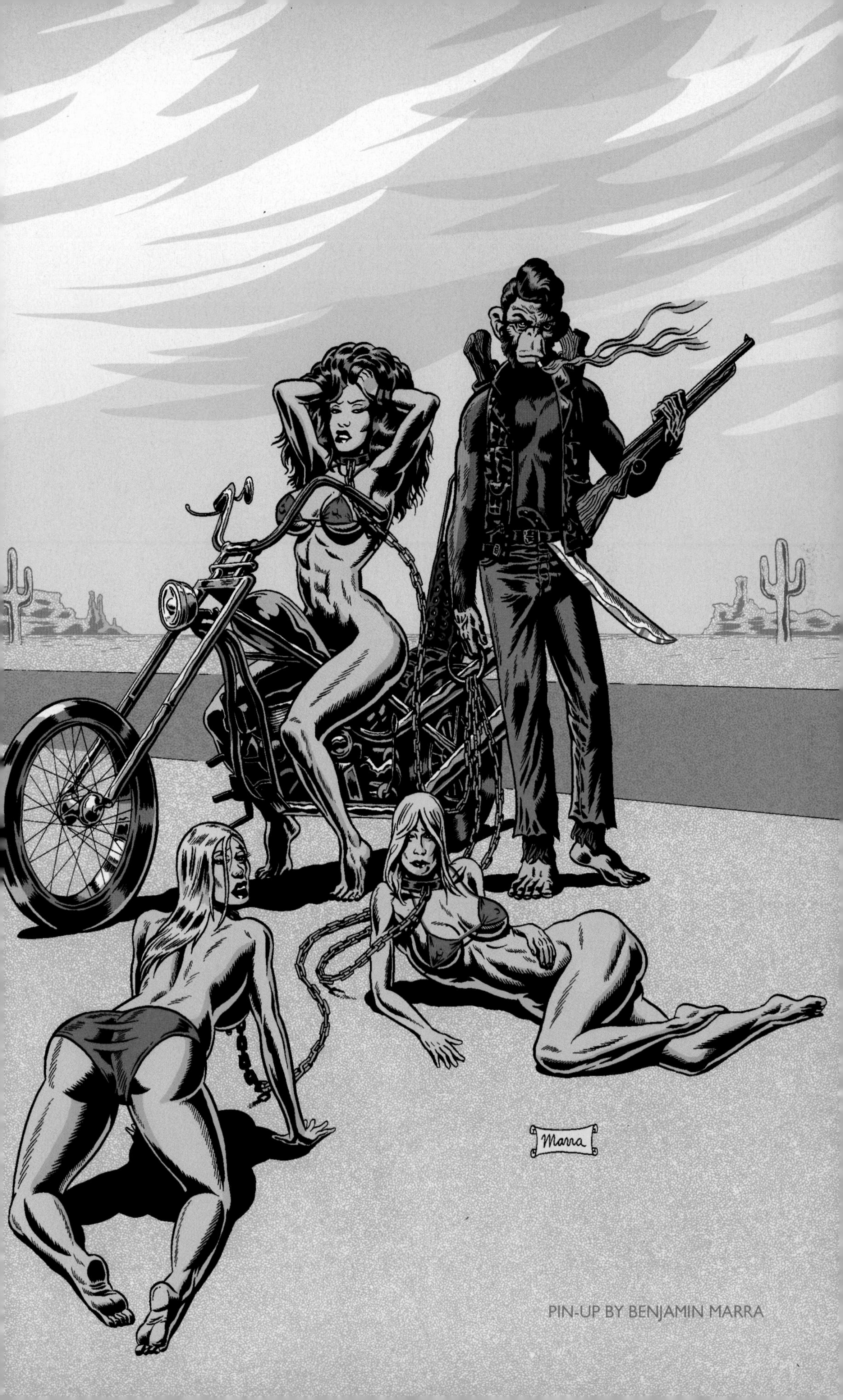
Marra

PIN-UP BY BENJAMIN MARRA

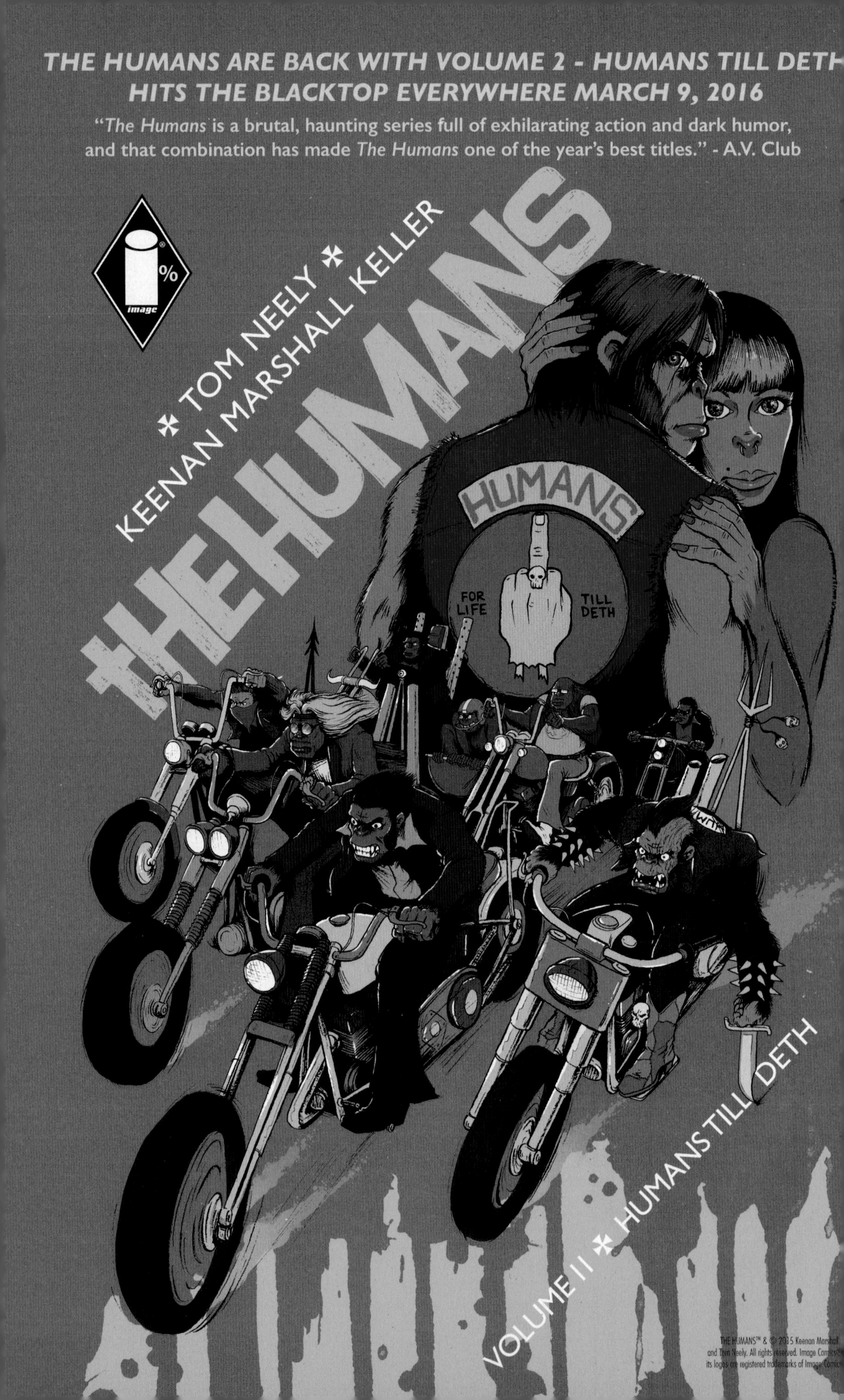
THE HUMANS ARE BACK WITH VOLUME 2 - HUMANS TILL DETH
HITS THE BLACKTOP EVERYWHERE MARCH 9, 2016
"*The Humans* is a brutal, haunting series full of exhilarating action and dark humor, and that combination has made *The Humans* one of the year's best titles." - A.V. Club
TOM NEELY
KEENAN MARSHALL KELLER
THE HUMANS
HUMANS
FOR LIFE
TILL DETH
VOLUME II
HUMANS TILL DETH
THE HUMANS™ & © 2015 Keenan Marshall
and Tom Neely. All rights reserved. Image Comics®
its logos are registered trademarks of Image Comic

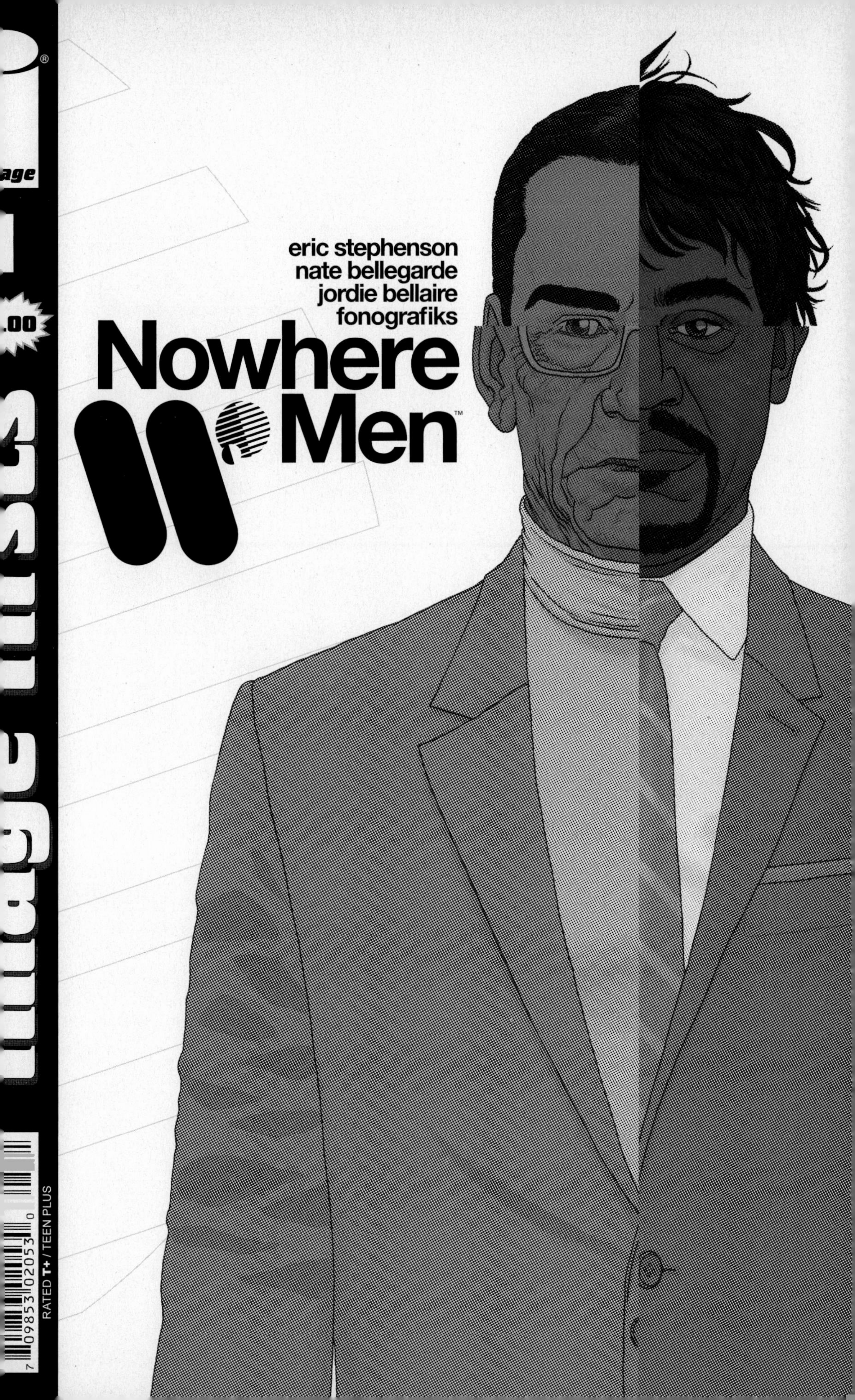
eric stephenson
nate bellegarde
jordie bellaire
fonografiks
Nowhere Men™
RATED T+ / TEEN PLUS

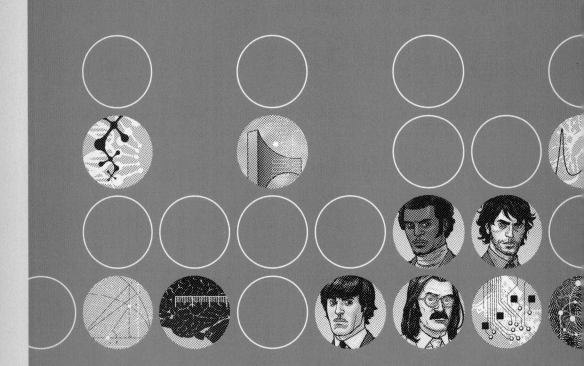

Join us.

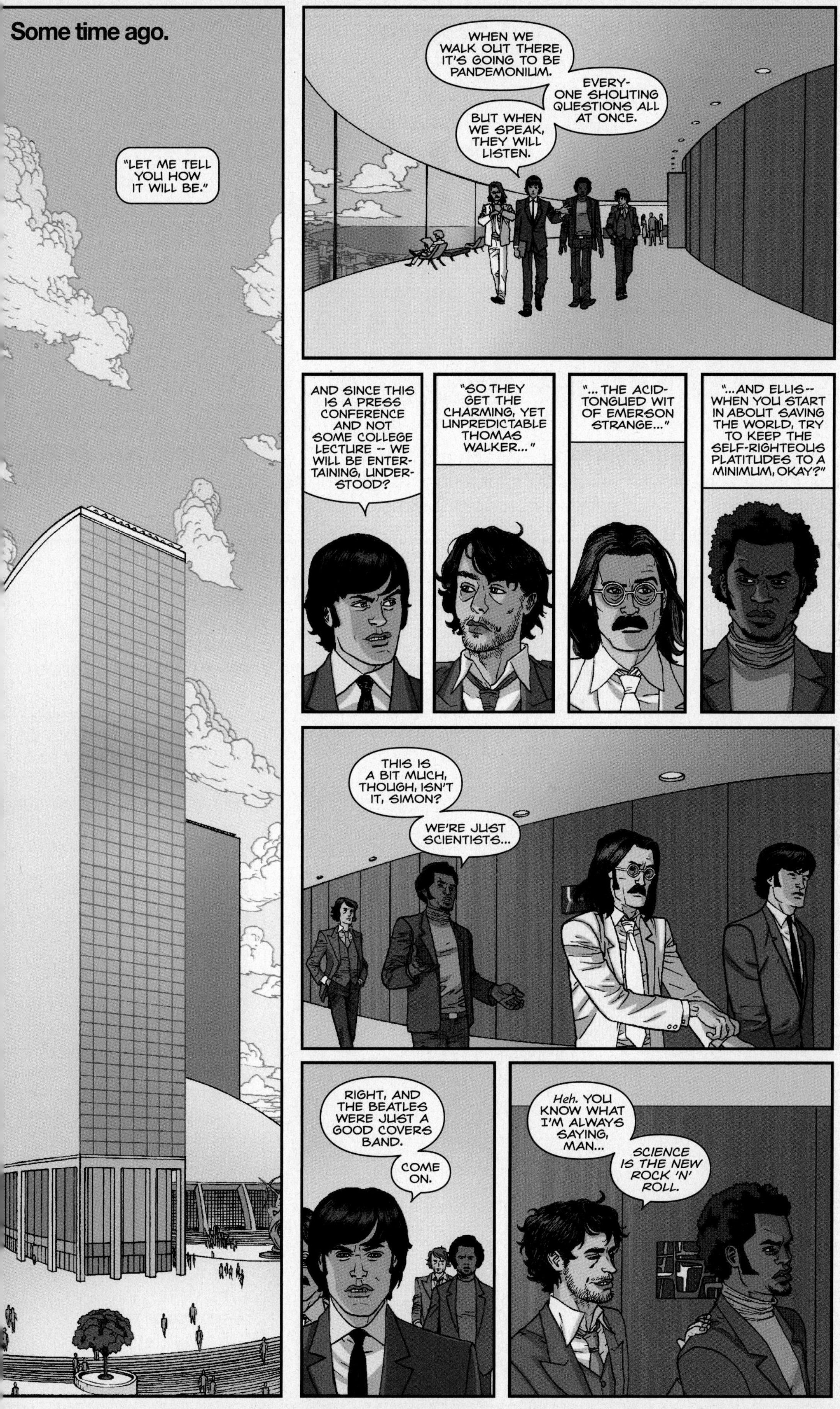
Some time ago.
"LET ME TELL YOU HOW IT WILL BE."
WHEN WE WALK OUT THERE, IT'S GOING TO BE PANDEMONIUM.
EVERY-ONE SHOUTING QUESTIONS ALL AT ONCE.
BUT WHEN WE SPEAK, THEY WILL LISTEN.
AND SINCE THIS IS A PRESS CONFERENCE AND NOT SOME COLLEGE LECTURE -- WE WILL BE ENTER-TAINING, UNDER-STOOD?
"SO THEY GET THE CHARMING, YET UNPREDICTABLE THOMAS WALKER..."
"... THE ACID-TONGUED WIT OF EMERSON STRANGE..."
"...AND ELLIS-- WHEN YOU START IN ABOUT SAVING THE WORLD, TRY TO KEEP THE SELF-RIGHTEOUS PLATITUDES TO A MINIMUM, OKAY?"
THIS IS A BIT MUCH, THOUGH, ISN'T IT, SIMON?
WE'RE JUST SCIENTISTS...
RIGHT, AND THE BEATLES WERE JUST A GOOD COVERS BAND.
COME ON.
Heh. YOU KNOW WHAT I'M ALWAYS SAYING, MAN...
SCIENCE IS THE NEW ROCK 'N' ROLL.

TSC *FACT FINDER

WORLD CORP.

Discover the detail

Dade Ellis. Simon Grimshaw. Emerson Strange. Thomas Walker. Separately, they are among the greatest thinkers in the world, but together, they comprise the all-out scientific supergroup known as World Corp. Though they've only been together briefly, their incredible new venture is sending shockwaves through the science community, so we're giving you the lowdown on what makes these sensational young men tick in the latest edition of our exclusive Fact Finders series!

DADE ELLIS

BORN: January 8
HOMETOWN: St. Louis, IL
EDUCATED: Yale University
FATHER: Joseph
MOTHER: Edith
BROTHERS: None
SISTERS: Kimberly
DEGREE: Neurobiology, Geophysics, Architecture
CAREER: Neuroscience
OTHER OCCUPATIONS: Library clerk
FAVORITE INVENTION: Just for the pure enjoyment it's given me over the years, I think I'd have to say the record player.
FAVORITE ARTICLE OF CLOTHING: Well-made shoes are indispensable.
FAVORITE SONG: *Stolen Moments* by Oliver Nelson
FAVORITE FILM: *Strangers on a Train*
FAVORITE BOOK: *Dandelion Wine* by Ray Bradbury
FAVORITE PERSON: My partners.
GREATEST INFLUENCE: No one person in particular, but music always inspires me.
GREATEST ACHIEVEMENT: The near-eradication of blindness through cyber-optics.
GREATEST AMBITION: Sustainable peace.
STATUS: Single
HEIGHT: 6'3"
WEIGHT: 165 lbs
HAIR: Brown
EYES: Brown
WHAT'S YOUR TIPPLE? Rye whiskey

of the visionary group at the epicenter of a science revolution!

SIMON GRIMSHAW

BORN: April 16
HOMETOWN: Barrytown, NY
EDUCATED: New York University
FATHER: Randall
MOTHER: Susan
BROTHERS: None
SISTERS: None
DEGREE: Molecular Biology, Mathematics in Finance
CAREER: Geneticist
OTHER OCCUPATIONS: None
FAVORITE INVENTION: The pencil.
FAVORITE ARTICLE OF CLOTHING: J. Press does really good ties.
FAVORITE SONG: I don't have a favorite song.
FAVORITE FILM: I don't have a favorite film.
FAVORITE BOOK: *Atlas Shrugged* by Ayn Rand
FAVORITE PERSON: No one I care to name. Just because I've given up my own privacy doesn't mean that extends to everyone I know.
GREATEST INFLUENCE: The prospect of failure or poverty.
GREATEST ACHIEVEMENT: World Corp.
GREATEST AMBITION: Perfection.
STATUS: Single
HEIGHT: 5'10"
WEIGHT: 152 lbs
HAIR: Brown
EYES: Blue
WHAT'S YOUR TIPPLE? I don't drink.

EMERSON STRANGE

BORN: October 9
HOMETOWN: Mountain View, CA
EDUCATED: Stanford University
FATHER: Alfred
MOTHER: Julia
BROTHERS: None
SISTERS: Victoria
DEGREE: Mechanical Engineering, Computer Science
CAREER: Inventor, designer
OTHER OCCUPATIONS: Systems Analyst, Programmer, Lecturer
FAVORITE INVENTION: Whatever new thing I'm working on at the moment.
FAVORITE ARTICLE OF CLOTHING: White suits
FAVORITE SONG: At the moment, I'd have to say something by The Beach Boys, probably *Surf's Up*.
FAVORITE FILM: *Lawrence of Arabia*
FAVORITE BOOK: *The Magus* by John Fowles
FAVORITE PERSON: My daughter, Monica.
GREATEST INFLUENCE: Thomas Edison
GREATEST ACHIEVEMENT: The actual name is yet to be determined, but for now, I'm calling it 'The Everything Box'— more news as it develops!
GREATEST AMBITION: Ubiquity.
STATUS: Divorced
HEIGHT: 6'3"
WEIGHT: 159 lbs
HAIR: Black
EYES: Blue
WHAT'S YOUR TIPPLE? Gin and tonic.

THOMAS WALKER

BORN: January 6
HOMETOWN: Cambridge, England
EDUCATED: Cambridge University
FATHER: Arthur
MOTHER: Matilda
BROTHERS: Roger, Nicholas, Richard, David
SISTERS: None
DEGREE: Astrophysics
CAREER: Theoretical Physicist
OTHER OCCUPATIONS: Sweeping up
FAVORITE INVENTION: LSD
FAVORITE ARTICLE OF CLOTHING: Corduroy
FAVORITE SONG: *Carnival of Light* by The Beatles
FAVORITE FILM: *Fantasia*
FAVORITE BOOK: *A Clockwork Orange* by Anthony Burgess
FAVORITE PERSON: Mother
GREATEST INFLUENCE: Keeping my mind occupied.
GREATEST ACHIEVEMENT: I suppose the theories I've put forward on wormholes and dark matter, but I've also learned to juggle whilst riding my bike, which is terribly useful, I've found.
GREATEST AMBITION: Space
STATUS: Single
HEIGHT: 5'11"
WEIGHT: 155 lbs
HAIR: Brown
EYES: Grey
WHAT'S YOUR TIPPLE? Brandy Alexander.

Years later.

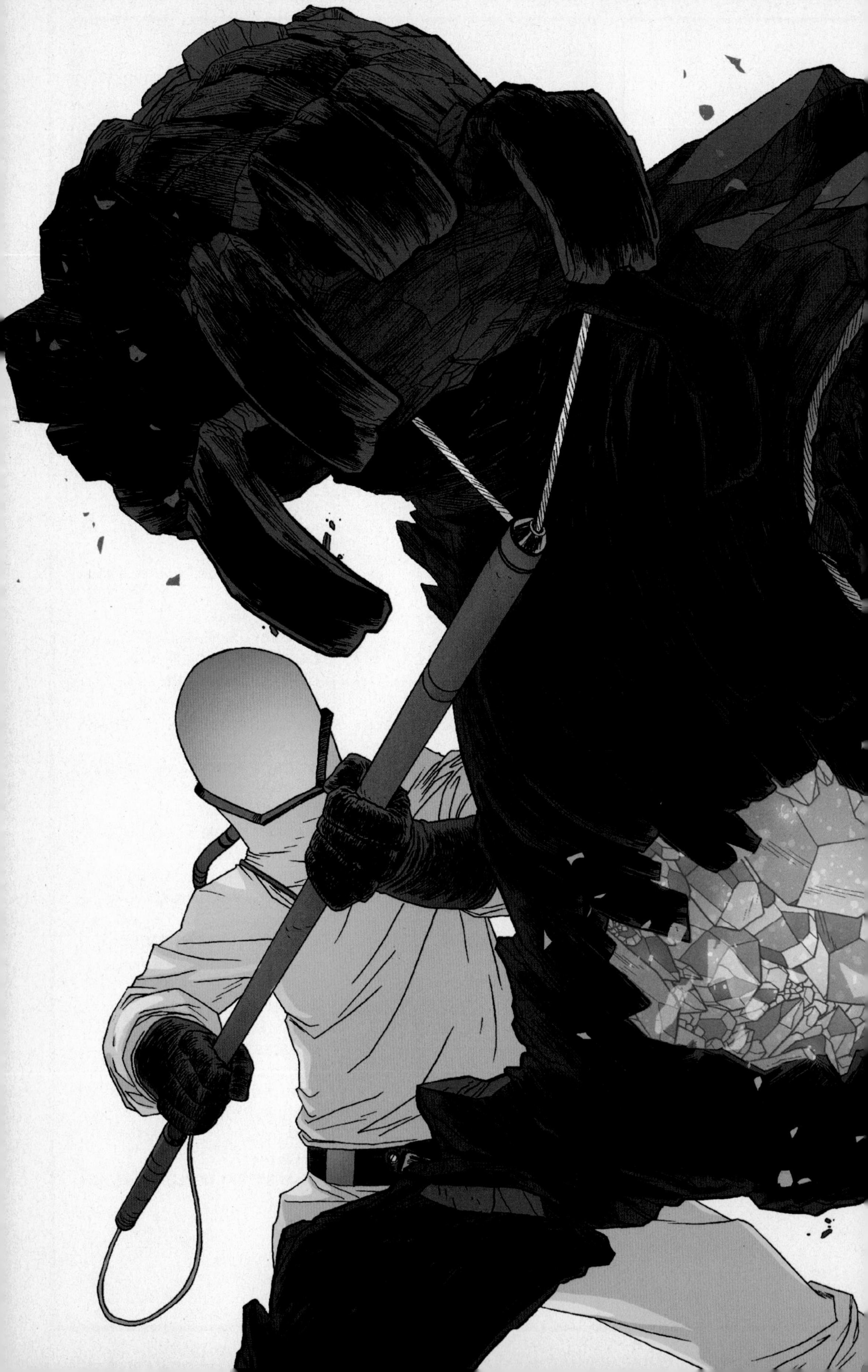

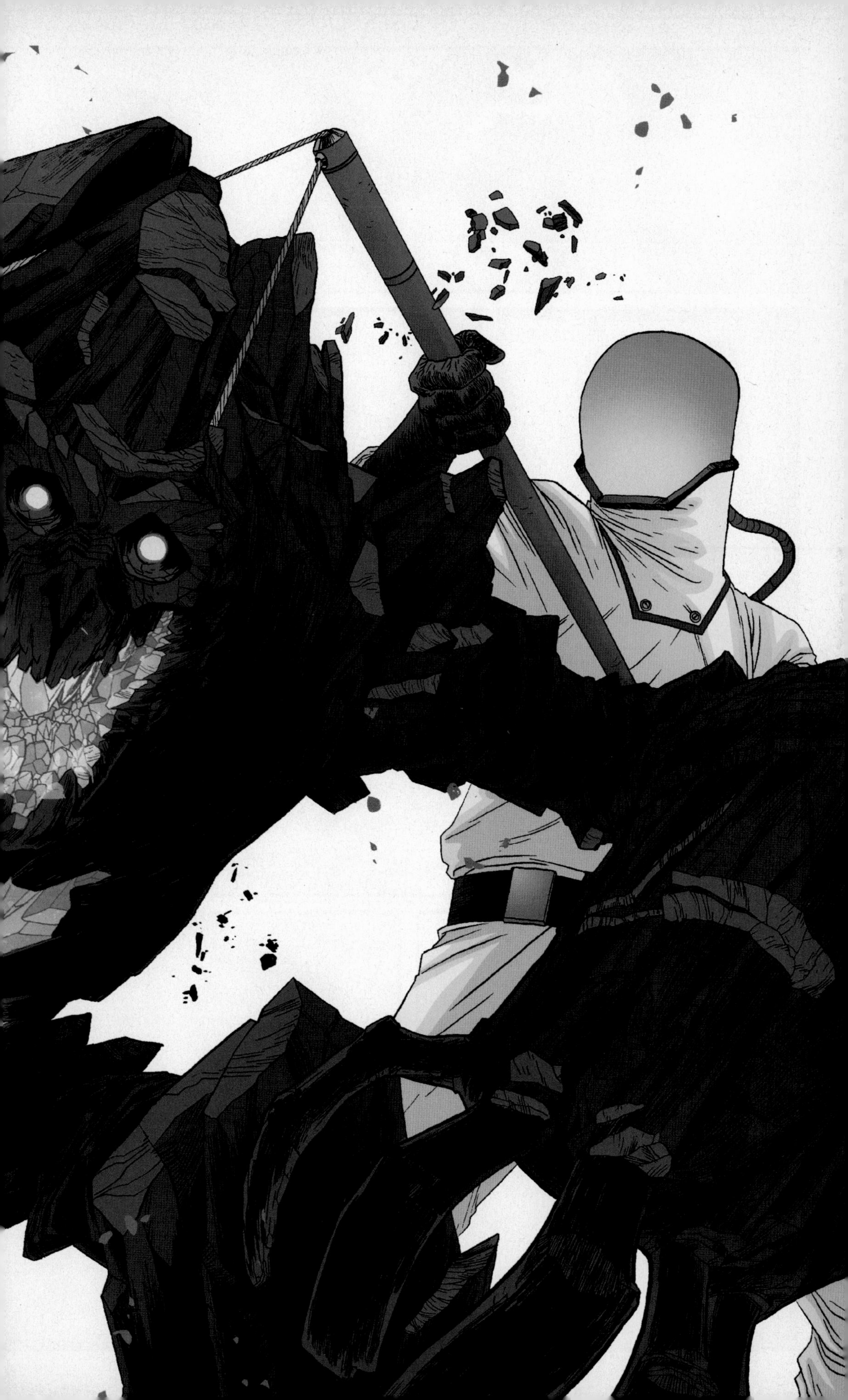

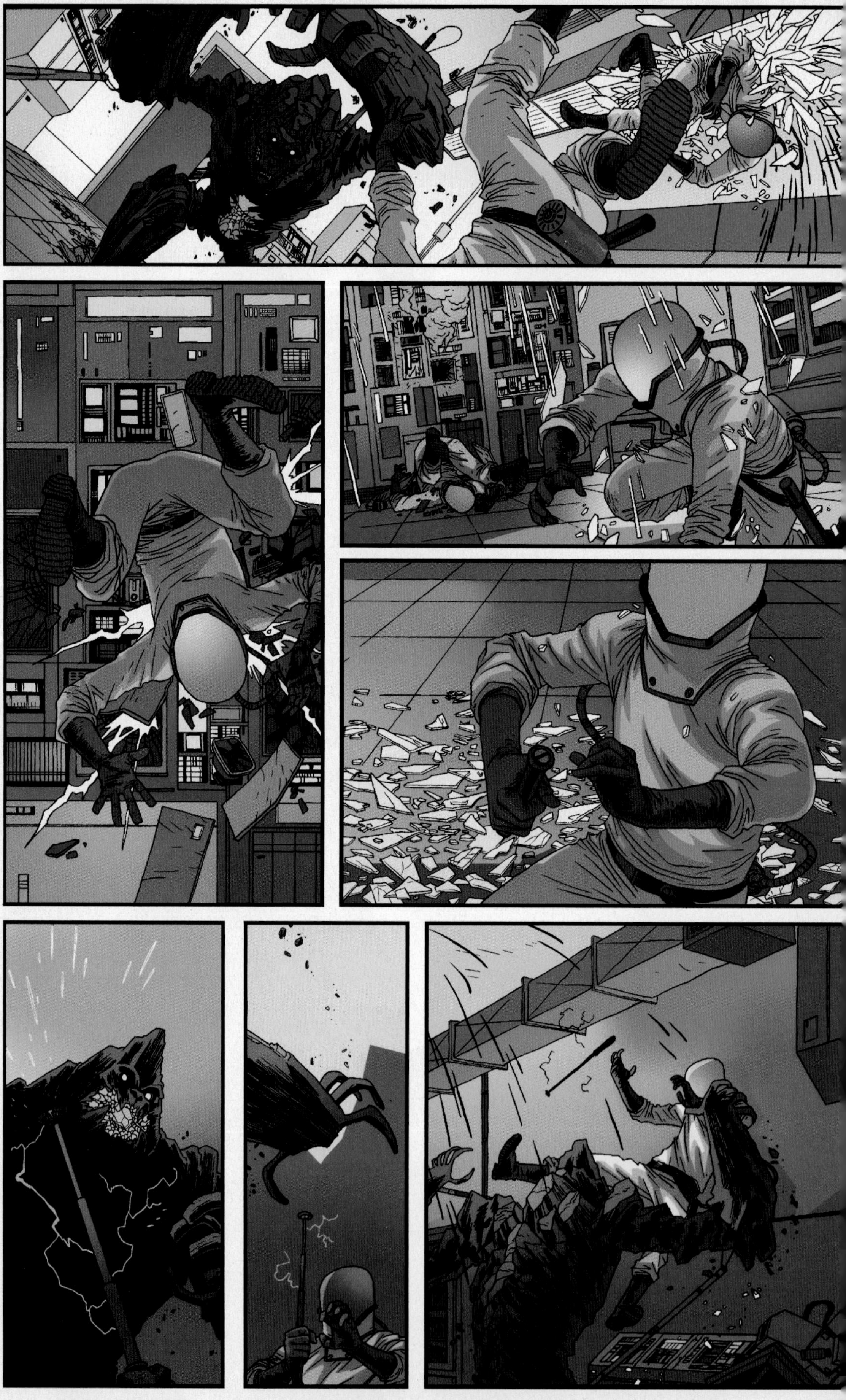

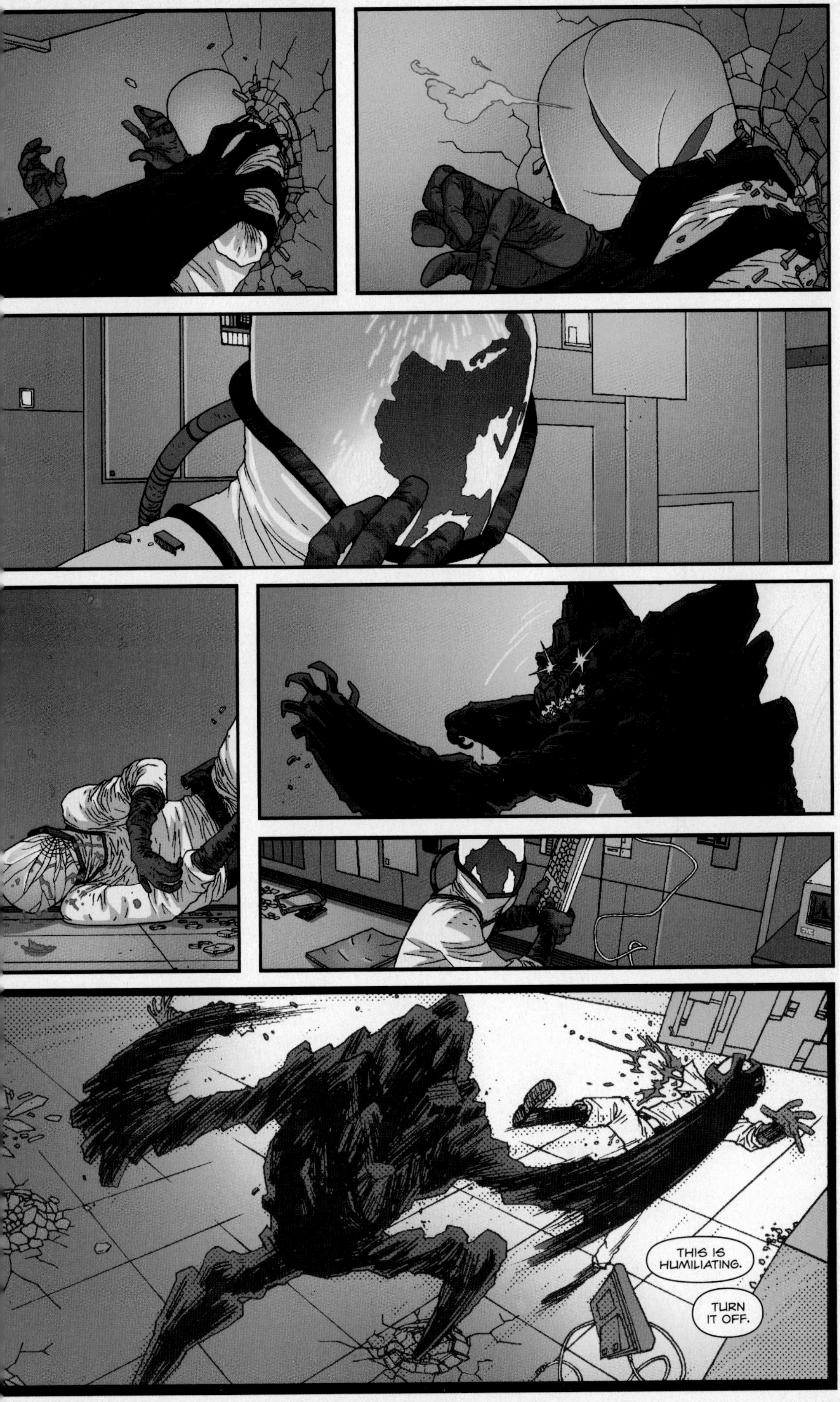
THIS IS HUMILIATING.
TURN IT OFF.

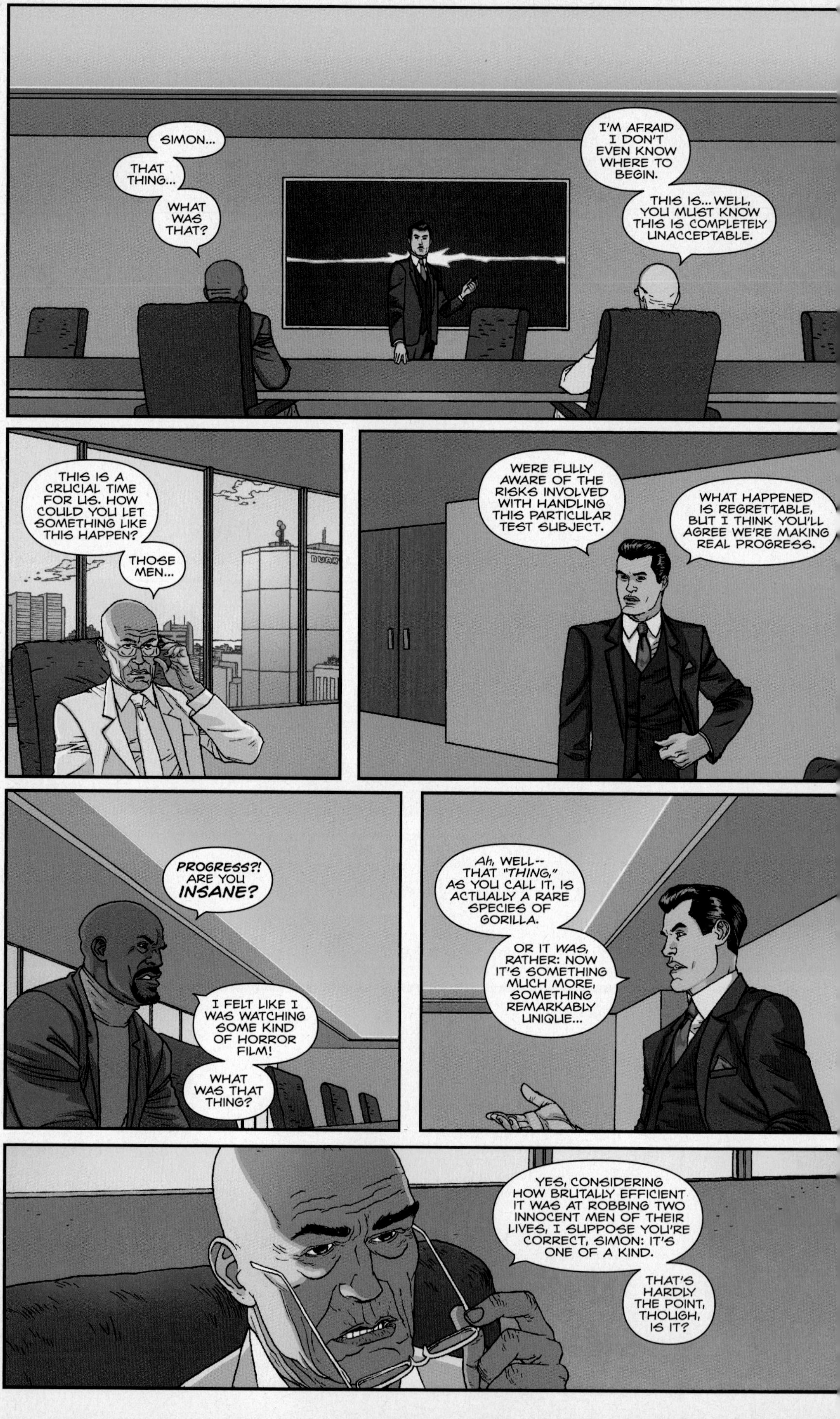
SIMON...
THAT THING...
WHAT WAS THAT?
I'M AFRAID I DON'T EVEN KNOW WHERE TO BEGIN.
THIS IS... WELL, YOU MUST KNOW THIS IS COMPLETELY UNACCEPTABLE.
THIS IS A CRUCIAL TIME FOR US. HOW COULD YOU LET SOMETHING LIKE THIS HAPPEN?
THOSE MEN...
WERE FULLY AWARE OF THE RISKS INVOLVED WITH HANDLING THIS PARTICULAR TEST SUBJECT.
WHAT HAPPENED IS REGRETTABLE, BUT I THINK YOU'LL AGREE WE'RE MAKING REAL PROGRESS.
PROGRESS?! ARE YOU INSANE?
I FELT LIKE I WAS WATCHING SOME KIND OF HORROR FILM!
WHAT WAS THAT THING?
Ah, WELL-- THAT "THING," AS YOU CALL IT, IS ACTUALLY A RARE SPECIES OF GORILLA.
OR IT WAS, RATHER: NOW IT'S SOMETHING MUCH MORE, SOMETHING REMARKABLY UNIQUE...
YES, CONSIDERING HOW BRUTALLY EFFICIENT IT WAS AT ROBBING TWO INNOCENT MEN OF THEIR LIVES, I SUPPOSE YOU'RE CORRECT, SIMON: IT'S ONE OF A KIND.
THAT'S HARDLY THE POINT, THOUGH, IS IT?

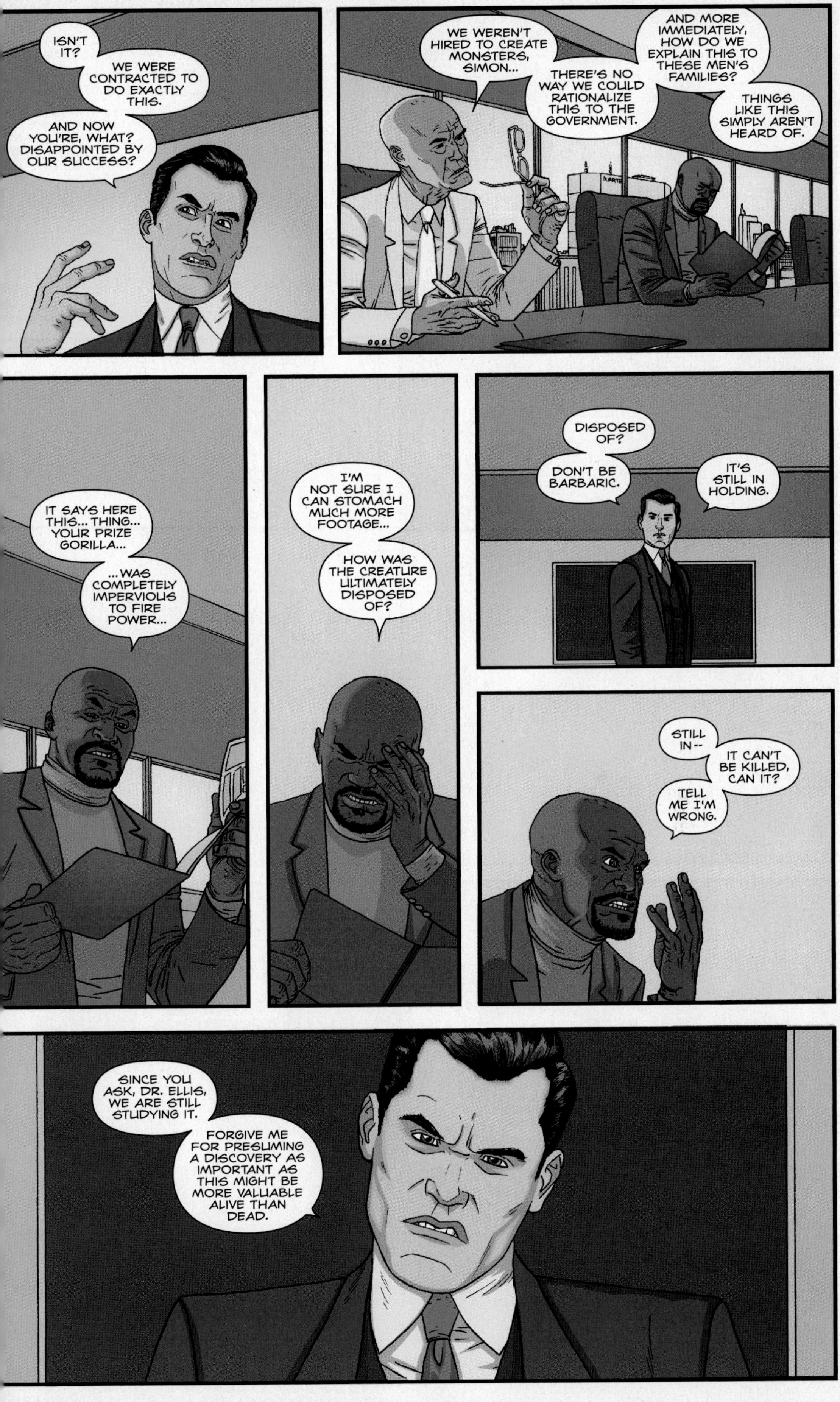

ISN'T IT?
WE WERE CONTRACTED TO DO EXACTLY THIS.
AND NOW YOU'RE, WHAT? DISAPPOINTED BY OUR SUCCESS?
WE WEREN'T HIRED TO CREATE MONSTERS, SIMON...
THERE'S NO WAY WE COULD RATIONALIZE THIS TO THE GOVERNMENT.
AND MORE IMMEDIATELY, HOW DO WE EXPLAIN THIS TO THESE MEN'S FAMILIES?
THINGS LIKE THIS SIMPLY AREN'T HEARD OF.
IT SAYS HERE THIS... THING... YOUR PRIZE GORILLA...
...WAS COMPLETELY IMPERVIOUS TO FIRE POWER...
I'M NOT SURE I CAN STOMACH MUCH MORE FOOTAGE...
HOW WAS THE CREATURE ULTIMATELY DISPOSED OF?
DISPOSED OF?
DON'T BE BARBARIC.
IT'S STILL IN HOLDING.
STILL IN--
IT CAN'T BE KILLED, CAN IT?
TELL ME I'M WRONG.
SINCE YOU ASK, DR. ELLIS, WE ARE STILL STUDYING IT.
FORGIVE ME FOR PRESUMING A DISCOVERY AS IMPORTANT AS THIS MIGHT BE MORE VALUABLE ALIVE THAN DEAD.

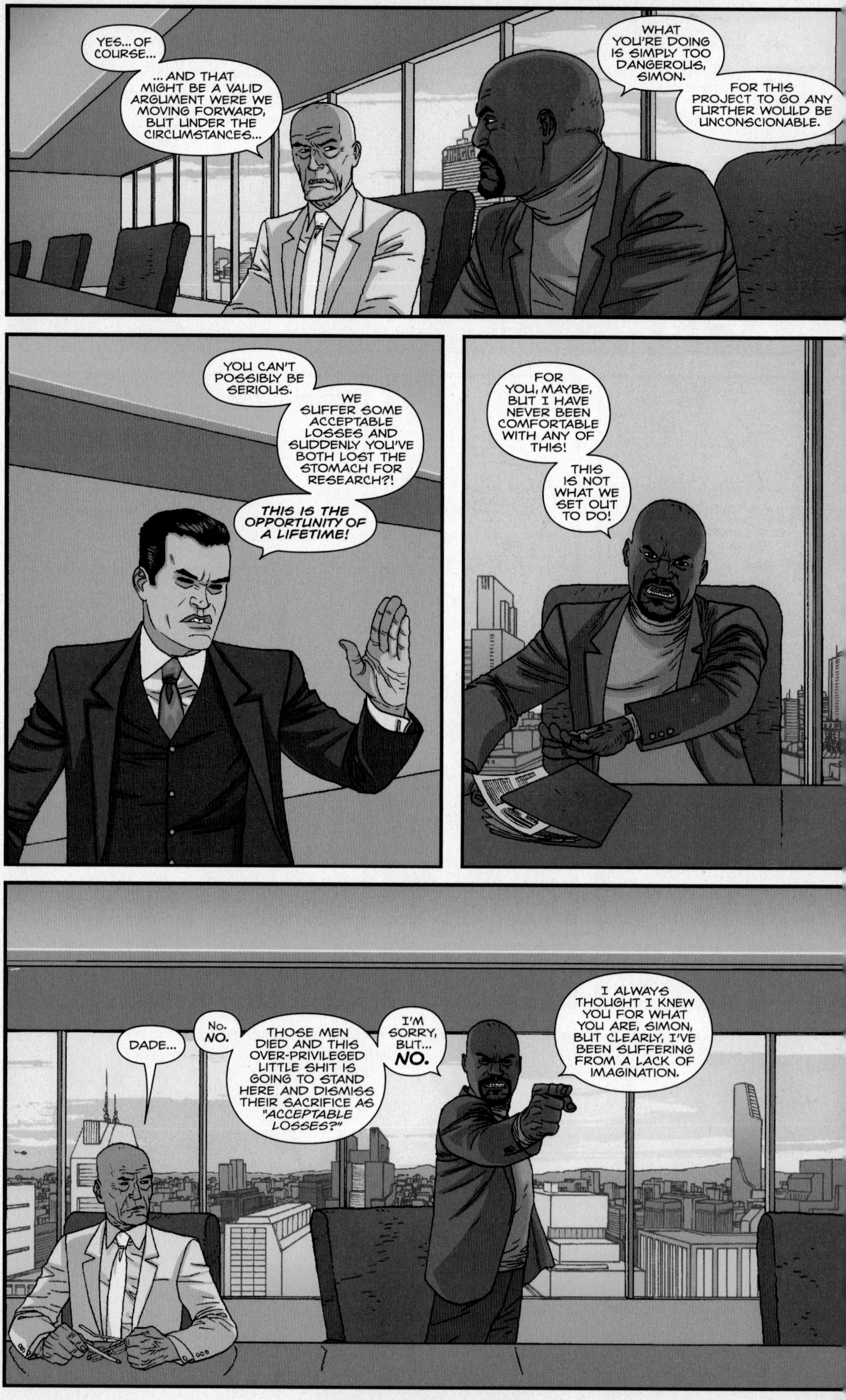
YES... OF COURSE...
... AND THAT MIGHT BE A VALID ARGUMENT WERE WE MOVING FORWARD, BUT UNDER THE CIRCUMSTANCES...
WHAT YOU'RE DOING IS SIMPLY TOO DANGEROUS, SIMON.
FOR THIS PROJECT TO GO ANY FURTHER WOULD BE UNCONSCIONABLE.
YOU CAN'T POSSIBLY BE SERIOUS.
WE SUFFER SOME ACCEPTABLE LOSSES AND SUDDENLY YOU'VE BOTH LOST THE STOMACH FOR RESEARCH?!
THIS IS THE OPPORTUNITY OF A LIFETIME!
FOR YOU, MAYBE, BUT I HAVE NEVER BEEN COMFORTABLE WITH ANY OF THIS!
THIS IS NOT WHAT WE SET OUT TO DO!
DADE...
No. NO.
THOSE MEN DIED AND THIS OVER-PRIVILEGED LITTLE SHIT IS GOING TO STAND HERE AND DISMISS THEIR SACRIFICE AS "ACCEPTABLE LOSSES?"
I'M SORRY, BUT... NO.
I ALWAYS THOUGHT I KNEW YOU FOR WHAT YOU ARE, SIMON, BUT CLEARLY, I'VE BEEN SUFFERING FROM A LACK OF IMAGINATION.

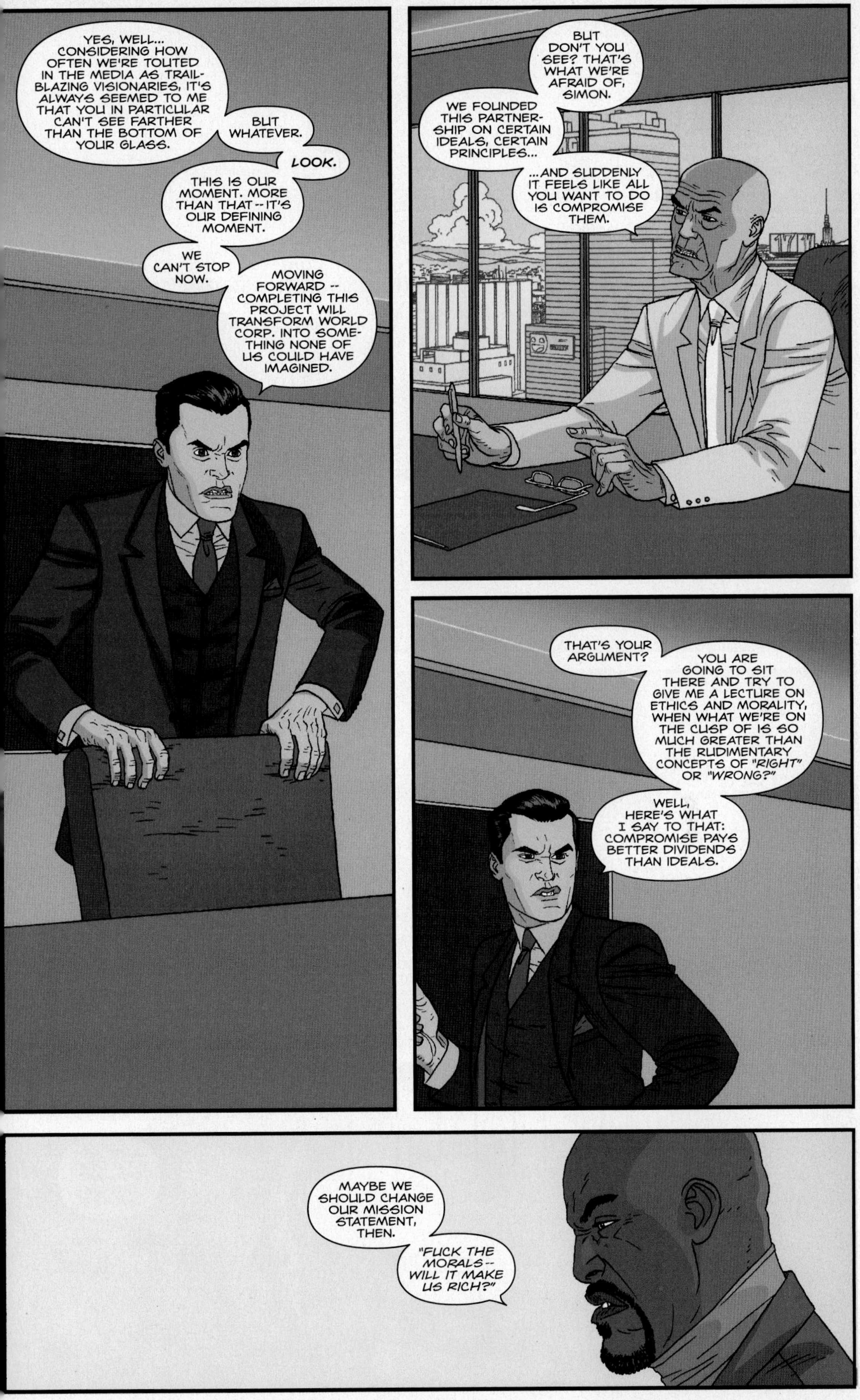
YES, WELL... CONSIDERING HOW OFTEN WE'RE TOUTED IN THE MEDIA AS TRAIL-BLAZING VISIONARIES, IT'S ALWAYS SEEMED TO ME THAT YOU IN PARTICULAR CAN'T SEE FARTHER THAN THE BOTTOM OF YOUR GLASS.
BUT WHATEVER.
LOOK.
THIS IS OUR MOMENT. MORE THAN THAT--IT'S OUR DEFINING MOMENT.
WE CAN'T STOP NOW.
MOVING FORWARD -- COMPLETING THIS PROJECT WILL TRANSFORM WORLD CORP. INTO SOMETHING NONE OF US COULD HAVE IMAGINED.
BUT DON'T YOU SEE? THAT'S WHAT WE'RE AFRAID OF, SIMON.
WE FOUNDED THIS PARTNERSHIP ON CERTAIN IDEALS, CERTAIN PRINCIPLES...
...AND SUDDENLY IT FEELS LIKE ALL YOU WANT TO DO IS COMPROMISE THEM.
THAT'S YOUR ARGUMENT?
YOU ARE GOING TO SIT THERE AND TRY TO GIVE ME A LECTURE ON ETHICS AND MORALITY, WHEN WHAT WE'RE ON THE CUSP OF IS SO MUCH GREATER THAN THE RUDIMENTARY CONCEPTS OF "RIGHT" OR "WRONG?"
WELL, HERE'S WHAT I SAY TO THAT: COMPROMISE PAYS BETTER DIVIDENDS THAN IDEALS.
MAYBE WE SHOULD CHANGE OUR MISSION STATEMENT, THEN.
"FUCK THE MORALS-- WILL IT MAKE US RICH?"

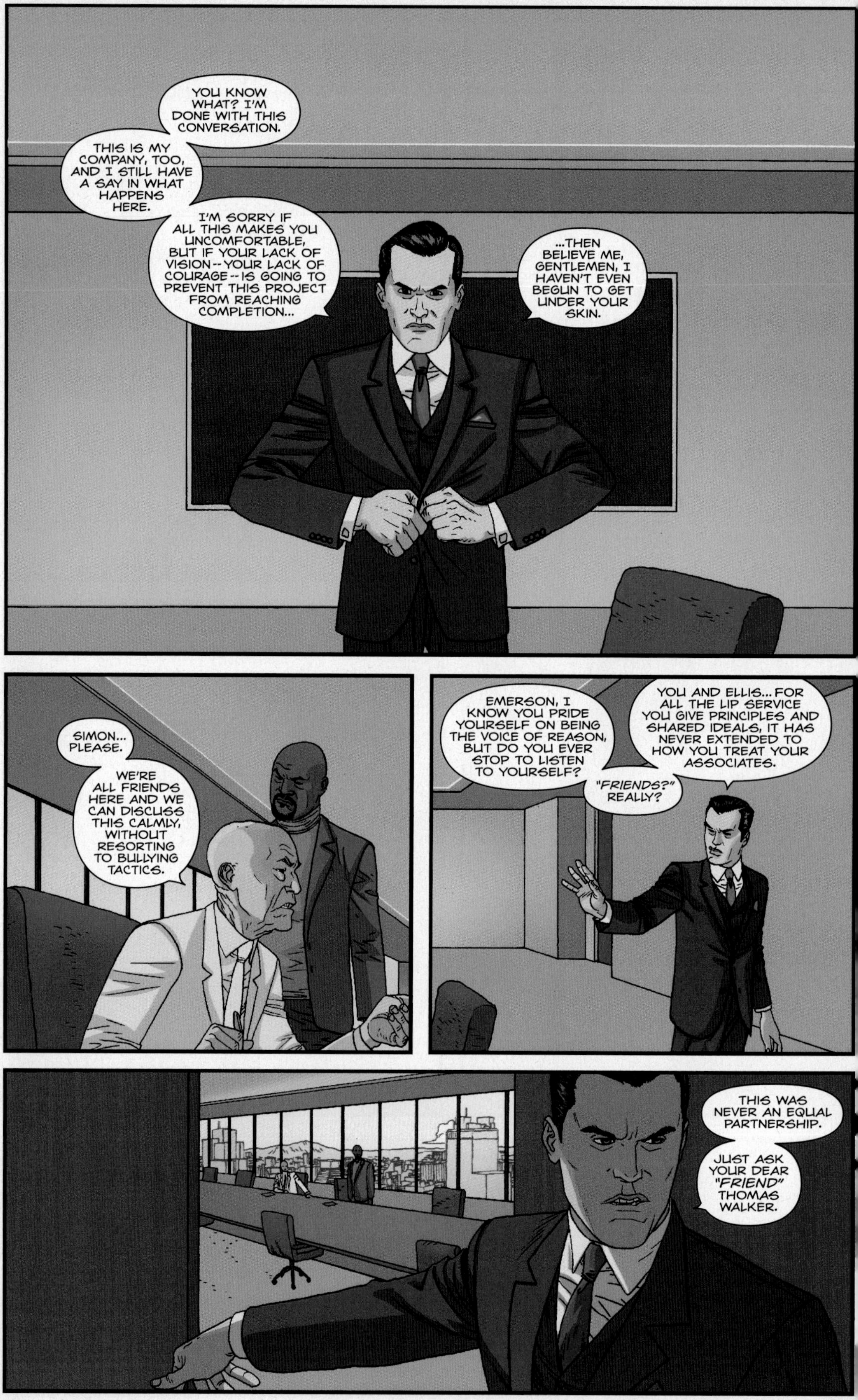
YOU KNOW WHAT? I'M DONE WITH THIS CONVERSATION.
THIS IS MY COMPANY, TOO, AND I STILL HAVE A SAY IN WHAT HAPPENS HERE.
I'M SORRY IF ALL THIS MAKES YOU UNCOMFORTABLE, BUT IF YOUR LACK OF VISION--YOUR LACK OF COURAGE--IS GOING TO PREVENT THIS PROJECT FROM REACHING COMPLETION...
...THEN BELIEVE ME, GENTLEMEN, I HAVEN'T EVEN BEGUN TO GET UNDER YOUR SKIN.
SIMON... PLEASE.
WE'RE ALL FRIENDS HERE AND WE CAN DISCUSS THIS CALMLY, WITHOUT RESORTING TO BULLYING TACTICS.
EMERSON, I KNOW YOU PRIDE YOURSELF ON BEING THE VOICE OF REASON, BUT DO YOU EVER STOP TO LISTEN TO YOURSELF?
"FRIENDS?" REALLY?
YOU AND ELLIS... FOR ALL THE LIP SERVICE YOU GIVE PRINCIPLES AND SHARED IDEALS, IT HAS NEVER EXTENDED TO HOW YOU TREAT YOUR ASSOCIATES.
THIS WAS NEVER AN EQUAL PARTNERSHIP.
JUST ASK YOUR DEAR "FRIEND" THOMAS WALKER.

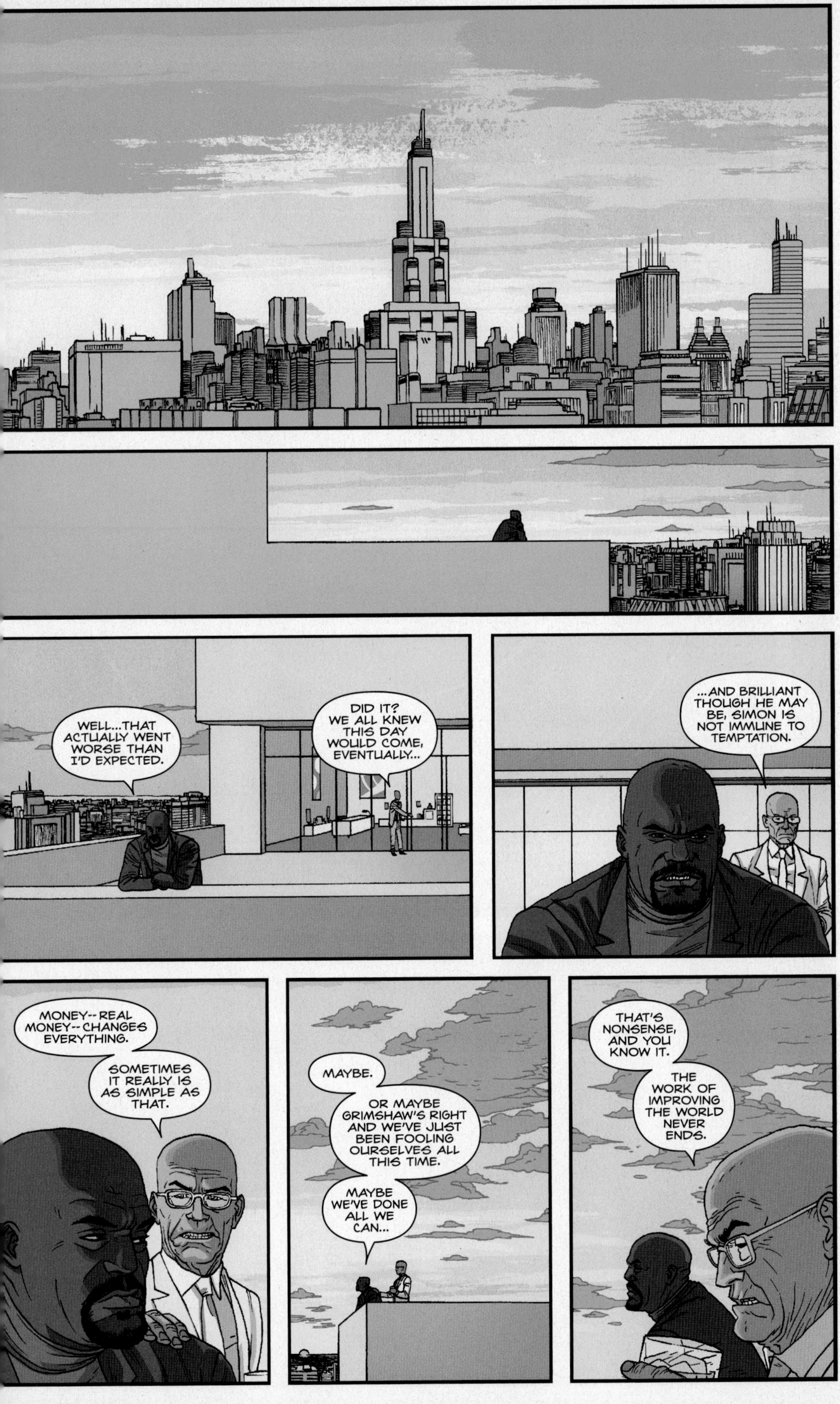
WELL...THAT ACTUALLY WENT WORSE THAN I'D EXPECTED.
DID IT? WE ALL KNEW THIS DAY WOULD COME, EVENTUALLY...
...AND BRILLIANT THOUGH HE MAY BE, SIMON IS NOT IMMUNE TO TEMPTATION.
MONEY-- REAL MONEY-- CHANGES EVERYTHING.
SOMETIMES IT REALLY IS AS SIMPLE AS THAT.
MAYBE.
OR MAYBE GRIMSHAW'S RIGHT AND WE'VE JUST BEEN FOOLING OURSELVES ALL THIS TIME.
MAYBE WE'VE DONE ALL WE CAN...
THAT'S NONSENSE, AND YOU KNOW IT.
THE WORK OF IMPROVING THE WORLD NEVER ENDS.

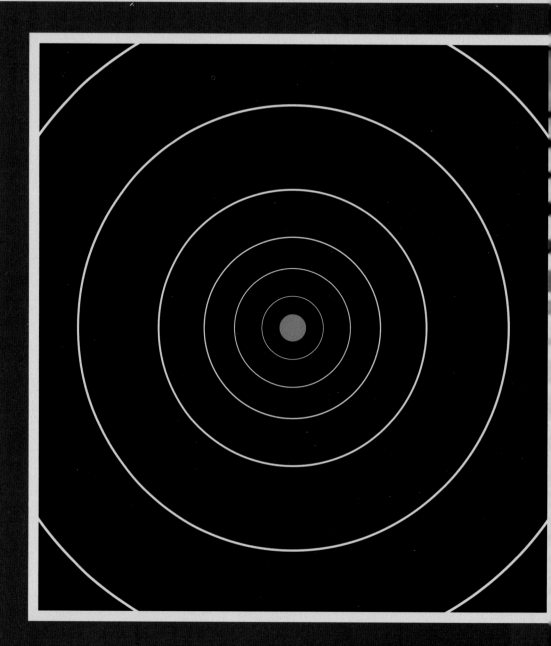

INTO
TOMORROW

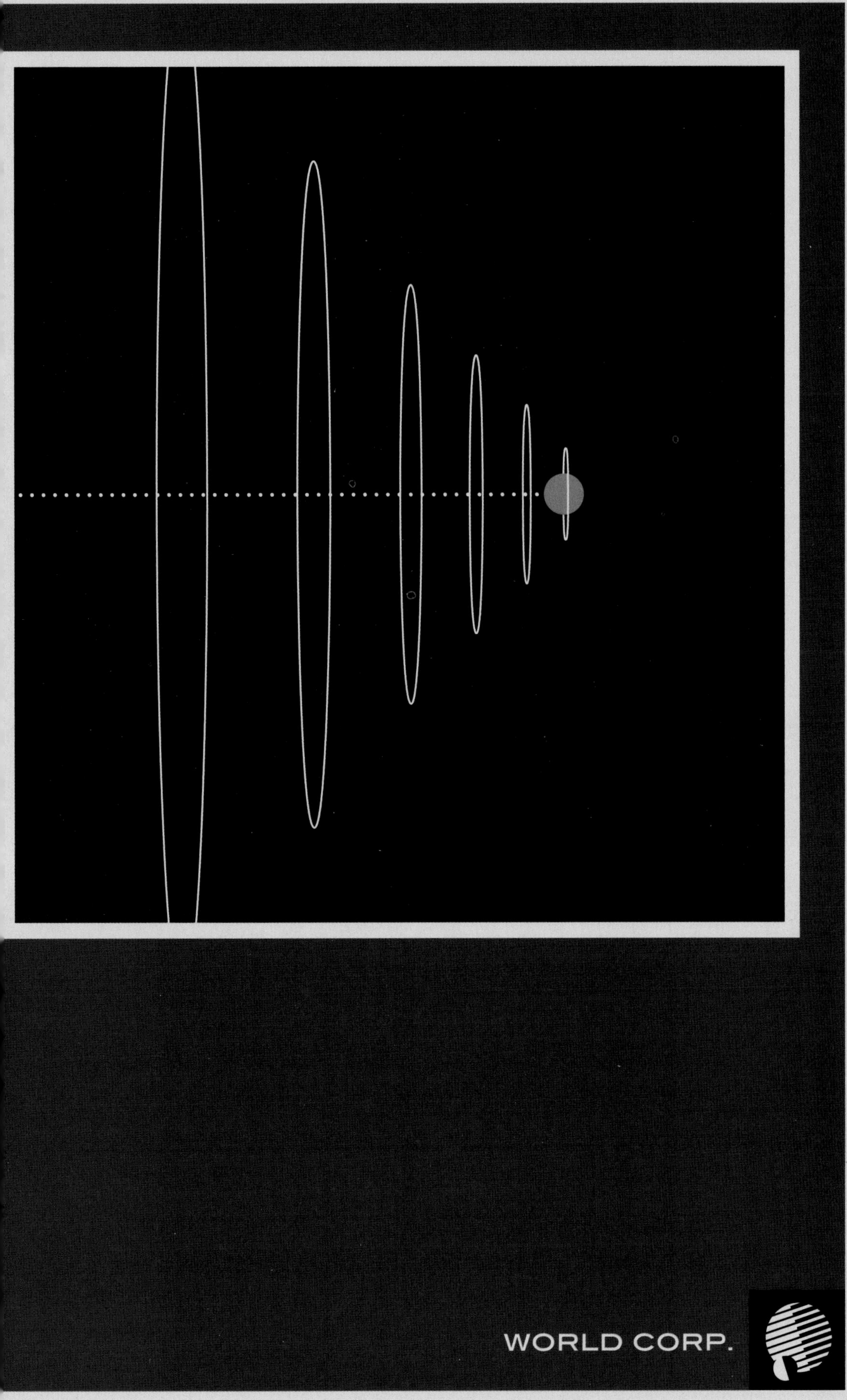
WORLD CORP.

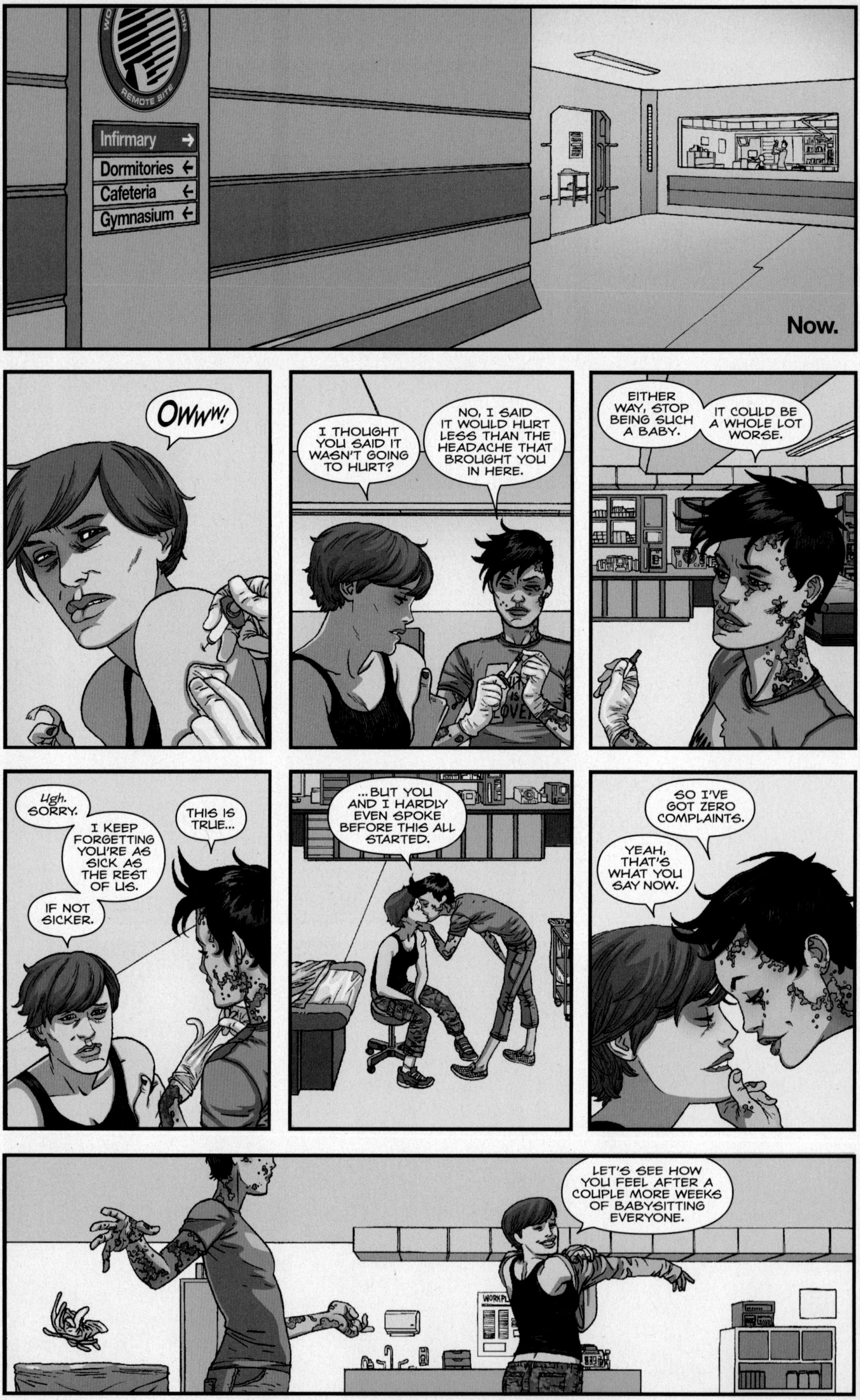

REMOTE SITE
Infirmary →
Dormitories ←
Cafeteria ←
Gymnasium ←
Now.
OWWW!
I THOUGHT YOU SAID IT WASN'T GOING TO HURT?
NO, I SAID IT WOULD HURT LESS THAN THE HEADACHE THAT BROUGHT YOU IN HERE.
EITHER WAY, STOP BEING SUCH A BABY.
IT COULD BE A WHOLE LOT WORSE.
Ugh. SORRY.
I KEEP FORGETTING YOU'RE AS SICK AS THE REST OF US.
IF NOT SICKER.
THIS IS TRUE...
...BUT YOU AND I HARDLY EVEN SPOKE BEFORE THIS ALL STARTED.
SO I'VE GOT ZERO COMPLAINTS.
YEAH, THAT'S WHAT YOU SAY NOW.
LET'S SEE HOW YOU FEEL AFTER A COUPLE MORE WEEKS OF BABYSITTING EVERYONE.

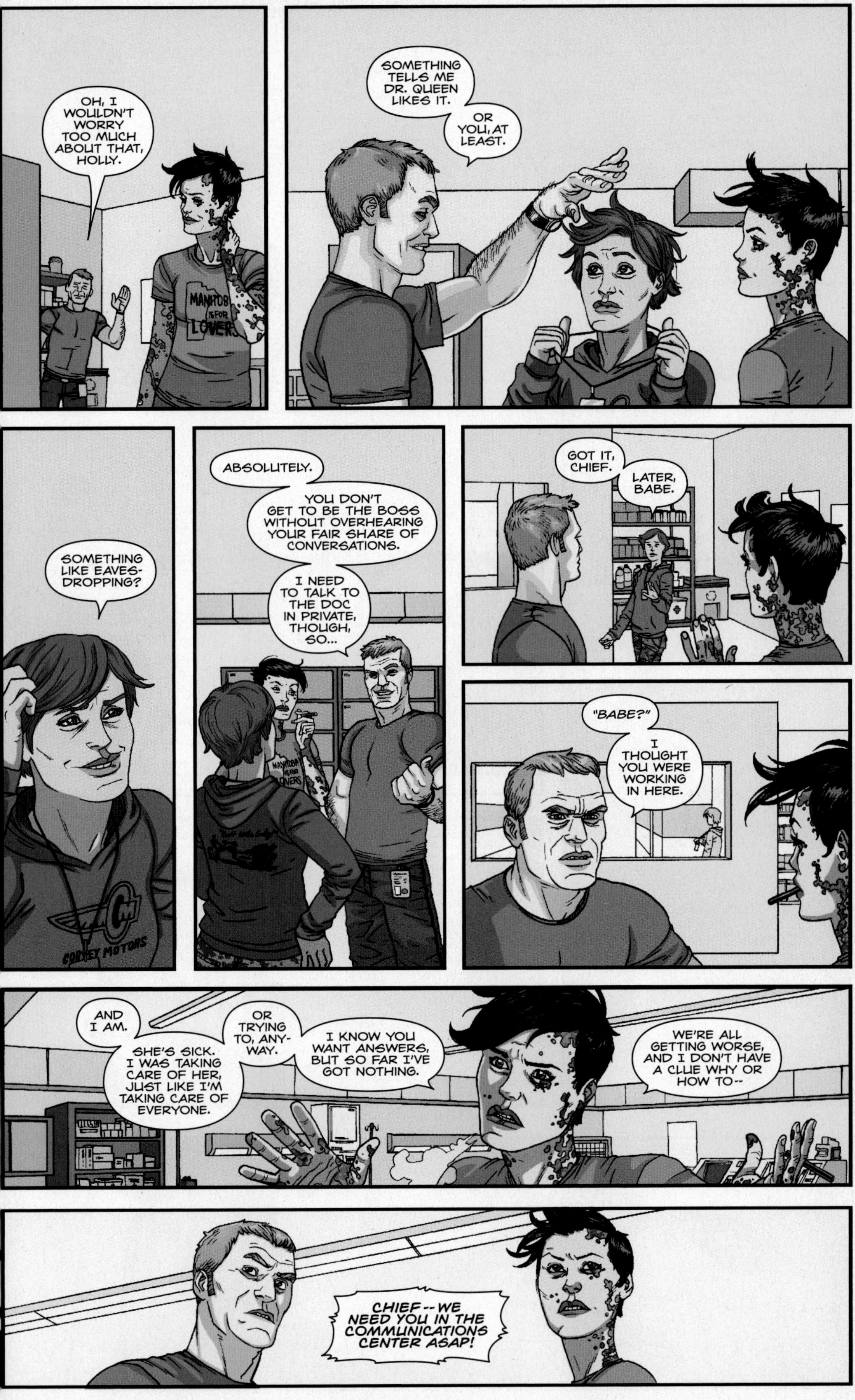
OH, I WOULDN'T WORRY TOO MUCH ABOUT THAT, HOLLY.
MANITOBA IS FOR LOVERS
SOMETHING TELLS ME DR. QUEEN LIKES IT.
OR YOU, AT LEAST.
SOMETHING LIKE EAVES-DROPPING?
ABSOLUTELY.
YOU DON'T GET TO BE THE BOSS WITHOUT OVERHEARING YOUR FAIR SHARE OF CONVERSATIONS.
I NEED TO TALK TO THE DOC IN PRIVATE, THOUGH, SO...
GOT IT, CHIEF.
LATER, BABE.
"BABE?"
I THOUGHT YOU WERE WORKING IN HERE.
AND I AM.
SHE'S SICK. I WAS TAKING CARE OF HER, JUST LIKE I'M TAKING CARE OF EVERYONE.
OR TRYING TO, ANY-WAY.
I KNOW YOU WANT ANSWERS, BUT SO FAR I'VE GOT NOTHING.
WE'RE ALL GETTING WORSE, AND I DON'T HAVE A CLUE WHY OR HOW TO--
CHIEF--WE NEED YOU IN THE COMMUNICATIONS CENTER ASAP!

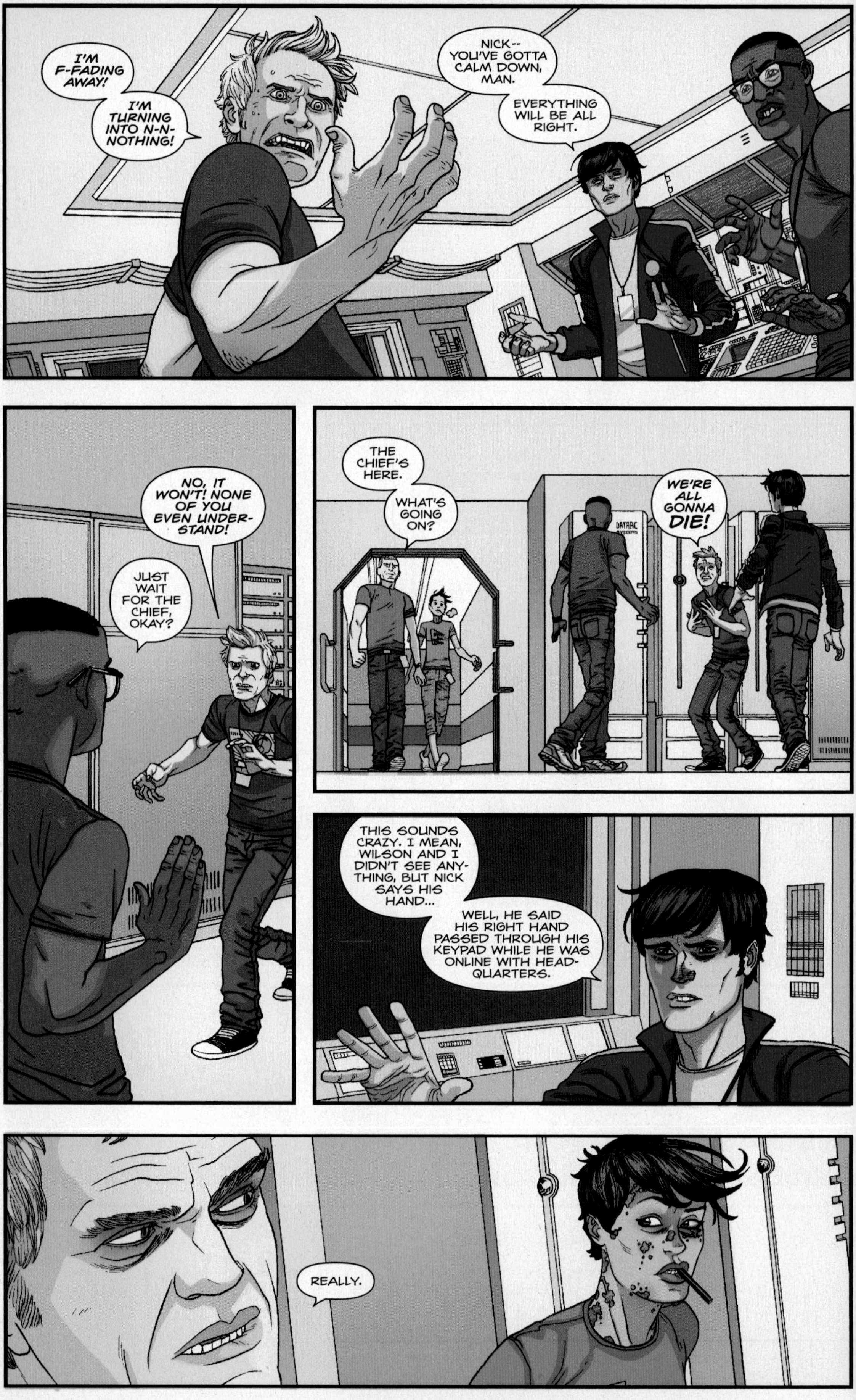
I'M F-FADING AWAY!
I'M TURNING INTO N-N-NOTHING!
NICK-- YOU'VE GOTTA CALM DOWN, MAN.
EVERYTHING WILL BE ALL RIGHT.
NO, IT WON'T! NONE OF YOU EVEN UNDERSTAND!
JUST WAIT FOR THE CHIEF, OKAY?
THE CHIEF'S HERE.
WHAT'S GOING ON?
WE'RE ALL GONNA DIE!
DATAAC SYSTEMS
THIS SOUNDS CRAZY. I MEAN, WILSON AND I DIDN'T SEE ANYTHING, BUT NICK SAYS HIS HAND...
WELL, HE SAID HIS RIGHT HAND PASSED THROUGH HIS KEYPAD WHILE HE WAS ONLINE WITH HEADQUARTERS.
REALLY.

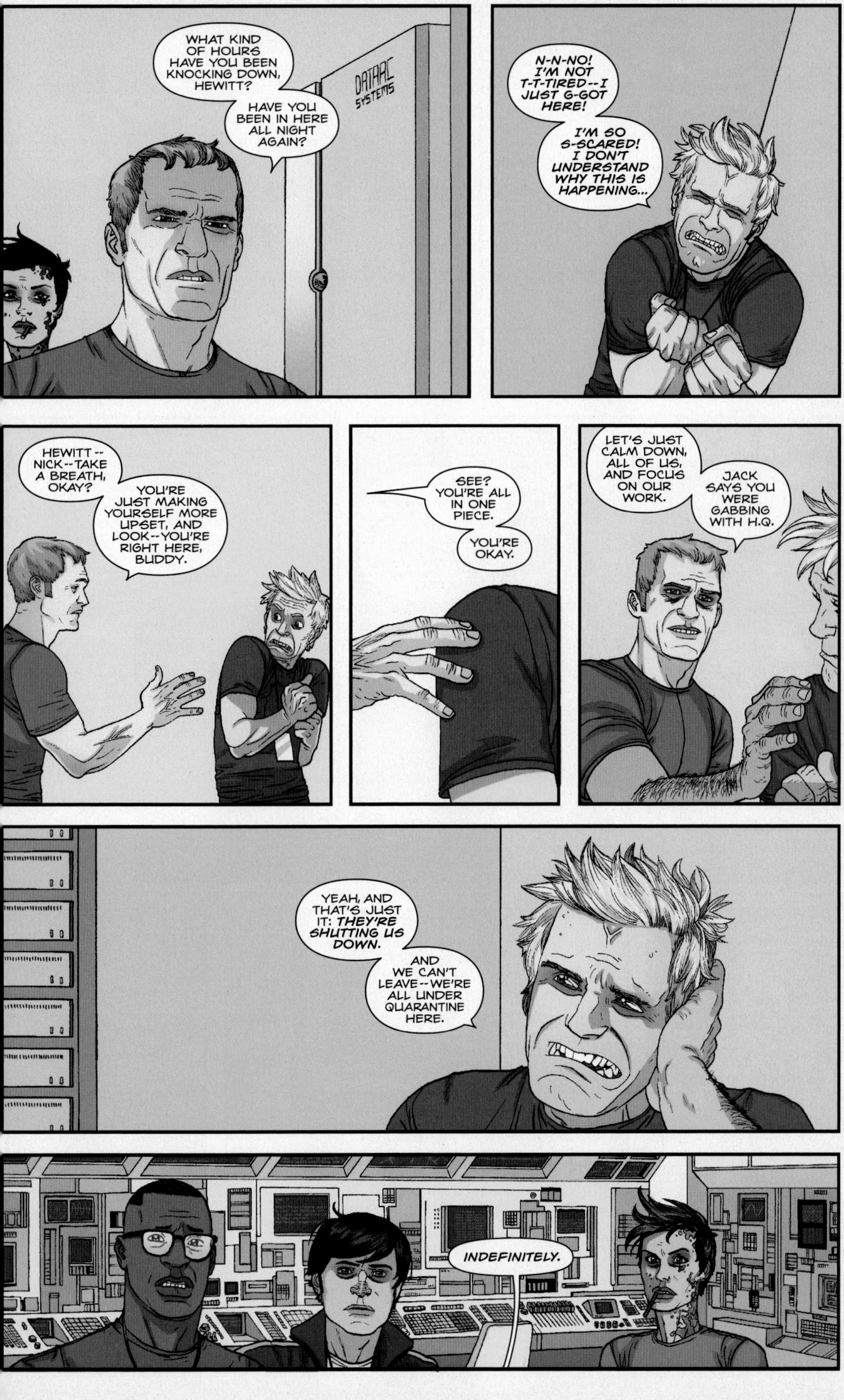
WHAT KIND OF HOURS HAVE YOU BEEN KNOCKING DOWN, HEWITT?
HAVE YOU BEEN IN HERE ALL NIGHT AGAIN?
DATARC SYSTEMS
N-N-NO! I'M NOT T-T-TIRED--I JUST G-GOT HERE!
I'M SO S-SCARED! I DON'T UNDERSTAND WHY THIS IS HAPPENING...
HEWITT-- NICK--TAKE A BREATH, OKAY?
YOU'RE JUST MAKING YOURSELF MORE UPSET, AND LOOK--YOU'RE RIGHT HERE, BUDDY.
SEE? YOU'RE ALL IN ONE PIECE.
YOU'RE OKAY.
LET'S JUST CALM DOWN, ALL OF US, AND FOCUS ON OUR WORK.
JACK SAYS YOU WERE GABBING WITH H.Q.
YEAH, AND THAT'S JUST IT: THEY'RE SHUTTING US DOWN.
AND WE CAN'T LEAVE--WE'RE ALL UNDER QUARANTINE HERE.
INDEFINITELY.

COME ON, KURT, TRY TO EAT A LITTLE MORE OF THIS.

AS SICK AS YOU ARE, THERE'S NO SENSE IN...

I'M SORRY, I COMPLETELY BLANKED.

THIS FEVER IS MAKING IT IMPOSSIBLE FOR ME TO FOCUS.

WHAT WAS I SAYING?

YOU'RE JUST TRYING TO GET ME TO EAT -- NO BIGGIE.

YOU KEEP FUSSING OVER ME, BUT YOU NEED TO TAKE CARE OF YOURSELF, ADRA.

I KNOW I LOOK LIKE I'VE BEEN TURNED INSIDE OUT AND I'M ABOUT AS USE-FUL AS A BUCKET OF WATER ON A RAINY DAY, BUT I ACTUALLY FEEL FINE.

WELL... GOOD.

I WAS TALKING TO HOLLY EARLIER AND SHE SAID SUSAN THINKS THIS VIRUS IS NON-LETHAL, SO I THINK WE'RE GOING TO BE OKAY IN THE LONG RUN.

IT'S JUST... LOOKING LIKE YOU DO -- IT'S HARD NOT TO WORRY THAT YOU MIGHT --

YEAH, I GOTCHA. AND I AM A MESS.

IT'S FUNNY, THOUGH, DYING ISN'T EVEN SOME-THING THAT'S CROSSED MY MIND.

MOSTLY, I JUST DON'T WANT CYNTHIA TO SEE ME LIKE THIS.

AND WHAT WOULD THE KIDS THINK, YOU KNOW?

me

no me soon!

I LOVE YOU DADDY

THAT THEIR SUPER-AWESOME DAD IS ONE OF THE BRAVEST GUYS EVER?

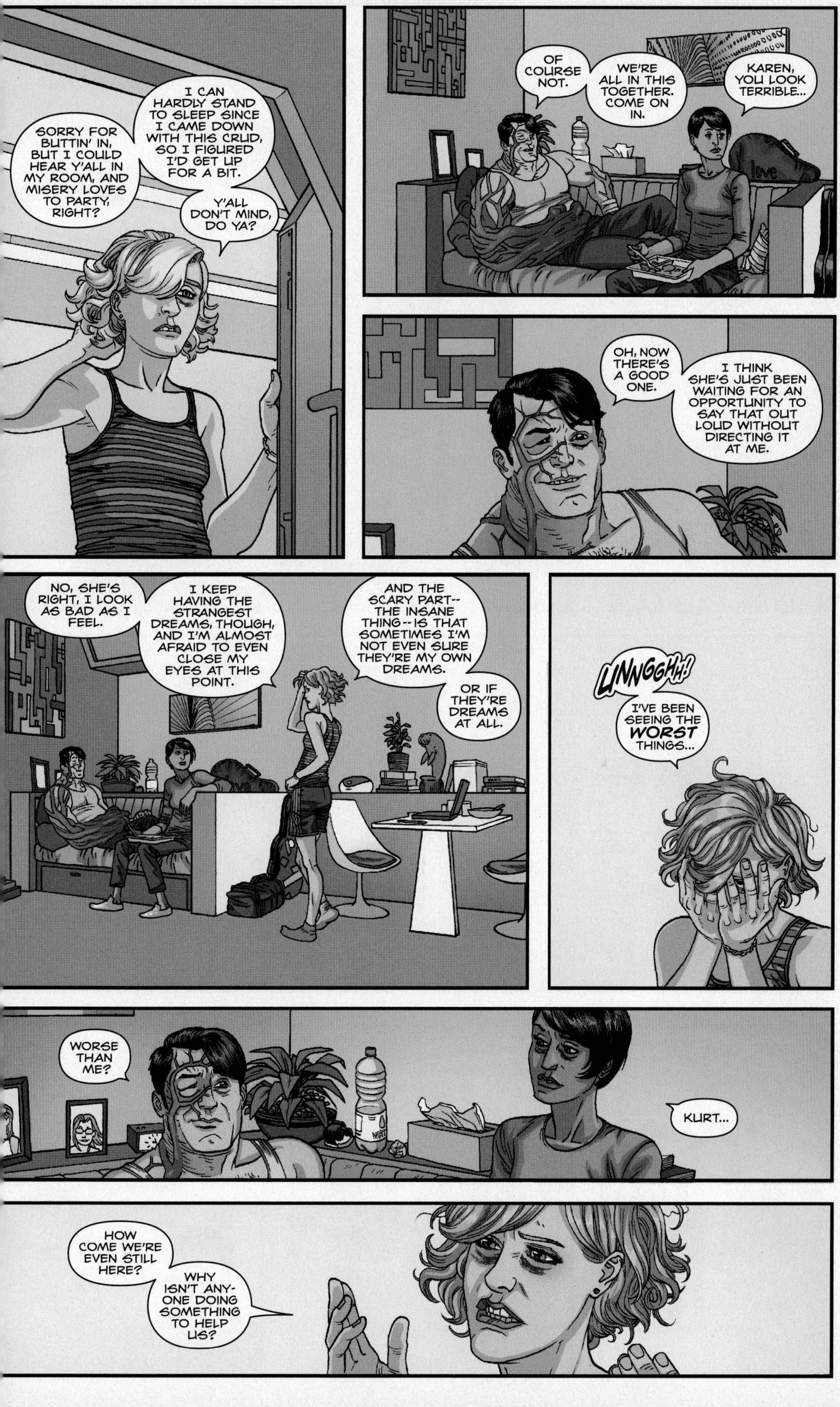
SORRY FOR BUTTIN' IN, BUT I COULD HEAR Y'ALL IN MY ROOM, AND MISERY LOVES TO PARTY, RIGHT?
I CAN HARDLY STAND TO SLEEP SINCE I CAME DOWN WITH THIS CRUD, SO I FIGURED I'D GET UP FOR A BIT.
Y'ALL DON'T MIND, DO YA?
OF COURSE NOT.
WE'RE ALL IN THIS TOGETHER. COME ON IN.
KAREN, YOU LOOK TERRIBLE...
OH, NOW THERE'S A GOOD ONE.
I THINK SHE'S JUST BEEN WAITING FOR AN OPPORTUNITY TO SAY THAT OUT LOUD WITHOUT DIRECTING IT AT ME.
NO, SHE'S RIGHT, I LOOK AS BAD AS I FEEL.
I KEEP HAVING THE STRANGEST DREAMS, THOUGH, AND I'M ALMOST AFRAID TO EVEN CLOSE MY EYES AT THIS POINT.
AND THE SCARY PART-- THE INSANE THING--IS THAT SOMETIMES I'M NOT EVEN SURE THEY'RE MY OWN DREAMS.
OR IF THEY'RE DREAMS AT ALL.
UNNGGHH!
I'VE BEEN SEEING THE WORST THINGS...
WORSE THAN ME?
KURT...
HOW COME WE'RE EVEN STILL HERE?
WHY ISN'T ANY-ONE DOING SOMETHING TO HELP US?

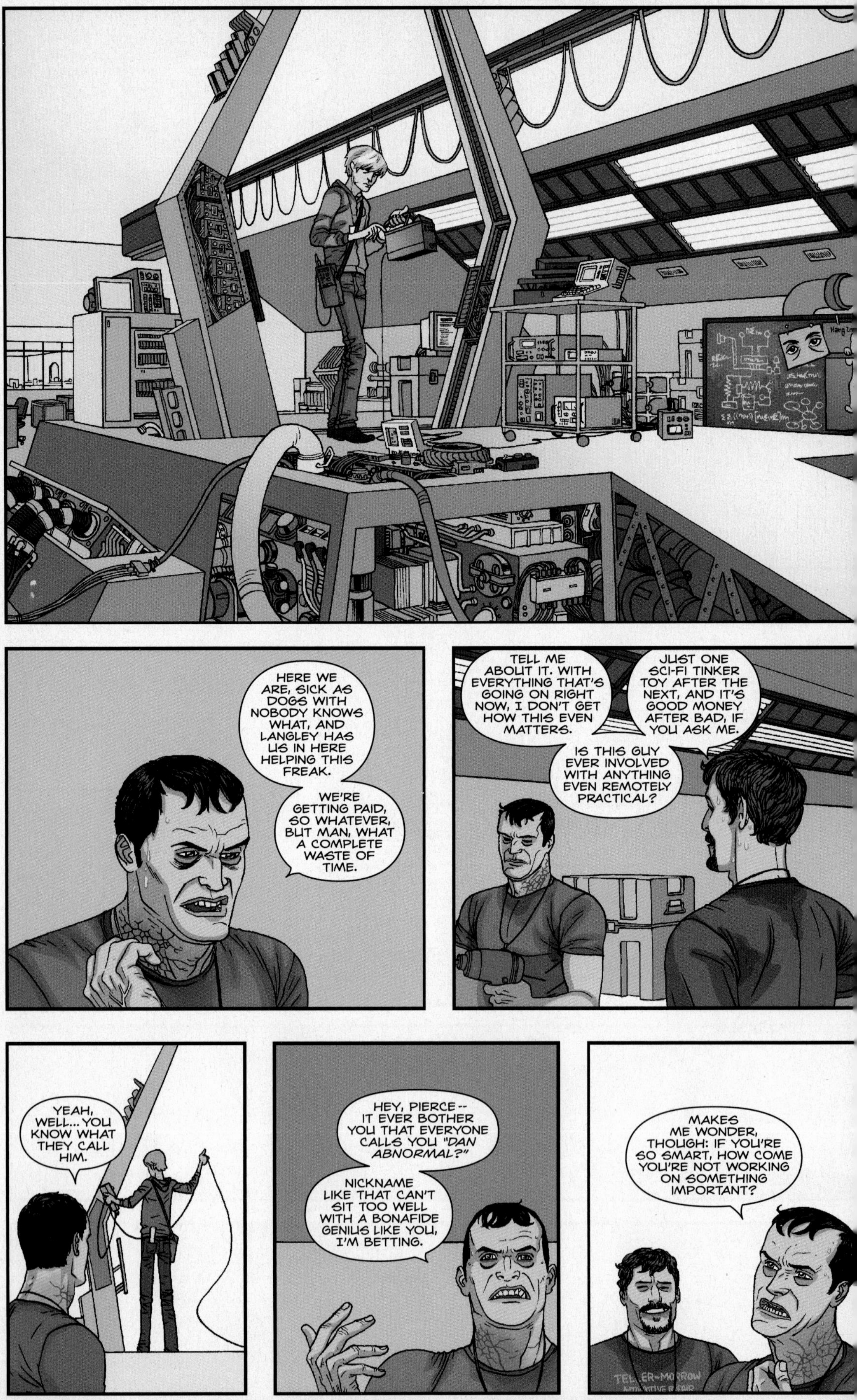
HERE WE ARE, SICK AS DOGS WITH NOBODY KNOWS WHAT, AND LANGLEY HAS US IN HERE HELPING THIS FREAK.
WE'RE GETTING PAID, SO WHATEVER, BUT MAN, WHAT A COMPLETE WASTE OF TIME.
TELL ME ABOUT IT. WITH EVERYTHING THAT'S GOING ON RIGHT NOW, I DON'T GET HOW THIS EVEN MATTERS.
JUST ONE SCI-FI TINKER TOY AFTER THE NEXT, AND IT'S GOOD MONEY AFTER BAD, IF YOU ASK ME.
IS THIS GUY EVER INVOLVED WITH ANYTHING EVEN REMOTELY PRACTICAL?
YEAH, WELL... YOU KNOW WHAT THEY CALL HIM.
HEY, PIERCE -- IT EVER BOTHER YOU THAT EVERYONE CALLS YOU *"DAN ABNORMAL?"*
NICKNAME LIKE THAT CAN'T SIT TOO WELL WITH A BONAFIDE GENIUS LIKE YOU, I'M BETTING.
MAKES ME WONDER, THOUGH: IF YOU'RE SO SMART, HOW COME YOU'RE NOT WORKING ON SOMETHING IMPORTANT?

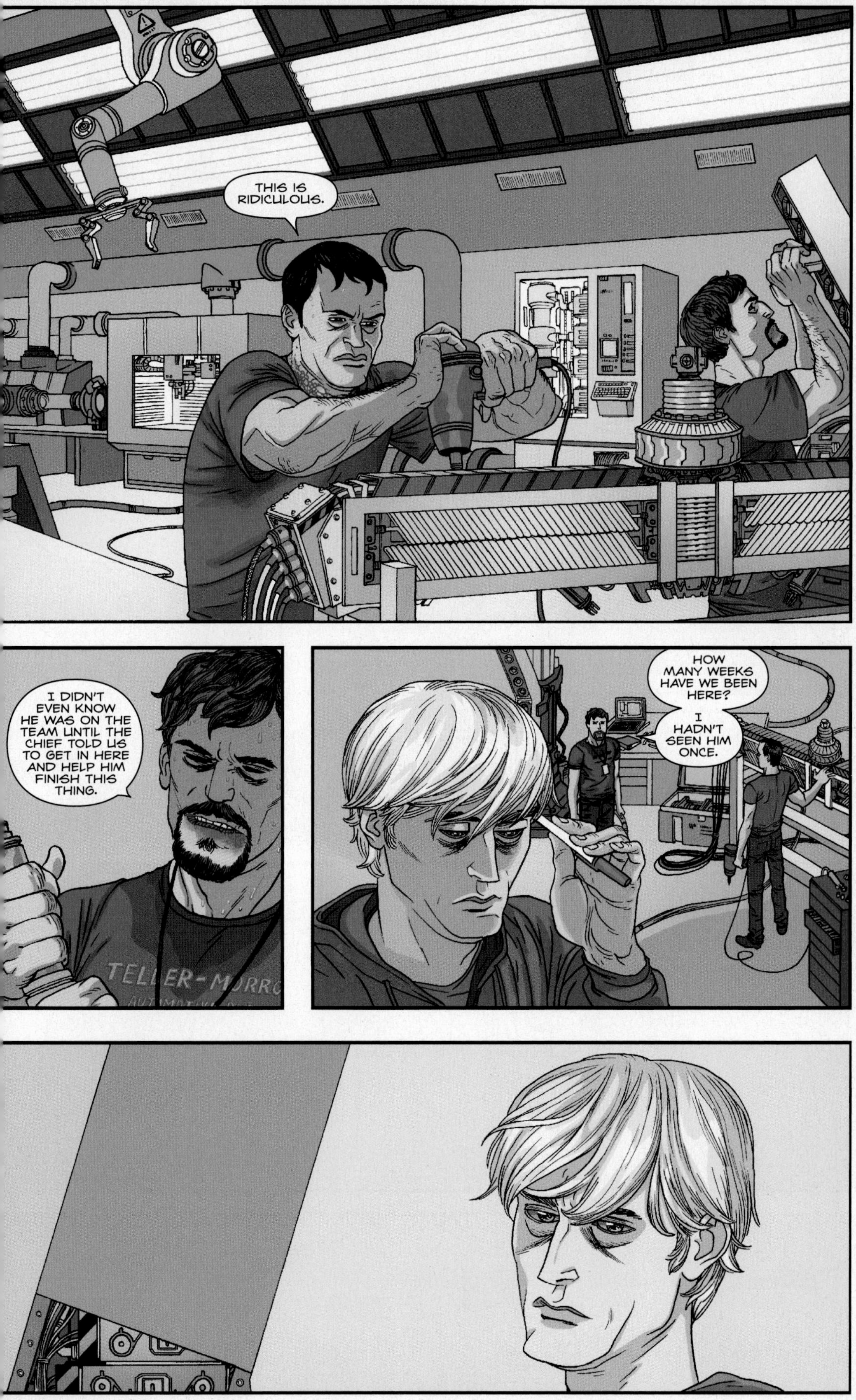
THIS IS RIDICULOUS.
I DIDN'T EVEN KNOW HE WAS ON THE TEAM UNTIL THE CHIEF TOLD US TO GET IN HERE AND HELP HIM FINISH THIS THING.
TELLER-MORRO
HOW MANY WEEKS HAVE WE BEEN HERE?
I HADN'T SEEN HIM ONCE.

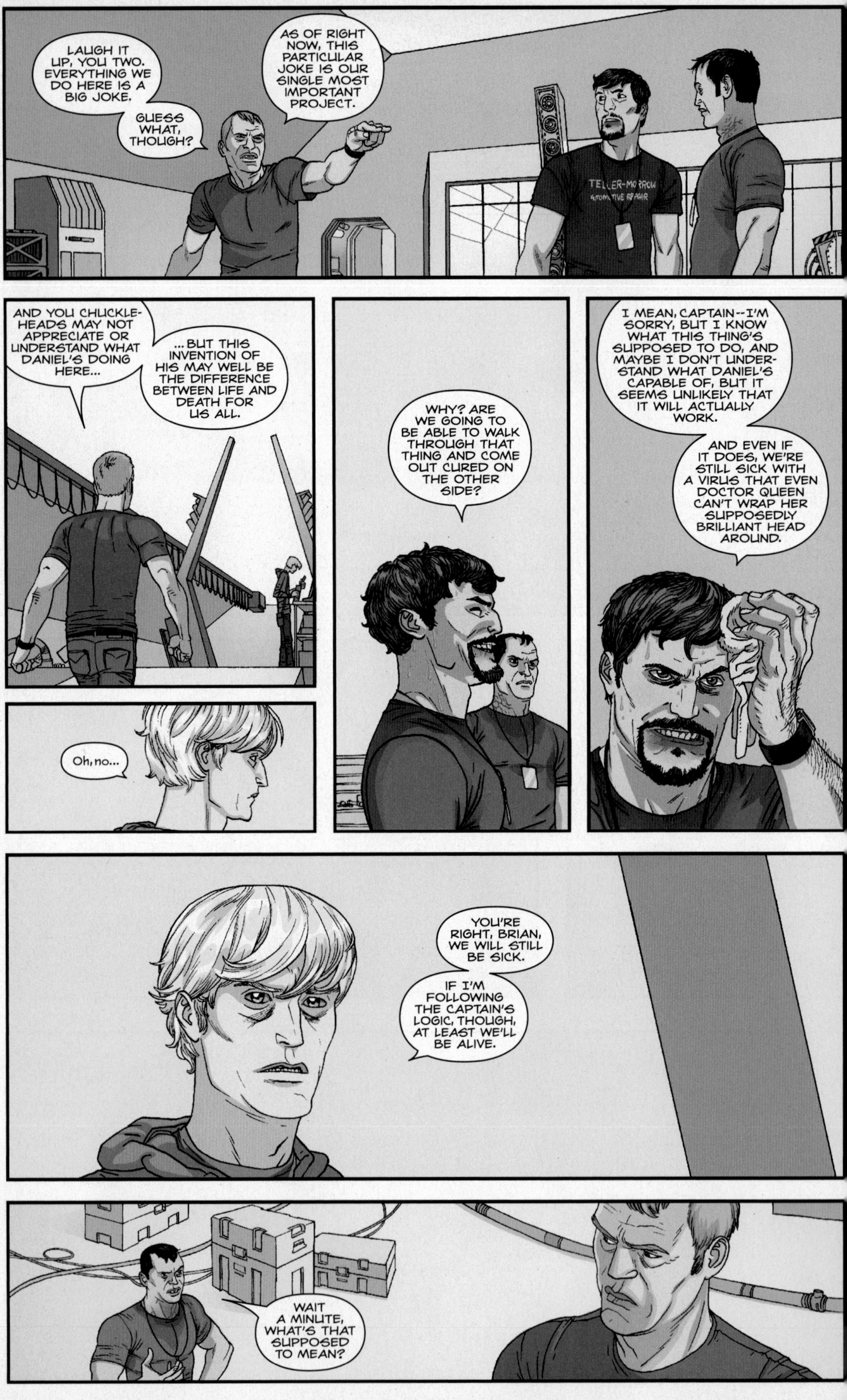
LAUGH IT UP, YOU TWO. EVERYTHING WE DO HERE IS A BIG JOKE.
GUESS WHAT, THOUGH?
AS OF RIGHT NOW, THIS PARTICULAR JOKE IS OUR SINGLE MOST IMPORTANT PROJECT.
TELLER-MORROW AUTOMOTIVE REPAIR
AND YOU CHUCKLE-HEADS MAY NOT APPRECIATE OR UNDERSTAND WHAT DANIEL'S DOING HERE...
...BUT THIS INVENTION OF HIS MAY WELL BE THE DIFFERENCE BETWEEN LIFE AND DEATH FOR US ALL.
Oh, no...
WHY? ARE WE GOING TO BE ABLE TO WALK THROUGH THAT THING AND COME OUT CURED ON THE OTHER SIDE?
I MEAN, CAPTAIN--I'M SORRY, BUT I KNOW WHAT THIS THING'S SUPPOSED TO DO, AND MAYBE I DON'T UNDERSTAND WHAT DANIEL'S CAPABLE OF, BUT IT SEEMS UNLIKELY THAT IT WILL ACTUALLY WORK.
AND EVEN IF IT DOES, WE'RE STILL SICK WITH A VIRUS THAT EVEN DOCTOR QUEEN CAN'T WRAP HER SUPPOSEDLY BRILLIANT HEAD AROUND.
YOU'RE RIGHT, BRIAN, WE WILL STILL BE SICK.
IF I'M FOLLOWING THE CAPTAIN'S LOGIC, THOUGH, AT LEAST WE'LL BE ALIVE.
WAIT A MINUTE, WHAT'S THAT SUPPOSED TO MEAN?

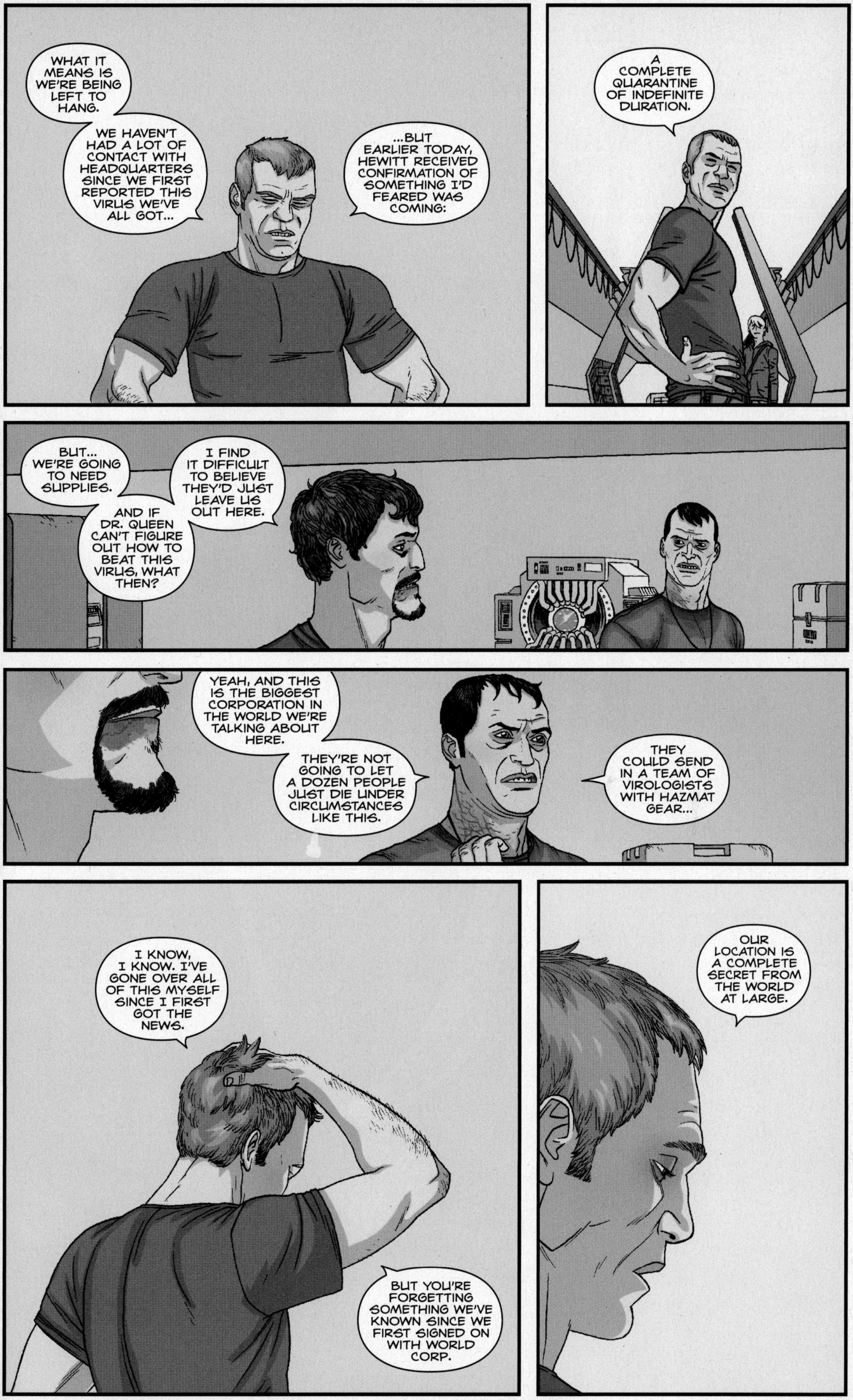
WHAT IT MEANS IS WE'RE BEING LEFT TO HANG.
WE HAVEN'T HAD A LOT OF CONTACT WITH HEADQUARTERS SINCE WE FIRST REPORTED THIS VIRUS WE'VE ALL GOT...
...BUT EARLIER TODAY, HEWITT RECEIVED CONFIRMATION OF SOMETHING I'D FEARED WAS COMING:
A COMPLETE QUARANTINE OF INDEFINITE DURATION.
BUT... WE'RE GOING TO NEED SUPPLIES.
AND IF DR. QUEEN CAN'T FIGURE OUT HOW TO BEAT THIS VIRUS, WHAT THEN?
I FIND IT DIFFICULT TO BELIEVE THEY'D JUST LEAVE US OUT HERE.
YEAH, AND THIS IS THE BIGGEST CORPORATION IN THE WORLD WE'RE TALKING ABOUT HERE.
THEY'RE NOT GOING TO LET A DOZEN PEOPLE JUST DIE UNDER CIRCUMSTANCES LIKE THIS.
THEY COULD SEND IN A TEAM OF VIROLOGISTS WITH HAZMAT GEAR...
I KNOW, I KNOW. I'VE GONE OVER ALL OF THIS MYSELF SINCE I FIRST GOT THE NEWS.
BUT YOU'RE FORGETTING SOMETHING WE'VE KNOWN SINCE WE FIRST SIGNED ON WITH WORLD CORP.
OUR LOCATION IS A COMPLETE SECRET FROM THE WORLD AT LARGE.

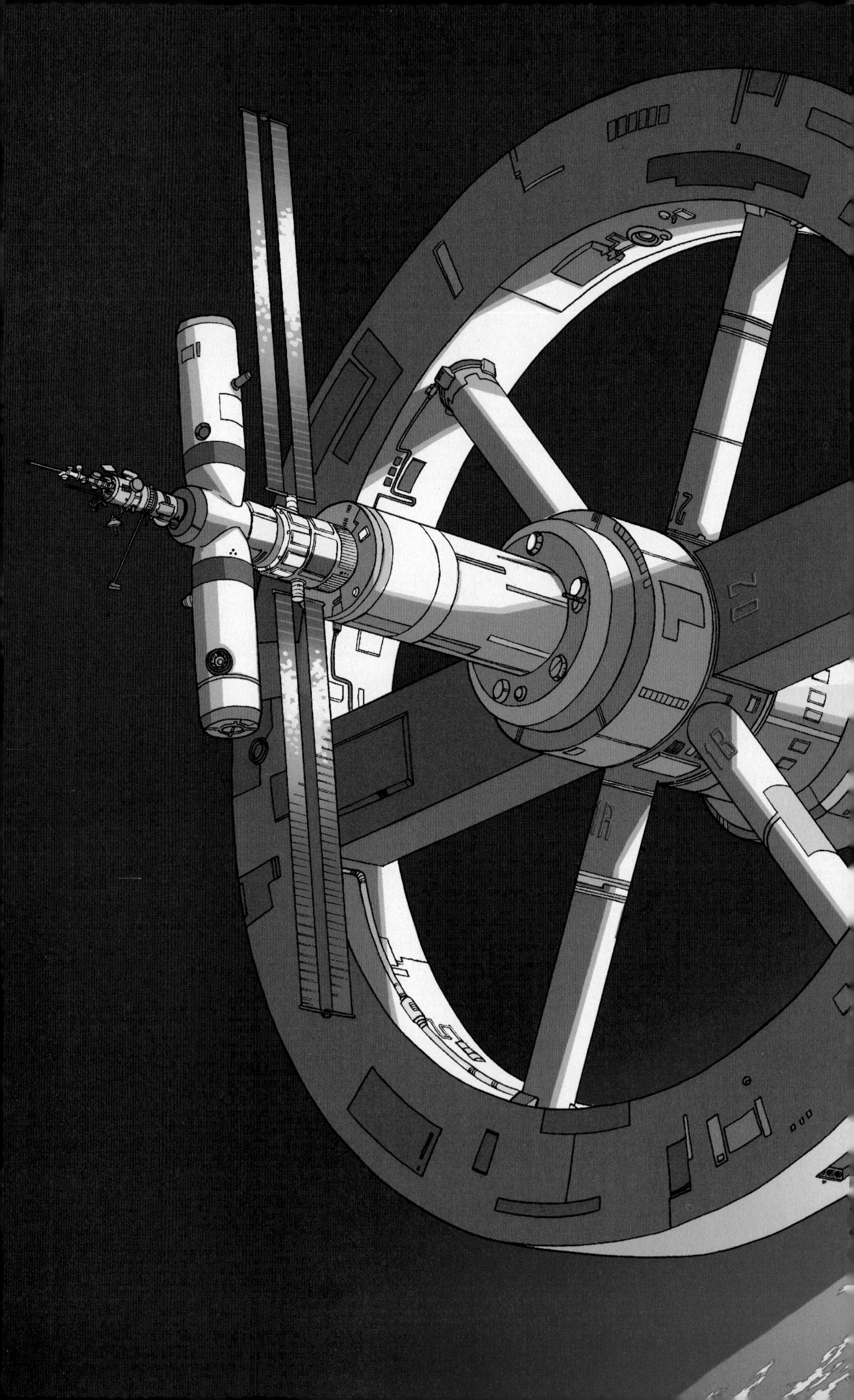

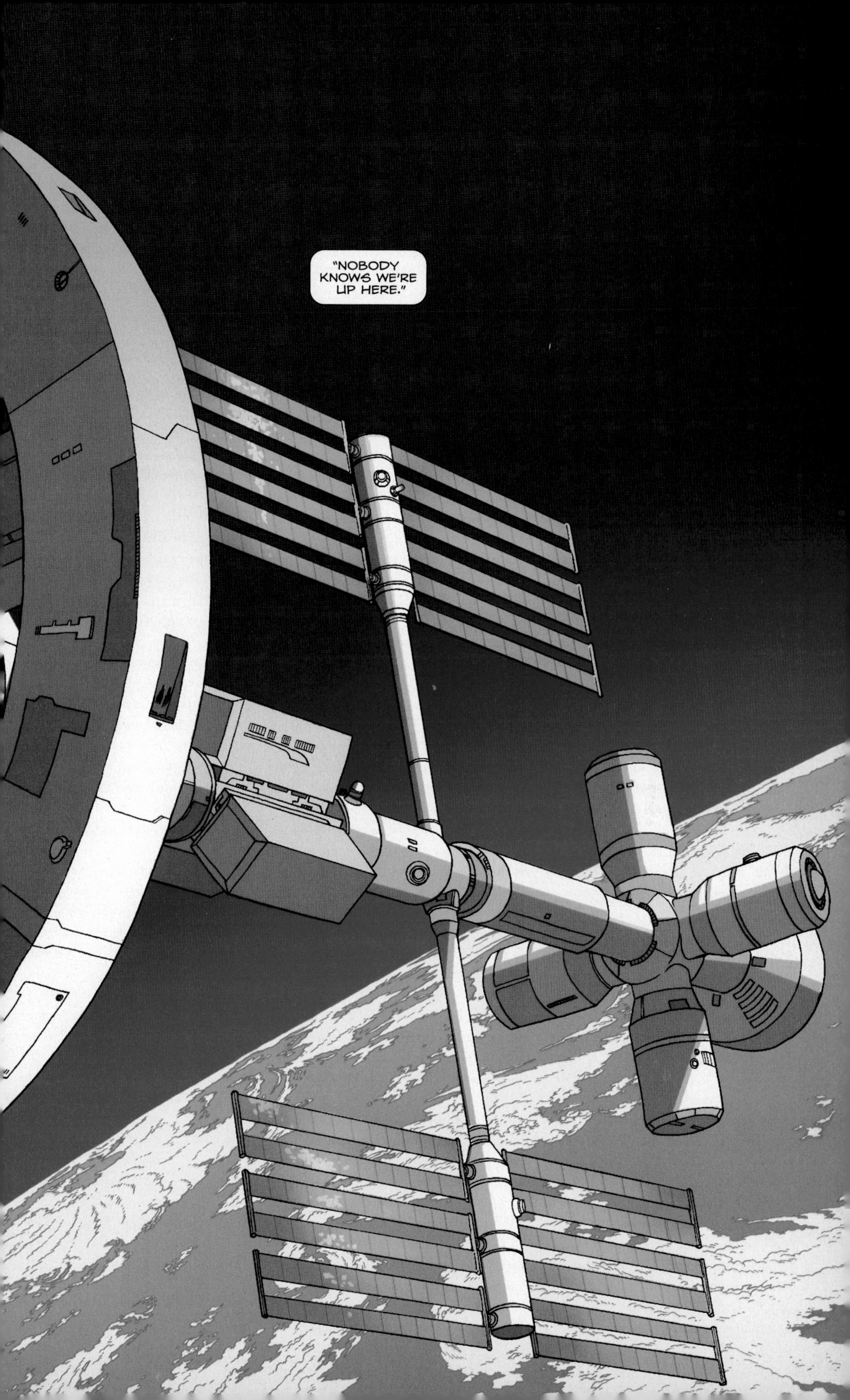
"NOBODY KNOWS WE'RE UP HERE."

WALKING IN THE SPIDERWEBS

the science chronicle interview THOMAS WALKER

It has long been suggested that Thomas Walker has always been something of an enigma, even to those who know him best, and that the qualities that so befuddle those around him are in fact the very same qualities that have made him one of the leading lights in theoretical astrophysics. It's certainly an interesting—not to mention entertaining—notion, but on the basis of current evidence, it's difficult to fathom how that might work in practice.

Walker was in town last week and though notoriously press-shy, he agreed to his first interview since leaving World Corp. amid a flurry of speculation. There has been talk of a falling out with his famous partners, specifically of a rift between himself and Dade Ellis, the man many view as the company's heart and soul. It has been said he has suffered severe psychological damage as the result of his long-rumored drug use. There are stories, too, that his focus on theory and research put him distinctly at odds with World Corp.'s increasing cachet as a producer of life-changing consumer products.

His appearance is quite different at this point, his hair shorn closer to the head than in years past, perhaps symbolic of his break with the company he refers to time and again as his "old group." He is also somewhat haggard, the apparent result of lack of sleep in the service of an unwavering commitment to meditation, and his frequently non-linear conversation is at times difficult to follow. One moment he seems thoughtful and alert, the next it's hard to tell if he's there at all...

TSC: *Of all the World Corp. founders, you are notoriously difficult to pin down for interviews. Do you have a particular aversion to the press?*

WALKER: *Interviews are more Simon's thing. Simon diamond. Diamond geezer. Simon says. It's helpful to have that kind of outlook for that kind of work. I have... other work.*

TSC: *Of course. I imagine you're quite busy.*

WALKER: *My own work is quite involved. There are many wheels to turn, and I've got a gaping hole in my head that needs to be filled... You know, with knowledge, and there's only so much time in each waking day. It's a lot of pressure. This interview is a lot of pressure.*

TSC: *Then why did you agree to it?*

WALKER: *That's the question, isn't it?*

TSC: *At the moment, yes. Do you have an answer?*

WALKER: *I think answers become apparent when you open your mind and listen. Different moments tell you different things. You have to be ready for it.*

TSC: *Does it perhaps have anything to do with your recent decision to step down from the board of directors at World Corp.? You're obviously at somewhat of a crossroads in your career at this point.*

WALKER: *My entire life is a crossroads. I mean, really... my entire life is a web. All ours lives are a living tapestry of webworks that we weave, one delicate strand at a time. One day, we climb this strand. Tomorrow we shimmy down another. Sometimes the strands intersect. We're all working away on our different webs, but often when they overlap, magical things happen. That's how my old group got started, but then they decided to cut some of the strands and here we are.*

TSC: *Are you saying it wasn't your decision to resign from the board?*

WALKER: *Decisions are made at a much higher level. You would have to climb up through a lot of webs to get to the heart of it, I think.*

TSC: *World Corp. issued a statement that you'd resigned from the board and would no longer be a part of the company's day-to-day business, though.*

WALKER: *I am resigned, very much so.*

TSC: *There are rumors there was tension between you and the other founders...*

WALKER: *Rumors are simple to weave. There wasn't really a battle of any kind. Just a matter of webs getting all tangled. I don't think World Corp. had any real trouble, but I had a difficult time adjusting as the others spun their webs. Perhaps you could say I created some of that difficulty myself, having visions and doing my own work. I don't know.*

TSC: *Can you tell me about these visions?*

WALKER: *I've been expanding my experience through meditation. I have learned to open my third eye and I can see and feel things on a different level. There are things we can't see with our physical eyes.*

TSC: *Can you give me an example?*

WALKER: *Well, after meditating a bit, I found I would awake in the middle of the night and see things I wasn't aware of before. The most startling discovery was all the webs. There were webs everywhere, all above my bed, and the first time I saw them, it was an awful scene. There were spider everywhere, skittering back and forth, spir ning their webs, climbing their strands. was so startled, I rolled out of bed and ont the floor, desperate for the light switch. was so shaken by the experience I had to ge out of my room and into the streets, becaus I didn't realize the true nature of the web yet.*

TSC: *Did you tell the others?*

WALKER: *I just dry-heaved in front of remarkably beautiful woman. We shared moment. One hopes she understood.*

TSC: *I'm not entirely sure I understand...*

WALKER: *I can't explain then. This med tation thing is making me a genius an a little bit insane. I close my eyes to try t sleep, but over time, I have developed th ability to see like a bat! Every sound boun es off nearby objects and creates a visua impression in the shape of what it is! I ca close my eyes and be very aware of what around me. I know this sounds crazy, bu it makes it impossible to sleep since I can turn it off. There are times I think perhap I should quit meditating for a bit, but it changed everything for me.*

TSC: *Did that change make your partner feel trepidation around you?*

WALKER: *Not everybody is ready for thi level of enlightenment.*

TSC: *Did it affect your role within the ove all structure of the company?*

WALKER: *Some might say. I don't know. only know that from my point of view, have always been the psychic equalizer.*

TSC: *There have been stories in the pres that some of your recent behavior is th result of excessive drug use, that you hav been taking acid trips in the name experimentation.*

WALKER: *I'm sure some people are chatte ing just to make themselves feel important*

TSC: *Are you saying you haven't taken aci then?*

WALKER: *Obviously, one does things tha pertain to one's work. I won't deny I was young person and as a member of a gener tion of switched-on young people, I thin I adopted a philosophy that allowed me t expand my boundaries. Not everyone wa so lucky, but I put my experiences to work.*

TSC: *You're a scientist. Your mind is you greatest tool. Don't you think drug use any kind is risky?*

WALKER: *You see risk. I see opportunity. A I had to do was open my mind to the po sibilities. It seemed like great fun to ent* his other world. It was something I hadn't explored before. It's the longest I've ever committed myself to this kind of work.

TSC: I want to talk a bit about the early days of World Corp. Dade Ellis, one of your former partners in the company, has said in the past he wasn't sure the company would survive more than a few years. Was that a feeling you shared?

WALKER: My memory of that time shifts and changes depending on the moment. Dade is older than I am. He has a degree in architecture. We met under challenging circumstances, but we shared common goals. You could say we were weaving similar webs. He was maybe two or three years older and already making an impact. It was an exciting time, but he was the dowdy one. He gets lost in his moods, one might say. I'm still figuring that out.

TSC: Ellis has also said he finds you rather strange.

WALKER: Strange is older still, but not in a bad way. I have tremendous fun working with him. Smiling Simon has all the words and Dade can always find his way, but Emerson Strange is the one I most admire.

TSC: Actually, what I meant is that Ellis regards you as something of an eccentric.

WALKER: He just doesn't like my bicycle in the hallways.

TSC: You've said before that cycling is part of your work.

WALKER: Yes, very much so.

TSC: Some of your colleagues have suggested it's more disruptive than productive.

WALKER: For them, perhaps. There's also a saying that goes "different spokes for different folks." Some people need to be confrontational. I'm not a troublemaker. I do my work my own way. It's hard to tell why some people react the way they do.

TSC: I think some might question how cycling and astrophysics are related…

WALKER: Yeah, I suppose.

TSC: As a theoretical astrophysicist, your contributions to the study of everything from evolution to dark matter has provided some genuinely thrilling insight into the secrets of the universe. Can you understand how the notion of you riding your bike through the World Corp. offices might be confounding or off-putting to some?

WALKER: I can't explain away anyone's confusion. I can only tell you what works for me. I have my own process as far as my work goes. I find other methods rather unexciting. Uninteresting, at the very least. One thinks of the best way to approach a job and then does it as well as one can. I mount my bike and ask questions. When I finish riding, I have answers, and I find that rather wonderful. Juggling is an interesting technique, as well, and I can also get spectacular results for a good round of pinball.

TSC: Do you think your success went to your head?

WALKER: I think my success went to Simon's head. I don't view any of that as particularly necessary. Simon likes publicity, and once he got involved in my old group he used that to his advantage.

TSC: Wouldn't you say it was to everyone's advantage? World Corp. is one of the most successful companies of all time.

WALKER: I don't have a problem admitting that. I'm proud of the old group and what we have accomplished. We have done some very exciting things. We haven't been restricted by what others think. We did things our own way, we created our scene, and we have done very well as a result. You probably have some of our ideas in your home. Some people have our ideas in their bodies.

TSC: Do you like how ubiquitous World Corp. has become then? At one point, your critics regarded the company's popularity as a fad.

WALKER: Rock and roll had critics who said the same thing and what do they say now?

TSC: Well, you yourself have been quoted on a number of occasions as saying, "Science is the new rock and roll," so wouldn't that suggest the critics were right?

WALKER: I still like rock and roll music, though. I never said it would whither and die or that its influence would fade. I was making an observation about how exciting science can be. That's all, really.

TSC: A great many people took that observation to heart, though. You must be aware that it's become a slogan—a rallying cry, if you will, for a whole underground movement in science…

WALKER: That's very nice, but I don't have any control over slogans. One could just as easily say, "violence is the new black," and put that on a t-shirt, but it doesn't have much to do with anything. It might look terrific on a red shirt, but really, it says nothing about me or my work. I could see something like that coming to pass, but I wouldn't necessarily support that cause.

TSC: What about the people you've inspired through your work? Is that a cause you would support?

WALKER: I suppose so, yeah.

TSC: Have you thought of meeting with any of them, now that you're no longer associated with World Corp.?

WALKER: Well, I haven't given it any thought. You see, I'm very focused on my own work, and none of my visions have indicated that's a strand I should follow. I think they're still building that particular web, and I'm into different things right now, you know?

TSC: I have one last question for you: If science is the new rock and roll, then what's the new science?

WALKER: Oh, that's simple. Understanding.

Dennis Blandon

Rumors are simple to weave. There wasn't really a battle of any kind. Just a matter of webs getting all tangled."

"My entire life is a web. All ours lives are a living tapestry of webworks that we weave, one delicate strand at a time."

"There's a saying that goes 'different spokes for different folks.' Some people need to be confrontational. I'm not a troublemaker."

PHOTOGRAPHY BY ROGER KEITH

NOWHERE Men™

Volume One // Fates Worse Than Death

Eric Stephenson // Nate Bellegarde // Jordie Bellaire // Fonografiks

Vol.1 // Fates Worse Than Death
collects issues #1-6 $9.99

Creators

Eric Stephenson
Writer

Nate Bellegarde
Artist

Jordie Bellaire
Colorist

Fonografiks
Lettering
& Design

Image Comics, Inc.

Robert Kirkman
Chief Operating Officer

Erik Larsen
Chief Financial Officer

Todd McFarlane
President

Marc Silvestri
Chief Executive Officer

Jim Valentino
Vice-President

Eric Stephenson
Publisher

Corey Murphy
Director of Sales

Jeff Boison
Director of Publishing
Planning & Book Trade
Sales

Jeremy Sullivan
Director of Digital
Sales

Kat Salazar
Director of PR &
Marketing

Emily Miller
Director of Operations

Branwyn Bigglestone
Senior Accounts
Manager

Sarah Mello
Accounts Manager

Drew Gill
Art Director

Jonathan Chan
Production Manager

Meredith Wallace
Print Manager

Briah Skelly
Publicity Assistant

Randy Okamura
Marketing Production
Designer

David Brothers
Branding Manager

Ally Power
Content Manager

Addison Duke
Production Artist

Vincent Kukua
Production Artist

Sasha Head
Production Artist

Tricia Ramos
Production Artist

Jeff Stang
Direct Market Sales
Representative

Emilio Bautista
Digital Sales Associate

Chloe Ramos-Peterson
Admin Assistant

IMAGECOMICS.COM

image

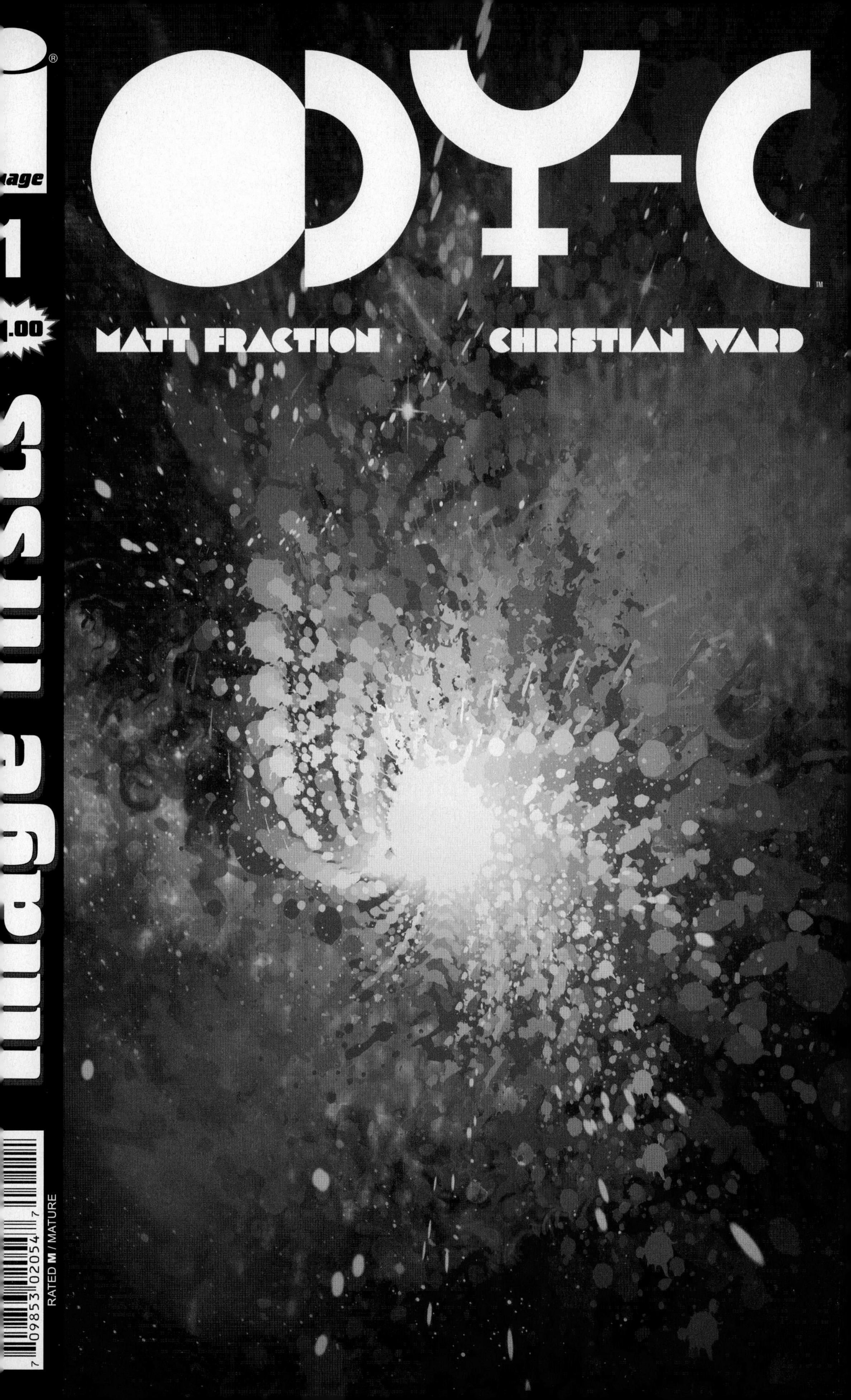
ODY-C
MATT FRACTION
CHRISTIAN WARD
1
image firsts
RATED M / MATURE

STORY **MATT FRACTION**

ART & COLORS **CHRISTIAN WARD**

FLATTING **DEE CUNNIFFE**

LETTERING **CHRIS ELIOPOULOS**

DESIGN **CHRISTIAN WARD & DREW GILL**

EDITOR **LAUREN SANKOVITCH**

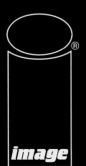

IMAGE COMICS, INC.
Robert Kirkman – Chief Operating Officer
Erik Larsen – Chief Financial Officer
Todd McFarlane – President
Marc Silvestri – Chief Executive Officer
Jim Valentino – Vice-President

Eric Stephenson – Publisher
Corey Murphy – Director of Sales
Jeff Boison – Director of Publishing Planning & Book Trade Sales
Jeremy Sullivan – Director of Digital Sales
Kat Salazar – Director of PR & Marketing
Emily Miller – Director of Operations
Branwyn Bigglestone – Senior Accounts Manager
Sarah Mello – Accounts Manager
Drew Gill – Art Director
Jonathan Chan – Production Manager
Meredith Wallace – Print Manager
Briah Skelly – Publicity Assistant
Randy Okamura – Marketing Production Designer
David Brothers – Branding Manager
Ally Power – Content Manager
Addison Duke – Production Artist
Vincent Kukua – Production Artist
Sasha Head – Production Artist
Tricia Ramos – Production Artist
Jeff Stang – Direct Market Sales Representative
Emilio Bautista – Digital Sales Associate
Chloe Ramos-Peterson – Administrative Assistant
IMAGECOMICS.COM

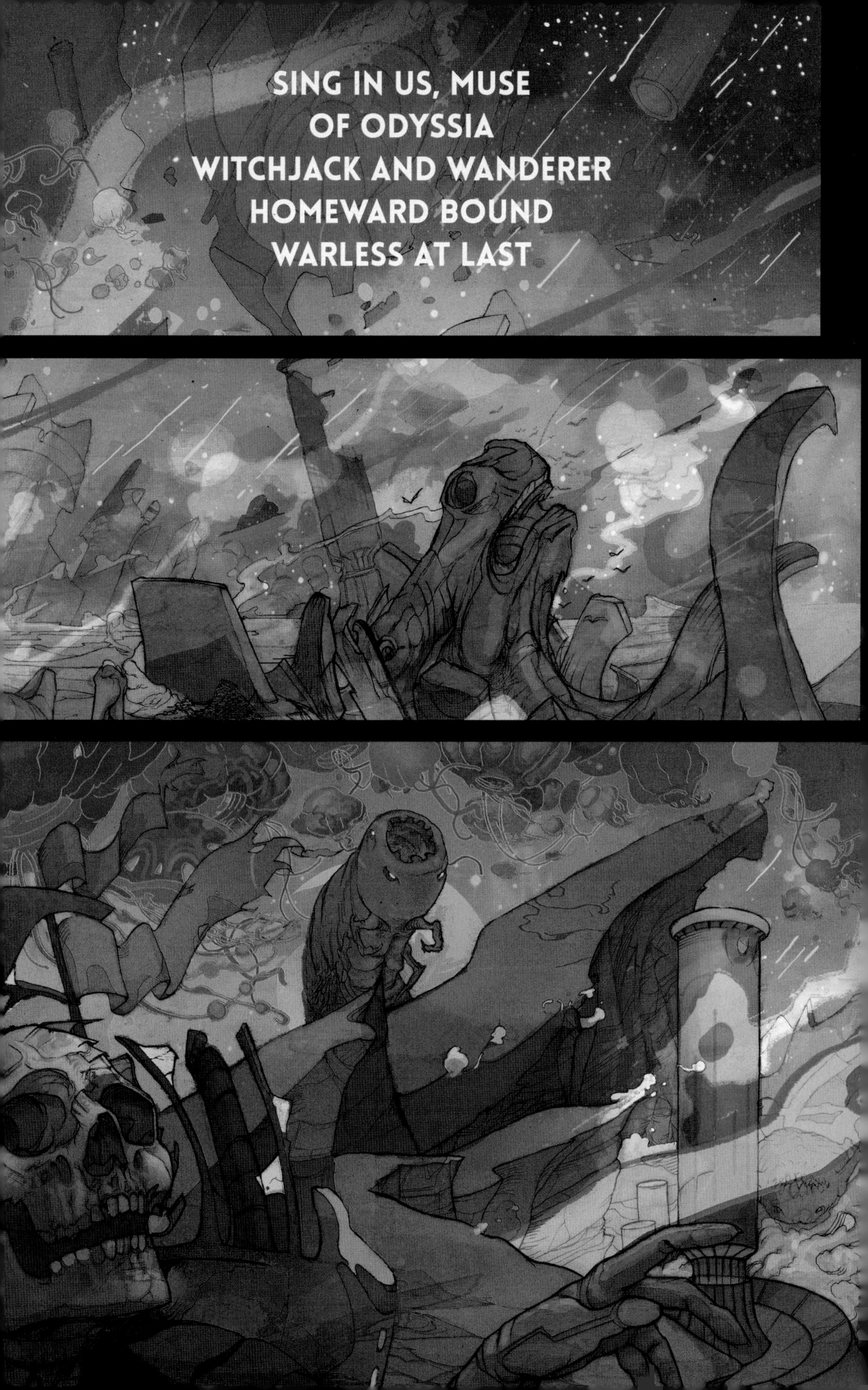
SING IN US, MUSE
OF ODYSSIA
WITCHJACK AND WANDERER
HOMEWARD BOUND
WARLESS AT LAST

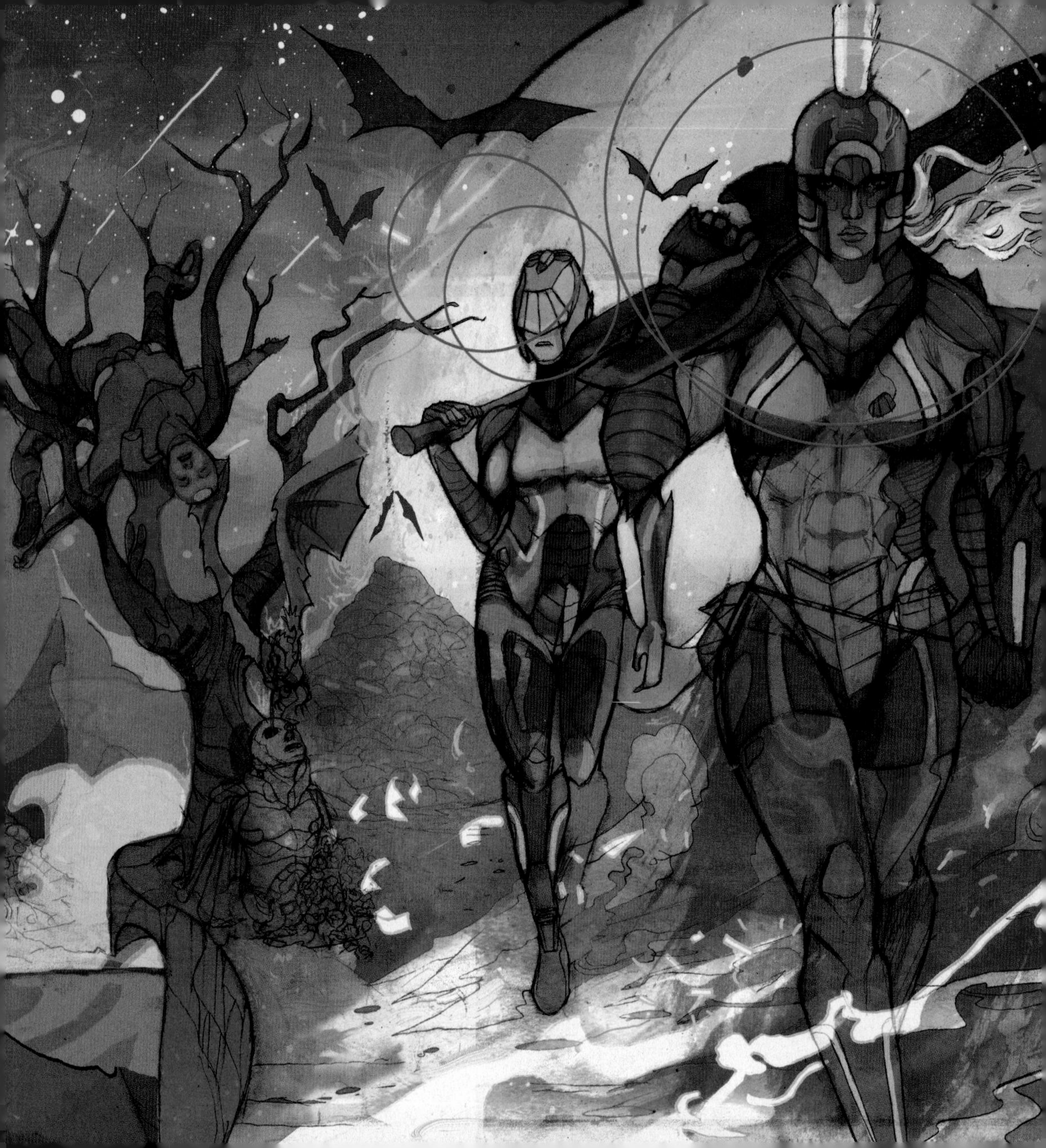

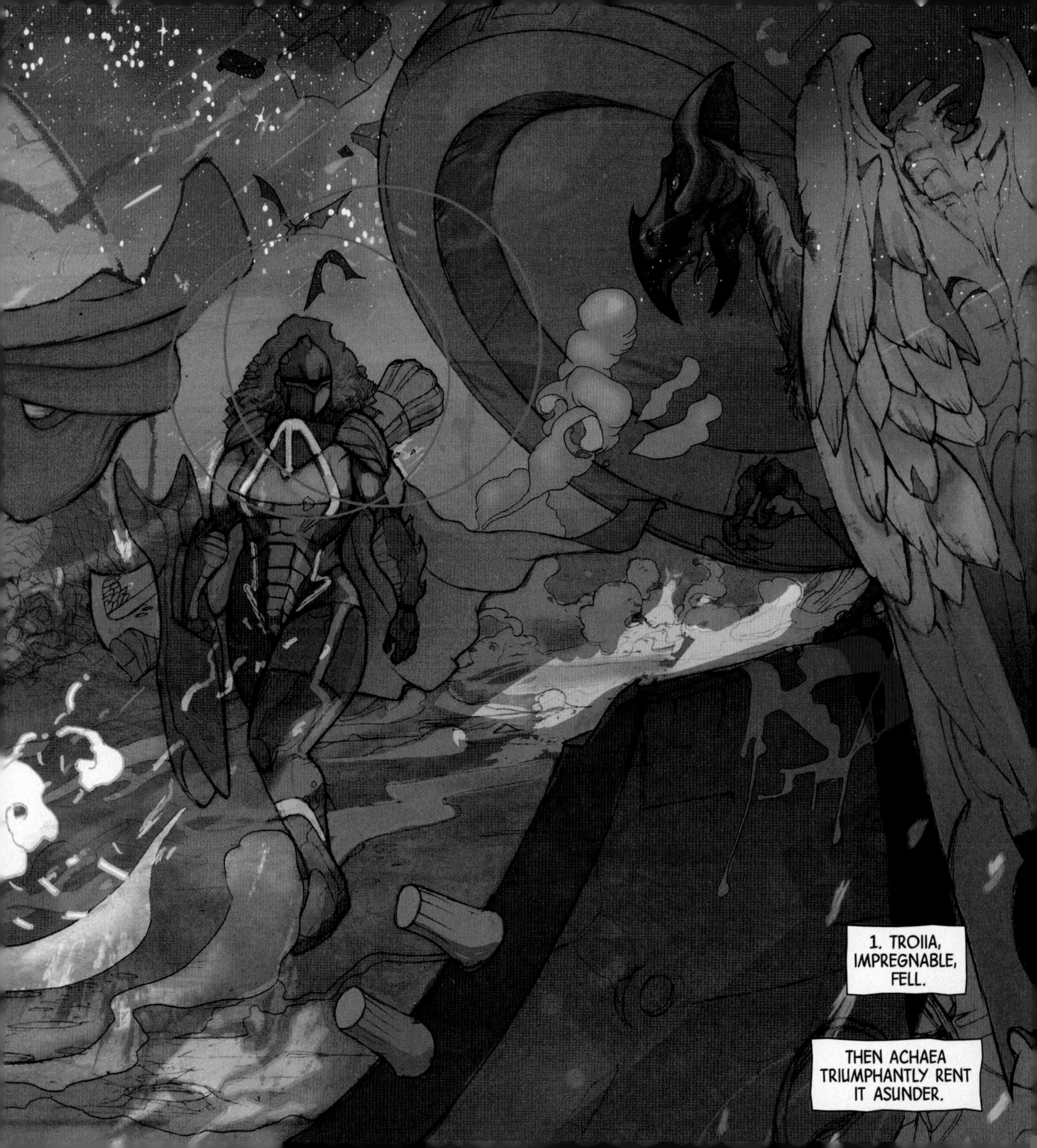
1. TROIIA, IMPREGNABLE, FELL.
THEN ACHAEA TRIUMPHANTLY RENT IT ASUNDER.

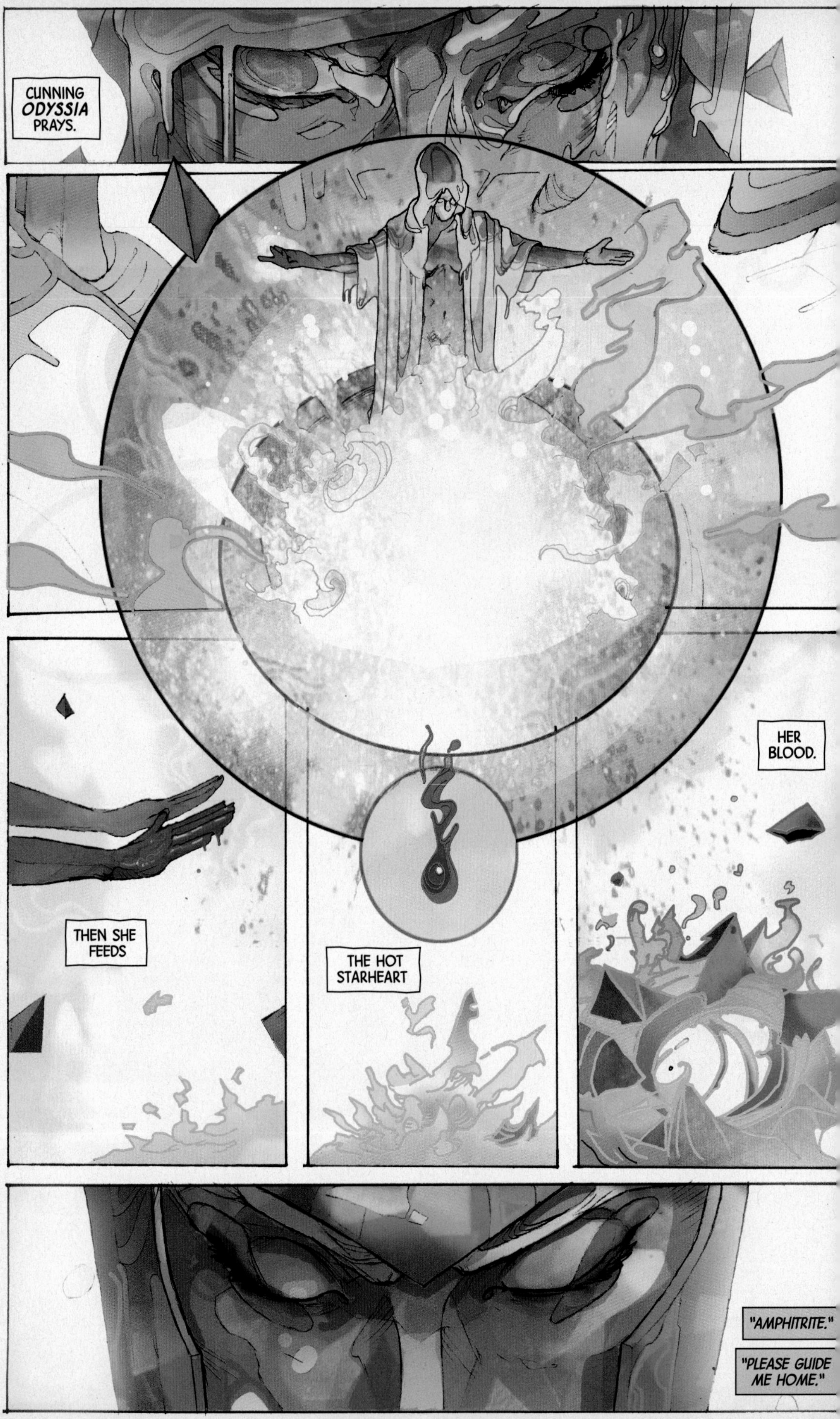

CUNNING *ODYSSIA* PRAYS.
THEN SHE FEEDS
THE HOT STARHEART
HER BLOOD.
"AMPHITRITE."
"PLEASE GUIDE ME HOME."

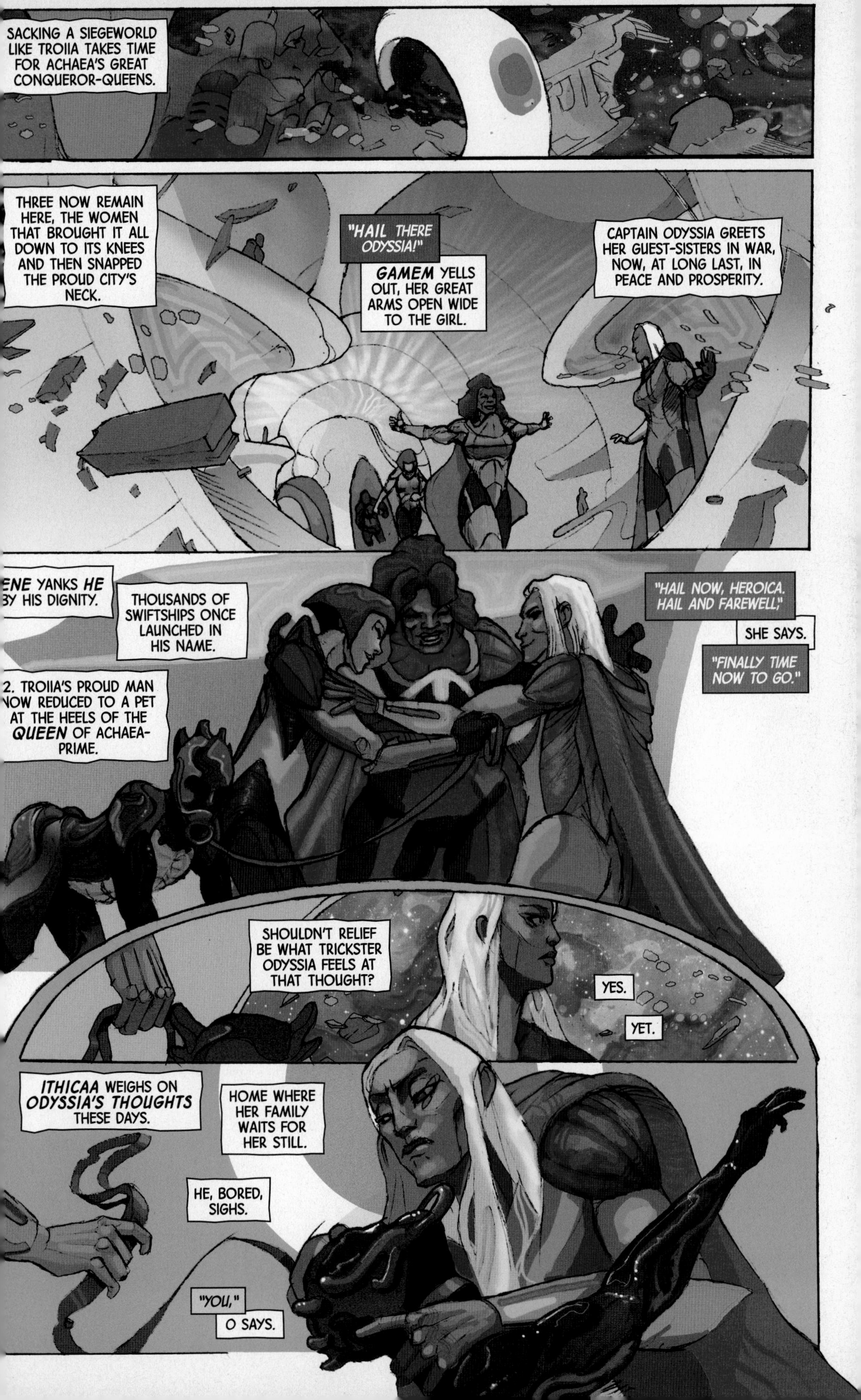
SACKING A SIEGEWORLD LIKE TROIIA TAKES TIME FOR ACHAEA'S GREAT CONQUEROR-QUEENS.
THREE NOW REMAIN HERE, THE WOMEN THAT BROUGHT IT ALL DOWN TO ITS KNEES AND THEN SNAPPED THE PROUD CITY'S NECK.
"HAIL THERE ODYSSIA!"
GAMEM YELLS OUT, HER GREAT ARMS OPEN WIDE TO THE GIRL.
CAPTAIN ODYSSIA GREETS HER GUEST-SISTERS IN WAR, NOW, AT LONG LAST, IN PEACE AND PROSPERITY.
ENE YANKS HE BY HIS DIGNITY.
THOUSANDS OF SWIFTSHIPS ONCE LAUNCHED IN HIS NAME.
2. TROIIA'S PROUD MAN NOW REDUCED TO A PET AT THE HEELS OF THE QUEEN OF ACHAEA-PRIME.
"HAIL NOW, HEROICA. HAIL AND FAREWELL,"
SHE SAYS.
"FINALLY TIME NOW TO GO."
SHOULDN'T RELIEF BE WHAT TRICKSTER ODYSSIA FEELS AT THAT THOUGHT?
YES.
YET.
ITHICAA WEIGHS ON ODYSSIA'S THOUGHTS THESE DAYS.
HOME WHERE HER FAMILY WAITS FOR HER STILL.
HE, BORED, SIGHS.
"YOU,"
O SAYS.

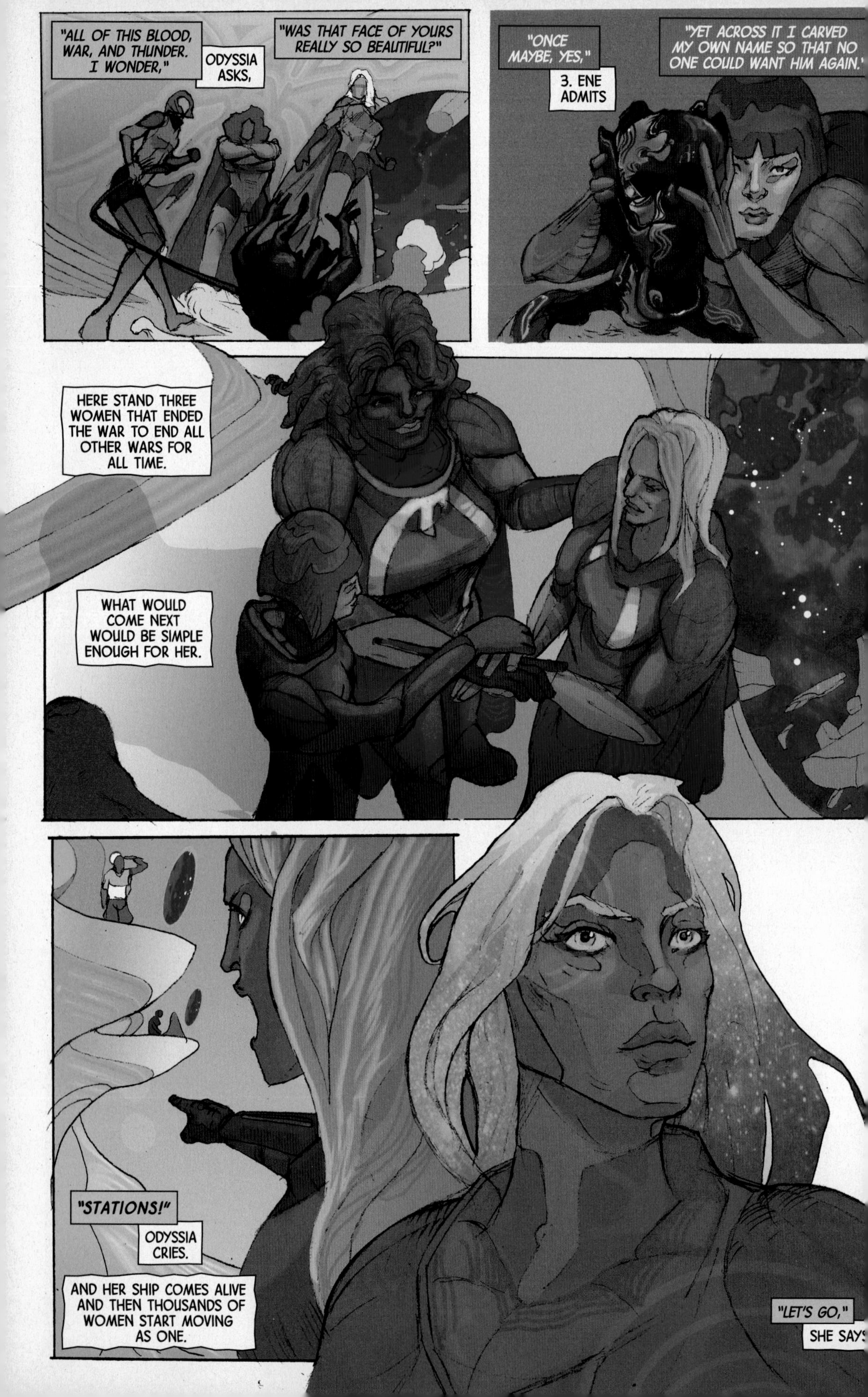
"ALL OF THIS BLOOD, WAR, AND THUNDER. I WONDER,"
ODYSSIA ASKS,
"WAS THAT FACE OF YOURS REALLY SO BEAUTIFUL?"
"ONCE MAYBE, YES,"
3. ENE ADMITS
"YET ACROSS IT I CARVED MY OWN NAME SO THAT NO ONE COULD WANT HIM AGAIN."
HERE STAND THREE WOMEN THAT ENDED THE WAR TO END ALL OTHER WARS FOR ALL TIME.
WHAT WOULD COME NEXT WOULD BE SIMPLE ENOUGH FOR HER.
"STATIONS!"
ODYSSIA CRIES.
AND HER SHIP COMES ALIVE AND THEN THOUSANDS OF WOMEN START MOVING AS ONE.
"LET'S GO,"
SHE SAYS

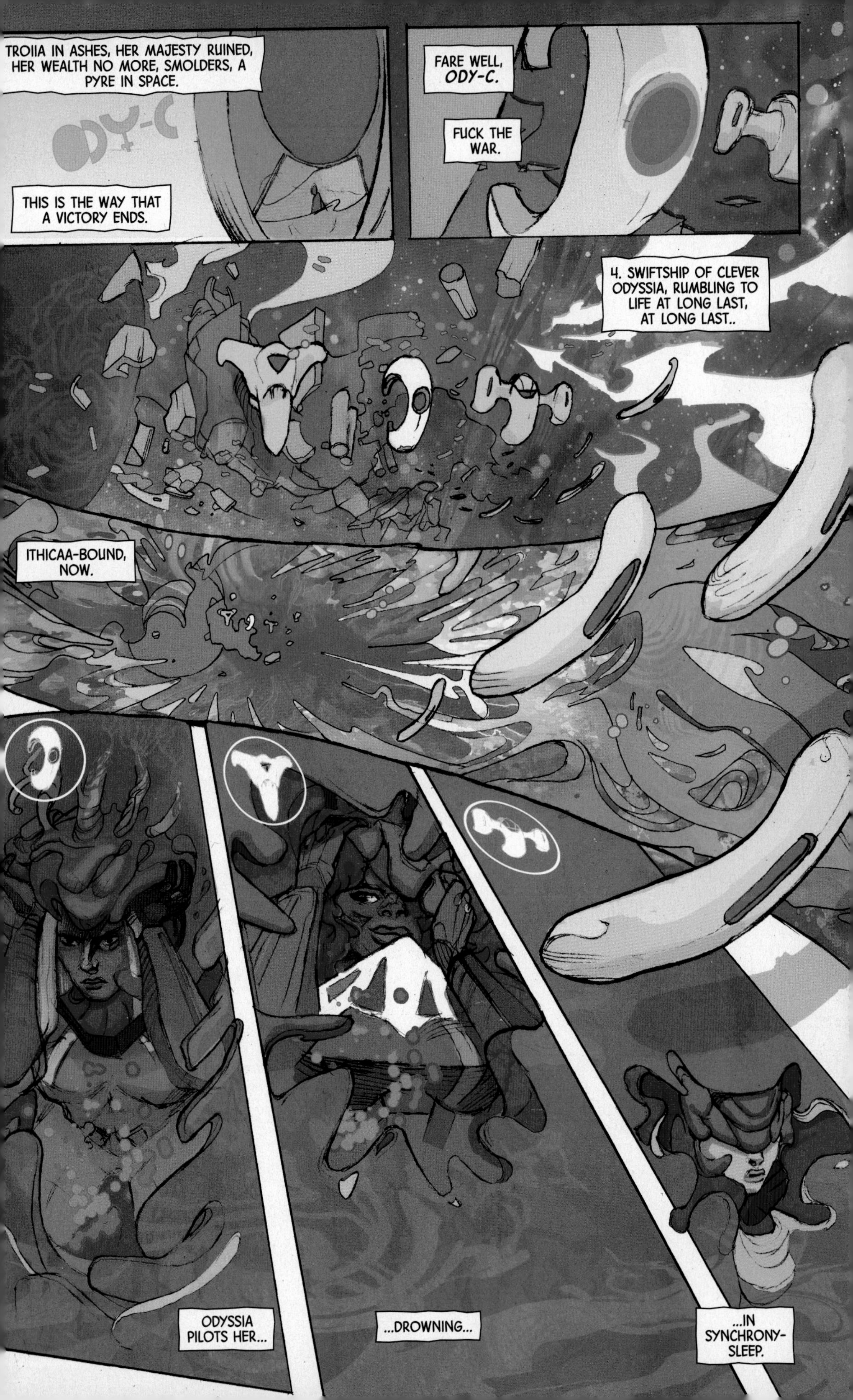
TROIIA IN ASHES, HER MAJESTY RUINED, HER WEALTH NO MORE, SMOLDERS, A PYRE IN SPACE.
ODY-C
THIS IS THE WAY THAT A VICTORY ENDS.
FARE WELL, ODY-C.
FUCK THE WAR.
4. SWIFTSHIP OF CLEVER ODYSSIA, RUMBLING TO LIFE AT LONG LAST, AT LONG LAST..
ITHICAA-BOUND, NOW.
ODYSSIA PILOTS HER...
...DROWNING...
...IN SYNCHRONY-SLEEP.

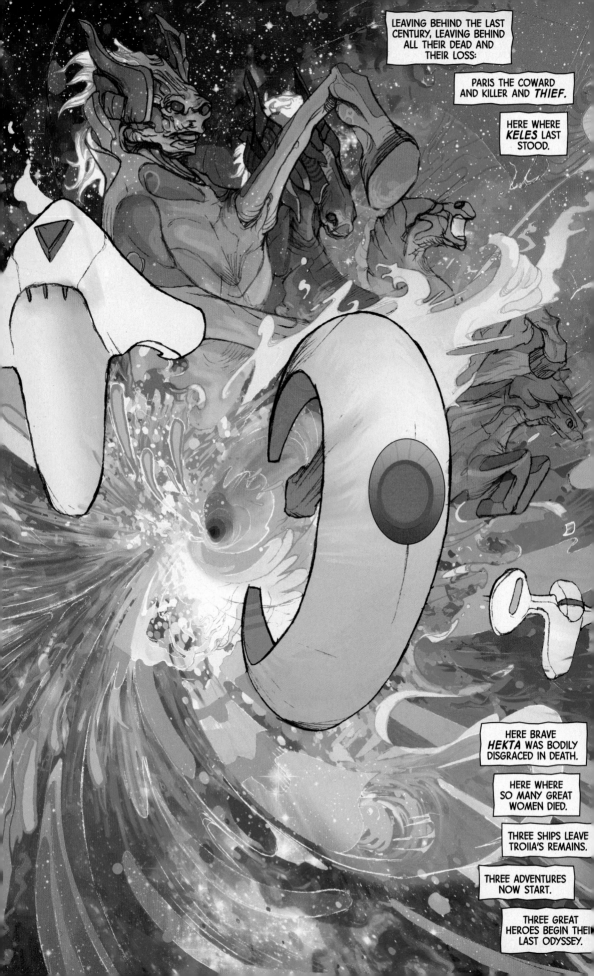

LEAVING BEHIND THE LAST CENTURY, LEAVING BEHIND ALL THEIR DEAD AND THEIR LOSS:

PARIS THE COWARD AND KILLER AND *THIEF.*

HERE WHERE *KELES* LAST STOOD.

HERE BRAVE *HEKTA* WAS BODILY DISGRACED IN DEATH.

HERE WHERE SO MANY GREAT WOMEN DIED.

THREE SHIPS LEAVE TROIIA'S REMAINS.

THREE ADVENTURES NOW START.

THREE GREAT HEROES BEGIN THEIR LAST ODYSSEY.

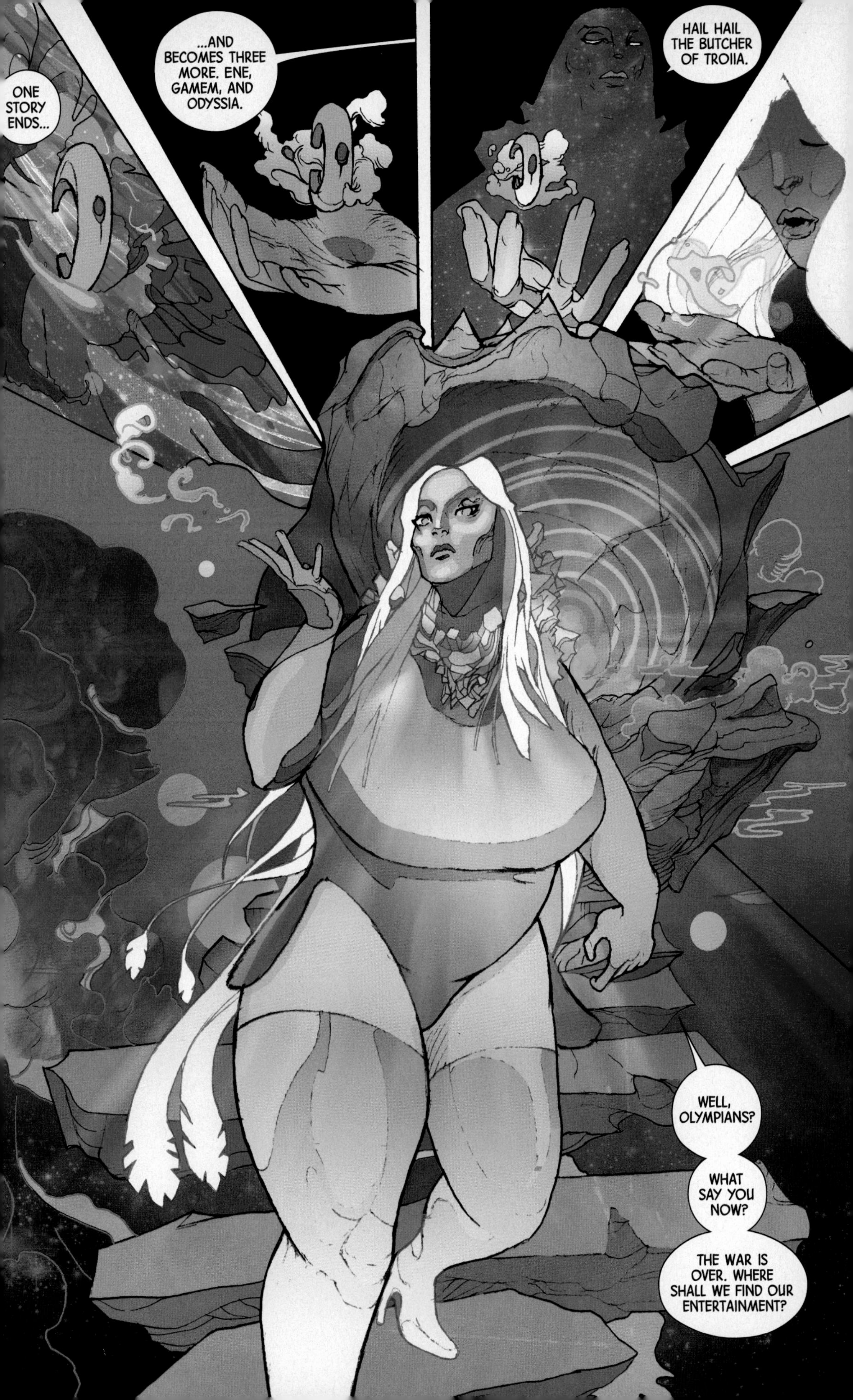
ONE STORY ENDS...
...AND BECOMES THREE MORE. ENE, GAMEM, AND ODYSSIA.
HAIL HAIL THE BUTCHER OF TROIIA.
WELL, OLYMPIANS?
WHAT SAY YOU NOW?
THE WAR IS OVER. WHERE SHALL WE FIND OUR ENTERTAINMENT?

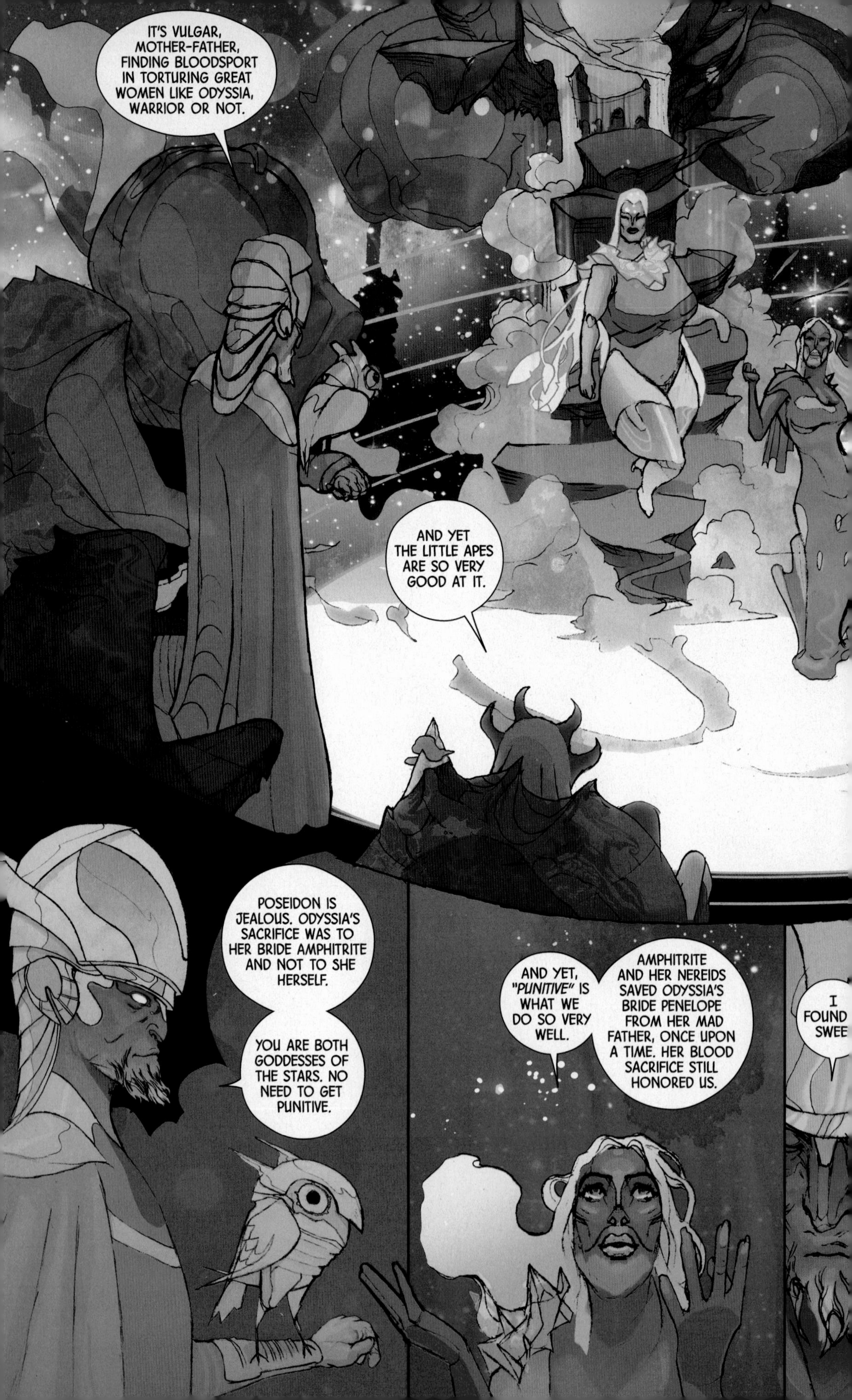
IT'S VULGAR, MOTHER-FATHER, FINDING BLOODSPORT IN TORTURING GREAT WOMEN LIKE ODYSSIA, WARRIOR OR NOT.
AND YET THE LITTLE APES ARE SO VERY GOOD AT IT.
POSEIDON IS JEALOUS. ODYSSIA'S SACRIFICE WAS TO HER BRIDE AMPHITRITE AND NOT TO SHE HERSELF.
YOU ARE BOTH GODDESSES OF THE STARS. NO NEED TO GET PUNITIVE.
AND YET, "PUNITIVE" IS WHAT WE DO SO VERY WELL.
AMPHITRITE AND HER NEREIDS SAVED ODYSSIA'S BRIDE PENELOPE FROM HER MAD FATHER, ONCE UPON A TIME. HER BLOOD SACRIFICE STILL HONORED US.
I FOUND SWEE

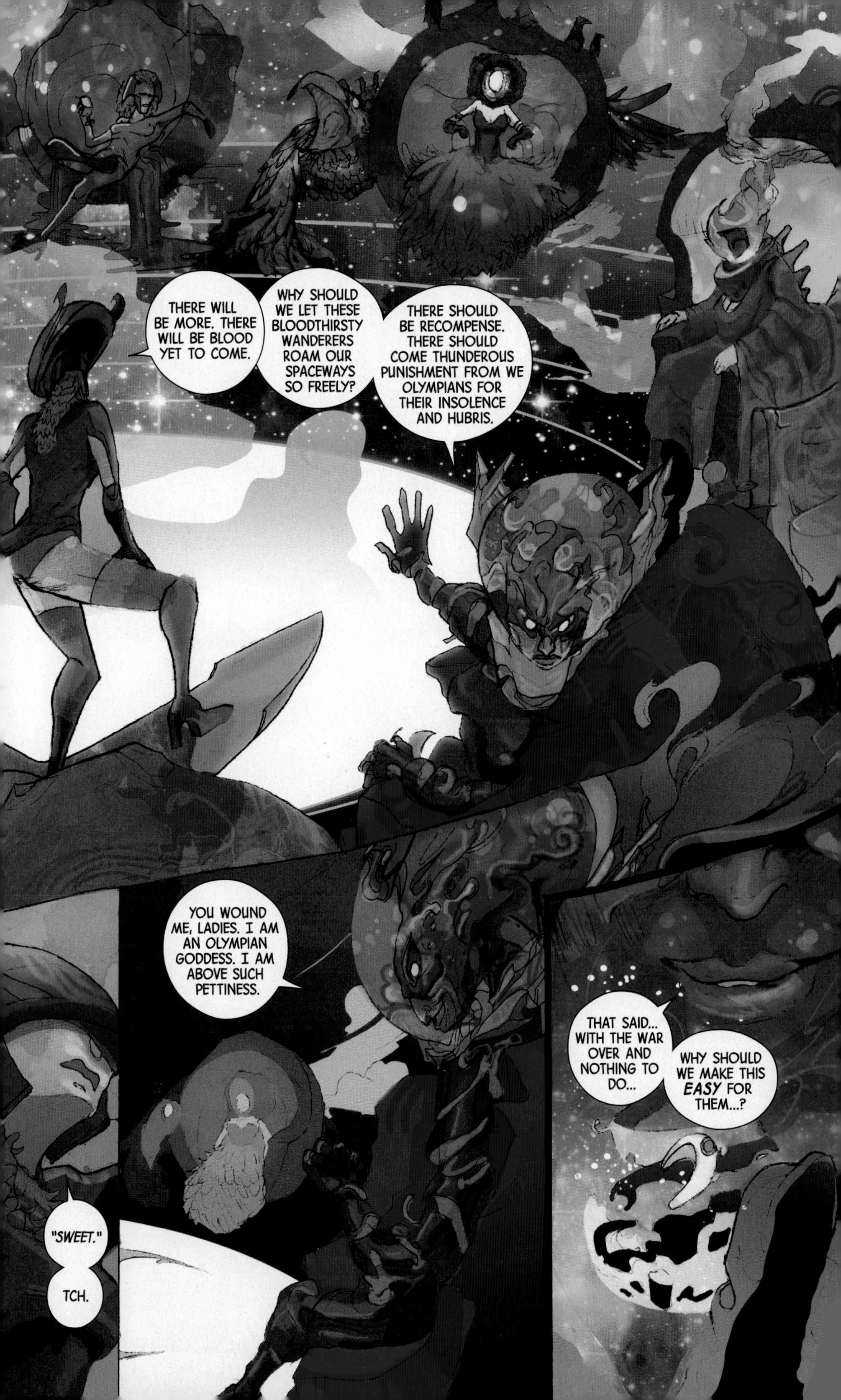
THERE WILL BE MORE. THERE WILL BE BLOOD YET TO COME.
WHY SHOULD WE LET THESE BLOODTHIRSTY WANDERERS ROAM OUR SPACEWAYS SO FREELY?
THERE SHOULD BE RECOMPENSE. THERE SHOULD COME THUNDEROUS PUNISHMENT FROM WE OLYMPIANS FOR THEIR INSOLENCE AND HUBRIS.
YOU WOUND ME, LADIES. I AM AN OLYMPIAN GODDESS. I AM ABOVE SUCH PETTINESS.
"SWEET."
TCH.
THAT SAID... WITH THE WAR OVER AND NOTHING TO DO...
WHY SHOULD WE MAKE THIS *EASY* FOR THEM...?

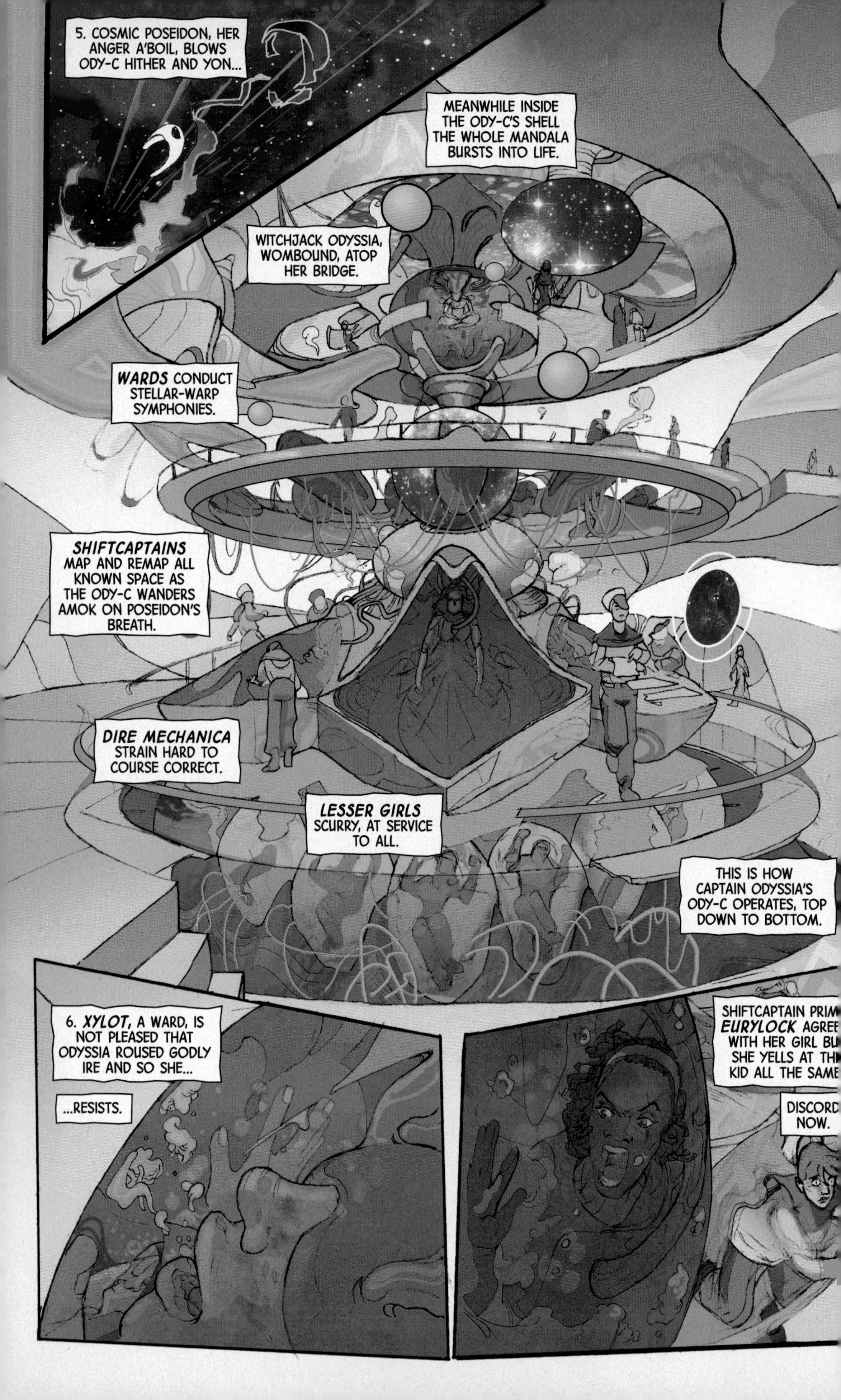
5. COSMIC POSEIDON, HER ANGER A'BOIL, BLOWS ODY-C HITHER AND YON...
MEANWHILE INSIDE THE ODY-C'S SHELL THE WHOLE MANDALA BURSTS INTO LIFE.
WITCHJACK ODYSSIA, WOMBOUND, ATOP HER BRIDGE.
WARDS CONDUCT STELLAR-WARP SYMPHONIES.
SHIFTCAPTAINS MAP AND REMAP ALL KNOWN SPACE AS THE ODY-C WANDERS AMOK ON POSEIDON'S BREATH.
DIRE MECHANICA STRAIN HARD TO COURSE CORRECT.
LESSER GIRLS SCURRY, AT SERVICE TO ALL.
THIS IS HOW CAPTAIN ODYSSIA'S ODY-C OPERATES, TOP DOWN TO BOTTOM.
6. XYLOT, A WARD, IS NOT PLEASED THAT ODYSSIA ROUSED GODLY IRE AND SO SHE...
...RESISTS.
SHIFTCAPTAIN PRIM EURYLOCK AGREE WITH HER GIRL BU SHE YELLS AT TH KID ALL THE SAME
DISCORD NOW.

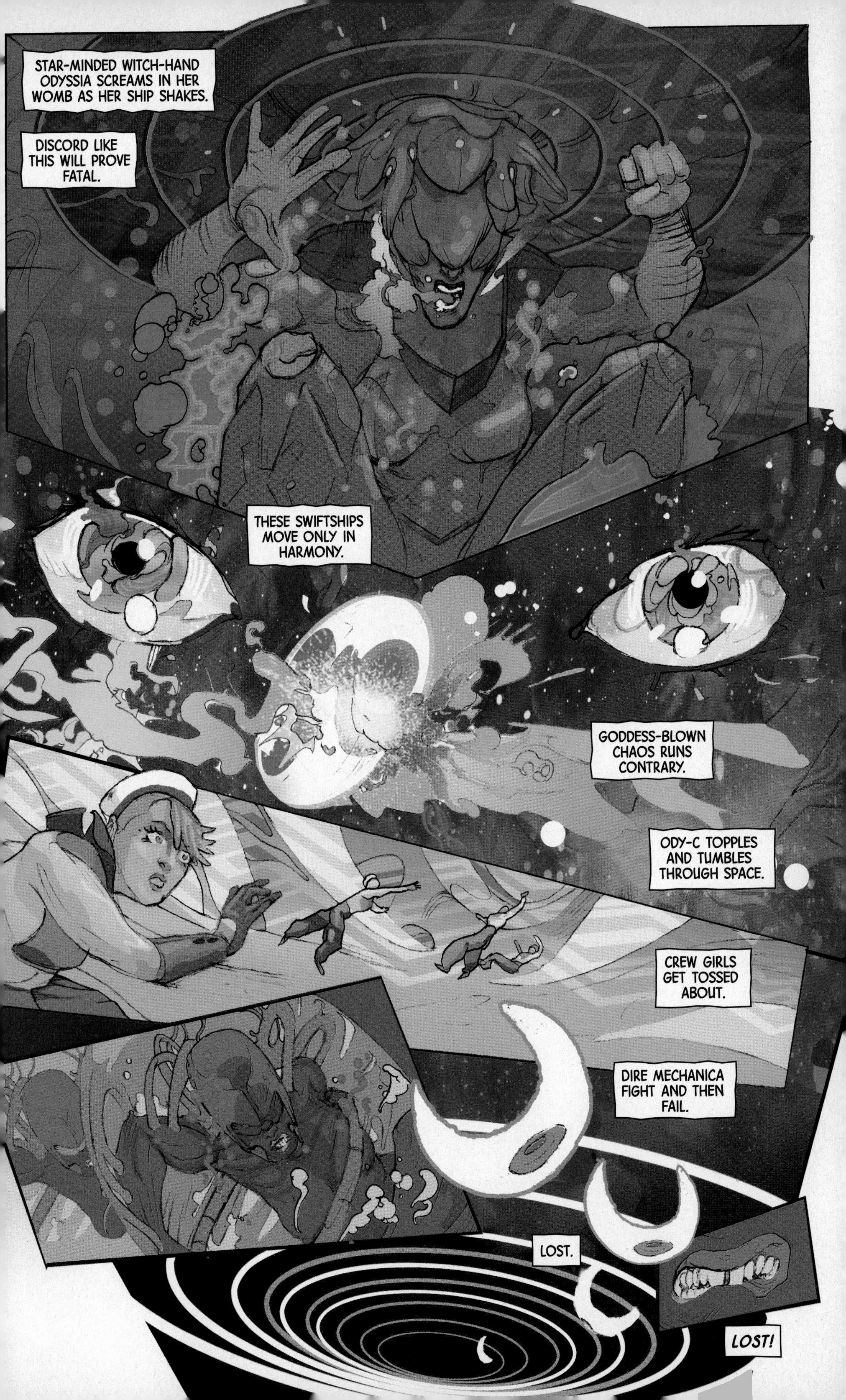
STAR-MINDED WITCH-HAND ODYSSIA SCREAMS IN HER WOMB AS HER SHIP SHAKES.
DISCORD LIKE THIS WILL PROVE FATAL.
THESE SWIFTSHIPS MOVE ONLY IN HARMONY.
GODDESS-BLOWN CHAOS RUNS CONTRARY.
ODY-C TOPPLES AND TUMBLES THROUGH SPACE.
CREW GIRLS GET TOSSED ABOUT.
DIRE MECHANICA FIGHT AND THEN FAIL.
LOST.
LOST!

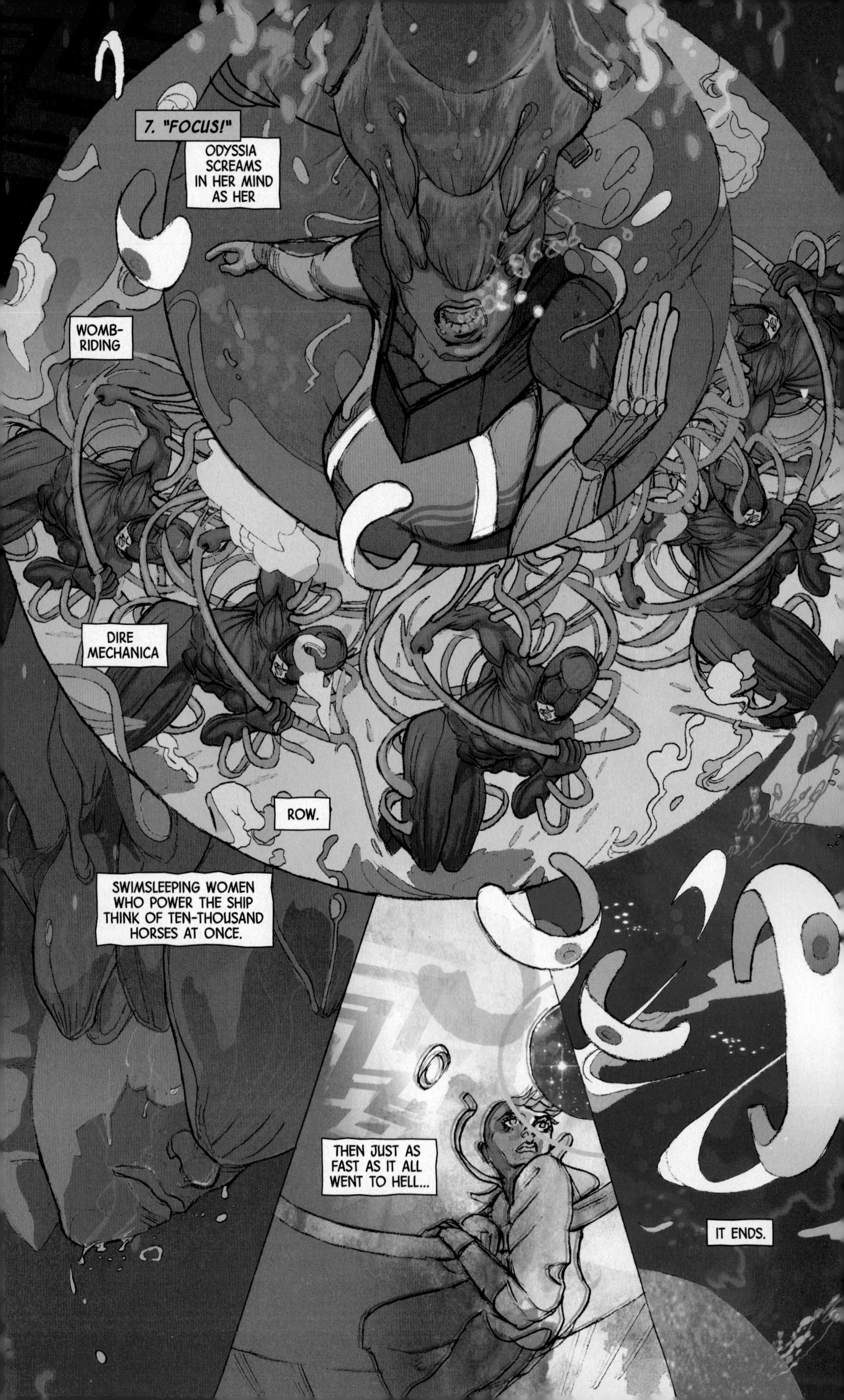
7. "FOCUS!"
ODYSSIA SCREAMS IN HER MIND AS HER
WOMB-RIDING
DIRE MECHANICA
ROW.
SWIMSLEEPING WOMEN WHO POWER THE SHIP THINK OF TEN-THOUSAND HORSES AT ONCE.
THEN JUST AS FAST AS IT ALL WENT TO HELL...
IT ENDS.

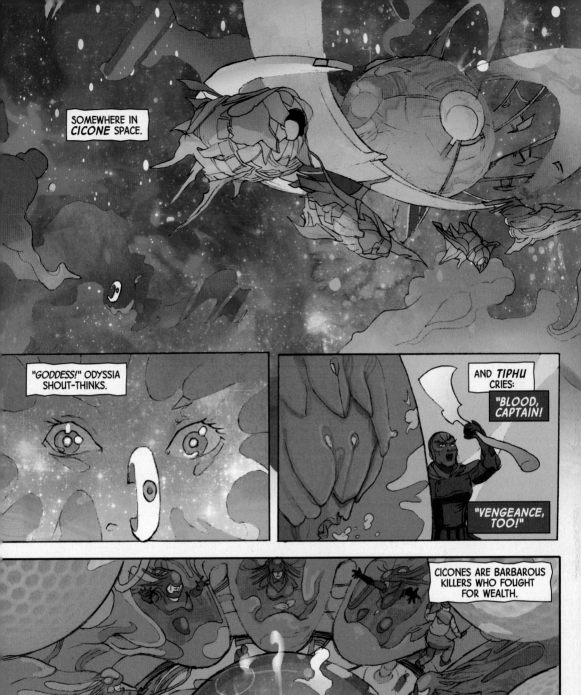

SOMEWHERE IN *CICONE* SPACE.

"GODDESS!" ODYSSIA SHOUT-THINKS.

AND *TIPHU* CRIES:

"BLOOD, CAPTAIN!"

"VENGEANCE, TOO!"

CICONES ARE BARBAROUS KILLERS WHO FOUGHT FOR WEALTH.

PAID BY THE TROIIAN REGIME.

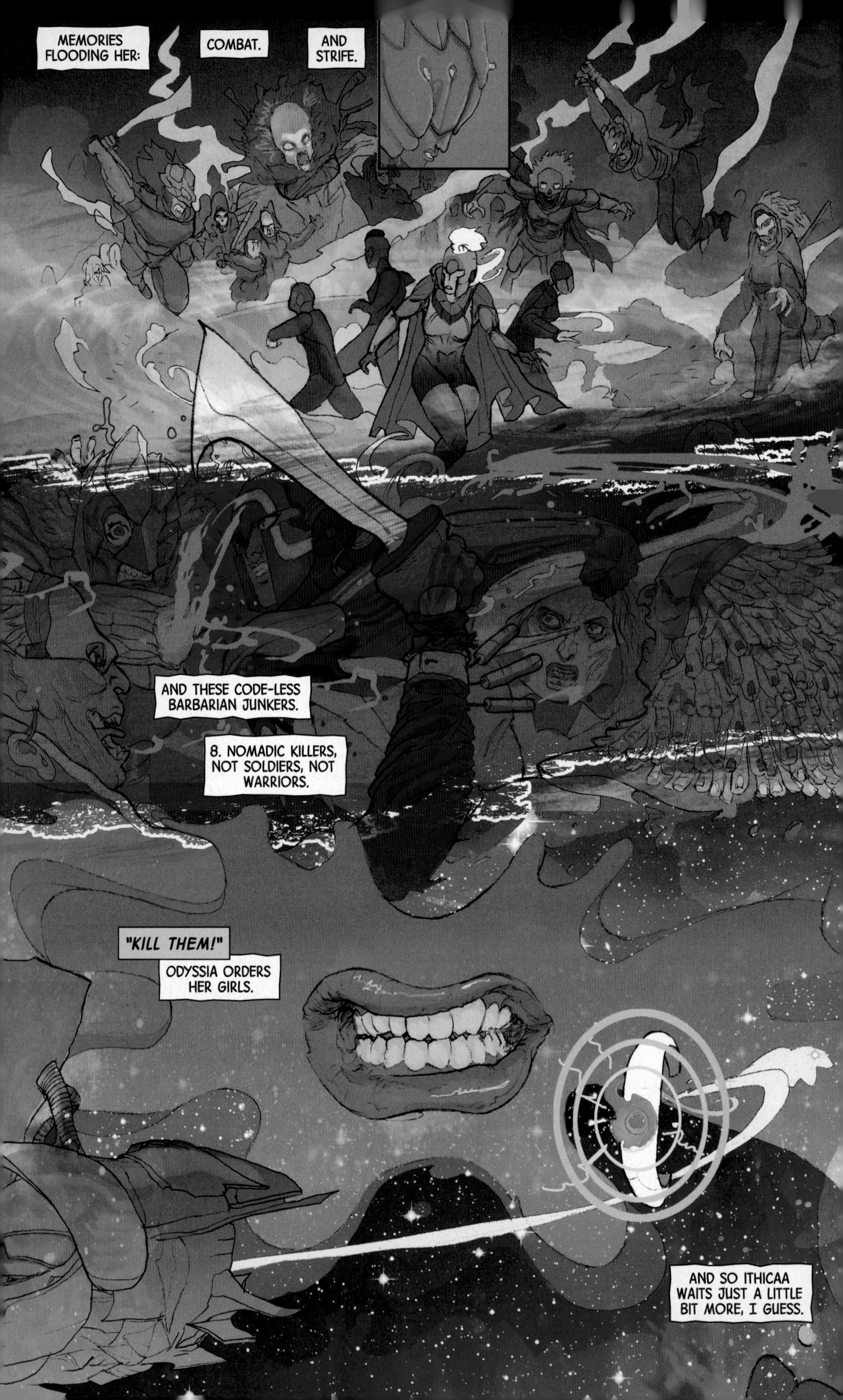
MEMORIES FLOODING HER:
COMBAT.
AND STRIFE.
AND THESE CODE-LESS BARBARIAN JUNKERS.
8. NOMADIC KILLERS, NOT SOLDIERS, NOT WARRIORS.
"KILL THEM!"
ODYSSIA ORDERS HER GIRLS.
AND SO ITHICAA WAITS JUST A LITTLE BIT MORE, I GUESS.

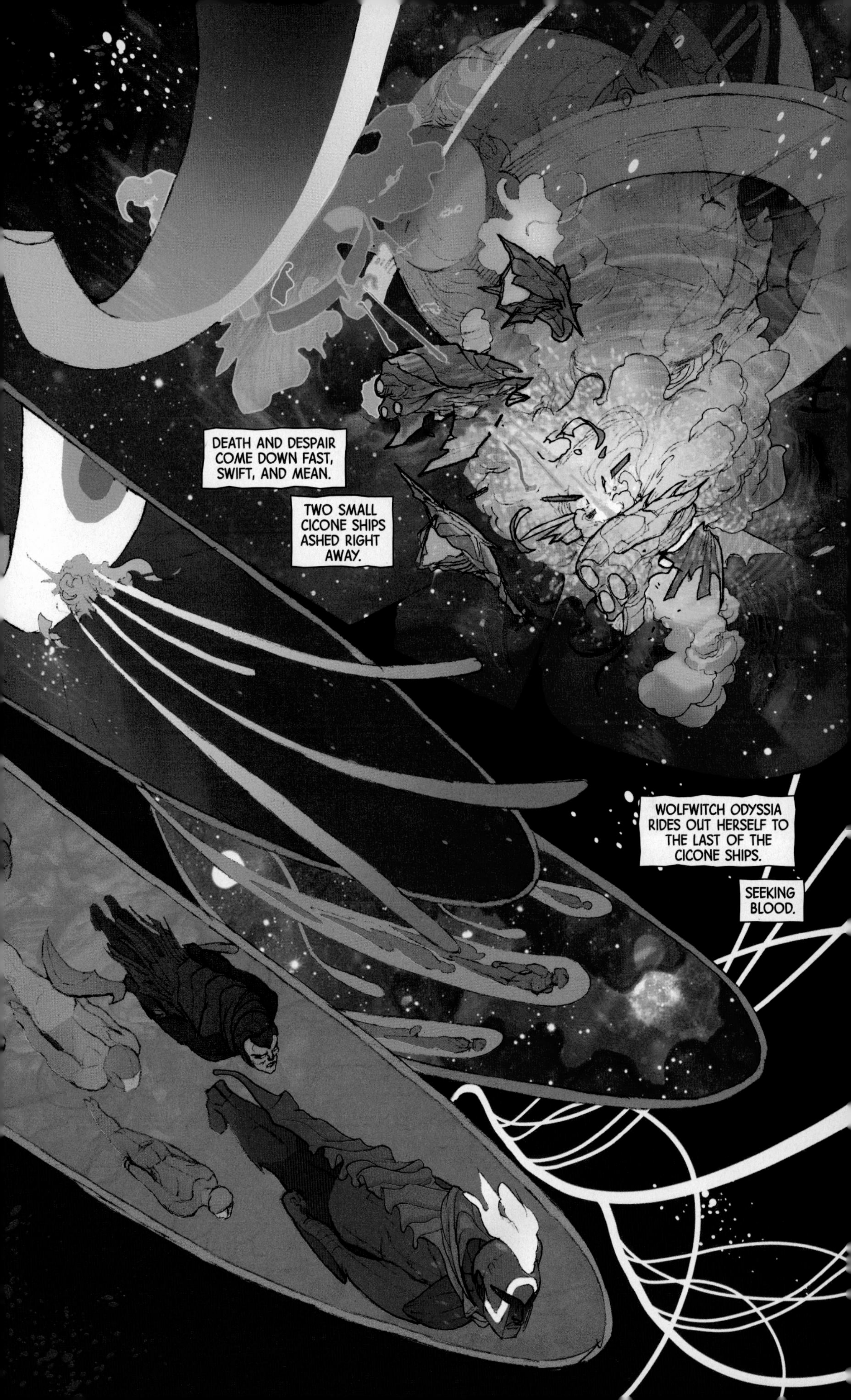
DEATH AND DESPAIR COME DOWN FAST, SWIFT, AND MEAN.
TWO SMALL CICONE SHIPS ASHED RIGHT AWAY.
WOLFWITCH ODYSSIA RIDES OUT HERSELF TO THE LAST OF THE CICONE SHIPS.
SEEKING BLOOD.

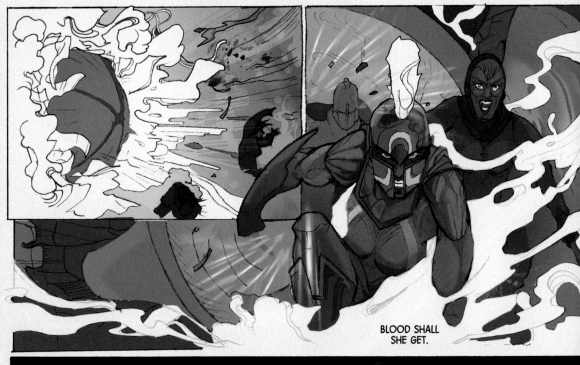

BLOOD SHALL
SHE GET.

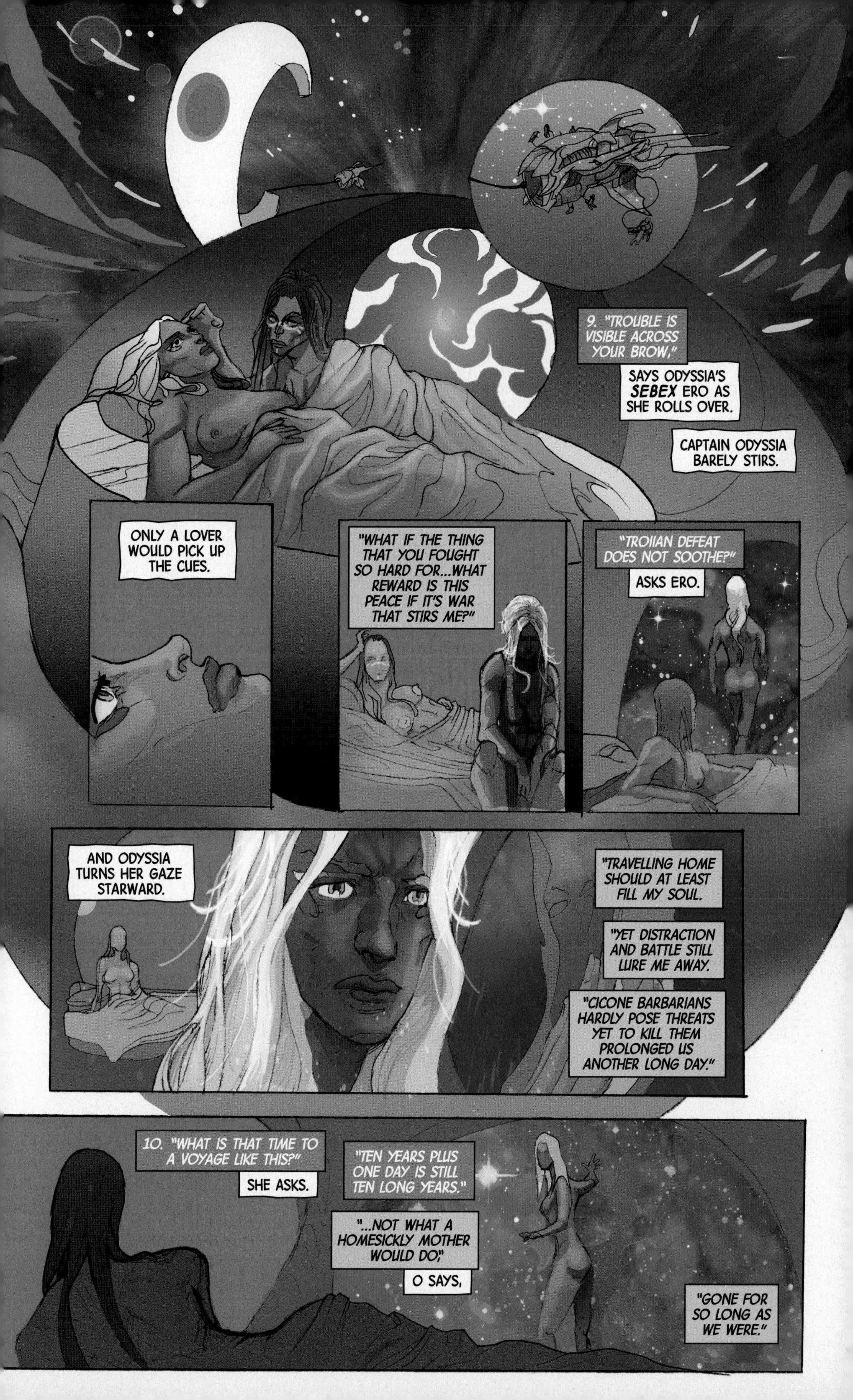
9. "TROUBLE IS VISIBLE ACROSS YOUR BROW,"
SAYS ODYSSIA'S **SEBEX** ERO AS SHE ROLLS OVER.
CAPTAIN ODYSSIA BARELY STIRS.
ONLY A LOVER WOULD PICK UP THE CUES.
"WHAT IF THE THING THAT YOU FOUGHT SO HARD FOR...WHAT REWARD IS THIS PEACE IF IT'S WAR THAT STIRS ME?"
"TROIIAN DEFEAT DOES NOT SOOTHE?"
ASKS ERO.
AND ODYSSIA TURNS HER GAZE STARWARD.
"TRAVELLING HOME SHOULD AT LEAST FILL MY SOUL.
"YET DISTRACTION AND BATTLE STILL LURE ME AWAY.
"CICONE BARBARIANS HARDLY POSE THREATS YET TO KILL THEM PROLONGED US ANOTHER LONG DAY."
10. "WHAT IS THAT TIME TO A VOYAGE LIKE THIS?"
SHE ASKS.
"TEN YEARS PLUS ONE DAY IS STILL TEN LONG YEARS."
"...NOT WHAT A HOMESICKLY MOTHER WOULD DO,"
O SAYS,
"GONE FOR SO LONG AS WE WERE."

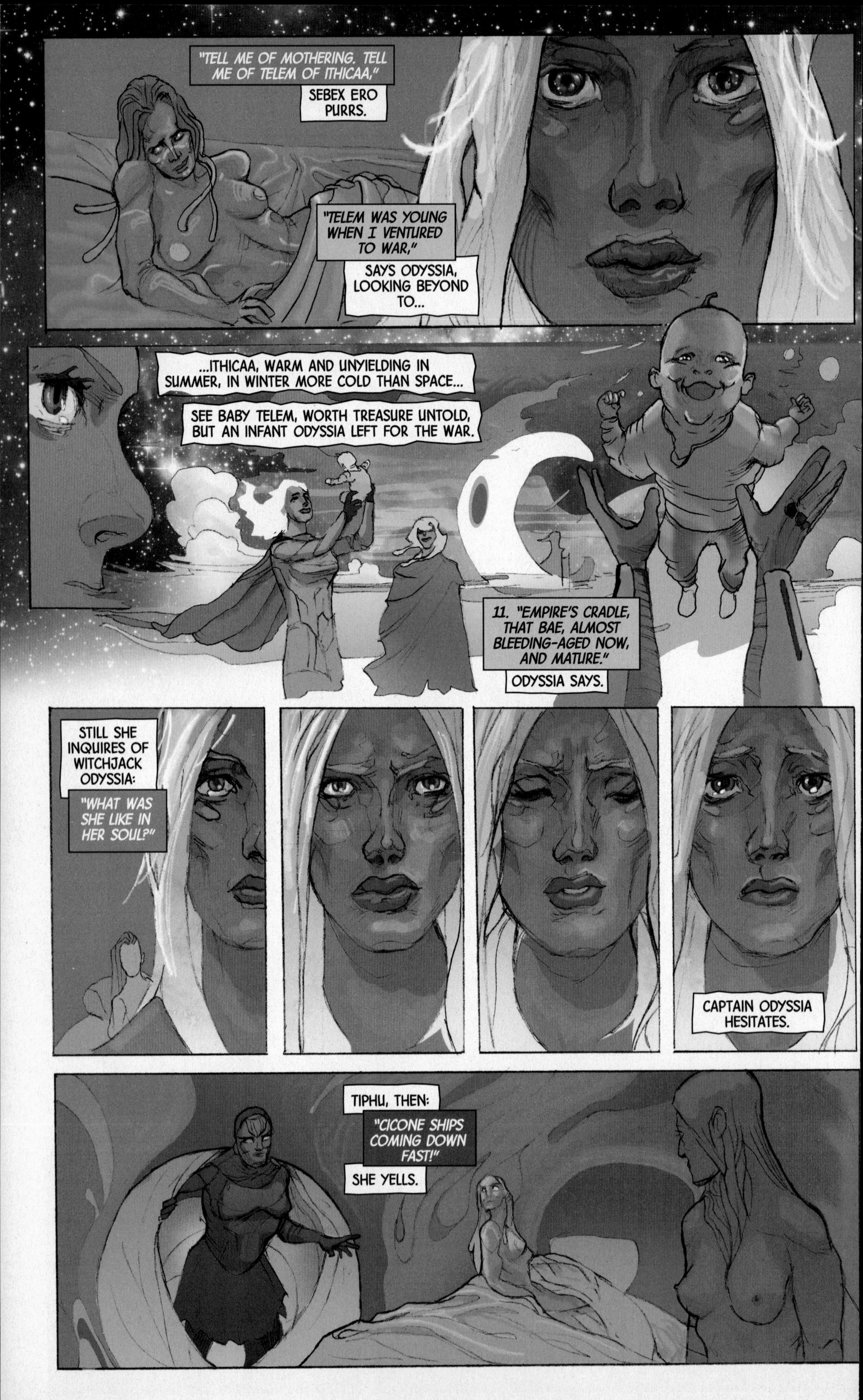
"TELL ME OF MOTHERING. TELL ME OF TELEM OF ITHICAA,"
SEBEX ERO PURRS.
"TELEM WAS YOUNG WHEN I VENTURED TO WAR,"
SAYS ODYSSIA, LOOKING BEYOND TO...
...ITHICAA, WARM AND UNYIELDING IN SUMMER, IN WINTER MORE COLD THAN SPACE...
SEE BABY TELEM, WORTH TREASURE UNTOLD, BUT AN INFANT ODYSSIA LEFT FOR THE WAR.
11. "EMPIRE'S CRADLE, THAT BAE, ALMOST BLEEDING-AGED NOW, AND MATURE."
ODYSSIA SAYS.
STILL SHE INQUIRES OF WITCHJACK ODYSSIA:
"WHAT WAS SHE LIKE IN HER SOUL?"
CAPTAIN ODYSSIA HESITATES.
TIPHU, THEN:
"CICONE SHIPS COMING DOWN FAST!"
SHE YELLS.

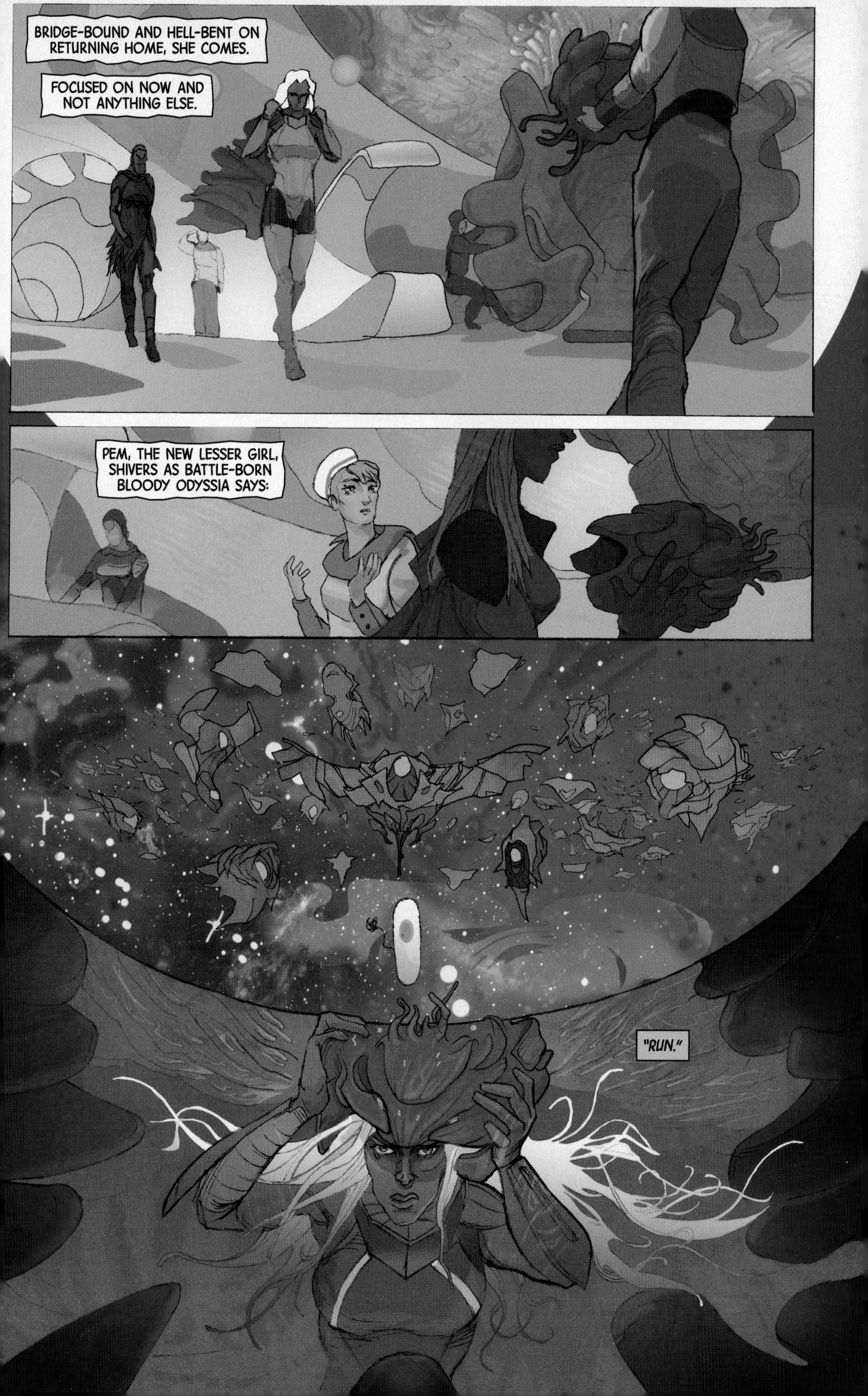
BRIDGE-BOUND AND HELL-BENT ON RETURNING HOME, SHE COMES.
FOCUSED ON NOW AND NOT ANYTHING ELSE.
PEM, THE NEW LESSER GIRL, SHIVERS AS BATTLE-BORN BLOODY ODYSSIA SAYS:
"RUN."

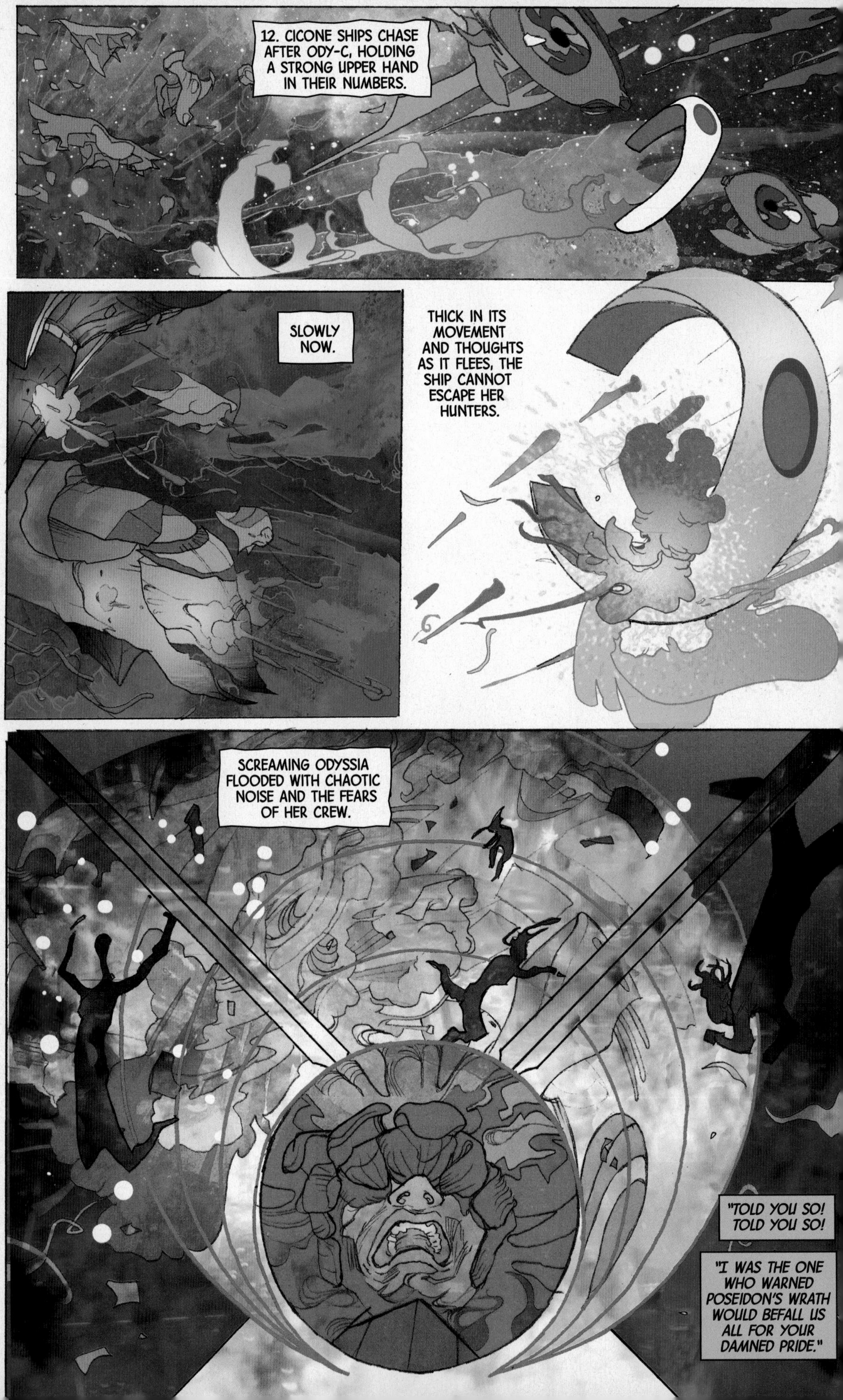
12. CICONE SHIPS CHASE AFTER ODY-C, HOLDING A STRONG UPPER HAND IN THEIR NUMBERS.
SLOWLY NOW.
THICK IN ITS MOVEMENT AND THOUGHTS AS IT FLEES, THE SHIP CANNOT ESCAPE HER HUNTERS.
SCREAMING ODYSSIA FLOODED WITH CHAOTIC NOISE AND THE FEARS OF HER CREW.
"TOLD YOU SO! TOLD YOU SO!
"I WAS THE ONE WHO WARNED POSEIDON'S WRATH WOULD BEFALL US ALL FOR YOUR DAMNED PRIDE."

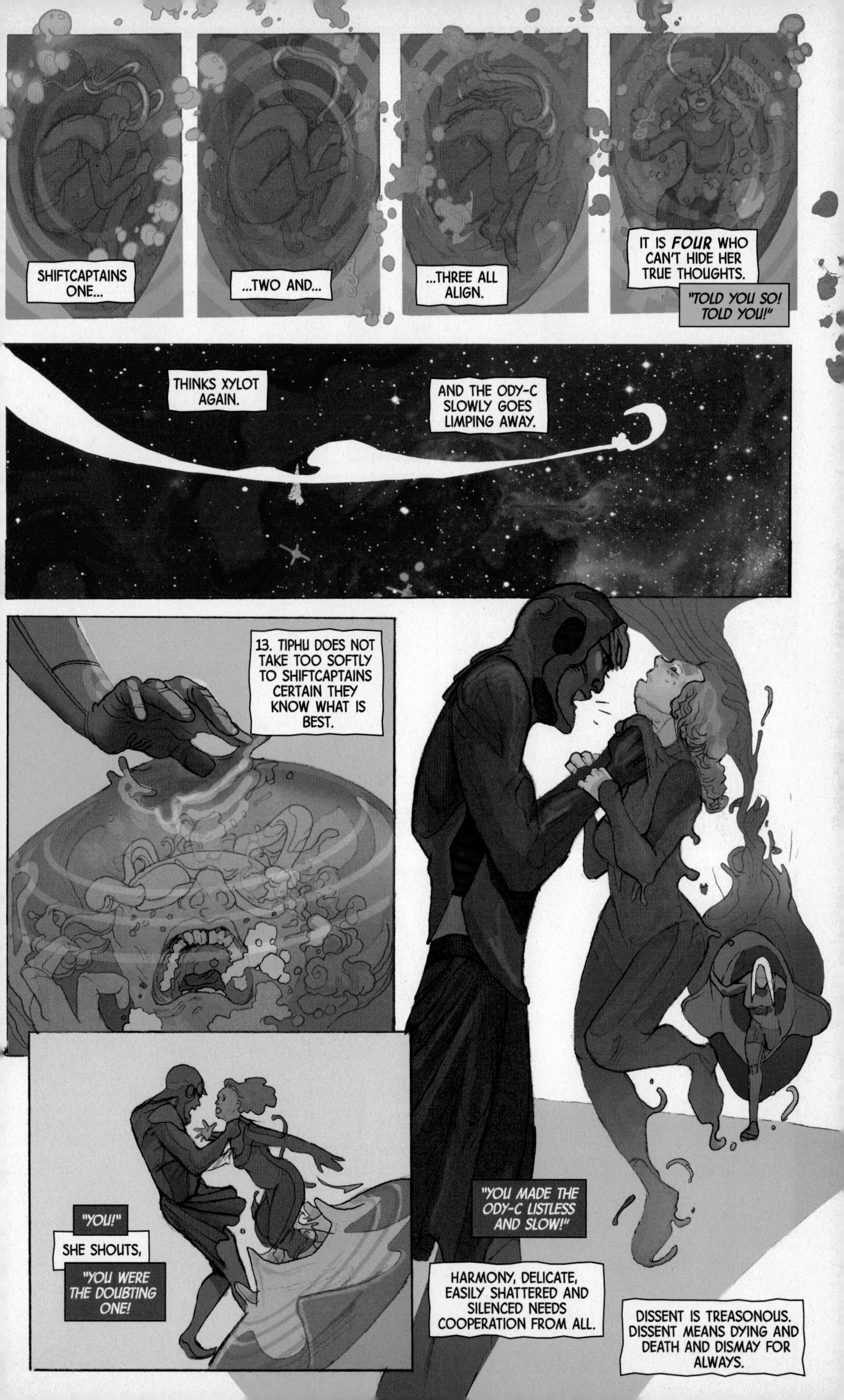
SHIFTCAPTAINS ONE...
...TWO AND...
...THREE ALL ALIGN.
IT IS FOUR WHO CAN'T HIDE HER TRUE THOUGHTS.
"TOLD YOU SO! TOLD YOU!"
THINKS XYLOT AGAIN.
AND THE ODY-C SLOWLY GOES LIMPING AWAY.
13. TIPHU DOES NOT TAKE TOO SOFTLY TO SHIFTCAPTAINS CERTAIN THEY KNOW WHAT IS BEST.
"YOU!"
SHE SHOUTS,
"YOU WERE THE DOUBTING ONE!
"YOU MADE THE ODY-C LISTLESS AND SLOW!"
HARMONY, DELICATE, EASILY SHATTERED AND SILENCED NEEDS COOPERATION FROM ALL.
DISSENT IS TREASONOUS. DISSENT MEANS DYING AND DEATH AND DISMAY FOR ALWAYS.

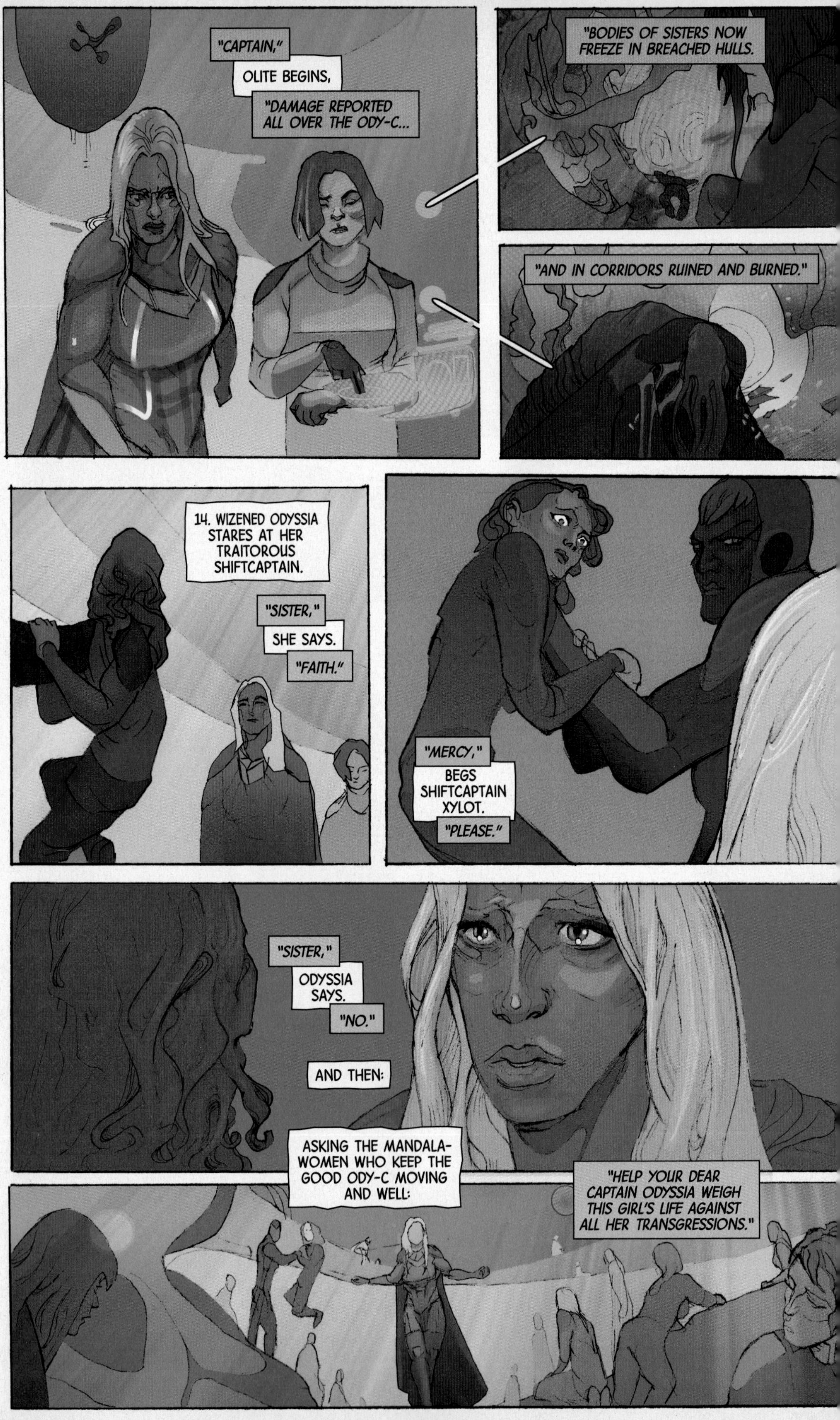
"CAPTAIN,"
OLITE BEGINS,
"DAMAGE REPORTED ALL OVER THE ODY-C...
"BODIES OF SISTERS NOW FREEZE IN BREACHED HULLS.
"AND IN CORRIDORS RUINED AND BURNED."
14. WIZENED ODYSSIA STARES AT HER TRAITOROUS SHIFTCAPTAIN.
"SISTER,"
SHE SAYS.
"FAITH."
"MERCY,"
BEGS SHIFTCAPTAIN XYLOT.
"PLEASE."
"SISTER,"
ODYSSIA SAYS.
"NO."
AND THEN:
ASKING THE MANDALA-WOMEN WHO KEEP THE GOOD ODY-C MOVING AND WELL:
"HELP YOUR DEAR CAPTAIN ODYSSIA WEIGH THIS GIRL'S LIFE AGAINST ALL HER TRANSGRESSIONS."

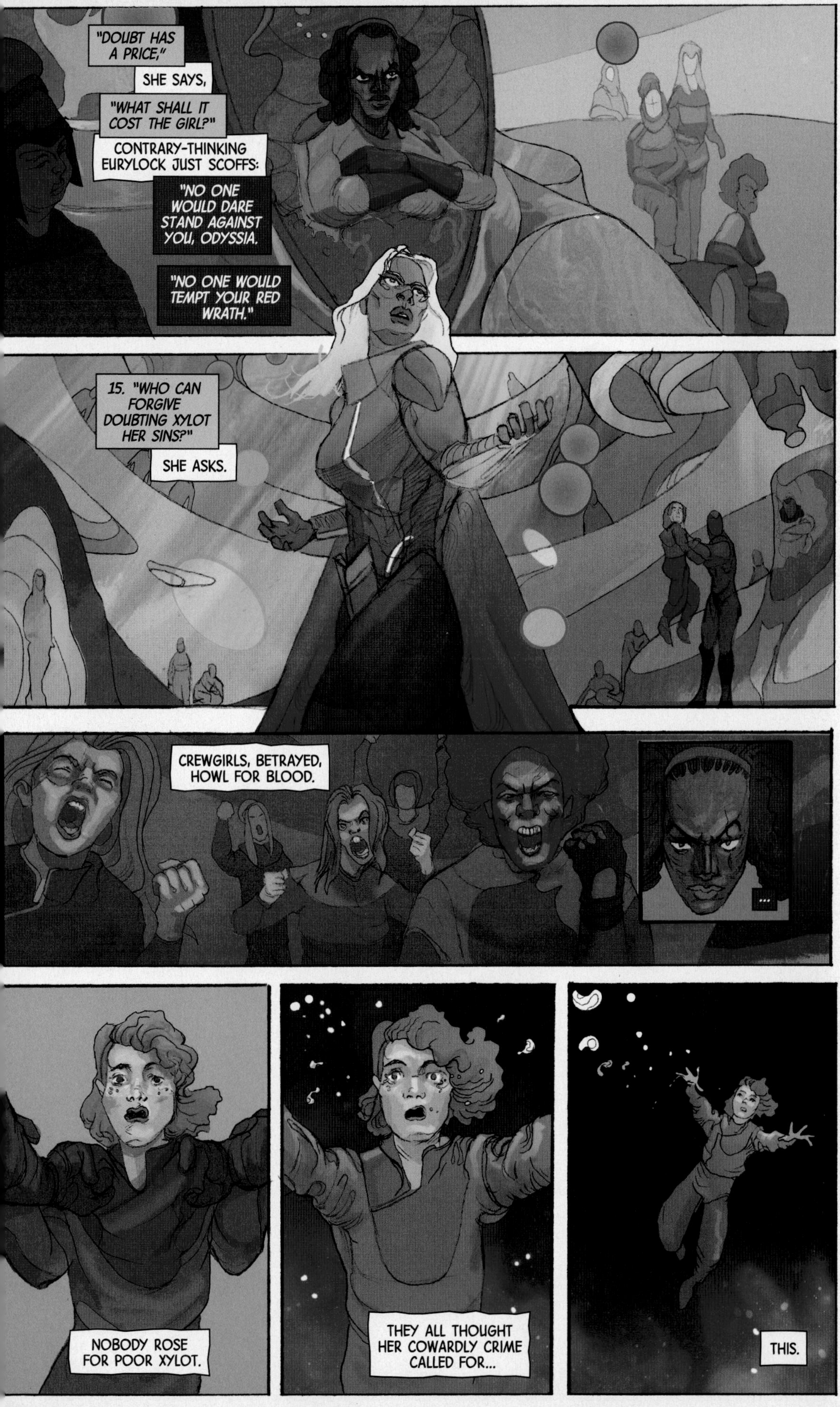
"DOUBT HAS A PRICE,"
SHE SAYS,
"WHAT SHALL IT COST THE GIRL?"
CONTRARY-THINKING EURYLOCK JUST SCOFFS:
"NO ONE WOULD DARE STAND AGAINST YOU, ODYSSIA.
"NO ONE WOULD TEMPT YOUR RED WRATH."
15. "WHO CAN FORGIVE DOUBTING XYLOT HER SINS?"
SHE ASKS.
CREWGIRLS, BETRAYED, HOWL FOR BLOOD.
...
NOBODY ROSE FOR POOR XYLOT.
THEY ALL THOUGHT HER COWARDLY CRIME CALLED FOR...
THIS.

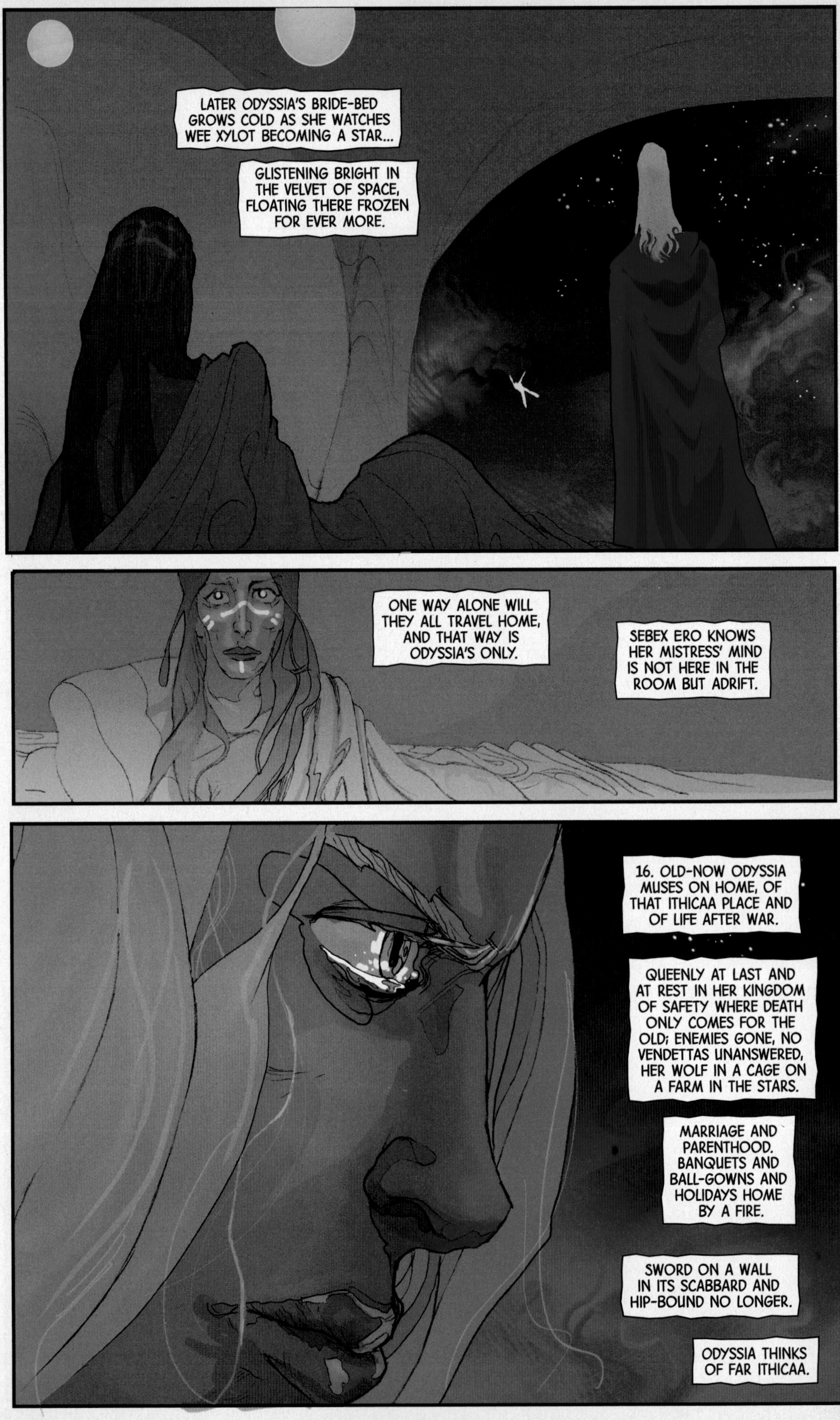
LATER ODYSSIA'S BRIDE-BED GROWS COLD AS SHE WATCHES WEE XYLOT BECOMING A STAR...
GLISTENING BRIGHT IN THE VELVET OF SPACE, FLOATING THERE FROZEN FOR EVER MORE.
ONE WAY ALONE WILL THEY ALL TRAVEL HOME, AND THAT WAY IS ODYSSIA'S ONLY.
SEBEX ERO KNOWS HER MISTRESS' MIND IS NOT HERE IN THE ROOM BUT ADRIFT.
16. OLD-NOW ODYSSIA MUSES ON HOME, OF THAT ITHICAA PLACE AND OF LIFE AFTER WAR.
QUEENLY AT LAST AND AT REST IN HER KINGDOM OF SAFETY WHERE DEATH ONLY COMES FOR THE OLD; ENEMIES GONE, NO VENDETTAS UNANSWERED, HER WOLF IN A CAGE ON A FARM IN THE STARS.
MARRIAGE AND PARENTHOOD. BANQUETS AND BALL-GOWNS AND HOLIDAYS HOME BY A FIRE.
SWORD ON A WALL IN ITS SCABBARD AND HIP-BOUND NO LONGER.
ODYSSIA THINKS OF FAR ITHICAA.

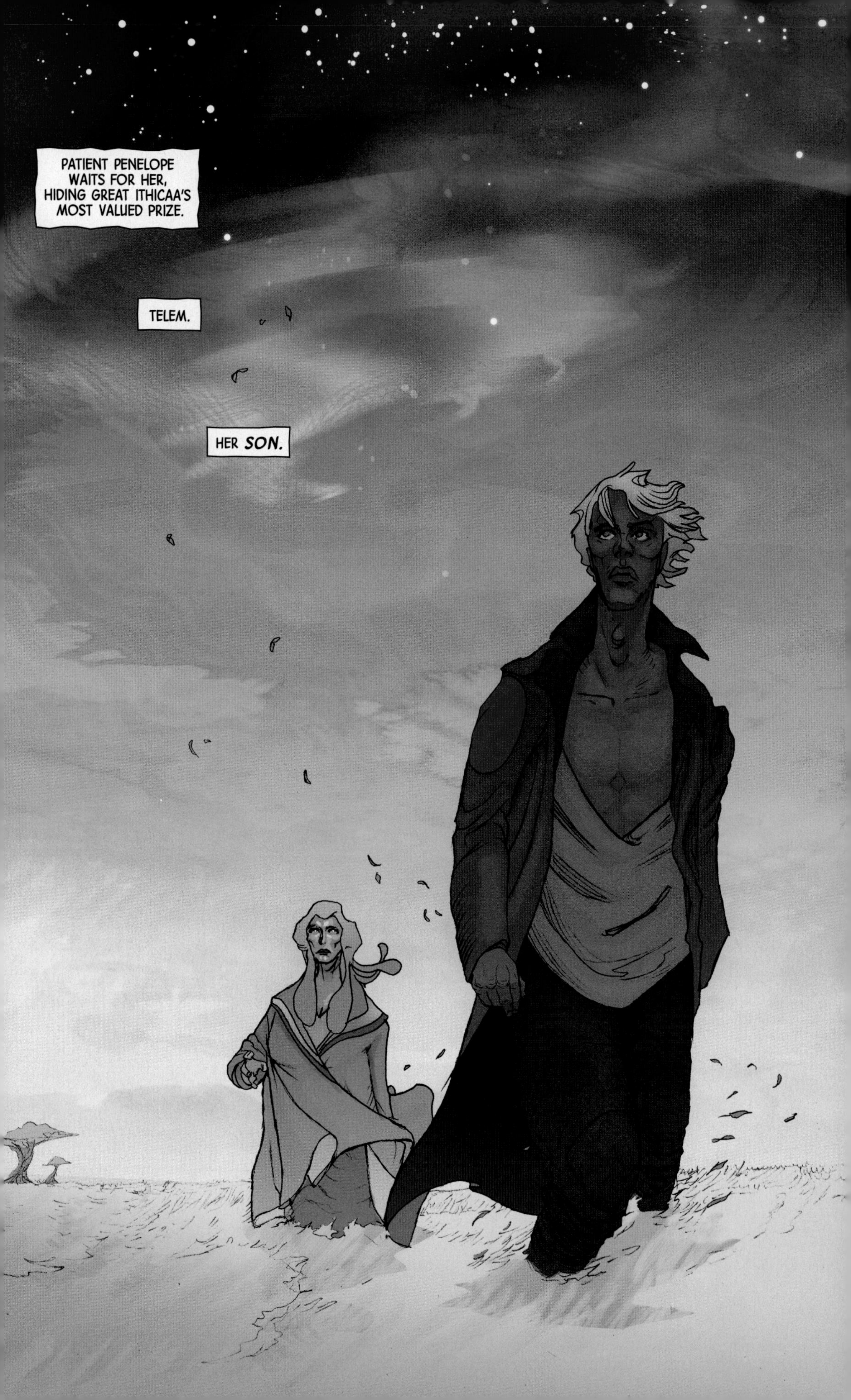
PATIENT PENELOPE WAITS FOR HER, HIDING GREAT ITHICAA'S MOST VALUED PRIZE.
TELEM.
HER SON.

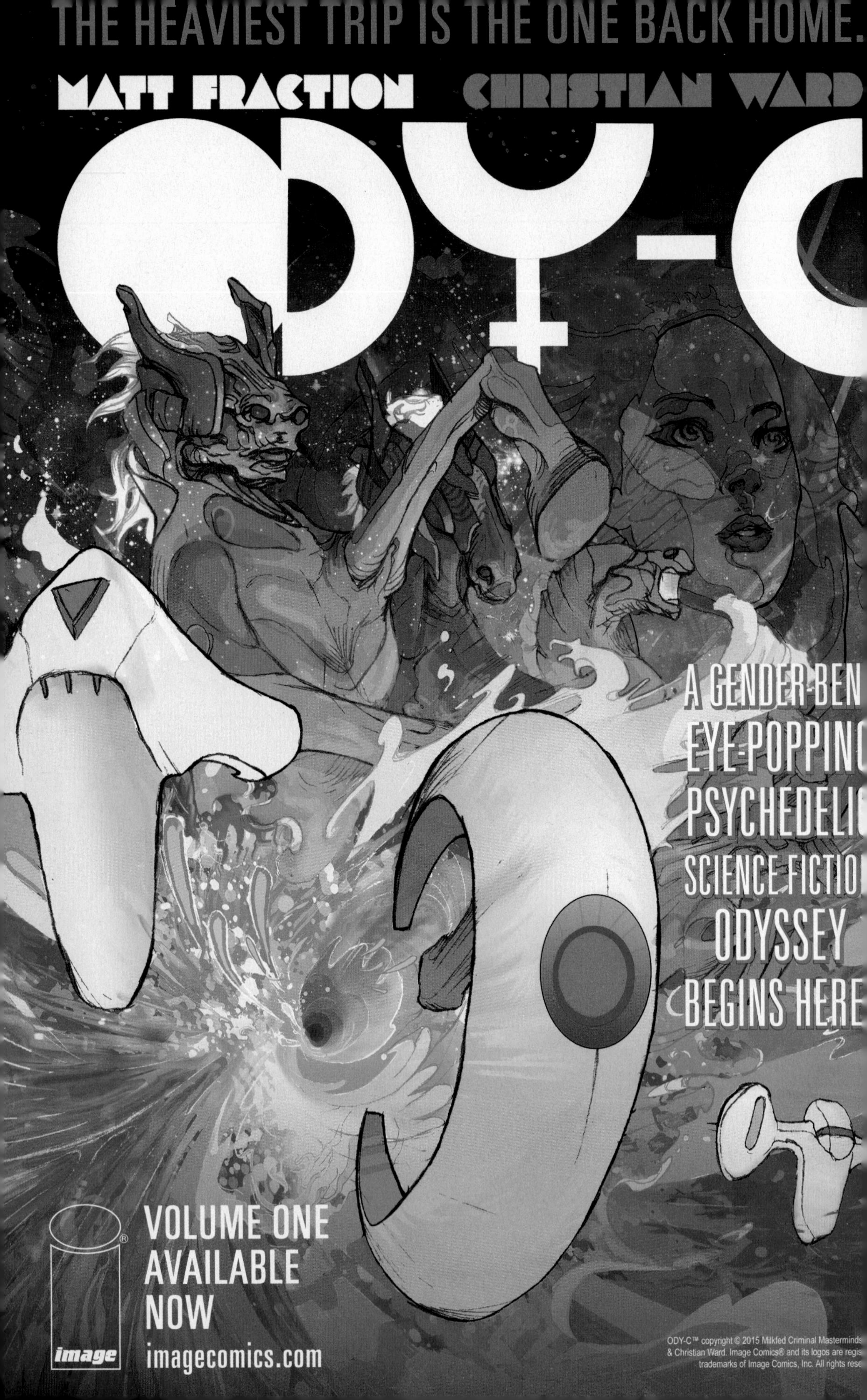
THE HEAVIEST TRIP IS THE ONE BACK HOME.
MATT FRACTION
CHRISTIAN WARD
ODY-C
A GENDER-BEN
EYE-POPPIN
PSYCHEDELI
SCIENCE FICTIO
ODYSSEY
BEGINS HERE
VOLUME ONE
AVAILABLE
NOW
image
imagecomics.com
ODY-C™ copyright © 2015 Milkfed Criminal Masterminds
& Christian Ward. Image Comics® and its logos are regis
trademarks of Image Comics, Inc. All rights rese

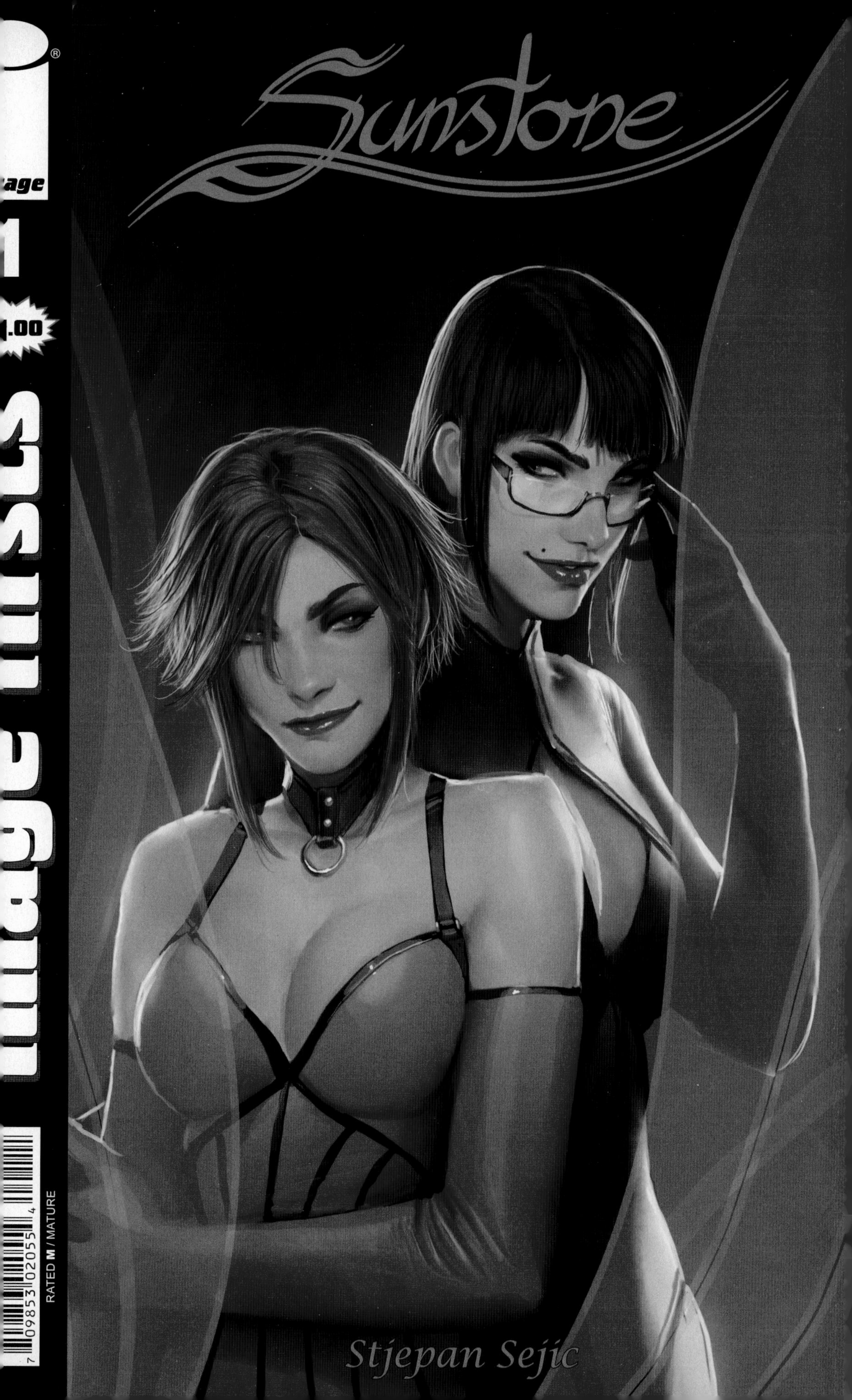Sunstone
image firsts
1
RATED M / MATURE
Stjepan Sejic

Top Cow Productions Presents...

Sunstone

Stjepan Sejic
Creater, Artist, and Writer

Stjepan Sejic
Cover Art

Betsy Gonia & Ryan Cady
Editors

Tricia Ramos
Production

For Top Cow Productions, Inc.

Marc Silvestri - *CEO* • Matt Hawkins - *President and COO*

Betsy Gonia - *Editor* • Bryan Hill - *Story Editor*

Elena Salcedo - *Operations Manager* • Ryan Cady - *Editorial Assistant*

Vincent Valentine - *Production Assistant*

To find the comic shop
nearest you, call:
1-888-COMICBOOK

Want more info? Check out:
www.topcow.com
for news & exclusive Top Cow merchand

IMAGE COMICS, INC.
Robert Kirkman – Chief Operating Officer
Erik Larsen – Chief Financial Officer
Todd McFarlane – President
Marc Silvestri – Chief Executive Officer
Jim Valentine – Vice-President
Eric Stephenson – Publisher
Corey Murphy – Director of Sales
Jeff Boison – Director of Publishing Planning & Book Trade Sales
Jeremy Sullivan – Director of Digital Sales
Kat Salazar – Director of PR & Marketing
Emily Miller – Director of Operations
Branwyn Bigglestone – Senior Accounts Manager
Sarah Mello – Accounts Manager
Drew Gill – Art Director
Jonathan Chan – Production Manager
Meredith Wallace – Print Manager
Briah Skelly – Publicity Assistant
Randy Okamura – Marketing Production Designer
David Brothers – Branding Manager
Ally Power – Content Manager
Addison Duke – Production Artist
Vincent Kukua – Production Artist
Sasha Head – Production Artist
Tricia Ramos – Production Artist
Jeff Stang – Direct Market Sales Representative
Emilio Bautista – Digital Sales Associate
Chloe Ramos-Peterson – Administrative Assistant
IMAGECOMICS.COM

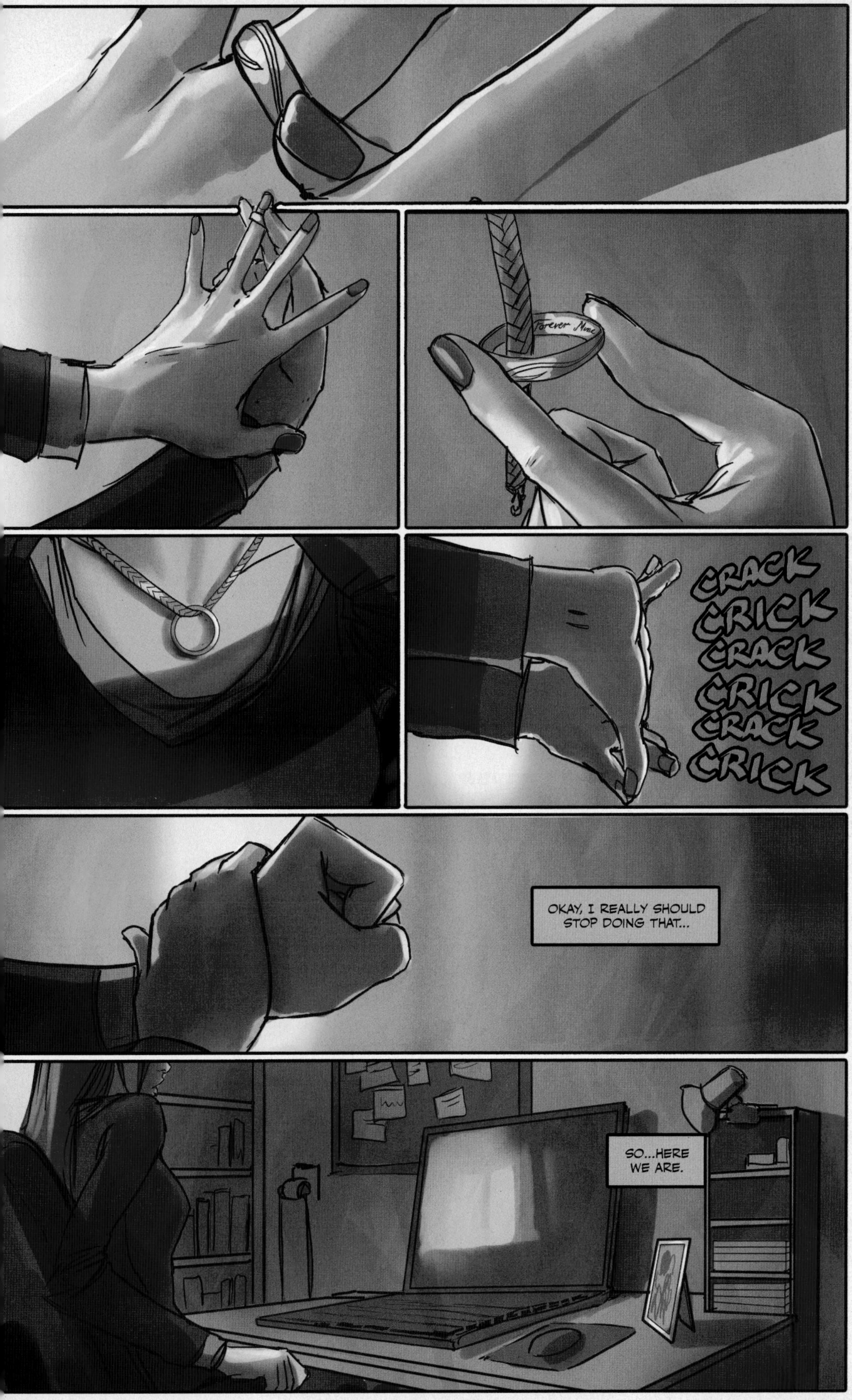
Forever Mine
CRACK
CRICK
CRACK
CRICK
CRACK
CRICK
OKAY, I REALLY SHOULD STOP DOING THAT...
SO...HERE WE ARE.

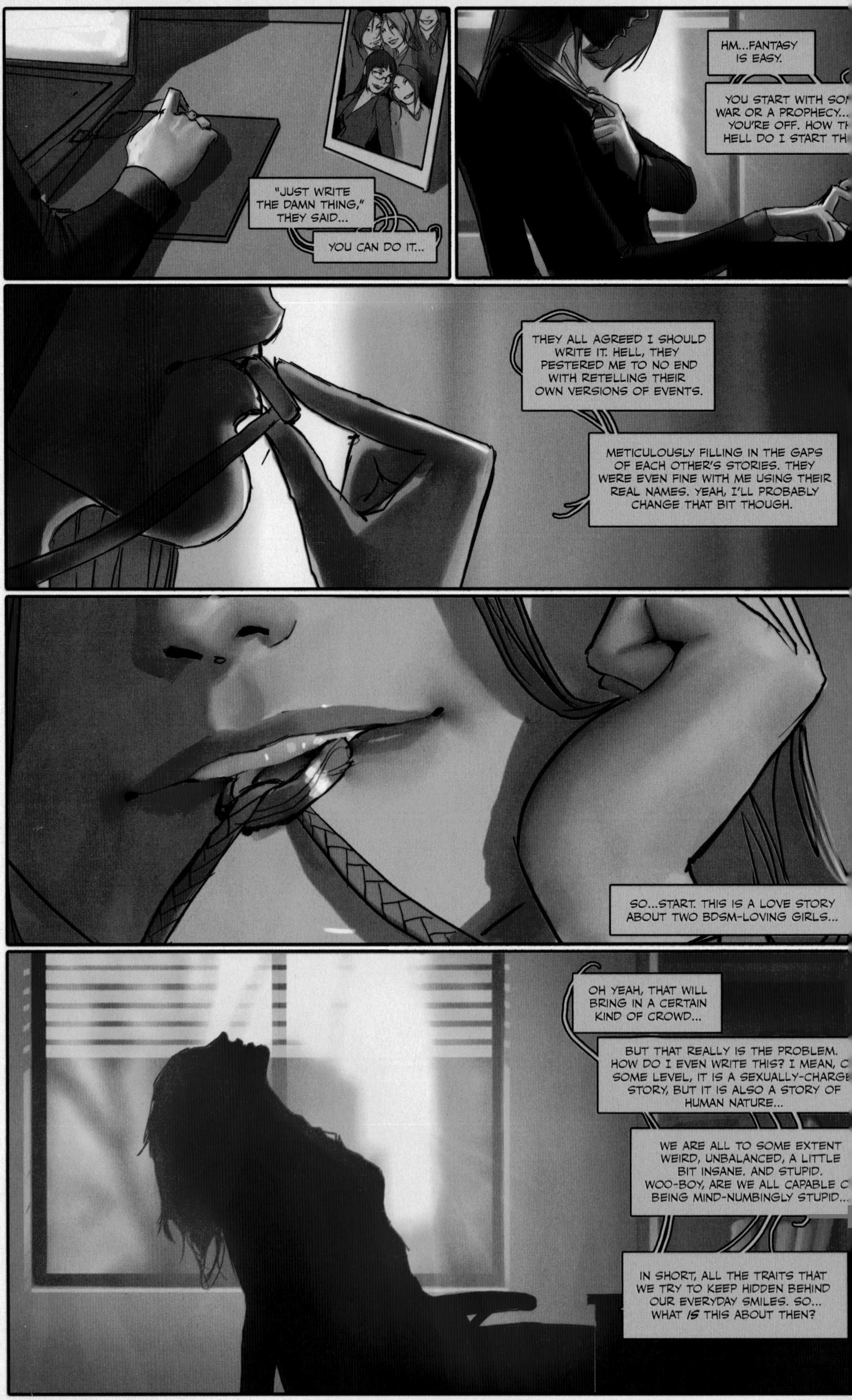
"JUST WRITE THE DAMN THING," THEY SAID...
YOU CAN DO IT...
HM...FANTASY IS EASY.
YOU START WITH SO WAR OR A PROPHECY... YOU'RE OFF. HOW T HELL DO I START TH
THEY ALL AGREED I SHOULD WRITE IT. HELL, THEY PESTERED ME TO NO END WITH RETELLING THEIR OWN VERSIONS OF EVENTS.
METICULOUSLY FILLING IN THE GAPS OF EACH OTHER'S STORIES. THEY WERE EVEN FINE WITH ME USING THEIR REAL NAMES. YEAH, I'LL PROBABLY CHANGE THAT BIT THOUGH.
SO...START. THIS IS A LOVE STORY ABOUT TWO BDSM-LOVING GIRLS...
OH YEAH, THAT WILL BRING IN A CERTAIN KIND OF CROWD...
BUT THAT REALLY IS THE PROBLEM. HOW DO I EVEN WRITE THIS? I MEAN, O SOME LEVEL, IT IS A SEXUALLY-CHARGE STORY, BUT IT IS ALSO A STORY OF HUMAN NATURE...
WE ARE ALL TO SOME EXTENT WEIRD, UNBALANCED, A LITTLE BIT INSANE. AND STUPID. WOO-BOY, ARE WE ALL CAPABLE O BEING MIND-NUMBINGLY STUPID...
IN SHORT, ALL THE TRAITS THAT WE TRY TO KEEP HIDDEN BEHIND OUR EVERYDAY SMILES. SO... WHAT *IS* THIS ABOUT THEN?

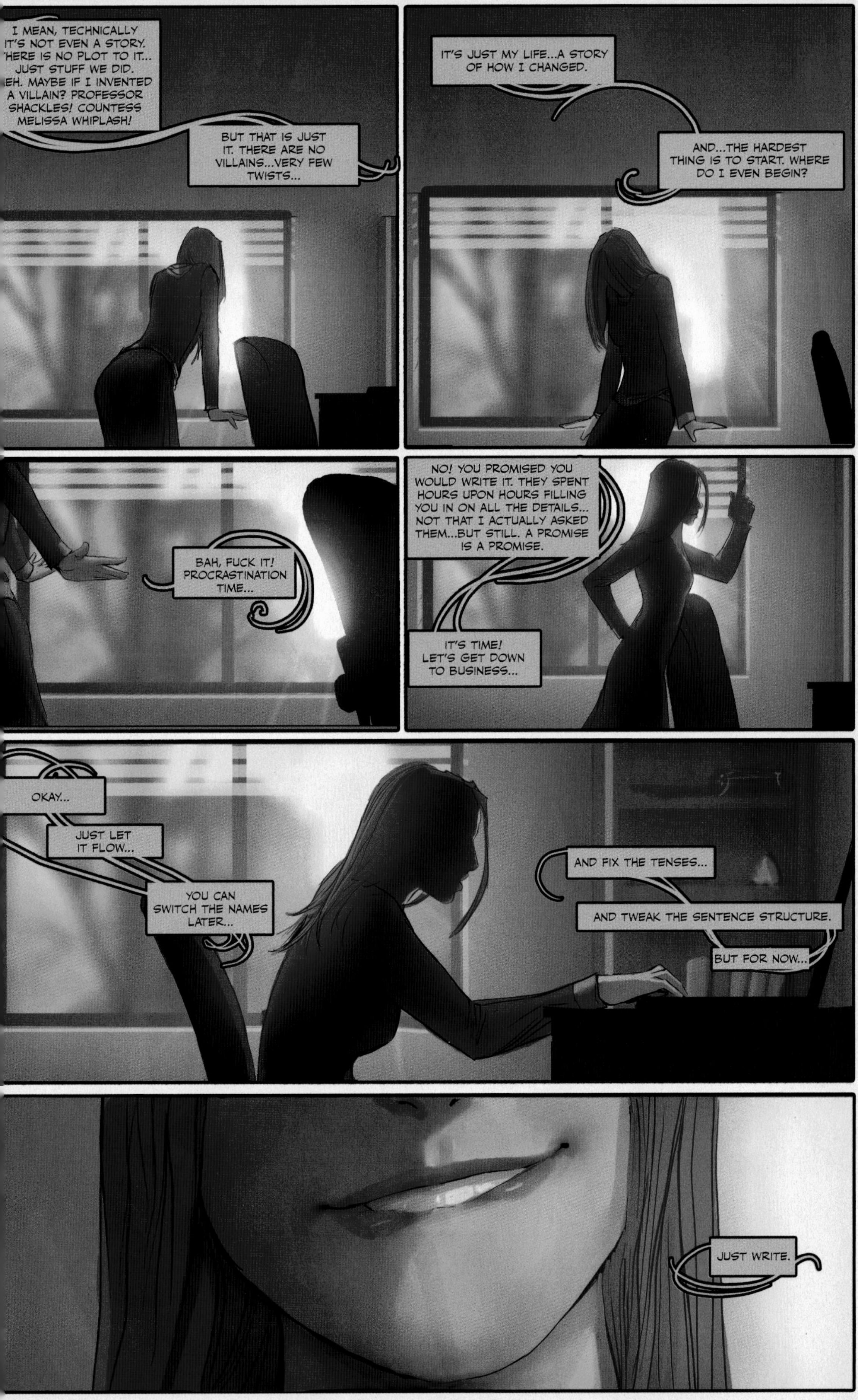
I MEAN, TECHNICALLY IT'S NOT EVEN A STORY. THERE IS NO PLOT TO IT... JUST STUFF WE DID. EH. MAYBE IF I INVENTED A VILLAIN? PROFESSOR SHACKLES! COUNTESS MELISSA WHIPLASH!
BUT THAT IS JUST IT. THERE ARE NO VILLAINS...VERY FEW TWISTS...
IT'S JUST MY LIFE...A STORY OF HOW I CHANGED.
AND...THE HARDEST THING IS TO START. WHERE DO I EVEN BEGIN?
BAH, FUCK IT! PROCRASTINATION TIME...
NO! YOU PROMISED YOU WOULD WRITE IT. THEY SPENT HOURS UPON HOURS FILLING YOU IN ON ALL THE DETAILS... NOT THAT I ACTUALLY ASKED THEM...BUT STILL. A PROMISE IS A PROMISE.
IT'S TIME! LET'S GET DOWN TO BUSINESS...
OKAY...
JUST LET IT FLOW...
YOU CAN SWITCH THE NAMES LATER...
AND FIX THE TENSES...
AND TWEAK THE SENTENCE STRUCTURE.
BUT FOR NOW...
JUST WRITE.

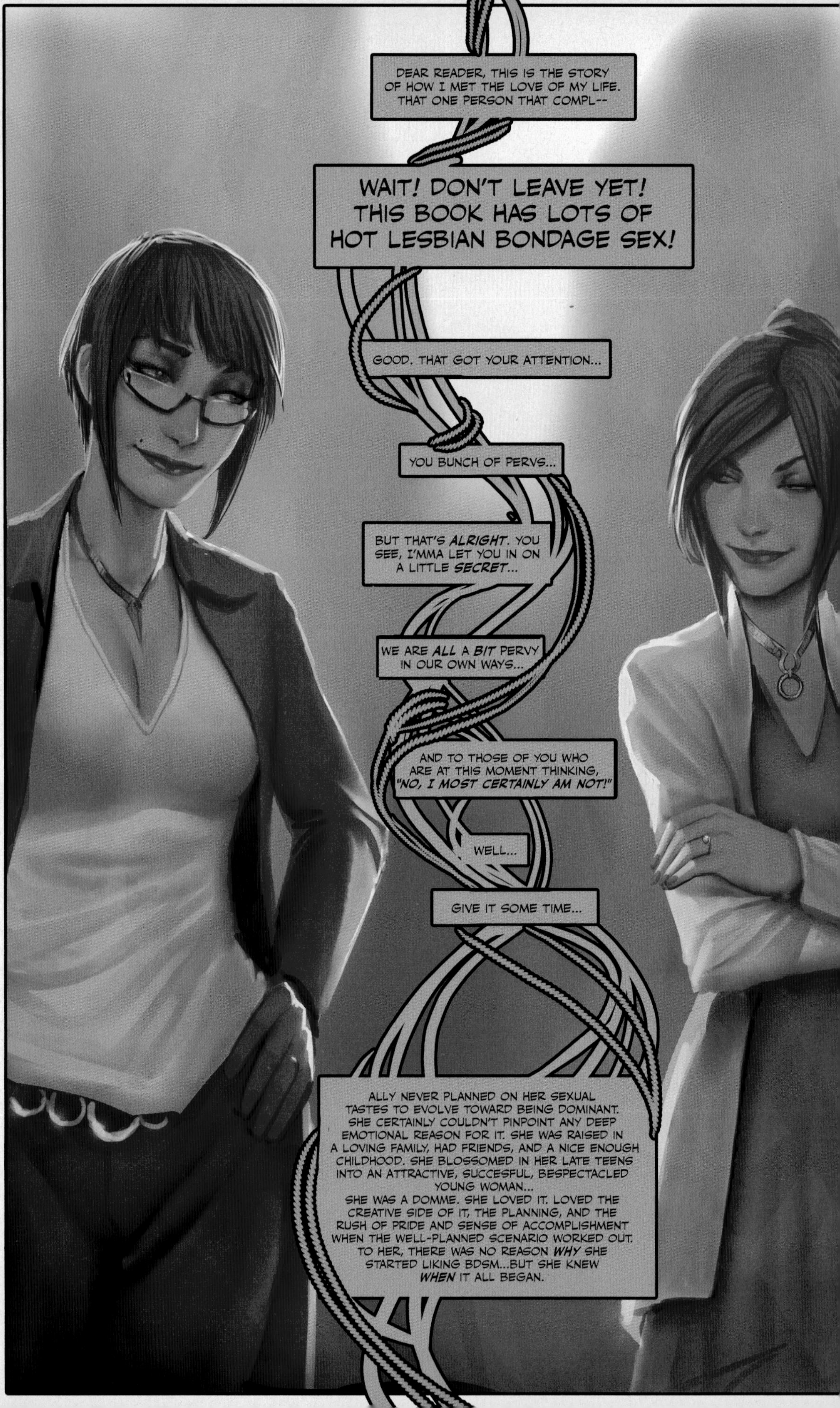
DEAR READER, THIS IS THE STORY OF HOW I MET THE LOVE OF MY LIFE. THAT ONE PERSON THAT COMPL--
WAIT! DON'T LEAVE YET! THIS BOOK HAS LOTS OF HOT LESBIAN BONDAGE SEX!
GOOD. THAT GOT YOUR ATTENTION...
YOU BUNCH OF PERVS...
BUT THAT'S *ALRIGHT*. YOU SEE, I'MMA LET YOU IN ON A LITTLE *SECRET*...
WE ARE *ALL* A *BIT* PERVY IN OUR OWN WAYS...
AND TO THOSE OF YOU WHO ARE AT THIS MOMENT THINKING, *"NO, I MOST CERTAINLY AM NOT!"*
WELL...
GIVE IT SOME TIME...
ALLY NEVER PLANNED ON HER SEXUAL TASTES TO EVOLVE TOWARD BEING DOMINANT. SHE CERTAINLY COULDN'T PINPOINT ANY DEEP EMOTIONAL REASON FOR IT. SHE WAS RAISED IN A LOVING FAMILY, HAD FRIENDS, AND A NICE ENOUGH CHILDHOOD. SHE BLOSSOMED IN HER LATE TEENS INTO AN ATTRACTIVE, SUCCESFUL, BESPECTACLED YOUNG WOMAN...
SHE WAS A DOMME. SHE LOVED IT. LOVED THE CREATIVE SIDE OF IT, THE PLANNING, AND THE RUSH OF PRIDE AND SENSE OF ACCOMPLISHMENT WHEN THE WELL-PLANNED SCENARIO WORKED OUT. TO HER, THERE WAS NO REASON *WHY* SHE STARTED LIKING BDSM...BUT SHE KNEW *WHEN* IT ALL BEGAN.

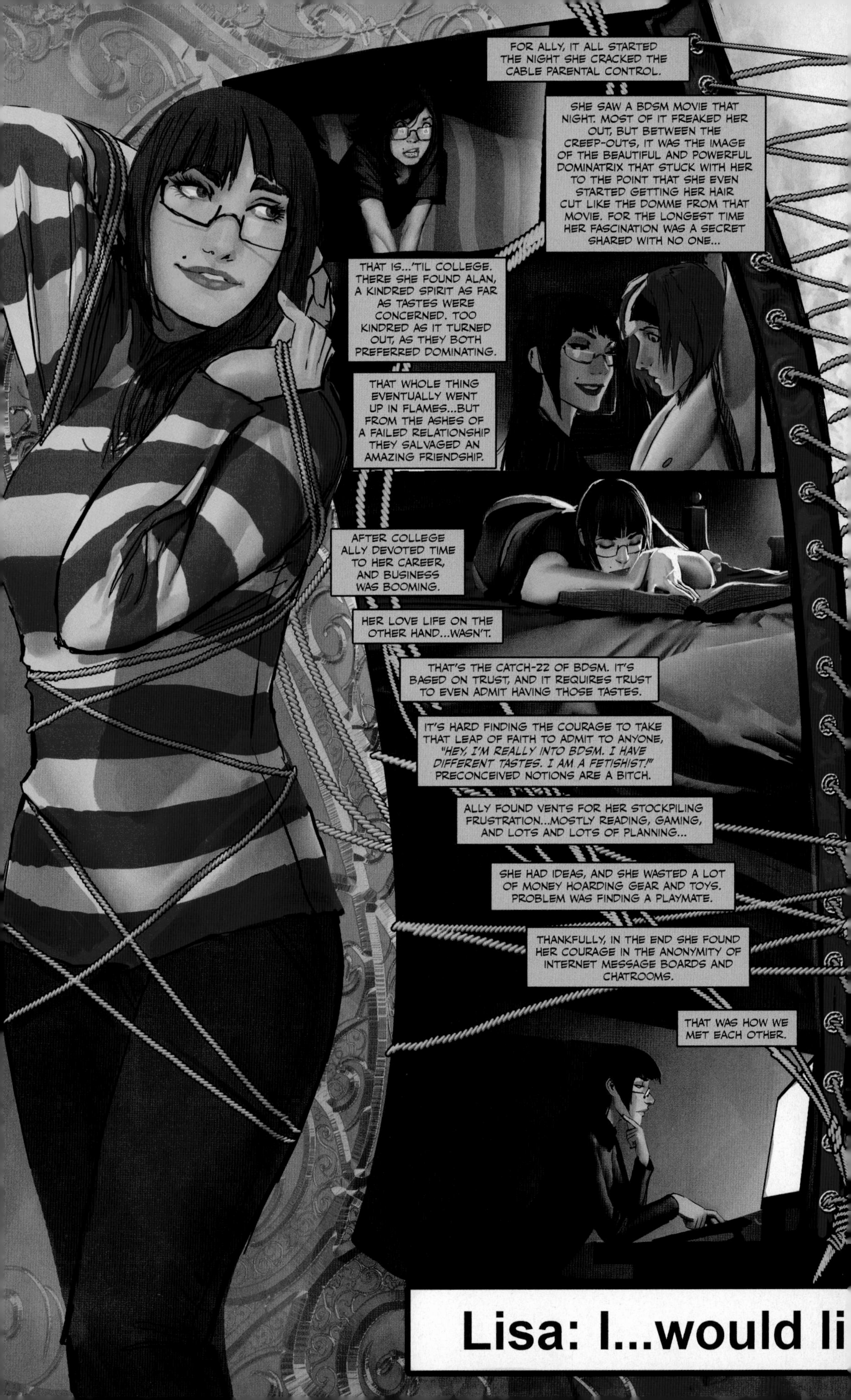
FOR ALLY, IT ALL STARTED THE NIGHT SHE CRACKED THE CABLE PARENTAL CONTROL.
SHE SAW A BDSM MOVIE THAT NIGHT. MOST OF IT FREAKED HER OUT, BUT BETWEEN THE CREEP-OUTS, IT WAS THE IMAGE OF THE BEAUTIFUL AND POWERFUL DOMINATRIX THAT STUCK WITH HER TO THE POINT THAT SHE EVEN STARTED GETTING HER HAIR CUT LIKE THE DOMME FROM THAT MOVIE. FOR THE LONGEST TIME HER FASCINATION WAS A SECRET SHARED WITH NO ONE...
THAT IS...'TIL COLLEGE. THERE SHE FOUND ALAN, A KINDRED SPIRIT AS FAR AS TASTES WERE CONCERNED. TOO KINDRED AS IT TURNED OUT, AS THEY BOTH PREFERRED DOMINATING.
THAT WHOLE THING EVENTUALLY WENT UP IN FLAMES...BUT FROM THE ASHES OF A FAILED RELATIONSHIP THEY SALVAGED AN AMAZING FRIENDSHIP.
AFTER COLLEGE ALLY DEVOTED TIME TO HER CAREER, AND BUSINESS WAS BOOMING.
HER LOVE LIFE ON THE OTHER HAND...WASN'T.
THAT'S THE CATCH-22 OF BDSM. IT'S BASED ON TRUST, AND IT REQUIRES TRUST TO EVEN ADMIT HAVING THOSE TASTES.
IT'S HARD FINDING THE COURAGE TO TAKE THAT LEAP OF FAITH TO ADMIT TO ANYONE, *"HEY, I'M REALLY INTO BDSM. I HAVE DIFFERENT TASTES. I AM A FETISHIST!"* PRECONCEIVED NOTIONS ARE A BITCH.
ALLY FOUND VENTS FOR HER STOCKPILING FRUSTRATION...MOSTLY READING, GAMING, AND LOTS AND LOTS OF PLANNING...
SHE HAD IDEAS, AND SHE WASTED A LOT OF MONEY HOARDING GEAR AND TOYS. PROBLEM WAS FINDING A PLAYMATE.
THANKFULLY, IN THE END SHE FOUND HER COURAGE IN THE ANONYMITY OF INTERNET MESSAGE BOARDS AND CHATROOMS.
THAT WAS HOW WE MET EACH OTHER.
Lisa: I...would li

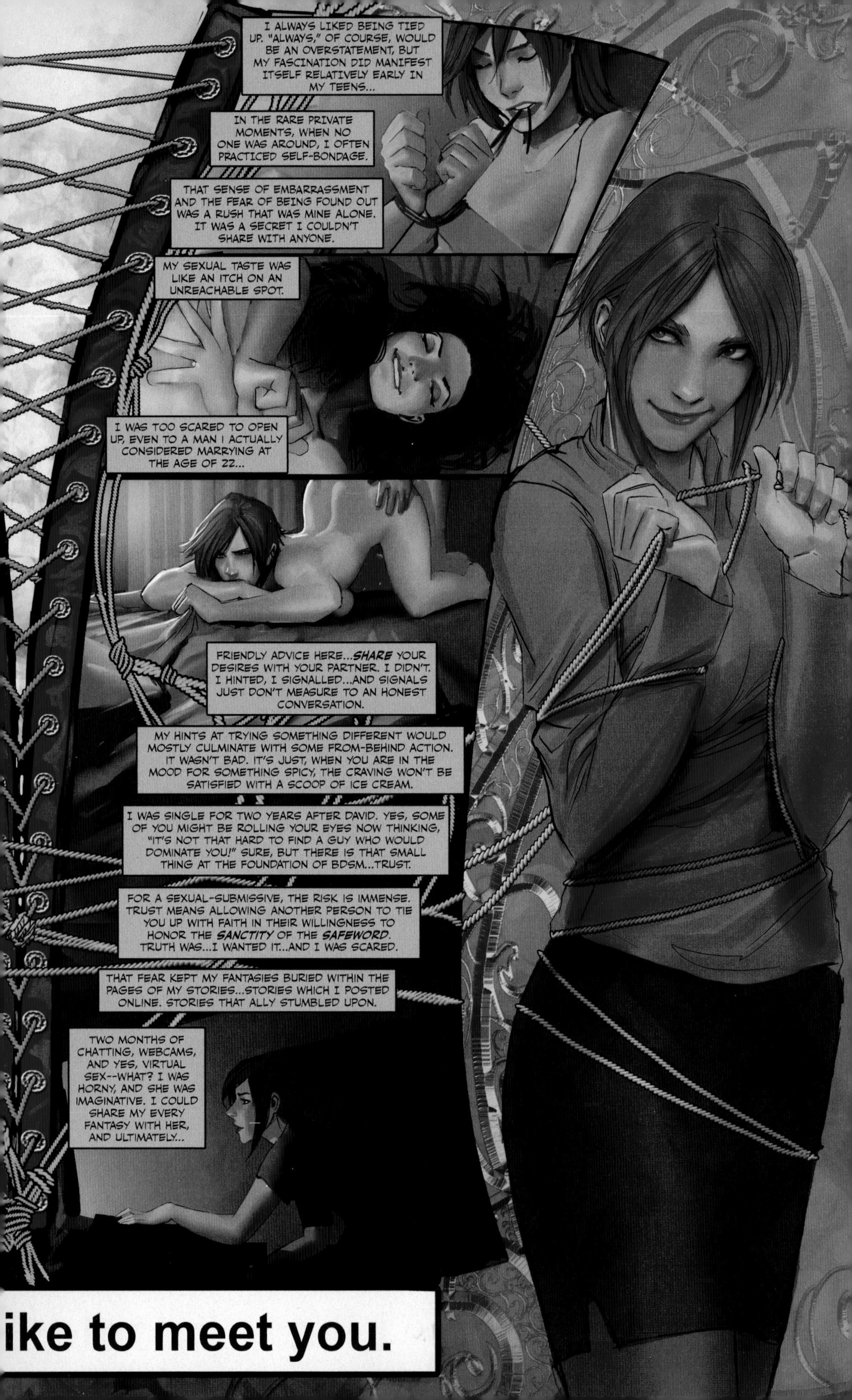
I ALWAYS LIKED BEING TIED UP. "ALWAYS," OF COURSE, WOULD BE AN OVERSTATEMENT, BUT MY FASCINATION DID MANIFEST ITSELF RELATIVELY EARLY IN MY TEENS...
IN THE RARE PRIVATE MOMENTS, WHEN NO ONE WAS AROUND, I OFTEN PRACTICED SELF-BONDAGE.
THAT SENSE OF EMBARRASSMENT AND THE FEAR OF BEING FOUND OUT WAS A RUSH THAT WAS MINE ALONE. IT WAS A SECRET I COULDN'T SHARE WITH ANYONE.
MY SEXUAL TASTE WAS LIKE AN ITCH ON AN UNREACHABLE SPOT.
I WAS TOO SCARED TO OPEN UP, EVEN TO A MAN I ACTUALLY CONSIDERED MARRYING AT THE AGE OF 22...
FRIENDLY ADVICE HERE...SHARE YOUR DESIRES WITH YOUR PARTNER. I DIDN'T. I HINTED, I SIGNALLED...AND SIGNALS JUST DON'T MEASURE TO AN HONEST CONVERSATION.
MY HINTS AT TRYING SOMETHING DIFFERENT WOULD MOSTLY CULMINATE WITH SOME FROM-BEHIND ACTION. IT WASN'T BAD. IT'S JUST, WHEN YOU ARE IN THE MOOD FOR SOMETHING SPICY, THE CRAVING WON'T BE SATISFIED WITH A SCOOP OF ICE CREAM.
I WAS SINGLE FOR TWO YEARS AFTER DAVID. YES, SOME OF YOU MIGHT BE ROLLING YOUR EYES NOW THINKING, "IT'S NOT THAT HARD TO FIND A GUY WHO WOULD DOMINATE YOU!" SURE, BUT THERE IS THAT SMALL THING AT THE FOUNDATION OF BDSM...TRUST.
FOR A SEXUAL-SUBMISSIVE, THE RISK IS IMMENSE. TRUST MEANS ALLOWING ANOTHER PERSON TO TIE YOU UP WITH FAITH IN THEIR WILLINGNESS TO HONOR THE SANCTITY OF THE SAFEWORD. TRUTH WAS...I WANTED IT...AND I WAS SCARED.
THAT FEAR KEPT MY FANTASIES BURIED WITHIN THE PAGES OF MY STORIES...STORIES WHICH I POSTED ONLINE. STORIES THAT ALLY STUMBLED UPON.
TWO MONTHS OF CHATTING, WEBCAMS, AND YES, VIRTUAL SEX--WHAT? I WAS HORNY, AND SHE WAS IMAGINATIVE. I COULD SHARE MY EVERY FANTASY WITH HER, AND ULTIMATELY...
ike to meet you.

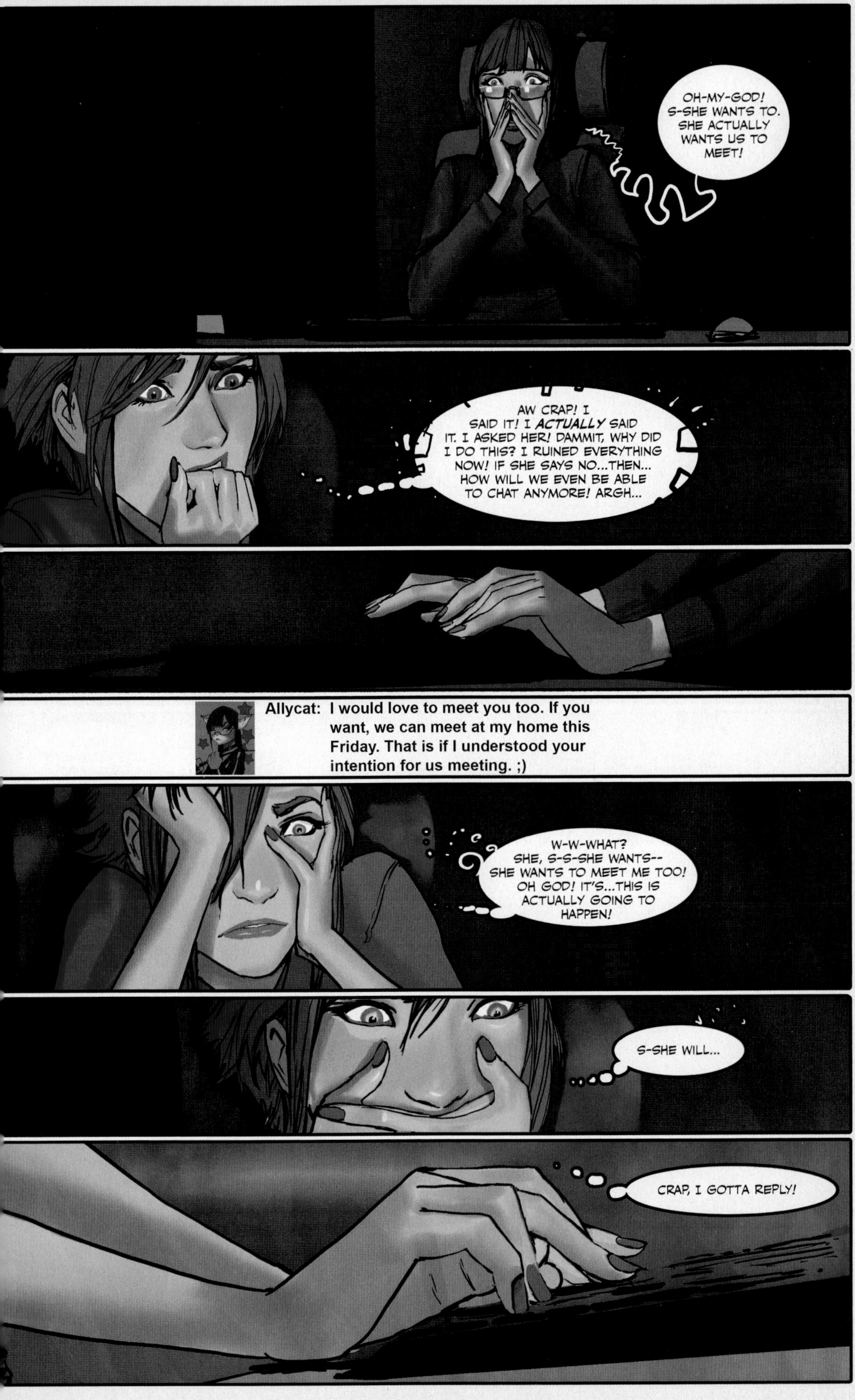
OH-MY-GOD! S-SHE WANTS TO. SHE ACTUALLY WANTS US TO MEET!
AW CRAP! I SAID IT! I ACTUALLY SAID IT. I ASKED HER! DAMMIT, WHY DID I DO THIS? I RUINED EVERYTHING NOW! IF SHE SAYS NO...THEN... HOW WILL WE EVEN BE ABLE TO CHAT ANYMORE! ARGH...
Allycat: I would love to meet you too. If you want, we can meet at my home this Friday. That is if I understood your intention for us meeting. ;)
W-W-WHAT? SHE, S-S-SHE WANTS-- SHE WANTS TO MEET ME TOO! OH GOD! IT'S...THIS IS ACTUALLY GOING TO HAPPEN!
S-SHE WILL...
CRAP, I GOTTA REPLY!

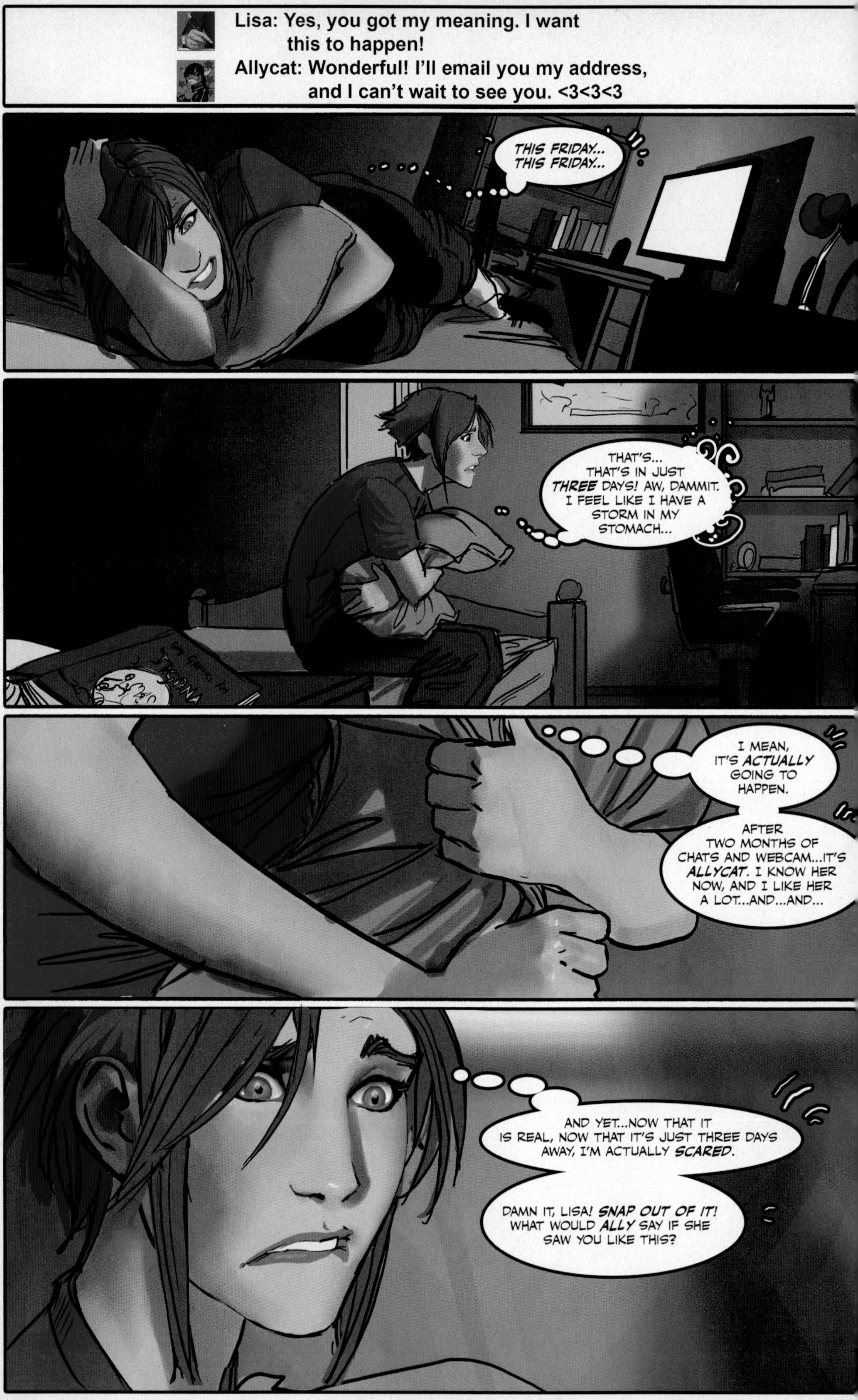
Lisa: Yes, you got my meaning. I want this to happen!
Allycat: Wonderful! I'll email you my address, and I can't wait to see you. <3<3<3
THIS FRIDAY... THIS FRIDAY...
THAT'S... THAT'S IN JUST THREE DAYS! AW, DAMMIT. I FEEL LIKE I HAVE A STORM IN MY STOMACH...
I MEAN, IT'S ACTUALLY GOING TO HAPPEN.
AFTER TWO MONTHS OF CHATS AND WEBCAM...IT'S ALLYCAT. I KNOW HER NOW, AND I LIKE HER A LOT...AND...AND...
AND YET...NOW THAT IT IS REAL, NOW THAT IT'S JUST THREE DAYS AWAY, I'M ACTUALLY SCARED.
DAMN IT, LISA! SNAP OUT OF IT! WHAT WOULD ALLY SAY IF SHE SAW YOU LIKE THIS?

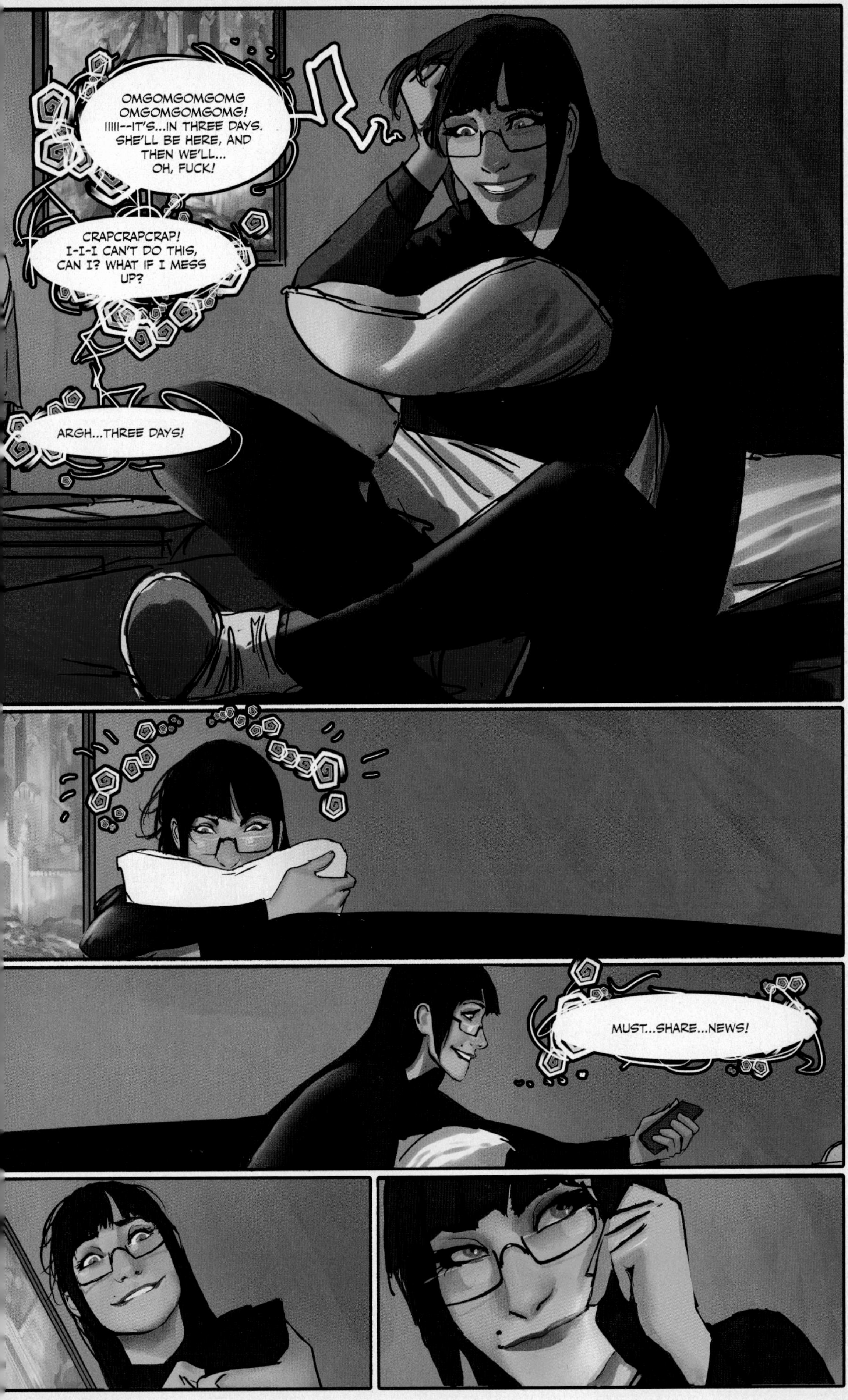
OMGOMGOMGOMG OMGOMGOMGOMG! IIIII--IT'S...IN THREE DAYS. SHE'LL BE HERE, AND THEN WE'LL... OH, FUCK!
CRAPCRAPCRAP! I-I-I CAN'T DO THIS, CAN I? WHAT IF I MESS UP?
ARGH...THREE DAYS!
MUST...SHARE...NEWS!

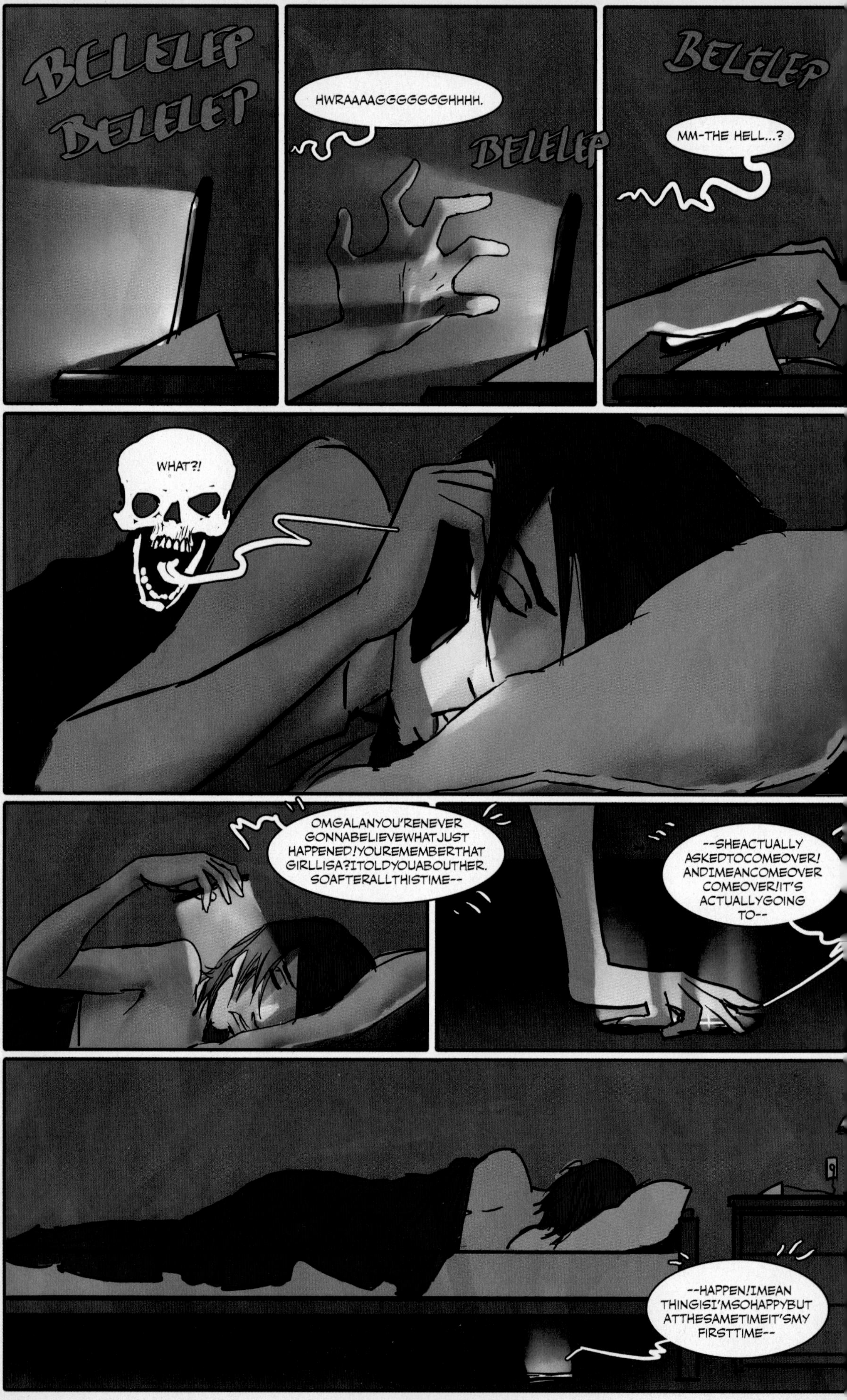
BELELEP
BELELEP
HWRAAAAGGGGGGGHHHH.
BELELEP
BELELEP
MM-THE HELL...?
WHAT?!
OMGALANYOU'RENEVER GONNABELIEVEWHATJUST HAPPENED!YOUREMEMBERTHAT GIRLLISA?ITOLDYOUABOUTHER. SOAFTERALLTHISTIME--
--SHEACTUALLY ASKEDTOCOMEOVER! ANDIMEANCOMEOVER COMEOVER!IT'S ACTUALLYGOING TO--
--HAPPEN!IMEAN THINGISI'MSOHAPPYBUT ATTHESAMETIMEIT'SMY FIRSTTIME--

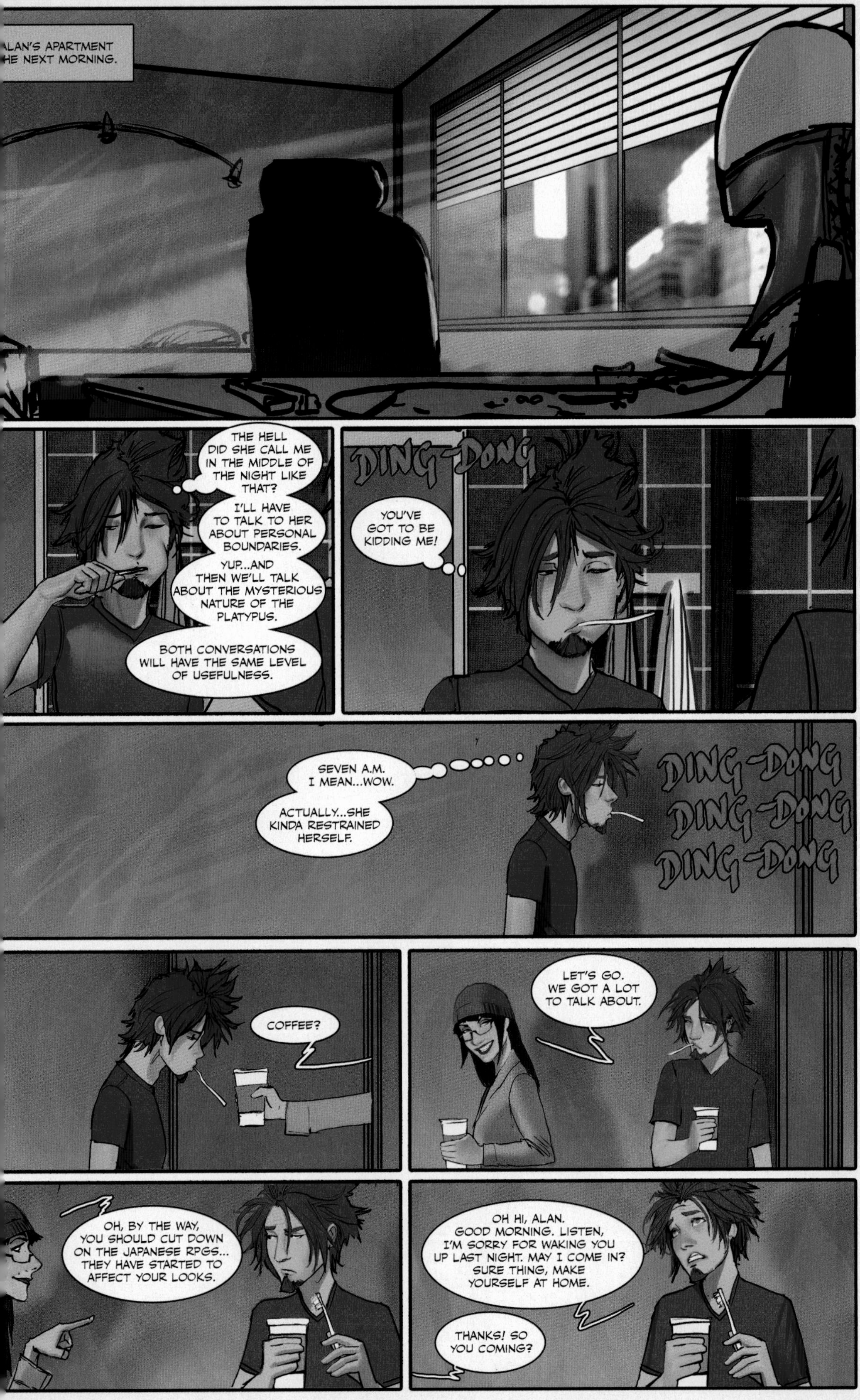
ALAN'S APARTMENT
HE NEXT MORNING.
THE HELL DID SHE CALL ME IN THE MIDDLE OF THE NIGHT LIKE THAT?
I'LL HAVE TO TALK TO HER ABOUT PERSONAL BOUNDARIES.
YUP...AND THEN WE'LL TALK ABOUT THE MYSTERIOUS NATURE OF THE PLATYPUS.
BOTH CONVERSATIONS WILL HAVE THE SAME LEVEL OF USEFULNESS.
DING-DONG
YOU'VE GOT TO BE KIDDING ME!
SEVEN A.M. I MEAN...WOW.
ACTUALLY...SHE KINDA RESTRAINED HERSELF.
DING-DONG
DING-DONG
DING-DONG
COFFEE?
LET'S GO. WE GOT A LOT TO TALK ABOUT.
OH, BY THE WAY, YOU SHOULD CUT DOWN ON THE JAPANESE RPGS... THEY HAVE STARTED TO AFFECT YOUR LOOKS.
OH HI, ALAN. GOOD MORNING. LISTEN, I'M SORRY FOR WAKING YOU UP LAST NIGHT. MAY I COME IN? SURE THING, MAKE YOURSELF AT HOME.
THANKS! SO YOU COMING?

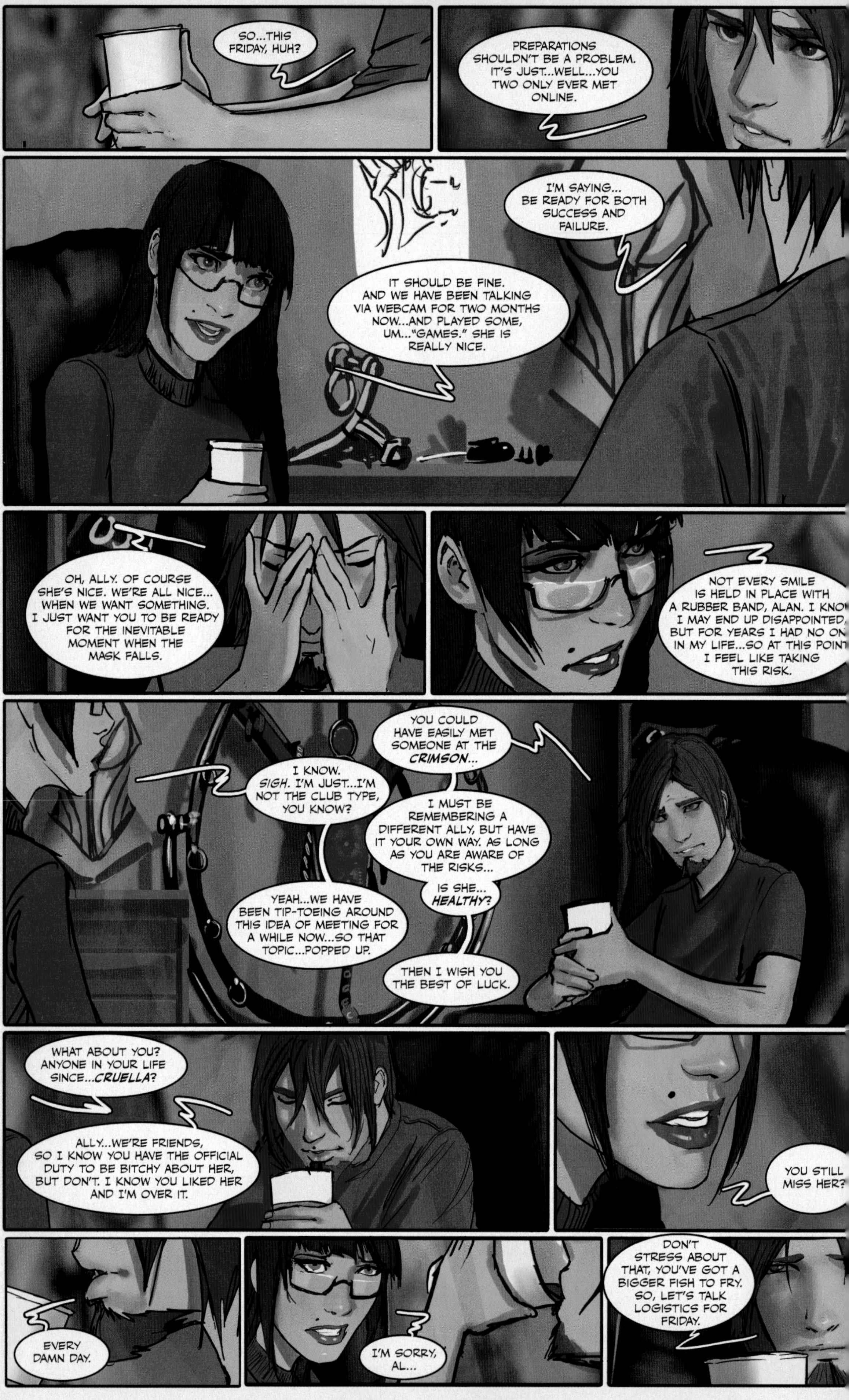
SO...THIS FRIDAY, HUH?
PREPARATIONS SHOULDN'T BE A PROBLEM. IT'S JUST...WELL...YOU TWO ONLY EVER MET ONLINE.
I'M SAYING... BE READY FOR BOTH SUCCESS AND FAILURE.
IT SHOULD BE FINE. AND WE HAVE BEEN TALKING VIA WEBCAM FOR TWO MONTHS NOW...AND PLAYED SOME, UM..."GAMES." SHE IS REALLY NICE.
OH, ALLY. OF COURSE SHE'S NICE. WE'RE ALL NICE... WHEN WE WANT SOMETHING. I JUST WANT YOU TO BE READY FOR THE INEVITABLE MOMENT WHEN THE MASK FALLS.
NOT EVERY SMILE IS HELD IN PLACE WITH A RUBBER BAND, ALAN. I KNO I MAY END UP DISAPPOINTED, BUT FOR YEARS I HAD NO ON IN MY LIFE...SO AT THIS POINT I FEEL LIKE TAKING THIS RISK.
YOU COULD HAVE EASILY MET SOMEONE AT THE CRIMSON...
I KNOW. SIGH. I'M JUST...I'M NOT THE CLUB TYPE, YOU KNOW?
I MUST BE REMEMBERING A DIFFERENT ALLY, BUT HAVE IT YOUR OWN WAY. AS LONG AS YOU ARE AWARE OF THE RISKS...
IS SHE... HEALTHY?
YEAH...WE HAVE BEEN TIP-TOEING AROUND THIS IDEA OF MEETING FOR A WHILE NOW...SO THAT TOPIC...POPPED UP.
THEN I WISH YOU THE BEST OF LUCK.
WHAT ABOUT YOU? ANYONE IN YOUR LIFE SINCE...CRUELLA?
ALLY...WE'RE FRIENDS, SO I KNOW YOU HAVE THE OFFICIAL DUTY TO BE BITCHY ABOUT HER, BUT DON'T. I KNOW YOU LIKED HER AND I'M OVER IT.
YOU STILL MISS HER?
EVERY DAMN DAY.
I'M SORRY, AL...
DON'T STRESS ABOUT THAT, YOU'VE GOT A BIGGER FISH TO FRY. SO, LET'S TALK LOGISTICS FOR FRIDAY.

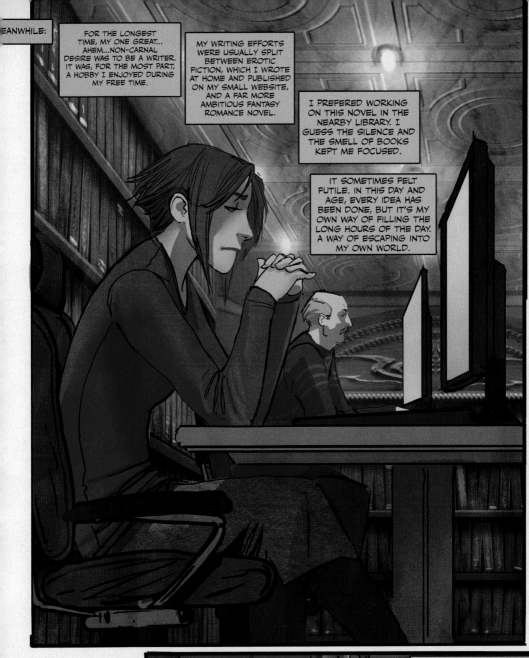

FOR THE LONGEST TIME, MY ONE GREAT... AHEM...NON-CARNAL DESIRE WAS TO BE A WRITER. IT WAS, FOR THE MOST PART, A HOBBY I ENJOYED DURING MY FREE TIME.

MY WRITING EFFORTS WERE USUALLY SPLIT BETWEEN EROTIC FICTION, WHICH I WROTE AT HOME AND PUBLISHED ON MY SMALL WEBSITE, AND A FAR MORE AMBITIOUS FANTASY ROMANCE NOVEL.

I PREFERED WORKING ON THIS NOVEL IN THE NEARBY LIBRARY. I GUESS THE SILENCE AND THE SMELL OF BOOKS KEPT ME FOCUSED.

IT SOMETIMES FELT FUTILE. IN THIS DAY AND AGE, EVERY IDEA HAS BEEN DONE, BUT IT'S MY OWN WAY OF FILLING THE LONG HOURS OF THE DAY. A WAY OF ESCAPING INTO MY OWN WORLD.

LET'S FACE IT...I HAD A FEW FREE HOURS TO BURN ON ANY GIVEN DAY, MY LOVE LIFE HAD BEEN IN A STATE OF PERPETUAL DROUGHT FOR THE LAST TWO YEARS...

AND YES...I GUESS THAT REALLY WAS MY OWN FAULT...

SO, FOR ONCE IN MY LIFE I DECIDED TO GO FOR IT. TO TAKE MY CHANCE...BE BRAVE AND FULFILL AT LEAST THIS ONE SECRET DESIRE!

NOOO....STOP IT! THIS BLANK SCREEN AIN'T GONNA FILL ITSELF...BACK TO WRITING! FOCUS!

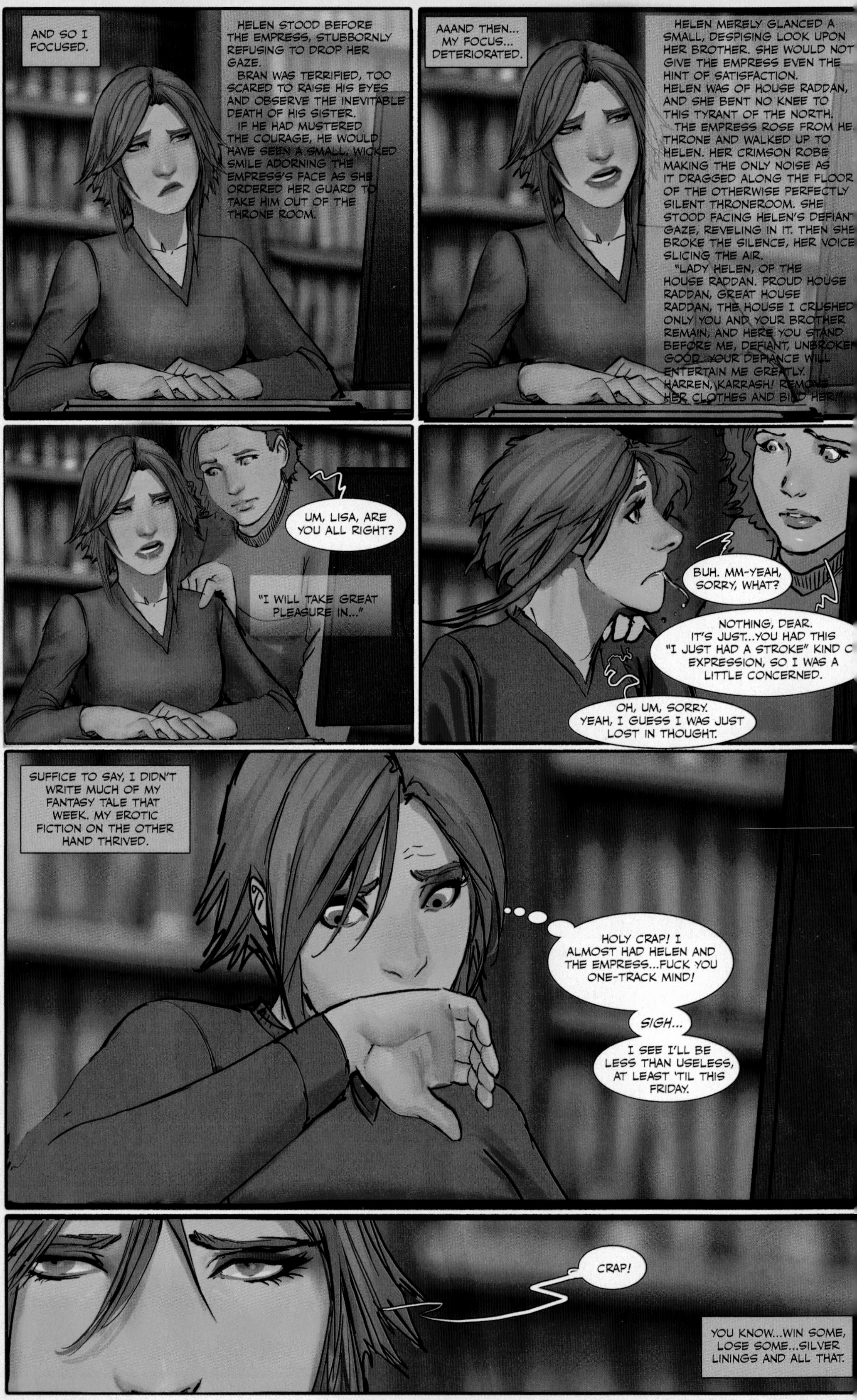
AND SO I FOCUSED.
HELEN STOOD BEFORE THE EMPRESS, STUBBORNLY REFUSING TO DROP HER GAZE.
BRAN WAS TERRIFIED, TOO SCARED TO RAISE HIS EYES AND OBSERVE THE INEVITABLE DEATH OF HIS SISTER.
IF HE HAD MUSTERED THE COURAGE, HE WOULD HAVE SEEN A SMALL, WICKED SMILE ADORNING THE EMPRESS'S FACE AS SHE ORDERED HER GUARD TO TAKE HIM OUT OF THE THRONE ROOM.
AAAND THEN... MY FOCUS... DETERIORATED.
HELEN MERELY GLANCED A SMALL, DESPISING LOOK UPON HER BROTHER. SHE WOULD NOT GIVE THE EMPRESS EVEN THE HINT OF SATISFACTION.
HELEN WAS OF HOUSE RADDAN, AND SHE BENT NO KNEE TO THIS TYRANT OF THE NORTH.
THE EMPRESS ROSE FROM HE THRONE AND WALKED UP TO HELEN. HER CRIMSON ROBE MAKING THE ONLY NOISE AS IT DRAGGED ALONG THE FLOOR OF THE OTHERWISE PERFECTLY SILENT THRONEROOM. SHE STOOD FACING HELEN'S DEFIANT GAZE, REVELING IN IT. THEN SHE BROKE THE SILENCE, HER VOICE SLICING THE AIR.
"LADY HELEN, OF THE HOUSE RADDAN. PROUD HOUSE RADDAN, GREAT HOUSE RADDAN, THE HOUSE I CRUSHED. ONLY YOU AND YOUR BROTHER REMAIN; AND HERE YOU STAND BEFORE ME, DEFIANT, UNBROKEN. GOOD. YOUR DEFIANCE WILL ENTERTAIN ME GREATLY. HARREN, KARRASH! REMOVE HER CLOTHES AND BIND HER!"
UM, LISA, ARE YOU ALL RIGHT?
"I WILL TAKE GREAT PLEASURE IN..."
BUH. MM-YEAH, SORRY, WHAT?
NOTHING, DEAR. IT'S JUST...YOU HAD THIS "I JUST HAD A STROKE" KIND O EXPRESSION, SO I WAS A LITTLE CONCERNED.
OH, UM, SORRY. YEAH, I GUESS I WAS JUST LOST IN THOUGHT.
SUFFICE TO SAY, I DIDN'T WRITE MUCH OF MY FANTASY TALE THAT WEEK. MY EROTIC FICTION ON THE OTHER HAND THRIVED.
HOLY CRAP! I ALMOST HAD HELEN AND THE EMPRESS...FUCK YOU ONE-TRACK MIND!
SIGH...
I SEE I'LL BE LESS THAN USELESS, AT LEAST 'TIL THIS FRIDAY.
CRAP!
YOU KNOW...WIN SOME, LOSE SOME...SILVER LININGS AND ALL THAT.

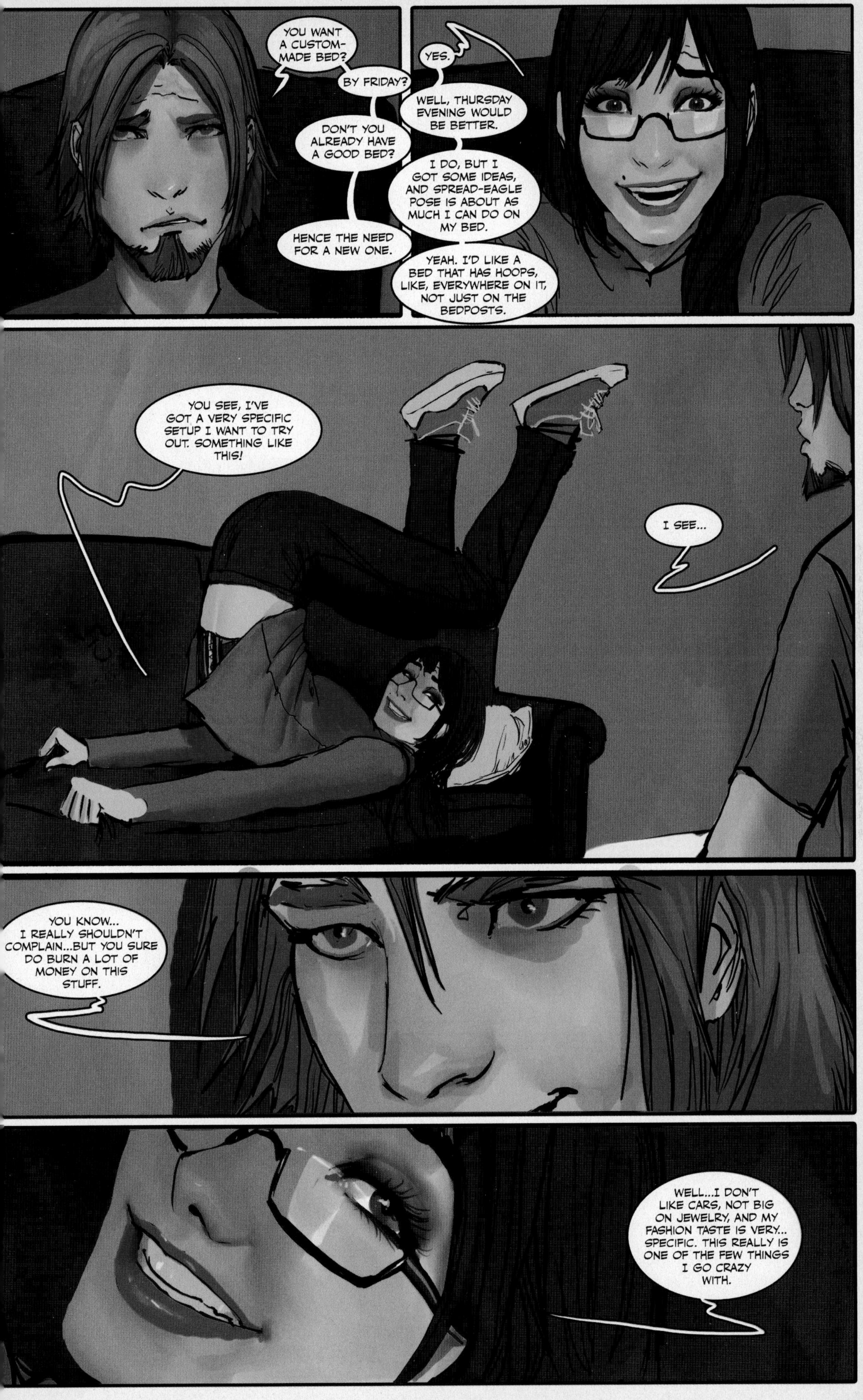
YOU WANT A CUSTOM-MADE BED?
YES.
BY FRIDAY?
WELL, THURSDAY EVENING WOULD BE BETTER.
DON'T YOU ALREADY HAVE A GOOD BED?
I DO, BUT I GOT SOME IDEAS, AND SPREAD-EAGLE POSE IS ABOUT AS MUCH I CAN DO ON MY BED.
HENCE THE NEED FOR A NEW ONE.
YEAH. I'D LIKE A BED THAT HAS HOOPS, LIKE, EVERYWHERE ON IT, NOT JUST ON THE BEDPOSTS.
YOU SEE, I'VE GOT A VERY SPECIFIC SETUP I WANT TO TRY OUT. SOMETHING LIKE THIS!
I SEE...
YOU KNOW... I REALLY SHOULDN'T COMPLAIN...BUT YOU SURE DO BURN A LOT OF MONEY ON THIS STUFF.
WELL...I DON'T LIKE CARS, NOT BIG ON JEWELRY, AND MY FASHION TASTE IS VERY... SPECIFIC. THIS REALLY IS ONE OF THE FEW THINGS I GO CRAZY WITH.

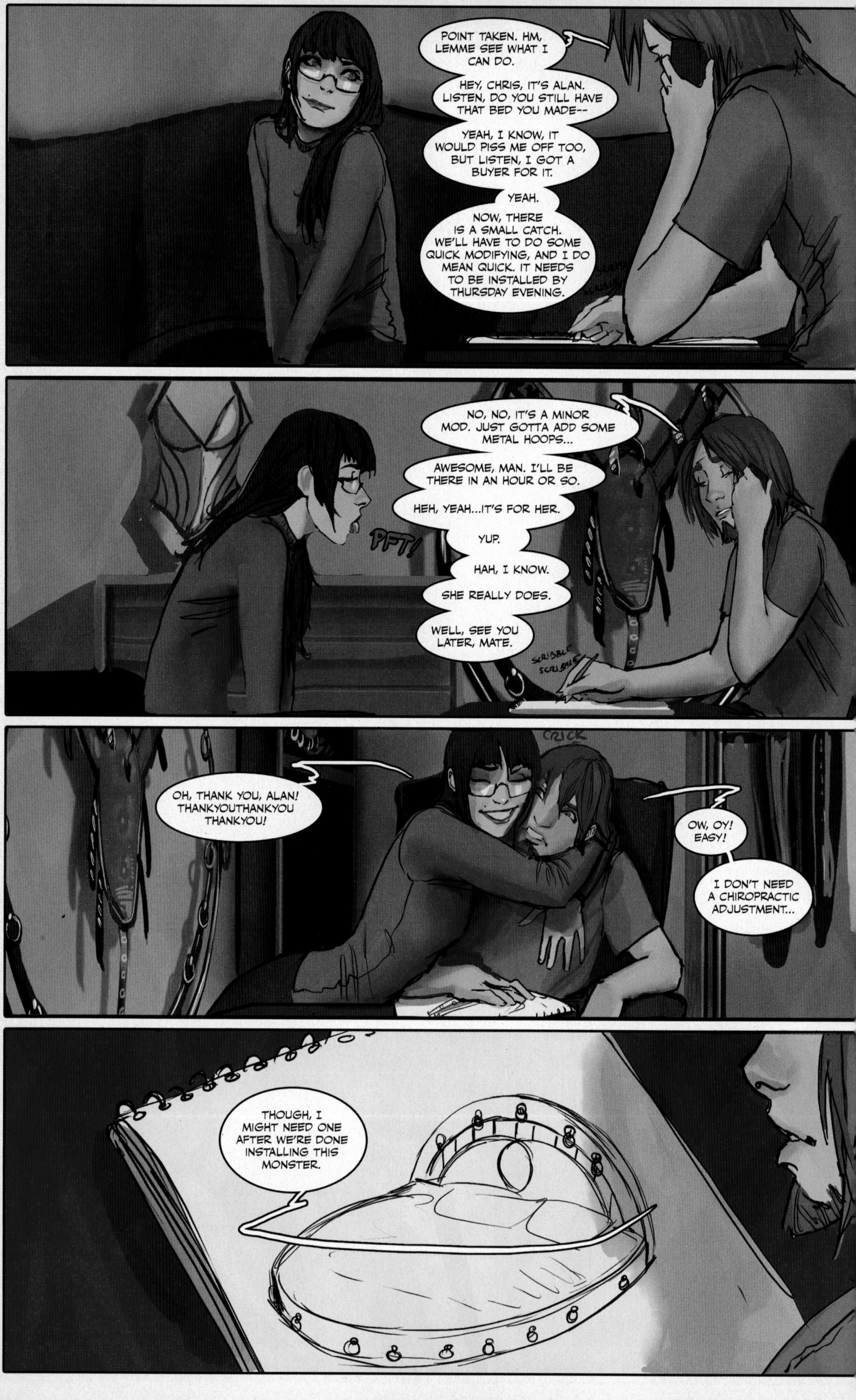
POINT TAKEN. HM, LEMME SEE WHAT I CAN DO.
HEY, CHRIS, IT'S ALAN. LISTEN, DO YOU STILL HAVE THAT BED YOU MADE--
YEAH, I KNOW, IT WOULD PISS ME OFF TOO, BUT LISTEN, I GOT A BUYER FOR IT.
YEAH.
NOW, THERE IS A SMALL CATCH. WE'LL HAVE TO DO SOME QUICK MODIFYING, AND I DO MEAN QUICK. IT NEEDS TO BE INSTALLED BY THURSDAY EVENING.
NO, NO, IT'S A MINOR MOD. JUST GOTTA ADD SOME METAL HOOPS...
AWESOME, MAN. I'LL BE THERE IN AN HOUR OR SO.
HEH, YEAH...IT'S FOR HER.
PFT!
YUP.
HAH, I KNOW.
SHE REALLY DOES.
WELL, SEE YOU LATER, MATE.
SCRIBBLE SCRIBBLE
CRICK
OH, THANK YOU, ALAN! THANKYOUTHANKYOU THANKYOU!
OW, OY! EASY!
I DON'T NEED A CHIROPRACTIC ADJUSTMENT...
THOUGH, I MIGHT NEED ONE AFTER WE'RE DONE INSTALLING THIS MONSTER.

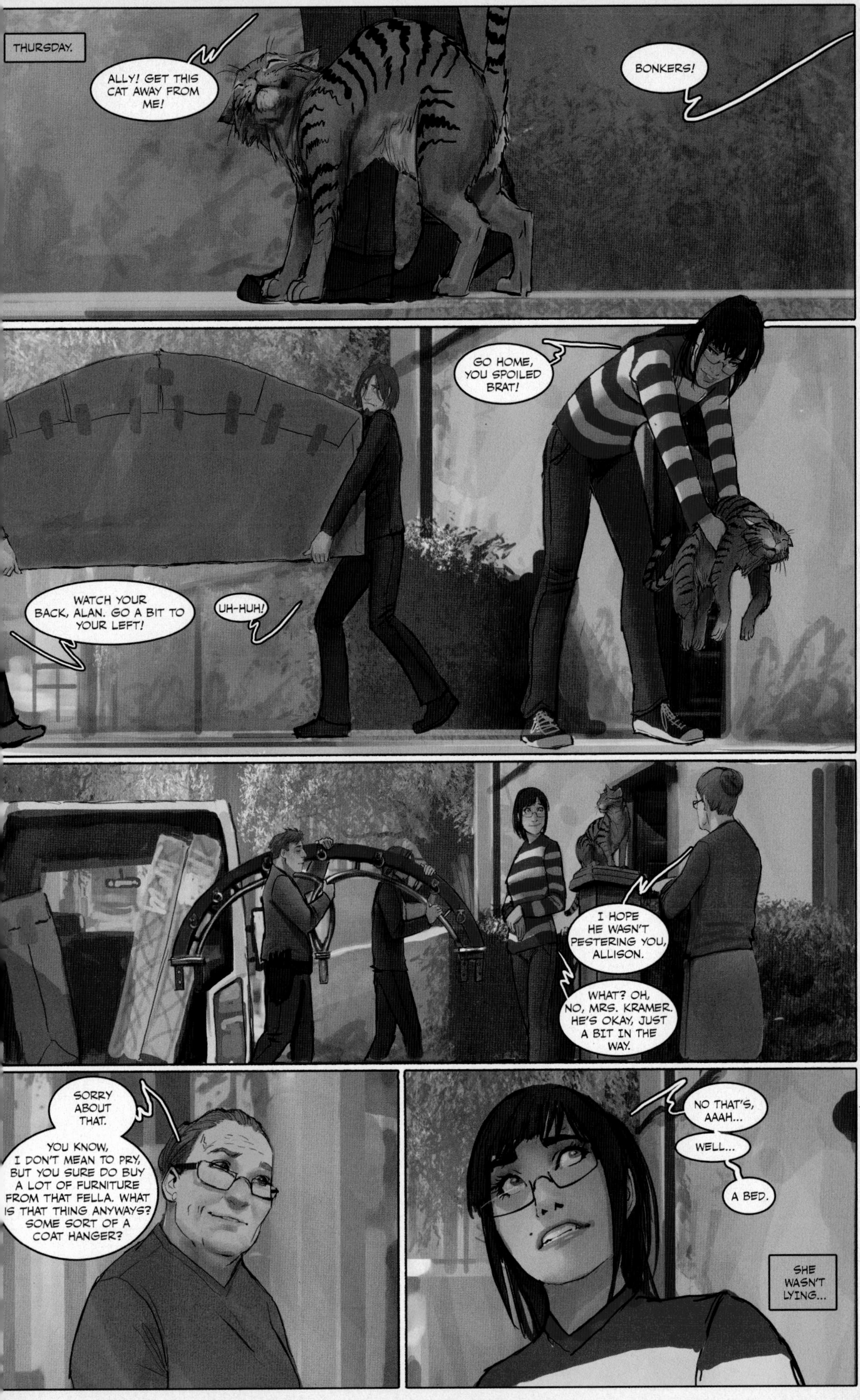
THURSDAY.
ALLY! GET THIS CAT AWAY FROM ME!
BONKERS!
GO HOME, YOU SPOILED BRAT!
WATCH YOUR BACK, ALAN. GO A BIT TO YOUR LEFT!
UH-HUH!
I HOPE HE WASN'T PESTERING YOU, ALLISON.
WHAT? OH, NO, MRS. KRAMER. HE'S OKAY, JUST A BIT IN THE WAY.
SORRY ABOUT THAT.
YOU KNOW, I DON'T MEAN TO PRY, BUT YOU SURE DO BUY A LOT OF FURNITURE FROM THAT FELLA. WHAT IS THAT THING ANYWAYS? SOME SORT OF A COAT HANGER?
NO THAT'S, AAAH...
WELL...
A BED.
SHE WASN'T LYING...

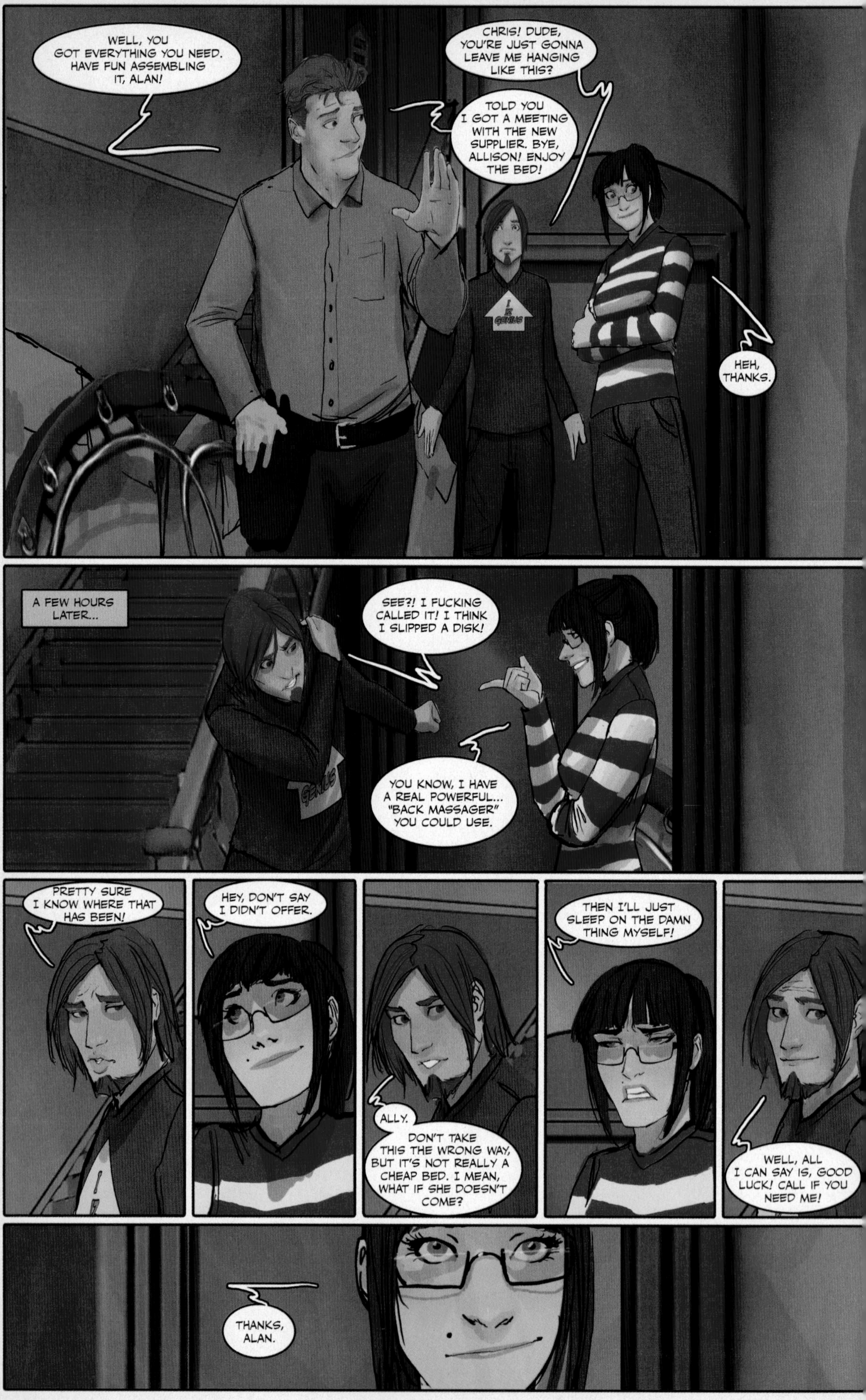
WELL, YOU GOT EVERYTHING YOU NEED. HAVE FUN ASSEMBLING IT, ALAN!
CHRIS! DUDE, YOU'RE JUST GONNA LEAVE ME HANGING LIKE THIS?
TOLD YOU I GOT A MEETING WITH THE NEW SUPPLIER. BYE, ALLISON! ENJOY THE BED!
HEH, THANKS.
A FEW HOURS LATER...
SEE?! I FUCKING CALLED IT! I THINK I SLIPPED A DISK!
YOU KNOW, I HAVE A REAL POWERFUL... "BACK MASSAGER" YOU COULD USE.
PRETTY SURE I KNOW WHERE THAT HAS BEEN!
HEY, DON'T SAY I DIDN'T OFFER.
ALLY.
DON'T TAKE THIS THE WRONG WAY, BUT IT'S NOT REALLY A CHEAP BED. I MEAN, WHAT IF SHE DOESN'T COME?
THEN I'LL JUST SLEEP ON THE DAMN THING MYSELF!
WELL, ALL I CAN SAY IS, GOOD LUCK! CALL IF YOU NEED ME!
THANKS, ALAN.

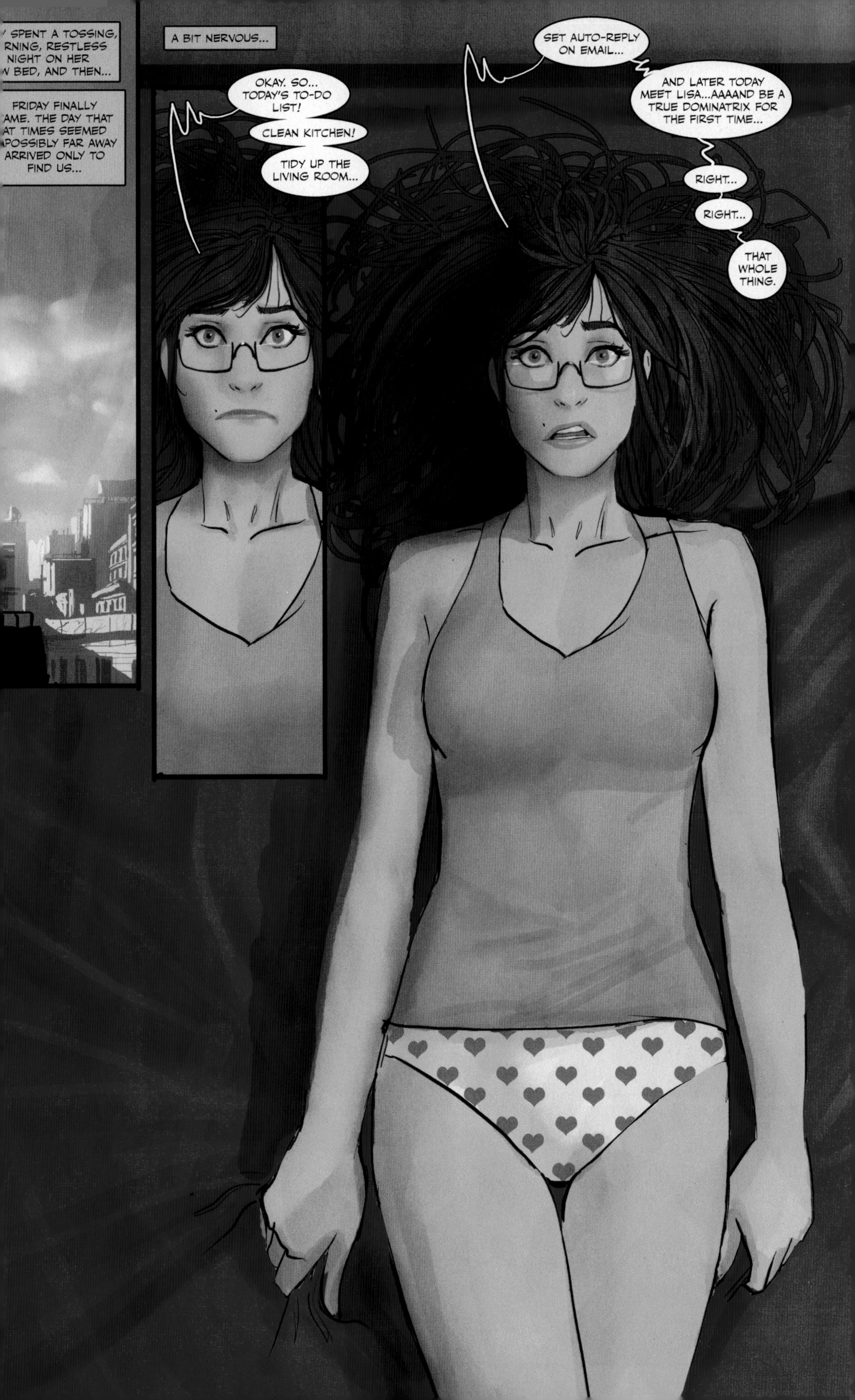

Y SPENT A TOSSING, RNING, RESTLESS NIGHT ON HER W BED, AND THEN...
FRIDAY FINALLY AME. THE DAY THAT AT TIMES SEEMED POSSIBLY FAR AWAY ARRIVED ONLY TO FIND US...
A BIT NERVOUS...
OKAY. SO... TODAY'S TO-DO LIST!
CLEAN KITCHEN!
TIDY UP THE LIVING ROOM...
SET AUTO-REPLY ON EMAIL...
AND LATER TODAY MEET LISA...AAAAND BE A TRUE DOMINATRIX FOR THE FIRST TIME...
RIGHT...
RIGHT...
THAT WHOLE THING.

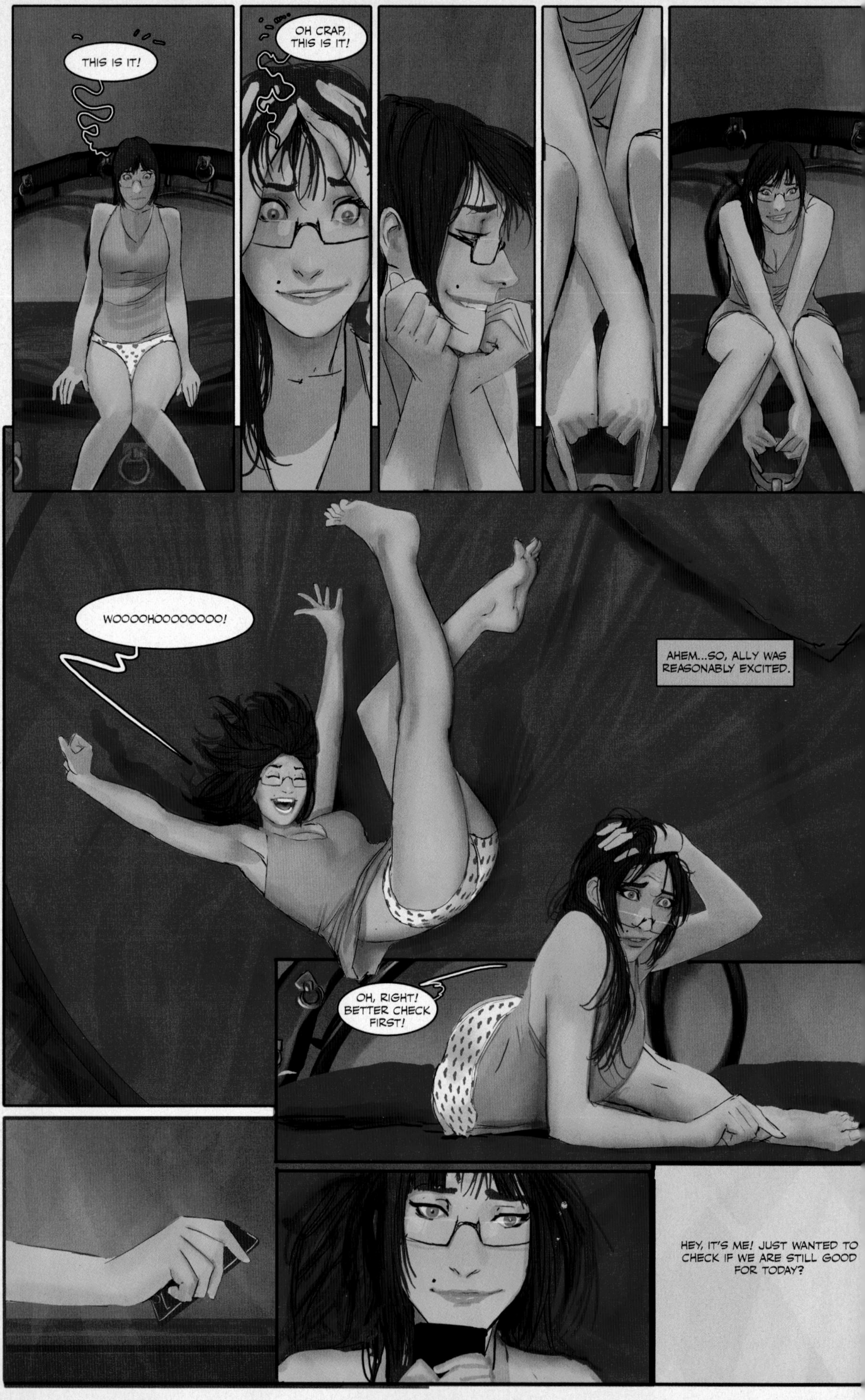
THIS IS IT!
OH CRAP, THIS IS IT!
WOOOOHOOOOOOOO!
AHEM...SO, ALLY WAS REASONABLY EXCITED.
OH, RIGHT! BETTER CHECK FIRST!
HEY, IT'S ME! JUST WANTED TO CHECK IF WE ARE STILL GOOD FOR TODAY?

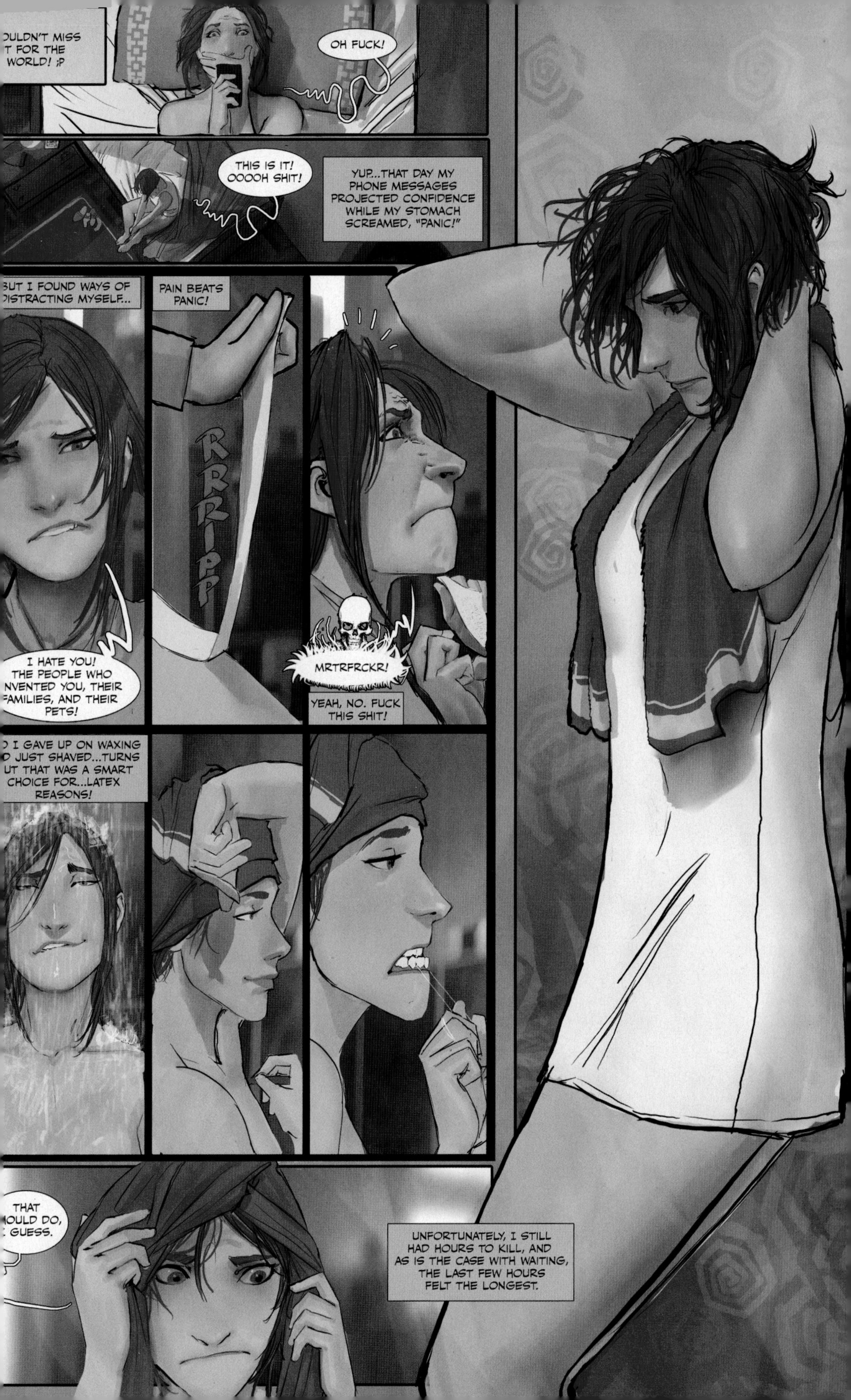
OULDN'T MISS
T FOR THE
WORLD! ;P
OH FUCK!
THIS IS IT!
OOOOH SHIT!
YUP...THAT DAY MY PHONE MESSAGES PROJECTED CONFIDENCE WHILE MY STOMACH SCREAMED, "PANIC!"
BUT I FOUND WAYS OF DISTRACTING MYSELF...
PAIN BEATS PANIC!
RRRIPP
I HATE YOU! THE PEOPLE WHO NVENTED YOU, THEIR FAMILIES, AND THEIR PETS!
MRTRFRCKR!
YEAH, NO. FUCK THIS SHIT!
O I GAVE UP ON WAXING D JUST SHAVED...TURNS UT THAT WAS A SMART CHOICE FOR...LATEX REASONS!
THAT OULD DO, GUESS.
UNFORTUNATELY, I STILL HAD HOURS TO KILL, AND AS IS THE CASE WITH WAITING, THE LAST FEW HOURS FELT THE LONGEST.

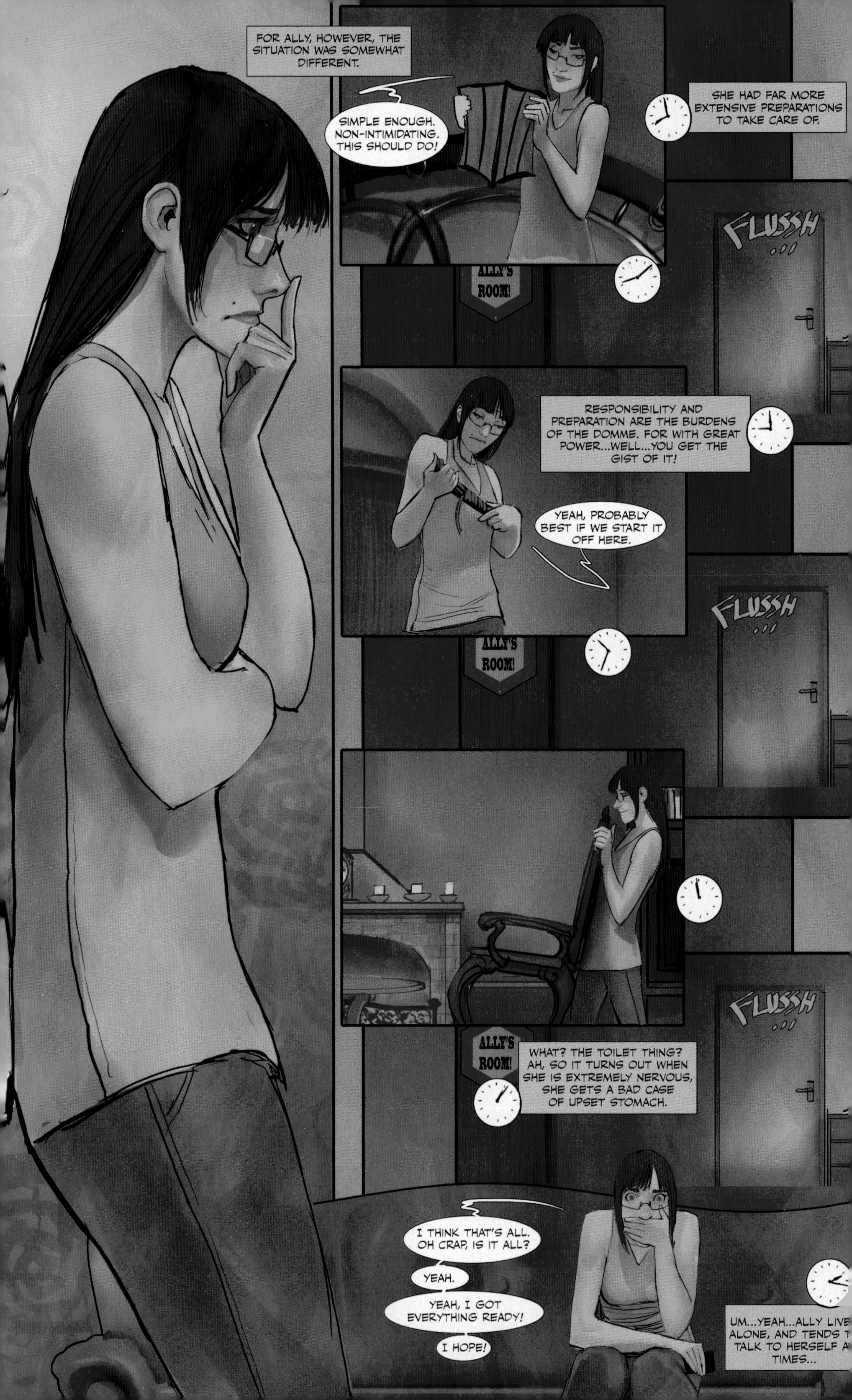
FOR ALLY, HOWEVER, THE SITUATION WAS SOMEWHAT DIFFERENT.
SIMPLE ENOUGH. NON-INTIMIDATING. THIS SHOULD DO!
SHE HAD FAR MORE EXTENSIVE PREPARATIONS TO TAKE CARE OF.
FLUSSH
ALLY'S ROOM!
RESPONSIBILITY AND PREPARATION ARE THE BURDENS OF THE DOMME. FOR WITH GREAT POWER...WELL...YOU GET THE GIST OF IT!
YEAH, PROBABLY BEST IF WE START IT OFF HERE.
FLUSSH
ALLY'S ROOM!
FLUSSH
ALLY'S ROOM!
WHAT? THE TOILET THING? AH, SO IT TURNS OUT WHEN SHE IS EXTREMELY NERVOUS, SHE GETS A BAD CASE OF UPSET STOMACH.
I THINK THAT'S ALL. OH CRAP, IS IT ALL?
YEAH.
YEAH, I GOT EVERYTHING READY!
I HOPE!
UM...YEAH...ALLY LIVE ALONE, AND TENDS T TALK TO HERSELF A TIMES...

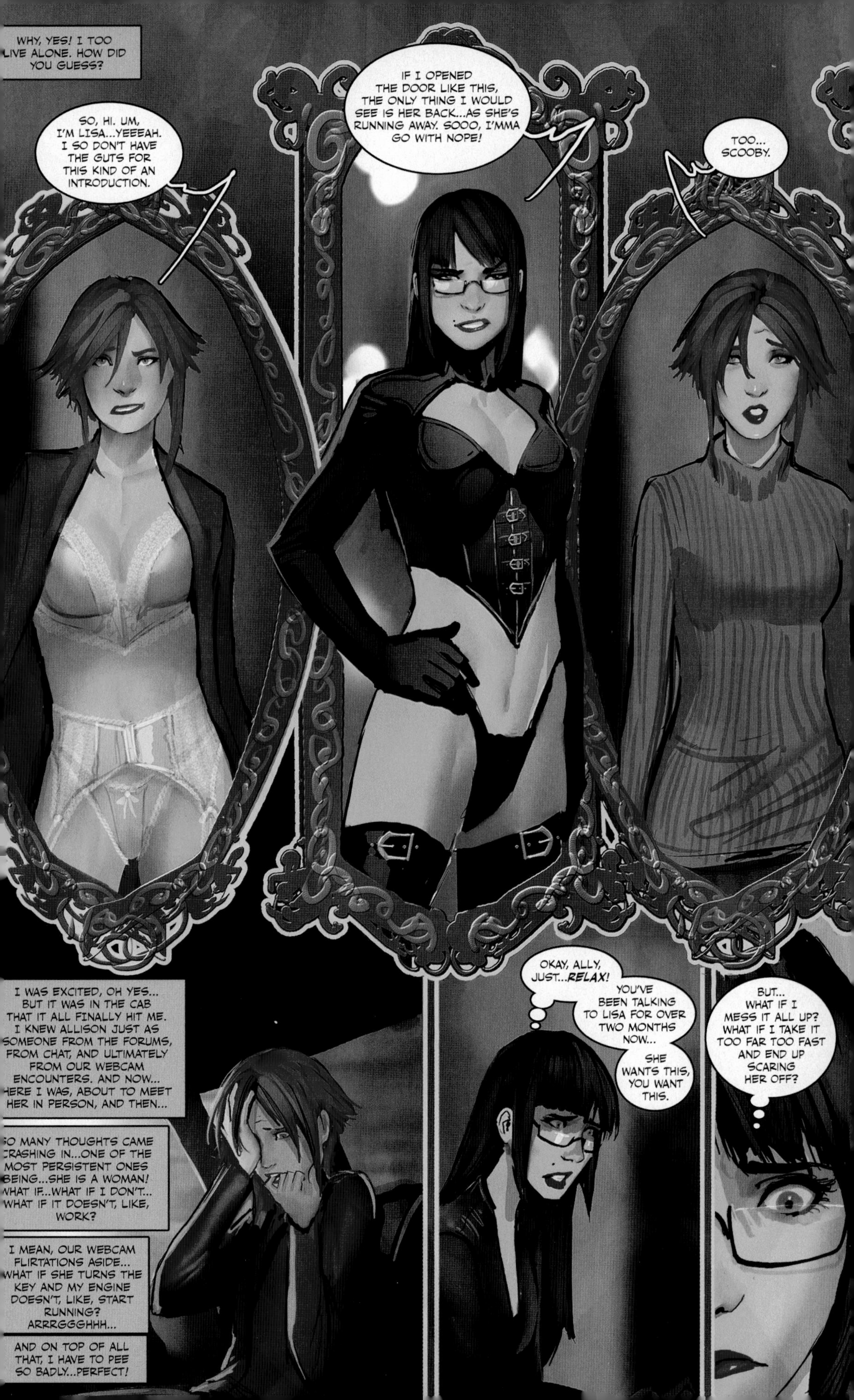
WHY, YES! I TOO LIVE ALONE. HOW DID YOU GUESS?
SO, HI. UM, I'M LISA...YEEEAH. I SO DON'T HAVE THE GUTS FOR THIS KIND OF AN INTRODUCTION.
IF I OPENED THE DOOR LIKE THIS, THE ONLY THING I WOULD SEE IS HER BACK...AS SHE'S RUNNING AWAY. SOOO, I'MMA GO WITH NOPE!
TOO... SCOOBY.
I WAS EXCITED, OH YES... BUT IT WAS IN THE CAB THAT IT ALL FINALLY HIT ME. I KNEW ALLISON JUST AS SOMEONE FROM THE FORUMS, FROM CHAT, AND ULTIMATELY FROM OUR WEBCAM ENCOUNTERS. AND NOW... HERE I WAS, ABOUT TO MEET HER IN PERSON, AND THEN...
SO MANY THOUGHTS CAME CRASHING IN...ONE OF THE MOST PERSISTENT ONES BEING...SHE IS A WOMAN! WHAT IF...WHAT IF I DON'T... WHAT IF IT DOESN'T, LIKE, WORK?
I MEAN, OUR WEBCAM FLIRTATIONS ASIDE... WHAT IF SHE TURNS THE KEY AND MY ENGINE DOESN'T, LIKE, START RUNNING? ARRRGGGHHH...
AND ON TOP OF ALL THAT, I HAVE TO PEE SO BADLY...PERFECT!
OKAY, ALLY, JUST...RELAX!
YOU'VE BEEN TALKING TO LISA FOR OVER TWO MONTHS NOW...
SHE WANTS THIS, YOU WANT THIS.
BUT... WHAT IF I MESS IT ALL UP? WHAT IF I TAKE IT TOO FAR TOO FAST AND END UP SCARING HER OFF?

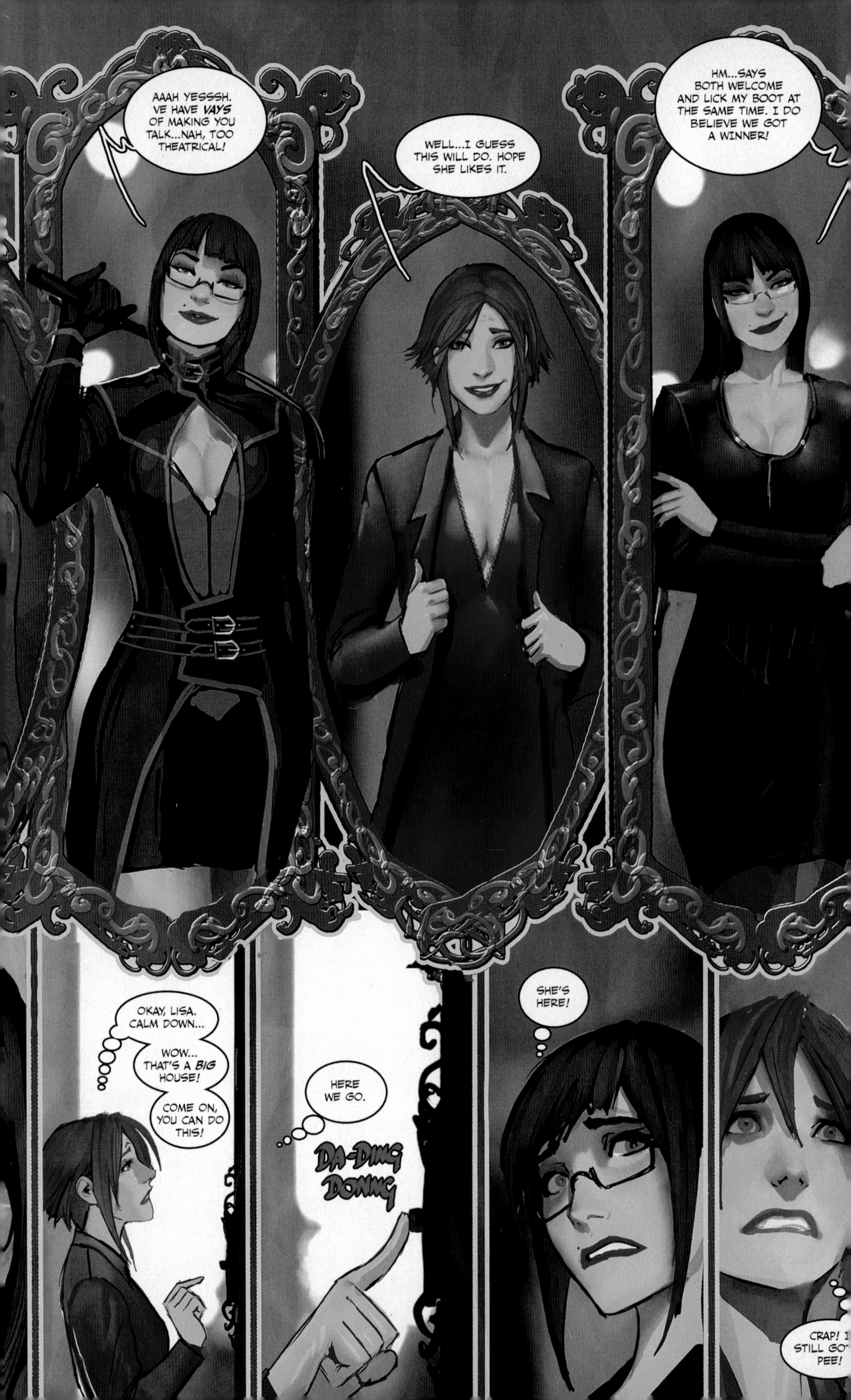
AAAH YESSSH. VE HAVE VAYS OF MAKING YOU TALK...NAH, TOO THEATRICAL!
WELL...I GUESS THIS WILL DO. HOPE SHE LIKES IT.
HM...SAYS BOTH WELCOME AND LICK MY BOOT AT THE SAME TIME. I DO BELIEVE WE GOT A WINNER!
OKAY, LISA. CALM DOWN...
WOW... THAT'S A BIG HOUSE!
COME ON, YOU CAN DO THIS!
HERE WE GO.
DA-DING DONNG
SHE'S HERE!
CRAP! I STILL GOT PEE!

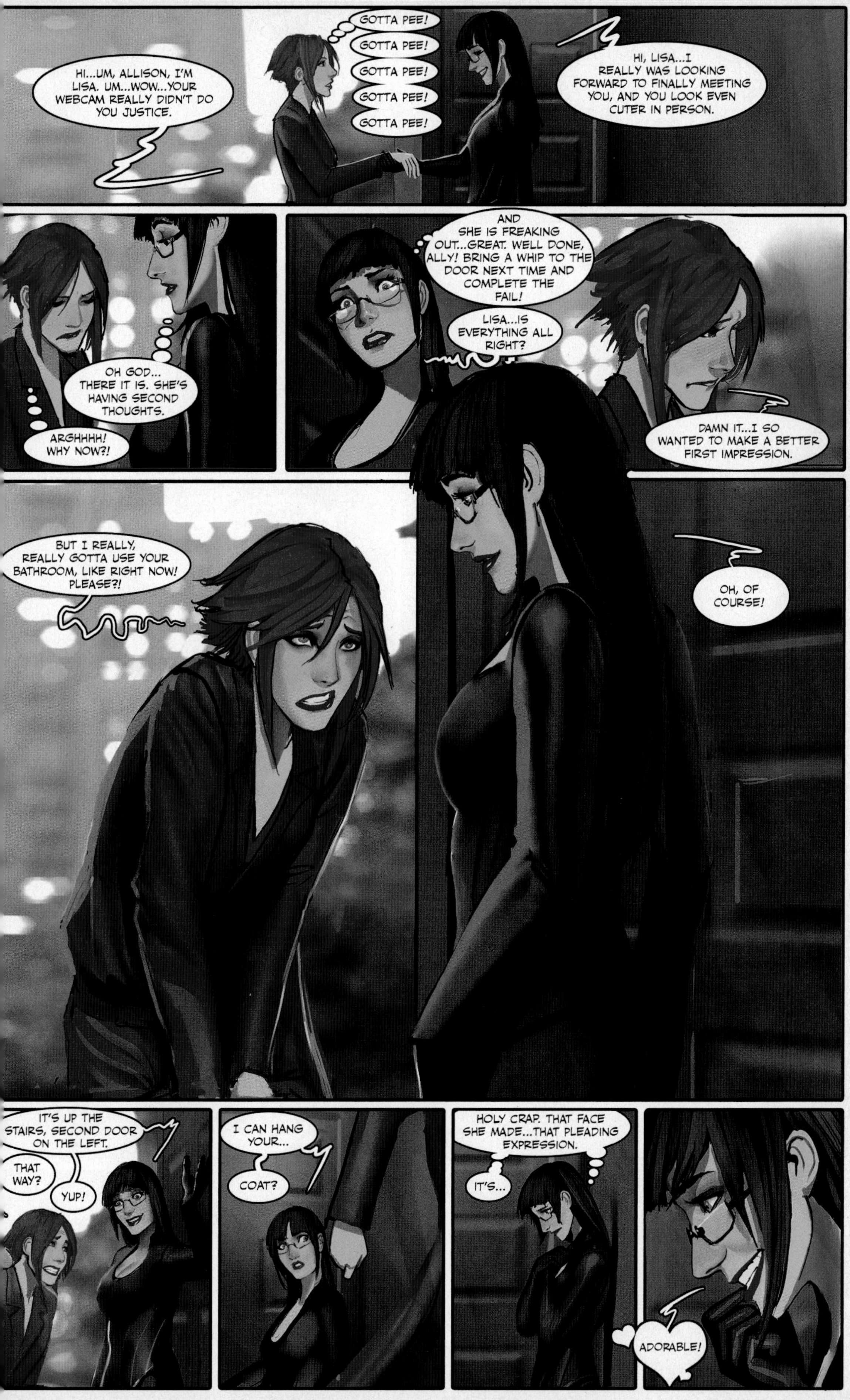
HI...UM, ALLISON, I'M LISA. UM...WOW...YOUR WEBCAM REALLY DIDN'T DO YOU JUSTICE.
GOTTA PEE!
GOTTA PEE!
GOTTA PEE!
GOTTA PEE!
GOTTA PEE!
HI, LISA...I REALLY WAS LOOKING FORWARD TO FINALLY MEETING YOU, AND YOU LOOK EVEN CUTER IN PERSON.
OH GOD... THERE IT IS. SHE'S HAVING SECOND THOUGHTS.
ARGHHHH! WHY NOW?!
AND SHE IS FREAKING OUT...GREAT. WELL DONE, ALLY! BRING A WHIP TO THE DOOR NEXT TIME AND COMPLETE THE FAIL!
LISA...IS EVERYTHING ALL RIGHT?
DAMN IT...I SO WANTED TO MAKE A BETTER FIRST IMPRESSION.
BUT I REALLY, REALLY GOTTA USE YOUR BATHROOM, LIKE RIGHT NOW! PLEASE?!
OH, OF COURSE!
IT'S UP THE STAIRS, SECOND DOOR ON THE LEFT.
THAT WAY?
YUP!
I CAN HANG YOUR...
COAT?
HOLY CRAP. THAT FACE SHE MADE...THAT PLEADING EXPRESSION.
IT'S...
ADORABLE!

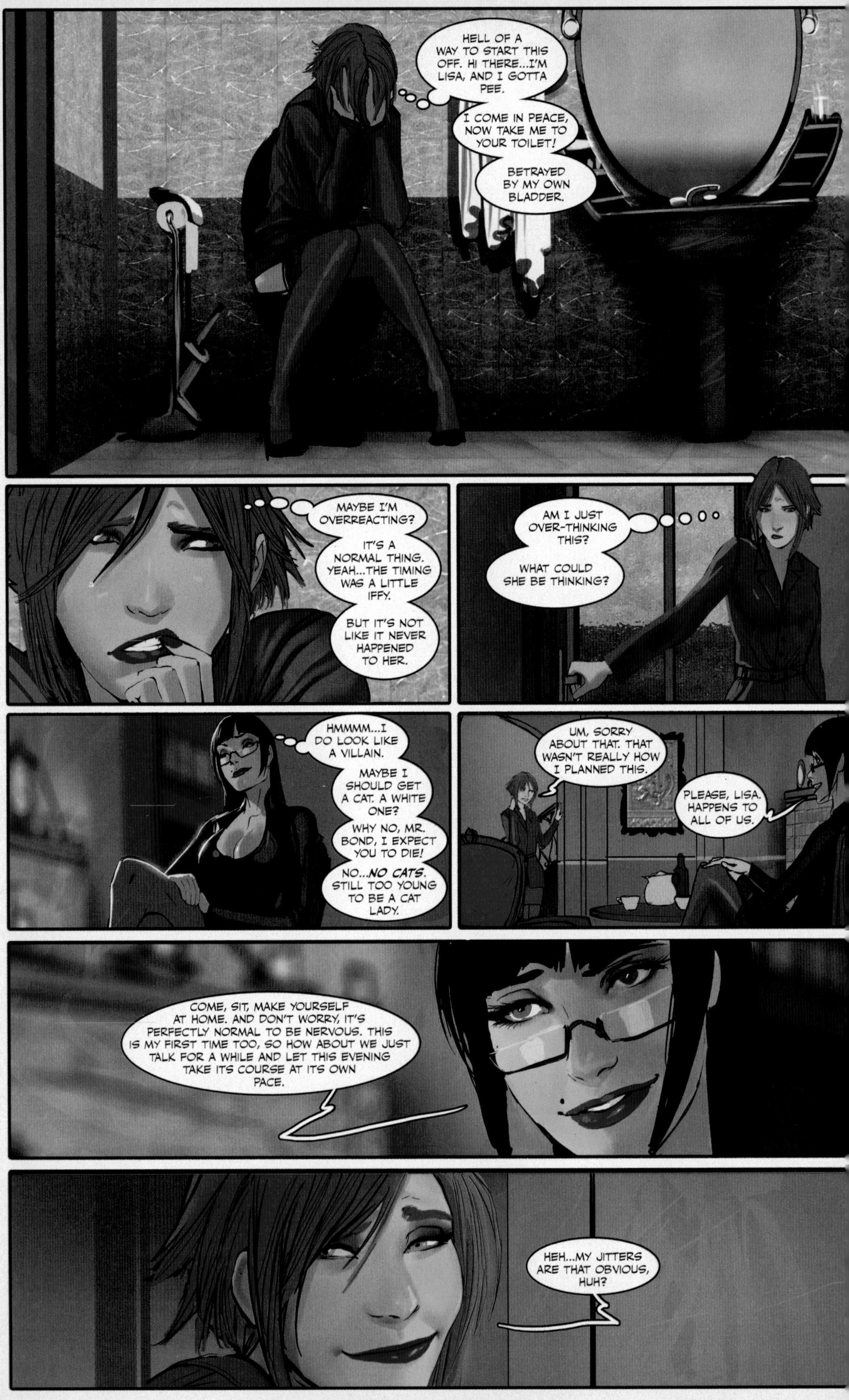
HELL OF A WAY TO START THIS OFF. HI THERE...I'M LISA, AND I GOTTA PEE.
I COME IN PEACE, NOW TAKE ME TO YOUR TOILET!
BETRAYED BY MY OWN BLADDER.
MAYBE I'M OVERREACTING?
IT'S A NORMAL THING. YEAH...THE TIMING WAS A LITTLE IFFY.
BUT IT'S NOT LIKE IT NEVER HAPPENED TO HER.
AM I JUST OVER-THINKING THIS?
WHAT COULD SHE BE THINKING?
HMMMM...I DO LOOK LIKE A VILLAIN.
MAYBE I SHOULD GET A CAT. A WHITE ONE?
WHY NO, MR. BOND, I EXPECT YOU TO DIE!
NO...NO CATS. STILL TOO YOUNG TO BE A CAT LADY.
UM, SORRY ABOUT THAT. THAT WASN'T REALLY HOW I PLANNED THIS.
PLEASE, LISA. HAPPENS TO ALL OF US.
COME, SIT, MAKE YOURSELF AT HOME. AND DON'T WORRY, IT'S PERFECTLY NORMAL TO BE NERVOUS. THIS IS MY FIRST TIME TOO, SO HOW ABOUT WE JUST TALK FOR A WHILE AND LET THIS EVENING TAKE ITS COURSE AT ITS OWN PACE.
HEH...MY JITTERS ARE THAT OBVIOUS, HUH?

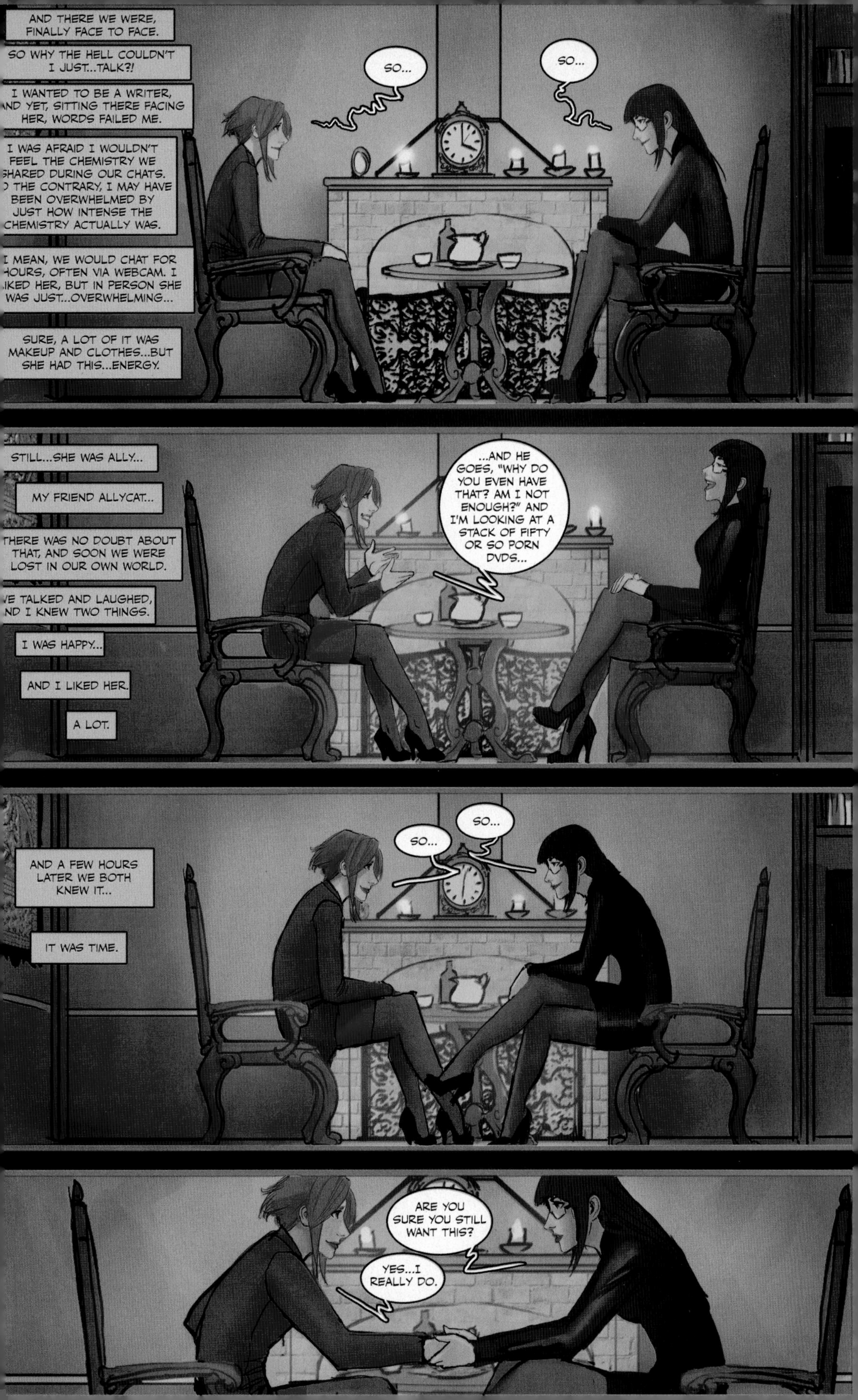
AND THERE WE WERE, FINALLY FACE TO FACE.
SO WHY THE HELL COULDN'T I JUST...TALK?!
I WANTED TO BE A WRITER, AND YET, SITTING THERE FACING HER, WORDS FAILED ME.
I WAS AFRAID I WOULDN'T FEEL THE CHEMISTRY WE SHARED DURING OUR CHATS. TO THE CONTRARY, I MAY HAVE BEEN OVERWHELMED BY JUST HOW INTENSE THE CHEMISTRY ACTUALLY WAS.
I MEAN, WE WOULD CHAT FOR HOURS, OFTEN VIA WEBCAM. I LIKED HER, BUT IN PERSON SHE WAS JUST...OVERWHELMING...
SURE, A LOT OF IT WAS MAKEUP AND CLOTHES...BUT SHE HAD THIS...ENERGY.
SO...
SO...
STILL...SHE WAS ALLY...
MY FRIEND ALLYCAT...
THERE WAS NO DOUBT ABOUT THAT, AND SOON WE WERE LOST IN OUR OWN WORLD.
WE TALKED AND LAUGHED, AND I KNEW TWO THINGS.
I WAS HAPPY...
AND I LIKED HER.
A LOT.
...AND HE GOES, "WHY DO YOU EVEN HAVE THAT? AM I NOT ENOUGH?" AND I'M LOOKING AT A STACK OF FIFTY OR SO PORN DVDS...
AND A FEW HOURS LATER WE BOTH KNEW IT...
IT WAS TIME.
SO...
SO...
ARE YOU SURE YOU STILL WANT THIS?
YES...I REALLY DO.

The Seduction Continues In...

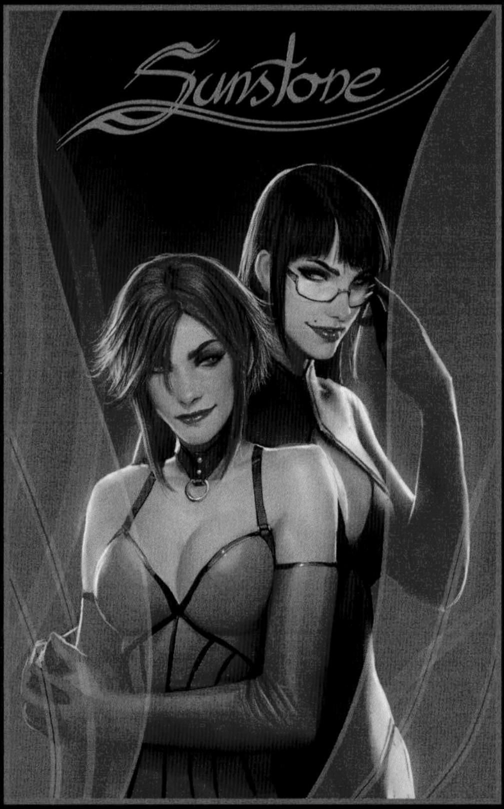
Sunstone

Volume 1

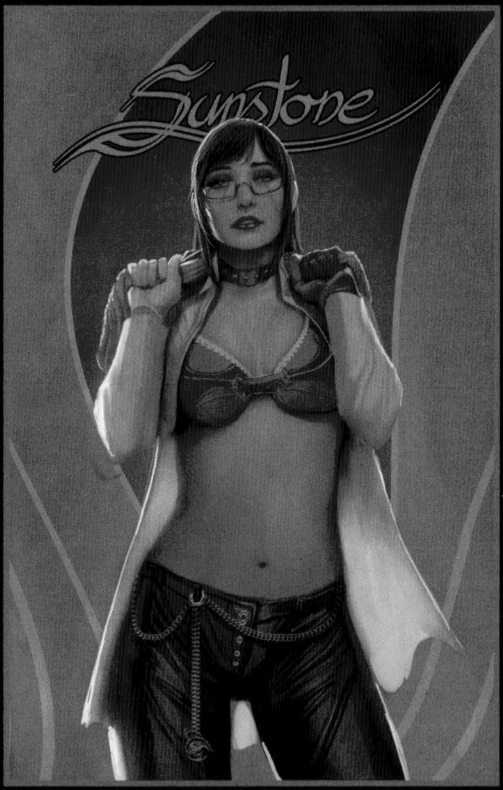
Sunstone

Volume 2

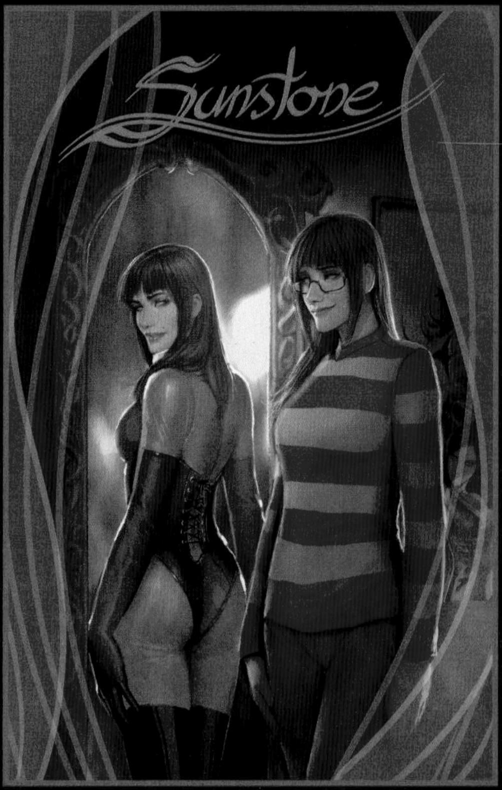
Sunstone

Volume 3

Available Now!

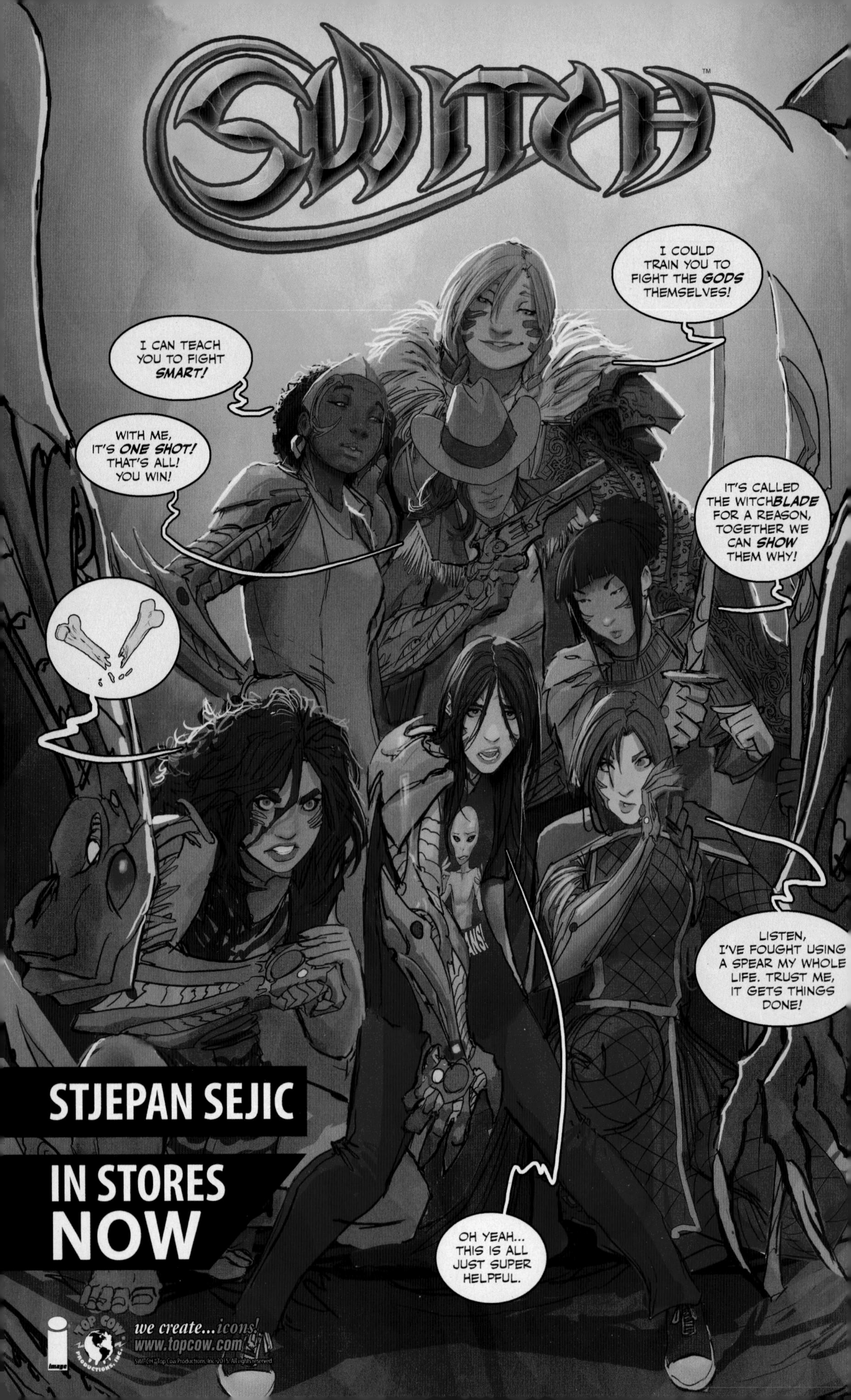
SWITCH™
I CAN TEACH YOU TO FIGHT SMART!
I COULD TRAIN YOU TO FIGHT THE GODS THEMSELVES!
WITH ME, IT'S ONE SHOT! THAT'S ALL! YOU WIN!
IT'S CALLED THE WITCHBLADE FOR A REASON, TOGETHER WE CAN SHOW THEM WHY!
LISTEN, I'VE FOUGHT USING A SPEAR MY WHOLE LIFE. TRUST ME, IT GETS THINGS DONE!
OH YEAH... THIS IS ALL JUST SUPER HELPFUL.
STJEPAN SEJIC
IN STORES NOW
we create...icons!
www.topcow.com
SWITCH™ Top Cow Productions, Inc. 2015. All rights reserved.

Zub • Cummings • Rauch • Dillon

Wayward™

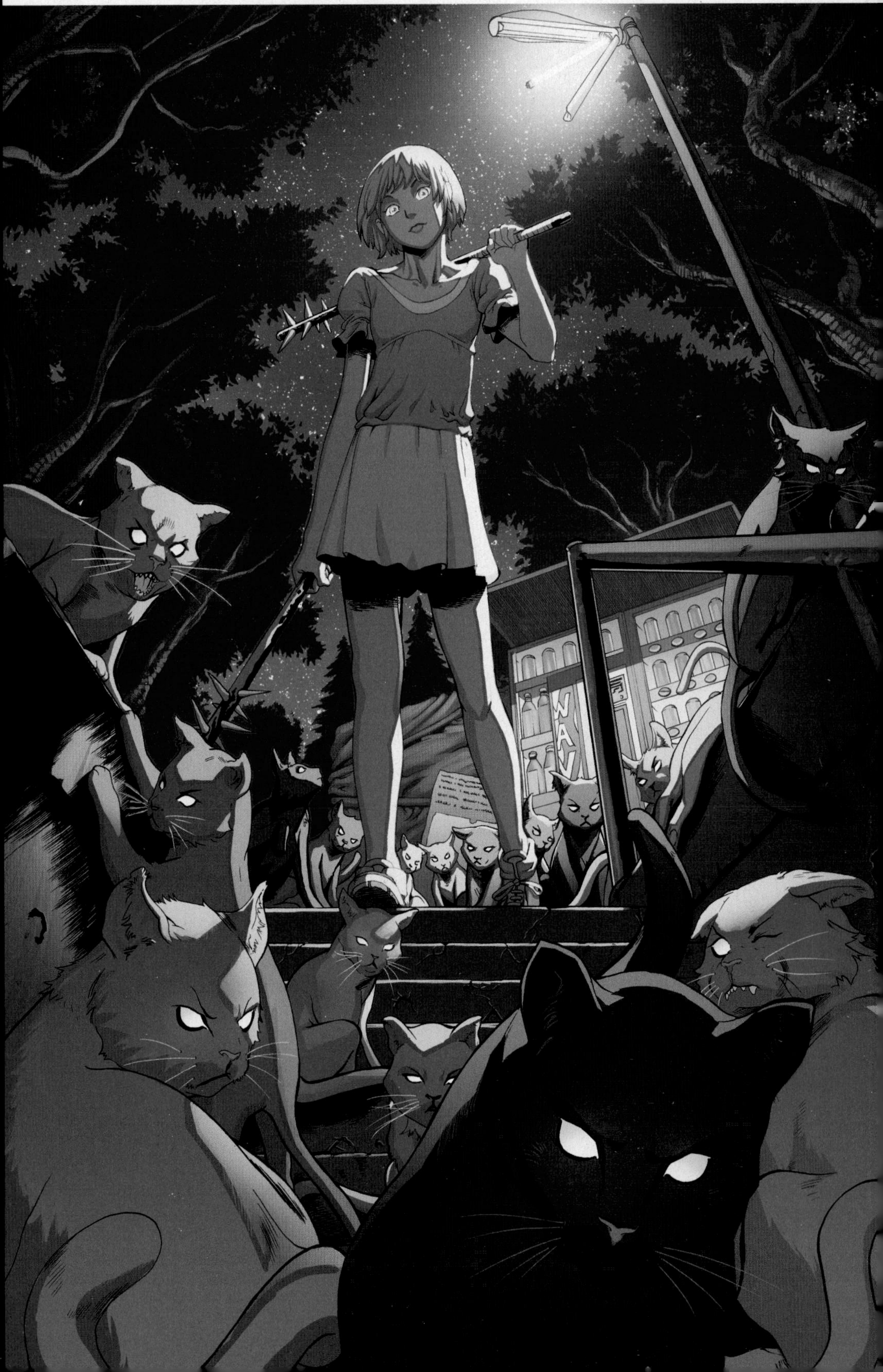

RATED T+ / TEEN PLUS

image firsts

Wayward

CHAPTER ONE

Story • Jim Zub
(Twitter: @jimzub)

Line Art • Steven Cummings
(Twitter: @stekichikun)

Colors • John Rauch and Jim Zub
(Twitter: @John_Rauch)

Letters • Marshall Dillon
(Twitter: @MarshallDillon)

Back Matter • Zack Davisson
(Twitter: @ZackDavisson)

Cover Art
Steven Cummings and Ross A. Campbell

IMAGE COMICS, INC.
Robert Kirkman – Chief Operating Officer
Erik Larsen – Chief Financial Officer
Todd McFarlane – President
Marc Silvestri – Chief Executive Officer
Jim Valentino – Vice-President
Eric Stephenson – Publisher
Corey Murphy – Director of Sales
Jeff Boison – Director of Publishing Planning & Book Trade Sales
Jeremy Sullivan – Director of Digital Sales
Kat Salazar – Director of PR & Marketing
Emily Miller – Director of Operations
Branwyn Bigglestone – Senior Accounts Manager
Sarah Mello – Accounts Manager
Drew Gill – Art Director
Jonathan Chan – Production Manager
Meredith Wallace – Print Manager
Briah Skelly – Publicity Assistant
Randy Okamura – Marketing Production Designer
David Brothers – Branding Manager
Ally Power – Content Manager
Addison Duke – Production Artist
Vincent Kukua – Production Artist
Sasha Head – Production Artist
Tricia Ramos – Production Artist
Jeff Stang – Direct Market Sales Representative
Emilio Bautista – Digital Sales Associate
Chloe Ramos-Peterson – Administrative Assistant
IMAGECOMICS.COM

Image Firsts: Wayward #1. December 2015. Published by Image Comics, Inc. Office of publication: 2001 Center St. 6th Floor, Berkeley, CA 94704. PRINTED IN USA. For information regarding the CPSIA on th printed material call: 203-595-3636 and provide reference RICH - 656685.
International Rights / Foreign Licensing - foreignlicensing@imagecomics.com.

Special Thanks
Charles Soule, Eric Stephenson, Ron Richards, Nishi Makoto (Edwin), Chris Butcher, Erik Ko, Brandon Seifert, Filip Sablik, Dafna Pleban, and our loving friends and families.

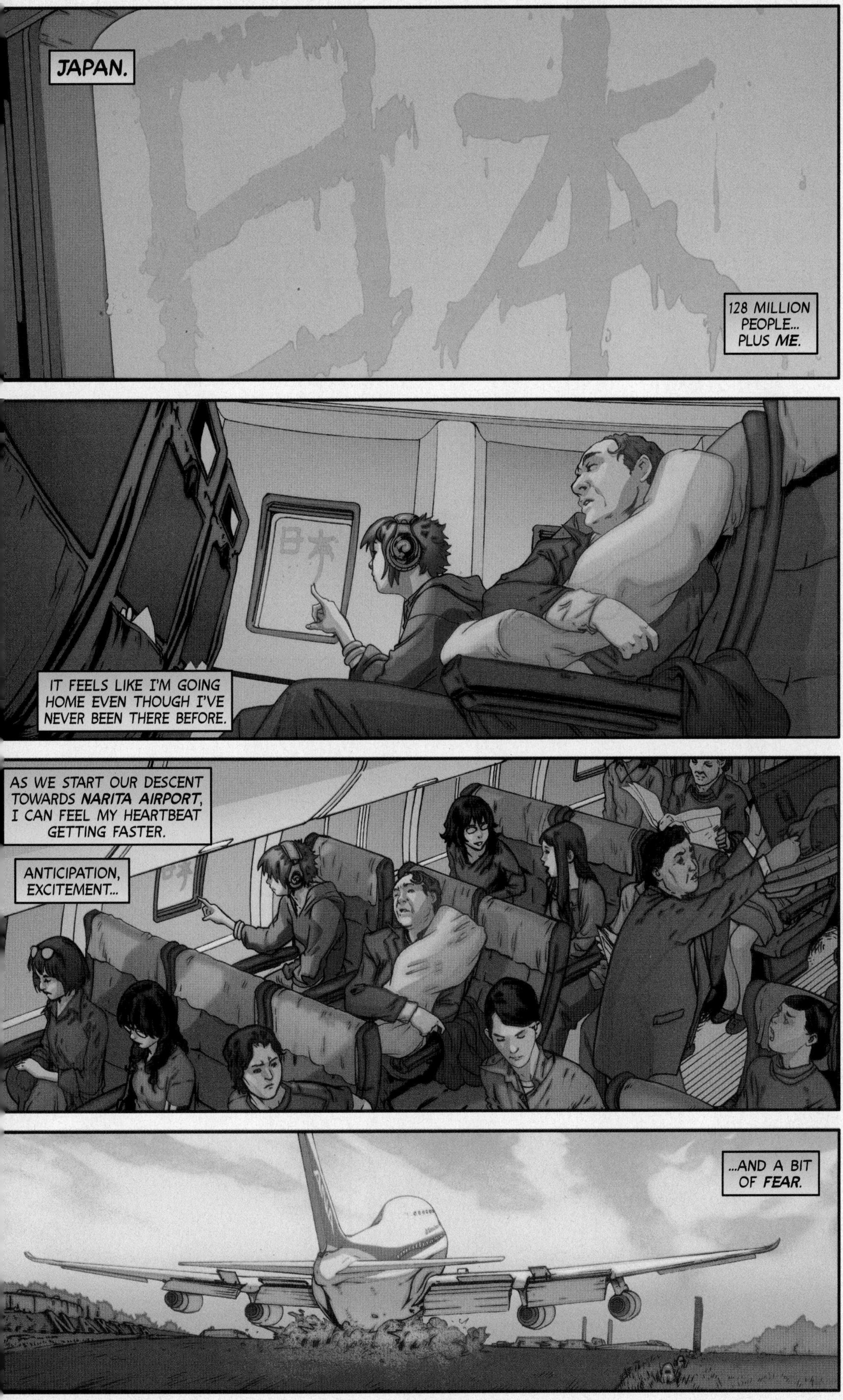
JAPAN.
128 MILLION PEOPLE... PLUS *ME*.
IT FEELS LIKE I'M GOING HOME EVEN THOUGH I'VE NEVER BEEN THERE BEFORE.
AS WE START OUR DESCENT TOWARDS *NARITA AIRPORT*, I CAN FEEL MY HEARTBEAT GETTING FASTER.
ANTICIPATION, EXCITEMENT...
...AND A BIT OF *FEAR*.

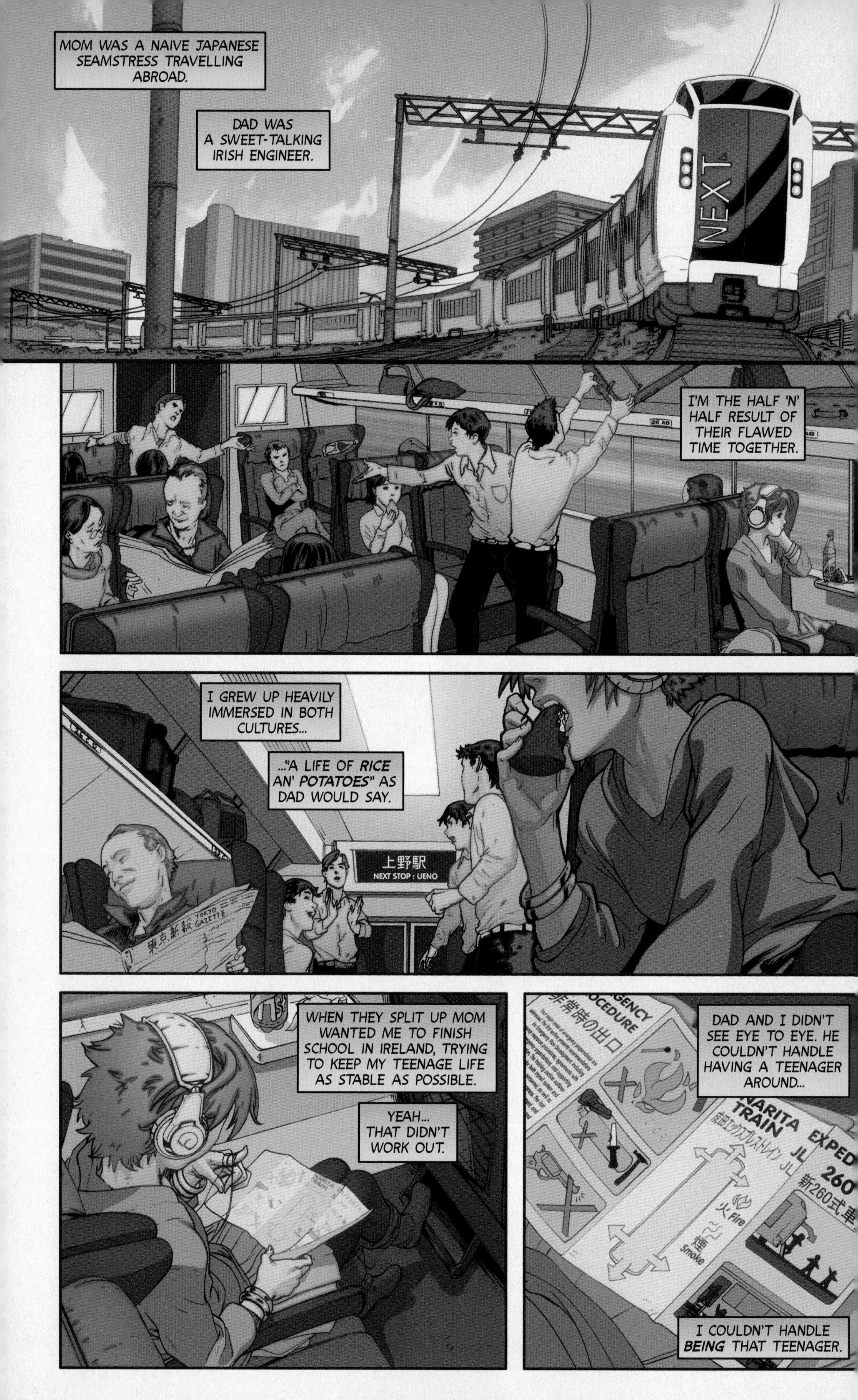
MOM WAS A NAIVE JAPANESE SEAMSTRESS TRAVELLING ABROAD.
DAD WAS A SWEET-TALKING IRISH ENGINEER.
NEXT
I'M THE HALF 'N' HALF RESULT OF THEIR FLAWED TIME TOGETHER.
I GREW UP HEAVILY IMMERSED IN BOTH CULTURES...
..."A LIFE OF RICE AN' POTATOES" AS DAD WOULD SAY.
上野駅
NEXT STOP : UENO
東京新報 TOKYO GAZETTE
WHEN THEY SPLIT UP MOM WANTED ME TO FINISH SCHOOL IN IRELAND, TRYING TO KEEP MY TEENAGE LIFE AS STABLE AS POSSIBLE.
YEAH... THAT DIDN'T WORK OUT.
DAD AND I DIDN'T SEE EYE TO EYE. HE COULDN'T HANDLE HAVING A TEENAGER AROUND...
非常時の出口
NARITA EXPRESS TRAIN
260
新260式車
火 Fire
煙 Smoke
I COULDN'T HANDLE BEING THAT TEENAGER.

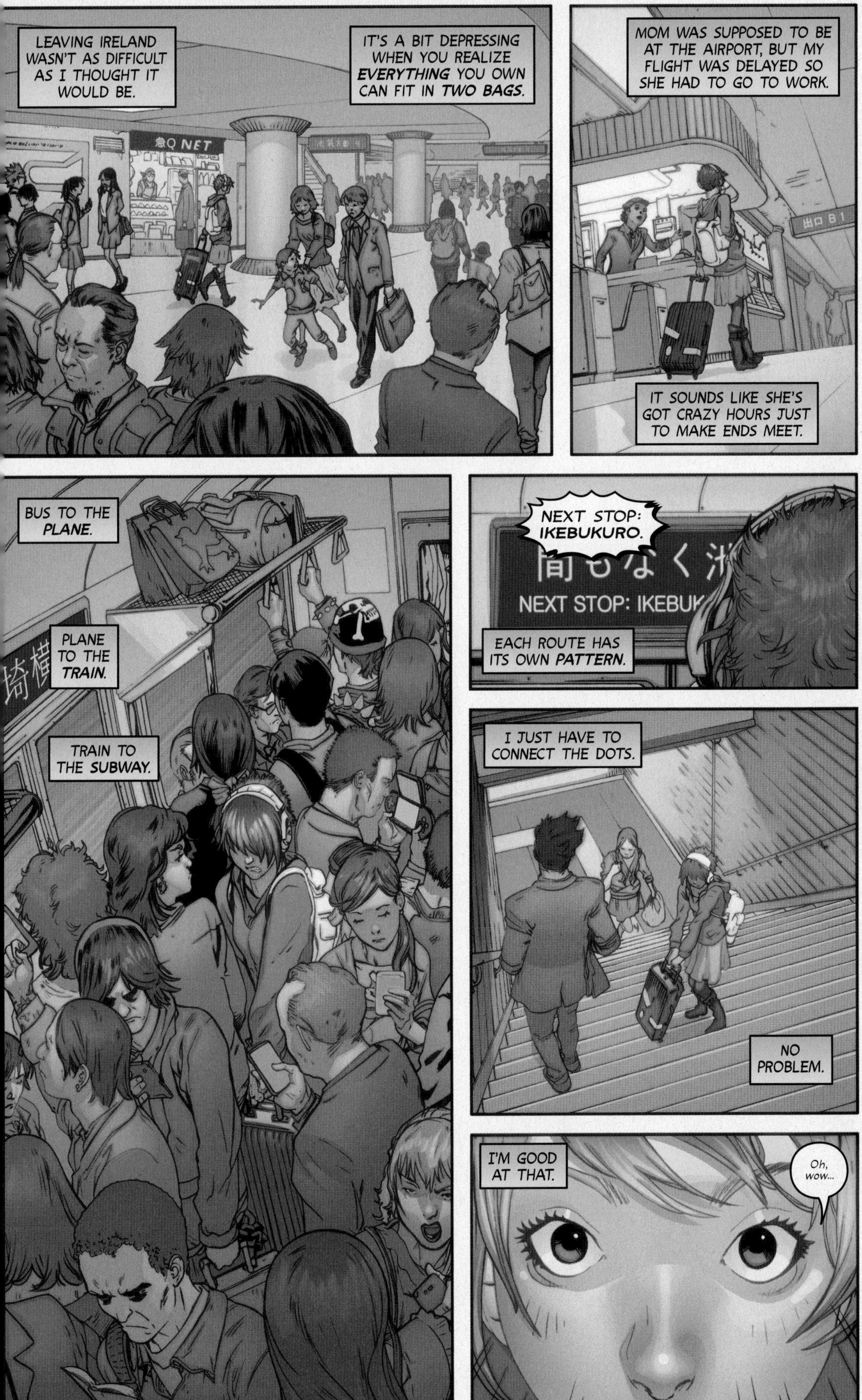
LEAVING IRELAND WASN'T AS DIFFICULT AS I THOUGHT IT WOULD BE.
IT'S A BIT DEPRESSING WHEN YOU REALIZE *EVERYTHING* YOU OWN CAN FIT IN *TWO BAGS*.
MOM WAS SUPPOSED TO BE AT THE AIRPORT, BUT MY FLIGHT WAS DELAYED SO SHE HAD TO GO TO WORK.
出口 B1
IT SOUNDS LIKE SHE'S GOT CRAZY HOURS JUST TO MAKE ENDS MEET.
BUS TO THE *PLANE*.
PLANE TO THE *TRAIN*.
TRAIN TO THE *SUBWAY*.
NEXT STOP: IKEBUKURO.
NEXT STOP: IKEBUK
EACH ROUTE HAS ITS OWN *PATTERN*.
I JUST HAVE TO CONNECT THE DOTS.
NO PROBLEM.
I'M GOOD AT THAT.
Oh, wow...

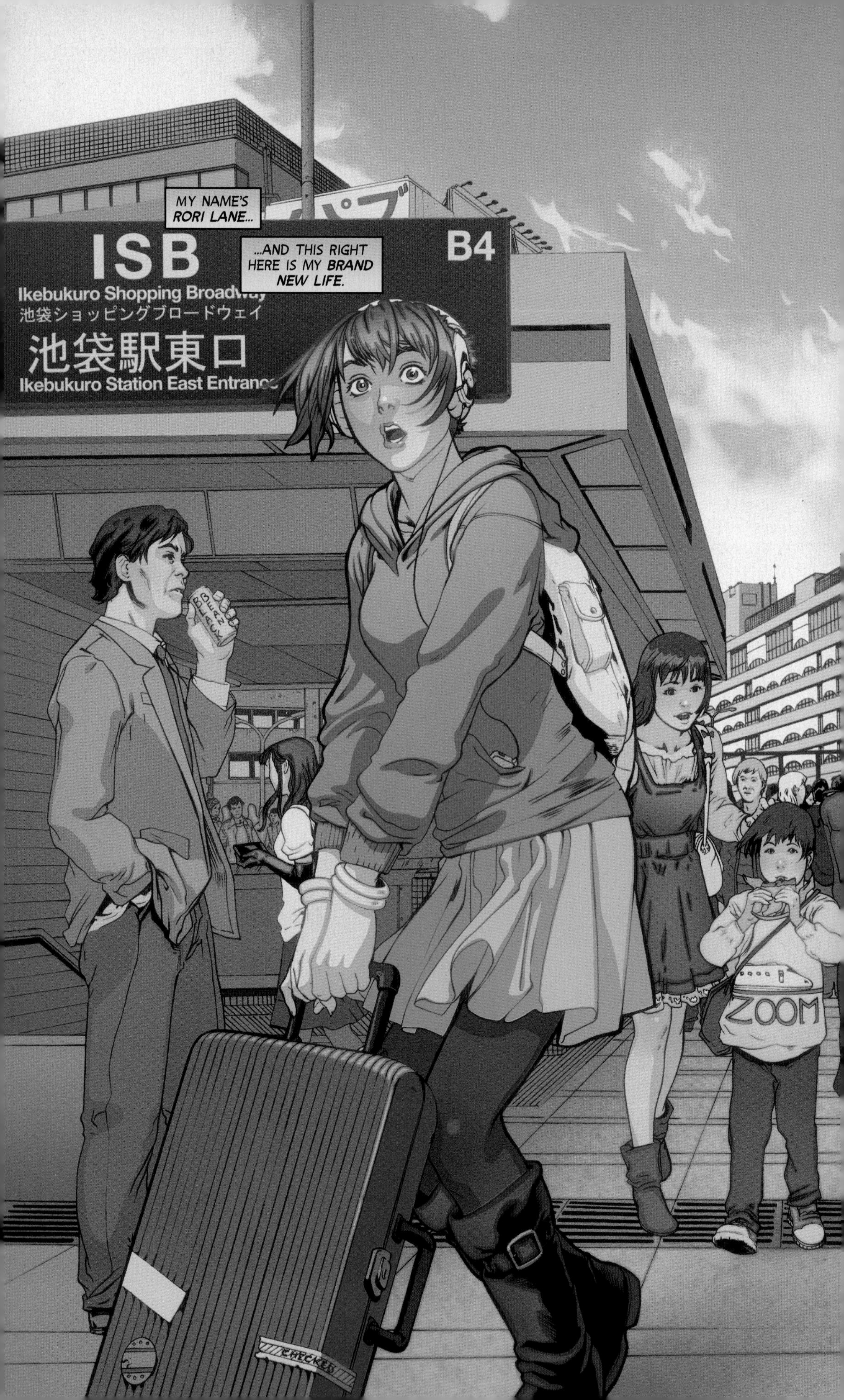

MY NAME'S *RORI LANE*...
...AND THIS RIGHT HERE IS MY *BRAND NEW LIFE*.
ISB
B4
Ikebukuro Shopping Broadway
池袋ショッピングブロードウェイ
池袋駅東口
Ikebukuro Station East Entrance
ZOOM
CHECKED

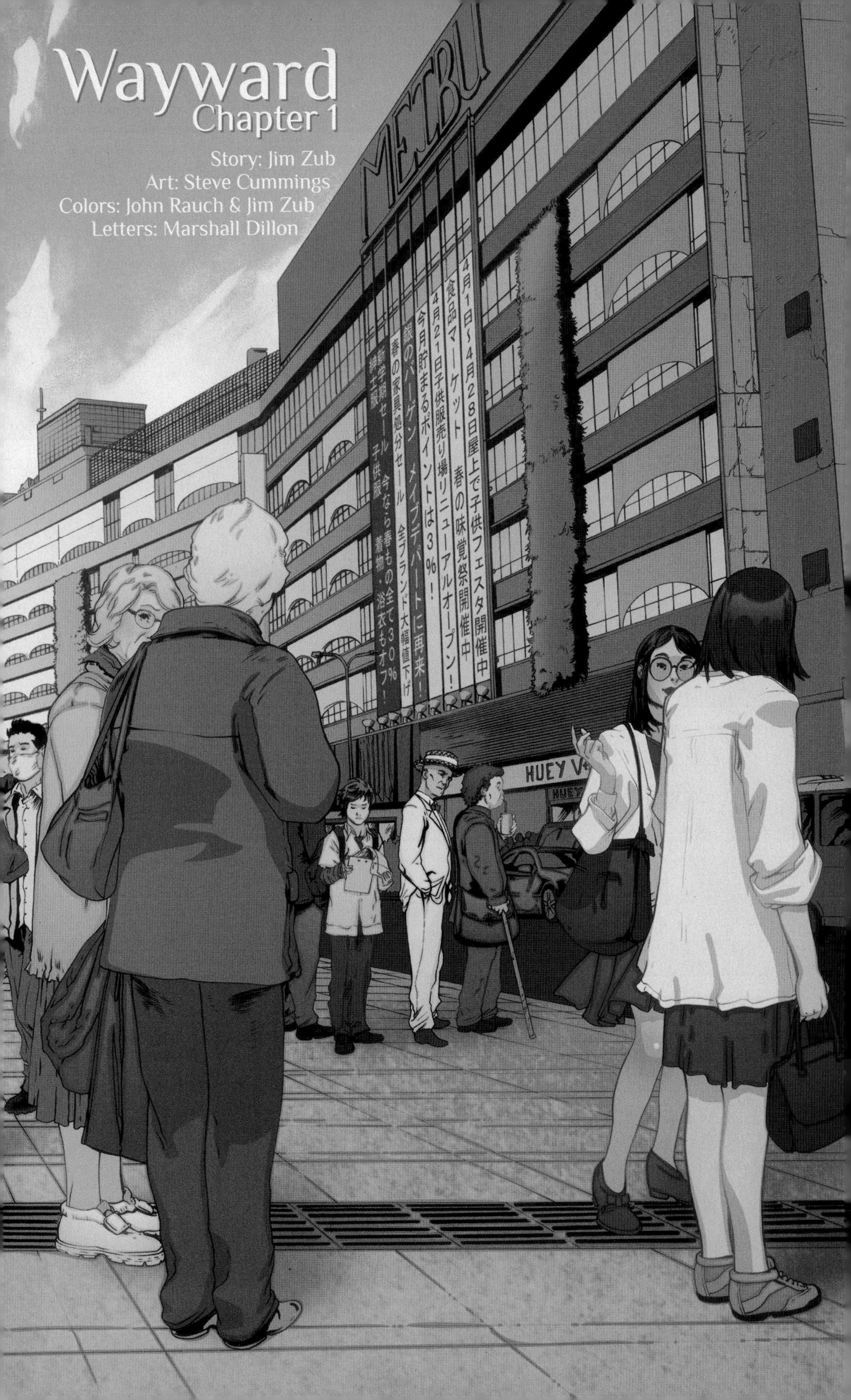

Wayward
Chapter 1
Story: Jim Zub
Art: Steve Cummings
Colors: John Rauch & Jim Zub
Letters: Marshall Dillon
METBU
4月1日～4月28日屋上で子供フェスタ開催中
食品マーケット　春の味覚祭開催中
4月21日子供服売り場リニューアルオープン！
今月貯まるポイントは3％！
銀のバーゲン　メイブデパートに再来！
春の家具処分セール　全ブランド大幅値下げ
新学期セール　今なら春もの全て30％
紳士服　子供服　着物・浴衣もオフ！

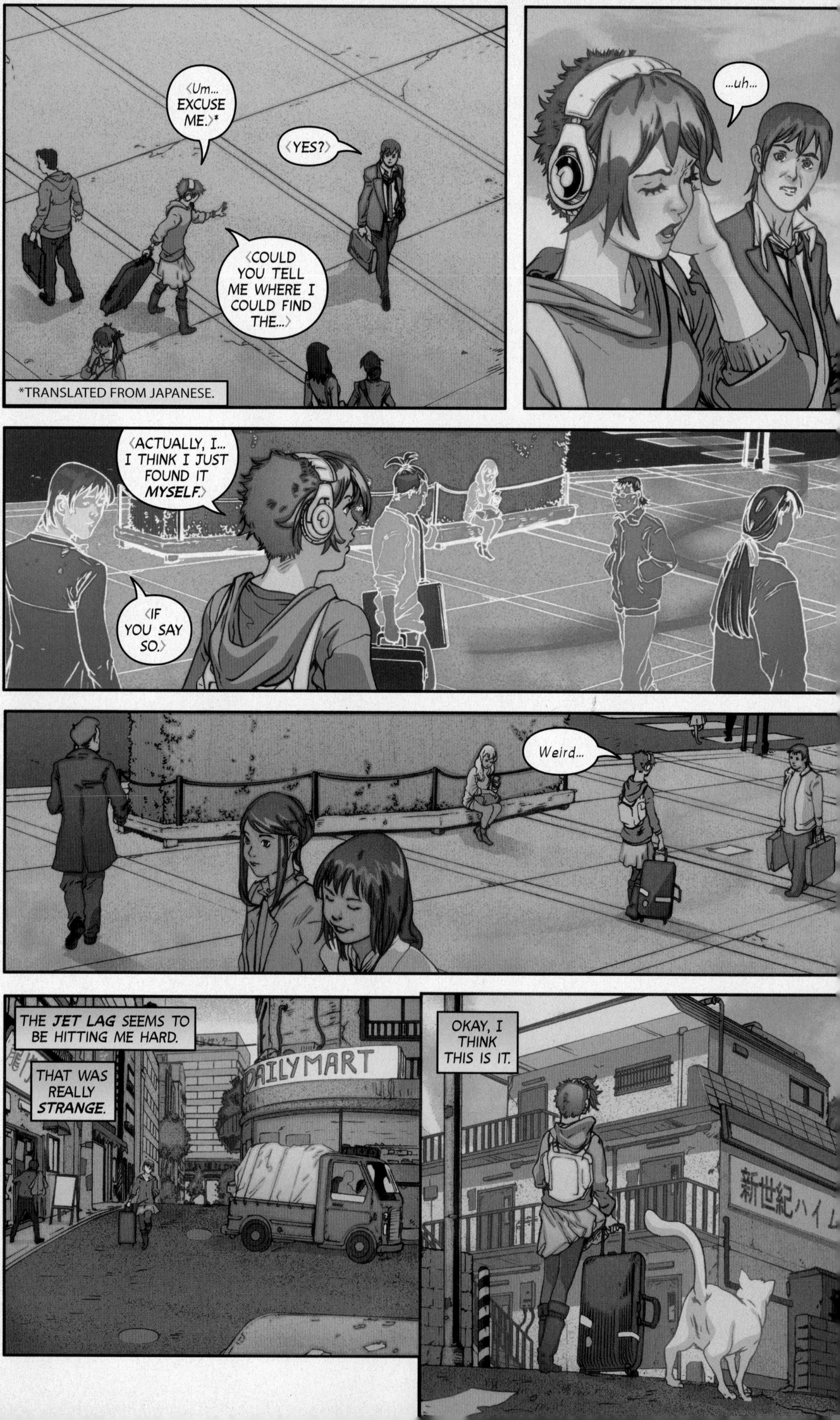
〈Um... EXCUSE ME.〉*
〈YES?〉
〈COULD YOU TELL ME WHERE I COULD FIND THE...〉
*TRANSLATED FROM JAPANESE.
...uh...
〈ACTUALLY, I... I THINK I JUST FOUND IT *MYSELF*.〉
〈IF YOU SAY SO.〉
Weird...
THE *JET LAG* SEEMS TO BE HITTING ME HARD.
THAT WAS REALLY *STRANGE*.
DAILY MART
OKAY, I THINK THIS IS IT.
新世紀ハイム

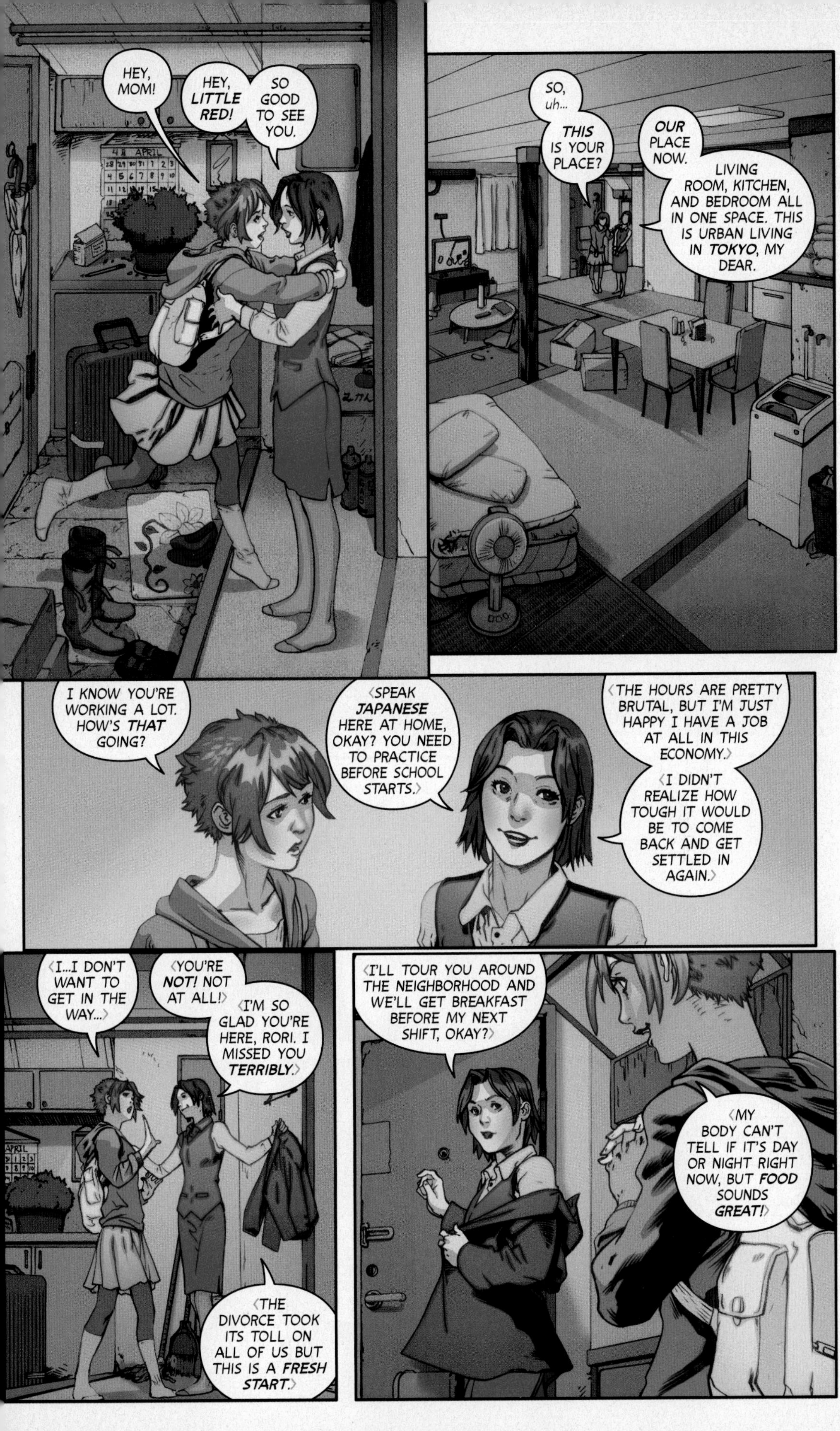
HEY, MOM!
HEY, *LITTLE RED!*
SO GOOD TO SEE YOU.
SO, uh... *THIS* IS YOUR PLACE?
OUR PLACE NOW.
LIVING ROOM, KITCHEN, AND BEDROOM ALL IN ONE SPACE. THIS IS URBAN LIVING IN *TOKYO*, MY DEAR.
I KNOW YOU'RE WORKING A LOT. HOW'S *THAT* GOING?
〈SPEAK *JAPANESE* HERE AT HOME, OKAY? YOU NEED TO PRACTICE BEFORE SCHOOL STARTS.〉
〈THE HOURS ARE PRETTY BRUTAL, BUT I'M JUST HAPPY I HAVE A JOB AT ALL IN THIS ECONOMY.〉
〈I DIDN'T REALIZE HOW TOUGH IT WOULD BE TO COME BACK AND GET SETTLED IN AGAIN.〉
〈I...I DON'T WANT TO GET IN THE WAY...〉
〈YOU'RE *NOT!* NOT AT ALL!〉
〈I'M SO GLAD YOU'RE HERE, RORI. I MISSED YOU *TERRIBLY*.〉
〈THE DIVORCE TOOK ITS TOLL ON ALL OF US BUT THIS IS A *FRESH START*.〉
〈I'LL TOUR YOU AROUND THE NEIGHBORHOOD AND WE'LL GET BREAKFAST BEFORE MY NEXT SHIFT, OKAY?〉
〈MY BODY CAN'T TELL IF IT'S DAY OR NIGHT RIGHT NOW, BUT *FOOD* SOUNDS *GREAT!*〉

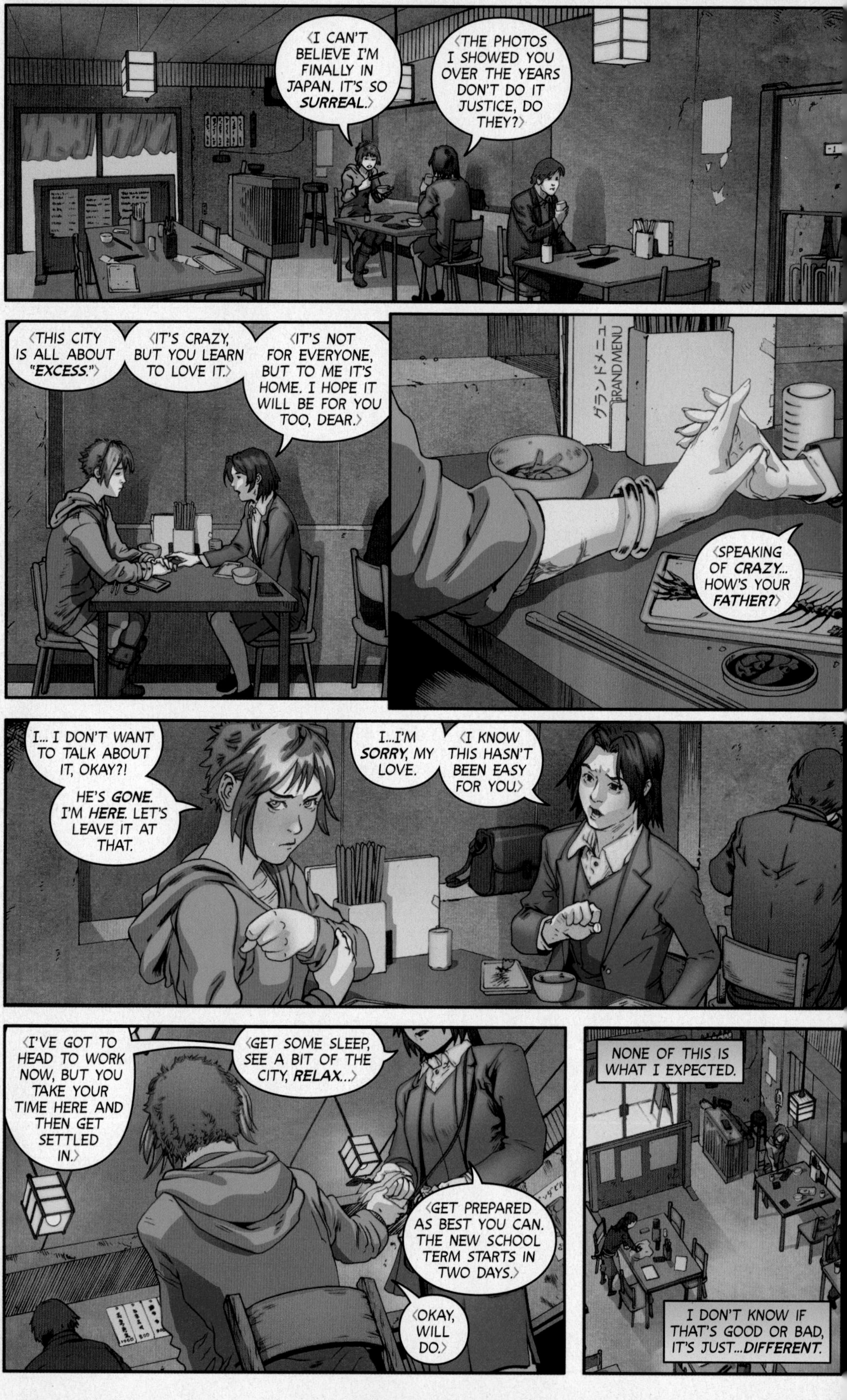

⟨I CAN'T BELIEVE I'M FINALLY IN JAPAN. IT'S SO SURREAL.⟩
⟨THE PHOTOS I SHOWED YOU OVER THE YEARS DON'T DO IT JUSTICE, DO THEY?⟩
⟨THIS CITY IS ALL ABOUT "EXCESS."⟩
⟨IT'S CRAZY, BUT YOU LEARN TO LOVE IT.⟩
⟨IT'S NOT FOR EVERYONE, BUT TO ME IT'S HOME. I HOPE IT WILL BE FOR YOU TOO, DEAR.⟩
グランドメニュー
GRAND MENU
⟨SPEAKING OF CRAZY... HOW'S YOUR FATHER?⟩
I... I DON'T WANT TO TALK ABOUT IT, OKAY?!
HE'S GONE. I'M HERE. LET'S LEAVE IT AT THAT.
I...I'M SORRY, MY LOVE.
⟨I KNOW THIS HASN'T BEEN EASY FOR YOU.⟩
⟨I'VE GOT TO HEAD TO WORK NOW, BUT YOU TAKE YOUR TIME HERE AND THEN GET SETTLED IN.⟩
⟨GET SOME SLEEP, SEE A BIT OF THE CITY, RELAX...⟩
⟨GET PREPARED AS BEST YOU CAN. THE NEW SCHOOL TERM STARTS IN TWO DAYS.⟩
⟨OKAY, WILL DO.⟩
NONE OF THIS IS WHAT I EXPECTED.
I DON'T KNOW IF THAT'S GOOD OR BAD, IT'S JUST...DIFFERENT.

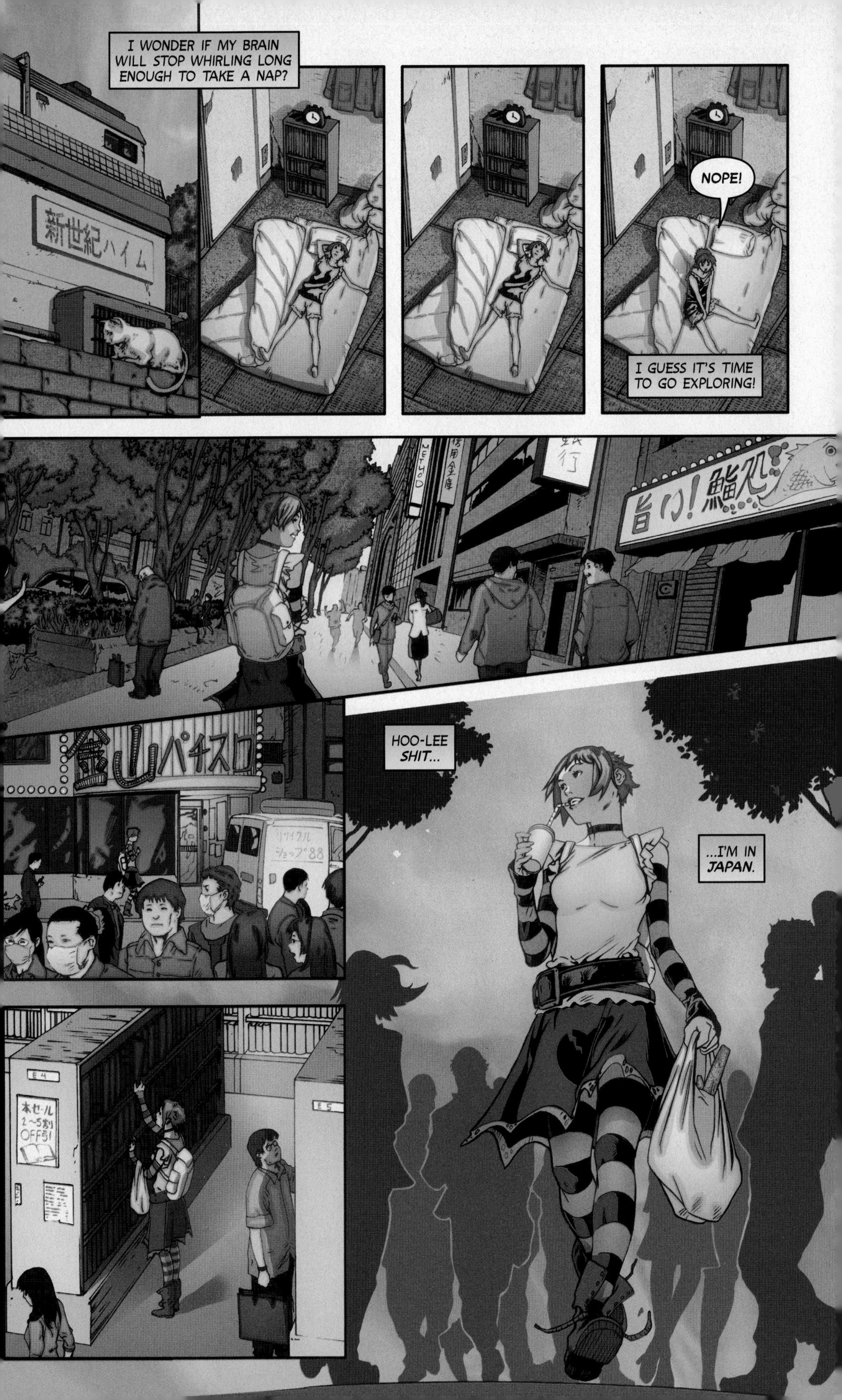
I WONDER IF MY BRAIN WILL STOP WHIRLING LONG ENOUGH TO TAKE A NAP?
新世紀ハイム
NOPE!
I GUESS IT'S TIME TO GO EXPLORING!
HOO-LEE SHIT...
...I'M IN JAPAN.

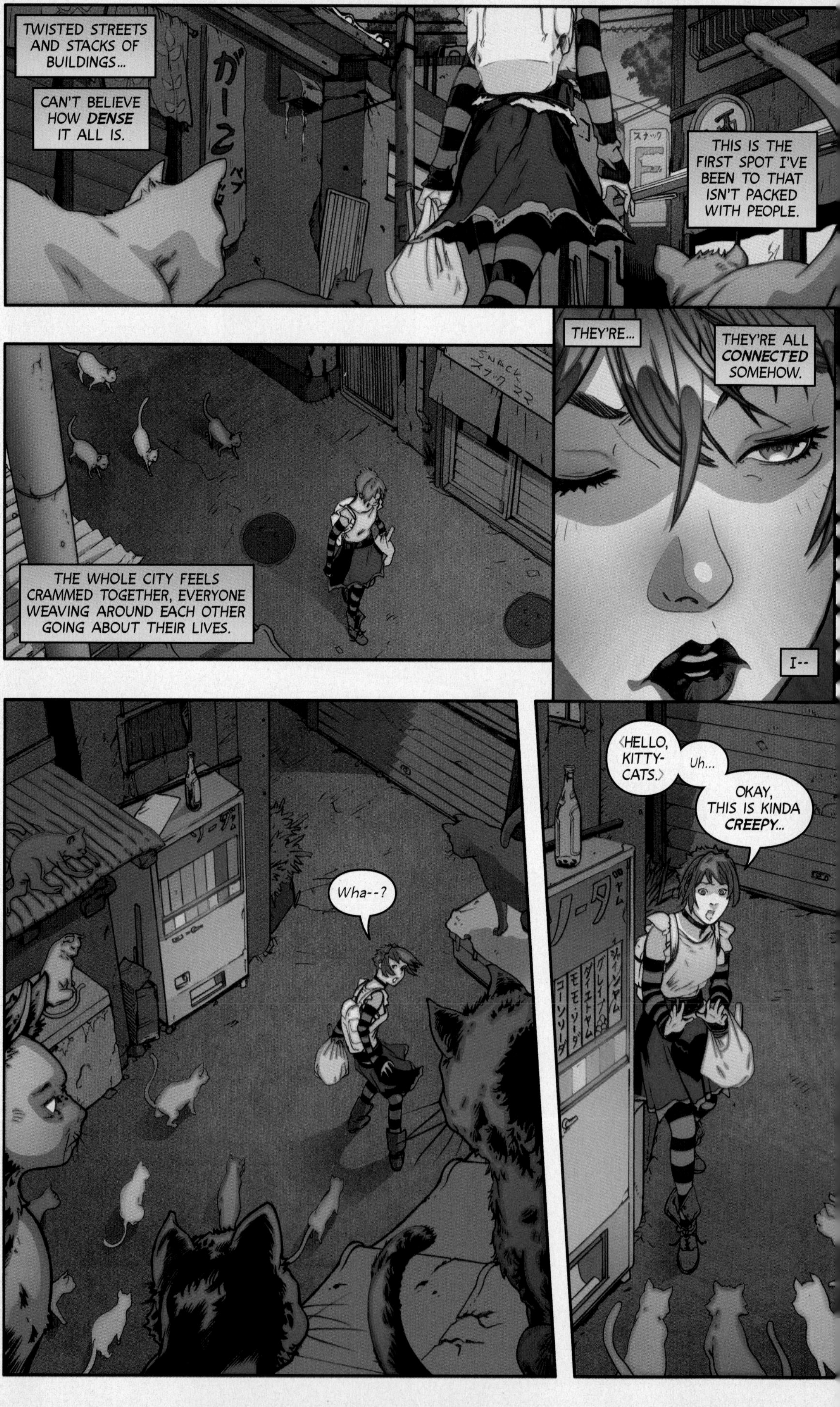

TWISTED STREETS AND STACKS OF BUILDINGS...
CAN'T BELIEVE HOW *DENSE* IT ALL IS.
THIS IS THE FIRST SPOT I'VE BEEN TO THAT ISN'T PACKED WITH PEOPLE.
SNACK
THE WHOLE CITY FEELS CRAMMED TOGETHER, EVERYONE WEAVING AROUND EACH OTHER GOING ABOUT THEIR LIVES.
THEY'RE...
THEY'RE ALL *CONNECTED* SOMEHOW.
I--
Wha--?
‹HELLO, KITTY-CATS.›
Uh...
OKAY, THIS IS KINDA *CREEPY*...

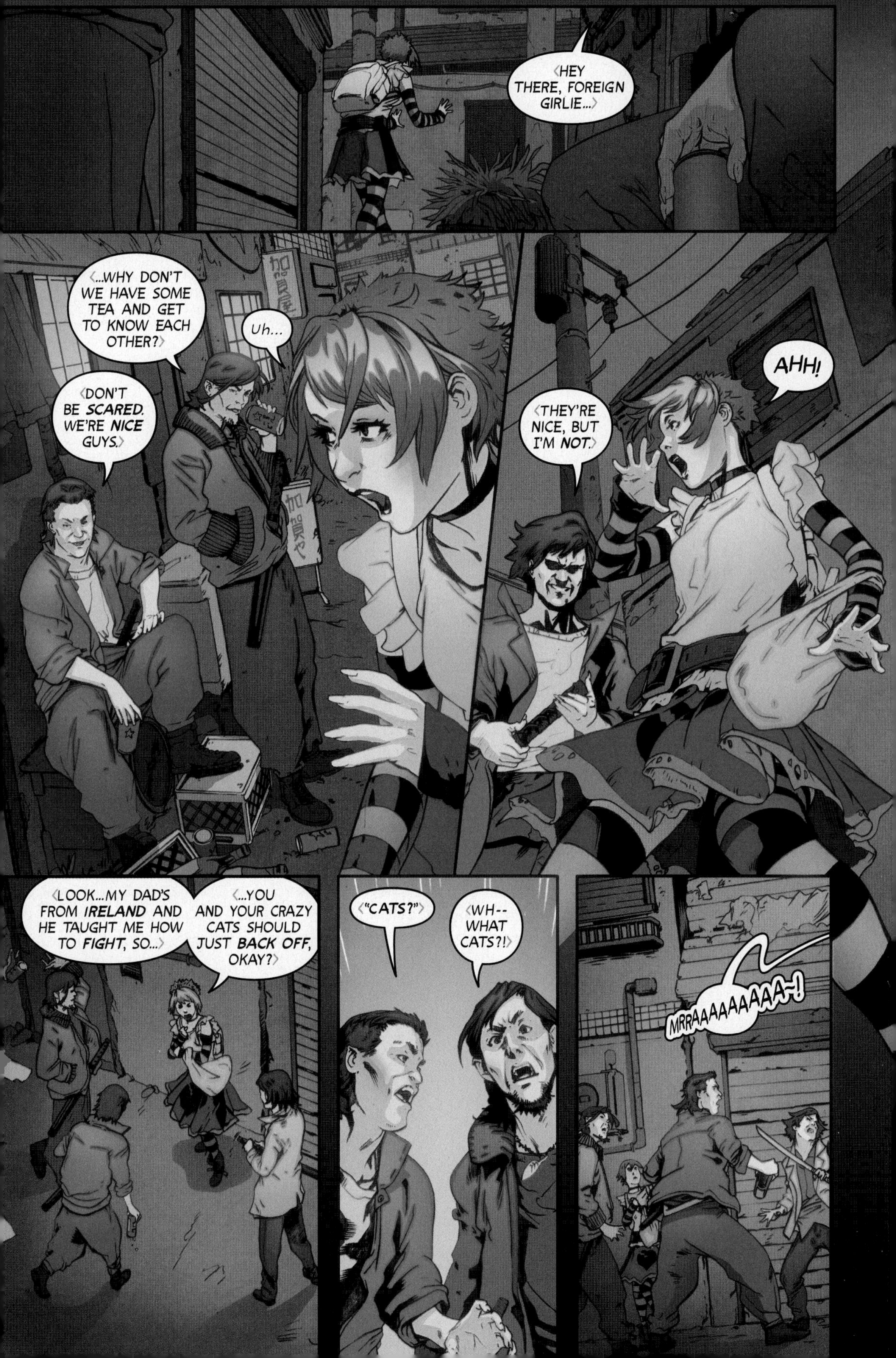

‹HEY THERE, FOREIGN GIRLIE...›
‹...WHY DON'T WE HAVE SOME TEA AND GET TO KNOW EACH OTHER?›
Uh...
‹DON'T BE *SCARED*. WE'RE *NICE* GUYS.›
‹THEY'RE NICE, BUT I'M *NOT*.›
AHH!
‹LOOK...MY DAD'S FROM *IRELAND* AND HE TAUGHT ME HOW TO *FIGHT*, SO...›
‹...YOU AND YOUR CRAZY CATS SHOULD JUST *BACK OFF*, OKAY?›
‹"CATS?"›
‹WH-- WHAT CATS?!›
MRRAAAAAAAAA--!

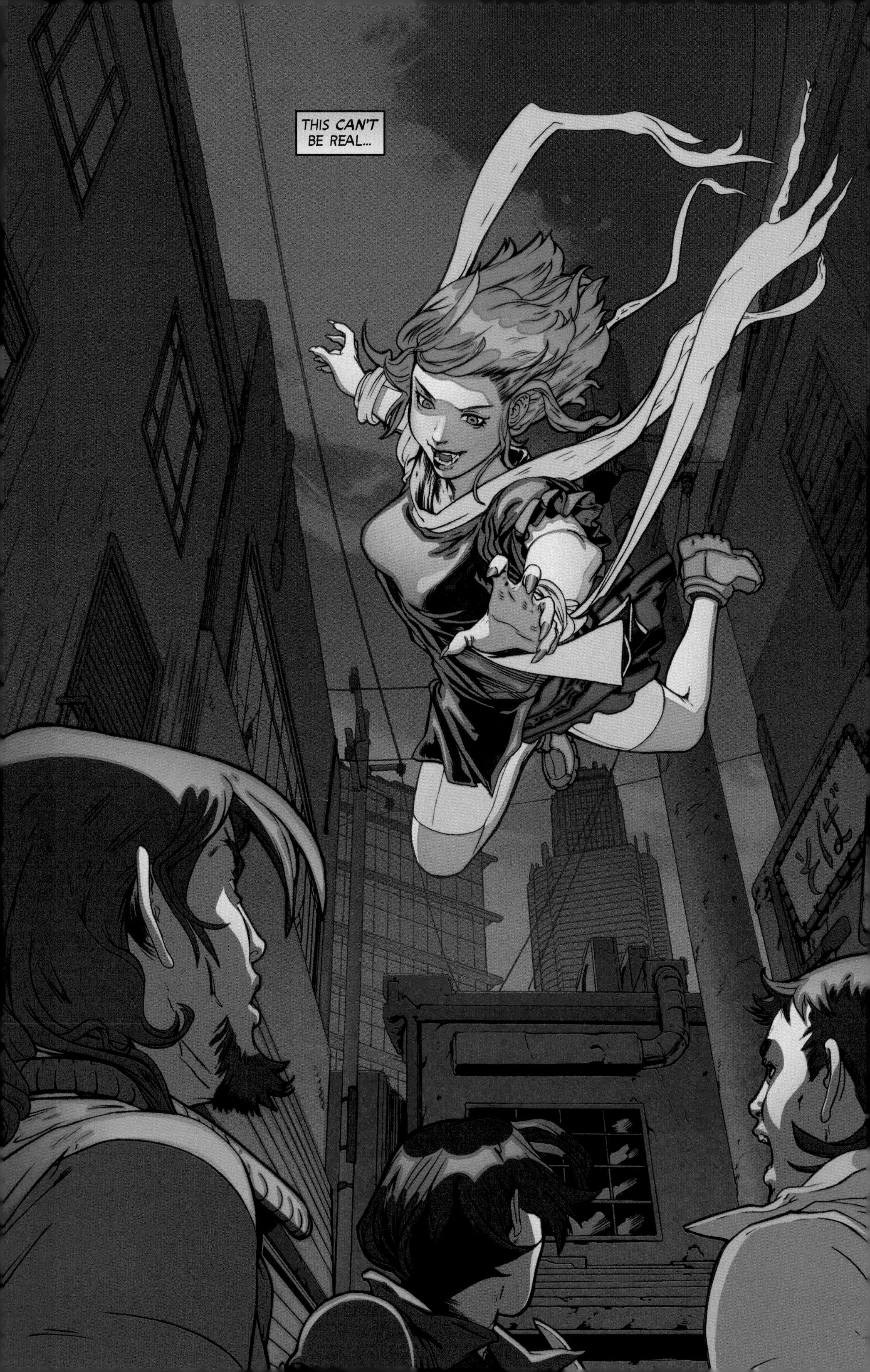
THIS CAN'T BE REAL...
そば

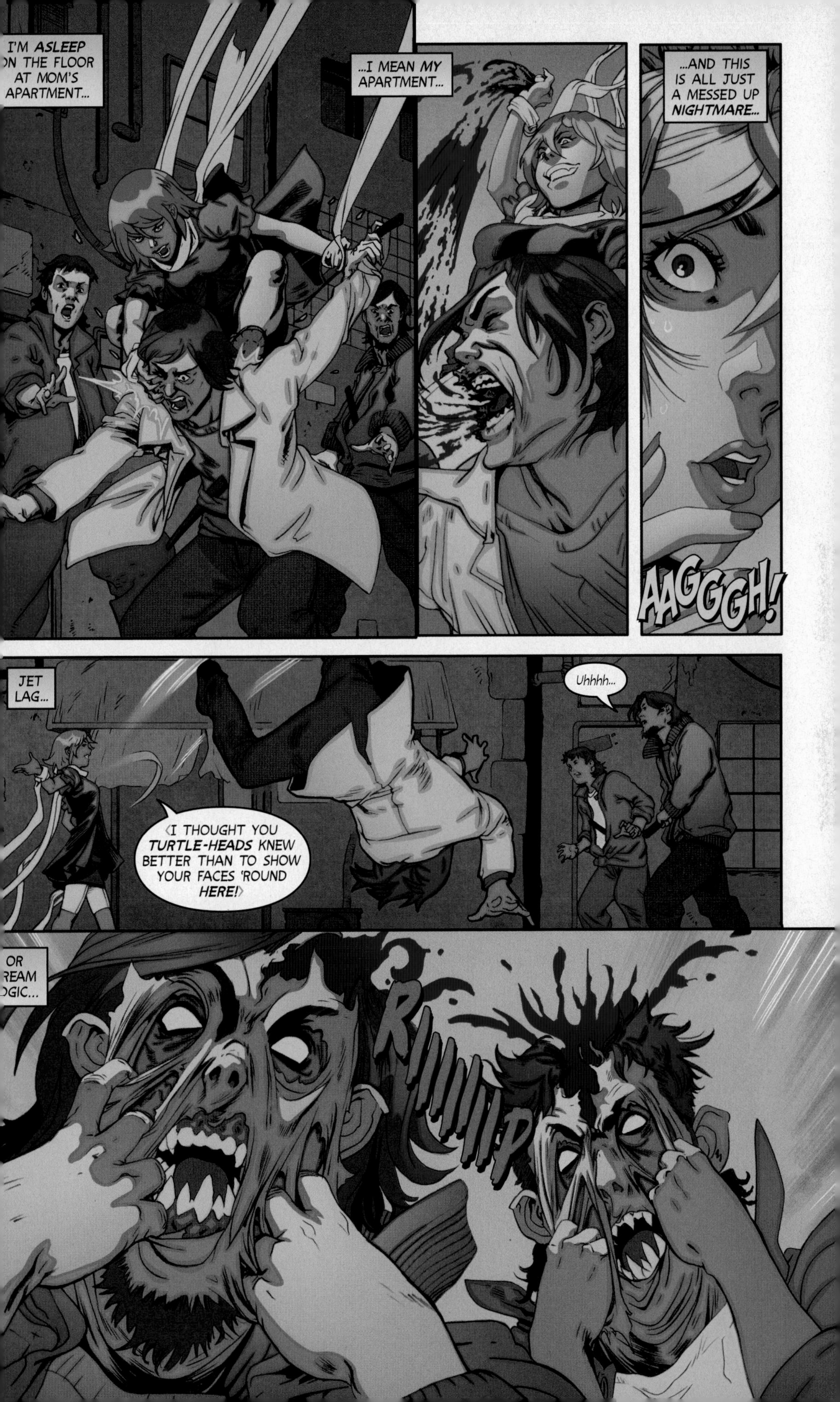
I'M ASLEEP
ON THE FLOOR
AT MOM'S
APARTMENT...
...I MEAN MY
APARTMENT...
...AND THIS
IS ALL JUST
A MESSED UP
NIGHTMARE...
AAGGGH!
JET
LAG...
‹I THOUGHT YOU TURTLE-HEADS KNEW BETTER THAN TO SHOW YOUR FACES 'ROUND HERE!›
Uhhhh...
OR
REAM
OGIC...
RIIIIIIIP

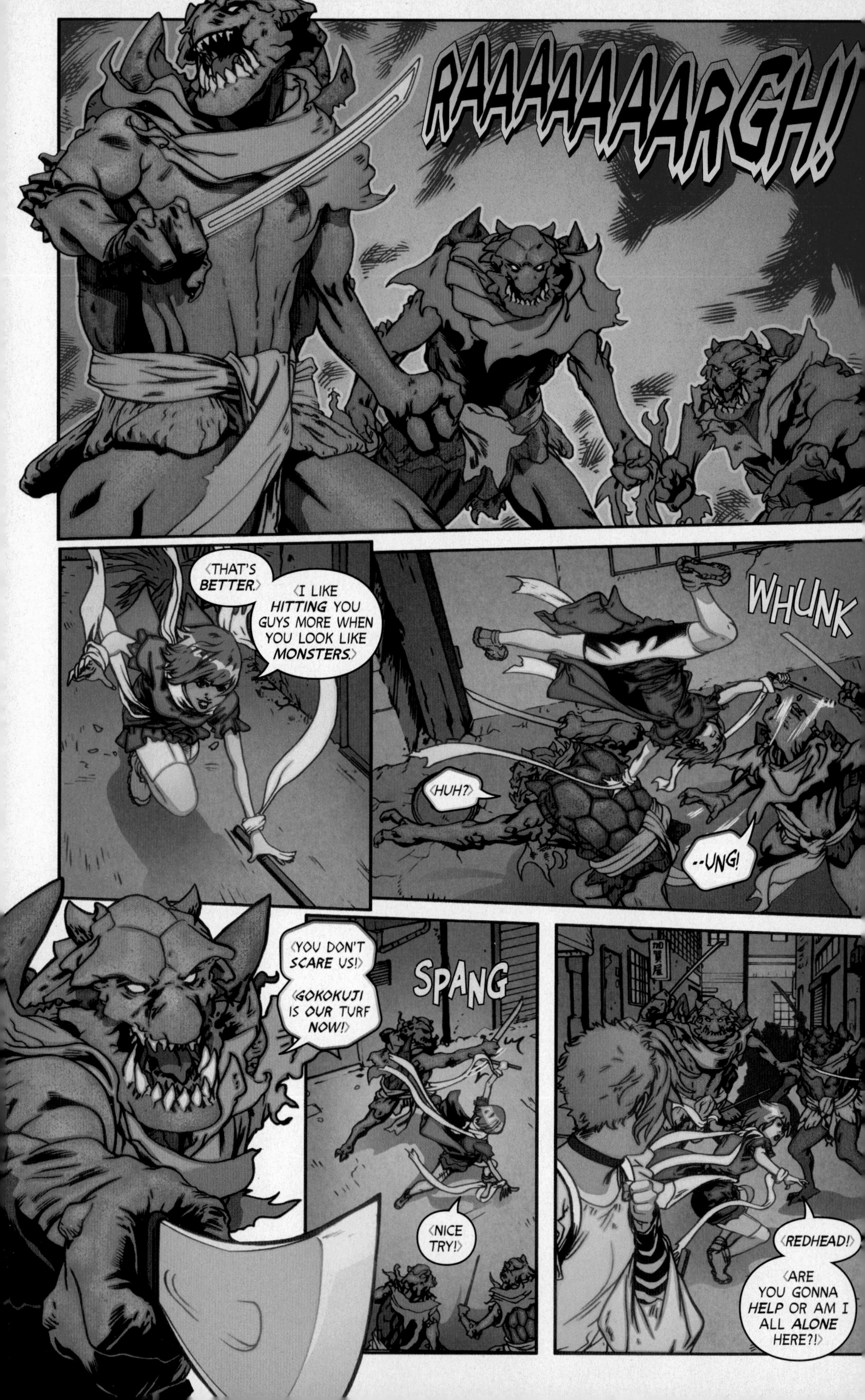
RAAAAAAARGH!
⟨THAT'S BETTER.⟩
⟨I LIKE HITTING YOU GUYS MORE WHEN YOU LOOK LIKE MONSTERS.⟩
WHUNK
⟨HUH?⟩
--UNG!
⟨YOU DON'T SCARE US!⟩
⟨GOKOKUJI IS OUR TURF NOW!⟩
SPANG
⟨NICE TRY!⟩
⟨REDHEAD!⟩
⟨ARE YOU GONNA HELP OR AM I ALL ALONE HERE?!⟩

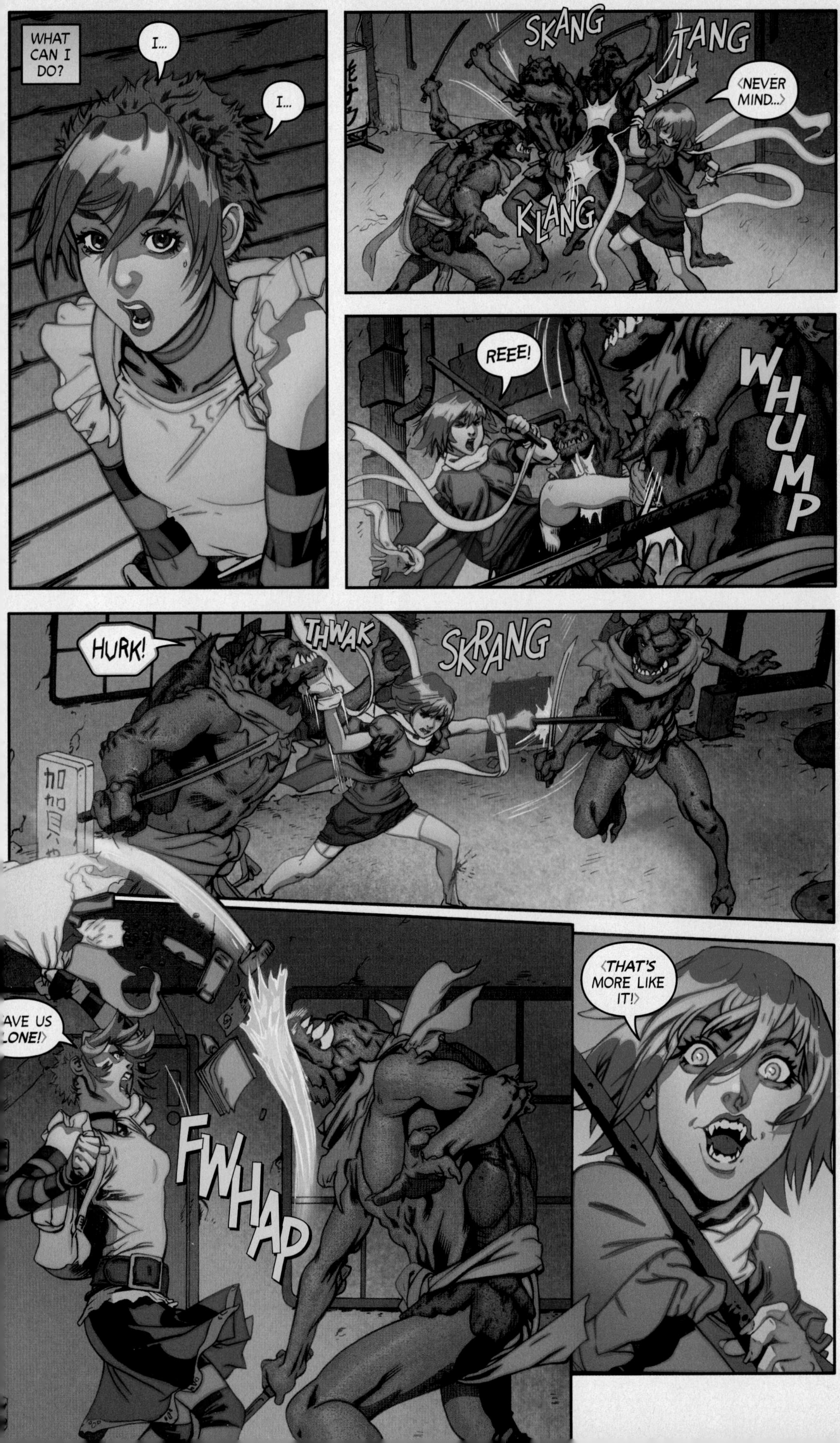
WHAT CAN I DO?
I...
I...
SKANG
TANG
〈NEVER MIND...〉
KLANG
REEE!
WHUMP
HURK!
THWAK
SKRANG
〈AVE US LONE!〉
FWHAP
〈THAT'S MORE LIKE IT!〉

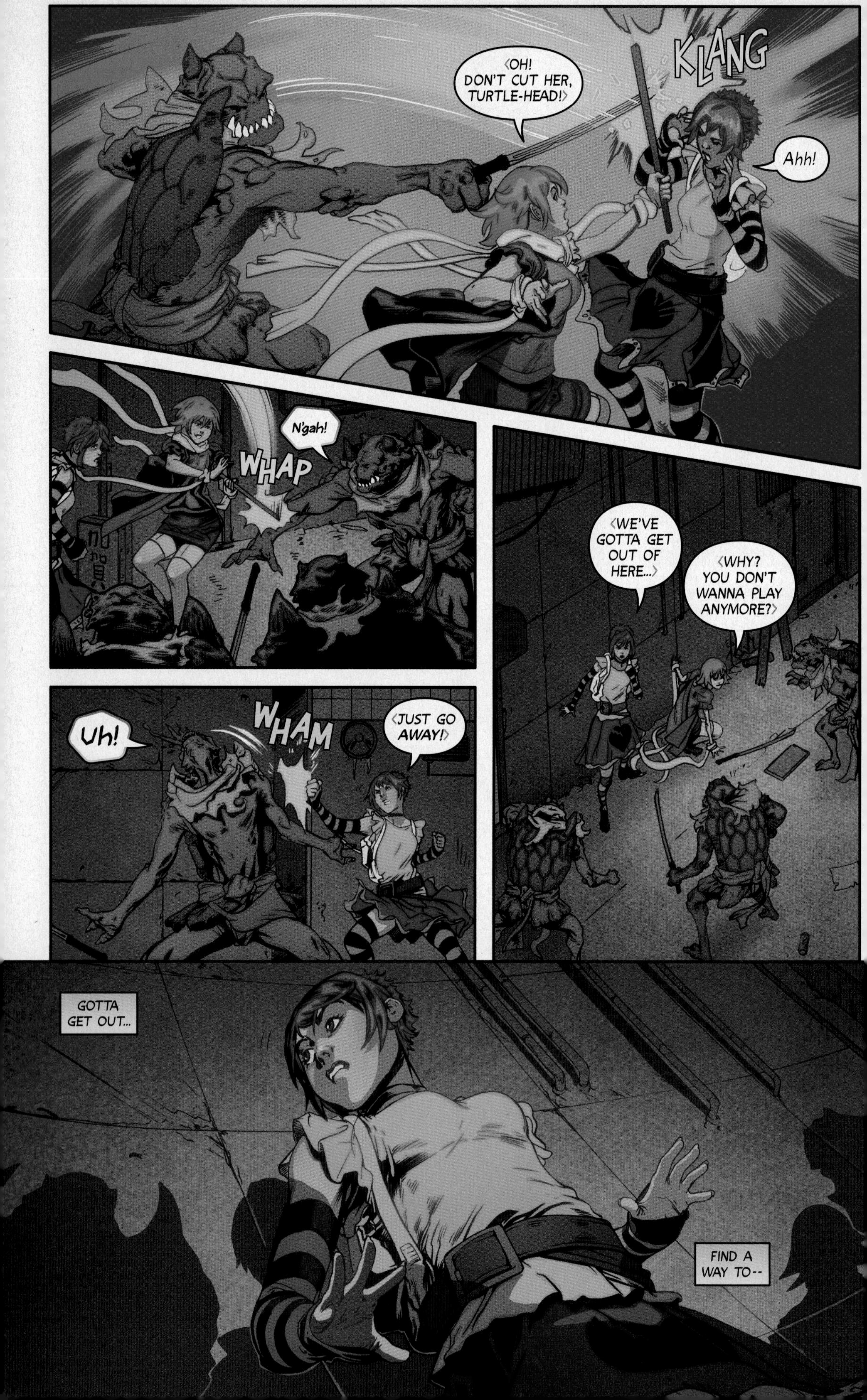
KLANG
‹OH! DON'T CUT HER, TURTLE-HEAD!›
Ahh!
N'gah!
WHAP
‹WE'VE GOTTA GET OUT OF HERE...›
‹WHY? YOU DON'T WANNA PLAY ANYMORE?›
Uh!
WHAM
‹JUST GO AWAY!›
GOTTA GET OUT...
FIND A WAY TO--

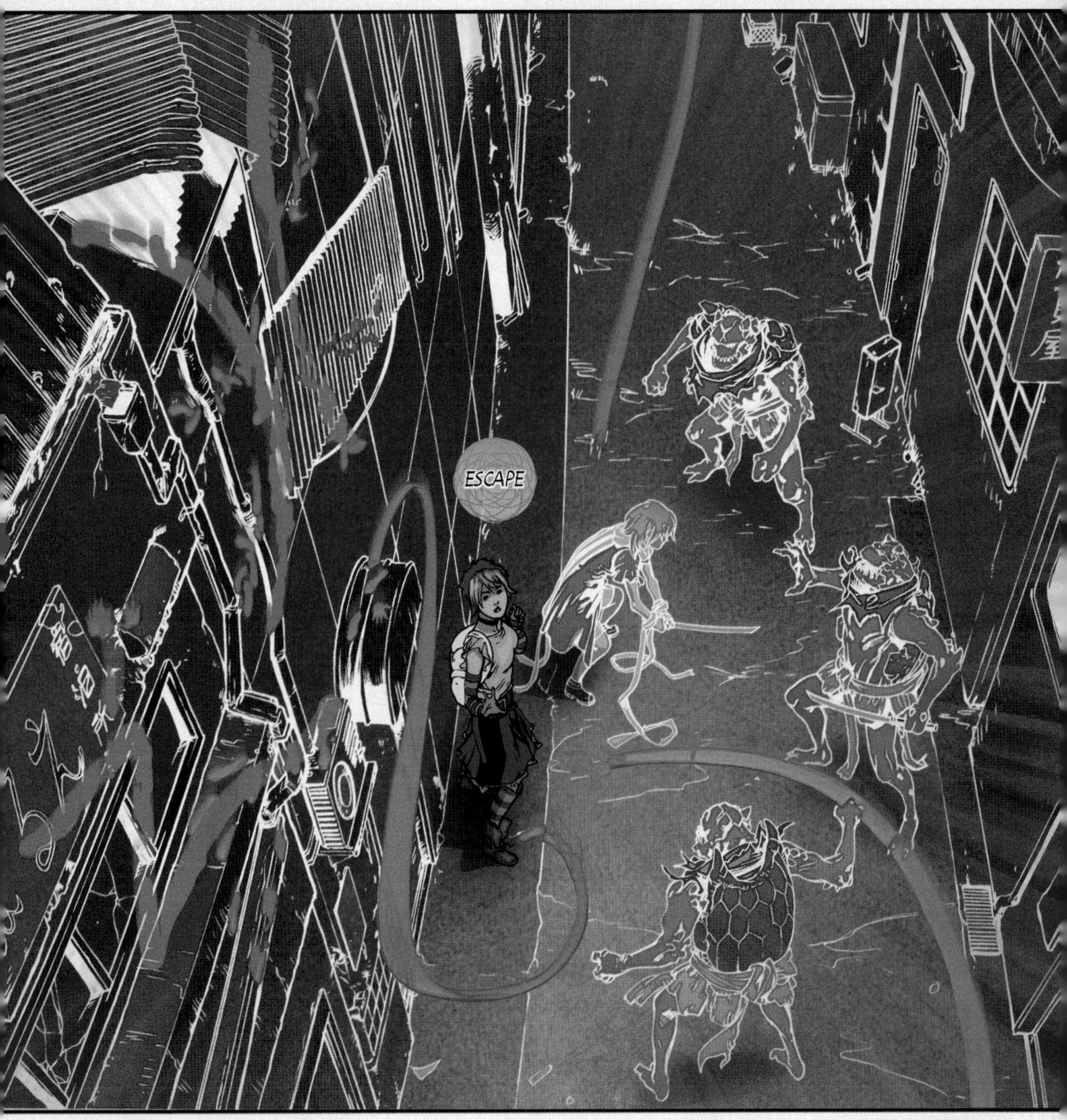
ESCAPE

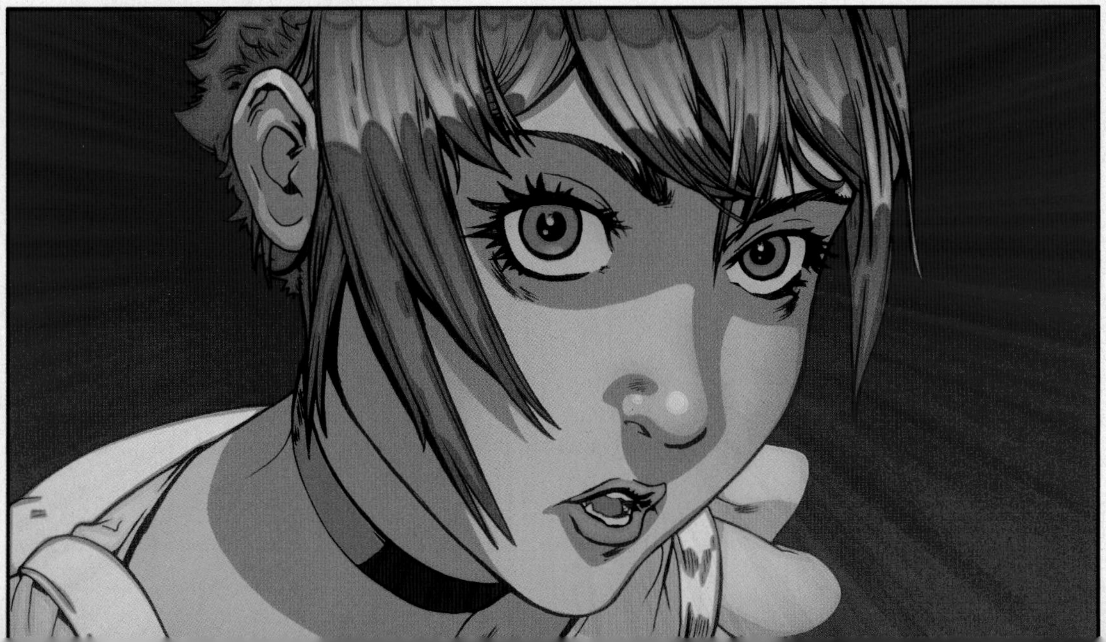

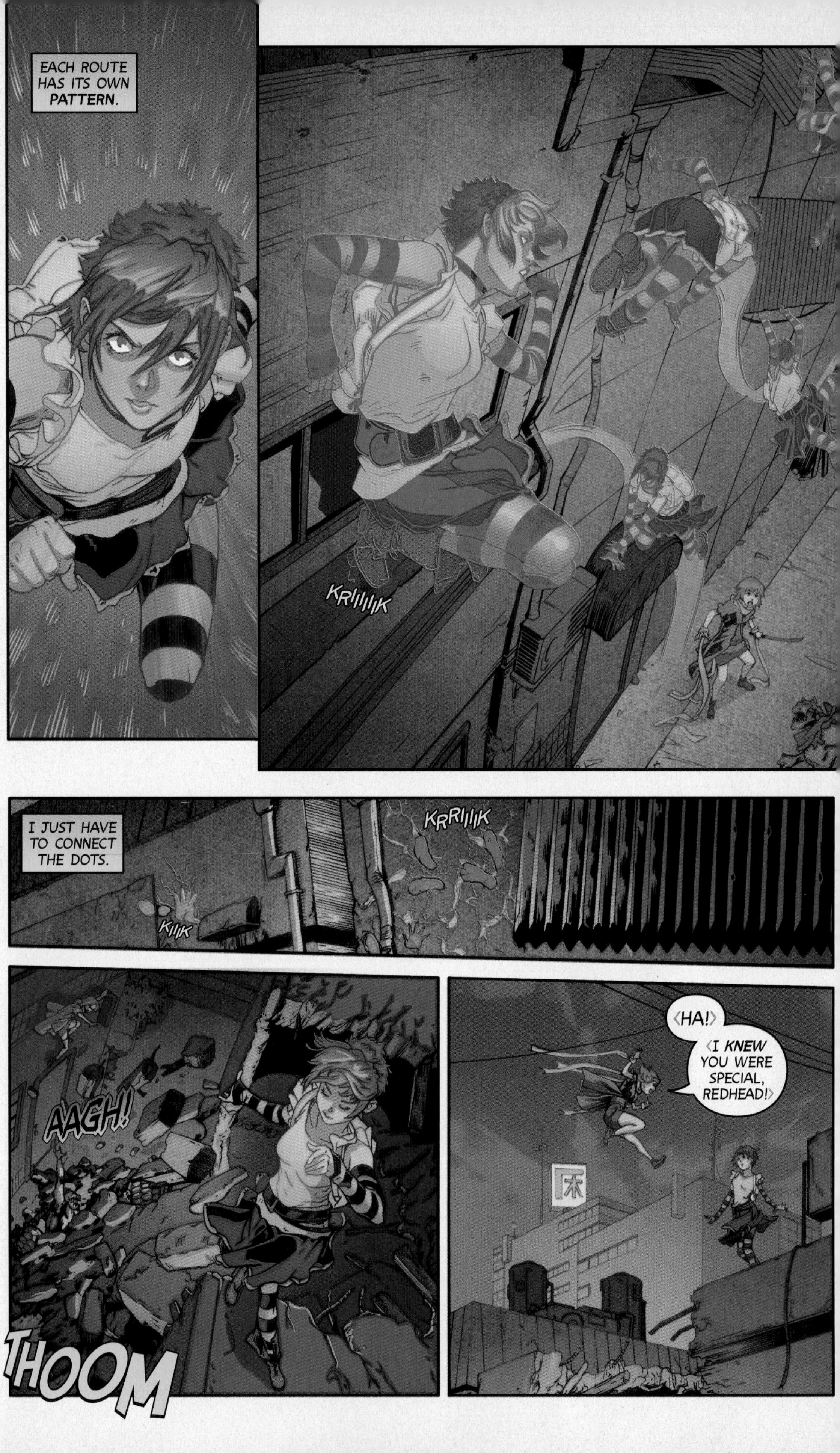
EACH ROUTE HAS ITS OWN PATTERN.
KRIIIIIK
I JUST HAVE TO CONNECT THE DOTS.
KIIIK
KRRIIIIK
AAGH!
THOOM
‹HA!›
‹I KNEW YOU WERE SPECIAL, REDHEAD!›

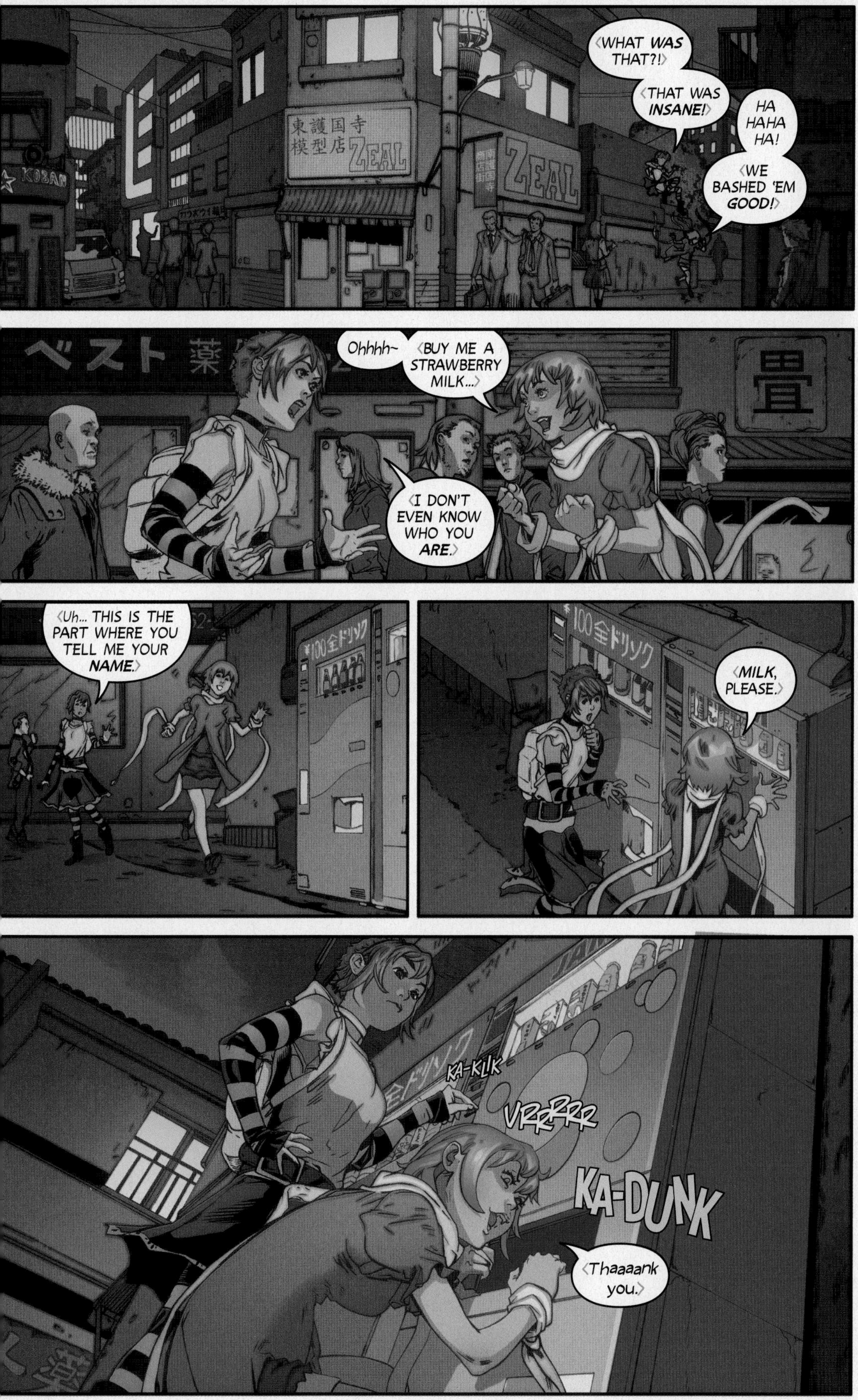

東護国寺
模型店
ZEAL
KOBAN
南護店街寺
ZEAL
⟨WHAT WAS THAT?!⟩
⟨THAT WAS INSANE!⟩
HA HAHA HA!
⟨WE BASHED 'EM GOOD!⟩
ベスト薬
畳
Ohhhh~
⟨BUY ME A STRAWBERRY MILK...⟩
⟨I DON'T EVEN KNOW WHO YOU ARE.⟩
¥100全ドリンク
⟨Uh... THIS IS THE PART WHERE YOU TELL ME YOUR NAME.⟩
100全ドリンク
⟨MILK, PLEASE.⟩
全ドリンク
KA-KLIK
VRRRRR
KA-DUNK
⟨Thaaaank you.⟩

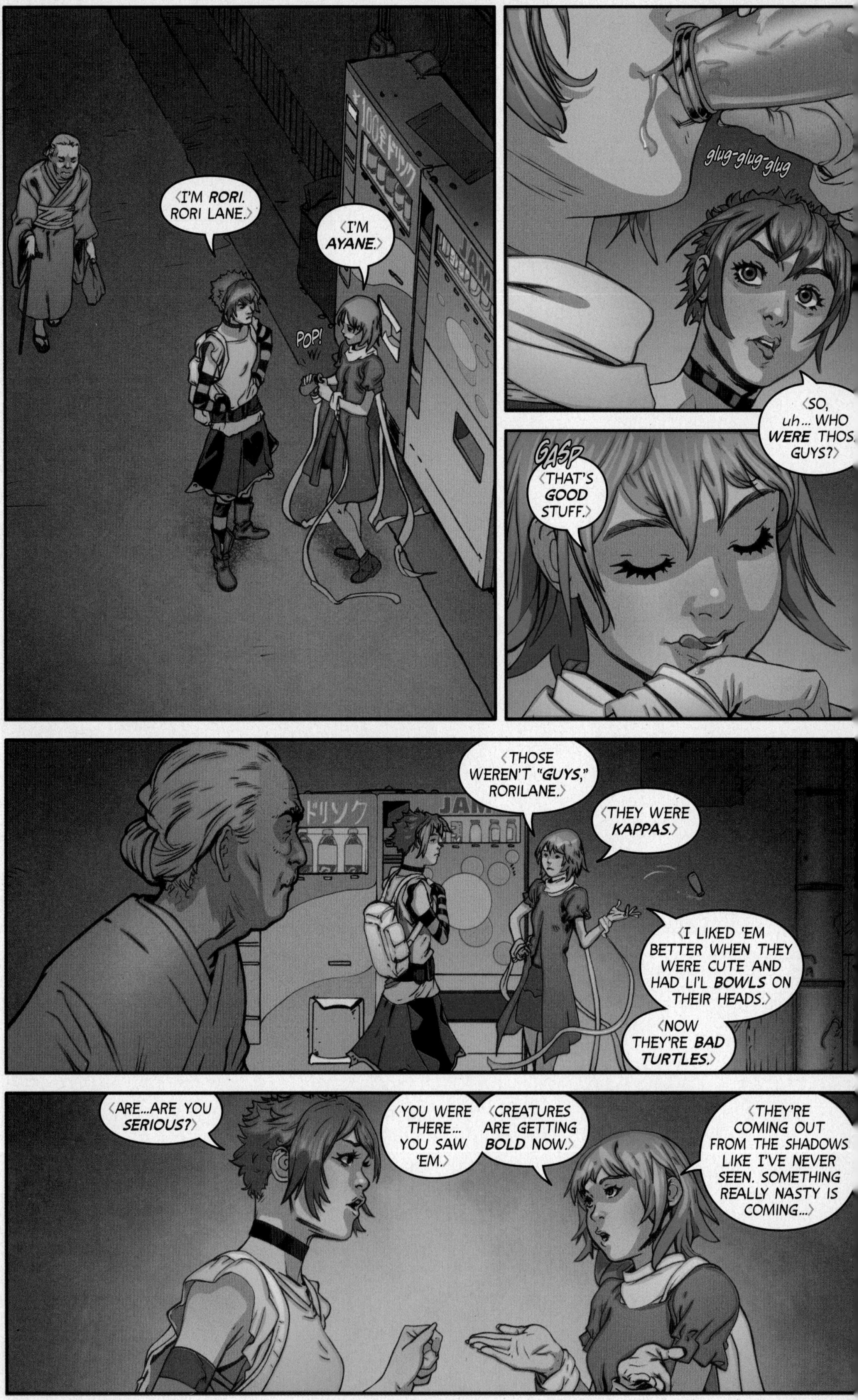

〈I'M RORI. RORI LANE.〉
〈I'M AYANE.〉
POP!
glug-glug-glug
〈SO, uh... WHO WERE THOS GUYS?〉
GASP
〈THAT'S GOOD STUFF.〉
〈THOSE WEREN'T "GUYS," RORILANE.〉
〈THEY WERE KAPPAS.〉
〈I LIKED 'EM BETTER WHEN THEY WERE CUTE AND HAD LI'L BOWLS ON THEIR HEADS.〉
〈NOW THEY'RE BAD TURTLES.〉
〈ARE...ARE YOU SERIOUS?〉
〈YOU WERE THERE... YOU SAW 'EM.〉
〈CREATURES ARE GETTING BOLD NOW.〉
〈THEY'RE COMING OUT FROM THE SHADOWS LIKE I'VE NEVER SEEN. SOMETHING REALLY NASTY IS COMING...〉

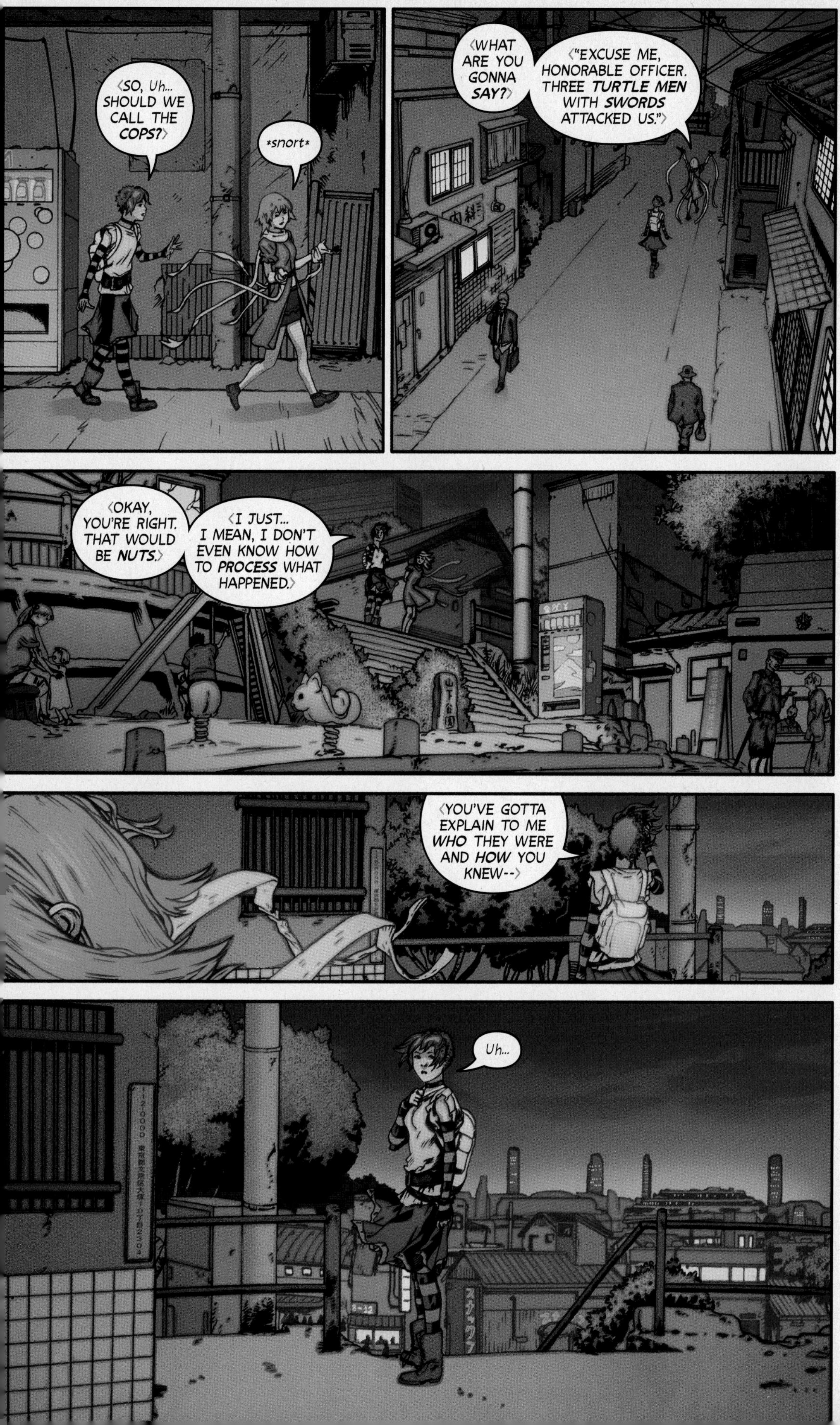

‹SO, Uh... SHOULD WE CALL THE COPS?›
snort
‹WHAT ARE YOU GONNA SAY?›
‹"EXCUSE ME, HONORABLE OFFICER. THREE TURTLE MEN WITH SWORDS ATTACKED US."›
‹OKAY, YOU'RE RIGHT. THAT WOULD BE NUTS.›
‹I JUST... I MEAN, I DON'T EVEN KNOW HOW TO PROCESS WHAT HAPPENED.›
‹YOU'VE GOTTA EXPLAIN TO ME WHO THEY WERE AND HOW YOU KNEW--›
Uh...

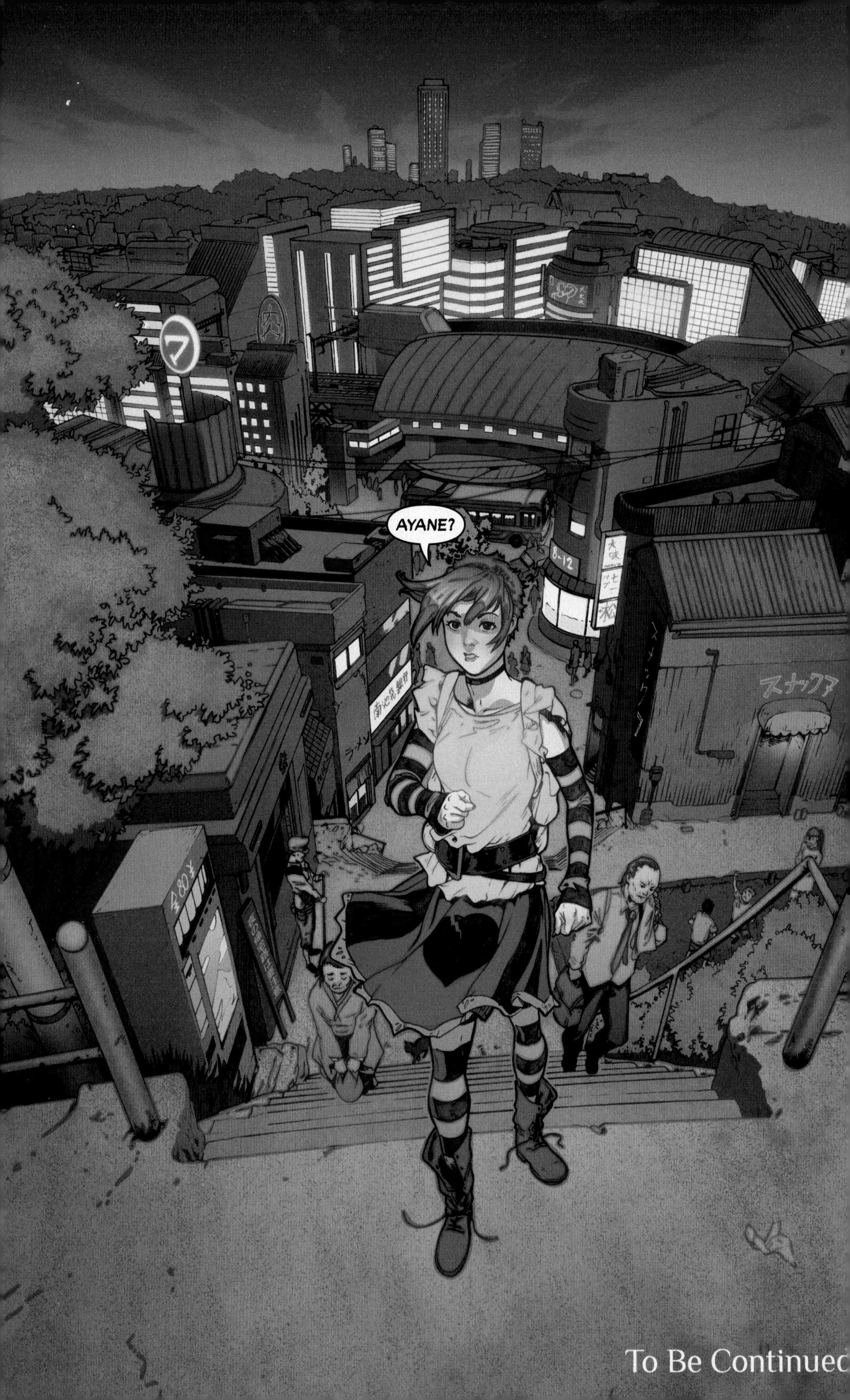
AYANE?
8-12
To Be Continued

Welcome to *Wayward*!

Jim Zub here. It's hard for me to put into words how proud I am to be launching a new creator-owned series at Image, especially one as incredible looking as Wayward. Steve Cummings and I have been plugging away on this for the past 8 months, slowly building a rich supernatural vision of Tokyo we hope will engage and entertain you. On the surface the story is a Buffy-esque action romp, but we hope you stick around to see bigger puzzle pieces we have planned slowly fitting together to make something unexpected.

Here's a few words from my skilled co-creator:

I'm Steven Cummings, the art half of the creative team behind Wayward. I have been drawing professionally since 2002 and have worked with publishers as varied as Marvel and DC, Kenzer and Udon, European and Japanese, and now I'm working with Jim on Wayward here at Image.

I have always wanted to do creator-owned so getting the opportunity to do this has been a dream come true. Monsters and myth and kids doing daring do all set in Tokyo makes for a great adventure to wake up each day to work on. Of course one of the greatest thrills about this is getting to draw my (almost) hometown as the setting for our epic adventure. So, please sit back and enjoy the creepy craziness of nasty creatures in the world's largest metropolis.

Steve and I want to hear what you think of our first issue! Send us your tweets/emails, send us photos of your cats or cool travel photos from Tokyo, chat with us in person at conventions we attend.

Here's where you can find the creative team on Twitter:

Writer - Jim Zub @JimZub
Line Artist - Steven Cummings @Stekichikun
Colorist - Tamra Bonvillain @TBonvillain
Letterer - Marshall Dillon @MarshallDillon
Lore Essays - Zack Davisson @ZackDavisson

Since this is the first issue we don't have any fanmail yet, so in the meantime I'll fill up this empty column space with a beautiful warm-up sketch of Rori done by Steve during our initial design phase of the series.

Okay, that's all for now. Thanks for supporting creator-owned comics. If you enjoy what you read here please check out the other issues and collections of *Wayward*!

-ZUB

Kappa. Kitsune. Oni. Or towering, post-war engines of destruction like Godzilla, Mothra, and Gamera. Even the endless parade of Pokémon—Japan is monster country. They write books about monsters; make movies about monsters; draw comics about monsters. From a young age, Japanese children wean themselves on folklore creatures with *Kitaro*. They graduate to modern, esoteric beasts with *Neon Genesis Evangelion* and *Attack on Titan*. When they head to college, *yōkaigaku* — monsterology —is a serious course of study.

It is a fact undeniable: Japan embraces the weird.

There's a reason why the country is in love with the supernatural. Monsters are a part of Japan's deep magic. They are found as far back as the creation myth and are threaded through all of Japanese history. And as Japan has evolved from a primitive tribal culture to a modern, scientific superpower, the monsters have kept pace.

The birth of Japan's gods and monsters is recorded in the 8th century *Kojiki* (*Record of Ancient Matters*) —the oldest known work of Japanese literature. The *Kojiki* tells of the god Izanagi, creator of the Japanese islands, freshly returned from the land of the dead. He purifies himself in a bath, and as he dries his body each falling drop of water soaks into the soil and imbues the land with latent supernatural potential.

For tens of thousands of years this supernatural potential manifested itself as invisible energy, a nameless, faceless, field that swaddled the islands. It was an elemental force that brought both life and death, in the same way that water both nourished the crops as a gentle rain and pounded villages in the form of typhoons. Like any natural resource this power could be harvested; shrines were built to contain and focus the energy, and used as spiritual batteries. When this energy was good and beneficial they named it *kami* (神). When it was wild and dangerous they referred to it by the euphemism stuff of mystery —*mononoke* (物の怪).

Things changed rapidly in the Heian period (794 – 1185) when contact with China brought the ideas of incarnate deities and organized religion. The influence of Buddhism forged that loose collections of folk beliefs and kami worship into the religion called Shinto. Simultaneously, new ideas created new beliefs that blended the ancient and the modern, like the ghost-religion *Goryō Shinko* and the sorcerous art of geomancy called *Onmyōdō*.

With this change, the mononoke first gained individual form and identities. Artists were at the forefront of this spiritual revolution, imagining a wild menagerie of thousands of forms and shapes that would shame Hieronymus Bosch with their variety. Heian period artists crafted long scrolls that would be unrolled to slowly reveal new and terrible monsters marching in a celebration of pandemonium called the *Night Parade of 100 Demons*—one of Japan's initial forays into sequential art.

The supernatural took a back seat for the next few centuries as Japan was ripped apart by civil wars and more physical horrors. Finally, peace arrived with conquest, as the shōgun Tokugawa Ieyasu took command and kick-started modern Japan with the Edo period (1603-1868). Many of the things Japanese —the aristocratic samurai and the artisanal geisha; the elegant theater of *bunraku* and the wild spectacle of kabuki; the floating world of *ukiyo-e* artists- sprouted and flowered during the Edo period. This era of peace and prosperity also gave birth to *yōkai* (妖怪).

The Edo period was marked by a mania for the supernatural. A popular parlor game, called *Hyakumonogatari Kaidankai*, gripped the nation. A hundred candles would be lit in a circle, and players would tell weird tales one after the other, extinguishing a single candle with each story. Players told stories of monsters—now called *yōkai*—expounding on those same beasts from the picture scrolls of the Heian period. Writers and storytellers filled in the details, giving the grotesqueries names and back stories, creating hierarchies and societies and mythologies. Kitsune and tengu were cast as aristocrats, while *kappa* and *tanuki* were earthier —the blue- collar yōkai. Others were just bizarre, like the *enjo-name* ceiling licker, or the one-eyed, one- footed umbrella monster called the *kasa obake*.

This enthusiasm lasted more than two hundred years, until war again silenced the supernatural. Japan's growing pains of the Meiji era (1868-1912) through the early Showa era (1926-1989) saw the militarization and mobilization of the country that lead to WWII. The government made a concentrated effort to suppress yōkai and superstition in favor of the new gods of science and industry.

It wouldn't last.

After Japan's defeat, the yōkai again crawled out of their dark holes, finding a new home and an appreciative audience in film and the emergent art form known as manga. Lead by the artist Shigeru Mizuki and his comic *Kitaro*, Japan underwent a yōkai boom that resurrected the lost monsters of previous generations.

And they evolved. Director Ishiro Honda combined science and the supernatural to create monsters for the new generation—*daikaiju*. Giant monsters like Godzilla and Rodan captured and continue to hold the imagination of monster-loving Japanese children. And Americans too.

Even now in 2014 the monsters of Japan are still there. Wander the streets of Tokyo—or anywhere in Japan—and you will find them. Whether it is the obvious sights like the statue of Godzilla in Ginza and the Kappa Bridge, or in the hidden power spots and energy zones laid out centuries ago by mystical onmyōji. Or even more esoteric wonders like the Sunset 60 ghost building or the shrine to the head of the samurai Taira no Masakado in the Otemachi financial district—one of the most expensive areas of land on Earth, but a place that no one will dare build over.

You just have to scratch the shiny, neon veneer of modern Japan to find the true skin of the country —the ancient soil infused with supernatural potential by the god Izanagi. Supernatural potential waiting to be tapped.

Zack Davisson is a translator, writer, and scholar of Japanese folklore, ghosts, and manga. He is the author of Yūrei: The Japanese Ghost, *the translator of the Eisner Award-winning* Showa: A History of Japan, *and creator of the Japanese folklore site* hyakumonogatari.com

Kappa

河童 (Lit: Water Child)

One of the most ubiquitous yōkai in Japan, kappa are found wherever there is fresh water, throughout the Japanese islands. Once worshiped as gods of the rivers (and indeed you can still find shrines dedicated to kappa across Japan), they are now viewed as little more than mischievous imps—albeit dangerous.

Traditionally about the size of a small person, kappa appear as humanized turtles, complete with shell and beak. Even with their small size, they are stronger than normal humans. Their skin is green and mottled, and their hands and feet are webbed and studded with claws. They reek of fish. The kappas' most distinctive feature is the bowl-shaped indentation on their heads. This small bowl holds a reservoir of water that is said to be the source of their powers. If the water is spilled, they have to return to their river or die—although some kappa adapted to wear metal plates over their bowl for protection.

Myths about kappa are myriad, and show their changeable nature. Their arms are detached from their bodies—pulling on one arm shortens the other. Their favorite foods are cucumbers and the elusive *shirikodama* —a magical ball that resides in the human anus which kappa forcibly rip out in brutal attacks.

Their level of civilization is also fluid. The 1910 *Tono Monogatari* portrays kappa as barbarians who raid fishing villages and rape women. Other folklore describes them as civilized and intelligent; they are said to have taught medicine and bone-setting to humans, and are masters of the strategy game *shogi*. In Ryunosuke Akutagawa's 1927 book Kappa, they are portrayed as having a society based on radical capitalism, where poor kappa are slaughtered as food for the wealthy class.

In modern Japan, kappa experienced a renaissance lately, depicted as children's toys or cute, harmless mascots for sushi restaurants. But underneath the plastic smiles and friendly waves lie the brutal monsters of folklore.

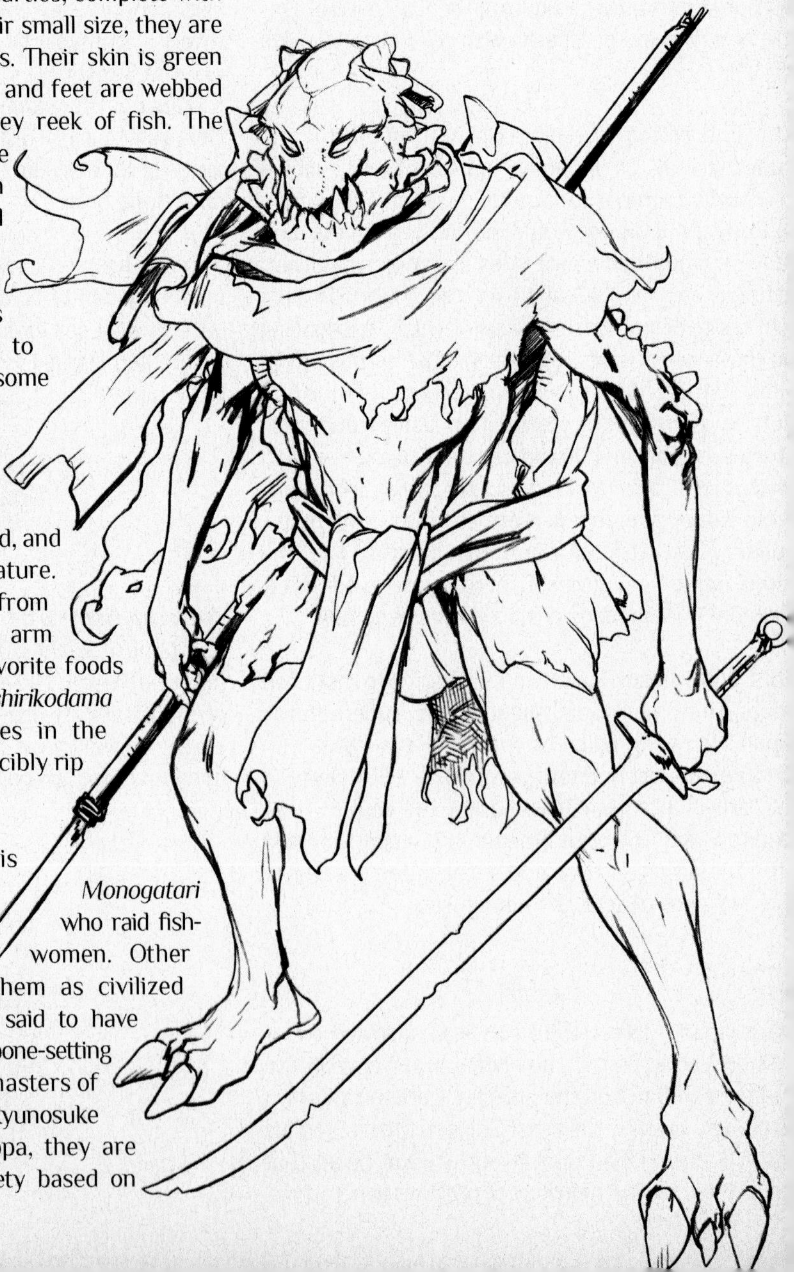

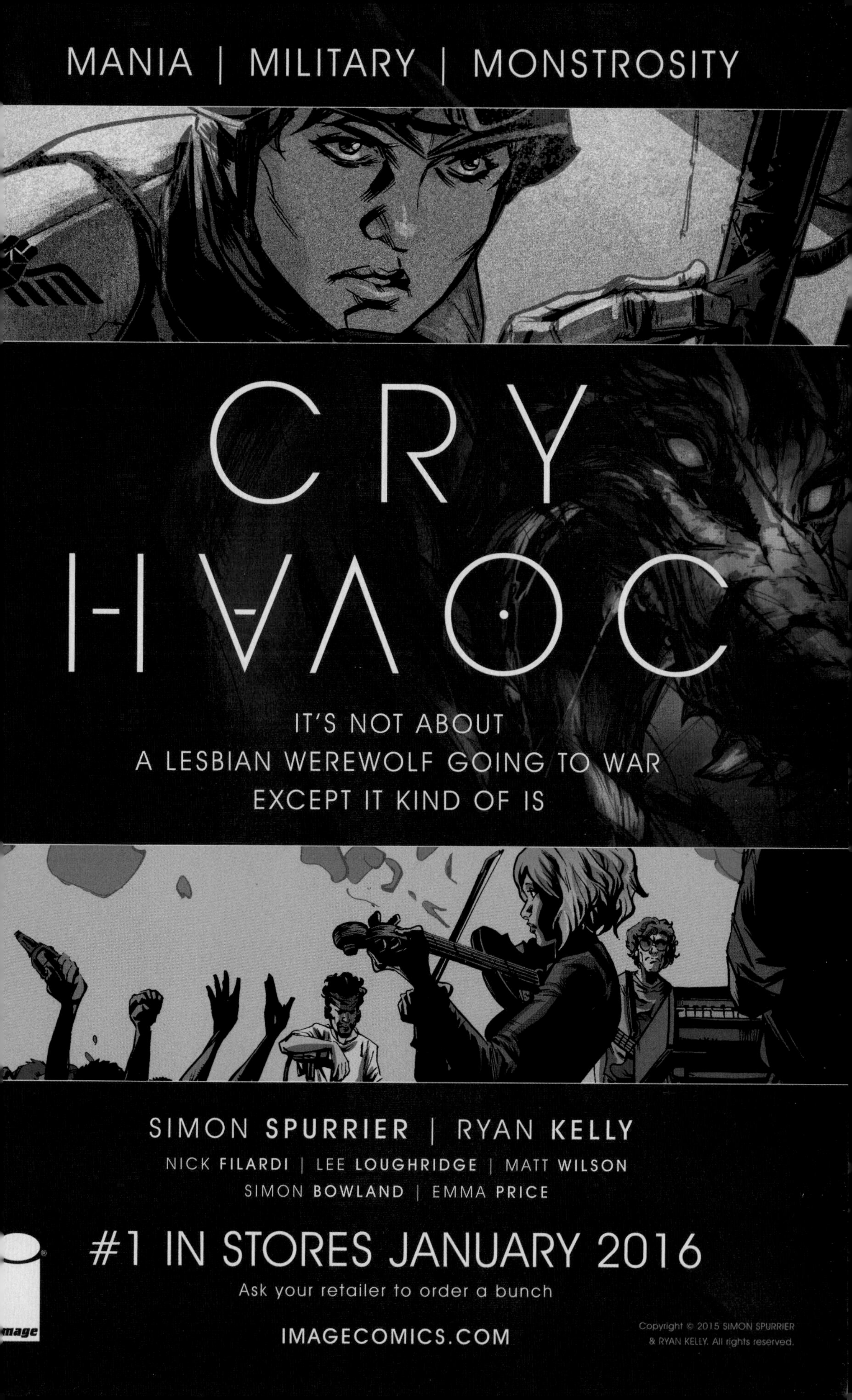
MANIA | MILITARY | MONSTROSITY
CRY HAVOC
IT'S NOT ABOUT
A LESBIAN WEREWOLF GOING TO WAR
EXCEPT IT KIND OF IS
SIMON SPURRIER | RYAN KELLY
NICK FILARDI | LEE LOUGHRIDGE | MATT WILSON
SIMON BOWLAND | EMMA PRICE
#1 IN STORES JANUARY 2016
Ask your retailer to order a bunch
IMAGECOMICS.COM
Copyright © 2015 SIMON SPURRIER & RYAN KELLY. All rights reserved.

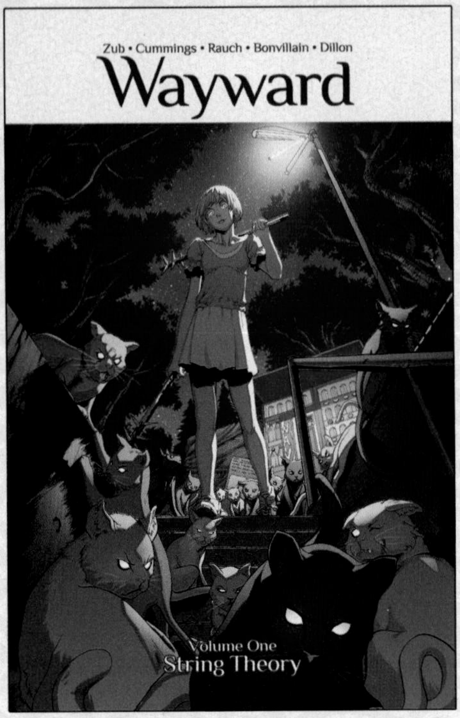
Zub • Cummings • Rauch • Bonvillain • Dillon
Wayward
Volume One
String Theory

Wayward Vol. 1: String Theory
(collects issues #1-5)
ISBN: 978-1-63215-173-5
136 pages / $9.99 USD

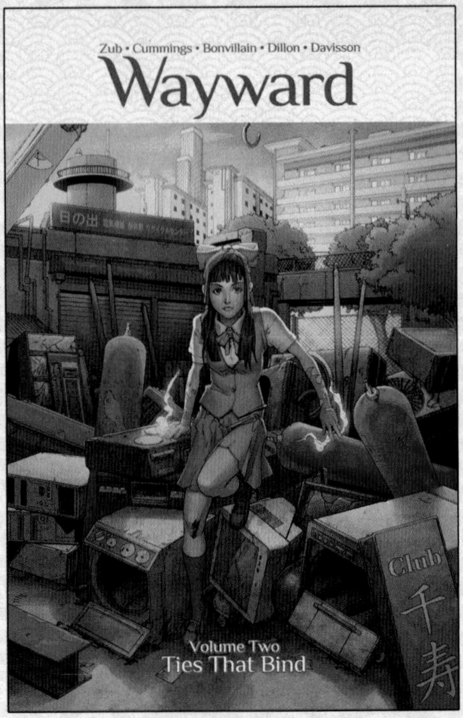
Zub • Cummings • Bonvillain • Dillon • Davisson
Wayward
Volume Two
Ties That Bind
Club
千寿

Wayward Vol. 2: Ties That Bind
(collects issues #6-10)
ISBN: 978-1-63215-403-3
136 pages / $16.99 USD

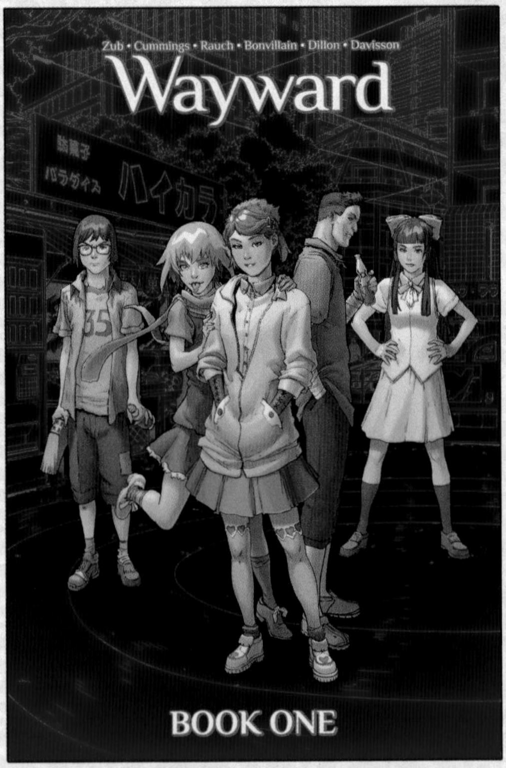
Zub • Cummings • Rauch • Bonvillain • Dillon • Davisson
Wayward
ハイカラ
BOOK ONE

Wayward Deluxe Hardcover Book 1
(collects issues #1-10 + Extras)
ISBN: 978-1-63215-473-6
320 pages / $39.99 USD

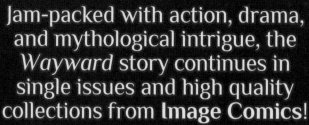

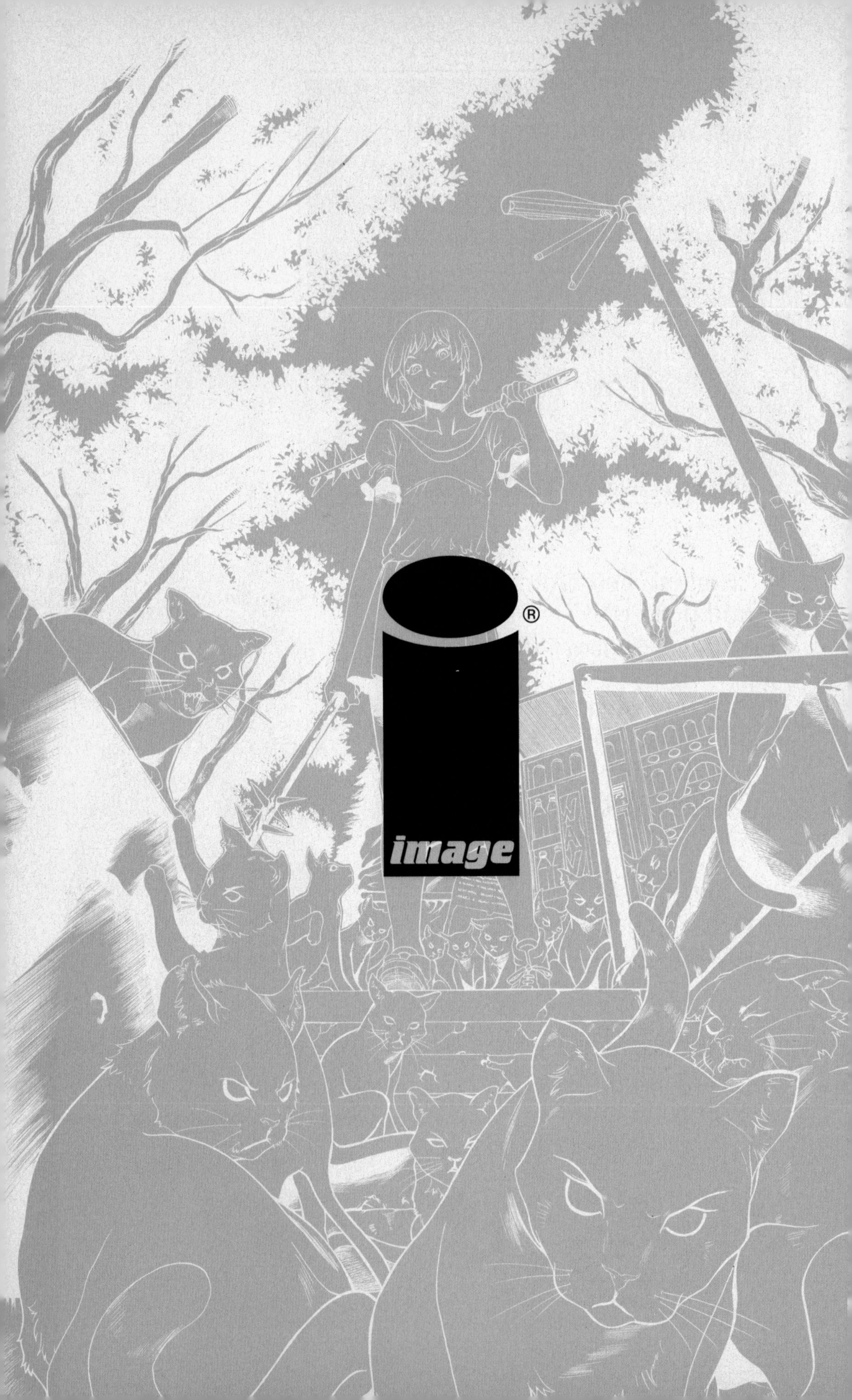
image